Perspectives on Population

Perspectives on Population

AN INTRODUCTION TO CONCEPTS AND ISSUES

Scott W. Menard and Elizabeth W. Moen

New York Oxford
OXFORD UNIVERSITY PRESS
1987

Oxford University Press

Oxford New York Toronto
Delhi Bombay Calcutta Madras Karachi
Petaling Jaya Singapore Hong Kong Tokyo
Nairobi Dar es Salaam Cape Town
Melbourne Auckland

and associated companies in
Beirut Berlin Ibadan Nicosia

Published by Oxford University Press, Inc.,
200 Madison Avenue, New York, New York 10016

Oxford is a registered trademark of Oxford University Press

Library of Congress Cataloging-in-Publication Data
Perspectives on population.
Bibliography: p.
Includes index.
1. Population. I. Menard, Scott W. II. Moen, Elizabeth.
HB871.P48 1987 304.6 86-23652
ISBN 0-19-504092-9
ISBN 0-19-504190-9 (pbk.)

10 9 8 7 6 5 4 3 2 1

Printed in the United States of America
on acid-free paper

Acknowledgments

Selections from works by the following authors and publications were made possible by the kind permission of their respective publishers and representatives:

"Regional Variations in Population Histories," by Scott Menard, prepared especially for this volume.

Excerpts from *Plagues and Peoples* by William H. McNeill. Copyright © 1976 by William H. McNeill. Reprinted by permission of Doubleday & Company, Inc.

"Demographic Impact of the Frontier" from *Victims of Progress* by John H. Bodley. Reprinted by permission of Mayfield Publishing Company. Copyright © 1982 Mayfield Publishing Company.

"Relevance of Demographic Transition Theory for Developing Countries," by Michael S. Teitelbaum, *Science* volume 188, pp. 420–425, 2 May 1975. Copyright © 1976 by the American Association for the Advancement of Science.

"The Theory of Change and Response in Modern Demographic History," by Kingsley Davis, originally published in *Population Index* 29(4), pp. 345–352 and 362, October, 1963.

"Toward a Restatement of Demographic Transition Theory," by John C. Caldwell, reprinted with the permission of the Population Council from John C. Caldwell, "Toward a Restatement of Demographic Transition Theory," *Population and Development Review* 2(3–4), pp. 321–366, December, 1976.

"Population Increase of States from 1970 to 1980 (%)." Copyright © The Population Reference Bureau, Inc., Washington, DC.

"Six Demographic Surprises of the 1970s," from "U.S. Population: Where We Are, Where We're Going," *Population Bulletin* 37(2), p. 33. Copyright © The Population Reference Bureau, Inc., Washington, DC, June, 1982.

"What's in Store for U.S. Population Trends in the 1980s?" in "U.S. Population: Where We Are, Where We're Going," *Population Bulletin* 37(2), p. 33. Copyright © The Population Reference Bureau, Inc., Washington, DC, June, 1982.

"U.S. Population Growth: Prospects and Policy," by Joseph A. McFalls, Jr., et al. Reprinted from *USA Today,* January, 1984. Copyright © 1984 by the Society for the Advancement of Education.

Thomas Robert Malthus, "An Essay on the Principle of Population" (1798), is in the public domain.

Excerpt from Friedrich Engels, *Outlines of a Critique of Political Economy,* from *Marx and Engels: Collected Works,* volume 3. New York: International Publishers Co., Inc. The edited version presented here originally appeared in *Marx and Engels on the Population Bomb,* edited by Ronald L. Meek, Ramparts Press, 1971.

"The Tragedy of the Commons," by Garrett Hardin, *Science* volume 162, pp. 1243–1248, 13 December 1968. Copyright © 1968 by the American Association for the Advancement of Science.

"Food First," by Frances Moore Lappe and Joe Collins, from *The New Internationalist,* volume 42, pp. 5–9. Copyright © 1976, Institute for Food and Development Policy.

The Global 2000 Report to the President (Washington, DC: U.S. Government Printing Office, 1980) is in the public domain.

"World Population Growth: An Anti-Doomsday View," by Julian L. Simon, reprinted from the *Atlantic Monthly,* August, 1981, by permission of the author and publisher.

"Ways of Life, Ways of Death," from *The Picture of Health: Environmental Sources of Disease,* by Erik P. Eckholm, reprinted by permission of W. W. Norton & Company, Inc. Copyright © 1977 by Worldwatch Institute.

"Sex, Marital Status, and Mortality," by Walter R. Gove, *American Journal of Sociology* 79(1), pp. 45–67, July, 1973.

"The Case of the Elusive Infant Mortality Rate," by Robert B. Hartford, *Population Today,* pp. 6–7. Copyright © The Population Reference Bureau, Inc., Washington, DC, May, 1984.

"Some Causes of Rising Mortality in the U.S.S.R. ," by S. Maksudov, reprinted by permission of the author.

"Why High Birth Rates Are So Low," Reprinted with the permission of the Population Council from John Bongaarts, "Why High Birth Rates Are So Low," *Population and Development Review,* 1(2), pp. 289–296, December, 1975.

"Frustrated Fertility: A Population Paradox," by Joseph A. McFalls, Jr., *Population Bulletin* 34(2), pp. 3–10. Copyright © The Population Reference Bureau, Inc., Washington, DC, May, 1979.

"Couples' Decision-Making Processes Regarding Fertility," by Linda J. Beckman, from *Social Demography,* edited by Karl E. Taeuber, et al., pp. 57–81. Copyright © Academic Press, Inc., 1978. All rights reserved.

"Building a Family: Unplanned Events." Reprinted with the permission of the Population Council from John Bongaarts, "Building a Family: Unplanned Events," *Studies in Family Planning* 15(1), pp. 14–19, February, 1984.

"The Asset Demand for Children During Agricultural Modernization." Reprinted with the permission of the Population Council from Oded Stark, "The Asset Demand for Children during Agricultural Modernization," *Population and Development Review* 7(4), pp. 671–675, December, 1981.

"Declining World Fertility: Trends, Causes, Implications," by Amy Ong Tsui and Donald J. Bogue, *Population Bulletin* 33(4), pp. 3–6 and 30–34. Copyright © The Population Reference Bureau, Inc., Washington, DC, October, 1978.

"The Relative Importance of Family Planning and Development for Fertility Reduction: Critique of Research and Development of Theory," by Scott Menard and Elizabeth W. Moen, *Studies in Comparative International Development* XVII(3–4), 1982. Copyright © 1982 by Transaction, Inc. Reprinted by permission of authors.

"The Holy War," by Patricia Donovan, reprinted with permission from *Family Planning Perspectives* 17(1), 1985.

"Eastern Europe: Pronatalist Policies and Private Behavior," by Henry P. David, *Population Bulletin* 36(6), pp. 3–13 and 43–44. Copyright © The Population Reference Bureau, Inc., Washington, DC, February, 1982.

"Fertility Policy in India," by Vina Mazumdar, from J. Lipman-Blumen and J. Bernard, *Sex Roles and Social Policy,* Sage, 1978.

"Resistance to the One-Child Family," by Jeffrey Wasserstrom, *Modern China* 10(3), pp. 345–358, July, 1984. Copyright © 1984 Sage Publications, Inc. Reprinted by permission of Sage Publications, Inc.

"What Does 'Control Over Our Bodies' Really Mean?" by Elizabeth W. Moen, *International Journal of Women's Studies* 2(2), pp. 129–143, 1979. Reprinted by permission of the author.

"Illegal Immigration and the International System, Lessons from Recent Legal Mexican Immigrants to the United States," by Alejandro Portes, *Social Problems* 24(4), pp. 425–438, April, 1979. Reprinted by permission of the Society for the Study of Social Problems and the author.

"Airborne Migrants Study Urged," *Intercom* 7(11–12), p. 3. Copyright © The Population Reference Bureau, Inc., Washington, DC, November/December, 1979.

"Refugees: The New International Politics of Displacement," by Kathleen Newland, Worldwatch Paper 43, March, 1981. Copyright © Worldwatch Institute, 1981.

"The Urbanization of the Human Population," by Kingsley Davis, *Scientific American,* September, 1965. Copyright © by Scientific American, Inc. All rights reserved.

Preface from *Urbanization in Latin America* by Jorge E. Hardoy. Copyright © 1975 by Doubleday & Company, Inc. Reprinted by permission of the publisher.

"The Migration Turnaround: End of a Phenomenon?" by Anthony Agresta, *Population Today* 13(1), pp. 6–7. Copyright © The Population Reference Bureau, Inc., Washington, DC, January, 1985.

"Sun Belt Growth: Not What It Seems?" by Carl Haub, *Population Today* 12(1), pp. 6–7. Copyright © The Population Reference Bureau, Inc., Washington, DC, January, 1984.

"Cross-National Comparisons of Population Density," by Alice Taylor Day and Lincoln H. Day, *Science* volume 181, pp. 1016–1023, 14 September 1973. Copyright © 1973 by the American Association for the Advancement of Science.

"Density-Intensity: A Theory of Crowding," from *Crowding and Behavior* by Jonathan L. Freedman. W. H. Freeman and Company. Copyright © 1975.

"How a Population Ages or Grows Younger" by Ansley J. Coale from *Population: The Vital Revolution,* edited by Ronald Freedman. Copyright © 1964 by Doubleday & Company, Inc. Reprinted by permission of the publisher.

"Progress of Depression Cohort, Baby Boom Cohort, and Baby Bust Cohort Through U.S. Population Age-Sex Pyramid: 1960–2050," by Leon F. Bouvier, *Population Bulletin* 35(1), pp. 18–19. Copyright © The Population Reference Bureau, Inc., Washington, DC, April, 1980.

"The 'Good Times' Cohort of the 1930s," by Carl L. Harter, *PRB Report* 3(3). Copyright © The Population Reference Bureau, Inc., Washington, DC, April, 1977.

"Children and the Elderly: Divergent Paths for America's Dependents," by Samuel H. Preston, *Demography* 21(4), pp. 435–457, November, 1984. Reprinted with permission of the Population Association of America.

"The Status of Majority and Minority Groups in the United States Today," from *Majority-Minority Relations,* by John E. Farley, Copyright © 1982, pp. 204–216, 218–222. Reprinted by permission of Prentice-Hall, Inc., Englewood Cliffs, NJ.

"Family Configuration and Intelligence," by R. B. Zajonc, *Science* volume 192, pp. 227–236, 16 April 1976. Copyright © 1976 by the American Association for the Advancement of Science.

Why Have a Census? (Washington, DC: U.S. Census Bureau, 1979) is in the public domain.

"The U.S. Census Undercount," by Philip M. Hauser, *Asian and Pacific Census Forum* 8(2), November, 1981.

"Trends and Prospects," by Everett S. Lee, with Harold F. Goldsmith, Michael Greenberg, and Donald B. Pittenger, from *Population Estimates: Methods for Small Area Analysis,* edited by Everett S. Lee and Harold F. Goldsmith. Copyright © 1982 Sage Publications, Inc. Reprinted by permission of Sage Publications, Inc.

"Voodoo Forecasting: Technical, Political, and Ethical Issues Regarding the Projection of Local Population Growth," by Elizabeth W. Moen, *Population Research and Policy Review,* volume 3, pp. 1–25, 1984. Copyright © Elsevier Science Publishers B. B., Amsterdam. Reprinted by permission of the author.

Using This Book

This reader is intended as a textbook to be used in undergraduate or graduate courses, either alone, as a supplement to a standard population text, or in conjunction with one or more supplementary paperback texts. In addition, it is designed to be a sourcebook for professionals in the field of population. To serve both of these ends, it has been necessary to include chapters of varying conceptual and technical difficulty; not all of them are appropriate for all levels of instruction. As a rough guide, chapters are classified below as "beginning," "intermediate," or "advanced" level. Classification as a beginning-level chapter does not mean that the chapter is inappropriate for use in a graduate course; it only means that the chapter is one which may readily be comprehended by readers with limited conceptual and technical background in population studies.

Beginning	*Intermediate*	*Advanced*
1–4	5, 7	6
8–15	16–18	
19, 20		21
22		23–25
26, 27	28	
29	30, 31	
32	33	
34, 35	36	37
38	39	
40	41	
42	43	
44	45	46
	47	

These classifications are, of course, rough and subjective, and instructors may wish to use some of the "advanced" chapters in a beginning class. This is entirely appropriate as long as the material is carefully explained.

We believe that the book can stand on its own or with limited supplementary material as the primary text in a course on population. To this end, we have included introductions to the sections which briefly summarize the basic material presented in most population textbooks. These introductions include material on the basic rates and measures used in demography, and also material which helps place the chapters in perspective with respect to the general field of population studies and social demography. References used in the part introductions are placed at the end of the book, following the readings.

FOR FURTHER READING

At the end of the introduction to each part of the book are several suggestions for further reading. These suggestions are, with few exceptions, books that provide more extensive detail on topics covered in that part of the book. Readings listed here are appropriate for beginning students unless otherwise noted. The principal criteria for selecting the recommended readings were readability and importance. Some readings were not selected, not because they fail either of these criteria, but because we thought something else was better or more appropriate as a next step after this reader.

Three agencies deserve special mention as sources of information on population. The Population Reference Bureau (from which are several selections included in this reader) is a nonprofit organization that publishes the *Population Bulletin* and *Population Today*. The *Population Bulletin* is published quarterly, and each edition examines a specific topic in detail, but at a level comprehensible by the general, nontechnical reader. *Population Today* is a bimonthly newsletter that provides brief, readable summaries of population news. For more advanced reading, the publications of the Population Council, including *Studies in Family Planning* and the *Population and Development Review* are two of the leading sources of articles on population. *Population and Development Review* is a quarterly journal with articles of varying, but often high, technical sophistication in the general area of population studies; *Studies in Family Planning* focuses on family planning programs and often has more of an appeal to family planning practitioners. Finally, for those who want exhaustive material at the highest level of sophistication, the publications of the Population Association of America include the journal *Demography,* with general articles in the various fields of population studies, and the *Population Index,* which often includes short articles but is primarily a bibliographic source that abstracts articles published on population. Also worth mentioning is the Worldwatch Association, which publishes a series of papers on environmental concerns, including many that are directly related to population.

Annotated Contents

Perspectives on Population

PART I

POPULATION GROWTH AND DECLINE IN HISTORY

Most of us are probably familiar with graphs that describe the growth of the human population. As shown in Figure 1.1, there is a long horizontal line that at first rises almost imperceptibly, then faster, and then starting fewer than fifty years ago it takes off into a nearly vertical flight. Those who dare to predict what might happen in the future come to radically different conclusions. The optimists, and those who consider the "S" shaped curve of exponential growth (of which population is an example) to be a natural law, predict (or hope) that the curve will become a horizontal line again as the result of reduced fertility rather than increased mortality, and that it will do so at a population size that can be sustained by its social systems and the earth's biophysical systems. The superoptimists envision a trouble-free continuation of the present vertical trend, with technology compensating for ever-larger population by providing increased access to the resources of the earth and the solar system, and substitutions for those which are non-renewable. The pessimists, by contrast, envision a population "crash" in which the upward vertical line is quickly reversed and becomes a downward plunge as the social and biophysical systems break down under the crushing weight of overpopulation.

The causes, consequences, pros, cons, and projections of population growth are topics of great importance and controversy that will be discussed throughout this book, and especially in Parts II and VII. In this part, we concentrate on the known part of the world population growth curve, but we also acknowledge three possible, but very different, population futures. One future, desired by many, is zero population growth (ZPG). The other two possibilities, considered in more detail in Part II, are those of continued growth envisioned by the superoptimists and of massive population decline envisioned by the pessimists.

MEASURING POPULATION GROWTH

Population growth or decline (often called "negative growth") can occur in only two ways: through *natural increase* (or decrease), the difference between the number of births and the number of deaths, and through *net migration,* the difference between the number of people who move into an area (immigration or in-migration) and the number who move out (emigration or out-migration). The relationship among these is illustrated in the *balancing equation* for population:

$$\text{Population growth} = \text{natural increase} + \text{net migration, or}$$
$$P_{\text{time 2}} - P_{\text{time 1}} = \text{Births} - \text{Deaths} + \text{Immigration} - \text{Emigration}$$

where the births, deaths, immigration, and emigration occur between time 1 and time 2. The equation can also be used for rates of growth, natural increase, and net migration, as long as all the terms in the equation are expressed in terms of rates. (Growth rates, unless otherwise specified, generally refer to a combination of natural increase and net migration. The term is also sometimes used, especially in nontechnical literature, to refer only to the rate of natural increase.)

Migration can have substantial influence on national population growth and decline (e.g., the massive migrations from the Old World of the Eastern Hemisphere to the New World of the West) as well as on subnational growth and decline (e.g., the historic movement in the United States from the East Coast to the Midwest and the West). Still, until we can live elsewhere in our solar system or until we have immigrants from outer space, migration cannot affect the size of the world's population.

In 1984, according to the population Reference Bureau (1984), the world population was growing at 1.7 percent per year. More developed countries (MDCs), those countries with higher levels of per capita gross national product, urbanization, industrialization, and so forth, had a rate of natural increase of 0.6 percent, while less developed countries (LDCs) had a 2.1 percent rate of natural increase (2.4 percent if China is excluded). Although national rates of growth seem to be very low, they are deceptive. This is because exponential growth is like a bank account with interest being calculated continuously and immediately added to the principal.

The momentum of exponential growth may be illustrated by *doubling time,* the time it takes a population to double itself. A simple and fairly accurate method for calculating the doubling time is to divide the number 70 by the annual rate of growth, expressed as a percentage. For example, a 2 percent annual growth rate means a doubling of the population in (70/2 =) 35 years, while a 3 percent growth rate causes the population to double in just over 23 years. In 1984, Kenya, the fastest growing population in the world, had a population of 194 million, a birth rate of 53 births per 1000 people, and a death rate of 13 deaths per 1000 people. The annual rate of growth by natural increase was (53 − 13)/1000 = 4 percent. With a doubling time of 70/4 = 17.5 years, if the growth rate remains stable, Kenya's population will reach 388 million sometime in the year 2001. If the 1984 world population growth rates were sustained into the next 80 years, the world population would increase from approximately 4.76 billion in 1984 to 12.5 billion in 2064 (Population Reference Bureau, 1984a).

In Chapter 1, Menard provides a brief history of world population growth and the major events that reduced (or sometimes increased) mortality. The main point of this chapter is that population growth has not taken a smooth, steady course, and that there has been considerable regional diversity in the timing and rates of population growth and decline.

THE DEMOGRAPHIC TRANSITION

The population dynamics of the now-MDCs that have moved from a low rate of growth with high mortality and high fertility to a very low rate of growth with low mortality and low fertility has been termed the *demographic transition.* Although Chapter 1 shows that there are exceptions to the general pattern, and the dates of the transition have varied considerably from country to country, in nearly every case there was a lag between the decline in mortality and the decline in fertility which created a period of rapid population growth.

Since World War II, many of the LDCs have experienced a rapid decline in mortality, without a corresponding decline in fertility, resulting in rapid population growth. During the last twenty years, demographers have anticipated (or hoped for) a decline in fertility as a "natural response" to mortality decline, or in response to the provision of birth control education and services (contraception, abortion, sterilization) to families who were presumed to have an "unmet need" for such services.

Fertility has declined in the LDCs, but mostly as a result of substantial declines in China and a handful of smaller countries. In 1984, natural increase in the LDCs ranged from 4 percent in Kenya to 0.9 percent in Uruguay. With a sustained growth rate at current levels (around 2 percent), the LDCs will double their population in just 35 years.

The history of the demographic transition and the theory as it applies particularly to LDCs are examined in Chapters 4 to 6. A common theme of these articles is that people behave rationally, and although fertility is not under perfect control, family size in different nations or cultures reflects choices made for rational reasons. When there is the right combination of economic, psychological, and cultural reasons and support for people to have smaller families, they do—even without modern family planning services. This suggests that we should not expect a voluntary decline in LDC fertility without social change conducive to such a decline.

As Kingsley Davis points out in Chapter 5, which was originally published in 1963, the reduction of fertility through the adoption of modern family planning methods is not the only response to increased population growth associated with reduced mortality. Migration, infanticide, delayed marriage, and periods of abstinence within marriage can all have the same effect. Teitelbaum and Caldwell in Chapters 4 and 6 show that the situation of the LDCs is much too complex and too different from the MDCs when they were undergoing their demographic transition to expect the people of these nations to behave in the same way, or to respond to those who offer modern family planning services in the same way as current residents of the MDCs. Teitelbaum, writing in 1975, provides a good summary of demographic transition theory, and a detailed examination of the differences between conditions in present-day LDCs and present-day MDCs prior to their fertility declines. Caldwell, writing in 1976, proposes a modification of demographic transition theory. He suggests that high fertility is characteristic of societies in which wealth flows from children to their parents. Fertility declines occur when the direction of this wealth flow shifts, when wealth flows instead from parents to their children. Historically, this has occurred in conjunction with economic modernization, but Caldwell notes that the social, rather than economic, process of *Westernization,* including the spread of mass education and mass media and the increasing nucleation of the family, is responsible for more recent declines in fertility. Caldwell's chapter also includes a good discussion of the history of demographic transition theory.

For all the modifications that have been proposed in transition theory, the key to the demographic transition is still mortality. As King et al. (1974:10) observed a decade ago,

> About 40 percent of the world's population live in countries with both high birth and death rates. The remainder are divided equally between (a) countries which have low mortality but high birth rates and (b) those which have low birth as well as death rates. No country has a birth rate below 30 and a death rate about 15; it appears that birth rates fall to low levels only after a decline in death rates.

King's observation concerning the relationship between mortality rates and fertility rates is as valid now as it was in 1974 (Population Reference Bureau, 1984a). We should not forget that the initial statement of demographic transition theory concerned only the long-term aggregate national relationship between mortality and fertility; that elementary statement of the theory may still be the most valid: before fertility rates decline, death rates must show a substantial, sustained decline. Although some may question this formulation, the cross-sectional (King et al., 1974) and longitudinal (Menard, 1983) relationship between mortality and fertility is something which must be explained in any complete theory of population change.

Preston (1978) describes two possible strategies people may adopt in response to infant and childhood mortality. The first, a *replacement* strategy, is when parents respond to the death of an infant or a child by having another child, in effect "replacing" the child that died. A second strategy is one Preston calls a *hoarding* strategy. Rather than wait to see if a child reaches adulthood, parents may have as many children as they think they will need to ensure that some reach adulthood. In a high-mortality society, the hoarding strategy is more rational, for it guards against the effects not only of mortality in infancy and early childhood, but also those that occur in later childhood, which are rare in low mortality societies but more common in societies with high mortality. For example, causes of mortality differ in more and less developed countries, as do rates of mortality (see Part III). In less developed countries, where there is higher risk of death at all ages, it may not be possible to "replace" older children lost to plague or famine (more likely to occur in less developed or high mortality societies). Not only may plague or famine kill women capable of bearing children, but it is also possible that women with older children may be past their childbearing years or otherwise unable to bear more children (see Chapters 19 and 20). As a result, those high mortality societies that adopt a replacement strategy are more vulnerable and less likely to survive than those that adopt a hoarding strategy. In terms of societal survival, then, it would be rational *not* to respond to short-term changes in mortality with immediate changes in fertility; instead, the rational course is to respond only to long-term, stable declines in mortality by reducing fertility.

DEPOPULATION

One important but often overlooked deviation from the general pattern of population growth is depopulation. Throughout history and even today parts of the world's population are declining. Such declines can result from migration as in the case of the Irish potato famine, which began in 1846. From 1846 to 1851, approximately 1 million people left Ireland, and the Irish population had fallen from a high of 8.5 million in 1845 to barely more than half that number, 4.5 million, in 1900. This decline, especially in the latter part of the nineteenth century, reflected falling birth rates as well as extensive emigration (McEvedy and Jones, 1978). The more usual cause of depopulation historically and today is that deaths exceed births.

Six countries (Denmark, East and West Germany, Hungary, Luxembourg, and Sweden) presently have a zero or negative rate of natural increase because of low levels of both fertility and mortality (Population Reference Bureau, 1984a). These countries are all in Europe, and while some (such as Denmark) are satisfied with a zero or negative growth rate, others (such as East and West Germany) are concerned that zero or negative natural increase will bring problems in the future. Because natural increase is only one component of growth, even countries with zero or negative natural increase may be growing because of migration into the country.

More tragic is the situation in which depopulation occurs through high mortality. Infectious diseases have ravaged nations and continents. As we write this, major famines are occurring or have recently occurred in sub-Saharan Africa: Niger, Mozambique, and Ethiopia are three recent, dramatic cases. Equally tragic has been the accidental and deliberate devastation of native populations in Africa, Asia, Oceania, and the Americas by European invaders, conquerors, and colonists. Chapters 2 and 3 deal with historical patterns of depopulation, both inadvertent and deliberate. For a contemporary example, see Davis' (1977) study of development and the Indians of Brazil.

Another potential source of depopulation is war. Historically, depopulation resulting solely from war has been temporary and has usually had local rather than global effects. Now, however, with over 50,000 nuclear weapons that are 50 to 1,000 times more powerful than those that devastated Hiroshima and Nagasaki, human extinction is a real possibility. Although governments speak of "limited" or "winnable" nuclear war and the U.S. Federal Emergency Management Agency (FEMA) proposed mass evacuation from ground zero to allegedly safer sites thirty or so miles away—we are told to pack as if for a two-week vacation (Scheer, 1982; Corbett, 1983)—civilian and military experts from the United States and the Soviet Union tell us that nuclear war cannot be limited, cannot be won, and cannot be survived (Kenan, 1982; LaRoque, 1983). One of the first groups in the United States to publicize the horrors of nuclear war was Physicians for Social Responsibility (PSR), led by Helen Caldicott. They declared that there could be no medical response to nuclear war because most health workers would be dead or dying, disease would be rampant, and water, sewage, food, shelter, and medical systems would be demolished. Life expectancy at birth in the industrialized countries after a large-scale nuclear war would "at best" be reduced to "40 or 50 years among the survivors, who might number about half the prewar population" (Coale, 1985:487). PSR concluded that the only morally responsible action for health workers would be to try to prevent nuclear war (Caldicott, 1980; Geiger, 1980).

Jonathan Schell, in *The Fate of the Earth* (1982) described the immediate effects of the blast waves, firestorms, heat, blinding light, electromagnetic pulse, and windstorms, as well as the longer-term sickness, death, and genetic damage from nuclear fallout and ozone depletion. He concluded that the atmospheric effects of fallout and smoke would create such an ecological catastrophe that earth could no longer sustain life. Studies of the "Nuclear Winter" effect (Raloff, 1983) are providing confirmation that even with less than full-scale nuclear war, worldwide fallout of dust and debris would block sunlight long enough that the resulting darkness and cold would not only make the earth inhospitable but would also block photosynthesis. With no plant life, there would be no animal life (Raloff, 1983; Turco et al., 1984; Weston, 1984; London and White, 1984). Schell concludes that the issue is no longer war or peace but extinction or peace.

No one knows for certain if all the predictions concerning the effects of a nuclear holocaust will come true. We hope no one ever will. In considering whether we are capable of initiating such destruction, and what effects it may have on the survivors, the chapters by McNeill and Bodley may, however, give some indication, based on historical experience. As history indicates, we are capable of inflicting incredible suffering, both deliberately and inadvertently. The slaughter of European Jews in the Holocaust of World War II, the devastation accompanying the creation of Pakistan and then Bangladesh, and more recent wars in Southeast Asia and the Middle East are all examples of the extent to which we are capable of massive extermination of our fellow human beings. The devastation of the famines in sub-Saharan Africa speak at one and the same time of the threat of traditional sources of depopulation even in the modern world, and our willingness to help those we perceive as innocent victims in need. What choices will we make in the future?

THE FUTURE OF U.S. POPULATION GROWTH

Even in technologically and statistically sophisticated MDCs, it is difficult to make accurate short-term predictions about population growth, much less formulate demographic policy that should be effective in the long run. Calvin Beale, writing for the Population Reference Bureau (1982) has identified six demographic trends in the United States in the 1970s that took demographers by surprise: fewer births, greater life expectancy, smaller household sizes, regional shifts in population, growth of the nonmetropolitan population, and larger numbers of illegal immigrants and refugees. Demographers who failed to forsee these trends in the 1970s, are able to do little more than predict a continuation of these trends into the 1980s and 1990s.

If the world manages to prevent violent depopulation and growth rates too high to be sustained, what will the future be like? As McFalls points out in Chapter 8, many believe that zero population growth (ZPG) is not only the preferred but also the only option. For them, the primary question is how soon and at what population size should ZPG be initiated. The Commission on Population Growth and the American Future (1972) concluded that this country would be better off in all ways with ZPG, and bioeconomists like Herman Daly believe that ZPG and zero economic growth are necessary because the environment, on which all human economic and social activities are dependent, cannot support and accommodate these activities at ever increasing rates. Global climate changes and the rapidly increasing costs of exploiting natural resources and natural pollution reservoirs are just two indications that there are social and environmental limits to growth (Brown, 1981; Brown et al., 1984; Daly, 1980; Commoner, 1972).

The generally preferred future, ZPG, is actually a return to the past, only now ZPG can be attained through low birth and death rates rather than high birth and death rates. ZPG occurs when the birth rate equals the death rate, as in Sweden where in 1984 there were 11 deaths and 11 births for every 1,000 population. (Sweden, however, continued to grow as a result of net migration.) ZPG is sustained in the long run through replacement fertility—when, on the average, each woman bears two children. Actually, to compensate for voluntary and involuntary infertility and the death of children before they replace themselves, replacement fertility must be a little more than two. In the United States and similar low-mortality nations, replacement fertility is about 2.1 children per woman. In Chapter 8, the implications of positive, negative, and zero growth are discussed, along with practical problems of attaining and maintaining ZPG.

FOR FURTHER READING

Colin McEvedy and Richard Jones. 1978. *Atlas of World Population History* (New York: Penguin) is the most complete overview of world population history and is broken down by regions. Although some of the data presented are no better than educated guesses, this is a valuable reference book. The information is presented in the form of graphs of population over time, to which the authors add limited commentary and extensive documentation of their sources.

Annabelle Desmond. 1962. "How Many People Have Ever Lived on Earth?" *Population Bulletin* 18(1):1–19; reprinted in Kenneth C. W. Kammeyer (ed.), *Population Studies,* second edition (Chicago: Rand McNally) is a short, readable summary of world population history.

Carlo Cipolla. 1978. *The Economic History of World Population* (New York: Penguin) is also a short, readable summary of world population history, more extensive in its coverage than the article by Desmond, and with the economic slant implied in the title.

1

Regional Variations in Population Histories

SCOTT MENARD

Most of the history of the human population on the earth is one of gradual increase in both absolute numbers and the rate of population growth. More recently, both growth rates and absolute numbers of the human population have skyrocketed. In a period variously estimated at 0.5 to 2 percent of the total amount of time since the first humans appeared on earth, over three-fourths of the growth in the human population has taken place (Coale, 1974:16; van der Tak et al., 1979:4). This long-term pattern and the more recent rapid growth are illustrated in Figure 1.1.

Such descriptions of world population growth tell an important part, but only a part, of human population history. They mask enormous declines in populations suffered by some regions, even as others experienced relatively rapid growth. They miss periods in some regions when populations doubled in as little as a century, although the world population as a whole was taking 600 to 1,000 years to double. Much of the apparent stability in world population size before 1750 A.D. represented a balance among regional stability, rapid growth, and decline in population.

Figure 1.1. World population growth over time.

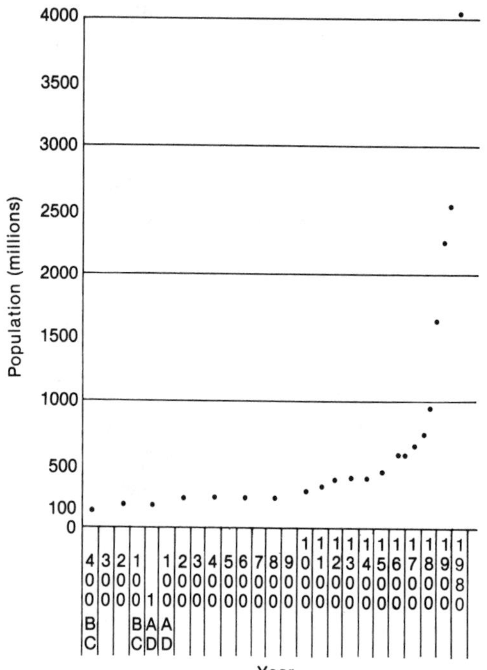

Human population history may conveniently be divided into four eras or periods. The first period is the paleolithic or Old Stone Age, which began about 1 million years ago (Desmond, 1962; Coale, 1974; Thomlinson, 1976:17; van der Tak et al., 1979), when humans first began using tools. From this earliest time in human prehistory until about 10,000 years ago, for 99 percent of human history, all human societies probably lived by hunting and gathering or, beginning perhaps 12,000 years ago, fishing and gathering (Lenski and Lenski, 1982:87–88). McNeill (1976:19–30) suggests that as long as 40,000 years ago, regional variations in population size, density, and growth rates may have been emerging. McNeill suggests (p. 25) that, "In leaving tropical environments behind, our ancestors also escaped many of the parasites and disease organisms to which their predecessors and tropical contemporaries were accustomed. Health and vigor improved accordingly, and multiplication of human numbers assumed a hitherto unparalleled scale."

Much of the population growth in this first era was made possible by the migration of hunting and gathering bands to new territory. From Africa, the population spread to West Asia, then northwest to Europe, eastward to India and China, and across the Bering Strait to the Americas. Aside from inferring a pattern of long-term growth and widespread migration, we can do little more than guess at patterns of population change during this period.[2] We cannot know for certain whether growth rates were fairly constant or whether they underwent a substantial increase in the last 20,000 years of this era.

Paleolithic hunting and gathering societies have existed for all of human history, and with them a characteristic pattern of moderate rates of births and deaths, slow rates of growth, and low population density (Dumond, 1975; Lenski and Lenski, 1982:111–113). The number of hunters and gatherers has been declining for the past 10,000 years, and hunting and gathering societies may be extinct by the end of this century (Lenski and Lenski, 1982:132–133). The beginning of their decline coincides with and was probably attributable to the development of a new means of subsistence for human populations: agriculture.

THE SECOND ERA

The beginning of agriculture about 10,000 years ago is widely accepted as the first major influence on human population size and growth since the development of tools during the paleolithic period (Coale, 1974; Thomlinson, 1976:17; Wrong, 1977:14; Cipolla, 1978:18–19; McEvedy and Jones, 1978:343). The increase in the rate of growth in population began in the Near East and spread to Europe, North Africa, and mainland Asia; by 5000 or 6000 B.C. (or B.C.E.) it was widespread enough to influence population size and growth rates for the world as a whole (Desmond, 1962; McEvedy and Jones, 1978:343). McEvedy and Jones call this the *primary cycle* of population growth. Growth began slowly at the beginning of the agricultural revolution (8000 B.C.), peaked at the beginning of the Iron Age (1000 B.C.), then gradually leveled off by about 500 A.D. (or C.E.). The agriculatural revolution may be considered complete around 1000 A.D., when it had spread through Europe, Asia, the Americas, Melanesia, and practically all of Africa (Bohannon and Curtin, 1971:221; Cipolla, 1978:18–27). The period from 8000 B.C. to 1000 A.D. is marked by slow growth of the world population as a whole and by sharp variations in regional patterns of population growth.

According to the data in McEvedy and Jones (1978), sub-Saharan Africa (roughly all of Africa except Egypt, Libya, Tunisia, Algeria, and Morocco) was increasing in population at a fairly substantial rate in the second demographic era. In the last 1,000 years of the second era, A.D. 1 to 1000, populations of all but the Kalahari desert region (Botswana and Namibia in present-day Africa) and the Sudan at least doubled. In the equatorial regions (from Cameroon and Gabon in the west to Tanzania and Kenya in the east), population size quadrupled in the west and increased tenfold in the east. In southeast Africa, it more than quintupled. The population of Madagascar appears to have doubled in a 200-year period from 800 to 1000 A.D. These rates of increase are the highest of any area during this period. North Africa, by contrast, was experiencing upswings and downswings in population during these last 1,000 years of the second era. Populations in present-day Algeria, Tunisia, Libya, and Egypt peaked under the Roman empire (200 A.D.), then declined as the empire began to fall apart. Around 600 A.D., just before the spread of Islam through North Africa, population in this region reached its low point. By 700 A.D., when the Arabs had conquered practically all of North Africa (Grun, 1979:68–70), population had once again started to increase, and the increase continued to the year 1000.

Those areas of Europe which did not come under Roman rule (Ireland, Scotland, Scandinavia, European Russia) experienced a slow, stable increase in the second era. The pattern was much like that of sub-Saharan Africa, but less dramatic. The Romanized part of Europe, by contrast, mirrored the North African pattern to varying degrees. The mass migrations of the German tribes—Franks into Gaul, Angles and Saxons into Britain, Goths and Vandals as far as Rome itself—and the expansion of the Slavs and Huns in eastern Europe combined with a general economic collapse (Greer, 1972:82) resulted in widespread depopulation. The effects were most severe in present-day France (38 percent population decline largely as a result of the Frankish invasions), Czechoslovakia (44 percent decline in the dispersion of the Slavs), the Balkan countries (40 percent decline in the wake of Slavic expansion and general economic decline), and Italy, where population may have declined by half, from a high of 7 million in 200 A.D. to a low of 3.5 million in 600 A.D. By the year 1000, European populations were once again increasing.

The Mediterranean coast of West Asia experienced the same pattern as North Africa and Roman Europe. Its population declined with the fall of Rome and increased after 600 or 700 A.D. The population of the Arabian peninsula maintained a pattern of increase until the eighth century A.D. Their subsequent decline in population coincided roughly with a period of military setbacks for the expanding Islamic empire: first, the destruction of the

Arab fleet by Leo III at Constantinople in 718, then Charles Martel's victory over the Arabs in France in 732 (Grun, 1979:72–74). Thereafter, Moslem expansion was halted and even reversed in Europe. The rest of the Near East during this period was marked by a series of irregular fluctuations in population, the most notable of which was the doubling of the population of present-day Iraq when the caliphate of al-Mansur moved from Damascus to Baghdad in 763 (Grun, 1979:80).

In eastern Asia, the vast waste of Siberia maintained a small, fairly stable population. China proper—that part of China bounded on the north and west by the Great Wall, and south and west by the Tibetan plateau—went through a period of fluctuation. Population size reached a peak under the Han dynasty, then declined as the dynasty declined. At the end of the second era, population was again increasing under the centralized and prosperous T'ang and Sung dynasties (Quale, 1966:265–267). The rest of Asia appears to have followed a pattern of fairly rapid population growth, with some populations (Korea and Japan) doubling in periods as short as 200 years, and most of the rest doubling over the first millennium of the Christian era. Oceania during the second era grew slowly, led by Melanesia, which entered the neolithic agricultural phase before its neighbors. The population of present-day Anglo-America (Canada and the United States) was small and growing slowly to moderately, as was that of Latin America and the Caribbean islands.

In summary, the second demographic era was marked by considerable diversity in patterns of population growth. Sub-Saharan Africa and much of eastern Asia experienced fairly rapid and continuous growth, while Oceania, Siberia, and the Americas experienced slower growth or stability. It is interesting to note that the areas that were suffering population declines toward the end of the second era were those dominated by the great empires, Rome in the west and China in the east. McNeill (1976:69–131) suggests that at the end of this period, increasing urbanization and trade facilitated the spread of infectious diseases from one geographic region to another, and that these diseases were more likely to result in epidemics in the more urbanized areas under imperial control than in the more sparsely settled outlying areas. The Roman epidemics of the second and third centuries (Desmond, 1962) may be examples of this phenomenon, and may have contributed to both the depopulation and the decline of the Roman empire.

THE THIRD ERA

The third era was a time of transition between the culmination of the agricultural revolution and the inception of the Industrial Revolution. By A.D. 1000, Venetian power in the Mediterranean was on the rise, Islam was solidly established in North Africa and the Middle East, Christianity had spread as far west as Iceland and Greenland, the Mayan and Tihuanaco civilizations were at their height in the Americas, and the Chinese had perfected gunpowder (Grun, 1979:124–125). India was divided between Moslem rule in the north and a unified Dravidian empire in the south (Quale, 1966:162–163). From 1000 A.D. to the industrial revolution, around 1750 A.D., world population twice went through a pattern of increase, followed by a leveling off and then a slight decline. Overall, the rate of growth was more rapid but less consistent than it was in the second era.

For sub-Saharan Africa, this was a period of continued but slower growth. The Ghana empire in the west and the Songhay empire in the western Sudan reached their respective heights during this period and then declined as trans-Saharan trade declined (Gugler and Flanagan, 1978). For North Africa, this was a period of fluctuation, increases, and declines with no clear upward trend in the long run. During this period, Mediterranean Africa was alternating between periods of invasion or pestilence and periods of recovery. In Europe, the fluctuation of the previous era continued, but a clear upward trend was established. Population declined dramatically twice during this era. The first decline occurred in the second half of the fourteenth century, as the Black Death devastated all of Europe. Then, between 1600 and 1650, economic setbacks in southern Europe and the Thirty Years War in central Europe led to a second, less dramatic decline in population. Despite these reversals, European population increased nearly fourfold during this era. African population, by contrast, had barely doubled. (In east and southeast Africa population trebled, and on Madagascar it increased by a factor of 6, but these figures represent *slower* growth than that of the second era.)

The Arabian peninsula ended a period of population decline in 1000. During the third era, the Arabian peninsula and the rest of the Middle East experienced the same pattern as that in North Africa: fluctuation with no clear trend. In the thirteenth and fourteenth centuries, Mongol invaders fought their way into the Middle East (Quale, 1966:58–59), and probably brought the bubonic plague with them (McNeill, 1976:165–167). The result was a decrease in population throughout the Middle East. In the seventeenth century, new trade routes around the southern tip of Africa brought a commercial collapse to the Middle East (except Turkey), and malnutrition and disease "cut the rural population to a fraction of its former size" (Quale, 1966:62). Only Turkey, of all the Middle Eastern countries, showed an increasing trend in population, coincident with the rise of the Ottoman empire.

Asiatic Russia in the third demographic era increased in population, again with the exception of Siberia, where population increased slightly only toward the end of the period. After an initial period of increase, the Mongolian population decreased as Ghengiz Khan led his horde out to conquer the world. After this decrease, the population appears to be stable, but the data are informed guesses at best.

China proper in the third period mirrors the European pattern, but with even more dramatic increases and decreases in population. The principal reason for population declines in China was a series of invasions, first the Mongols in the thirteenth century, and then the Manchu in the seventeenth. The Mongol invasion is estimated to have cost the Chinese one-fourth to one-third of their total population; the Manchu invasion resulted in a loss of one-sixth of the population (McEvedy and Jones, 1978:170–172). Despite these massive losses, Chinese population increased between threefold and fourfold during the third demographic era. The Mongol and Manchu invasions also resulted in some depopulation in Korea, but the rest of East Asia, Southeast Asia, and the Indian subcontinent appears to have experienced slow but steady growth comparable to that of the second era.

Oceania in the third era continued its slow, steady growth. Anglo-America maintained stable (in Canada) or growing population (in the United States), but this stability and growth masks a substantial decrease in the native population and the replacement of the native population with European colonists. The same pattern is true of the southern and eastern part of South America (Argentina, Brazil, Chile, and Paraguay). In the rest of South America, and in Central America, the Caribbean islands, and Mexico, the invasion of European colonists is more clearly reflected in the population declines these areas experienced. The declines were a result more of diseases passed from the Europeans to the native Americans than from military action, but both pestilence and war played a part (McNeill, 1976; Bodley, 1982).

THE INDUSTRIAL REVOLUTION AND THE FOURTH DEMOGRAPHIC ERA

The fourth and current era is characterized by population growth in all areas at a more rapid rate than before. The rapid upturn in population occurs earliest (1750 to 1850) in Europe, Anglo-America, the Caribbean, the Indian subcontinent, and China proper. Other areas followed around 1900, and by 1950 the population of the world and all its major areas had increased dramatically over levels circa 1750. Central to the explanation of the increase is the industrial revolution around 1750 and the declining mortality brought about by improved living conditions, particularly better nutrition and later better public health (Wrigley, 1969:168–181).[3] Most recently, fertility and population growth have declined for the European countries. The fertility decline began shortly after the decline in mortality, but was smaller in magnitude than the decline in the death rate. At present, most of these populations continue to increase, but at a slower rate than in other areas of the world. (Wrigley, 1969:207; United Nations, 1979).

An important difference between the fourth demographic era and previous eras is the source of population growth and decline. In previous eras, population appears to have grown during times of political stability and economic prosperity, and declined as a result of famine and pestilence during times of political and economic decline. This pattern is seen in the rise and decline of the Roman, Islamic, and Ottoman empires and in the Han, T'ang, and Sung dynasties. A third reason for population decline, intimately related to political stability and military strength, was the invasion of nomadic conquerors (Germanic tribes, Mongols) and colonizers (the Europeans in the Americas). In the fourth era, the relationship between economic and political strength and population growth has been reversed. The more politically powerful and economically stable areas of Europe, European and Asiatic Russia, Japan, Oceania, and Anglo-America have the lowest rates of population increases, while the less developed countries of Africa and most of Asia, the Caribbean, and Latin America continue to grow at a rapid pace. The overall pattern from the first to the fourth era is presented in Table 1.1.

Although famine, pestilence, and war have not been eliminated as causes of population reduction, their influence has been reduced. The population reductions in China during the Taiping rebellion (1850 to 1865) and in France, the battleground for two world wars (1914 to 1918 and 1939 to 1945) were minor in comparison to reversals previously suffered in those areas, in terms of both absolute numbers and proportion of the population. Pestilence appears to be largely under control in the more developed nations and has become increasingly so in the less developed nations as well, thanks to improvements in public health, nutrition, and medical care. Of the traditional sources of population reduction, famine seems to pose the greatest threat, barring nuclear war.

Future historians of population may find in the present times the beginning of a worldwide leveling off of world population size and population growth rates. There is wide affirmation of the necessity and inevitability of such a change (Desmond, 1962; Coale, 1974:25; Cipolla, 1978:123–136; McEvedy and Jones, 1978:350–351; van der Tak et al., 1979). For most, the question is when population will stabilize and whether population stabilization will come as the result of gradual reduction in growth rates or precipitous reduction in population size. In view of the differences in regional patterns historically, it is appropriate to ask *where* population growth rates will stabilize and where population will experience declines because of famine, pestilence, and war. The world in the past has not adhered to a single uniform pattern, and there is no reason to expect it to do so in the future.

Table 1.1. Patterns of Population Growth for Various World Regions

Region	First Era	Second Era	Third Era	Fourth Era
Sub-Saharan Africa	Stability/slow growth	Moderate growth	Slow to moderate growth	Very rapid growth
North Africa	Stability/slow growth	Fluctuation, no clear trend	Fluctuation, upward trend	Very rapid growth
Europe	Slow growth	Mixed: slow growth or fluctuation	Fluctuation, upward trend	Very rapid growth, then very slow growth
West Asia (Middle East)	Stability/slow growth	Fluctuation, upward trend	Fluctuation, no clear trend	Very rapid growth
Arabian peninsula	Stability/slow growth	Rapid increase then rapid decrease	Fluctuation, no clear trend	Very rapid growth
Indian subcontinent	Slow growth	Moderate growth	Moderate growth	Very rapid growth
China proper	Slow growth	Fluctuation, no clear trend	Moderate growth with periods of sharp decline	Very rapid growth with some periods of decline; appears to be stabilizing
Siberia	Slow growth then stability	Stability	Stability then slight growth	Rapid growth
East Asia except Siberia and China	Slow growth	Moderate growth	Slow to moderate growth	Very rapid growth, stabilizing in some areas
Oceania	Unpopulated for most of era, then slow growth	Slow growth	Slow growth	Slight decline, then stability, then rapid growth
Anglo-America	Unpopulated for most of era, then slow growth	Slow to moderate growth	Stability or moderate growth	Very rapid growth, then slow growth
Caribbean Islands	Unpopulated for most of era, then slow growth	Slow to moderate growth	Decline, then stability	Very rapid growth
Latin America	Unpopulated for most of era, then slow growth	Slow to moderate growth	Mixed: stability or decline and then stability	Very rapid growth

NOTES

1. Prepared especially for this volume. Population data, unless otherwise noted, are from McEvedy and Jones (1978).
2. Even for the modern era, population figures are generally estimates. For a discussion of the accuracy of population estimates for primitive societies, see McArthur (1970). More general discussion of the accuracy of global and national population estimates is presented by Coale (1974:15) and Cole (1979:18–19), as well as by McEvedy and Jones (1978).
3. Even in the industrial era, however, agricultural populations are still faced with the threat of famine. The Irish potato famine of 1848–1852 resulted in high mortality at the time it occurred. This high mortality, along with late marriage (which restricted fertility) and high rates of emigration, led to a decline in the Irish population from 8 million in 1846 to less than 3 million a century later (Morris, 1975:133). Similar depopulation may be occurring in sub-Saharan Africa as this is being written, in 1985.

REFERENCES

Bodley, John H. 1982. *Victims of Progress.* Menlo Park, CA: Benjamin/Cummings.
Bohannon, Paul, and Philip Curtin. 1971. *Africa and Africans.* Garden City, NY: Natural History Press.
Cipolla, Carlo M. 1978. *The Economic History of World Population.* New York: Penguin.
Coale, Ansley J. 1974. "The History of the Human Population," pp. 13–25 of Scientific America, ed., *The Human Population.* San Francisco: W. H. Freeman.
Cole, J. P. 1979. *Geography of World Affairs.* New York: Penguin.
Desmond, Annabelle, 1962. "How Many People Have Ever Lived on Earth?" *Population Bulletin* 18(1):1–19.
Dumond, Don E. 1975. "The Limitation of Human Population: A Natural History, " *Science* 187:713–721.
Greer, Thomas H. 1972. *A Brief History of Western Man,* second edition. New York: Harcourt Brace Jovanovich.
Grun, Bernard. 1979. *The Timetables of History.* New York: Simon and Schuster.
Gugler, Josef, and William G. Flanagan. 1978. *Urbanization and Social Change in West Africa.* Cambridge, England: Cambridge University Press.
Lenski, Gerhard, and Jean Lenski. 1982. *Human Societies: An Introduction to Macrosociology.* New York: McGraw-Hill.
McArthur, Norma. 1970. "The Demography of Primitive Populations," *Science* 167:1097–1101.
McEvedy, Colin, and Richard Jones. 1978. *Atlas of World Population History.* New York: Penguin.
McNeill, William H. 1976. *Plagues and Peoples.* Garden City, NY: Anchor.
Morris, Judy K. 1975. "Professor Malthus and His Essay," Pp. 114–134 of Kenneth C. W. Kammeyer, *Population Studies,* second edition. Chicago: Rand McNally.
Quale, G. Robina. 1966. *Eastern Civilizations.* New York: Appleton-Century-Crofts.
Thomlinson, Ralph. 1976. *Population Dynamics: Causes and Consequences of Demographic Change,* second edition. New York: Random House.
United Nations. 1979. *Concise Report on the World Population Situation in 1977: New Beginnings and Uncertain Ends.* New York: United Nations.
van der Tak, Jean, Carl Haub, and Elaine Murphy. 1979. "Our Population Predicament: A New Look," *Population Bulletin* 34(5):2–41.
Wrigley, E. A. 1969. *Population and History.* New York: McGraw-Hill.
Wrong, Dennis H. 1977. *Population and Society,* fourth edition. New York: Random House.

2
Transocеanic Exchanges of Disease

WILLIAM H. McNEILL

Nearly twenty years ago, as part of my self-education for writing *The Rise of the West: A History of the Human Community,* I was reading about the Spanish conquest of Mexico. As everyone knows, Hernando Cortez, starting off with fewer than six hundred men, conquered the Aztec empire, whose subjects numbered millions. How could such a tiny handful prevail? How indeed? All the familiar explanations seemed inadequate. If Montezuma and his friends first thought the Spaniards were gods, experience soon showed otherwise. If horses and gunpowder were amazing and terrible on first encounter, armed clashes soon revealed the limitations of horseflesh and of the very primitive guns the Spaniards had at their disposal. Cortez's skill in finding allies among the Indian peoples of Mexico and rallying them against the Aztecs was certainly important, but his Indian allies committed themselves to the Spanish side only when they had reason to think Cortez would win.

The extraordinary story of the conquest of Mexico (soon to be followed by Pizarro's no less amazing conquest of the Inca empire in South America) was really only part of a larger puzzle. Relatively few Spaniards ever were able to cross the ocean to the New World, yet they succeeded in impressing their culture on an enormously larger number of Amerindians. The inherent attraction of European civilization and some undeniable technical superiorities the Spaniards had at their command do not seem enough to explain wholesale apostasy from older Indian patterns of life and belief. Why, for instance, did the old religions of Mexico and Peru disappear so utterly? Why did villagers not remain loyal to deities and rituals that had brought fertility to their fields from time immemorial? The exhortation of Christian missionaries and the intrinsic appeal of Christian faith and worship seem insufficient to explain what happened, even though, in the eyes of the missionaries themselves, the truth of Christianity was so evident that their success in converting millions of Indians to the faith seemed to need no explanation.

A casual remark in one of the accounts of Cortez's conquest—I no longer can tell where I saw it—suggested an answer to such questions, and my new hypothesis gathered plausibility and significance as I mulled it over and reflected on its implications afterward. For on the night when the Aztecs drove Cortez and his men out of Mexico City, killing many of them, an epidemic of smallpox was raging in the city. The man who had organized the assault on the Spaniards was among those who died on that *noche trista,* as the Spaniards later called it. The paralyzing effect of a lethal epidemic goes far to explain why the Aztecs did not pursue the defeated and demoralized Spaniards, giving them time and opportunity to rest and regroup, gather Indian allies and set siege to the city, and so achieve their eventual victory.

Moreover, it is worth considering the psychological implications of a disease that killed only Indians and left Spaniards unharmed. Such partiality could only be explained supernaturally, and there could be no doubt about which side of the struggle enjoyed divine favor. The religions, priesthoods, and way of life built around the old Indian gods could not survive such a demonstration of the superior power of the God the Spaniards worshiped. Little wonder, then, that the Indians accepted Christianity and submitted to Spanish control so meekly. God had shown Himself on their side, and each new outbreak of infectious disease imported from Europe (and soon from Africa as well) renewed the lesson.

The lopsided impact of infectious disease upon Amerindian populations therefore offered a key to understanding the ease of the Spanish conquest of America—not only militarily, but culturally as well. But the hypothesis swiftly raised other questions. How and when did the Spaniards acquire the disease experience that served them so well in the New World? Why did the Amerindians not have diseases of their own with which to mow down the invading Spaniards? Tentative answers to such questions soon began to uncover a dimension of the past that historians have not hitherto recognized: the history of humanity's encounters with infectious diseases, and the far-reaching consequences that ensued whenever contacts across disease boundaries allowed a new infection to invade a population that lacked any acquired immunity to its ravages.

Looked at in this way, world history offered a number of parallels to what happened in the Americas in the sixteenth and seventeenth centuries. . . . My conclusions will startle many readers, since events but little noticed in traditional histories assume central importance for my account. This is because the long line of learned scholars whose work it was to sift surviving records from the past has not been sensitive to the possibility of important changes in disease patterns.

To be sure, a couple of spectacular examples of what can happen when an unfamiliar infection attacks a population for the first time have never been expunged from European memory. The Black Death of the fourteenth century was the chief example of this phenomenon, and the cholera epidemics of the nineteenth century constitute a second, far less destructive, but more recent and better-documented instance. Historians, however, never saw these as belonging to a more general class of critically important epidemiological breakthroughs because earlier examples of disastrous encounters with new diseases lay buried deeper in the past where records were so imperfect that both the scale and the significance of what happened were easy to overlook.

In appraising ancient texts, historians were naturally governed by their own experience of epidemic infection. Living amid disease-experienced populations, where relatively high levels of immunity to familiar infections damped any ordinary epidemic outbreak very quickly, critically trained historians were impelled to discount as exaggeration any remark about massive die-off from infectious disease. Failure to understand the profound difference between the outbreak of a familiar disease amid an experienced population and the ravages of the same infection when loosed upon a community lacking acquired immunities is, indeed, at the bottom of the failure of previous historians to give adequate attention to the whole subject. Assuming that infections had always been present in much the same fashion as they were in Europe before the advent of modern medicine, there seemed nothing much to say about epidemics, and historians tended, therefore, to pass such matters by with only the sort of casual mention I found in the account of Cortez's victory.

In view of what happened after the Spaniards inaugurated free exchange of infections between the Old World and the New, it seems certain that Amerindian encounters with disease before Columbus had been unimportant from an epidemiological point of view. The inhabitants of the New World were bearers of no serious new infection transferable to the European and African populations that intruded upon their territory—unless, as some still think, syphilis was of Amerindian origin—whereas the abrupt confrontation with the long array of infections that European and African populations had encountered piecemeal across some four thousand years of civilized history provoked massive demographic disaster among Amerindians.

Reasons for this disbalance are not far to seek. The New World was, by comparison with the mass and ecological complexity of the Old, no more than an enormous island. Forms of life were, in general, more highly evolved in Eurasia and Africa, having responded to a wider range of variability arising in the larger land mass. Consequently, plants and animals from the Old World introduced by Europeans to the Americas often displaced native American species, and disturbed pre-existing ecological balances in explosive and, at least initially, highly unstable ways. We seldom realize, for instance, that Kentucky blue grass, dandelions, and daisies, so familiar in contemporary North American landscapes, are all of Old World origin. Similarly, runaway swine, cattle, and horses developed into vast wild herds in the New World with results that were sometimes destructive to the vegetable cover and soon led to serious erosion of topsoil. American food plants had far-reaching importance for the peoples of Europe, Asia, and Africa after 1500, but few organisms of American provenance were successful in competing in the wild with Old World life-forms—though some examples do exist (e.g., the spread of the plant louse, *phylloxera*) that nearly destroyed European vineyards in the 1880s.

The undeveloped level of Amerindian disease was, therefore, only one aspect of a more general biological vulnerability, but one that had peculiarly drastic consequences for human life. Precise information about disease in the

Americas before Columbus is difficult to come by. Bone lesions can be found on pre-Columbian skeletons indicating some sort of infection. These have sometimes been interpreted as syphilitic by doctors seeking to confirm the American origins of that disease. But such identifications are controversial, since the way one micro-organism attacks a bone is very similar to the way another is likely to do so; and tissue reactions to such invasions are also similar, no matter what the infectious agent may be. Unambiguous proof of the presence of intestinal worms and protozoa has been discovered at pre-Columbian burial sites, but even so the array of parasitic worms fell considerably short of varieties abounding in the Old World.

Indication of disease and epidemic death have been found in Aztec codices; but these seem related to famine and crop failure and may not have been the result of the sort of human-to-human infectious chain that existed in the Old World. Moreover, disasters came far apart in time, only three being discernible in surviving texts. After the Spanish conquest, old men even denied that disease had existed in any form in the days of their youth. If looks, therefore, as though Amerindian communities suffered little from disease, even though in both Mexico and Peru, the size and density of settlement had reached far beyond the critical threshold at which contagious disease organisms could sustain a simple human-to-human chain of infection indefinitely. In this, as in some other respects, the Amerindian civilizations seem comparable to ancient Sumer and Egypt, rather than to the epidemiologically scarred and toughened communities of sixteenth-century Spain and Africa.

Several centuries—perhaps more than a thousand years—had passed since favored regions of Mexico and Peru had begun to carry human populations dense enough to sustain human-to-human disease chains indefinitely. Yet such infections do not seem to have established themselves. Presumably the reason was that the domesticable animals available to the Amerindians did not themselves carry herd infections of a sort that could transfer their parasitism to human populations when those populations became sufficiently large. This sort of transfer is what must have happened in the Old World, where massive herds of wild cattle and horses, dispersed across the steppe and forest lands of Eurasia, were sufficiently numerous and made close enough contact with one another in a wild state to be able to sustain infections that passed from animal to animal without any sort of intermediate host. By comparison, wild llamas and alpacas lived high in the Andes in small and dispersed groups. These were too few and too isolated to sustain such infections in the wild. There seems to be no plausible reconstruction of the style of life of the wild ancestors of the guinea pig—the other distinctive Amerindian domesticated animal. And as for dogs, mankind's oldest domesticated animal, though they today share many infections with humans, it is clear enough that in their wild state they, too, must have existed in relatively small and isolated packs. Thus with the possible exception of the guinea pig, the Amerindians' domesticated species, like the human hunting bands that had initially penetrated the Americas, were incapable of supporting infectious chains of the sort characteristic of civilized diseases. No wonder, then, that once contact had been established, Amerindian populations of Mexico and Peru became the victims, on a mass scale, of the common childhood diseases of Europe and Africa.

The scope of the resultant disaster reflected the fact that both central Mexico and the heartlands of the Inca empire were very densely settled at the time of the European discovery of America. The two most important American food crops, maize and potatoes, were more productive of calories per acre than any Old World crops except rice. This allowed denser populations per square mile of cultivated ground in the Americas than was attainable anywhere in the Old World outside of the East Asian rice paddy region.

Moreover, Amerindian customary ways of preparing maize for food obviated some of the nutritional disadvantages of a diet in which that cereal plays the principal role. The kernels were soaked in a lime solution, which broke down some of the molecules of the maize in a way that allowed human digestion to synthesize needed vitamins that are absent from the maize itself. Without such treatment, a diet of maize leads to niacin deficiency. Symptoms of this deficiency, known as pellagra, were often seriously debilitating among European and African populations that took to maize cultivation. But Amerindians escaped pellagra by soaking maize to make "hominy grits," and by supplementing their diet with beans in those regions where hunting was no longer possible because human populations had become too dense.

Ecological adjustment in Mexico and Peru

showed signs of strain, even before the Spaniards arrived and upset everything so radically. In Mexico, erosion was already a serious problem; and in some irrigated coastal areas of Peru, salting of the soil seems to have led to population collapse not long before Pizarro appeared. Everything points to the conclusion that Amerindian populations were pressing hard against the limits set by available cultivable land in both Mexico and Peru when the Spaniards arrived. Moreover, the absence of any considerable number of domesticated animals meant that there was a smaller margin between the sum of agricultural productivity in the Americas and direct human consumption than was commonly the case in the Old World. In time of crop failure or other kind of food crisis, Eurasian flocks and herds constituted a sort of food bank. They could be slaughtered and eaten; and in times and places when overpopulation started to be felt, human beings always displace herds by turning pastureland into cropland—at least for a while. No such cushion existed in the Americas, where domesticated animals played a merely marginal part in human food patterns.

All these factors therefore conspired to make Amerindian populations radically vulnerable to the disease organisms Spaniards and, before long, also Africans, brought with them across the ocean. The magnitude of the resultant disaster has only recently become clear. Learned opinion before World War II systematically underestimated Amerindian populations, putting the total somewhere between eight and fourteen million at the time Columbus landed in Hispaniola. Recent estimates, however, based on sampling of tribute lists, missionary reports and elaborate statistical arguments, have multiplied such earlier estimates tenfold and more, putting Amerindian population on the eve of the conquest at about one hundred million, with twenty-five to thirty million of this total assignable to the Mexican and an approximately equal number to the Andean civilizations. Relatively dense populations also apparently existed in the connecting Central American lands.

Starting from such levels, population decay was catastrophic. By 1568, less than fifty years from the time Cortez inaugurated epidemiological as well as other exchanges between Amerindian and European populations, the population of central Mexico had shrunk to about three million (i.e., to about one tenth of what had been there when Cortez landed). Decay continued, though at a reduced rate, for another fifty years. Population reached a low point of about 1.6 million by 1620. Recovery did not definitely set in for another thirty years or so and remained very slow until the eighteenth century.

Similarly drastic destruction of preexisting Amerindian societies also occurred in other parts of the Americas, continuing even into the twentieth century. Disaster is to be expected whenever some previously remote and isolated tribe comes into contact with the outside world and there encounters a series of destructive and demoralizing epidemics. A relatively recent case history will illustrate how ruthless and seemingly irresistible such process can be. In 1903 a South American tribe, the Cayapo, accepted a missionary—a single priest—who bent every effort to safeguard his flock from the evils and dangers of civilization. When he arrived the tribe was between 6,000 and 8,000 strong, yet only five hundred survived in 1918. By 1927 only twenty-seven were alive and in 1950 two or three individuals tracing descent to the Cayapo still existed, but the tribe had totally disappeared—and this despite the best intentions and a deliberate attempt to shield the Indians from disease as well as other risks of outside contacts.

Other examples of swift and irretrievable disaster abound. In 1942 to 1943, for instance, the opening of the Alcan highway exposed a remote Indian community in Alaska to measles, German measles, dysentery, whooping cough, mumps, tonsillitis, meningitis, and catarrhal jaundice in a single year! Yet thanks to airlift into modern hospitals, only 7 of 130 individuals actually died. A little more than a century before, in 1837, the Mandan tribe of the high plains found itself cooped up in two defended camps by their Sioux enemies when epidemic broke out. As a result their numbers were reduced from about 2000 to a mere 30 to 40 survivors in a matter of weeks; and those survivors were promptly captured by enemies so that the Mandan tribe ceased to exist.

In an age of almost worldwide population growth, it is hard for us to imagine such catastrophes. Even without total disruption of the sort that came to the Mandan and Cayapo, a 90 percent drop in population within 120 years (i.e., across five to six human generations), as happened in Mexico and Peru, carries with it drastic psychological and cultural consequences. Faith in established institutions and beliefs cannot easily withstand such disaster; skills and knowledge disappear. This, indeed, was what allowed the Spaniards to go as far as they did in transferring their culture and language to the New World, making it normative even in regions where millions of Indians had previously lived according to standards and customs of their own.

Labor shortage and economic retrogression was another obvious concomitant. The development of forms of compulsory labor and dispersal from cities (where disease losses concentrate) to rural estates are necessary responses if social hierarchies are to survive at all. Late Roman institutions and those of seventeenth-century Mexico have an uncanny likeness in this respect, which Spain's heritage of the Roman law only partially explains. Landlords and tax collectors, facing a radically decaying population from which to derive support, can be counted on to react in parallel fashion; and this seems to be what happened in both the late Roman and the seventeenth-century Spanish empires.

It is not really surprising, therefore, to discover how much alike the late Roman system of compulsory labor and Mexican debt peonage were in practice, even though legal forms were different. The rise of haciendas in seventeenth-century Mexico exactly parallels the rise of villas in the late Roman times. Both societies also saw a massive emptying out of older urban centers. To be sure, there were differences. Rome faced a serious problem of border defense, whereas the Spanish empire of the New World was threatened only by sea and was therefore spared the expense of trying to maintain any but the most sketchy sort of armed forces on its landward frontiers. On the other hand, Roman encounters with epidemic disease were undoubtedly less crippling than the concentrated exposure to the Old World's full repertory of infections proved to be for Amerindians. Consequently, Roman authorities had a less radically decaying population base upon which to draw than the labor force that remained available for the support of the Spanish imperial structure in the New World.

Wholesale demoralization and simple surrender of will to live certainly played a large part in the destruction of Amerindian communities. Numerous recorded instances of failure to tend newborn babies so that they died unnecessarily, as well as outright suicide, attest the intensity of Amerindian bewilderment and despair. European military action and harsh treatment of laborers gathered forcibly for some large-scale undertaking also had a role in uprooting and destroying old social structures. But human violence and disregard, however brutal, was not the major factor causing Amerindian populations to melt away as they did. After all, it was not in the interest of the Spaniards and other Europeans to allow potential taxpayers and the Indian work force to diminish. The main destructive role was certainly played by epidemic disease.

The first encounter came in 1518 when smallpox reached Hispaniola and attacked the Indian population so virulently that Bartoleme de Las Casas believed only a thousand survived. From Hispaniola, smallpox traveled to Mexico, arriving with the relief expedition that joined Cortez in 1520. As a result, at the very crisis of the conquest, when Montezuma had been killed and the Aztecs were girding themselves for an attack on the Spaniards, smallpox raged in Tenochtitlán. The leader of the assault, along with innumerable followers, died within hours of compelling the Spaniards to retreat from their city. Instead of following up on the initial success and harrying the tiny band of Spaniards from the land, therefore, as might have been expected had the smallpox not paralyzed effective action, the Aztecs lapsed into a stunned inactivity. Cortez thus was able to rally his forces, gather allies from among the Aztecs' subject peoples, and return for the final siege and destruction of the capital.

Clearly, if smallpox had not come when it did, the Spanish victory could not have been achieved in Mexico. The same was true of Pizarro's filibuster into Peru. For the smallpox epidemic in Mexico did not confine its ravages to Aztec territory. Instead, it spread to Guatemala, where it appeared in 1520, and continued southward, penetrating the Inca domain in 1525 or 1526. Consequences there were just as drastic as among the Aztecs. The reigning Inca died of the disease while away from his capital on campaign in the North. His designated heir also died, leaving no legitimate successor. Civil war ensued, and it was amid this wreckage of the Inca political structure that Pizarro and his crew of roughnecks made their way to Cuzco and plundered its treasures. He met no serious military resistance at all.

Two points seem particularly worth emphasizing here. First, Spaniards and Indians readily agreed that epidemic disease was a particularly dreadful and unambiguous form of divine punishment. Interpretation of pestilence as a sign of God's displeasure was a part of the Spanish inheritance, enshrined in the Old Testament and in the whole Christian tradition. The Amerindians, lacking all experience of anything remotely like the initial series of lethal epidemics, concurred. Their religious doctrines recognized that superhuman power lodged in deities whose behavior toward men was often angry. It was natural, therefore, for them to assign an unexampled effect to a supernatural cause, quite apart from the Spanish missionary efforts that urged the same interpretation of the catastrophe upon dazed and demoralized converts.

Secondly, the Spaniards were nearly immune from the terrible disease that raged so mercilessly among the Indians. They had almost always been exposed in childhood and so developed effective immunity. Given the interpretation of the cause of pestilence accepted by both parties, such a manifestation of divine partiality for the invaders was conclusive. The gods of the Aztecs as much as the God of the Christians seemed to agree that the white newcomers had divine approval for all they did. And while God thus seemed to favor the whites, regardless of their mortality and piety or lack thereof, his wrath was visited upon the Indians with an unrelenting harshness that often puzzled and distressed the Christian missionaries who soon took charge of the moral and religious life of their converts along the frontiers of Spain's American dominions.

From the Amerindian point of view, stunned acquiescence in Spanish superiority was the only possible response. No matter how few their numbers or how brutal and squalid their behavior, the Spaniards prevailed. Native authority structures crumbled; the old gods seemed to have abdicated. The situation was ripe for the mass conversions recorded so proudly by Christian missionaries. Docility to the commands of priests, viceroys, landowners, mining entrepreneurs, tax collectors, and anyone else who spoke with a loud voice and had a white skin was another inevitable consequence. When the divine and natural orders were both unambiguous in declaring against native tradition and belief, what ground for resistance remained? The extraordinary ease of Spanish conquests and the success a few hundred men had in securing control of vast areas and millions of persons is unintelligible on any other basis.

Even after the initial ravages of smallpox had passed, having killed something like one third of the total population, nothing approaching epidemiological stability prevailed. Measles followed hard upon the heels of smallpox, spreading through Mexico and Peru in 1530 to 1531. Deaths were frequent, as is to be expected when such a disease encounters a virgin population dense enough to keep the chain of infection going. Still another epidemic came fifteen years later, in 1546, whose character is unclear. Perhaps it was typhus. Probably typhus was a new disease among Europeans, too; at least the medical men who first described it clearly enough to make diagnosis possible thought it was new when it broke out among troops fighting in Spain, in 1490.

Hence if the pestilence of 1546 in the Americas was in fact typhus, the Amerindians were beginning to participate in epidemic diseases that also affected the populations of the Old World. This becomes unambiguous in course of the next American disease disaster: an influenza epidemic that raged in 1558 to 1559. This epidemic, which broke out in Europe in 1556 and lasted on and off till 1560, had serious demographic consequences on both sides of the Atlantic. One estimate places die-off in England from the influenza at no less than 20 per cent of the entire population, for instance, and comparable losses occurred elsewhere in Europe. Whether the influenza outbreak of the 1550s was a genuinely global phenomenon, like its more recent parallel, 1918 to 1919, cannot be said for sure, but Japanese records also mention an outbreak of "coughing violence" in 1556 from which "very many died."

The incorporation of Amerindian populations into the circle of epidemic disease that happened to be current in Eurasia in the sixteenth century did not relieve them of special exposure to still other infections coming across the ocean. Relatively trifling endemic afflictions of the Old World regularly became death-dealing epidemics among New World populations that were totally lacking in acquired resistances. Thus diphtheria, mumps, and recurrent outbreaks of the first two great killers, smallpox and measles, appeared at intervals throughout the sixteenth and seventeenth centuries. Whenever a new region or hitherto isolated Amerindian population came into regular contact with the outside world, the cycle of repeated infections picked up renewed force, mowing down the helpless inhabitants. The peninsula of Lower California, for instance, began to experience drastic depopulation at the very end of the seventeenth century, when a first recorded epidemic broke out there. Eighty years later the population had been reduced by more than 90 percent, despite well-intentioned efforts by Spanish missionaries to protect and cherish the Indians assigned to their charge.

Obviously, where European records are lacking, it is difficult to follow the course of disease and depopulation. There is no doubt that epidemics often ran ahead of direct contact with Europeans, even in the thinly occupied lands north and south. Thus, because the French had already established a post at Port Royal in what is now Nova Scotia, we happen to know that in 1616 to 1617 a great pestilence of some sort swept through the Massachusetts Bay area. Thus God prepared the way, as Englishmen and Indians agreed, for the arrival of the Pilgrims just three years later. A subsequent outbreak of smallpox, starting in 1633, convinced the colonists (if they needed convincing) that Divine Providence was indeed on their side in conflicts with the Indians.

Similar experiences abound in Jesuit missionary records from Canada and Paraguay. The smaller and more isolated populations of North and South America were just as vulnerable to European infections as the denser populations of Mexico and Peru, even though their numbers were insufficient to maintain a chain of infection on the spot for very long at a time. The judgment a German missionary expressed in 1699 is worth repeating: "The Indians die so easily that the bare look and smell of a Spaniard causes them to give up the ghost." If he had said "breath" instead of "smell" he would have been right.

The long and lethal series of European diseases was not all that Amerindians had to face. For in tropical regions of the New World climatic conditions were suitable for the establishment of at least some of the African infections that made that continent so dangerous to the health of strangers. The two most significant African diseases to establish themselves in the New World were malaria and yellow fever. Both of them became important in determining human patterns of settlement and survival in tropical and subtropical parts of the New World.

Overall, the disaster to Amerindian populations assumed a scale that is hard for us to imagine, living as we do in an age when epidemic disease hardly matters. Ratios of 20:1 or even 25:1 between pre-Columbian populations and the bottoming-out point in Amerindian population curves seem more or less correct, despite wide local variations. Behind such chill statistics lurks enormous and repeated human anguish, as whole societies fell apart, values crumbled, and old ways of life lost all shred of meaning. A few voices recorded what it was like:

> Great was the stench of death. After our fathers and grandfathers succumbed, half the people fled to the fields. The dogs and vultures devoured the bodies. The mortality was terrible. Your grandfathers died, and with them died the son of the king and his brothers and kinsmen. So it was that we became orphans, oh, my sons! So we became when we were young. All of us were thus. We were born to die!

3
Demographic Impact of the Frontier

JOHN H. BODLEY

Wherever the European has trod, death seems to pursue the aboriginal.

Charles Darwin, cited Merivale, 1861:541

Severe depopulation of tribal peoples is a characteristic feature of the frontier process and has been reported by observers from all parts of the world over the past 150 years. As early as 1837 the members of the Select Committee found tribal populations to be declining at alarming rates in areas influenced by British colonists. They noted that the Indians of Newfoundland had been completely exterminated by 1823 and that the Canadian Cree had declined from 10,000 to 200 since 1800. They also found "fearful" depopulation in the Pacific where reportedly the Tasmanians would soon be extinct, and that the Australian Aborigines were simply vanishing from the earth.

In retrospect, it is now clear that what the Select Committee was seeing at that time was only the beginning of a truly catastrophic decline in tribal populations that continued in most areas of the world for another hundred years. Table 3.1 represents an attempt to indicate the scale of at least some of this depopulation. According to these figures, tribal populations in lowland South America (east of the Andes and exclusive of the Caribbean) and North America (north of Mexico) were reduced by almost 95 percent or by nearly 18 million by 1930. It is noteworthy that in these areas much of this reduction occurred *since* 1800 and can be only partly attributed to the Spanish and Portuguese conquests, which, of course, decimated large populations in the Orinoco, the lower Amazon, and eastern Brazil and Bolivia prior to 1800. Certainly in North America, with the exception of some portions of the southwest and California, and the eastern seaboard, most of the depopulation was again after 1800. In Polynesia, Micronesia, and Australia, where fairly complete, although conservative, estimates have been made, the population was reduced by approximately 80 percent, or more than 1.25 million since 1800. If moderate allowances are made for further depopulation in areas not included in Table 3.1, such as Siberia, southern Asia, island southeast Asia, southern Africa, and Melanesia, and if Morel's modest estimate for the Congo is accepted, it might be conservatively estimated that during the 150 years between 1780 and 1930 world tribal populations were reduced by at least 30 million as a direct result of the spread of industrial civilization. A less conservative and probably more realistic estimate would place the figure at perhaps 50 million. Such an incredible loss has no parallel in modern times and must certainly have been a major factor in the "acculturaation" of tribal peoples.

These population losses have perhaps greater meaning when their impact on specific tribal groups is examined, because it is clear that countless groups were never able to recover from such massive depopulation and simply became extinct while those that did survive were seriously weakened. The speed with which many groups were engulfed by the frontier was certainly a critical factor in the ultimate outcome. The Tasmanians, for example, were reduced by almost 98 percent from a population of 5,000 to 111 within thirty years. In western Victoria the aboriginal population of perhaps 4,000 was reduced to 213 full bloods after less than forty years of settlement, and within fifty years anthropologists could find no one who could reliably describe their traditional culture (Corris, 1968). In California, 75 percent of an estimated 85,000 Yokut and Wintun Indians were swept away by epidemic diseases in 1830 to 1833 (Cook, 1955). In recent times there have been reports of extremely rapid rates of decline for many South American tribal groups. In Tierra del Fuego, for example, the nomadic Indians such as the Ona and Yahgan, who may have numbered more than 8,000 as recently as 1870, were effectively extinct by 1950. It is estimated that in Brazil alone 87 of 230 groups known to be in existence in 1900 were extinct by 1957 (Ri-

Table 3.1. World Survey of Tribal Depopulation

	Precontact Population	Population Lowpoint	Depopulation
North America (U.S. and Canada)[a]	9,800,000	490,000	9,310,000
Lowland South America[b]	9,000,000	450,000	8,550,000
Oceania			
Polynesia[c]	1,100,000	180,000	920,000
Micronesia[d]	200,000	83,000	117,000
Melanesia			
Fiji[d,e]	300,000	85,000	215,000
New Caledonia[f]	100,000	27,000	73,000
Australia[g]	300,000	60,500	239,500
Africa			
Congo[h]			8,000,000
	Estimated Total Depopulation		27,860,000

[a,b]Dobyns, 1966:415.

[c,d]Keesing, 1941.

[e,fe,f]Roberts, 1927.

[g] Rowley, 1970:384.

[h] Morel in Louis and Stengers, 1968:123. (Suret-Canale, 1971:36–37, gives a much more liberal estimate of some 12 million for the depopulation of the French Congo alone between 1900 and 1921).

beiro, 1957), while many other surviving groups experienced drastic declines following white contacts. Some of the most dramatic cases recorded for Brazil are the Caraja, estimated to number 100,000 in 1845, 10,000 in 1908, and 1,510 in 1939 (Lipkind, 1948:180). The Araguaia Kayapo, who numbered 8,000 in 1903, were reduced to 27 by 1929 (Dobyns, 1966). More recently, the Kreen-Akarore were reduced from 300 to 35 in 1979, just 6 years after agreeing to establish permanent contact with the national society (Davis, 1977:69–73, Latin America Political Report 1979, Vol. 13(3):19). Depopulation of this magnitude would clearly constitute a major source of stress for any culture, and particularly when it occurs in the context of conquest and economic exploitation.

The causes of tribal depopulation have generally been well understood, at least since the Select Committee's 1837 Report clearly designated frontier violence, disease, alcohol, firearms, and demoralization as the principal causes. Since that time, however, there have been some ethnocentric attempts to attribute depopulation to inherent tribal decadence and racial inferiority, and to suggest that civilization merely accelerated a decline that was already occurring. This view has been supported by some missionaries and government inquiries, and by not a few scholars, such as the historian Roberts, who spoke vaguely of "a general racial decline, an indefinable *malaise* of the stock itself" (Roberts, 1927:59). This explanation is no longer regarded seriously by anthropologists and was vigorously rejected years ago by the British anthropologists Rivers (1922) and Pitt-Rivers (1927), who examined the depopulation of the Pacific and showed how culture contact was responsible.

The only real problem remaining for more recent writers to debate has been the difficulty of assessing *which* contact factors are the most critical. Some would place special emphasis on the role of disease; others stress the importance of direct physical violence. Certainly both of these factors were important, but they should not distract attention from other indirect factors, because there seem to be very complex interrelationships and feedback mechanisms operating among all the variables leading to depopulation. For example, dispossession often forced enemy groups into severe competition for greatly reduced resources, and the availability of firearms made the resulting conflicts far more destructive than previous conflicts. These increased conflicts, combined with other new disturbances in economic and social patterns (such as those related to debt peonage), often placed new stresses on tribal societies and weakened them to the point that they willingly accepted outside control and welfare. Even depopulation itself is a form of stress that can lead to further depopulation by threatening the subsistence base. Rivers (1922) speculated that the sudden total transformation experienced by many tribes caused a form of shock that made people stop producing or desiring children, and in some cases they simply died because life was no longer worth living. While this explanation is now in disrepute, it would seem difficult to disprove.

It appears that increased mortality alone does not account for the complete disappearance of so many tribal peoples: other cultural variables must be involved. Ironically, the special adaptive mechanisms of primitive cultures designed to prevent *overpopulation,* such as abortion, infanticide, and the not infrequent ideal of a small family, may have actually contributed to *depopulation* and even extinction when frontier conditions drastically elevated mortality rates. There is little reliable data on this point because the importance of these population-regulating devices has only recently been recognized, but anthropologists have specifically cited these factors to explain the depopulation of the Tapirape in Brazil (Wagley, 1951), and for Yap in Micronesia (Schneider, 1955).

WE FOUGHT WITH SPEARS

Nothing much is said about the sufferings on our side. Yet we fought with spears, clubs, bows and arrows. The foreigners fought with cannons, guns and bullets.

F. Bugotu, 1968, Solomon Islands

The early anthropologists who have studied the culture change process did not generally place sufficient emphasis on the role of military force in bringing about the initial breakdown of tribal autonomy. According to the standard definition presented in the famous "Memorandum for the Study of Acculturation" (Redfield, et al., 1936), *acculturation* is the result of groups with different cultures entering into "continuous firsthand contact, with subsequent changes in the original cultural patterns of either or both groups." The memorandum indicated that the contact situation could be friendly or hostile, but certainly it gave no hint that force might be a major cause of acculturation. Even some modern anthropology textbooks continue to stress that acculturation often results from demands for change coming from tribal peoples themselves, due to their exposure to higher standards of living or the idea of progress—almost as if such "demonstration effects" were the basic cause of culture change (Starr, 1971:514, 516). Considered in a different light, giving full weight to the historical record, acculturation can in many cases be seen as the direct outcome of the defeat of individual tribes in separate engagements in a very long war fought between all tribal peoples and industrial civilization throughout the world.

While it is not appropriate here to attempt a major history of military actions against tribal peoples, this essay does emphasize the extent and nature of this military pressure, and shows how it has frequently initiated culture change by destroying tribal autonomy.

In many parts of the world, tribal peoples fought back fiercely when they saw their traditional cultures threatened by outsiders and when they realized that those outsiders had come to stay and intended to impose their will on them. Often they were forced into one-sided battles to defend their lives against militarily superior enemies, and in most cases the outcome was never long in doubt when natives were engaged with regular troops armed with modern weapons. Defeat on the battlefield was invariably followed by the surrender of cultural autonomy and the imposition of government administrative control leading ultimately to further culture change.

In general, two major varieties of military action against tribal peoples can be distinguished: punitive raids and wars. The difference between these categories is that punitive raids tend to be short punishments for specific offenses committed by the natives and the intent is merely to establish administrative control. Wars, however, may involve protracted campaigns, often for the purpose of extermination or the forced removal of native populations that are not in themselves of direct economic value. Both approaches have been widely applied and have had profound impacts on tribal culture, as is discussed in the following sections.

THE PUNITIVE RAID

The basic purpose of a punitive raid is to impress a tribal population with the overwhelming force at the government's disposal, and to thereby gain their "cooperation." It is simply a form of intimidation, always with the threat of greater force in the background, and it normally does not intend the total annihilation of a people.

The punitive raid has been used widely in New Guinea and throughout the Pacific, where the native population was too valuable as a source of labor to risk its extermination. The Germans conducted frequent raids in their

New Guinea colony and frequently carried them to excessive lengths. When two white men and eight native laborers were killed by unpacified natives, the government responded by sending an expedition that killed eighty-one people, destroyed houses and canoes, and carried off women and children as prisoners (Reed, 1943:136–137). Such overreaction was a common feature of punitive raids. In 1928, when two native policemen in Australian New Guinea were killed by the Kwoma in a dispute over the rape of a village woman, the government massacred seventeen villagers in return (Reed, 1943:154–155). By coincidence, in the same year Australian police killed seventeen Aborigines near Alice Springs (Rowley, 1967:73). Even if these raids were considered a necessary form of retribution for specific "crimes" committed by the natives, there was seldom any effort to determine who the guilty parties were or to balance the punishment to fit the crime.

Naval battleships and cruisers were often used in the Pacific by the French, Germans, British, and Americans to impress recalcitrant natives. This occurred as late as 1920, when the Americans stopped a revolt in Samoa with naval guns (Keesing, 1941:173). The Germans made regular use of their warships in New Guinea but did not always gain the intended result. The natives may have been impressed with the noise, but often merely returned to their villages when the barrage was over and planted taro in the shell holes (Reed, 1943:136).

Punitive raids were also institutionalized in colonial Africa. In South Africa they were known as *commandos,* and were often conducted by detachments of armed settlers whose leaders were officially acknowledged by both the government and the military. The usual excuse for a raid was to regain "stolen" cattle, but they often resulted in the indiscriminant destruction of tribal life and property.

Perhaps the most raided tribal group in Africa were the Nuer of the Sudan, who Evans-Pritchard found to be arrogant and suspicious in 1930. The British usually sent expeditions or patrols against tribes in the Sudan that refused to submit to government administration or that were fighting among themselves. The Nuer proved to be one of the most difficult of such groups to subdue because they simply refused to be humbled and had abundant empty land in which to hide. According to the count of a recent historian, armed force was used against the Nuer and related tribes sixteen times between 1902 and 1932 (Beshir, 1968:19).

Such raids probably accomplished several things: they caused loss of life, which was a significant disruption of tribal society in itself, and they seriously disturbed the subsistence economy when stored food or gardens were destroyed. The psychological impact of such displays of overwhelming force would also do much to undermine native morale and the self-confidence necessary for tribal autonomy. When these disturbances were combined with the other difficulties characteristic of the uncontrolled frontier, the surrender of tribal peoples to the government becomes quite understandable.

It should be emphasized that punitive raids are not a thing of the past and were never restricted to colonial governments. It is well known that such raids were a common tactic of the U.S. Army in the Indian Wars and were widely applied in Latin America. In Brazil, organized irregular troops, known as *bandeiras,* often punished Indian tribes in the nineteenth century. Thanks to modern technology, punitive raids can now be conducted more easily and much more effectively. In 1965 newspapers reported that Brazilian air, naval, and ground forces were used against the Marubo, a small Indian tribe in Amazonas that attacked settlers who had invaded their territory (Bowman, 1965). At about the same time in the Peruvian Amazon, the Peruvian air force used napalm to punish Campa Indians who were thought to be in support of leftist rebels. Bombing raids and armed patrols were also used by the Indonesian government in 1965 to 1966 to control 4,000 "disaffected" Arfak people in West Irian (Indonesian New Guinea); they reportedly left 1,200 dead (Hastings, 1968:17).

WARS OF EXTERMINATION

Major campaigns and wars of extermination waged against tribal peoples have usually been for the purpose of removing the population so that their territory could be utilized by outsiders to benefit the national economy. The immediate justification for such action, as with punitive raids, has often been the need to protect settlers or colonists from "marauding savages," or to quell tribal rebellions, or it has simply been viewed as a quick means of spreading civilization and progress. It is generally acknowledged that in most cases rebellions and raids by tribal peoples were the direct result of pressures exerted against them by outsiders and could have been prevented if they had been left alone—but that policy was not often economically advantageous.

Wars against tribal peoples became extremely frequent throughout the world as European expansion began, and probably reached a high point in the period between 1850 and 1910. It is well known that the Indian Wars in the United States continued almost without respite from 1820 to 1890, but it is not often realized that similar wars were occurring in South America at the same time, and sometimes on just as large a scale as in North America. Africa, particularly the southern and eastern regions, was also the scene of almost continual military action during the same period. In Asia, campaigns were conducted against tribal peoples in Formosa by the Japanese; in the Philippines by the Spanish and then by the Americans; in Indochina by the French; and in Burma and Assam by the British. In the Pacific, the Maori Wars of 1860 to 1872 and the New Caledonia revolt of 1878 to 1879 were the most significant major military actions. These tribal wars have received relatively little attention in history texts because they were overshadowed by other political and economic events occurring in Europe and America at the same time, but they were nevertheless extremely dramatic and critical struggles for the peoples most directly involved.

GUNS AGAINST SPEARS

Half measures do not answer with natives. They must be thoroughly crushed to make them believe in our superiority. . . . I shall strive to be in a position to show them how hopelessly inferior they are to us in fighting power although numerically stronger.

(Lord Chelmsford, British Commander in the Zulu Campaign, cited Furneaux, 1963:32)

It is generally true, of course, that modern weapons gave government forces a distinct advantage in conflicts with tribal peoples, particularly in large-scale battles between troops and natives still unfamiliar with the effects of firearms. Conventional forms of resistance were usually futile and often ended tragically, like the Matabele rebellion in Rhodesia in 1896, which was decisively ended when machine gun fire mowed down spear-carrying warriors by the hundreds with "bullets that came like hail in a storm" (Wellington, 1967:245). In many areas, magical as well as thoroughly empirical defenses were developed by tribal peoples to counteract such weapons. In New Guinea a special salve was invented that was supposed to deflect bullets (Reed, 1943:134), while on the American plains, the "ghost dance" shirt was intended to turn bullets to water, and in the Amazon Campa shamans attempted to blow at the bullets as protection. Guerrilla tactics generally proved more effective, however, and better still was the acquisition of firearms.

While these campaigns were often short, one-sided affairs, tribal peoples were not infrequently capable of incredibly stubborn resistance and sometimes struck back major blows against their enemies. In Burma, the British spent more than ten years suppressing rebellious tribesmen (La Raw, 1967:131), and the Naga were even more troublesome, as will be shown. The odyssey of Chief Joseph and the Nez Perce in 1877 is well known, as well as the massacre of General Custer and 264 men of the Seventh Cavalry in 1876. Perhaps even more dramatic, though less familiar, was the destruction of more than 800 of the British forces sent against the Zulu in 1879 at Isandhlwana and Rorke's Drift. The soldiers were attempting to teach the Zulu that they were "hopelessly inferior," but in this case spears prevailed against guns. That same year in nearby Basutoland, 300 rebellious Pluthi warriors, armed with a few guns, managed to withstand a siege of their fortified hilltop refuge for eight months against 1,800 soldiers with artillery. The most stubborn cases of resistance often occurred when tribal people were able to obtain firearms from traders and learned to use them before major conflicts broke out. This availability of firearms certainly prolonged the Maori Wars and was an important factor in many other areas as well.

The distinction between these wars and the wars that Europeans waged among themselves was not merely the usual one-sidedness of the fighting, but rather that their purpose was often the total destruction of a way of life and the subjugation if not destruction of entire populations. Military defeat of tribal peoples by industrial states involves far more than a mere change in political structure. When the Pluthi were defeated, their cattle and land were immediately taken from them, and their women and children became involuntary laborers for white farmers. In effect, the Pluthi ceased to exist as a distinct tribal entity.

REFERENCES

Beshir, Mohamed Omer. 1968. *The Southern Sudan: Background to Conflict.* New York: Praeger.

Bowman, James D. 1965. "They Like White Men—Broiled." (Associated Press) *Eugene Register-Guard* (Oct. 7): 2B.

Cook, Sherburne F. 1955. "The Epidemic of 1830–33 in California and Oregon." *University of California Publications in American Archaeology and Ethnology* 43:303–326.

Corris, Peter, 1968. *Aborigines and Europeans in Western Victoria.* Occasional Papers in Aboriginal Studies No. 12, Ethnohistory Series No. 1. Canberra: Australian Institute of Aboriginal Studies.

Davis, Shelton H. 1977. *Victims of the Miracle: Development and the Indians of Brazil.* Cambridge: Cambridge University Press.

Dobyns, Henry F. 1966. "Estimating Aboriginal American Population: An Appraisal of Techniques With a New Hemispheric Estimate." *Current Anthropology* 7(4):395–399.

Furneaux, Rupert. 1963. *The Zulu War: Isandhlwana and Rorke's Drift.* Philadelphia and New York: J. B. Lippincott Co.

Hastings, Peter. 1968. "West Irian—1969." *New Guinea* 3(3):12–22.

Keesing, Felix M. 1941. *The South Seas in the Modern World.* Institute of Pacific Relations International Research Series. New York: John Day.

La Raw, Maran. 1967. "Toward a Basis for Understanding the Minorities in Burma: the Kachin Example." *Southeast Asian Tribes, Minorities, and Nations,* edited by Peter Kunstadter, 125–146. Princeton: Princeton University Press.

Lipkind, William. 1948. "The Caraja." In *Handbook of South American Indians,* edited by Julian Steward, 179–191, Vol. III. Bulletin 143, Bureau of American Ethnology. Washington, D.C.: Smithsonian Institution.

Louis, Roger, and Jean Stengers. 1968. *E. P. Morel's History of the Congo Reform Movement.* Oxford: Clarendon Press.

Pitt-Rivers, George H. 1927. *The Clash of Culture and the Contact of Races.* London: George Routledge and Sons.

Redfield, Robert, Ralph Linton, and M. J. Herskovits. 1936. "Memorandum on the Study of Acculturation." *American Anthropologist* 38:149–152.

Reed, Stephen W. 1943. *The Making of Modern New Guinea.* Philadelphia: The American Philosophical Society.

Ribeiro, Darcy. 1957. *Culturas e Linguas Indigenas do Brasil.* Separata de Educacao e Ciencias Socais No. 6. Rio de Janeiro: Centro Brasiliero de Pesquisas Educacionais.

Rivers, W. H. R. 1922. *Essays on the Depopulation of Melanesia.* Cambridge: Cambridge University Press.

Rowley, Charles D. 1967. "The Villager and the Nomad: Aboriginals and New Guineans." *New Guinea* 2(1):70–81.

———. 1970. *The Destruction of Aboriginal Society.* Aboriginal Policy and Practice, Vol. 1. Canberra: Australian National University Press.

Schneider, David. 1955. "Abortion and Depopulation on a Pacific Island: Yap." In *Health, Culture, and Community,* edited by B. D. Paul, 211–235. New York: Russel Sage.

Starr, Cecie, ed. 1971. *Anthropology Today.* Del Mar, Calif.: Communications Research Machines, Inc.

Suret-Canale, Jean. 1971. *French Colonialism in Tropical Africa 1900–1945.* New York: Pica Press.

Wagley, C. 1951. "Cultural Influences on Population." *Revista do Museu Paulista* 5:95–104.

Wellington, John H. 1967. *South West Africa and Its Human Issues.* Oxford: Clarendon Press/Oxford University Press.

4

Relevance of Demographic Transition Theory for Developing Countries

MICHAEL S. TEITELBAUM

The theory of the demography transition is by now a well-known feature of discussions of human population phenomena, and recently it has also become an element of international politics. In the debates at the World Population Conference in Bucharest in 1974 the theory of the demographic transition was an active, if usually implicit, participant. It lay behind some of the most attractive and confident sentiments expressed ("Take care of the people and population will take care of itself." "Development is the best contraceptive"), and there is no reason to think that the proponents of these views believed they were espousing anything but the revealed wisdom of demographic science.[1]

Yet popular adoption of a scientific theory usually lags far behind the elaboration of the theory itself. The theory of the demographic transition was originally developed nearly a half-century ago, and ironically its explanatory and predictive power has come into increasing scientific doubt at the very time that it is achieving its greatest acceptance by nonscientists. In scientific circles, only modest claims are now made for transition theory as an explanation of the very demographic experiences from which the theory was originally drawn—those of nineteenth-century Europe. When applied to the markedly different social and economic circumstances of modern-day Asia, Africa, and Latin America, the explanatory and predictive power of transition theory is open to further scientific questions.

Hence the credence given to assertions based upon transition theory that development will "take care of" population matters as it did in Europe justify an assessment of (i) what is known about what *did* happen in Europe and (ii) the extent to which the same processes may be expected in developing countries, given their similarities and dissimilarities from the countries of 19th-century Europe.

THE THEORY OF THE DEMOGRAPHIC TRANSITION

The theory[2] of the demographic transition[3] is a descriptive interpretation of the transformations that took place in European demographic patterns during the nineteenth century. It seeks to characterize three "stages" of fertility and mortality levels, viewed as derivative from the fundamental economic and social changes of "development" of "modernization."

According to the theory, stage I of the demographic transition is that which has been characteristic of the human species throughout most of its history—an equilibrium of population size over the long term achieved by high birth rates and high death rates. Infant mortality is high and fertility is similarly high, although perhaps never at the biological maximum of the species. The high rate of mortality is taken as inevitable in the absence of modern forms of sanitation, agriculture, transport, and medicine. Given this high rate of mortality, a similarly high birth rate is required (by definition) of any population which has persisted. In order to maintain high fertility, societies in stage I of the demographic transition are characterized by powerful pronatalist norms supported by popular values both sacred and secular, and effectively enforced by a variety of societal sanctions, that is, by a pronatalism which is highly institutionalized and slow to change.

In contrast to the stable societal maintenance of a high birth rate, transition theory views control of the death rate as beyond the reach of preindustrial societies. However, since most people desire health and long life, new methods of reducing mortality are readily adopted as they become known, resulting in a gradual decline in mortality. Both high fertility and low mortality are viewed as blessings.

Stage II of the demographic transition [is]

characterized by declining mortality with fertility remaining at previous high levels under the control of traditional social institutions. This is the stage of the "population explosion," that is, the rapid growth of population resulting from an imbalance between birth rates and death rates.

Finally, individuals begin consciously to control their fertility, marking the onset of stage III of the demographic transition in which the birth rate gradually declines toward equilibrium with the now low death rate. The reduction of fertility typically lags behind the mortality decline because it cannot occur until the traditional social and economic institutions supporting fertility are weakened and new institutions emerge favoring a reduction in fertility to levels more commensurate with the lower levels of mortality. The theorists of the demographic transition explain the adoption of this new smaller family ideal by reference to the industrial and urban transformations of the nineteenth century. Industrial and urban life are seen as modifying substantially the role of the family in production, consumption, education, and recreation. The reduced importance of the family weakens the social pressures favoring high fertility, since it is through the extended agrarian family that many of these pressures are funneled by the society. The economic value of children is lowered by the growth of widespread or compulsory education, which removes children from the potential labor force. People come to perceive that mortality (especially infant mortality) has declined substantially, and that fewer births are required to achieve a certain family size of live children.

Through this multitude of major social transformations, the pressures for high fertility weaken and the idea of conscious control of fertility gradually gains strength.[4] In the early stages no elaborate technology of fertility control is required, but there is more knowledgeable and effective use of folk methods such as coitus interruptus, abortion, and various crude devices. Later, pressures arise for more effective and less objectionable means of fertility control, leading to the development of more modern methods.

CURRENT STATUS OF TRANSITION THEORY

As has been noted above, the theory of the demographic transition is essentially a plausible description of complex social and economic phenomena which took place in nineteenth-century Europe. It is notably lacking in such components of theories as a specifiable and measurable mechanism of "causation" and a definite time scale. It has, however, generated some very general hypotheses which have been affirmed by subsequent events, for example, the proposition that mortality generally responds more quickly than fertility to the forces of medicine and development, and the prediction of the 1950s that regions such as Asia could therefore be expected to experience large population increases in the decades following.[5]

It is notable, however, that only limited efforts have been made to examine the more specific and "explanatory" propositions of transition theory, especially those concerning the factors associated with the European *fertility* decline.

One important finding of the Princeton studies[6] is that overall fertility levels in pretransition Europe were far from uniform, but instead varied considerably from province to province and from country to country. This was due in part to differences in marriage patterns, but, when this factor is controlled, the fertility variation remains large—the lowest fertility levels are only two-thirds as large as the highest. A variety of explanations may be offered. Two possibilities are that fecundity (defined in demography as the biological capacity to reproduce) was affected by nutritional factors[7] or by the prevalence, duration, and intensity of nursing,[8] or both. Another strong contender is the view that many pretransitional subpopulations were in fact practicing conscious fertility control.[9]

The Princeton studies clearly document the importance to the overall level of fertility in Europe of the proportions married. The Western European marriage pattern[10] of late marriage and of extensive nonmarriage stands out in sharp relief from that of Eastern Europe, and is even more distinctive when compared with the very early and nearly universal marriage patterns of many modern developing countries.

When the cluster of socioeconomic variables to which transition theory attributes the European fertility decline (industrialization, urbanization, education, mortality decline, and other factors) are quantified and examined, it becomes quickly apparent that a number of confident propositions in some versions of transition theory are overly facile. In some areas such as parts of France, fertility began to decline before the spread of industrialization and urbanization, and prior to or simultaneously with the declines in mortality. Certain socioeconomic factors were associated with (but not necessarily causes of) demographic changes in some countries, but in others these relationships were not apparent at all. Indeed, in most countries the data show subnational regional clusters which tend to correspond more to cultural and linguistic groups than to the socioeconomic variables central to transition theory. Hence the causal model posited by transition theory has proven to be more elusive in the empirical data than in the theoretical propositions.

Coale (6, p. 65) summarizes the generalization of transition theory that remains in terms of three broad preconditions for a substantial decline of fertility within marriage:

1. Fertility must be within the calculus of conscious choice. Potential parents must consider it an acceptable mode of thought and form of behavior to balance advantages and disadvantages before deciding to have another child—unlike, for example, most present-day Hutterites or Amish, who would consider such calculations immoral, and consequently do not control marital fertility.
2. Reduced fertility must be [seen as] advantageous. Perceived social and economic circumstances must make reduced fertility seem an advantage to individual couples.
3. Effective techniques of fertility reduction must be available. Procedures that will in fact prevent births must be known, and there must be sufficient communication between spouses and sufficient sustained will, in both, to employ them successfully.

The European data show that a high level of development was ultimately *sufficient* to establish these three preconditions for a decline in marital fertility across Europe. However, there is no evidence of any threshold levels of development which were *necessary* for this to happen, and it is apparent that the preconditions for fertility decline existed under situations of little social and economic development, as in parts of rural France and Hungary.[11]

RELEVANCE OF TRANSITION THEORY FOR DEVELOPING COUNTRIES

The relevance of transition theory for the present situation of developing countries is an important issue of both science and policy. From a scientific perspective, the weaknesses and ambiguities of transition theory in explaining European experience may be further examined if one follows the current and future demographic processes of developing countries. For example, it is possible that the explanatory failures of the theory for Europe may be due in part to lack of adequate data on potentially important factors, since explanation of the ongoing fertility decline was not contemplated at the time these data were being collected. The application of modern techniques of demographic and socioeconomic measurement on a prospective basis in the developing countries may provide better opportunities to validate or refute (at least for those countries) the hypothesized relationships among mortality, fertility, and various social and economic changes.[12]

The relevance of transition theory to the modern era may be of even greater interest to policy formulation. If it can be shown that within a reasonable period of time social and economic development cause a "natural" decline in fertility, as is predicted by some on the basis of transition theory, the underlying assumptions on population issues held by many national leaders will have been validated. If, on the other hand, it appears that the theory of the demographic transition (whatever its validity for Europe) is not appropriate for the conditions of the modern developing countries, revised assumptions will be very much in order as leaders seek the correct policy stance on population issues.

In considering the relevance of transition theory to contemporary developing countries, the theory's general explanatory difficulties are compounded by very substantial differences between developing countries and nineteenth-century Europe in certain of the socioeconomic and demographic variables central to the theory. The situation is a mixed one: in some respects the different circumstances in developing countries suggest great obstacles to the timely completion of the transition by means of a "natural" decline in fertility along the European pattern. In other respects these differences provide reasons to anticipate an unusually rapid completion of the transition in these countries.

The differences which cumulatively militate against "natural" and timely fertility declines in the developing countries include at least the following:

A1. *Pace and source of mortality decline.* The declines in mortality of European countries were gradual, and were generally related to the social and economic forces of development and industrialization. The same is not true for many developing countries, where mortality declines have been far more dramatic and have often resulted largely from imported technologies which can be transferred with relative ease and are only marginally related to the pace and level of general development. The result is that mortality levels in developing countries are much lower than those of early industrial Europe, but the factors which brought this about may be less indigenous and hence have less impact upon fertility.

A2. *Fertility levels before decline.* Fertility in most developing countries today is much higher than in pretransition Europe. For example, the birth rate in early nineteenth-century Britain is estimated to have been generally less than 35 per thousand, whereas in many countries today (such as Tanzania and Iran) it is over 45 per thousand, and in some (such as Afghanistan) possibly over 50. These higher birth rates are due primarily to the practice in most developing countries of early and near-universal marriage, in distinct contrast to the nineteenth-century European pattern of late marriage and extensive nonmarriage.

A3. *International migration.* The untoward effects of too-rapid population growth in a given country can, in theory, be mitigated by international migration. In the nineteenth century the countries of Europe "exported" tens of millions of their citizens to the "new" continents of the Americas and Oceania and to overseas colonies elsewhere. Yet the political and economic realities of today mean that substantial international migration is no longer a potential outlet for excessive population growth.

A4. *Rate of population growth.* As a result of the above differences, all of which operate in the same direction, population growth in most developing countries is literally extraordinary—quite unprecedented in human experience, including that of the European transition. Growth rates of developing countries today range as high as 3.4 percent (e.g., in Algeria, Colombia, and the Dominican Republic, among others), with an average of about 2.5 percent. At the former rate a population would double in size in only 20 years (and would increase 32-fold in a century): at the latter rate doubling would take less than 30 years. In contrast, European nations undergoing their demographic transitions rarely experienced doubling times of less than 50 years, and the average was about 90 years. Hence, at no point in their transitions did European countries sustain the rates of population-related growth in demand for basic necessities and for social investment that are now confronted daily by the leaders of many developing countries. Such demands often compete with those for investment in key physical resources in industry and agriculture, and can thereby serve to impede social and economic development. The perversely circular effect may be to slow or even short-circuit any underlying "natural" tendencies toward completion of the demographic transition which result from the forces of development.

A5. *Momentum for further growth.* The rapid growth of developing countries will be more difficult to halt than the slower growth of transitional Europe. As a result of their much higher fertility, modern developing countries have very much "younger" age structures than Europe had, and therefore a far greater momentum for further growth. For example, even in the unlikely event that fertility in developing countries declined *within the next decade* to the "replacement" level now characteristic of developed countries, the population of the developing world would nonetheless continue to grow for 60 to 70 years, and by the year 2050 would have reached a size nearly 90 percent greater than its 1970 level. If replacement fertility is deferred until 20 years later, the increase would be over 150 percent. For specific developing countries with unusually young age structures, the force of growth momentum under these two assumptions would, of course, be even larger.[13]

A6. *Opportunities for occupational and rural-to-urban mobility.* Occupational mobility away from agriculture and spatial migration from rural to urban areas provided alternative life opportunities for the increased rural population during the European Transition.[14] The much more rapid natural increase of modern developing countries presents great difficulties to the provision of comparable opportunities for occupational and spatial mobility. The increase in demand for nonagricultural employment often exceeds the increase in supply, and the extraordinarily rapid rates of urban growth in many developing countries are threatening to overwhelm their capacities of accommodation. Indeed, in some cases policies are being sought to *reduce* rural-to-urban migration flows although the population remains predominantly rural, thereby limiting the hypothesized effects of urban life upon family and reproductive values.[15]

A7. *Fewer opportunities for female participation in the labor force.* There is some evidence that the increased entry of women into the nonagricultural labor force in Europe was a factor in fertility decline. If this is true, the more rapid rate of natural increase in developing countries today means that the entering labor force is growing faster as well. Ceteris paribus, this would tend to limit the growth in the demand for female labor.

A8. *Difficulties of providing universal education.* With school-age cohorts doubling in only two or three decades, many developing countries are understandably experiencing difficulties in expanding educational facilities at a rapid enough rate to provide educational opportunities for a growing proportion of those eligible. This means deferment of the goal of universal education, along with its hypothesized effects upon fertility behavior in the transition.

There are also differences between the situations of the European transition and those of modern developing countries which tend to favor more prompt and rapid fertility declines in the developing countries:

B1. *Pace of social and economic development.* For many developing countries, social and economic development has been more rapid than in nineteenth-century Europe. To the extent that such development "causes" or expedites the decline in marital fertility, this suggests more rapid completion of the demographic transition as well.

B2. *Methods of fertility control.* The European fertility declines appear to have been based upon increased and more effective use of traditional fertility control measures such as coitus interruptus and abortion, although by modern standards the effectiveness of the former was not high and the danger of the latter was great. Improved contraceptive technology and safe abortion techniques have now been developed, and additional approaches such as safe and acceptable voluntary sterilization are available for the first time in history. At any given level of motivation to control fertility, access to such improved methods is likely to mean more frequent and effective practice, with consequently greater demographic effects.

B3. *Greater latitude of deferment of marriage and increased nonmarriage.* The European demographic transition began in the context of late marriage and extensive nonmarriage. In developing countries today marriage is generally early and almost universal. Hence, although the nineteenth-century European transition relied primarily upon reduction of marital fertility (indeed, marriage occurred earlier and became more frequent, which tended to *increase* overall fertility), fertility in developing countries may be reduced via changes both in marriage practices and fertility within marriage[16], and will at least not tend to increase as a result of earlier marriages and higher marital frequencies.

B4. *Increased legitimacy of the small family norm.* The large family was taken as "normal" in most of nineteenth-century Europe: there were few obvious examples of alternatives, and cultural diffusion was in any case relatively limited. In contrast, the "demonstration effect" of the European transition has provided modern legitimacy for the small family norm and evidence that its achievement is feasible, and many factors (such as improved international communication and expanded trade) have accelerated the processes of cultural and intellectual diffusion.

B5. *Increased interest and planning capability of government.* Population growth rates in nineteenth-century Europe, high by historical standards (although low by twentieth-century standards), were not considered to be excessive. Modern leaders are better aware of the fundamental importance of rapid population growth as a variable in development than their nineteenth-century predecessors, and governments representing 81 percent of the *population* of the developing world (although still a minority of developing *countries*) have now declared their population growth rates to be excessive.[17] In addition, many developing countries now have economists and planners able in principle to foresee future problems, whereas such planning at a national level was little known in nineteenth-century Europe.

B6. *Governmental ability to permeate subnational linguistic/cultural barriers.* Evidence from the Princeton European Fertility Study demonstrates the importance of subnational linguistic/cultural barriers in limiting or delaying the spread of the European demographic transition. Unlike much of nineteenth-century Europe, most modern developing countries have the administrative and technological infrastructure (for example, central planning and administration, widespread publication in multiple languages, improved transport, telecommunications, radio and TV, and postal systems) to enable them to better permeate such barriers.

B7. *International assistance.* The present availability of international assistance (via the United Nations and other agencies) means that governments of developing countries may call upon substantial outside resources and expertise. Such assistance, if employed properly, can reduce delays in development processes which might otherwise result from indigenous shortages of capital, materials, technology, and know-how.

B8. *More rapid pace of fertility decline.* Kirk[18] and Beaver[19] among others, have noted that countries that *have* experienced fertility declines in recent decades have shown a more rapid pace of decline than in nineteenth-century Europe. This phenomenon may be attributable to varying combinations of the factors described above, especially more rapid development, sharper declines in mortality, greater governmental interest and capability, and the availability of effective contraception and safe abortion and sterilization.

SUMMARY AND CONCLUSIONS

When the available data on the 19th-century decline in European fertility are analyzed on a systematic basis, some major propositions of transition theory are empirically supported, but only those at a high level of generality. From a broad macrohistorical view it is correct to say that in the two centuries from the mid-1700s onward there were widespread and substantial declines in marital fertility which were associated with major social and economic transformations in European societies. However, the more specific and explanatory propositions derived from transition theory cannot explain all of the salient features of the European experience. In particular, the theory fails to explain fundamental phenomena such as variations in pretransition levels of fertility and in the timing of onset and the pace of the fertility decline which eventually became universal.

A recent study suggests that transition theory can achieve a similar moderate level of success in Latin America, especially when the traditional theory is substantially modified and additional causal variables including cultural factors are introduced. Once again the (modified) theory achieves considerable predictive power at a high level of generality—those Latin American countries with relatively high levels of development are more likely to experience the beginning of fertility decline than others. Again as in the European case, however, little success is achieved in predicting the timing of onset and the date of progress of fertility decline on the basis of transition theory.[20]

Hence at high levels of generality the basic causal structure of transition theory appears sound. When the process of development is carried to the high levels achieved in Europe and some parts of Latin America, it appears to be sufficient to establish the preconditions for a natality decline. It cannot, however, be said to be necessary to this end, for these preconditions also arose in contexts of quite low social and economic development.

The substantially different socioeconomic and demographic characteristics of modern developing countries leave little doubt that their patterns of fertility decline will differ markedly from those of Europe. Still, there is no reason to think that a *high* level of development will prove to be any less sufficient or any more necessary for the establishment of the preconditions for fertility reduction; indeed, there is already good evidence that fertility declines have occurred in areas of both high and low development.

It must be recognized, however, that the high levels of development of Europe and parts of Latin America are not a realistic prospect for many developing countries, at least over the next few years or decades. When transition theory is applied to such circumstances, it fails to provide adequate answers to two questions of fundamental scientific and policy significance:

1. Sufficiency: Will the moderate levels of development to which many developing countries can realistically aspire in the medium-term future be sufficient to establish the preconditions for "natural" fertility decline?
2. Timeliness: If such declines do occur, will they occur soon enough and at a pace rapid enough to compensate for the sharply increased pace of mortality decline and higher initial fertility levels of these countries as compared with transitional Europe?

The current international debate hinges on these matters of sufficiency and timeliness. Those arguing that development will "take care of" population believe that development is sufficient (and also necessary) to bring about adequately prompt fertility reductions at an acceptable tempo. Those arguing in favor of voluntary population policies and programs—as additions to, not substitutes for, maximal efforts in the development sphere—emphasize the importance of development but doubt its sufficiency and timeliness for many countries, and hence call for direct efforts to enhance and accelerate its demographic impacts. Those urging coercive population policies accept the significance of development, approve of policies encouraging voluntary restraint, but hold that both of these are neither sufficient nor adequately rapid to meet the pressing need. All agree with the general proposition of transition theory that high levels of social and economic development will eventually have important downward effects upon fertility. Hence the structure of these theoretical postures is pyramidal, with each finding scientific support in different aspects of the same basic orthodoxy.

If this be so, it may well be asked why the debate about the modern relevance of transition theory is so strident, so lacking in scientific objectivity. The answer is the familiar one of politics, for over the past decade population has willy-nilly become an important issue of international affairs. In this arena, perspectives deriving from political rather than scholarly considerations have been wrapped in the scientific mantle of transition theory.

The politicization of population issues is, in principle, not a bad thing. Indeed, if policies are to be considered, it will have to be done via the political process. But politicization is not a friend of science, particularly when, as with transition theory, the empirical evidence is ambiguous and may be interpreted as supportive of diverse political perspectives.[21] At present in the field of population policy, decisions must respond primarily to political priorities and constraints rather than to the demands of scientific validity. In particular, it is clear that there is great political virtue in a simplistic interpretation of transition theory asserting that in all circumstances development will "take care of" population matters. Nonetheless, scientists are obligated to report that close examination of transition theory in both historical and modern perspective shows that policy-makers would be ill-advised to adopt such a simplistic and deterministic view.[22] In dealing with the intertwined issues of population and development, the challenge facing both scientists and policy-makers is to gain greater understanding of the processes of the demographic transition in their full subtlety and complexity and thereby to seek a more informed basis for policy.

NOTES AND REFERENCES

1. An extensive report on the Bucharest debates is presented in W. P. Mauldin, N. Choucri, F. W. Notestein, M. S. Teitelbaum [*A Report on Bucharest* (Population Council, New York, 1974); *Stud. Fam. Plann.* 5, 357 (1974)]. For a discussion of the bewildering variety of extant positions on population and development, see M. S. Teitelbaum [*Foreign Aff.* 52, 742 (1974)]. The importance for policy of theories on the relation between fertility and development is discussed in H. Leibenstein [*Int. Labour Rev.* 109, 443 (1974)].
2. The term "theory" is used in a qualified manner throughout this chapter, since it can be argued that the theory of the demographic transition is not a theory in a strict scientific sense.
3. The generalization of transition theory developed gradually from the work of a number of scholars, including W. S. Thompson [see *Am. J. Sociol.* 34, 959 (1929)] and A. Landry, A. M. Carr-Saunders, F. W. Notestein, and C. P. Blacker [see citations in D. V. Glass, in *Public Health and Population Change,* M. C. Sheps and J. C. Ridley, Eds. (Univ. of Pittsburgh Press, Pittsburgh, 1965), pp. 13–14]. More extensive summaries of the theory are presented by F. W. Notestein [in *Proceedings of the Eighth International Conference on Agricultural Economics* (Oxford Univ. Press, London, 1953), pp. 15–31] and G. J. Stolnitz [in *Population: The Vital Revolution,* R. Freedman, ed. (Doubleday-Anchor, New York, 1964), pp. 30–46].
4. The adoption of this idea is not uniform across all segments of society. It is usually embraced initially by the elite, whose social situation makes them better aware of the changing social milieu and who also have greater access to knowledge of methods required, for reasonably effective fertility control.
5. See, for example, the discussion in Notestein [(n. 3), pp. 22–23].
6. A. J. Coale, in *Proceedings of the IUSSP International Population Conference* (International Union for the Scientific Study of Population, Liège, Belgium, 1973), pp. 53–72.
7. R. E. Frisch and J. W. McArthur, *Science* 185, 949 (1974).
8. The evidence on this subject has been reviewed by J. Knodel and E. van de Walle [*Popul. Stud.* 21. 109

(1967)]. They report that in their German data the high correlation between breast-feeding and fertility nearly disappears when statistical control is provided for infant mortality, thereby raising some doubt as to the demographic impact of lactation practices.

9. See, for example, the following: N. E. Himes, *Medical History of Contraception* (Williams & Wilkens, Baltimore, 1936); P. Demeny, in *Population and Social Change,* D. V. Glass and R. Revelle, Eds. (Arnold, London, and Crane, Russak, New York, 1972), pp. 153–172; D. E. Dumond, *Science* 187, 713 (1975); and D. E. C. Everseley, in *Population in History,* D. V. Glass and D. E. C. Everseley, Eds. (Aldine, Chicago, 1965), pp. 46–52.
10. See J. Hajnal, in *Population in History,* D. V. Glass and D. E. C. Everseley, Eds. (Aldine, Chicago, 1965), pp. 101–143.
11. The so-called "threshold hypothesis" [supported in *Popul. Bull.* 7, 134 (1963)] was also found to be wanting when subjected to the empirical test of European data [see E. van den Walle and J. Knodel, in *Contributed Papers of the IUSSP Sydney Conference* (International Union for the Scientific Study of Population, Liège, Belgium, 1967), pp. 47–55]. It must be emphasized that, although very high levels of development appear to be sufficient to establish the preconditions for marital fertility decline, such declines do not necessarily ensue. For example, in Central Asian republics of the U.S.S.R. such as Tadzhik S.S.R., Turkmen S.S.R., and Usbek S.S.R., high levels of marital fertility have persisted up to 1970, and indeed the 1970 levels may be higher than those of 1926 (A. J. Coale, personal communication).
12. See the discussion of these possibilities in R. Freedman [*Popul. Index* 31, 425 (1965)]. A recent publication presents an interesting attempt to apply transition theory on a retrospective basis to Latin American data (see S. E. Beaver, *Demographic Transition Theory Reinterpreted* (Lexington Books, Lexington, MA, 1975)].
13. For example, under the two alternative assumptions described, by the year 2050 the population of Nigeria would have increased by 108 and 205 percent, that of Bangladesh by 125 and 248 percent, and that of Mexico by 118 and 229 percent, respectively [see Teitelbaum (n. 1), pp. 747–749].
14. See, for example K. Davis [*Popul. Index* 29, 345 (1963)].
15. In addition, the patterns of urbanization observed in some developing countries differ in several important respects from those in other developing countries and in 19th-century Europe, and hence urbanization may not represent the same force for value change in all cases. See, for example, the discussion in *The Determinants and Consequences of Population Trends* [United Nations, New York (1973)], vol. 1, pp. 97–98. See also S. Kusnets, *Proc. Am. Phil. Soc.* 118 (No. 1), 1 (1974).
16. The population policy of the People's Republic of China apparently places great emphasis upon increasing age at marriage [see A. Faundes and T. Luukkainen, *Stud. Fam. Plann.* 3, 172 (1972); J. S. Aird, in *People's Republic of China: An Economic Assessment* (Joint Economic Committee, Congress of the United States, Washington, DC, 18 May. 1972, 92nd Congress, 2nd Session), pp. 301, 316].
17. See Mauldin et al. (n. 1), p. 392.
18. D. Kirk, in *Rapid Population Growth* (National Academy of Sciences, Washington, DC, 1971), pp. 123–147.
19. See Beaver [(n. 12), (p. 89)].
20. See Beaver, [(n. 12), (especially pp. 145–152)]. Unfortunately this study of Latin American fertility patterns does not separate the effects of nuptiality from those of marital fertility, which may raise problems in dealing with some Latin American data. The level of analysis is also highly aggregated, that is, the nation-state as opposed to the province-level employed in the Princeton studies of the European fertility decline.
21. Scientists have had much experience with the facile application of inadequate evidence to social policy for political reasons. One need only mention the cases of social Darwinism, eugenics, and Lysenkoism, and the more recent excesses on subpopulation differences in intelligence.
22. Indeed, it may be argued that no current theory of fertility decline provides definitive guides to policy. For a discussion, see T. K. Burch, *Soc. Order,* in press.
23. I gratefully acknowledge the helpful comments of many colleagues, who unfortunately are too numerous to mention individually here. The European Fertility Study of the Office of Population Research, Princeton University, is supported by the National Institute of Child Health and Human Development.

5
The Theory of Change and Response in Modern Demographic History

KINGSLEY DAVIS

The process of demographic change and response is not only continuous but also reflexive and behavioral—reflexive in the sense that a change in one component is eventually altered by the change it has induced in other components; behavioral in the sense that the process involves human decisions in the pursuit of goals with varying means and conditions. As a consequence, the subject has a frightening complexity—so much so that the temptation is great to escape from its intricacies. One method of escape is to eschew any comprehensive theory, simply describing computations or working on a single hypothesis at a time. Another is to adopt some convenient oversimplification, such as the assumption that population is simply a matter of two capacities—a "reproductive urge" on the one side and "means of subsistence" on the other—or, at an opposite extreme, that demographic behavior is a function of a "traditional culture" or "value system."

My purpose here is to try to encompass some of the complexities in an overall analysis of demographic change in the industrialized countries. To do this, I prefer to start with Japan. Not only does Japan, the sole fully industrialized non-Western country, furnish a perspective that no other country can furnish, but some phases of its population change are statistically better documented.

ABORTION AS A DEMOGRAPHIC RESPONSE

The phenomenon most discussed—and one commonly regarded as peculiarly Japanese—is the rapid rise of the registered abortion rate from 11.8 per 1,000 women aged 15 to 49 in 1949 to a peak of 50.2 per 1,000 in 1955,[1] although at the latter date the registration of abortions is estimated to have been only 50 to 75 percent complete.[2] The resort to abortion has been the leading cause of probably the fastest drop in the birth rate ever exhibited by an entire nation, births per 1000 women aged 10 to 49 falling by 41 per cent between 1950 and 1957. Westerners profess to be astonished by this phenomenon, but they should not be. The behavior of the Japanese is essentially the same in kind as the behavior of West Europeans at a similar time in their social and demographic history. The main difference is that Japanese tolerance permits the abortion rate to be reasonably well known, whereas in the past of Europe the abortion rate has never been known and, for this reason, is usually ignored in population theory.

Yet there is indirect and approximate evidence that in the late nineteenth and early twentieth centuries in Western Europe abortion played a great role. David Glass, who in 1940 summarized the findings for eight northwest European countries, cited the records of women under a German sickness benefit fund which show a gradual climb in abortions from 38 per 100 births in 1908 to 113 per 100 in 1932.[3] In Belgium "there were many books explaining how to induce abortion and any woman could buy, for 60 centimes, a uterine syringe and use this to induce an abortion."[4] In both France and Germany advertisements by abortionists were freely published. In fact, one gets the impression that the attitude toward abortion in West European society was much less intolerant between 1900 and 1935 than it is today. A study of maternity cases in Israel in 1958 showed that, for women born in Europe, America, and Australia-New Zealand, 32 percent of those having a third birth admitted having resorted to induced abortion.[5]

Finally, in five of the People's Republics in Eastern Europe, which have legalized abortion, the subsequent history of the rise of registered abortions, as summarized by Tietze,[6] is amazingly like that of Japan. In Hungary, for example, medical boards were established about 1953 for authorizing therapeutic abortions.

"That these boards progressively liberalized their policies is reflected in the growing numbers of legal abortions from 1953 onward." After the decree of 1956 permitting "the interruption of pregnancy on request, the number of legal abortions increased rapidly until in 1959 it exceeded the number of live births."[7] Not only did the legal abortion rate rise rapidly in all four countries but also, as in Japan again, there was a substantial nonlegal rate. The number of abortions per 100 births in 1961 was in Hungary, 145; Czechoslovakia, 55; Poland, 35; and Yugoslavia (1960), 34.

If, then, abortion was once a widespread practice in the most advanced countries of Western Europe, if it is now widespread in Eastern Europe, where it is legal and subject to record, and where economic development is behind that of Western Europe, there is no reason to regard the resort to abortion as peculiarly Japanese. It is not an outgrowth of ancient tradition in Tokugawa times; not an outgrowth of the absence of Christian ideology. It is a response to social and economic conditions arising in country after country at a particular time in the process of modernization. The fact that abortion was not safe earlier in the century shows how determined the people of northwest Europe were in their reproductive control. Now that it is reasonably safe when legalized,[8] it is an effective means of family limitation for Hungary and Poland as well as for Japan.

If Western prudery and Oriental realism have led to an exaggeration of the role of abortions in Japan, this tendency has been helped by a statistical illusion. Not only have abortions increased as births have fallen, but the sum of births and registered abortions for each year yields a combined rate per 1,000 population that has changed little during the big fertility drop.[9]

This seems to say that an abortion was responsible for each birth saved. Actually, of course, abortions can and do occur much more frequently than births can.[10] Other factors must therefore have played a role in Japan's falling birth rate.

OTHER RESPONSES IN JAPAN

One such factor was contraception. Irene Taeuber points out that this practice increased rapidly after 1950 although abortions were available, relatively safe, and cheap.[11] Use prior to that time is shown by a 1950 national survey which found that a fifth of all couples were currently practicing contraception and that nearly a third had done so at some time. Furthermore, the age-pattern of change in marital fertility shows that, before the great rise in reported abortions began, couples were increasingly controlling their births, especially at the older ages.[12]

Of late, further control has been achieved by sterilization. Reported operations, totaling 5,695 in 1949, averaged 42,843 per year during 1955 to 1959, at which time they equalled 3.8 per cent of the reported abortions. There is even some indication of a small amount of infanticide.[13]

In addition, the Japanese migrated from their homeland in sizable numbers. The proportion of Japanese persons aged 15 to 59 outside to those inside the home islands were 2.8 percent in 1920; 3.2 percent in 1930; and 5.6 percent in 1940.[14]

Finally, the Japanese have exhibited still another adjustment—postponement of marriage. The proportion ever married among girls aged 15 to 19 fell from 17.7 in 1920 to 1.8 percent in 1955, and for women 20 to 24 it fell from 68.6 to 33.9.

The shift for men was also drastic. Indeed, it may be that the age at marriage rose faster in Japan than in any other country in history. By 1959 the nation had a marital age higher than that of most Western countries. In the United States in that year nearly half the brides in first marriages were under 20, but in Japan only one-nineteenth of them were that young. However, the Japanese concentrate their marriages more heavily in the modal ages—20 to 24 for brides and 25 to 29 for grooms—than Western countries do.

The one adjustment the Japanese have not adopted is celibacy. In 1955 the proportion of women aged 40 to 44 who had never married was only 2.4 percent, whereas in the United States in 1950 it was 8.1, and in Italy in 1951 it was 15.7 percent. It looks as though the age at marriage is flexible in Japan, but not the decision to marry or not to marry. However, even this may change. The women who in 1955 were aged 40 to 44 represent a generation whose marriages, occurring mainly in 1930 to 1940, were still almost wholly arranged by parents. As the age at marriage gets later, and as mating becomes more a matter of individual selection, a rising contingent of women may never succeed in attracting a man they are willing to marry.

THE THEORY OF THE MULTIPHASIC RESPONSE

What, then, is the picture that Japan presents? It is the picture of a people responding in almost every demographic manner then known to some powerful stimulus. Within a brief period they quickly postponed marriage, embraced contraception, began sterilization, utilized abortions, and migrated outward. It was a determined, *multiphasic response,* and it was extremely effective with respect to fertility. It brought down the gross reproduction rate, with only a brief wartime interruption, from 2.7 in 1920 to 0.99 in 1959.[15] A change that took at least 60 years in the United States required only 40 years in Japan.

What was the stimulus that caused such a massive response? In my view, the demographic stimulus was the decline in mortality and the sustained natural increase to which it gave rise. The data prior to 1920, though not entirely trustworthy, do at least suggest a declining death rate.[16] This is consistent with the better established trend after 1920, when, in not quite 30 years, mortality dropped to an extent that had required, starting at the same level, 76 years in Sweden and 37 years in Germany. The resulting natural increase climbed above 10 per 1,000 around the turn of the century and averaged 12.8 from 1900 to 1959. When these rates are plotted on the same chart as those for three Scandinavian countries averaged together (Denmark, Norway, and Sweden), with Japan lagged 50 years, the latter appears to be reenacting the history of natural increase in northwestern Europe, but more abruptly.[17]

But why the multiphasic reaction to sustained natural increase? Were the Japanese experiencing increased poverty? Were their "means of subsistence" disappearing under the impact of increased millions? No, such an explanation—of a type often called upon in demographic theory—has no relation to the facts. During the 45 years from 1913 to 1958 the average rate of growth of industrial output in Japan rose by 5.4 percent per year, thus exceeding the 5 percent rate of Germany, Italy, and the United States from 1880 to 1913, and greatly exceeding the performance of the United Kingdom and France in any sustained period.[18] Obviously the demographic response of the Japanese is not to be explained in terms of spreading poverty or diminishing resources. Nor were the people influenced in their behavior by concern about national "overpopulation," for they let their government proclaim a policy of population expansion during the "Coprosperity" era. In short, an explanation of the vigorous Japanese response to sustained natural increase must account for the antagonism between such increase and prosperity, in terms of behavior prompted by personal rather than national goals.

Was the Northwest European Response Similar?

Since the northwest European countries, years ahead of Japan, also had a sustained natural increase, did they manifest a similar multiphasic response? The answer is undeniably yes. Although generally overlooked because of our preoccupation with the contraceptive issue, the fact is that every country in northwest Europe reacted to its persistent excess of births over deaths with virtually the entire range of possible responses. Regardless of nationality, language, and religion, each industrializing nation tended to postpone marriage, to increase celibacy, to resort to abortion, to practice contraception in some form, and to emigrate overseas. The timing and relative importance of the reactions were not identical in the various countries, and of course methods could not be used that were not then technically feasible for the public at large (e.g., harmless sterilization); but the remarkable thing is that all of the northwest European countries reacted, that they did so in each case with the reappearance of the whole range of responses, and that virtually the entire panorama was later repeated in Japan.

The Theory of How the Stimulus Produces Response

But how were the stimulus and the response connected? It was not true in Europe, any more than in Japan, that the connecting link was poverty. From 1860 to 1900, the gross domestic product grew on the average at almost 3 percent per year in Denmark and Sweden, and almost 2 percent in Norway.[19]

The answer to the central question about modern demographic history cannot be posed, then, in the framework of ordinary population theory, which assumes the sole "population factor" to be some relation between the population resources ratio and the collective level of living. It is doubtful that any question about demographic behavior can be satisfactorily posed in such terms, because human beings are not motivated by the population-resources ratio even when they know about it (which is seldom).

My own view is that no society has been geared to a sustained high rate of natural increase except by conquest. Under a prolonged drop in mortality with industrialization, people in northwest Europe and Japan found that their accustomed demographic behavior was handicapping them in their effort to take advantage of the opportunities being provided by the emerging economy. They accordingly began changing their behavior. Thus it was in a sense the rising prosperity itself, viewed from the standpoint of the individual's desire to get ahead and appear respectable, that forced a modification of his reproductive behavior.

Mortality decline impinged on the individual by enlarging his family. Unless something were done to offset this effect, it gave him, as a child, more siblings with whom to share whatever derived from his parents as well as more likelihood of reckoning with his parents for a longer period of life; and, as an adult, it gave him a more fragmented and more delayed share of the patrimony with which to get married and found his own family, while at the same time it saddled him, in founding that family, with the task of providing for more children—for rearing them, educating them, endowing their marriages, etc.—in a manner assuring them a status no lower than his. The obligations of marriage and expanded parenthood were not easy, as Banks has shown so convincingly for nineteenth-century Britain,[20] in a changing society where one's position was threatened from every side and where one's children had to acquire new and costly forms of education. The parent needed to conserve some means for himself, because of longer life expectancy and because of the importance of capital for seizing opportunities or staving off disaster in the fluid situation of the times.

The inappropriateness of the old demographic behavior was not confined to one segment of society, such as the "middle class" or the towns and cities. Nor was it characteristic of some societies and not others. Whenever and wherever mortality declined on a sustained basis, there the continuation of old demographic patterns brought a train of disadvantages.

CONCLUSION

My thesis is that, faced with a persistent high rate of natural increase resulting from past success in controlling mortality, families tended to use every demographic means possible to maximize their new opportunities and to avoid relative loss of status. An understanding of this process in population theory has been hindered by a failure to see the multiphasic character of the response and by an interpretation of demographic behavior as a response either to absolute need or to some cultural idiosyncracy such as a particular "value system" or "custom." When the demographic history of industrialized nations is analyzed comparatively, an amazing similarity of the response syndrome seems to me to emerge. An explanation of a country's demographic behavior by reference to a peculiarity or accident of its culture fails to cope with this basic similarity of response. Curiously, we do not adopt such an easy way out with respect to mortality. We do not "explain" India's high death rate and Sweden's low death rate by saying that the one "values" high mortality and the other low mortality. Yet we sometimes come perilously close to this in regard to other aspects of human demography, especially fertility.

As for the view that the motivational linkage between change and response depends on fears of absolute poverty, we have seen that it fails to account for the fact that the multiphasic effort to reduce population growth occurs simultaneously with a spectacular economic growth. Fear of hunger as a principal motive may fit some groups in an extreme stage of social disorganization or at a particular moment of crisis, but it fits none with which I am familiar and certainly none of the advanced peoples of western Europe and Japan. The fear of invidious deprivation apparently has greater force, and hence the absolute level of living acts more as an environmental condition than as a subjective stimulus. If each family is concerned with its prospective standing in comparison to other families within its reference group, we can understand why the peoples of the industrializing and hence prospering countries altered their demographic behavior in numerous ways that had the effect of reducing the population growth brought about by lowered mortality.

NOTES

1. Masabumi Kimura, "A Review of Induced Abortion Surveys in Japan." Paper No. 43 mimeographed proceedings of the 1961 conference of the International Union for the Scientific Study of Population, p. 1.
2. Minoru Muramatsu, "Effect of Induced Abortion on the Reduction of Births in Japan," *Milbank Memorial Fund Quarterly,* XXXVIII, No. 2 (April, 1960), 152–166.
3. D. V. Glass, *Population Policies and Movements in Europe* (Oxford: Clarendon Press, 1940), pp. 278–280. Other health-fund data showed more abortions than births in the late 1920s.
4. Ibid., pp. 444–445.
5. Roberto Bachi and Judah Matras, "Contraception and Induced Abortions among Jewish Maternity Cases in Israel," *Milbank Memorial Fund Quarterly,* XXXX, No. 2 (April, 1962), 227.
6. Christopher Tietze, "Legal Abortion in Eastern Europe," *Journal of the American Medical Association,* CLXXV (April, 1961), 1149–1154; idem, "The Demographic Significance of Legal Abortion in Eastern Europe," paper presented at annual meeting, Population Association of America, April 25–27, 1963. Mimeographed.
7. Tietze, "Legal Abortion in Eastern Europe," pp. 1149–1154.
8. In Denmark and Sweden, 1953–57, there were only 6 or 7 deaths per 10,000 legal abortions. See Christopher Tietze, "The Current Status of Fertility Control," *Law and Contemporary Problems,* XXV (Summer, 1960), 442.
9. The combined rate would doubtless remain even more unchanging if the number of unregistered abortions were known.
10. According to surveys in 1949–50 and 1953–54, the gestation preceding abortions in Japan lasted between 9 and 11 weeks, depending on the order of the abortion. Kimura, op. cit., pp. 3, 9.
11. Irene B. Taeuber, *The Population of Japan* (Princeton: Princeton University Press, 1958), p. 274.
12. Legitimate births per 1,000 married women:

Age of married women	1950 rate as % of 1925 rate
15–19	92.8
20–24	96.4
25–29	93.3
30–34	75.4
35–39	54.4
40–44	40.5
45–49	13.2

Derived from data in: Taueber, op. cit., p. 265.

13. Ibid., pp. 278–282.
14. Ibid., p. 203.
15. Annual gross reproduction rates, 1920–55 from Taeuber, op. cit., p. 232. Annual gross reproduction rates, 1956–1959 from *Population Index,* XXVIII, No. 2 (April, 1962), 205.
16. Taeuber, op. cit., pp. 50–51.
17. Dudley Kirk pointed out in 1944 the similarity between the Japanese birth and death rates of 1921–41 and those of England and Wales in 1880–1900. ["Population Changes in the Postwar World," *American Sociological Review,* IX (Feb., 1944), 34.]
18. Surendra J. Patel, "Rates of Industrial Growth in the Last Century, 1860–1958," *Economic Development and Cultural Change,* IX (April 1961), 317–318.
19. Based on average rates of growth over various specified periods, with constant prices, as given in Simon Kuznets, "Quantitative Aspects of the Economic Growth of Nations: VI. Long-term Trends in Capital Formation Proportions," *Economic Development and Cultural Change,* IX (July, 1961), 76, 82, 88.
20. J. A. Banks, *Prosperity and Parenthood* (London: Routledge and Kegan Paul, Ltd., 1954).

6
Toward a Restatement of Demographic Transition Theory

JOHN C. CALDWELL

Our interpretation of past population movements and our expectations about future trends rest primarily on a body of observations and explanations known as "demographic transition theory." The conventional wisdom of this theory has had a deep impact and guides the work programs of international organizations, technical assistance decisions by governments, and popular analyses in the media.

The theory has changed little in the last 20 years. Indeed the period has seen a plethora of analyses of differentials in fertility, especially those found in contemporary American society, which have tended to obscure the all-important distinction between the origins of fertility decline and the subsequent demographic history of societies experiencing such decline.[1] This failure to update the theory is curious because the last two decades have provided researchers with far more experience of pretransitional and early transitional societies than they had previously been able to obtain.

It is also unfortunate because it has led to unnecessary misunderstandings, misinterpretations, and frustrations. It will be argued here that an inadequate understanding of the way in which birth levels first begin to fall has led both to premature gloom about the success of family planning programs and unnecessary hysteria about the likely long-term size of the human race, as well as to antagonisms at such forums as the Bucharest World Population Conference between countries at different stages of demographic transition.

DEVELOPMENT AND TESTING OF THE THEORY

The thrust of the paper is that there are only two types of fertility regime, with the exception of the situation at the time of transition: one where there is no economic gain to individuals from restricting fertility; and the second where there is often or eventually economic gain from such restriction. In both situations behavior is not only rational but economically rational. Another corollary is that there is not a whole range of economically rational levels of fertility in different societies, but instead only two situations, the first where the economically rational response is an indefinitely large number of children and the second where it is to be childless. It is admitted that in many societies at different times there is not a steep economic gradient between different levels of fertility; however, maximum and minimum family sizes in these societies are determined by personal, social, and physiological reasons, not economic ones. Further, it will be posited that the movement from a society characterized by economically unrestricted fertility to a society characterized by economically restricted fertility is essentially the product of social, rather than economic, change, although with economic implications. It will also be argued that the forces sustaining economically unrestricted fertility are frequently strengthened by economic modernization unaccompanied by specific types of social change and that this is the explanation for sustained high fertility in a situation in which "modernization"—urbanization, increase in the proportion of nonagricultural production, and so on—is demonstrably occurring. The social revolution—one of familial relationships and particularly of the direction of intrafamilial flows of wealth dictated by familial obligations—need not by its nature accompany economic modernization. However, it almost inevitably will occur either simultaneously with, or to a considerable degree preceding and perhaps hastening, economic modernization in the contemporary world. This is due largely to the phenomenon of Westernization, an essentially social process with a range of mechanisms for its spread (which have depended on economic advance in the West and to a more limited extent elsewhere, but which have not been dictated or formed by economic growth).[2]

The discussion will cover three types of society: (1) primitive societies where food gatherers, nomadic pastoralists or agriculturalists live in largely self-sufficient communities feeling little or no impact from a national state or a world religion; (2) traditional societies, predominantly agrarian, where the apparatus of a state government or the attitudes, and often the structure, of an organized religion make an impact on both community and individuals, especially in giving guarantee of safety or assistance; (3) transitional societies where rapid change in way of life towards that followed by people in lands with a "modern" economy usually in recent times has been catalyzed by outside contacts. It will be maintained that, at least in the contemporary world, the supports for unlimited fertility finally crumble in the transitional society, and that the analysis of this crumbling and of its preconditions is largely unrelated to the analysis of the frequently slow and sometimes vicissitudinous reduction in family size that subsequently occurs in transitional and modern societies. Much of the argument draws primarily on African examples, both because of my experience in Africa, and because all three types of society are well represented on the continent.

DEMOGRAPHIC TRANSITION THEORY

By the end of the nineteenth century it was common knowledge that fertility levels were falling in many Western countries and there was a presumption that birth rates would stabilize at lower levels (although there was no agreement about what the new levels would mean in terms of natural increase). An attempt was made by Warren Thompson in 1929 to divide this transition into three phases and by C. P. Blacker in 1947 to distinguish five phases.[3] Neither could be said to be the father of demographic transition theory in that neither suggested an explanation for fertility change.

Modern demographic transition theory was born almost in mature form in a paper written by Frank Notestein in 1945. Notestein offered a twofold explanation for why fertility had begun to decline. Fertility in premodern countries had been kept, if not artificially high, then high only by the maintenance of a whole series of props: "religious doctrines, moral codes, laws, education, community customs, marriage habits and family organizations . . . all focused towards maintaining high fertility."[4] High fertility was necessary for survival because otherwise the very high mortality rate would have led to population decline and extinction. But eventually in country after country mortality began to decline, and the props were no longer needed or were not needed at their original strength. One could leave the explanation here and argue that the props would inevitably wither, as social adjustments were made in response to other changes. However, Notestein put forward the view that, in the West at least, more positive forces (arising out of the same process of modernization that had brought the death rates down) were at work destroying the props. Fundamental was "the growth of huge and mobile city populations," which tended to dissolve the largely corporate, family-based way of life of traditional society, replacing it with individualism marked above all by growing personal aspirations. Large families became "a progressively difficult undertaking; expensive and difficult for a population increasingly freed from older taboos and increasingly willing to solve its problems rather than accept them."[5]

Again in 1953 Notestein pointed to the "urban industrial society" as the crucible of demographic transition and stated, "It is difficult to avoid the conclusion that the development of technology lies at the root of the matter." Once again he placed emphasis on the erosion of the traditional family, "particularly the extended family," and on the growth of individualism, but he also drew attention to other important social movements; "the development of a rational and secular point of view; the growing awareness of the world and modern techniques through popular education; improved health; and the appearance of alternatives to early marriage and childbearing as a means of livelihood and prestige for women." However, this time the description of pretransitional society was not drawn largely from the experience of the West but was generalized to include the developing world:

> The economic organization of relatively self-sufficient agrarian communities turns almost wholly upon the family, and the perpetuation of the family is the main guarantee of support and elemental security. When death rates are high the individual's life is relatively insecure and unimportant. The individual's status in life tends to be that to which he was born. There is, therefore, rather little striving for advancement. Education is brief, and children begin their economic contributions early in life. In such societies, moreover, there is scant opportunity for women to achieve either eco-

nomic support or personal prestige outside the roles of wife and mother, and women's economic functions are organized in ways that are compatible with continuous childbearing.[6]

The mainstream arguments of the theory are that fertility is high in poor, traditional societies because of high mortality, the lack of opportunities for individual advancement, and the economic value of children. All these things change with modernization or urban industrialism, and individuals, once their viewpoints become reoriented to the changes that have taken place, can make use of the new opportunities.[7]

The argument appears at first clear and convincing, but it has elements and implications that are more complex or debatable and that have had an enormous effect on our way of looking at demographic change. The most fundamental issue is whether the theory actually deals with reactions and accommodations to material circumstances. There is a persistent strain in demographic transition theory writings that claims that rationality comes only with industrial, urban society, and a related strain that regards traditional agrarian societies as essentially brutish and superstitious. This arises in two distinct ways.

The first is from the references to pre-demographic-transition society. The concept of the brutishness of the poor, and their inability and unwillingness to help themselves, is a fundamental proposition of Malthus. But the origin of the view in modern demographic transition theory is the argument that, in spite of the high mortality, insecurity, and lack of cost of children in pre-demographic-transition societies, all kinds of religious and social institutions and preserves were needed to keep fertility high. This is why demographic transition literature is full of references not to the behavior or reactions of such people but to *attitudes, beliefs, traditions,* and *irrationality.* Kingsley Davis wrote of the contrast between traditional societies and "the growing rationalism of modern life" and, again, describing sex and reproduction in the former, that "towards this aspect of life the woman has mainly a nonrational approach—religious, superstitious and incurious"[8]; George Stolnitz described "a shift in attitudes from the traditional fatalism of peasant societies"[9]; Eva Mueller observed that, "it is difficult to influence deep-seated attitudes"[10]; William Rich believed that "large-scale fertility declines cannot be expected until the living conditions of the majority of the population improve enough so that they no longer *consider* large families necessary for economic reasons"[11]; Stephen Enke deduced that, "many simple peoples understand very little about why reproduction occurs and how it can be prevented"[12]; Michael Endres has written recently, "people directed by tradition resist rational intervention and choice between behavioral patterns," and "to urge upon a traditional people a rational technical means of birth control is to challenge the tenacious hold of a hard-won culture to which choice and change are the enemy"[13]; while G. T. Trewartha indicted the irrationality of premodern society for causing not only high fertility but also maldistribution of settlement: "Indeed, much of the distribution does not appear to be particularly rational . . . Tradition, which is unusually strong among the tribal peoples of Negro Africa, plays a more than ordinary role."[14]

The second respect in which an implicit assumption of pretransition irrationality enters into the theory is through references to cultural lags in making fertility adjustments to the arrival of the new urban, industrial conditions. Such references are plausible in a way because a period of change is under consideration instead of an extended stable situation. Several of the quotations above do refer also to such lags, but the concept is both implicit and explicit in Notestein's 1945 paper. There he argued that the supports for high fertility "change only gradually and in response to the strongest stimulation" and described "a population increasingly freed from older taboos and increasingly willing to solve its problems rather than accept them."[15]

That the central tradition of demographic transition theory is still very much that of Notestein's 1945 and 1953 formulations and that the belief in increasing rationality with modernization is still an integral element has been demonstrated vividly by the publication of the most recent United Nations *Population Studies,* which justifies the latest United Nations population projections. The argument is worth quoting at some length:

> The entire process of economic and social development . . . itself changes people's outlooks from traditions and fatalism towards modern concepts and rationalism. . . . The past record in the more developed countries demonstrates . . . that it [fertility decline] can . . . be expected to occur in the normal course of the modern development process . . . the deliberate regulation of fertility defies age-old custom. . . . A high frequency of child-

birth ... was necessary for the continuation and security of families and this found emphatically strong support in the prevailing values and customs. In many cultures it has also been considered that children provide a much needed insurance against destitution in old age. Associated with such cultural norms has been the regard for women in their seemingly principal function as bearers and rearers of children, limiting thereby their participation in economic and social roles held to be mainly the prerogative of men. Interwoven with such attitudes there can also be a fatalistic refusal, or even an abhorrence, to contemplate any regulatory interference with the reproductory process. It is not to be wondered at that such a traditional outlook on life can be highly resistant to change. But as shown by the earlier experience of the more developed regions ... change is possible or eventually to be expected.[16]

Much of the argument for demographic transition concepts as they are now widely held turns on the definition of rational. The term "economically rational" is frequently substituted so as to avoid having to judge "social rationality" with the possibility of having to agree that a certain mode of behavior was rational in a given setting in that it met the ends of religious beliefs or of community obligations. Even so, the criteria employed are highly ethnocentric and are laden with Western values. It is assumed that it is rational for a man or a couple to maximize the expenditure on the individuals in his or their nuclear family; but there are any number of non-Western societies in which there is greater pleasure in spending on some relatives outside the nuclear family (adult brothers for instance) than on some within it, and in which children are happier to spend on parents than are parents on children. Obviously the fundamental choices are social ones and economic behavior is rational only insofar as it is rational within the framework established by social ends. What demographic transition theory has always regarded as rational are primarily Western social ends with economically logical steps to maximize satisfactions given those ends.

The underlying assumption of this study is that all societies are economically rational. The point is a simple one, but its acceptance is absolutely necessary if we are to arrive at an adequate theory of demographic transition, if we are to understand the contemporary population changes, and if we are going to make adequate predictions for planning purposes. It is, in fact, difficult to have a rigorous analysis on any other assumption. Social ends differ but can be largely explained on a rational basis—usually even in economic terms. Furthermore, change in social ends can often be observed, measured, explained, and predicted. The view that the fertility behavior of the Third World arises largely from ignorance and should be combatted with education and guidance is held strongly by many family planning movements and leads to friction and even confrontation; the same reaction arising out of much the same origins was witnessed writ a little larger at the Bucharest Conference. Indeed the view that peasants are usually mistaken in evaluating the effect of their fertility on their own economic well-being has recently been seriously argued in a paper by Mueller.[17]

A second implication of demographic transition theory, at least as originally conceived by Notestein, is that industrialization and concomitant urbanization are preconditions to development. Notestein placed stress on "urban industrial living" (in 1945) and later on "urban industrial society" (in 1953), as the context in which the social changes leading to fertility decline occur. Similarly Thompson (in 1946) referred to "industrialization" as the necessary condition. In the last 20 years such terms have largely been replaced by "modernization" or near synonyms like "the modern development process" as it became clear that great numbers of people in the Third World were unlikely to be living in industrial cities for generations. The demographic transition theory did allow for the possibility that the new way of life and the consequent new fertility behavior might be generated in the urban industrial setting and then be exported to nonurban and nonindustrial populations either by exporting some of its institutions (such as schools, women's rights legislation or a full market economy) or by simply exporting its attitudes or ideas. This tenet received historical support from the decline in fertility among rural populations in the West. The theory did not specify whether the urban industrial melting pot from which the changes were derived had to be in the same society or whether a global economy and society was beginning to operate that could export the necessary ideas and institutions from the economically developed countries to the commercial cities of Asia and Africa and on to the rural hinterlands. (Demonstrably this has long been happening with regard to governmental institutions and more recently in terms of schools and political ideology.) In any case the link with the emphasis on the props for high fertility is clear. If high fertility in developing countries were a wholly rational response to economic circumstances, then the small family pattern could never be exported; but, if the large family were to a considerable extent the product of beliefs and attitudes sustained largely by religion and shibboleth in order to compete with high mortality rather than to meet the needs of the economic system, then export was quite possible. Those who doubted the validity of a theory based only on the transmission of ideas but who were prepared to accept the possibility that the spread of small families could be achieved by the spread of institutions made little progress in identifying those institutions that were minimally necessary for fertility transition—schools? nonagricultural employment?

A third problem lurked in demographic transition theory but was not specifically identified. Was it primarily modernization that was being exported? Is there a specific form of social modernization that is a necessary adjunct to economic modernization? Or is the export Westernization, which by historical accident has been tailored to fit the world's first economic modernization and which is easily exportable partly because of the West's economic strength (clearly visible in its earlier ability to colonize) and partly because this tailoring makes it easily adaptable to modernizing economies? Notestein wrestled with problem areas in his 1953 paper and the whole question of Westernization almost arose: why had fertility fallen steeply between World Wars I and II in almost wholly agricultural Bulgaria while failing to do so during the 1950s in the larger urban areas of Egypt and the Far East?[18]

Suggested Modifications to the Theory

Without actually saying as much, Davis argued in 1955 and again, with Judith Blake, in 1956 that the props were not needed. High fertility was a perfectly rational response to socioeconomic conditions in a traditional agrarian society: the extended family means that the cost and care of children are shared; children, once past infancy, may in fact pay for their costs, especially in conditions of cottage industry, but more generally in any farming situation; both husbands' and wives' families of origin may help establish the newly married couple, often on a farm of their own; large families may bring economic strength through political strength in the local decision-making organizations.[19]

Recently this aspect of the demographic transition debate has been summarized and evaluated by Thomas Burch and Murray Gendell, who demonstrated that research findings from India and Taiwan fail to show the predicted fertility contrasts between families residing as nuclear families and those living together in larger agglomerations of relatives.[20] The point is an important one, and, in order to clear the way for the subsequent argument in this chapter, should be dealt with here. The research in India and Taiwan is almost certainly irrelevant for three reasons, of which the second is most important. The first is that survey or census data do not accurately measure even residential family size. The building materials, mud and stone in contrast to bamboo and thatch for instance, often determine whether considerable numbers of people can be housed in a single structure or alternatively in several smaller structures adjacent or close by. The second (a point to be elaborated later) is that family residence arrangements have little or nothing to do with the true extended family of mutual obligations, at least as long as residence outside the traditional community is not specified. It is the size and ramifications of this family of obligations that may well help to determine fertility. The third is that family residential patterns are often a function of the life cycle; in some societies nuclear residence is most likely to be found immediately after husband and wife (often with children of their own by this time) first move away from their parents to a farm or business of their own. What demographers should really be interested in are the families of this type who are unlikely to subsequently attract or retain many other relatives (except perhaps aged parents or nephews and nieces undergoing education) often because they have moved to a city or have been fairly highly educated and so have opted for a different way of life from their relatives.

Family sociologists added some riders to the picture. William Goode decided that the nuclear family's fundamental demographic characteristic was not that it leaned toward small size but that it was more flexible than the extended family in reacting to economic conditions favoring high or low fertility; thus at much the same time (eighteenth and early nineteenth centuries) European populations had chosen high fertility in frontier North America and moderate fertility in their homelands in Europe.[21] This had, of course, been a major contention of Malthus. Some, Colin Clark, for example, went further and identified nuclear families with advanced economies and extended families with nonindustrial societies—probably, as will be argued later, a fundamental mistake at least in terms of European history.[22]

Another attack on the props came from David Heer and Dean Smith who argued that the props had at every stage been wholly rational because of high mortality and had withered as the death rates fell.[23]

Recent Ideas

An important contribution in the 1950s was that of the economists, especially Ansley Coale and Edgar Hoover in 1958 with a major analysis of India, together with Mexico. What is apt to be overlooked is that Coale and Hoover accepted as their starting point the existing demographic transition theory,[24] and that most of the subsequent economic analysis is independent of theories about when and if fertility is likely to fall. Coale and Hoover spelled out the economic implications of transition theory but they did not test its basic assumptions. Their analyses were essentially those of macroscopic data, and their main conclusion was that national economic growth is impaired if fertility levels too greatly exceed mortality levels. However, most nonspecialists received the message that they had shown convincingly that high fertility is considered the ideal family size. The concept of "norms" had been one of the basic planks of modern sociology, and in the early 1960s Ronald Freedman applied it to fertility studies in a way that seemed to have implications not only for behavioral rationality but for behavioral economic rationality: "family size norms will tend to correspond to a number which maximizes the net utility to be derived from having children in the society or stratum." In developing countries, he concluded, "there may be a delicate balance of pressures towards higher fertility to ensure at least a certain minimum number of children and counter pressures to minimize or eliminate an intolerable surplus of children under difficult subsistence conditions."[28]

During the mid-1960s, knowledge, attitude, and practice (KAP) surveys were used to measure desired or "ideal family size" in the developing world using questions about the "best" or "ideal" number of children or the family size that would be desired if the respondent were to start her reproductive history all over again. Comparisons made in 1965 between "desired" and actual fertility prompted W. Parker Mauldin to state, "although it is not yet true that people in the developing areas share the small family ideal, it is true that most of them no longer want very large families,"[29] and Bernard Berelson to calculate that, while ideal family size in the United States was 97 percent of the achieved size, it ranged in a number of developing countries between 60 and 92 percent.[30]

The whole question of ideal family size is of the utmost importance for the discussion of demographic transition theory in this paper. It is not necessary to regard the gap between ideal and achieved size as evidence of irrational behavior; indeed Berelson regarded it as arising from "lack of information, services and supplies" and this was the most common position taken during the 1960s by technical aid organizations in the family planning field. Indeed the significant gap—that created by the props, according to demographic transition theory—is essentially that between the family size which would be dictated by economically rational behavior and ideal family size. In fact there is little relationship between the demographic transition concern with the attainment of economic rationality and the KAP study attention to ideal family size; KAP studies essentially attempt to measure potential consumer demand, and in this they ignore the issue of rationality except to the extent that it seems reasonable for a person to do what he wants to do. Some researchers appear to take it for granted, however, that a movement in ideals is almost inevitably a movement toward rationality and, hence, evidence of the decay of the props.

There are three fundamental questions.

The first is whether there are "norms" at all in the high-fertility situation. It will be argued here that economically there is no ceiling in primitive and traditional societies to the number of children who would be economically beneficial; the actual number is kept down because physiological and social problems arise from too frequent childbirth and the failure to cease childbearing at a certain stage. Achieved fertility is a product of this conflict and can hardly be described as approximating a norm.[31]

The second question is whether fertility behavior must be regarded as mainly economically motivated, or whether social motivations are also important or even dominant—whether norms, if they exist, and fertility behavior can be taken as an approximate measure of the individual's reaction to economic circumstances. Simon argues that fertility can be taken to be primarily economically motivated and justifies "an important omission [from his study] . . . , social norms and values. The reason . . . is that in the context of long-run analysis, culture and values do *not* have independent lives of their own."[32] This, it will be noted, is a direct assault on the props. This proposition differs from that put forward in this paper in that the argument here is that fertility is economically rational only between certain limits that are set by noneconomic factors; that there are two types of society, one in which it is economically rational for fertility to be ever lower, but in which a floor is interposed by noneconomic considerations, and the other, in which it is rational for it to be ever higher, restrained only by a noneconomic ceiling.

The third question is whether fertility can be used as a measure of desired behavior. The apparent demonstration by the KAP surveys that there is a wide gulf between what Third World people want to do and what they succeed in doing introduced a large element of chance (and not random chance at that) into the whole matter. It is perhaps impossible to study the motivation behind fertility decline if the populations of the Third World habitually exhibit fertility well above what both economic rationality and the attitudes molded by the props dictate. I suggest that this apparent gap is partly the product of the present unusual circumstances, but largely an artifact of the method of investigation. Change is at present so rapid in many societies that there is a fast increase in the number of people who will economically benefit from lower fertility. However, the "ideal family" questions ultimately fail to measure likely fertility behavior even under conditions of adequate access to contraception because they are imported almost undigested from Western society and contain a range of assumptions about non-Western societies that will not bear up under examination. The fundamental problem is the questioning of a woman about the "best" number of children, as if the chief cultural thrust were optimization of family size instead of a range of other concerns such as meeting the expectations of husband and other relatives, conforming with peer group behavior, and so on. In many surveys most respondents probably do not fully understand the question. They know what the words mean, but they also know that they are being economically disadvantageous for every size of population unit, and the view that high-fertility agrarian families were behaving irrationally was given a powerful boost.

It is possible to extrapolate part of the argument from national populations to individual families: to suggest that lower fertility will produce a family age structure with a higher ratio of potential adult producers to child consumers than will high fertility and that fewer children will allow mothers to participate more in economic activity.[25] For reasons analyzed below all these arguments ring somewhat hollowly in an actual agrarian society: children work at young ages; often the peasant's analysis is dynamic in contrast to the demographer's static one in that the peasant is thinking less of the present and more of safeguarding the future; and, in many societies, the peasant's wife already works long hours (freed from minding the product of her recent fertility by the child care being practiced by the product of her earlier fertility).

Two years before Coale and Hoover's study appeared, R. Nelson had produced his "low-level equilibrium trap model." Subsequently Harvey Liebenstein made the model more specifically demographic, suggesting that in "backward areas" people are merely caught by circumstances: they lack the inducement to save or invest and are unlikely to make quantum jumps in technology; as a result, per capita income remains static, mortality does not decline, and, hence, population does not grow.[26] The model does imply at least short-term rationality, although it could also be taken to mean that the society as a whole was incapable of planning its course to a better future. A more important limitation is that the model seems to have no real significance for social theory (except for historical studies) in a world where societies are no longer isolated from each other and where imported health technology means that population is growing increasingly fast, even in many societies with largely subsistence economies.

In 1974 Julian Simon summarized and assessed much of the research evidence available on fertility and stage of economic development, concluding that "fertility is everywhere subject to much rational control." He largely avoided the question of why—within the framework of rational decision—fertility decline sets in, contenting himself with pragmatically observing that "we may rely on the fact that, as education rises, fertility will fall" and that "if one wishes to reduce fertility, one should think about raising educational levels as well as aiding birth control."[27]

Since the 1950s, sociologists have contributed powerfully—not always intentionally—to the thesis of irrationality by apparently showing a substantial gap between desired and achieved fertility in the Third World (together with a smaller gap in developed economies). The origin of this formulation dated from the beginning of fertility studies, when the Indianapolis Survey of 1941 asked American respondents what they asked to define "best" in a modernizing sense by interviewers (and behind them, some institution) who interpret "best" in a futuristic sense or in the sense of the elites. The "politeness response" is only a small part of the reaction.[33] The "ideal family" question was shaped by Western, middle-class researchers, living in conjugal families in which husbands and wives consult each other over matters of reproduction and sex, and it achieves its greatest reliability among such people. In this paper it will be taken that achieved fertility everywhere comes close to being a rational response to the circumstances of the society.

In 1965 the publication of a United Nations study directed the attention of researchers to the prime importance of the changing conditions that lead to fertility decline at a point identified as the "threshold." The analysis distinguished six levels of fertility, in what was essentially a cross-sectional and not an historical analysis, but for further analysis combined the levels into two groups, one in which relatively low fertility had been achieved and the other in which it had not. Every Asian and African population, except Japan, was in the high-fertility group, while, with the exception of Albania, every European population in Europe, North America, and Oceania was in the low-fertility group. In Latin America, only Argentina and Uruguay were among the low-fertility countries. The United Nations recognized that it was "perhaps no coincidence that most of the countries where fertility is low . . . are in Europe and European-settled regions," concluding that "fertility levels might . . . be due . . . at least partly to culturally determined circumstances affecting the interactions between fertility and economic and social changes."[34] This dichotomy had the disadvantage that the nations identified as being beyond the threshold had in many cases passed it long ago; and neither the nature of the actual threshold nor the changes sufficient to ensure movement across it were actually detected.[35]

Other attempts to apply or develop threshold analysis have been made. Etienne van de Walle and John Knodel failed to find it a usable tool when analyzing fertility decline in France and Germany.[36] Dudley Kirk proclaimed the value of such an approach in 1971, and in 1975, together with Frank Oechsli, applied it to Latin America, calculating a "Development Index" and relating it to declines in both mortality and fertility.[37] But Oechsli and Kirk's data unmistakably evidence a cultural dichotomy: most of the countries with reduced fertility either are areas of almost purely European settlement in the extreme south or are Caribbean Islands with very mixed cultures and population origins. Island nations have been conspicuous in recent fertility declines, and the United Nations has identified ten and attempted to explain the change in terms of their small size and hence the easy penetration of ideas and health measures.[38] Yet seven of the island nations were settled entirely by immigrant populations while under European control: Réunion, Jamaica, Maruitius, Trinidad and Tobago, Guadeloupe, Martinique and Puerto Rico; one has been entirely Christianized: American Samoa; one is a mixture of an immigrant population and a fully Christianized indigenous one: Fiji; and one has achieved universal Western-style education: Sri Lanka.

In contrast to the approach of the thresholders, there has recently been renewed interest in the innovational explanation. (In the late nineteenth and early twentieth centuries, governments and other institutions almost invariably explained fertility control innovationally, as the spread of pernicious ideas.) Much of this has arisen from the Princeton Office of Population Research European fertility project and its demonstration that fertility declines spread fairly rapidly through linguistic or religious units only to be halted at their borders.[39]

The threshold and innovational approaches share a common problem in explaining the onset of fertility decline. Their data are usually for considerable aggregates of population, and, hence, it is difficult to determine whether the measured drop in fertility is attributable to a single socioeconomic group or not. If it is, then the threshold explanation holds up (provided that the threshold indices are meant to apply to subsections of a society), but the spread of innovation is shown to have an impact only on groups that have already reached some potential state of receptivity as measured by socioeconomic indices and not by attitudinal changes; if it is not, then the threshold indices can be discarded as measures of the sufficient conditions that must be met for demographic change to occur. In any case both approaches have failed as yet to specify the kinds of change necessary for individuals or couples to alter their fertility behavior and why such alterations take place.

Attempts have of course been made to investigate these changes around the beginning of transition, the most ambitious to date for developing countries being the East-West Population Institute's Value of Children Study.[40] So far the published national reports (on the Philippines and Hawaii) have had a strong social psychological orientation toward beliefs and values—stronger even than the questionnaires upon which they are based. The approach is clearly an aspect of innovational theory and has a good deal in common with explanations that rely heavily on the props; and, although it does not spell it out, the Philippines report could be described as an analysis of the import and diffusion of non-indigenous cultural values. So far, the project has insufficiently investigated the changing material aspects of life and the extent to which changing values could be said to be rationally moving parallel to economic realities.

New Experience

Increasingly massive family planning programs in Asia and parts of Africa, Latin America, and Oceania over the last quarter of a century have presented an enormous increase in opportunities to watch and measure fertility transition and to identify the innovators. This should have allowed demographic transition theory to be rewritten with the sureness that arises from large-scale field experiments. This has not happened, and one of the keys to the whole problem may be why it has not happened.

An important reason is undoubtedly described by the well-known precept in other areas of endeavor: applied science has increasingly limited returns, unless based on continuing fundamental research. Too much of the research has taken as its starting point and framework the preexisting conclusions of demographic transition theory. Too many frustrated family planning fieldworkers and administrators have been only too willing to blame the props for the failure to achieve program targets. Most indigenous and all expatriate administrators and advisors are in circumstances in which they economically benefit from controlling their own fertility, and they find it hard to understand why this should not be so for everyone else—irrationality is an easy answer especially when it can be demonstrated that education and demand for the family planning services are highly positively correlated. Probably too much of the research has been program-based instead of concentrating on the mechanisms of change in the society as a whole. Yet this is not the whole explanation. The operational research has permitted the identification of large numbers of innovators—at least in terms of using contraception, if not always in terms of deciding to restrict family size—but research has not clearly established the basic changes that have affected these people. On the face of it this seems hard to believe, and yet it is true for a number of reasons. One (as will be seen below) is that the innovators do not really know themselves; they differ in various ways from their parents and these differences make fertility control rational, but they usually cannot identify the essential differences. Another reason for the failure to identify preconditions is that comparison of the characteristics of family planning acceptors and nonacceptors shows that the former are much more likely to exhibit not merely one "modern" characteristic but a whole interrelated set (more education, nonagricultural employment, higher incomes, and so on), so that there is a chicken-and-egg problem. There has also been a research failure: failure to investigate in detail the way of life and circumstances of individual acceptors parallel to similar studies of the population as a whole.

In relation to the last point it might be noted that there has been over the last half century a considerable advance in economic anthropology, which has been almost entirely ignored by demographers.[41] Fierce debate has raged in economic anthropology between the Formalists and the Substantivists, the former claiming that Western economic analysis can be applied unchanged to all economic life and the latter maintaining that economics serves social ends and that every culture has its own economic theory. The Formalists narrowly define the subject of modern economics as allocation of scarce resources between either unlimited or numerous ends, while the Substantivists contend that rational economic behavior is rational only within a given social context and that these contexts are diverse and often startlingly different from those of the modern West. The Substantivists have also established that, even where money and markets exist, these may embrace only part of a society, and, more importantly, only part of the life of much of the population. The rest of the society, and perhaps the bulk of the life of most of its citizens, falls in the more traditional sector, where it is not rational, and usually not possible, to act out the life of market-economy man. The implications for demographic transition theory are that transition is made possible only by profound changes in the social structures of such societies, and that analyses of the economic rationality of high fertility reach different conclusions in different social structures.

Fundamental Problems of Research

Part of the failure to advance demographic transition theory can undoubtedly be blamed on inadequate research. The basic problem has not been inadequate methodology but rather poor application, especially in the application of methods in cultures other than those for which they were developed. The problems will only be summarized here as they have been treated more adequately elsewhere. The general failing, and one that encompasses the others, has been ethnocentricity. Too much research has been done too quickly and on too large a scale with research instruments, and often researchers, brought directly from contemporary Western society. Too often, the representatives of the non-Western society in the research have been completely inculcated with Western research approaches and conclusions in Western universities. As a result, the research approach often predetermines the range of findings and asks questions that provide the appropriate answers almost by an echo effect.[42] What prevents the researcher from worrying about the extent to which the pattern of responses fails to represent the society is the magnitude and flowchart nature of modern social scientific research: the large sample, the hierarchy of command, the precoded questionnaire, the responses as invisible magnetic recordings on a computer tape, computer editing, the computer print-outs of marginals and cross-tabulations that necessarily balance to the last unit, the written report in a predetermined pattern, and finally the cross-cultural international comparison with other research using similar or even identical instruments.

Four pitfalls of current research have particularly contributed to misunderstanding of the nature of demographic transition.

1. The magnitude and direction of wealth (money, goods, services, guarantees) flows and potential flows are areas of research that often are neglected or misunderstood. Such research is difficult. In premodern societies much of the wealth is still outside the monetized economy. Often money-equivalents are not visualized; services usually have an element of obligation; investments in future security may be discounted in the opposite direction to that to which Western economics is accustomed (discussed further below); the details about wealth have often not been disclosed even to immediate relatives (who exert competing demands and from whom details must often be hidden, more to prevent resentment and to allow equity to prevail, than to deprive people of their just deserts); and there is sometimes also a fear about tax officials and other authorities knowing about earnings. In these circumstances, small-scale, painstakingly thorough research is needed by investigators with a thorough knowledge of the society. Hardly any good research has yet been done. There is a temptation to quote inadequate or incomplete research, with highly misleading results. There would be less danger if the errors were random, but, without question, there is a great understatement of all flows of wealth and potential wealth.

2. The "family" of the fertility survey is often an artifact of the survey. Women are asked about their own reactions and their husbands' reactions, and of course, the women answer in these terms. No one describes the role in decision-making of the husbands' and wives' lineages; no one explains that the husband regards his brother as a nearer relation than his wife in the sense of that close inner circle where one no longer regards expenditure as depriving one personally of wealth; no one explains the intricate system of decision-making and obligations that may far exceed the nuclear family or residential group and in which the nuclear family may not even be a recognizable subunit.

3. The nature of family formation and of related decisions in developing countries is frequently misunderstood. Family size decisions are usually out of the respondents' hands for several reasons: both the physiological side of reproduction and the obeying of cultural practices may seem (sensibly enough) to them to be something they cannot control and hence there is an element of fatalism; family size is often the product of decisions taken for family reasons not primarily aimed at determining fertility; and, where there are decisions to be made, they may not be primarily decisions of the "couple." All these factors must be taken into account when interpreting "Up to God" and "Don't know" responses, which may be closer to the truth than the numerical ones. In these circumstances the value of any "ideal family" type of question is debatable, and the employment of the concept of "norms" misleading.

4. While fertility transition research is essentially a study of change, such investigations

have been impeded by too much emphasis on modernization. Change can be understood only if emphasis is given to studying the fundamental nature of the society that is being subjected to new forces. Too many survey questions are focused on the modernizing features, and too many of them have a built-in assumption that everyone is reaching for such change. Demographers have been far too rarely concerned with familiarizing themselves with the knowledge other social scientists have already accumulated about the society being examined. Perhaps even more serious is the fact that modernization has been accorded such respect (by all development researchers, but specifically by population researchers, in that they regard modernization as being the chief mechanism for reducing fertility and hence eventually containing global population growth) that its components have usually not been analyzed and the all-important distinction has not been made between Westernization, which may proceed at a rate unrelated to economic change, and residual modernization, which must go hand in hand with economic change because it is either a necessary condition or a necessary product.

What we obtain from research that is vitiated by these weaknesses is a reflection of the way a poorer version of our own society might be expected to behave if set down in a Third World context. We fail to appreciate significantly different social and economic structures and the extent to which these yield rewards to the highly fertile.

A SOCIETY EXPERIENCING CHANGE

The observations in this section are primarily of Nigerian Yoruba society. The Yoruba are the indigenous inhabitants of Nigeria's Western State (recently subdivided into Ogun, Ondo, and Oyo States) and Lagos State, as well as considerable parts of Kwara State in Nigeria and Southern Benin, or Dahomey. The Western and Lagos States are believed to have contained about 8.5 million people in 1962[43] and contain perhaps 13 million now, of whom over 11 million are Yoruba, out of a total of 13 million Yoruba in Nigeria and Benin. The Yoruba of the Western and Lagos States have been the focus of the largest segment of the Changing African Family Project and of the Nigerian Family Study, and many of the data used here are drawn from that study.[44] The area is well suited to this kind of investigation, because a primitive society (as defined here) existed over most of it until the latter part of the nineteenth century (and aspects of it can still be studied in any rural area); the traditional society is now paramount; and some of the population—largely the urban population and especially the middle classes of the cities (Lagos probably has over 2 million inhabitants and Ibadan 750,000)—are part of transitional society.

The Primitive Society

A primitive society is one in which the largest organizational institution is the tribe, the clan, or the village. No overall responsibility is taken by the larger apparatus of State or Church, which means that security within the groupings that exist is not augmented or guaranteed by an outside entity. Indeed, security outside the group is minimal; nearly everyone continues to live among their people of origin; and the size of that group is often the measure of safety.

Several aspects of such a society are of prime importance for understanding all pre-demographic-transition societies.

Perhaps the foremost is that the society or economy (for they cannot be separated) of the group is a single system in which the participants have time-honored roles and duties. There is usually communal land (which is essential in nomadic, food-gathering, and most shifting-cultivation systems); residence in propinquity to large numbers of people—mostly relatives—with whom one has lived all one's life; government by these same people; and a simple economy where much cooperation is needed for the larger tasks. The absolute right of individual ownership is unknown. In fact economic relations and social relationships intermingle. Edward Evans-Pritchard wrote of the Sudan, "One cannot treat Nuer economic relations by themselves, for they always form part of direct social relationships of a general kind,"[45] and C. K. Meek of Nigeria, "One of the main distinctions between Native systems of holding land and those of Western societies is that the former are largely dominated by personal relationships, whereas the latter are subject to the impersonal legal conception of 'contract'."[46] Marshall Sahlins summarized the position as, "A material transaction is usually a momentary episode in continuous social relations."[47] Transactions and gifts are not in fact markedly differentiated, especially as the latter are almost invariably also the cause of two-way flows of wealth.

Gifts of goods or services and later reciprocation allow the creation of a security system of mutual obligations (which will be dealt with in this review of the primitive society, even though such systems are of fundamental economic and demographic importance in traditional and transitional societies and survive even into modern society[48]). In all primitive and most traditional societies the maximization of profit or other ends in good times is of small importance compared with the minimization of risks (which often means ensuring survival) in bad times. Describing the Fulbe (or Fulani) of northern Nigeria, C. Edward Hopen reported that they "have an almost pathological concern (and often fear) for the future. Their conversation abounds with such expressions as 'tojaango' (what of tomorrow) and 'gam jaango' (because of tomorrow).... The prospect of a secure and relatively carefree old age under the care of their sons will often restrain young women from deserting or divorcing their husbands. Both men and women in many respects show a remarkable disposition to forego present convenience (or pleasure) in the interests of future benefit."[49] Such attitudes are universally reported by field researchers, even among the businessmen of Ghana's capital, Accra.[50]

The fertility implications are obvious. It is in such conditions, where one lives with almost all one's relations and possibly with other families whose ancestors have dwelt near one's own for generations, and where one has no other social environment and no other source of cooperation, and where social organization tends towards gerontocracy, that it is inconceivable that the nuclear family should crystallize out and that such a unit should attempt to gain economic advantage over other units.[51]

It is the survival of the extended family system as economic change occurs that helps to sustain high fertility. This survival is rendered more likely by a system of mechanisms that retain the full rigor of the extended family system even through the primitive and traditional societies. After the observations above, it might seem unlikely that primitive society would need such mechanisms, yet they exist throughout sub-Saharan Africa.[52] The reason is society's awareness that conjugal sexual relations can intensify conjugal emotional relationships, and that parent-child emotions can also become of overriding importance. Therefore, African cultures successfully weaken both types of relationship, because communal residence and occupational cooperation would be endangered if men listened to what their wives said was in their mutual interest rather than what their brothers or fathers said, while matrilineal societies would disintegrate if preference were to be shown for sons and daughters over nephews and nieces. In fact (and this is important in terms of demographic transition), relationships between spouses, even in monogamous marriages, are not very strong in traditional Yoruba society and parents do not exclusively focus their attention on their biological children. Even in 1973 only one-third of Yoruba spouses slept in the same room or ever ate together (admittedly indexes of affection regarded as less significant by Yorubas than by outsiders), and fewer still identified the person to whom they felt closest as their spouse, while children were commonly brought up by a number of kinsmen.[53] This should be seen in the context of traditional Yoruba residence in extended family compounds, which persisted even in Ibadan until only a few years ago.

Networks of relatives are important in the primitive society and remain so in the traditional society. They increase the size of the security system and of the cooperating group in less serious situations; they increase the number of close allies in the political contest in the traditional political system in which success is due to the ability to tap more or better communal resources; they increase the number of relatives who can attend family ceremonies and hence magnify one's social importance and sheer consumption pleasure. In rural Yoruba society it is still taken as one of the immutable facts of existence that family numbers, political strength, and affluence are not only interrelated but are one and the same thing. Furthermore, such a base still forms an excellent springboard to success for young aspirants in the modern sector of the economy.[54] There are only two ways of increasing the size of one's network of relatives and they are interrelated: by reproduction and by the marriage of one's children. Data from the second survey in the Nigerian segment of the Changing African Family Project show that 80 percent of all Yoruba still hold that children are either better than wealth or are wealth, while those who maintain that on balance they consume wealth fall to 6 percent in rural areas; 96 percent agree that increasing the number of relatives by means of marriage is a good thing and 83 percent that they can ask relatives by marriage for help with material things or services to a greater extent than they can ask nonrelatives.

But, if this is the way to wealth and power, why do extra children not press more on resources, especially on the supply of food? The question seems to have no meaning in most primitive societies and in traditional society among the Yoruba, even in densely settled rural areas or among urban populations. Part of the answer is that each new pair of hands helps to feed the extra mouth (to paraphrase the kind of proverb that seems to be found widely in Africa and Asia). Part is the nature of the communal economy, where "a man does not acquire more objects than he can use; were he to do so he could only dispose of them by giving them away."[55] Indeed, in such an economy underuse of resources may be far more common than pressure upon them, a situation generalized in Sahlins' rephrasing of Chayanov's rule: "the intensity of labour varies inversely to the relative working capacity of the producing unit [i.e., the household or family]."[56] Lorimer constructed a model for agrarian societies, which apparently showed that, even if belt-tightening was caused in some families by the birth of extra children, it was only to a small extent while the children were young.[57] Less than one-fifth of Yoruba respondents in the second survey of the Nigerian segment of the Changing African Family Project believed that the birth of an extra child would have even an immediate impoverishing effect.

African children certainly work (except perhaps in the transitional society), beginning at age 5 to 7 years, as they imitate ever more what their elders of the same sex do. It is often difficult, even among adults, to distinguish work completely from way of life. Nevertheless, the traditional patriarch appreciated that work had to be done, that it was often onerous, and that more could be done and others could perhaps take a larger share of the burden if the family were large. C. Edward Hopen relates that he discussed with a Fulani of northern Nigeria whether the Fulani, who supposedly are filled with joy by fathering large families, would have many children in the happy Moslem Heaven that they describe, only to be told: "No, why will we want children? All the work will be done by the servants of Allah."[58] Pierre de Schlippe, reporting on the Zande of southwest Sudan states that, "The prestige of extensive fields and full granaries was to a great extent achieved by family despotism," including "cruel punishments inflicted on wives and children."[59] This is not now the case among either the Zande or the Yoruba, but in rural areas wives and children obey male instructions to work (see below on the question of schoolchildren). Yoruba children work as they have always done helping to provide nonmarket goods and services, as well as helping with market production. That a man benefits economically in such a society by polygyny is now widely affirmed[60]; it is a small step from this to recognizing that he also gains if he has a large number of children.

Traditional Society

In Yoruba society the difference between primitive and traditional society is hardly worth making when analyzing demographic trends; but the establishment of the latter was undoubtedly the necessary precursor for fertility change in the transitional society. However, this has not been the case in all traditional societies, many of which evolved slowly over a long period,[61] and indeed the beginning of fertility transition can almost certainly be found in Europe at a time when it was still very largely premodern. State and Church, long before the advent of the Welfare State, were able to provide some assurance that they would intervene to try to prevent unnecessary deaths at times of community disaster—in Europe, with intermissions, since the time of the Ancient World, and over considerable parts of China over the centuries. This may well have weakened the need for the extended family in that the family was no longer the ultimate guarantor of survival. This was probably particularly the case where the authority of the State impinged most strongly and for the longest periods: for instance, in the Ancient World, in Metropolitan Rome, and, especially, in the City of Rome. It is difficult to examine Augustus's marriage laws without concluding both that the extended family at least was under pressure and that a subsequently reversed fertility decline was under way. Rome, as Gibbon so eloquently related, never really died away in Europe: the Church inherited the marriage laws and the attitudes that framed them, as well as responsibility for those in critical circumstances; the manor guaranteed employment and set conditions on access to land, which not only implied that family nucleation (in the economic sense of responsibilities) was well advanced but also reinforced that nucleation (and possibly held fertility in check by preventing early marriage).[62]

Traditional societies with their greater overall organization either introduced or increased the use of money. This, together with their greater guarantees of security to the traveler, expanded trade. With their national legal systems, they were more likely to move toward freehold tenure of land, although the demographic transition theorist should note how recently communal tenure has been important in non-European parts of the world. In fact, in most of sub-Saharan Africa freehold land still exists on only a very limited scale. All these changes had implications for the family.

Wealth Flows in Primitive and Traditional Societies[63]

As analyzed by an outsider from a modern society, children have demonstrable values of several different types in primitive and traditional societies. They do a great deal of work for or with their parents not only when young but usually during adulthood as well; they accept responsibility for the care of parents in old age; they eventually bolster the family's political power and hence give it economic advantages; they ensure the survival of the lineage or family name and in many societies undertake the necessary religious services for the ancestors.

This list, like much value of children research, obscures two very important points.

The first is that such disaggregation is a product of external observation or, even more significantly, of hindsight. In relatively unchanging societies no one sees these separate bonuses conferred by fertility. The society is made of a seamless cloth: children fit into an unintrospective society where they behave as their parents behaved and where their role is to work when young and to care for the old. This is why they may have great trouble in listing any good things (or bad things) about large families when asked by the researcher. Indeed, the respondents' ability to see clearly the separate aspects of children's roles are not as certain as before. These roles, then, become important in what is now the transitional society and help to explain the options and decisions of such a society.

The second point is that the value of children to the lineage and ancestors is not really a prop with a strength of its own. Rather, this aspect of the role of children reflects the fact that the other aspects conducive to high fertility are positive as well. When the other props begin to deteriorate in the transitional society, so does the concern for ancestors (often with the help of imported religions, or new interpretations of existing religions, or the spread of secularism).

Nevertheless it is important for the analyst of a society moving toward transition (and this is true of most developing countries) to identify the nature and magnitude of the intergenerational wealth flows in the society. In pretransitional and essentially rural societies, at least six different economic advantages of children to one or both parents can be distinguished: (1) Situational gain is of particular importance to patriarchal males. The obsession with per capita analysis has obscured this type of gain. In Yoruba society there is nothing approaching an equal division of wealth or consumption within the family: there are inequalities by sex, age, and family status. As the number of children beyond infancy grows, and, indeed, as the number of wives and ultimately the number of children-in-law increases, it is inevitable that the person on top of the pyramid controls more resources and has access to more services (as well as enjoying more obvious power), even if per capita income remains static. (2) Children work in the household and on the farm not only producing goods but providing a range of services that adults regard as wholly or partly children's work and that they are loath to do themselves: carrying fuel, water, messages, and goods; sweeping; looking after younger siblings; caring for the animals; weeding the crops; and so on. (3) Adult children usually assist their parents, especially with labor inputs into farms (which frequently increase as the parents age) and with gifts, to a much greater extent than the older generation readily admits or than is spontaneously reported to survey interviewers by either parents or children. (4) Adult children provide particular assistance in making up the family contributions to community festivities and to such family ceremonies as marriages, funerals, and celebrations connected with births. (5) The care of aged parents, who may insist on having their farms, businesses and households propped up as if they were still running them, can be a major undertaking. (6) Parents can invest in training or education of children so as to increase their ability to make returns (although the motive is usually only partly economic and is much more complex than is baldly stated here).

The key issue here, and, I will argue, the fundamental issue in demographic transition, is the *direction and magnitude of intergenerational wealth flows* or the net balance of the two flows—one from parents to children and the other from children to parents—over the period from when people become parents until they die. In premodern society much of the flow is indirect, because of the existence of extended families, clans, and even villages that share in these flows, and because the child's contribution to the parent may be largely by the augmentation of political strength to allow the tapping of a larger share of the communal wealth. The concept of a net balance is still valid, however, even if difficult to measure. It may even be closer to the truth in the older traditional village to speak of the flow being from the younger to the older in the community as a whole with the parent-child relationships in each family playing only a secondary role.

In all primitive societies and nearly all traditional societies the net flow is from child to parent. This is often partly obscured (especially in recent times) from the researcher by the very mechanisms that help to keep it working and to some degree determine the magnitude of the flow. Parents continually point out to children how much they have done for them and how much the children owe (not specifically as money or goods, but more as duty, which in the end means much the same thing). Such protestations may not have been needed in primitive society; to a large extent they help to provide guarantees in a changing and increasingly uncertain society. Three points should be noted. First, such protests are heard most in societies where the wealth flow is still from child to parent; they are much less a feature of a society where the flow has been firmly established toward the child. Second, the protests are not likely to bear much relation to the size of the family and hence to the size or reality of the outlay. Third, the researcher is likely, on hearing the protests and recording them as responses in his questionnaire, to take them as evidence of the economic disadvantages or even irrationality of high fertility. The protests are likely to be supported by details of actual expenditure, without equal concern for details of the returns, and these the researcher may regard as quantified data. There is evidence from one study of a region adjacent to Nigeria that the work of single, adult sons is so important to fathers that they deliberately use their control of bride wealth and marriage ceremonies to space out and postpone sons' marriages so as to organize an even flow of the labor first of unmarried sons and eventually of grandchildren.[64]

There is then a great divide, a point where the compass hesitatingly swings around 180 degrees, separating the earlier situation in which the net flow of wealth is toward parents and in which hence high fertility is rational and the later situation in which the flow is toward children and in which hence no fertility is rational. Why the divide is where it is, and why the compass swings, will be our major concern when investigating the transitional society.[65]

What this means is that before the divide economic rationality dictates unlimitedly high fertility. On the whole, discussion and even survey work in African primitive and traditional society seem to support this. Fertility is limited for all kinds of noneconomic reasons (some of which, however, like child survival, have economic implications). In Yoruba society, the Nigerian segment of the Changing African Family Project found that easily the most important reason is the spacing of births so as to contain infant and early childhood mortality and, hence, to maximize the number of living children. The second most important reason (at least in the past, because it has now been displaced in importance by delayed marriage) has been the cessation of sexual relations by a woman on the birth of the first grandchild so as to avoid the social and psychological tension arising from competing maternal and grandmaternal obligations. Other reasons have been the cessation of sexual relations in some cases when the husband takes another wife or when he moves elsewhere to work or because the woman feels increasingly old or battered by reproduction. Increasingly, fertility is being held in check by postponed age at marriage, which in the case of females already averages several years past puberty; this postponement arises out of competition with education or job opportunities and holds fertility in check because it is accompanied by continence, less sexual activity than in marriage, contraception, or abortion. When the numbers of children become really large, they raise problems of control, noise, and emotional deprivation even in rural societies. The list of noneconomic reasons is quite formidable and is incontrovertible evidence that economic rationality alone is unlikely to determine fertility in any society.

Similarly, after the economic divide, economic rationality dictates zero fertility. This does not happen, and fertility often falls slowly and even irregularly, again for social and psychological reasons—the extent to which alternative roles are available to women, the degree to which child-centeredness renders children relatively expensive, the climate of opinion, and so on.[66] Fertility does not reach zero for reasons that are entirely psychological and social.

It is then necessary to attempt to measure intergenerational wealth flows, an endeavor that is rendered difficult in pretransitional society by a host of problems: much of the flow is not direct but is derived from the extra political power exerted by a man with many children, especially grown-up sons and daughters married into other families; much of the flow is not money but goods and services; some of the flow forms part of family contributions to meet community obligations and does not reach the parents at all; most people have good reason for diffidence about revealing the total flow of wealth, or at least that received. All of these difficulties except the last diminish as the economy becomes more monetized and society more urbanized, and hence transitional society allows easier measurement. Attempts to measure the near-lifetime return on investment in children as well as the outflow from older children were made in Ghana in 1963, and a more comprehensive attempt to examine intergenerational money flows was made in Nigeria's Western State in 1974 to 1975. Both showed clearly that returns from children are substantial.[67]

It is essential to emphasize that the divide is not mechanistically determined by economic conditions. On the contrary it is almost entirely a social phenomenon (except that parent-child net flows of wealth, with the exception of labor and other services such as care for the very young and very old, are hardly possible in subsistence conditions or in the primitive society), and can be reached only when the economy of the nuclear family has been largely isolated from that of the extended family and when a subsequent change of balance has occurred within the nuclear family. The necessity for economic nucleation arises in several ways: the change of economic balance inside the nuclear family is essentially one of emotion and sentiment, which requires emotional nucleation (and other changes of emotional balance within the family) that is incompatible with the extended family economic system, which also needs a parallel system of emotional obligations to work; the change of economic balance in the nuclear family really means that the parents of the family are wholly in charge of their own family economy.

Even if the divide would probably eventually be reached in any urban-industrial society, attitudes and social organization could long delay its advent. Alternatively, a different set of circumstances could bring it on early, even, in fact, before the creation of the modern economy. This seems to be what happened in Western Europe.[68] The feudal system, built on the inherited ruins of the urbanized civilizations of the ancient world, went far toward making a nuclear family economically viable. Doubtless, economic obligations existed to more distant relatives. But these obligations were supported by moral forces and were susceptible to the weakening or reversal of those forces. This seems to have happened with the rise of Protestantism, which put much store on self-sufficiency of all types and on moderation in expenditure and desires. It allowed a man to tell his relatives that they should be more careful in their expenditures, more frugal in their wants, and more foresighted in planning for times of need. More importantly, it allowed him to do this and cautiously refuse to give any (or much) assistance, while retaining his pride and even preaching his practice. Given that the divide had been reached, fertility could be increasingly controlled, even if, at first, mostly by postponed marriage.

In Africa, substantial support for the thesis that emotional nucleation precedes economic nucleation comes from a study in Ghana where Oppong showed among male undergraduates at two universities a significant correlation between the kind of family and kinship obligations the students believed in and the number of children they wanted and an earlier study by the writer that presented evidence on the extent to which urban elite families were emotionally turning in upon themselves.[69]

The Transitional Society

An increasing proportion of the Third World population lives in transitional societies that are laboratories for the study of demographic change and lack of change and for determining the origins of demographic transition. "Transitional" here refers to rapid changes in the way of life, especially changes in the impact of children and in the possibilities available to parents for limiting the number of their children.

Nigeria's second largest city, Ibadan, is such a laboratory.[70] Its population is almost 750,000. Although agricultural links are still strong, only one-sixteenth of males report farming as their main occupation; one-third work in nonmanual occupations and another one-third work as soldiers, policemen, or craftsmen, or in similar jobs requiring a degree of training or imported skills and often with an orientation toward the nontraditional world. One-twelfth of women work in nonmanual occupations; but a similar proportion is employed in skilled occupations and over one-half in marketing, often of a somewhat different order from similar employment in rural areas. Three-quarters of the men and one-half the women have been to school; of the latter, one-quarter have experienced some secondary education and almost one-eighth have completed secondary school. More importantly, in terms of the strains on families frequently depicted by demographers, nearly all their children are now receiving some formal education and the majority are proceeding on to secondary schooling. It is rapidly becoming easier to limit fertility if that is the aim. Sexual abstinence has long been widely known as an approved method of avoiding pregnancy. Modern contraceptives are now available from several clinics, a large number of pharmacies, and other retail outlets; in 1973 one-sixth of all women aged 15 to 59 years had used modern contraception and one-ninth were currently doing so, while the doubling time for the levels of each category of behavior (i.e., the time taken for the proportions behaving in this way to double) had for many years been only four years.

However, fertility (and "ideal family size") appear to have changed little. Significant differentials exist neither between Ibadan and Yoruba rural areas nor within Ibadan society (except that the small group of very highly educated women exhibit lower fertility at younger ages). Nor were contraceptors less fertile than noncontraceptors within Ibadan.[71] The conventional answer in terms of accepted demographic transition theory would be that attitudinal lags prevented parents from fully assessing the new economic situation, that innovation is not fully accepted and implemented at once because the props do not disintegrate at once, and that insufficiently motivated contraceptors are inefficient. None of these propositions appears to hold good in Ibadan, nor are they likely to elsewhere: the parents' assessment of the economic situation appears to be realistic with no time-lag involved; the innovators (as discussed in the section below) do not seem to be aware of their courage in disregarding the props; the contraceptors are mostly doing precisely what they meant to do with the contraceptives.

High fertility remains rational in nonagricultural urban conditions as long as the flow of wealth is predominantly from the younger to the older generation.[72] This is still overwhelmingly the case in Ibadan. The 1974 to 1975 Survey of the Intra-Family Flow of Money and Assistance in Nigeria's Western State surprised us by showing that the return from investment in children is greater for urban than rural residents and is the greatest of all among the city white-collar and professional class. Yet the reason is not far to seek. The urban population working in the modernized economy have both the means and the understanding of the system to keep their children moving up the educational ladder to the top positions in the modern society—positions with high salaries and fringe benefits, as well as control of the levers of power and hence access to opportunities for more wealth, some, but not all, fraudulently obtained. The parents can provide a background suited to continued study, and they know the headmasters and the people who allocate jobs. Perhaps more unexpectedly, the younger generation do not resent the system because they expect to receive wealth in turn from their own, even more successful children. In fact, as Adepoju has shown, it is the more successful children who would feel most guilt about not sharing their wealth and who visit their parents most often to share it.[73] Furthermore, as the Nigerian Family Study's biographies of the successful clearly demonstrated, a major joy (perhaps the single most important consumption good for the successful) is meeting all family obligations in a more than generous way—in (as they repeatedly said) seeing distant relatives and even nonrelatives recognize the donor's success and generosity.

This picture of the success of the urban middle class is but a segment of a wider picture of a whole modernizing society existing in a situation where wealth flows predominantly from the young to the old and where there are marked differentials in earning powers by rural-urban division and by education. The route from the rural area to the job in the modern sector of the economy is almost solely by extended education. Most parents can no longer manage to travel this way, but their children can. To get children far up the educational ladder and into the high-salary positions three stratagems are necessary: relatives outside the nuclear family must be encouraged to help with school fees or with accommodation and subsistence at centers where the right educational institutions exist; older children must help the younger ones in the same way (the sibling chain of educational assistance); and priority must be given to channeling the most assistance, at least early in the establishment of the sibling chain, to the children with the most chance of success—usually the brightest but occasionally those with unusual application, although the distinction is not often made. The first and second stratagems depend on the retention of the system of mutual obligations; the second and third work best with high fertility. The society, like many others in the Third World, believes that the birth of bright and potentially successful children is a matter of capricious fate to which some kind of probability can be assigned (the lucky dip, or lottery, principle) and that large families are likely to have one or more of such children whose existence far outweighs any disadvantages arising from a larger number of less successful siblings. Poor people have limited investment opportunities in such societies, and economic and political caprice can upset what appears to exist, so educational investment in children is thought to be the best investment in both Nigeria and Ghana, and doubtless in many similar societies. The child who has broken through to a job in the modern economy can assist the parents through flows of wealth (sent regularly and at times of crisis, brought on visits, or spent on visiting parents and siblings) or through influencing authorities and manipulating power; the child can bring honor to the parents by visiting them; and can give them access to the joys of the modern world during their visits or final retirement to the child's house. Children in urban areas are usually needed to bring earnings into the household, in circumstances where the total income of a poor household is often the sum of many small parts.[74]

Contraception may in the future be used largely to limit family size, but for the time being there is a substantial and increasing demand for contraceptives in Ibadan for other, more pressing reasons: to substitute for female sexual abstinence after birth (in a world where the message of the enjoyment of sexual relations is increasingly being heard); to permit sexual relations during the increasingly long period before marriage in a situation in which pregnancy might destroy the investment in education or dictate a marriage regarded as less than desirable by the family; or to allow safe extramarital sexual relations in a society in which long periods of abstinence, substantial age gaps between spouses, and late marriage of males have meant that discreet relations of this kind have been to a large measure condoned.

More work needs to be done on individuals and families in dire poverty in both traditional and transitional societies. We have investigated a considerable number of cases in West Africa and one point seems clear: they are most likely to be products of an atypically inadequate family structure—often one that has been greatly eroded by mortality and that was vulnerably small in the first place because of accident or subfertility.

Identification of the Primary Forces of Change

The transitional nature of Ibadan society also allows the identification of the extent, nature, and cause of fertility transition. This is best done by identifying the innovators. Two methods were employed in the Changing African Family Project. The first was the isolation of all those women in Ibadan (together with their husbands where the marriage was a first, monogamous one with the husband still present) who had indubitably succeeded in demographic innovation: women already over age 40 years with fewer than six live births achieved by intention and any method of restricting fertility.[75] The second was the examination of all women in the three 1973 Nigerian surveys who, regardless of age at the time, had had fewer than six live births, but desired no more and were at the time employing modern contraception to try to ensure this.

The first point established was that there are still very few demographic innovators. Ibadan contains about 62,500 women over age 40 years, but only 438 or 0.7 percent had intentionally and successfully restricted fertility to less than six births.[76] Women of all ages with fewer than six live births and using modern contraception to avoid further pregnancies numbered less than 2,000 in Ibadan, out of about 153,000 women aged 15 to 49 (or 1.3 percent) or about 128,000 aged 20 to 44 (about 1.5 percent). The size of this demographically innovating group (i.e., under 2,000) can be compared with the number of so-called family planning innovators, for in 1973 the number of Ibadan women practicing modern contraception was over 17,000 or almost nine times as many. In the whole of the Western and Lagos States (which include rural areas but which also contains Lagos with its 2 million people and rapidly changing society as well as many other towns), only 0.5 percent of women are currently demographic innovators according to the first Nigerian survey. The 1.5 percent of demographic innovators in Ibadan can also be compared with the number of socioeconomic innovators: 46 percent of women have had schooling, and 15 percent have experienced at least some secondary education; most have their children of school age in full-time education; one-tenth are employed in the modern sector of the economy; one-third of the husbands work in nonmanual occupations, while no more than one-fourth could be said to be employed in the traditional sector of the economy. Clearly, continuing high fertility is not explained by lack of access to or even use of contraception, or by only limited modernization, or by children still maintaining the occupational roles they filled in traditional rural society.

The problem is, then, to study the demographic innovators in depth and to find out how and when they separated themselves from the rest of the community. The quest should be easy. One might infer from demographic transition theory that the decision to do without the props might well be traumatic, and some demographers have wished that they could talk to the eighteenth-century French couples who first daringly decided to innovate. In fact, at first the most frustrating and then the most illuminating discovery was that the demographic innovators are for the most part unaware that they have done anything unusual. After all, contracepting is no longer unusual, particularly in the educational and social groups to which most belong. The use of such contraception to limit family growth just seemed an obvious thing to do in their economic circumstances.

The fundamental question is then: What were the economic circumstances of this group and how did they differ from others who were supporting children at school? The first hint is given by some of their characteristics: demographic innovators compared with noninnovators are 1.6 times as likely to have been to school and 2.7 times as likely to have been to secondary school; they are 2.0 times as likely to have husbands in nonmanual occupations, 4.5 times as likely to be in such occupations themselves, and 2.5 times as likely to have had fathers in such occupations; they are 6.5 times as likely to have all these characteristics—to have fathers and husbands in nonmanual occupations and to be in such occupations themselves and to have had secondary education. Background and education are more important than current occupational experience or indeed any other contemporary circumstance or experience.

These findings could be said to be consonant with the knocking away of the props. However, the Nigerian segment of the Changing African Family Project contained a battery of questions and propositions of a psychosocial kind, relating to phrases taken from Yoruba proverb or song and of a type that could be made in a semi-philosophic way in everyday conversation. The responses showed clearly that what distinguished the demographic innovators from others was not their lack of superstition or their rationalism but their attitudes toward family and children. They have emotionally nucleated their families; they are less concerned with ancestors and extended family relatives than they are with their children, their children's future, and even the future of their children's children. They are more likely to have been "spoilt" themselves in the sense that their parents gave them more emotion and wealth than they expected back, and this is the way they tend, although usually to a greater extent, to treat their own children.[77]

What causes this emotional nucleation of the family whereby parents spend increasingly on their children, while demanding—and receiving—very little in return? Not the urban-industrial society, at least to the extent that it has developed in Ibadan. The majority of the society, even among the elite, is still one where net wealth flows over a lifetime from child to parent. Nor is that majority system buffeted by the institutional requirements of the modern economy; on the contrary it can adapt not only well but profitably to such a society. It might well be able to continue and improve the adaption for decades, or perhaps generations, except for the factor that has already brought about change among the small minority of demographic innovators.

That factor is undoubtedly the import of a different culture; it is Westernization. Just as Western ethnocentricity has bedeviled Third World research and introduced wholly inappropriate attitudes, assumptions and methods, it has in a perversely negative way upset the whole study of "modernization" (i.e., the social changes that seem to precede, accompany, or follow economic development). Western researchers have all too frequently decided to become "objective" or at least "non-self-centered" by achieving the almost incredible feat of omitting transmitted European cultural traditions from the study of modernization; it is like leaving Hellenization out of an examination of social change in fifth century B.C. Macedonia or leaving Roman social influences out of a treatise on Britain in the second century A.D. This may sound like hyperbole, but it is not. In one of the major texts on social change in the Third World, Alex Inkeles and David Smith fleetingly recognized that the difference in their division of the world into that which was modernized and that which was not was almost entirely a contrast between the West and the rest: "With the exception of Japan . . . all the major nations which we can consider modernized are part of the European tradition."[78] Rather than pursue this theme, they decided not to be "arrogant" and instead broke up the Western tradition into components that could be used for measuring not "Westernization" but "modernization."[79] Throughout William Goode's important study, *World Revolution and Family Patterns,* with its investigation of recent family changes in the Arab, sub-Saharan African, Indian and Chinese worlds, "revolution," except in the discussion of slower growth over a longer period in the West, is a synonym for "Westernization."[80]

Curiously, it is only the well-trained, oversensitive Western researcher who does not see and hear the obvious. In West Africa, survey respondents (as well as the conversationalist met in the street, the villager in the compound, and the Lagos newspaper) speak continually of adopting European ways—often, in fact, embarrassing the researcher in rural areas by going on to summarize this as "becoming civilized."

How, then, is the European concept of family relationships and obligations imported? The answer is that the import has been on such a massive scale that the slow erosion of traditional family structures is a measure of cultural durability.

Sailors, traders, and slavers may have disrupted some families, but they preached little and few took their examples as a model. However, in the mid-nineteenth century British colonial administration reached Lagos (less than 160 kilometers from Ibadan) and missionaries arrived at Ibadan itself. According to the Changing African Family project, by 1973 nearly one-half the population of Ibadan were Christian and only 0.5 percent still described themselves as adhering to traditional African beliefs; two-thirds of those who had achieved small families were Christian. Missionaries and their successors have for over a century preached the Western family as the Christian family: monogamy as God's way instead of polygyny; husbands and wives looking after their children.[81] Administrators tended to take the same viewpoint, and nearly all Europeans in the developing colonial society advertised the Western family by example and viewpoint.

The mass infusion of European manners, however, has been relatively recent and it has had two interrelated vehicles: mass education and the mass media. Schooling for a very small minority, mostly male, dates back in Ibadan for over a century, but the movement toward some schooling for most children got under way in Yorubaland only in the 1950s. "The family," as taught by the school is almost entirely the Western family. Textbooks either come from England or are local products modeled on English prototypes. Readers, used in the first years of schooling, are very much concerned with the family and generally tell of a house with a father who goes out to work, a mother who stays home and looks after the children, and the children themselves, who are good and who can expect help and gifts to rain upon them from their two parents. School teachers, even when their own family lives are not fully Westernized, are unlikely to offer non-Western family precepts to their pupils.[82] Researchers have sometimes tried to relate fertility change to the Westernized context of the syllabus,[83] while activists have introduced a "population awareness" ingredient into existing syllabuses; almost certainly such formal ingredients are trivial compared with the inbuilt assumptions of the system and its teachers. Education systems are not easily changed, and are much more likely to be imported intact. In much of the Third World they are essentially a reflection of the modern West, both in their origins and messages, and rarely mirror life in a largely communal and subsistence village. By the mid-1980s many of the women who flooded as youngsters in the late 1950s into the new primary schools may well be faced with the question of calling a halt to family size rather than continuing to reproduce. Then we will discover what impact their schooling had on their families' social and economic structure and what impact this has for their fertility.

Mass media in Nigeria have only had a marked impact since Independence in 1960.

Only the newspapers and magazines require the literacy that comes from schooling, but education is likely to lead to the higher income that facilitates the purchase of a radio or a television set or a cinema ticket and to the interest in the nontraditional world that makes these purchases more probable. All cinema films, most television films that portray family life, much of the magazine content, and a considerable proportion of the newspaper feature content are imported, and the models on which they are based are wholly imported from the West. The same message of nuclear family structure is relayed as is imparted by the schools. But another message is also presented in Nigeria: the great importance of sexual relations. This is luridly presented in newspaper and magazine features, news stories, and question and answer sections. Taking a single important example, the emphasis on sex in the widely read *Lagos Weekend* must boost the market for contraceptives, because until recently the main interpretation has been on the excitement of relations outside marriage. But, with the increase in the proportion of educated (and partly Westernized) wives, it is inevitable that the message will be increasingly interpreted to mean also sexual relations within marriage. Such a change, certainly already well under way among the elite, cannot fail to affect the traditional system of family relationships (as has always been recognized in the society) and by strengthening the conjugal emotional bond will tend to nucleate the family, at first emotionally and ultimately economically.

TRANSITION THEORY RESTATED

In general, in societies of every type and stage of development, fertility behavior is rational, and fertility is high or low as a result of economic benefit to individuals, couples, or families in its being so. Whether high or low fertility is economically rational is determined by social conditions: primarily by the direction of the intergenerational wealth flow. This flow has been from younger to older generations in all traditional societies; and it is apparently impossible (or, at least, examples are unknown) for a reversal of flow—at the great divide—to occur before the family is largely nucleated both emotionally and economically. A fair degree of emotional nucleation is needed for economic nucleation; and considerable amounts of both are required before parents are free to indulge in ever greater expenditures on their children.

Pre-divide populations do not aim at females conceiving as frequently as possible during the full reproductive span, and post-divide populations do not favor childlessness. The reasons are not basically economic; they are social, psychological, and physiological. It is possible, however, that the marginal economic advantage of each additional child in pre-divide society and disadvantage in post-divide society in some circumstances modifies the impact of the noneconomic determinants. Nevertheless, economic analysis on its own can do nothing to predict the timing of the divide and very little to explain the levels of fertility on either side of it—probably the course of fertility in the twentieth century West owes less to the economics of each additional child born than it does to the extent to which parental emotional and expenditure patterns have become focused on the children and the degree to which their society renders such focusing expensive in terms of alternative uses for money, emotion, and time. Similarly, demographic evidence of fertility change may be valueless in terms of deducing movement toward the divide or estimating the probable timing of the reversal of the intergenerational wealth flow; the fertility change may well represent an adjustment of changing social, psychological, or physiological circumstances.[84]

Extreme external factors may influence this pattern. Pre-divide fertility may be restricted in the Kalahari Desert or on Tikopia because of very finite resources; and post-divide fertility was temporarily very high on the American frontier, where the wealth flow to children was relatively insignificant and where there were few alternative sources of labor and even company. The analysis carried out here has been largely based on Africa where access to land has been fairly unrestricted. The position may be somewhat more like Tikopia in densely settled agrarian areas in Asia. However, the little available evidence suggests that it is not, and that even there farming families do not on the whole see the extra birth as impoverishing and do not tighten their belts as the child grows. The explanation may be partly that we are deceived by a static analysis and see the household or family too little in terms of the coming and going of people over time; partly that the extra child does in due course add sufficiently to production; and partly that in the contemporary world the existence of urban employment takes sufficient strain off the need for providing more land.

For reasons that lie deep in its history, the family was increasingly economically nucleated in Western Europe centuries ago; indeed some social groups may have crossed the divide reversing the intergenerational wealth flow as early as the seventeenth century.[85] This phenomenon had two demographic effects: a direct one, namely that Europe's population growth rate was lower than it would otherwise have been once mortality began to decline; an indirect one, in that European culture accepted the nuclear family as the basic unit of society and included a range of values associated with it among exports to other parts of the world.

An emphasis must be placed here on the export of the European social system as well as its economic system. It is as absurd to deny that this is the central feature of our times as to deny the significance of the Hellenization of southwest Asia, the Romanization of the Mediterranean and western Europe, and the Sinoization of much of southeast and central Asia in other periods. The issue is not whether Western social structure is better or even whether it is more suited to modernization; it is merely that the West has been able to export it because of the overwhelming economic strength it derived from the industrial revolution.

From the demographic viewpoint, the most important social exports have been the concept of the predominance of the nuclear family with its strong conjugal tie and the concept of concentrating concern and expenditure on one's children. The latter does not automatically follow from the former, although it is likely to follow continuing Westernization; but the latter must be preceded by the former. There probably is no close relationship in timing between economic modernization and fertility—and, if true, this may be the most important generalization of our time. If another culture had brought economic development, a culture with a much less nucleated family system, industrialization might well have proceeded far beyond its present level in the Third World in the next half century, almost independently of the success of industrialization, and, almost inevitably, they will guarantee slower global population growth.

Several subsidiary points about the export of the Western economic and social systems should be made. First, this export has made both mortality and fertility declines possible in the Third World. Public health measures were acceptable deep in traditional society, and this has been taken as evidence of the reality of the props, which were so constructed as to encourage the desire for low mortality and high fertility. The props are in fact needless: in pre-divide society economic prosperity increased with the number of surviving children—the noneconomic restraints on fertility were more on the number of pregnancies and on the time-span of reproduction than on numbers of survivors. Second, the whole system of extended family obligations and the flow of wealth from younger to older generations may be disrupted by political means (China is the clearest example) with exactly the same effect in reducing fertility (although net wealth flows in a commune are probably relatively low, they are almost certainly from the old to the young). Third, the imminence of the reversal of the wealth flow and of declining fertility is usually hidden because of the increased economic benefits from high fertility in the modernizing economy of pre-divide transitional society. And fourth, the attempts to slow associations over time between mortality decline and various economic development indices on one hand and fertility decline on the other are probably valueless; even where there are direct relationships they usually cannot be proved because of the tendency for so many economic and social changes to move together.

A final note should perhaps be added on the more theoretical aspect of population growth in primitive societies. It can be argued that mortality is determined by environment, way of life, and technology, and varies widely among primitive and traditional societies. Yet, demonstrably, population growth rates over long periods have been very low, thus establishing that fertility levels must have approximated mortality levels. One can go further and maintain that this means that mortality levels determined fertility levels, an argument that not only supports the concepts of props but implies that they were subject to strengthening or relaxing until the right level was reached. A more plausible reading of the African tribal situation, however, is that fertility levels were established independently. Where they were above mortality levels, population grew, and the tribe expanded its area through warfare with its neighbors. When expansion was successfully opposed, mortality rates climbed to meet fertility rates: first, because of increasingly unsuccessful warfare and, subsequently, because of growing pressure on limited resources. Where fertility levels were below mortality levels, the tribe died out.

RESEARCH IMPLICATIONS

If the society is at every stage rational, and economically rational at that, then it can be studied employing tools, as long as it is understood that the researchers must accept the society's own ends. Those ends can be researched only by students of society, and their techniques alone—and not those of economic inquiry—can attempt to predict the approach to the divide where the wealth flow reverses.

First-class fieldwork on wealth flows in predivide societies is urgently needed, and that research must start with the identification of all possible types of mobile wealth and the development of methods for detecting flows. A good study of a single village would be worth a great deal; defective work on a nation could be dangerously misleading. Cross-sectional studies have some value, but it will be necessary to build up life-cycle models. Specialized investigations might attempt to discover why children do not seem to press on resources in agrarian areas even when these areas are densely settled.

Sociological and anthropological work is needed to define the extent of the true extended families of obligation and to measure the internal wealth flows. It will also be necessary to measure the strength of each obligation bond—the circumstances (and the likelihood of those circumstances occurring) that will bring it into play and the probable volume of the wealth flow under given conditions. The study of the changing family and the measurement of movement toward the social, emotional, and economic nucleation of the conjugal family are important.

A combined social science assault will probably be needed on the circumstances and conditions of the reversal of the wealth flow—and on the time taken for the flow from the older to the younger generation to grow to such an extent that it exerts a real impact on fertility control decisions.

We also need studies that can easily be done in association with family planning action programs. We must find out the real reasons people want contraceptives and the extent to which contraception has anything to do with restricting fertility. Subtle and sympathetic studies in depth of both demographic innovators and contraceptive innovators are essential for action programs.

Finally, we need to know a lot more about the effect on the family of the lessons learned from the media and in school. Much effort has gone into distinguishing the population content of high school lessons but little study has been done on the family structure almost inadvertently taught in the elementary school.

The major implication of this analysis is that fertility decline in the Third World is not dependent on the spread of industrialization or even on the rate of economic development. It will of course be affected by such development in that modernization produces more money for schools, for newspapers, and so on; indeed, the whole question of family nucleation cannot arise in the nonmonetized economy. But fertility decline is more likely to precede industrialization and to help bring it about than to follow it.

NOTES

1. See Harvey Leibenstein, "An interpretation of the economic theory of fertility: Promising path or blind alley?", *Journal of Economic Literature* 12 (1974): 457–479, for a survey of primarily economic theory that brings out the lack of concern of that theory with the onset of fertility decline.
2. Although many European countries remained in a state of transition for a long period, such conditions are not likely to recur, partly because of the existence of mass schooling. In contemporary transitional societies, families tend to be clearly in one fertility situation or the other, and hence fertility differentials appear; even whole societies are likely to move rather rapidly through the transition as the social and economic calculus changes.
3. Warren S. Thompson, "Population," *The American Journal of Sociology* 34, no. 6 (May 1929): 959–975: C. P. Blacker, "Stages in population growth," *The Eugenics Review* 39, no. 3 (October 1947): 88–101. In his 1946 publication, *Population and Peace in the Pacific* (Chicago: University of Chicago Press), Thompson largely supported the view put forward by Notestein in 1945.
4. Frank W. Notestein, "Population: The long view," in Theodore W. Schultz (ed.), *Food for the World* (Chicago: University of Chicago Press, 1945), p. 39. The term "demographic transition" is first employed on page 41 of this article, after reference has been made to "demographic evolution" and "transitional growth."
5. Notestein, "Population: The long view," pp. 40–41.
6. Frank. W. Notestein, "Economic problems of population change," *8th International Conference of Agricultural Economists, 1953* (London: Oxford University Press, 1953), pp. 15–18.
7. Some social scientists emphasized isolated parts of the argument: In "Population and family planning programs in newly developing countries" [in Ronald Freedman (ed.), *Population: The Vital Revolution*

(Chicago: Aldine, 1965)], J. Mayone Stycos emphasized the possibility of advancement in life. W. F. Ogburn and M. F. Nimkoff [*Technology and the Changing Family* (Cambridge, Mass.: Houghton Mifflin, 1955)] stressed the great departure in the city from rural household economy. And Gösta Carlsson in "The decline of fertility: Innovation or adjustment process" (*Population Studies* 20 (November 1966), wrote of the new life style of the urban industrial society and the export of that style. Others, notably Philip M. Houser and Otis Dudley Duncan, complained that too many explantions had been given, and that some of the supposed causes were material changes, while others were ones of ideas. [See "Demography as a body of knowledge," in Philip M. Hauser and Otis Dudley Duncan, *The Study of Population: An Inventory and Appraisal* (Chicago: University of Chicago Press, 1959), p. 94.]

8. Kingsley Davis, *Human Society* (New York: Macmillan, 1949), pp. 599–600, and "Institutional patterns favoring high fertility in underdeveloped areas," *Eugenics Quarterly* 2, no. 1 (March 1955): 37.
9. George J. Stolnitz, "The demographic transition: From high to low birth rates and death rates," in Freedman (ed.), *Population: The Vital Revolution* (Garden City, New York: Anchor Books, 1964), pp. 33–34.
10. Eva Mueller, "Economic motives for family limitation: A study conducted on Taiwan," *Population Studies* 27, no. 3 (November 1972): 383.
11. William Rich, *Smaller Families Through Social and Economic Development* (Washington, DC: Overseas Development Council, 1973), p. 2. Emphasis added.
12. Stephen Enke, "The economic aspects of slowing population growth," *The Economic Journal* 76, no. 1 (March 1966): 54.
13. Michael E. Endres, "Underdeveloped countries and the birth control alternative," in *On Defusing the Population Bomb* (Cambridge, MA: Halstead Press, 1975), p. 74.
14. Glenn Thomas Trewartha, *The Less Developed Realm: A Geography of Its Population* (New York: Wiley, 1972), pp. 182–183.
15. Notestein, "Population: The long view," pp. 39–41.
16. United Naitons, *Concise Report on the World Population Situation in 1970–75* (New York: United Nations, 1974). Quotations from pp. 17, 2, and 14.
17. Eva Mueller, "The economic value of children in peasant agriculture," in Ronald G. Ridker (ed.), *Population and Development* (Baltimore: Johns Hopkins University Press, 1976).
18. Notestein, "Economic problems of population change," pp. 17–18.
19. Davis, "Institutional patterns favoring high fertility"; Davis and Judith Blake, "Social structure and fertility: An analytic framework," *Economic Development and Cultural Change* 4 (April 1956): 211–235. The relationship of fertility to kinship was stressed a year earlier by Lorimer, but he retained the religious and cultural props. See Frank Lorimer, *Culture and Human Fertility: A study of the Relation of Cultural Conditions to Fertility in Non-Industrial and Transitional Societies* (Paris: UNESCO, 1954).
20. Thomas K. Burch and Murray Gendell, "Extended family structure and fertility: Some conceptual and methodological issues," in Stephen Polgar (ed.), *Culture and Population: A Collection of Current Studies* (Chapel Hill: Carolina Population Center, 1971), pp. 87–104.
21. William J. Goode, "Industrialization and family change," in Bert F. Hoselitz and Wilbert E. Moore (eds.), *Industrialization and Society* (Mouton: UNESCO, 1963), p. 240. It is possible to argue, at least in the Australian context, that they opted not for high fertility but for early female marriage in frontier conditions where women were scarce, but had an important role to play and that high fertility was the unplanned consequence [L. D. Ruzicka and J. C. Caldwell, *The End of Demographic Transition in Australia* (in preparation)].
22. Colin Clark, *Population Growth and Land Use* (London: Macmillan, 1967), pp. 186–187. It is true, however, that some preindustrial peoples appear to have a family structure nucleated not only in residence, but in closeness of relationships; but nevertheless they shared food and animal skins for clothing on a basis going beyond even distant relatives at the same camp. See Nelson H. Graburn, "Traditional economic institutions and the acculturation of the Canadian Eskimos," in George Dalton (ed.), *Studies in Economic Anthropology* (Washington, D.C.: American Anthropological Association, 1971), pp. 107–111. For the argument that the true extended family is largely a product of agrarian societies, see R. L. Blumberg and R. F. Winch, "Societal complexity and familial complexity: Evidence for the curvilinear hypothesis," *American Journal of Sociology* 77, no. 4 (January 1972): 898–920.
23. David M. Heer and Dean O. Smith, "Mortality level and desired family size," Contributed Papers: *Sydney Conference, International Union for the Scientific Study of Population, 21–25, August 1967* (Canberra: 1967), pp. 26–36.
24. Ansley J. Coale and Edgar M. Hoover, *Population Growth and Economic Development in Low-Income Countries: A Case Study of India's Prospects* (Princeton: Princeton University Press, 1958), pp. 11–12. Their summary is essentially based on Notestein, "Economic problems of population change."
25. See Deborah S. Freedman (with Eva Mueller), "Economic data for fertility analysis," *Occasional Paper* no. 11, World Fertility Survey (August 1974): 7–8.
26. Richard Nelson, "A theory of the low-level equilibrium trap in underdeveloped economies," *American Economic Review* 46, no. 1 (1956): 894–906; Harvey Leibenstein, *Economic Backwardness and Economic Growth: Studies in the Theory of Economic Development* (New York: Wiley, 1957), pp. 170–173.

27. Julian L. Simon, *The Effects of Income on Fertility* (Chapel Hill: Carolina Population Center, 1974), pp. 163–164 and 130.
28. Ronald Freedman, "The sociology of human fertility: A trend report and bibliography," *Current Sociology* 10/11, no. 3 (1961–2): 40 and 48.
29. W. Parker Mauldin, "Fertility studies: Knowledge, attitude and practice," *Studies in Family Planning* 1, no. 7 (June 1965): 6.
30. Bernard Berelson, "KAP studies on fertility," in *Family Planning and Population Programs,* Berelson et al. (eds.) (Chicago: University of Chicago Press, 1966), p. 658.
31. This view is also at odds with Lorimer's attempt to produce a more sophisticated interpretation of fertility levels, a kind of "plural society" way of looking at the world, when he argued that there is not a simple contrast between the low fertility of developed countries and the high fertility of developing countries but that the latter exhibit a wide range of fertility levels reflecting their social and economic structures and presumably their norms. See Frank Lorimer, *Culture and Human Fertility: A Study of the Relation of Cultural Conditions to Fertility in Non-Industrial and Transitional Societies* (Westport, Conn.: Greenwood Press, Inc., 1954). Carr-Saunders had earlier argued that societies might be able to sustain different levels of fertility and that "the evidence . . . shows that the mechanism whereby numbers may be kept near to the desirable level is everywhere present" [A. M. Carr-Saunders, *The Population Problem: A Study in Human Evolution* (Oxford: Clarendon Press, 1922), p. 230].
32. Simon, *The Effects of Income on Fertility,* p. 105. He buttresses this by deciding that fertility behavior is rational, largely on the basis of the Princeton Office of Population Research demonstration that fertility is nearly everywhere substantially lower than it would be if presumably largely uncontrolled Hutterite fertility behavior were prevalent (see, e.g., p. 11).
33. See Emily L. Jones, "The courtesy bias in South-East Asian surveys," *International Science Journal* 15, no. 1 (1963): 70–76.
34. United Nations, Department of Economic and Social Affairs, *Population Bulletin of the United Nations, No. 7—1963, with Special Reference to Conditions and Trends of Fertility in the World* (New York: 1965), p. 143.
35. Among Western European countries, the first declines in fertility paralleled the beginning of marriage postponement perhaps as early as the seventeenth century [see J. Hajnal, "European marriage patterns in perspective," in D. V. Glass and D. E. C. Eversley (eds.), *Population in History: Essays in Historical Demography* (London: Arnold, 1965), pp. 101–143]; and even the restriction of fertility within marriage began a century ago. Therefore, at the threshold itself, many of the post-threshold societies identified in the study exhibited different index values (a range of socioeconomic and demographic indices was calculated) than their current ones—most, indeed, were then within the range of the contemporary pre-threshold societies. (This assumes that the UN studies mean the threshold to be between Groups 3 and 4. There is some tendency to alternate between the concept of a threshold and that of a continuum.)
36. Etienne van de Walle and John Knodel, "Demographic transition and fertility decline: The European case," *Contributed Papers: Sydney Conference, International Union for the Scientific Study of Population, 21–25 August 1967,* pp. 47–55.
37. Dudley Kirk, "A new demographic transition?" in National Academy of Sciences, *Rapid Population Growth: Consequences and Policy Implications* (Baltimore: Johns Hopkins Press, 1971), pp. 123–147: Frank W. Oechsli and Dudley Kirk, "Modernization and the demographic transition in Latin America and the Caribbean," *Economic Development and Cultural Change* 23, no. 3 (April 1975): 391–419.
38. United Nations, *Concise Report on the World Population Situation.*
39. A. J. Coale, "The demographic transition reconsidered," *International Population Conference, Liege, 1973* Vol. I (Liege: IUSSP, 1973), pp. 62–63.
40. The only two national survey reports published at the time of writing were Rodolfo A. Bulatao, *The Value of Children: A Cross-National Study, II, Philippines* (Honolulu: East-West Population Institute, 1975), and Fred Arnold and James T. Fawcett, *The Value of Children: A Cross-National Study, III, Hawaii* (Honolulu: East-West Population Institute, 1975). The emphasis on a psychological approach is set out in Fred Arnold et al., *The Value of Children: A Cross-National Study, I, Introduction and Comparative Analysis* (Honolulu: East-West Population Institute, 1975), pp. 5–6. The report on the original workshop is also available but it is more economically oriented than the subsequent project [James T. Fawcett (ed.), *The Satisfactions and Cost of Children: Theories, Concepts, Methods* (Honolulu: East-West Center, 1972)]. There have been separate Value of Children projects, such as the survey carried out as part of the 1973 Nigerian segment of the Changing African Family Project to be describe later in this paper.
41. The origins of economic anthropology lie, appropriately for the demographic transition theorist, in pre-modern European history and economic history, but its genesis as a separate field is to be found in German ethnographic studies of the second half of the nineteenth and the first quarter of the twentieth centuries and French studies of the 1920s. In English a literature also began to develop from the 1920s with the work of Malinowski and Firth, leading to the attempt by Herskovits at the end of the 1930s to compile and synthesize what was known. Controversy and new studies have found a renewed vitality

in recent years. For a good review of the field, see Raymond Firth (ed.), *Themes in Economic Anthropology* (London: Tavistock, 1967), with references to the syntheses of Wilhelm Koppers in 1915–16 and Max Schmidt in 1920–21 and the later work by Richard Thurnwald. And on more recent studies, see also, for instance, George Dalton, *Studies in Economic Anthropology* (Washington, D.C.: American Anthropological Association, 1971): Marshall Sablins, *Stone Age Economics* (Chicago: Aldine-Atherton, 1972): and Scarlett Epstein, "The data of economics in anthropological analysis," in A. L. Epstein (ed.), *The Craft of Social Anthropology* (London: Tavistock, 1967).

42. For example, in the Nigerian Segment of the Changing African Family Project, respondents were asked, "If someone offered you a good job for three years, but you could only take it if you put off having a baby for that time, would you be prepared to try to stop having a baby for three years?" Only one-quarter of both women and men replied "No" and that response was not much higher even in remote villages. Very few Nigerians would be offered a good job (defined by most as meaning one in the modern, white-collar sector) and fewer still with a guaranteed period of employment. In practically no case would a woman have to agree not to have a child (and never in the case of men). Should such an extraordinary offer ever be made, of course many might opt for the good job. The fundamental fact about developing economies is that choices of this kind do not exist and, therefore, a question of this kind is not appropriate.

43. Chukuka Okonjo, "A preliminary medium estimate of the 1962 mid-year population of Nigeria," in John C. Caldwell and Chukuka Okonjo (eds.), *The Population of Tropical Africa* (London: Longman, 1968), pp. 78–96.

44. The argument will not repeat that of the various research papers from that work but will draw on them: primarily, John C. Caldwell, "Fertility and the household economy in Nigeria," *Journal of Comparative Family Studies,* Special Issue, 1976, and "The economic rationality of high fertility," with supporting data from J. C. Caldwell and Pat Caldwell. "The role of marital sexual abstinence in determining fertility: A study of the Yoruba in Nigeria," *Population Studies* 30, no. 2 (July 1977, forthcoming) and "Demographic and contraceptive innovators: A study of transitional African society," *Journal of Biosocial Science* 8, no. 4 (October 1976): "The achieved small family: Early fertility transition in an African city" (in press); J. C. Caldwell and H. Ware, "The evolution of family planning in an African city: Ibadan, Nigeria," *Population Studies* 31, no. 3 (November 1977) (forthcoming): F. O. Okediji et al., "The Changing African Family Project: A report with special reference to the Nigerian segment"; Pshomha Imoagene, *Social Mobility in Emergent Society: A Study of the New Elite in Western Nigeria,* Changing African Family Monograph, No. 2, Department of Demography, Australian National University and Department of Sociology, University of Ibadan, Canberra, 1976.

45. Edward E. Evans-Pritchard, *The Nuer: A Description of Livelihood and Political Institutions of a Nilotic People* (Oxford: Clarendon, 1940), p. 90.

46. C. K. Meek, *Land Law and Custom in the Colonies* (Oxford: Oxford University Press, 1949), p. 16.

47. Sahlins, *Stone Age Economics,* pp. 185–186: see also Mauss (esp. pp. 37–41).

48. See Larissa Lomnitz, "Reciprocity of favors in the urban middle class of Chile," in Dalton, *Studies in Economic Anthropology,* for a description of the extensive system of reciprocity still existing among the Chilean middle class.

49. C. Edward Hopen, *The Pastoral Fulbe Family in Gwandu* (Oxford: International African Institute, Oxford University Press, 1958), pp. 113–114. For examples from other cultures, see, for instance, Clifton R. Wharton, Jr., "Risk, uncertainty and the subsistence farmer: Technological innovation and resistance to change in the context of survival," and Allen W. Johnson, "Security and risk taking among poor peasants: A Brazilian case," both in Dalton, *Studies in Economic Anthropology.*

50. Peter C. Garlick, *African Traders and Economic Development in Ghana* (Oxford: Clarendon Press, 1971), pp. 110–118.

51. Although this conclusion seems obvious, misinterpretations on this issue abound. Thus, one economist/demographer, Julian Simon, arrived at the right conclusion by making the unfounded assumption that in high-risk situations one cannot afford to worry about the future and, hence, is irresponsibly fertile. George Peter Murdock's analysis of family types from the Yale cross-cultural survey file in *Social Structure* (New York: Macmillan, 1949) confused the whole position by placing emphasis on such simple characteristics as residence units and groupings during movement, so that his successors began to draw parallels between independent, nucleated families found on the one hand among food gatherers and herders and on the other in industrial societies, and to contrast these with the extended family of settled agriculturists. (See, for example, M. F. Nimkoff and Russell Middleton, "Types of family and types of economy," *The American Journal of Sociology* 66, no. 3 (November 1960): 215–225.) Nothing, as we will see, could be less illuminating. The inward-turning nuclear family where obligations exist largely between spouses and toward their nonadult children is a very recent phenomenon almost everywhere except in the West. In spite of Murdock's followers' attempts to show resemblances between Eskimo and Western Families, the former in fact have traditionally shared all the food they caught, and it is hardly possible that a nuclear family could improve its diet at the expense of others (see Graburn, cited in note 22 above).

52. Max Gluckman, *Custom and Conflict in Africa* (Oxford: Basil Blackwell, 1955). See also, on the breaking of the emotional bond between a mother and her first-born in Hausa-Fulani society of northern Nigeria, Jean Trevor, "Family change in Sokoto: A traditional Moslem Fulani/Hausa city," in John C. Caldwell (ed.), *Population Growth and Socioeconomic Change in West Africa* (New York: Columbia University Press, 1975).
53. Data from CAFN 2 (Changing African Family Project: Nigerian Segment, Survey 2). On the traditional upbringing of children by a number of kinsmen, see L. P. Mair, "African marriage and social change," in Arthur Phillips (ed.), *Survey of African Marriage and Family Life,* Part 1 (London: Oxford University Press, 1953), p. 2; and, for survey figures showing fewer than half of children in the Ivory Coast to be with their biological parents, see Remi Clignet, *Many Wives Many Powers: Authority and Power in Polygymous Families* (Evanston: Northwestern University Press, 1970), p. 171.
54. The new elite are more likely to have come from larger rural families than from smaller rural families even when allowance is made for the anticipated differential between the two in the number of children supplied to the succeeding generation (see Imoagene).
55. Evans-Pritchard, *The Nuer,* p. 91.
56. Marshall Sahlins, "The intensity of domestic production in primitive societies: Social inflections of the Chayanov Slope," in Dalton, *Studies in Economic Anthropology,* pp. 30–51. S. P. Reyna, "Pronatalism and child labor: Chadian attitudes to birth control and family size," in *Population Growth and Socio-economics Change in West Africa,* argues that, even in primitive society, the unit with greater working capacity is able to diversify its activities, thus making use of windfall gains and distant economic opportunities and raising its per capita income.
57. Frank Lorimer, "The economics of family formation under difficult conditions," in *Proceedings of the World Population Conference, Belgrade, 30 August-10 September 1965* (New York: United Nations, 1967). II, pp. 92–95.
58. Hopen, p. 124, fn. 1.
59. Pierre de Schlippe, *Shifting Cultivation in Africa: The Zande System of Agriculture* (London: Routledge and Kegan Paul, 1956), p. 235.
60. Boserup, *Woman's Role in Economic Development* (London: Allen and Unwin, 1970), pp. 27–52.
61. An analysis of the startlingly rapid change that occurred in another southern Nigerian society (the Ibos) with the imposition of colonial government found massive development in trading and other economic adaptations, but nothing worth reporting on the family and reproduction. See Simon Ottenberg, "Ibo receptivity to change," in William R. Bascom and Melville J. Herskovits (eds.), *Continuity and Change in African Cultures* (Chicago: University of Chicago Press, 1959), pp. 130–143.
62. Josiah C. Russell, "Demographic values in the Middle Ages," in George F. Mair (ed.), *Studies in Population: Proceedings of the Annual Meeting of the Population Association of America at Princeton, New Jersey, May 1949* (Princeton: Princeton University Press, 1949), pp. 103–107.
63. Strictly speaking, economists describe these "wealth flows" as "income flows," retaining the word "wealth" for a stock rather than a flow. However, most social scientists assume that "income" excludes the giving of a helping hand in the house and many other items included in this discussion. Hence, it seemed necessary to use a new term.
64. Stephen P. Reyna, "Making do when the rains stop: Adjustments of domestic structure to climate variations among the Barma," *Ethnology* 14, no. 4 (October 1975): 405–417.
65. This will be discussed by the author at greater length in a book on *The Condtions of Fertility Decline* (in preparation) and in a set of studies which he is editing, *The Persistence of High Fertility: Population Prospects in the Third World, Changing African Family Project Monograph no. 3* (Canberra: Department of Demography, Australian National University, 1977).
66. This pattern is being examined toward the end of fertility transition in Australia in a book by L. D. Ruzicka and John C. Caldwell, *The End of Demographic Transition in Australia* (in preparation). Reported child-centeredness in this population is noted in John C. Caldwell, "Family size norms," in Helen Ware (ed.), *Fertility and Family Formation: Australasian Bibliography and Essays, 1972,* Australian Family Formation Project Monograph No. 1 (Canberra: Department of Demography, Australian National University, 1973), pp. A3–A13.
67. See John C. Caldwell, "The erosion of the family," "Extended family obligations and education," and "Fertility and the household economy in Nigeria," especially the section entitled, "An investigation into the inputs into children and the returns from adult children and from education."
68. It is doubtful if this happened in the traditional stage of any other society, although in Japan families did exhibit "rapid segmentation in each generation," partly because of a kind of primogeniture system, and because fertility levels were probably moderate. [See Ezra F. Vogel, "Kinship structure, migration to the city, and modernization," in R. P. Dore (ed.), *Aspects of Social Change in Modern Japan* (Princeton: Princeton University Press, 1967), pp. 91–92; and Irene B. Taueber, *The Population of Japan* (Princeton: Princeton University Press, 1958), pp. 52–53.] Extended family help was the rule in India and China [Olga Lang, *Chinese Family and Society* (New Haven: Yale University Press, 1946), p. 169], while in northern Nigeria it could be institutionalized into the *gandu* [Polly Hill, *Rural Hausa: A Village and a setting* (New York: Cambridge University Press, 1972)].

69. Christine Oppong, "Attitudes to family type and family size in West Africa: A study of norms among a Ghanaian student population," *International Journal of the Sociology of the Family* 4, no. 2 (1974): Caldwell, *Population Growth and Family Change in Africa.*
70. Data from the Changing African Family Project, mostly from the first survey in the Nigerian segment.
71. John C. Caldwell and Helen Ware, "The evolution of family planning in an African city: Ibadan, Nigeria." Comparisons were made by age at given parities and changes in parity, and age-specific birth rates were also estimated.
72. This is a different argument from that put forward in Davis, "Institutional patterns favoring high fertility," p. 4, where it is argued that the growth of cities at first reinforces high fertility in rural areas by providing greater outlets for agricultural produce.
73. Aderanti Adepoju, "Migration and socioeconomic links between urban migrants and their home communities in Nigeria," *Africa* 44, no. 4 (October 1974): 385–387.
74. On the economic impact of rural-urban migrant children in Ghana, see John C. Caldwell, *African Rural-Urban Migration: The Movement to Ghana's Towns* (New York: Columbia Univeristy Press, 1969); for a discussion of the role of children in the family economy in India, see Mahmood Mamdani, *The Myth of Population Control, Family, Caste, and Class in an Indian Village* (New York: Monthly Review Press, 1972); for a description of the situation in a cloth-weaving town in south India, see V. P. Pethe, "Attitudes toward family planning: Case studies," in *Demographic Profiles of an Urban Population* (Bombay: Popular Prakashan, 1964), p. 112.
75. CAFN 3, Changing African Family Project: Nigerian Segment, Survey 3. The latitude allowed with regard to contraception, namely the use of any method, including abstinence, to achieve the small family was necessary because the survey was restricted to older women who had relatively little access to modern contraception.
76. This is a very conservative definition of fertility innovation; however, even some of these women might have achieved this fertility by chance and then have rationalized the position [see R. Lesthaege and H. J. Page, "Relating individual fertility to other variables: Common problems and pitfalls," *Seminar on Marriage, Parenthood, and Fertility in West Africa, Lomé, January 3–9, 1976.* International Sociological Association].
77. There has been previous evidence pointing this way from studies in Ghana. The author, drawing on a 1962–64 research program, emphasized that the family-building practices and attitudes of the new urban elite could be understood only in terms of relationships restructured in terms of a fusion of an existing culture with an imported one (*Population Growth and Family Change in Africa,* especially pp. 52–73 and 1983–188). Oppong has shown how presumably rational decisions about desired family size among younger members of this elite reflect the type of family situation they desire and will probably try to construct (see "Attitudes to family type and family size in West Africa," a study of university students).
78. Alex Inkeles and David H. Smith, *Becoming Modern: Individual Change in Six Developing Countries* (London: Heinemann, 1974), pp. 17–18.
79. Their index lists "European influence" only to suggest "See Western bias," and, on following this into the text, we find them preparing a defense because "some of our critics would be prepared to argue that the use of the O. M. [Overall Modernity] scale borders on being a social science form of cultural colonialism" (p. 297). Their scale is of little use for the demographer trying to relate modernization to family and fertility change, for two of its important components are "kinship obligations" and "family size" (both measured negatively) (pp. 25–27 and 34).
80. William J. Goode, *World Revolution and Family Patterns* (Glencoe: Free Press, 1963).
81. There has been some revolt against the identification of Christianity with the West, and the African pentecostal churches, which do not preach Western values, have attracted about one-quarter of Ibadan's Christians (CAFN 1).
82. A comprehensive study of teachers, their family lives and problems, their attitudes, and their fertility will be available when Christine Oppong analyzes the Ghanaian Segment of the Changing African Family Project.
83. Norman H. Loewenthal and Abraham S. David, *Social and Economic Correlates of Family Fertility: An Updated Survey of the Evidence* (North Carolina: Research Triangle Institute, 1972), p. 42.
84. See, for example, past fertility declines reported in William Brass et al., *The Demography of Tropical Africa* (Princeton: Princeton University, Press, 1968), pp. 178, 181, 346–347, 512–513.
85. Louis Henry, *Anciennes Familles Genevoises: Etude Dêmographique XVI–XX Siècle,* INED, Travaux et Documents, Cahier no. 26 (Paris: Presses Universitaires de France, 1956): Sigismund Peller, "Births and deaths among Europe's ruling families since 1500," in D. V. Glass and D. E. C. Eversley (eds.), *Population in History: Essays in Historical Demography.*

Population Increases of States from 1970 to 1980 (%)

POPULATION REFERENCE BUREAU

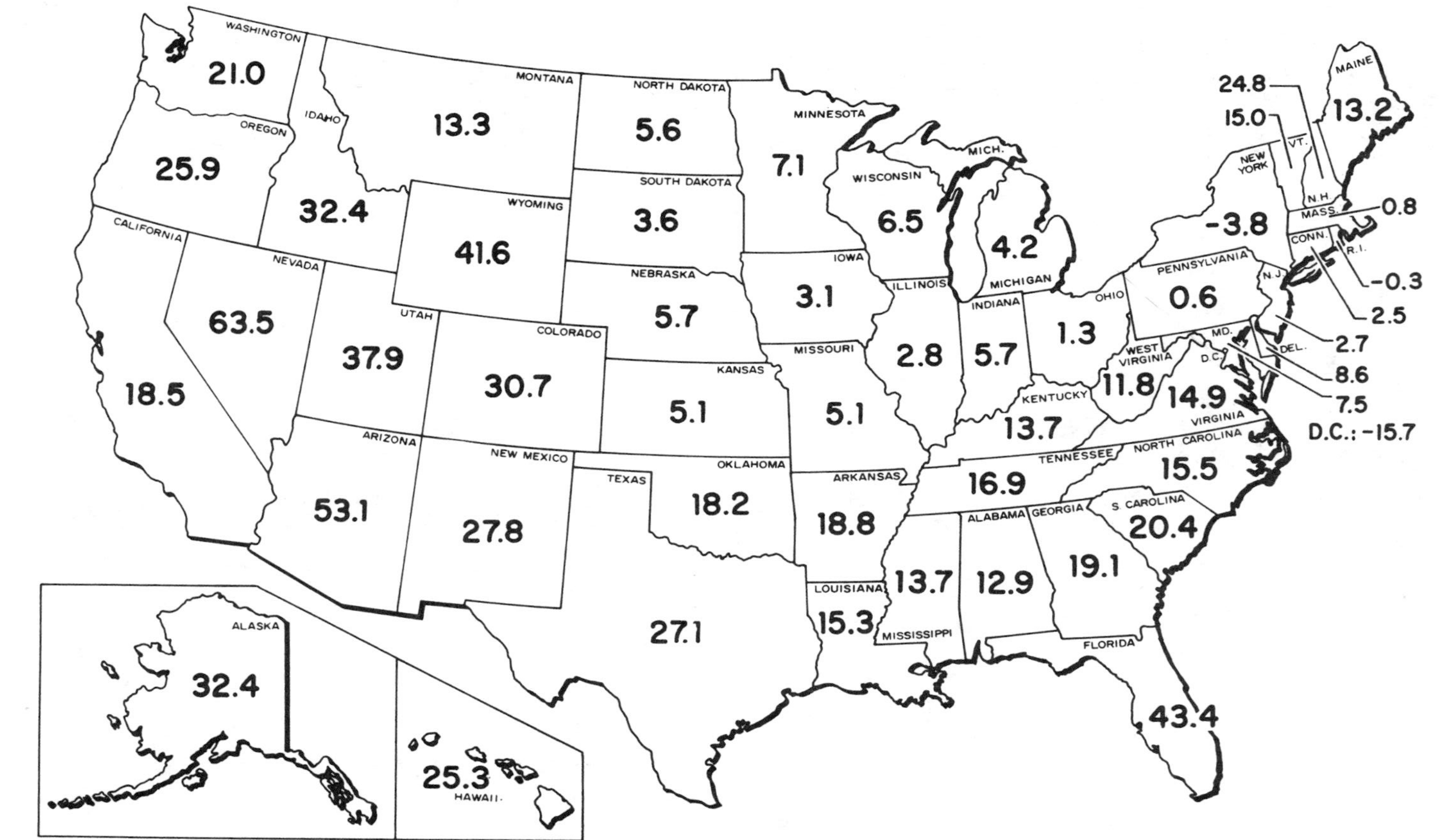

1980 Census Totals Show U.S. Grew 11.4 Percent During 1970s.
Population Reference Bureau, Inc., 1337 Connecticut Ave., NW, Washington, D.C. 20036.

Six Demographic Surprises of the 1970s

CALVIN L. BEALE

It is instructive (and chastening) to review ways in which the course of American demographic trends deviated from what had been foreseen at the beginning of the 1970s despite the increased sophistication of projection models. To my mind, there were at least six major demographic surprises.

1. ***The Birth Rate.*** In 1971, the Bureau of the Census issued four projections of births for the 1970s, ranging from 40.1 to 49.3 million. Actual births for the decade proved to be only 33.2 million, 17 percent below the lowest projection, and 23 percent below the lowest widely accepted series. Deferred marriage and childbearing and increased abortion all contributed to produce this result.

2. ***The Death Rate.*** In the same Census Bureau projections, deaths for the decade were forecast at about 21 million. The observed number was 19.3 million. Life expectancy was projected to increase by only a half a year; instead it rose by 3.4 years. Major gains were made in reducing mortality from heart disease and strokes.

3. ***Household Size.*** A third surprise of the 1970s was the accelerated decline in average household size. In 1970 the average was 3.14 persons per household. In 1968, the Bureau of the Census issued eight projections, the lowest of which for 1980 was 3.88 persons per household, but the two most favored series ranged from 3.08 to 3.19 persons. By 1980, however, actual average household size had plummeted to 2.76 persons. In particular, the creation of small nonfamily households and one-parent households had proceeded far more rapidly than had been foreseen.

4. ***The Regional Shift in Population.*** Migration to the South and West in the 1970s proved much greater than expected. The most ambitious set of regional projections was a seven-volume work prepared by the Bureau of Economics Analysis (BEA) in 1972. Population growth in the Southern New England, Mid-Atlantic, and East North Central states from 1970 to 1980 was only 1.1 million against a projected 7.6 million, whereas the West grew by double the predicted rate (8.3 vs 4.0 million) and the South rose by three-fifths more than expected (12.5 million vs. 7.8 million.)

5. ***Growth of Nonmetropolitan Population.*** Perhaps the most surprising trend of all was the revival of rural and small town population growth. No one seems to have been on record as forecasting the nonmetropolitan growth rate to be higher than the metropolitan rate in the 1970s. The BEA projection, referred to above, foresaw metropolitan growth of 11.4 percent and nonmetropolitan of 5.3 percent. Instead, metropolitan countries grew by 9.8 percent, but nonmetropolitan growth was 15.8 percent, or triple the projected rate.

6. ***The Role of Illegal and Refugee Immigration.*** By its nature, illegal immigration is difficult to estimate, much less to predict. Whatever its true amount, the consensus seems to be that it rose to major proportions during the 1970s, and became a significant factor in population growth. A further source of unanticipated growth was the influx of refugees—Indochinese in particular.

It is not my point in recounting these surprises to imply criticism of the forecasters, although I think some is merited in particular cases. I view the problem as generic. The demand for projections is insatiable. But, the ability to project inflections and changes in human behavior is limited—and will probably continue to be so.

7

What's in Store for U.S. Population Trends in the 1980s?

POPULATION REFERENCE BUREAU

Continued low fertility and declining mortality, slowdowns in rising rates of divorce and nonmarital cohabitation, somewhat less mobility and internal migration, and increases in both legal and illegal immigration—these are among the predictions of five population experts for the rest of the decade.

At a February 17, 1982, seminar at the Population Reference Bureau in Washington, D.C., called to consider "What's in store for U.S. population trends in the 1980?" the five experts bravely voiced their expectations that most current trends will continue, if moderated in some cases. None foresaw surprises in the decade ahead to rival the 1970s turnaround in net rural-to-urban migration, the tripling of the number of unmarried couples living together, the surge in refugees and illegal immigration, and the faintness of the baby boom echo. However, they also agreed, as one panelist put it, that "many questions asked of demographers are not knowable." Among the "unknowables" that could affect U.S. demographic trends in the 1980s are: the outcome of current cutbacks in social welfare programs and "new federalism" proposals to shift responsibility for many such programs to individual states, the depth and duration of the current economic recession, and new immigration legislation. Energy shortages and technological innovations could affect demographic trends over the long run.

The five panelists, who spoke in their private capacity on their fields of expertise, are:

Calvin Beale (Leader, Economic Research Service, U.S. Department of Agriculture)—internal migration;

Leon Bouvier (Director, Demographic Research and Policy Analysis, Population Reference Bureau)—international migration;

Paul Glick (Senior Demographer, Population Division, Bureau of the Census, retired)—marriage, divorce, and household composition;

Marilyn McMillen (Statistician, Social Security Administration)—mortality;

Martin O'Connell (Chief, Fertility Statistics Branch, Population Division, Bureau of the Census)—fertility;

Jacob Siegel (Senior Statistician, Demographic Research and Analysis, Bureau of the Census) served as moderator.

Following are highlights of their predictions, including their responses to questions from the overflow audience:

CHANGES IN COHORT SIZES (Siegel)

Warning of coming changes in cohort sizes that result from past fluctuations in numbers of births is the main contribution demographers can make to planning for changes in such areas as school enrollment, labor force participation, and marketing. The changes to prepare for in the 1980s are: a small increase in the 0 to 14 age group and a drop in the 15 to 29 age group, reflecting the birth rate decline of the 1960s and 1970s; a sharp increase in the group aged 30 to 44—the baby boom generation; a decline in numbers of persons aged 55 to 64, reflecting the birth decline from the mid-1920s to the mid-1930s; and a moderate increase in the number of elderly, aged 65 and over.

FERTILITY (O'Connell)

Assuming no major changes in contraceptive technology and availability of abortion and family planning services, period fertility will continue low during the 1980s, fluctuating between 1.8 and 2.1 births per woman. Although women in the childbearing ages are projected to reach a record 55 million by the mid-1980s, annual births should peak at 3.9 to 4 million in the decade and then decline.

Continued delayed marriage will keep fertility rates low for teenagers and women in their early twenties, although cutbacks in publicly funded family planning and abortion services could after the proportion of premaritally conceived, but legitimated, births compared to the proportion of out-of-wedlock births among women of these ages. Fertility rates among women aged 25 to 34 will continue their recent slight rise, especially among urban, highly educated, professional women who have been delaying marriage and childbearing. However, birth rates among women in their thirties will continue at about half the level of rates for women in their twenties.

The fertility rate of black women will continue about 30 percent higher than the rate for white women, as it has for the past 50 years. Migration might narrow regional differences in the crude birth rate, but in 1990, as in 1980, the birth rate is likely to be highest in the West, where both economic growth and proportions of people in the childbearing ages are currently highest.

The first wave of baby boom women, born between 1946 and 1950 and now in their early to mid-thirties, will have had about 2 children per woman, on average, and 15 percent will still be childless when their childbearing is ended about 1990. Women now in their twenties, born in the 1950s and early 1960s, will probably complete their childbearing with 1.8 to 2.0 children per woman and as many as 20 to 25 percent could remain childless. In Census Bureau surveys, women aged 18 to 24 now report that they expect eventually to have slightly more children than this (2.0 births each, on average) and that only 11 percent will remain childless. Currently, however, two-thirds of this age group are still single and since 1976, when the Census Bureau began collecting birth expectations data for single women, women aged 18 to 24 who have remained single have been revising their expectations downward. Marriage is the big unknown for single women in responding to survey questions on birth expectations.

MORTALITY (McMillen)

Death rates will continue to decline in the 1980s as they did from 1968 to 1978 when the age-adjusted mortality rate fell from 7 to 8 deaths per 1,000 population—the level at which it had hovered between 1954 and 1968—to 6 deaths per 1,000 population. This latest mortality decline reflects the combined effects of changes in life style—improved diets, more exercise, less smoking, etc.—and increased access to medical screening and care.

In 1978, life expectancy at birth was 69.5 years for U.S. males and 77.2 for females. By the end of the 1980s, males will pass the 70-year mark and females will reach 80 according to most federal and private researchers. Projections made by the Social Security Office of the Actuary in 1981, the latest available, show male life expectancy at 71.9 in 1990 and 72.9 in the year 2000, and female life expectancy at 80.0 in 1990 and 81.1 in 2000.

That mortality will continue to decline is supported by international comparisons which show that there is still room for improvement in U.S. mortality levels; internationally, U.S. males ranked 18th and females ranked ninth in life expectancy in 1975. Except for infant mortality, the decline in death rates may very well continue even if the 1980s see a repeat of the great depression of the 1930s, predicted Siegel, also an expert in mortality, in response to a question from the floor. Health conditions did not deteriorate in the 1930s and mortality declined far more than it did during the period of maximum expansion of public health programs in the late 1950s and early 1960s, Siegel said.

McMillen predicted a continued narrowing of the racial gap in mortality for the 1980s, reflecting the faster fall in death rates for non-whites than for whites that resumed as general mortality began to decline again about 1968. Similarly, improvements in female mortality have slowed somewhat compared to the gains for males since 1968, so that the sex differential in mortality is likely at least to stabilize in the 1980s, rather than continuing to widen as it did from 1900 to 1968.

MARRIAGE, DIVORCE, AND HOUSEHOLD COMPOSITION (Glick)

In 1982, the number of people in the ages where first marriages generally occur—18 to 25 for women and 20 to 27 for men—has peaked. As the numbers go down, numbers of first marriages should also decline gradually, although the "marriage squeeze" will reverse to favor easier marriage for women—(i.e., by 1990, there will be 5 percent more men than women in the main ages of first marriage compared to the 10 percent excess of women in the mid-1960s).

Delayed first marriages may increase during the 1980s, but 8 to 10 percent of women now in their twenties will never marry, compared with only 4 percent of women who were in their twenties during the 1950s. These delayed marriages would involve more of the large numbers of people born at the end of the baby boom: thus, the median age at first marriage should continue to rise moderately in the 1980s. Deteriorating economic conditions could contribute to continuing declines in the rates of first marriage and remarriage.

Annual divorces will continue to rise during the 1980s until the number of persons in the main age range for divorce (25 to 40) reaches a peak around 1990. However, the rise in divorces should moderate, partly because the increase in women's employment—a prime, though indirect, factor in divorce—is also likely to slow.

Changing norms are speeding up the time between first marriage and divorce and between divorce and remarriage. This increases the likelihood of second divorces and third marriages.

Marriage and divorce rates are lowered by the steep rise in the number of unmarried couples living together, which tripled from 523,000 in 1970 to 1.8 million in 1981. This number will still rise steeply but may not triple again in the 1980s. By 1990, however, unmarried couples should constitute 7 percent of all couple households, compared to 3.5 percent in 1981.

During the 1980s, the number of households will again increase far more than the total U.S. population (21 versus 9 percent). However, the annual addition is projected to peak at 1.8 million in 1982 and decline to 1.6 million in 1990. Some 43 percent of the 1980s increase in households will occur among nonfamily households, now about one-fourth of all households. Nine-tenths of nonfamily households are currently persons living alone: unmarried couples constitute over one-half of the remainder.

Mean household size was 3.14 persons in 1970, 2.76 in 1980, and is expected to decline to 2.47 in 1990. Most of the decline will be due to fewer children under age 18.

The proportion of children under 18 living with one parent will continue to increase, reaching 25 percent in 1990 compared to 20 percent in 1980.

The gap between median incomes of black and white families, which stabilized in the 1970s, could widen again in the 1980s because of rising unemployment which particularly affects black families, a large proportion of which are headed by women at the lower end of the employment scale.

INTERNAL MIGRATION (Beale)

Gross mobility—the proportion of people changing households in a year—may drop to 16 to 17 percent in the 1980s, or slightly below the recent American "standard" of 20 percent. This will be due to a diminishing supply of people in the prime moving ages (22 to 25), which is at a peak in 1982 (reflecting the peak baby boom years of 1957 and 1961), the high cost and inadequate supply of housing, and the preponderance of two-earner families, which inhibits migration. Migration may be little affected by the shift of social welfare responsibilities to states ("new federalism") if that comes to pass, because migration rates are generally low among people entirely dependent on social security, e.g., welfare and unemployment insurance. However, less state support for people with economic problems might stimulate migration to areas promising more jobs.

The population shift to the South and West will continue, but not accelerate as it did in the 1970s. Movement to the North cannot be reduced much further, but substantial outmovement is still possible from many northern industrial areas. Growth is also likely to be slow in similar areas in the South (e.g., Delaware, Maryland, the District of Columbia, and the Carolinas). Migration will continue rapid to the Mountain states of the West (Arizona, Colorado, Idaho, Montana, Nevada, New Mexico, Utah, Wyoming). Coal gasification and more complex forms of oil extraction (e.g., from shale) should provide continued impetus to mining-related migration. However, most population boom areas will still be related to resort-retirement growth and suburbanization. Diminishing water supplies will eventually restrain population growth in the West, but not yet in the 1980s.

The net flow of migration from urban areas to small towns and rural areas—a demographic surprise of the 1970s—will continue until popular perceptions of life in large urban areas improve and/or the ideological underpinning of the shift to small communities weakens (environmentalism, counter-culture values, homesteading, etc.). However, the size of the net flow may lessen in the 1980s, because some of the bloom is off the economic surge that facilitated nonmetropolitan population growth in the 1970s: unemployment rates are now higher and job growth has been lower since 1978 in nonmetropolitan areas than in metropolitan areas. But higher energy costs for transportation are not a limiting factor in nonmetropolitan growth.

INTERNATIONAL MIGRATION (Bouvier)

The doubling of Mexico's young adult population over the next 20 years and continuing improvements in transportation and communication are among the forces that will keep the potential for migration to the United States at a high pitch during the 1980s. How many will actually enter depends partly on legislation which is unlikely to change substantially during the decade with reference to the three principal types of immigration—legal immigration, refugees, and illegal immigration.

In 1980, some 800,000 people entered the United States legally under the limited or unlimited categories for legal immigration or as refugees. The 270,000 slots currently available in the limited category will remain unchanged. Beyond that, however, are those unlimited categories which consist of spouses and minor children of U.S. citizens, parents of U.S. citizens aged 21 and over, and small special groups, such as former U.S. citizens who wish to return to the United States. The number admitted in these categories was about 130,000 per year until recently, rose to 151,000 in 1980, and is likely to increase substantially to between 200,000 and 250,000 per year during the 1980s as the large number of refugees become legal residents and many opt for citizenship after four years as legal residents and begin bringing in close relatives under the categories now exempt from numerical restrictions. This would bring the total of legal immigrants in the limited and unlimited categories to 470,000 to 520,000 a year. These estimates are considerably higher than the limit in the immigration reform bill recently introduced in the Congress which recommends an upper limit of 425,000 legal immigrants a year, *including* those presently entering under the categories exempt from the 270,000 numerical restriction.

Current legislation permits 50,000 refugee admissions a year. The number can be raised by executive order in consultation with Congress and has been around 200,000 in recent years: 140,000 slots are allocated for 1982. Although political turmoil continues to erupt around the globe, refugee levels are likely to fall to between 75,000 and 100,000 in the next few years because of Americans' increasing resistance to large numbers of refugees.

As refugees may apply for legal residence status after one year in this country, care must be taken not to double-count these people—first as refugees and second when they become legal residents. The immigration and Naturalization Service (INS) only records them as they become legal residents under the numerically exempt status. The predictions above for the exempt category do not include refugees who adjust their status. It does take into consideration the fact that when refugees eventually acquire citizenship, they are in a position to sponsor their immediate relatives for entrance as legal immigrants under that same exempt category.

Illegal immigration will probably increase somewhat during the 1980s. The urge to migrate remains high in the Latin American and Caribbean countries where most illegals originate: the young adult population is growing rapidly and unemployment has not been reduced. On the U.S. side, a consensus about limiting illegal immigration seems to be emerging. On the other hand, many businesses benefit from employing illegals: the administration is concerned with, among other things, maintaining smooth relations with Mexico and other countries for whom illegal migration represents a safety valve. Also, enforcement of laws curbing illegal immigration will not be easy. Past levels of illegal immigration are unknown; estimates range from 100,000 to half a million a year. Forced to pick a number for the coming years. Bouvier estimated between 350,000 and 500,000 a year.

The sum of the various categories of immigrants comes to about 900,000 a year under the low assumptions and just over 1.1 million under the high assumptions (see Table 7.1). Subtracting emigration of legal residents estimated at 100,000 to 150,000 annually (following estimates by Robert Warren and Jennifer Peck of the Census Bureau) results in a prediction of net immigration for the 1980s ranging from three-quarters of a million to almost one million a year.

Immigration at these levels rules out the possibility of reaching a quasi-stationary population in the near future and promises a change in the makeup of U.S. society that presents Americans with a challenge similar to that of the large numbers of European immigrants who entered at the beginning of the twentieth century. Today's base population is far larger than it was then, but by 1990 Hispan-

Table 7.1. Projections of Annual Migration to the U.S. in the 1980s: Leon Bouvier

Type of Migration	Low Assumptions	High Assumptions
Legal—Limited	270,000	270,000
Unlimited[a]	200,000	250,000
Refugees[b]	75,000	100,000
Illegal	350,000	500,000
Gross migration, total	895,000	1,120,000
Minus emigration of legal residents	100,000	150,000
Net migration, total	795,000	970,000

[a]Exempt from legal migration numerical limitations: spouses and minor children of U.S. citizens and parents of U.S. citizens aged 21 and over.

[b]Refugees adjust their status to legal immigrants after one or two years. They are only counted as "refugees" in these estimates.

ics will comprise a significant minority of 10 percent of the population. Siegel observed that the problems of adjustment for the immigrants of today could be greater than at the turn of the century, because the cultural gap between Hispanics and the many immigrants from Asia and the present U.S. population is wider than it was between the earlier West and East European immigrants, and, unlike those earlier immigrants. Hispanics in particular appear to want to preserve their own culture and language, rather than assimilating.

PROSPECTS FOR FUTURE GROWTH

U.S. population growth has been spurred in the recent past by both the high birth rates of the baby boom era and by immigration. Together these factors have given the United States a rate of growth about four times higher than those of the industrialized countries of Northern and Western Europe. Yet the 1970s witnessed a decline in the U.S. fertility rate to a level nearly as low as that of Western Europe. If the fertility rate remains low. U.S. population growth could be expected to follow the "European model" to eventual zero, and then negative, growth. But one major spur to population growth will remain: immigration. The United States, along with Australia and Canada, has been an important "receiving" country in the more developed world for immigrants and refugees. No other country takes in more new residents on a regular basis.

What would U.S. population size be in the future if no immigration were allowed? If our fertility rate remains below the replacement level of 2.1 children per woman. U.S. population size would eventually begin to decline, as Austria's and West Germany's already have. With a total fertility rate of 1.8 children per woman (0.1 child below the current rate) and no immigration, U.S. population would begin declining just before 2030, and by 2080 would be about 202 million, approximately the level at the time of the 1970 census (see Table 7.2, top panel). But if we add half a million immigrants a year (somewhat above the annual net

Table 7.2. Projected U.S. Population Size, by Total Fertility Rate and Net Annual Immigration: 2000, 2030, 2050, 2080

(Numbers in millions)

Total Fertility Rate	2000	2030	2050	2080
	No immigration			
1.8	243.7	244.8	227.3	201.6
2.0	250.3	267.8	265.9	260.8
2.2	257.7	295.0	311.6	341.3
	Annual net immigration = 500,000			
1.8	255.5	277.6	274.1	268.2
2.0	262.3	302.1	315.0	335.1
2.2	269.9	331.0	365.6	425.1
	Annual net immigration = 750,000			
1.8	261.3	294.1	297.5	301.5
2.0	268.3	319.2	340.0	372.2
2.2	276.0	349.0	392.6	467.1
	Annual net immigration = 1 million			
1.8	267.1	310.4	320.9	334.8
2.0	274.2	336.3	365.1	409.3
2.2	282.1	367.0	416.6	509.1

Source: Leon F. Bouvier, *The Impact of Immigration on U.S. Population Size,* Population Trends and Public Policy Series No. 1 (Washington, D.C.: Population Reference Bureau, 1981) Table 2.

Note: These projections assume a base 1980 U.S. population of 222 million, about 4.5 million below the actual April 1, 1980, census count of 226.5 million (which was announced only on January 1, 1981, after the projections were prepared). Adjustment for this discrepancy would not significantly change the projections shown here.

legal immigration average of 420,000 in the 1970s) while fertility remains at 1.8 children per woman, the population would begin to decline only about 2050 and would be about 268 million in 2080 (Table 7.2, panel 2)

But what if fertility does not remain at this low level? While the birth rate may not rise much in the future, even rather small changes can have large long-term effects. Even if immigration were zero. U.S. population could still reach 260 million by 2080 if women had 2.0 children, on average, instead of 1.8 (top panel, Table 7.2). And with no immigration, but above-replacement fertility of 2.2 children per woman (as some demographers are now predicting for future decades), the population would top the 340 million mark by 2080!

Perhaps the one aspect that sets the United States apart from other developed countries so far as future population size is concerned is the complete uncertainty as to what that size will be. While fertility rates of some low-fertility European countries might well rise somewhat, only the United States must also try to deal with such potentially large numbers of immigrants in projecting its future size. With an annual net immigration of 750,000 (close to Bouvier's low assumptions for the 1980s described in the preceding section) and 2.0 children per woman, U.S. population could be about 372 million by 2080; with net annual immigration of one million (just over Bouvier's high assumptions) and fertility of 2.2 children per woman, the figure goes over 500 million (see bottom two panels of Table 7.2).

While a few other developed countries have moderately high immigration *rates,* no other country accepts such large *numbers* of immigrants. Thus, it is possible to speculate about future U.S. population size using very reasonable assumptions about future fertility rates and immigration—both legal and illegal—and be *wrong by several hundred million.*

In looking to the future, we must also keep in mind that the world of the next hundred years will be vastly different from that of the past hundred. The stage of international relations will be joined by more and more actors—many with nuclear clout. The people of the United States can no longer make decisions independently, cushioned by the safety of geographic isolation and a strong economy. Political unrest, caused in part by the strain of development in Third World nations, may increase the numbers of refugees seeking asylum. The increasing interdependence of the world economy will affect us all, including our decisions about family size.

Early population growth in the United States was essentially a product of a vibrant nation, needing a population to develop its seemingly limitless resources. Both the causes of future population growth and our policy toward it will be very different from the past. How we handle them will determine the future of the United States.

8

U.S. Population Growth: Prospects and Policy

JOSEPH A. MCFALLS, JR.
BRIAN JONES
BERNARD J. GALLAGHER III

The effect of population growth on the well-being of society has been debated for several hundred years. Experts now agree that population growth must cease sooner or later, because infinite growth can not occur in a finite world. At the current 2 percent rate of world population growth, there would be one individual for every square foot on the Earth's surface in less than 700 years. Although the experts agree that population growth must ultimately stop, there is disagreement about when this should occur. Some analysts hold that population growth can proceed, at least at a low rate, almost indefinitely, because additional resources will be discovered when existing supplies are exhausted or, better yet, substitutes will be developed. Most experts believe, however, that population growth must come to a halt within several hundred years. Moreover, several global studies on population and resources such as *The Global 2000 Report* and the Club of Rome projects have concluded that population growth must stop almost immediately if the current world population—and future populations of similar size—are to be able to subsist on the world's resources.

An even more hotly debated issue is whether an affluent nation like the U.S. should cease its population growth, and this issue has been the focus of much debate among the experts over the last 15 years. Rising concern about U.S. population growth was expressed by the public during the 1960s. At that time, the stresses caused by the baby boom generation were mounting and many people became anxious about the problems society would face if the baby boom generation itself had large families. During that decade, "zero population growth" (ZPG) turned into a household phrase. Public concern about future population growth was so great that it led Pres. Nixon to create the President's Commission on Population Growth and the American Future. However, this public concern dissipated rapidly in the 1970s, when it became clear that the baby boomers were reproducing at such record-low levels that they were not even having enough children to take their place in the population. Both the media and the public thought that this meant zero population growth had been achieved, but this was not true because the number of births and immigrants still exceeded the number of deaths and emigrants by a wide margin. Indeed, more people were actually added to the U.S. population during the 1970s than during any other decade. This is an especially good example of the sociological principal that the objective reality and subjective perception of a problem can move in opposite directions from each other.

Despite the atrophy of public concern, most demographers and a variety of organizations such as Zero Population Growth, Inc. have continued to advocate policies to terminate U.S. population growth. Among the most prominent bodies supporting this position was the Commission on Population Growth and the American Future, which concluded that population growth threatens severe problems for American society—and for the rest of the world—and "found no convincing argument for continued population growth." It recommended that the United States adopt the attainment of zero population growth as its national policy.

There are many problems posed by continued population growth. The major negative effect is its tendency to intensify or aggravate other types of problems. It leads to more congestion and crowding in metropolitan areas; increases pollution of the air, water, and land; places a great demand on energy re-

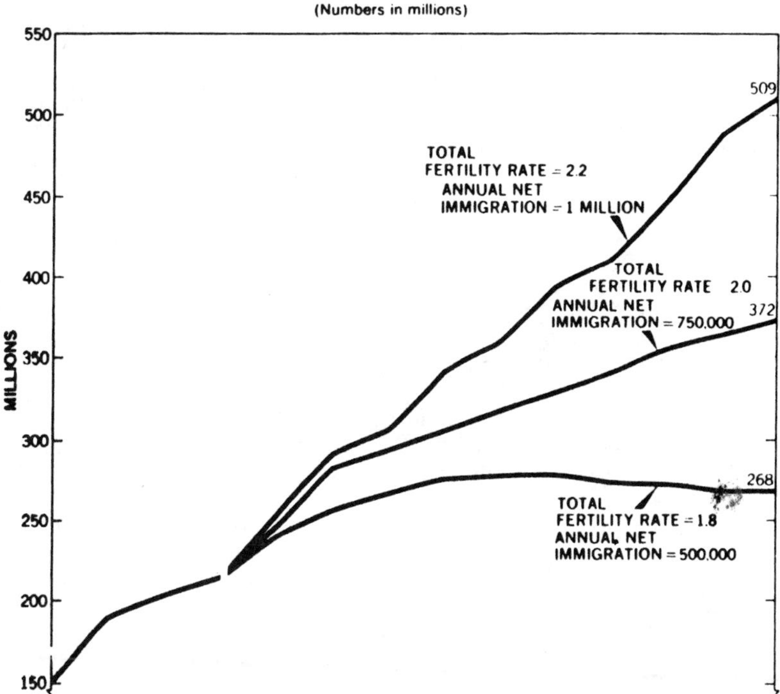

Figure 8.1. U.S. Population size, 1950–1980, and three scenarios for 1990–2080.

Figure 8.2. Total Fertility Rate: 1917–1981

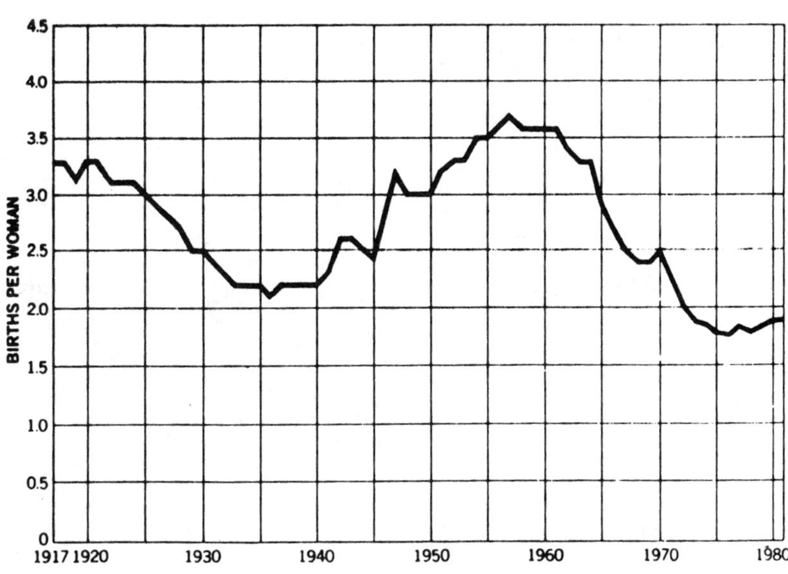

Tables courtesy of Population Reference Bureau, Inc.

sources; requires the development of new sources of food, minerals, lumber, and other raw materials; increases demand for water which is even now running short in many states; requires the duplication, rather than the improvement, of existing facilities such as nursing homes, hospitals, schools, and roads; leads to the destruction of agricultural land through urban and industrial expansion; and intensifies pressure on the fragile ecosystem. The Commission on Population and the American Future searched for the economic benefits of continued population growth, but was unable to find any. Rather, it found that, in the absence of population growth, the overall quality of life would improve and that many of our domestic problems would be easier to solve. More generally, the commission concluded:

> [Zero population growth] can contribute to the nation's ability to solve its problems . . . by providing an opportunity to devote resources to the quality of life rather than its quantity, and by "buying time"—that is, slowing the pace at which problems accumulate so as to provide opportunity for the development of orderly and democratic solutions.

In considering the desirability of continued population growth in the United States, we must also take into account its impact on the rest of the world. An additional American consumes and pollutes far more than an additional person in a poor country. Consequently, an American's impact on the well-being of the planet is much more adverse. Even though the United States makes up only about five per cent of the world's population, it uses up about 35 percent of its natural resources and creates about 50 percent of its pollution. Indeed, based on the threat the United States poses to the ecology of the planet, it is, for all intents and purposes, already the most overpopulated country in the world. According to environmentalist G. Tyler Miller, the United States's population is now equivalent to a pollution population of somewhere between 5,000,000,000 and 10,000,000,000, due to an environmental impact factor 25 to 50 times that of poorer countries. Our population growth problem is also the world's problem.

Population growth in the United States also increases our dependence on other countries for raw materials. In 1940, the United States was a net exporter of raw materials, but now, only four decades later, we import more than half of the raw materials necessary to maintain our current standard of living. If present, trends continue, within 25 years United States will be dependent on developing countries for most essential raw materials. This dependence makes us economically and politically vulnerable, as we have already experienced in our relations with oil-producing countries. More importantly, it is extremely risky to rely on poor nations for our raw materials when they themselves have rapidly growing populations which may need most or all of these resources in the future. By the same token, many nations of the world rely on us for our agricultural surplus. If we continue to expand our population to the point where this surplus disappears, these nations would not be able to obtain needed food and the United States would have fewer assess to trade for needed resources.

It is important to stress that the elimination of population growth in the United States will not eradicate the problems that it intensifies or aggravates—it just makes their solutions easier and less costly. As demographer Lincoln Day notes, a nongrowing population only makes the "good life" more attainable; it does not, in itself, produce it.

NEGATIVE GROWTH

To this point, we have been concentrating on the problems associated with positive population growth, largely because this is the actual problem faced by the vast majority of the nations of the world, including the United States. However, once positive population growth is eliminated and ZPG is achieved, there is no homeostatic mechanism that keeps a society at ZPG. It can easily slip back into a positive growth mode or into a negative one.

A variety of things happen to a society that is experiencing negative population growth. One is that the proportion of older people increases markedly. Another is that shortages develop in the labor force. Consequently, there are strains on systems such as Social Security. Most demographers agree that, if a nation declines in size very gradually, the objective damage of such problems is minimal. If the decline is rapid, however, it can produce severe economic and social dislocations.

Nevertheless, regardless of the actual objective damage caused by negative population growth, there is tremendous subjective concern about it. According to demographer Charles Westoff, the few countries that are at or near negative growth—for example, East

Germany, West Germany, Austria, Luxembourg, and Great Britain—are already giving signs of being very uncomfortable with it. In West Germany, where there have been more deaths than births since the mid 1970s, the growing subjective concern was evidenced by a recent television show entitled "Are the Germans Dying Out?" According to the program, the answer to this question is yes. Indeed, one German demographer has remarked: "Beneath the blankets we are a dying people." Similarly, in France, where fears of losing population have long been of concern both as a matter of national prestige and of national security, population growth is now the theme of a national debate. Former President Giscard d'Estaing recently cautioned that France could not aspire to grandeur if it were losing population, and former Premier Michel Debre regards a declining population as a national peril.

Such subjective concerns are understandable in a world in which population size has traditionally been correlated, though not perfectly, with military power and security. Although this correlation has lost some significance in the nuclear age, it still has some meaning in the face of nuclear equivalency and deterrence, and it would regain strength if nuclear disarmament becomes a reality.

The United States is not immune to the types of fears about negative growth prevalent in France and other European countries. Consider for a moment what the average American's reaction might be if the population (and armies) of our enemies continued to grow while ours declined—particularly if our nuclear armaments were strategically neutralized or dismantled. Many American citizens and military leaders would almost certainly call for increased population growth.

Examining demographic trends for the 12-month period from July 1, 1981, to June 30, 1982, shows that the United States is presently nowhere near zero population growth. The population grew by nearly 2,800,000 individuals, because the number of births and immigrants (4,800,000) exceeded the number of deaths and emigrants (2,000,000) by that amount, and ZPG occurs only when the quantity of births and immigrants is equal to the quantity of deaths and emigrants. How can this be achieved in the United States?

Before answering that question, it should be pointed out that it is not practical to try to achieve ZPG in the near future. Such an objective would require drastic alterations in our average family size, even if immigration were halted altogether. For example, couples would have to limit themselves to only about one child for the next 20 years or so. Obviously, most couples would view that requirement as a greater problem than the negative effects of population growth. The reason that such drastic requirements would be necessary now is that the U.S. population already has built-in momentum for growth resulting from its relatively young population. The United States has a relatively young population because of the post-World War II baby boom and the baby boomlet that generation is now parenting. However, once these large cohorts grow old, they will yield a relatively large number of deaths, making ZPG easier to attain in the future—all things being equal.

It is more realistic to think of achieving ZPG gradually over the next 50 to 100 years. Population growth would, of course, continue over this interval, but at least the goal of ZPG would ultimately be attained. Moreover, the problems posed by growth during this time span would be less troublesome than those caused by the unusually small cohorts resulting from trying to achieve ZPG immediately.

ATTAINING ZPG

To achieve ZPG in the future, the United States must keep fertility and net immigration (immigration minus emigration) relatively low. Just how low can be seen in Table 8.1, which presents projected U.S. population size and growth rates for various combinations of fertility and net immigration. It also assumes that life expectancy will continue to increase over the period, although at a slower rate than in recent decades. The fertility measure used is the total fertility rate (TFR), and indicator of average number of children per couple. The TFR indicates how many children women would average during their lifetimes if the rate of childbearing in a given year persisted. For example, the TFR in the United States in 1982 was 1.9 children. This means that, if the rate at which women were having children in 1982 does not change, teenagers just entering the childbearing ages in that year would average 1.9 children during their lifetimes. The TFR is our best answer to the question: How many children are women having "nowadays"? These projections were prepared by Leon Bouvier of the Population Reference Bureau.

Panel A of Table 8.1 permits us to observe the impact of growth of different levels of fertility if no immigration were allowed. Two

Table 8.1. Projected U.S. Population Size and Growth Rate, 2000 to 2080, by Level of Annual Immigration and Total Fertility Rate

	Year							
	2000		2030		2060		2080	
Total Fertility Rate	Total Population (1,000s)	Pop. Growth Rate (%)	Total Population (1,000s)	Pop. Growth Rate (%)	Total Population (1,000s)	Pop. Growth Rate (%)	Total Population (1,000s)	Pop. Growth Rate (%)
			(A) Annual Net Immigration 0					
1.8	243,677	0.3	244,835	−0.2	277,315	−0.4	201,563	−0.4
2.0	250,348	0.4	267,797	0.03	264,851	−0.06	260,790	−0.06
2.2	257,722	0.5	295,010	0.3	311,603	0.3	341,266	0.3
			(B) Annual Net Immigration 250,000					
1.8	249,538	0.4	261,219	−0.07	250,720	−0.2	234,870	−0.2
2.0	256,318	0.5	284,928	0.2	289,904	0.06	297,927	0.1
2.2	263,809	0.6	312,998	0.4	338,612	0.4	383,209	0.4
			(C) Annual Net Immigration 500,000					
1.8	255,402	0.5	277,603	0.06	274,125	−0.08	268,177	−0.06
2.0	262,287	0.6	302,059	0.3	314,957	0.2	335,066	0.2
2.2	269,896	0.8	330,986	0.5	365,620	0.5	425,149	0.5
			(D) Annual Net Immigration 750,000					
1.8	261,265	0.6	293,967	0.2	297,530	0.04	301,485	0.05
2.0	268,257	0.7	319,190	0.4	340,009	0.3	372,204	0.3
2.2	275,983	0.9	348,974	0.6	392,631	0.6	467,006	0.6
			(E) Annual Net Immigration 1,000,000					
1.8	267,127	0.7	310,371	0.3	320,935	0.1	334,792	0.1
2.0	274,226	0.8	336,321	0.5	365,063	0.4	409,343	0.4
2.2	282,070	1.0	366,962	0.7	419.641	0.7	509,039	0.6
			(F) Annual Net Immigration 2,000,000					
1.8	290,578	1.1	375,907	0.6	414,555	0.5	468,022	0.4
2.0	298,104	1.2	404,844	0.8	466,305	0.7	558,011	0.6
2.2	306,419	1.4	438,915	1.0	527,677	0.9	676,806	0.8

points stand out. First, the seemingly small four-tenths of a child difference between two low fertility rates—1.8 and 2.2—leads to an enormous difference in total population in the future. A TFR of 1.8 will result in a population of only 201,000,000 by the year 2080, while a TFR of 2.2 will produce a population of 341,000,000, a difference of 140,000,000 persons. In addition, the demographic and social profiles of the two populations would be radically dissimilar. The first population (TFR = 1.8) would be declining rapidly in size, dropping, for instance, by 76,000,000 people in the 30 years between 2050 and 2080. If this rate were to remain the same, this population would continue to attenuate and would eventually flicker out. The second population (TFR = 2.2) would still be growing, and although this growth would be slow, it would never end. The point is, therefore, that slight differences in the level of fertility in an advanced society like the United States are profoundly consequential in terms of resultant population growth. (If such a small difference in the TFR can have such a profound effect on the rate of population growth, it is easy to understand why the much larger differences in the TFR's of the major racial and ethnic groups in the United States—whites, 1.7; blacks, 2.3; Hispanics, 3.0—would, if they were to persist, result in widely disproportionate rates of growth between the three population subgroups and a radically different admixture of racial and ethnic types in the United States in the future.)

The second point that can be drawn from Panel A is that, even in the absence of immigration, a low average number of children of only 2.2—just one-tenth of a child above the 2.1 rate needed for population replacement—will lead to massive population growth over the next 100 years. (A population that averages exactly two children does not lead to population replacement. An average of 2.1 live births per woman are necessary for one female to live to replace her mother. This is due to two factors: more males are born than females and not all women live through their childbearing years.) Thus, the achievement of ZPG is not just a matter of avoiding a return to the moderate level (TFR = 3.7) the United States experienced during the post-World War II baby boom. Achieving ZPG is a matter of avoiding a return to a level not much higher than the current U.S. rate (TFR = 1.9), which is only one-tenth higher than the nation's all-time low. Hence, in order to achieve ZPG, the United States must avoid a return to a level of *low* fertility that is "too high."

Fortunately, there is not much chance that the United States will permanently return to high or even moderate fertility levels in the foreseeable future. Women report in surveys that they intend to continue to have low fertility, and the reasons for the current low fertility level would also hinder any movement toward moderate or large families. These reasons include the increasing cost of bearing and raising children; the fact that individuals are spending increasingly fewer of their prime reproductive years in a stable marital union, the place were most childbearing occurs; the growing economic independence of women from men, which means women now have more practical and viable alternatives to marriage and motherhood; the availability of sophisticated and versatile birth control methods, especially the pill, induced abortion, and sterilization; and the decline in religious authority and the expansion of education of women—both trends being powerful antifertility forces.[1] For the birth rate to rise to high or moderate levels in the future, many of these trends would have to be reversed, but there seems little likelihood of that. It is safe to say, for instance, that the cost of raising children will not decline, that women will not relinquish their hard-won occupational and social gains, that birth control will not become less effective, and that individuals will not spend more time in stable marital unions.

Although the factors above are probably strong enough to prevent a return to moderate or high fertility, they are not necessarily strong enough to ward off a return to "too high" low fertility—that is, fertility in the 2.2 to 2.6 TFR range. This means that massive population growth is still quite possible, even in the absence of immigration. However, there is reason to believe that future fertility will remain very low, as it has since the mid-1970s, or fall even lower. The reason for this is that the trends discussed above, rather than reversing or just holding steady, are more likely to continue. Contraception, for instance, will be even more sophisticated and versatile in the future, with available methods including easily reversible sterilization and long-term pills or injections. It is difficult to predict fertility, but it is probably fair to say that the chances that the birth rate will fall to an extremely low level, let us say 1.5, are probably as good as the chances of it rising to 2.6. If the birth rate did fall to 1.5 in the absence of immigration, the U.S. population would stop growing early in the twenty-first century and, if this rate persisted, it would then begin a rapid decline toward extinction.

Thus, in the absence of immigration, a birth rate above 2.1 would lead to substantial population growth; a rate of 2.1 would yield ZPG; and one lower than 2.1 would result in negative growth. Therefore, if ZPG is society's goal, the fertility level must be kept at or below 2.1 children per woman. If it is below 2.1, the difference between the actual birth rate and 2.1 determines the number of immigrants that can be admitted if ZPG is to be attained.

Table 8.1 also shows roughly how many net immigrants the United States could accept while still achieving ZPG. If our fertility rate drops to and remains at 1.8, we could accept 750,000 net immigrants a year and still achieve a growth rate near zero (i.e., 0.05) by the year 2080 (Panel D). If our birth rate increases to and remains at 2.0, we would have to accept fewer than 250,000 net immigrants in order to achieve ZPG in 100 years (Panel B). Of course, if our fertility rate stabilizes at 2.2, we would not be able to achieve ZPG without substantial net emigration (Panel A). (The United States has only had substantial emigration once in its history, during a few years of the Great Depression.) It is clear from this analysis that fertility is the major determinant of zero population growth. Very slight changes in fertility result in large differences in the number of new immigrants that can be accepted.

Table 8.1 also permits us to observe how much popualtion growth results from combinations of fertility and net immigration which do not produce ZPG. For instance, a birth rate of 2.2 and net immigration of 2,000,000 per year would dramatically increase the U.S. population from 232,000,000 in 1982 to 677,000,000 in less than 100 years (see Panel F). Net immigration of 2,000,000 per year is admittedly almost twice the current 1,100,000 record level, but it is by no means inconceivable, given that the demand for immigration to the United States is building up in the developing world. Of course, a TFR of 2.2 is still a low birth rate, one which we could very easily adopt as a long-term average. Thus, while this combination is not a likely scenario for the United States, neither is it an outlandish one.

A POSSIBLE SOLUTION

After a comprehensive evaluation of the pros and cons of positive, negative, and zero population growth, the Commission on Population Growth and the American Future concluded that the achievement of ZPG is in the best interest of the United States. However, the United States does not have zero population growth now, and our current demographic behavior will not lead us to it in the future. If our present annual levels of fertility (1.9) and net immigration (1,100,000) continue, the U.S. population will rise dramatically from 232,000,000 in 1982 to almost 400,000,000 by the year 2080—an increase of about 70 percent. Moreover, the population would still be growing rapidly in 2080. Thus, if the United States is going to attain ZPG in the next 100 years, our demographic behavior must change. What is needed is an over-all population growth policy designed to achieve ZPG.

This policy would recognize that it is impractical to try to reach ZPG immeditely. Its goal would be to attain ZPG at a particular time in the future, recognizing that the size of the population then will be substantially larger than it is today. Given the United States's present built-in momentum for population growth, the lowest realistic goal to aim for at this time is constant-size population of about 300,000,000 to be reached within the next 50 to 100 years. This goal would then determine the combinations of fertility and net immigration levels that would be necessary to achieve ZPG by that time. These combinations would also be based on the usual mortality assumption that life expectancy will continue its gradual increase over the period. Obviously, under this policy, the levels of fertility and net immigration would be inversely related—the higher the level of fertility, the lower the level of net immigration, and vice versa. The levels of fertility and net immigration would have to be monitored throughout the transition period to make sure they did not collectively exceed or fall short of the intermediate growth goals. If they threatened to do so, then fertility and/or net immigration levels would be raised or lowered.

This policy would work by permitting the birth rate to seek its own level, as long as it did not exceed 2.1. If it settled at 2.1, there would be no net immigration allowed; if the birth rate rose above 2.1, programs would be introduced to lower it; if it fell below 2.1, net immigration would be permitted to fill in the gap between the actual birth rate and 2.1; or programs to encourage individuals to have more children could be introduced in place of, or in tandem with, increases in net immigration. Thus, this policy would regulate fertility and/or net immigration, depending upon the circumstances prevailing at any given time during the transition to ZPG.

A likely future scenario is that the birth rate will hover between 1.8 and 2.1. If this does occur, the government could pursue its ZPG goals by manipulating its legal immigration quotas to make up the deficit in the number of births. This is certainly technically feasible, because the United States has manipulated quotas in the past. Indeed, the concept of adjusting legal immigration to suit our national interest—demographic or otherwise—already exists in our immigration laws.

It is also possible to severely curtail the flow of illegal immigration. While illegal aliens can not be prevented from entering the country at remote border points, much of the incentive to do so is eliminated if there are no jobs. One effective regulatory measure would be to hold employers strictly accountable for hiring "undocumented" workers. A bill which passed the U.S. Senate in 1982 takes this approach. Another measure that would probably work is the adoption of a counterfeit-resistant worker I.D. card.

While it is possible to regulate net immigration, the process would not be problem-free, especially if it led to substantial cuts in customary levels of legal and even illegal immigration. There are several reasons for this. One is that a severe curtailment of immigration would violate the humanitarian proimmigration values of many Americans. These values are symbolized by the oft-quoted inscription on the Statue of Liberty and are particularly common among immigrants and the descendants of recent immigrants. However, most Americans are discontented with current immigration levels and favor reducing immigration of all kinds, so there are bound to be value conflicts. As with most policies, immigration of all kinds, so there are bound to be value conflicts. As with most policies, immigration policy will probably be determined ultimately by the value of the most powerful interest groups—and in this case, those groups are not opposed to substantial immigration cuts. A social segment which would be against curbing immigration are the businessmen who presently find it profitable to hire immigrants. There is also strong opposition in this country to worker I.D. cards because of fears that they would be a step toward a "Big Brother" society. Finally, any major action by the United States to curb immigration will impose hardships and inconvenience on the principal countries from which the immigrants come. Since most of these source countries are neighbors of the United States, Mexico being by far the largest source, many severe adverse effects on them would have negative repercussions on U.S. foreign policy interests in the Western Hemisphere.

However, it must be remembered that immigration would only be terminated when the birth rate is 2.1 or greater. Much of the time, the birth rate may be below this, and at those times large numbers of legal immigrants could be admitted. A birth rate of 1.8, for instance, would leave room for about 500,000 immigrants per year.

PRACTICAL PROBLEMS

To this point, we have focused on the practical problems of implementing an immigration cut when fertility is relatively high, but there are also practical problems involved in expanding immigration when fertility is relatively low. As Westoff notes:

> Immigrants . . . arrive in various colors and nationalities and speaking different languages. Any country with substantial immigration seems sooner or later to experience problems, arising from differences in language, customs, religion, or race, that tend to offset many of the economic and long-term cultural advantages.

The United States has experienced many of these problems in the past, and they may be sufficient to keep the public from accepting a high level of immigration as a means of attaining ZPG. It is especially noteworthy that none of the European nations presently at or below ZPG have yet opted for immigration to increase their growth rate. Instead, they have all chosen to try to boost the birth rate through a variety of policies including economic and social incentives to have children and restrictions on induced abortion. The U.S. public might prefer this path also.

Finally, if the birth rate exceeds 2.1, there are two methods that can be used to reduce it: family planning, which could be targeted mainly at those age groups or cultural subgroups which have especially high fertility; and the use of incentives to encourage people to voluntarily limit their fertility. These incentives are often just the reverse of those used to boost fertility. For instance, China's ZPG-oriented program to bring down the birth rate is based on a system of rewards and penalties designed to encourage couples to have only one child. Parents who pledge to do so receive a monthly allowance for their child's health care, priority enrollment in nursery schools, and exemption from school tuition. On the other hand, families with more than one child commonly have their salaries reduced by 10 percent for as long as 14 years.

There are a number of possible social changes which might bear on the future functioning of this policy. In looking into the future, we must keep uppermost in our minds that the world of the next 100 years will be immensely different from that of the last 100 years. Political and economic turmoil in Third World nations, due in part to their population explosions and the pressure of development, will almost certainly swell the numbers of refugees and emigrants seeking a new home. Our decision about how to manage our own population size in light of our prevailing fertility rate and the possibly large numbers of immigrants and refugees seeking entry into the United States will not be made in a vacuum, considering only the interests of the United States. The increasing economic interdependence of the world economy could radically affect our population policies. An overpopulated nation with a precious resource could demand that the United States admit part of its population overflow. Moreover, the expansion of nuclear capability to more and more countries, some of whom are already overpopulated, introduces the threat of nuclear blackmail for space on this planet. Even in the absence of such economic and military tyranny, the world is changing such that more and more countries will make their presence felt in international relations and will have the power to influence our population policies. The time has passed when the United States could make demographic and other decisions independently and unilaterally, relying on the cover of geographic isolation and a robust economic system.

NOTE

1. Joseph A. McFalls, Jr., "Where Have All the Children Gone?: The Future of Reproduction in the United States," *USA Today*, March 1981, pp. 30–33.

PART II

POPULATION THEORY AND POLICY: POVERTY, POLLUTION, RESOURCES, AND DEVELOPMENT

POPULATION THEORY

What are the causes and consequences of population growth? Is the world a population bomb ready to explode? Are there famine, poverty, war, pestilence, and environmental calamities because there are too many people in the world? Or is population growth to be welcomed—even encouraged—because it will increase the pool of potential geniuses? Is population pressure the driving force behind invention and innovation that will enable the technological accommodation of ever more people at an ever higher standard of living? Is childbearing haphazard or is it a rational response to immediate economic and social needs and demands? How can societies influence population growth? In Part I, we discussed the theory of demographic transition, a twentieth-century theory concerning the impact of mortality and development on fertility. Here, we consider two theoretical perspectives which have their roots in the eighteenth century, and which are concerned with the reasons for population growth and its impact on development or national prosperity and individual well-being.

The Classic Debate

T. R. Malthus was born in 1766 and wrote his famous "Essay on the Principle of Population" in 1798. The essay was written following five years of poor harvest (1792 to 1797), in a period of food shortages that continued into the 1800s. True to his own prescriptions, Malthus married in 1804, after receiving a degree in mathematics, taking holy orders, and accepting an appointment to a rectory. He had three children, two of whom survived to maturity. Shortly after the publication of the second edition of his essay in 1803, he became the first professor of political economy in the English-speaking world (Appleman, 1976:xi to xiii; Morris, 1966).

Malthus (Chapter 9) was concerned primarily with the relationships among family size, poverty, and food supply. He argued that while food supply could increase at a steady rate, population could increase at a rate that was not steady but that increased over time: linear or arithmetic growth of food supply as opposed to exponential or geometric growth of population. Ultimately, Malthus warned, the power to reproduce people would overtake the power to produce the necessities of life, unless the former were somehow checked. Historically, he argued, this usually meant what he called *positive checks* on population, events like famine, plague, and war, which decreased the population by increasing the death rate. An alternative, he suggested, would be to decrease population growth by means of the *preventive* check of remaining celibate until marriage and postponing marriage until one could afford children.

Unlike many of those who accept his arguments regarding population and food supply today, Malthus was strongly opposed to any form of birth control other than abstinence; he regarded artificial birth control as a form of vice, akin to prostitution. He also opposed the English Poor Laws, which provided sustenance to the poor, arguing that the administration of the Poor Laws was mismanaged and corrupt, and that their end effect was only to increase the number in poverty by encouraging higher fertility among those who could not otherwise afford to have children. In so doing, Malthus came to be known as an apologist for existing political and social inequality. In fact, although he considered such measures as agricultural development and land reform desirable, he believed them altogether unlikely to occur. His pessimism about the possibility of political reform and his belief in the inherent imperfectibility of human beings earned him the title (at least among his detractors) of "the gloomy parson" (Morris, 1966). In his later writings, following a period of relative prosperity in England, Malthus developed a less pessimistic tone and suggested that universal education might help decrease fertility by altering tastes and habits.

Malthus' principal opponent in the classical debate was William Godwin. Godwin's essays in 1797 and 1820 took what we have labeled the superoptimist position that "there is no evil under which the human species can labour, that man is not competent to cure" (Appleman, 1976:143). This line of argument was subsequently taken by Engels (Chapter 10) and has become identified with the Marxian position on population. Karl Marx, born nearly fifty years after Malthus, and Friedrich Engels, seven years younger than Marx, wrote at a time when the industrial revolution was well under way, a time when the United States was expanding westward and opening up the Great Plains to agriculture, and Latin American nations were obtaining their independence from Europe by violent revolution. Marx received his doctorate at Jena in 1842 and, the following year, while working as a journalist in Paris, met Friedrich Engels. Their collaboration laid the foundation for most modern forms of socialism and communism. Although the influence of Malthus came primarily from his writings, which were directed primarily at other scholars, Marx and Engels exerted a wider influence that was not limited to their writings. Marx founded the International Workingman's Association, an early labor union, and Engels helped organize revolutionary movements in Europe.

Marx and Engels were much more forceful than Malthus in pointing out that people were poor because the economy and society were organized in such a way that they did not have the opportunity to be anything else but poor. They were also much more optimistic than Malthus about the potential for technological development and the productivity of workers. They believed that under a fair and just social organization in which technology was designed and used for the benefit of all people, unlimited population growth could be accommodated at a healthy and comfortable standard of living (Meek, 1971; Anderson, 1976). Where Malthus emphasized diminishing returns to labor, Marx and Engels emphasized the greater prosperity possible with economies of scale. For Marx and Engels, the solution to problems such as poverty, hunger, and unemployment was massive social and economic change to a socialist (and eventually communist) society, which they believed could happen primarily through violent revolution.

The Contemporary Debate

Time has proven the Malthusian and Marxian theories to be both right and wrong, at least in part. Technology has enabled the world to accommodate a population much larger than Malthus thought possible. Since Malthus' death in 1834, world population has quadrupled from 1 billion to over 4 billion. On the grimmer side, according to United Nations estimates (U.N. Food and Agriculture Organization, 1983), nearly half a billion are chronically undernourished. As many as 2 billion—half the current world population and twice the total world population in Malthus' time—may be either undernourished or malnourished, and it is estimated that about 700 million people in just the rural areas of LDCs live in absolute poverty (Higgins et al., 1983). Although China has proven that even a poor nonindustrialized society which emphasizes the well-being of all of the people can provide basic needs and employment for a large and rapidly growing population, it has also had to acknowledge that resources and ingenuity can only be stretched so far. Now China has adopted a neo-Marxian position that in a planned society it is just as essential to plan reproduction as it is to plan agricultural and industrial production. The Marxian position has also been broadened by neo-Marxians to recognize that there are technological and environmental constraints on population growth. Meanwhile, the Malthusian position has been broadened by neo-Malthusians to include artificial birth control as an acceptable means of limiting population and a recognition that factors other than population growth contribute to poverty, pollution, and other social ills. The emphases of each perspective, however, remain the same: Malthusians still emphasize the need for reduced population growth and Marxians the need for political and economic reform.

From a liberal, though not necessarily Marxian, perspective, the neo-Malthusians are criticized for presenting much too simple answers to complex problems (ul Haq, 1981; Durham, 1979; George, 1979; Faaland, 1982; Commoner, 1972; Bondestam and Bergstrom, 1980). Some point out, for example, that nations with the highest rates of population growth are not the nations that consume the most resources or cause the greatest amount of environmental damage, per capita or in total. Less developed countries in Africa, Asia, and Latin America, with 75 percent of the world's population, produce 30 to 40 percent of the world's energy, but consume only 15 to 21 percent (World Bank, 1981:36; U.S. Department of Commerce, 1984, tables 982, 1541, 1542). Comparing the consumption of commercial energy in just two countries, in 1982 China, with a population of about one billion, used 17.9 exajoules (one exajoule equals one billion joules), and the United States with a population of about 230 million used 74 exajoules (Chandler, 1985a). Although the LDCs consume more food calories in total than the more developed countries, they consume considerably less on a *per capita* basis (Population

Reference Bureau, 1983; World Bank, 1984). As noted previously, malnutrition is common in less developed countries, despite the fact that "[a]t the global level, if income were distributed differently, present output of grain alone could supply every man, woman, and child with more than 3,000 calories and 65 grams of protein per day—far more than the highest estimates of requirements" (World Bank, 1980). Each additional birth in a more developed, low fertility country places more of a burden on world resources than each birth in a less developed, high fertility country.

The chapters by Hardin (Chapter 11) and by Lappe and Collins (Chapter 12) take the debate into the twentieth century. Hardin presents a neo-Malthusian position with which Malthus himself would probably had disagreed (Malthus never advocated coercive measures to control fertility, and he considered moderate growth in population desirable), while Lappe and Collins point to an alternative interpretation of contemporary food shortages.

In an analysis of environmental degradation of the European "commons," or common grazing ground (akin to the "open range" in the nineteenth-century United States), Hardin, writing in 1968, concludes that although high fertility may benefit individual households, the aggregate impact creates enormous problems for society as a whole, including the high-fertility families. The tragedy of the commons is that individuals, acting to maximize their personal welfare, ultimately act to worsen conditions for themselves as well as for others. To prevent this tragedy, Hardin advocates "mutual coercion mutually agreed upon" to control birth rates and usage of natural resources.

In Chapter 12, Lappe and Collins, writing in 1976, identify and debunk some common myths about hunger. Others have also concluded that although weather and rapid population growth may have contributed to hunger, malnutrition, and famine in the world, the root of these problems is political, economic, and social; therefore, the solution lies not in population alone, but in social, political, and economic change. (See, e.g., Eckholm, 1979; Murdoch, 1980; Higgins et al., 1983; Faaland, 1982; and especially Garcia, 1981). Kleinman (1980), for example, in a specific response to Hardin, argues that neither the poverty of the European peasants nor the degradation of the commons were caused by overpopulation, but rather by the expropriation and privatization of once commonly held resources. In other words, the peasants were made poorer because their means of livelihood were taken away by the rich and powerful and the formerly public resources were *then* overutilized and degraded.

The Modern Simulation Debate

In 1971, a new element was added to the population debate with the publication of Jay W. Forrester's *World Dynamics* (Forrester, 1971). This was subsequently followed by a series of reports under the auspices of the Club of Rome, an international group with the purpose of studying the interaction of major global systems including population, industrial production, pollution, natural resources, and agricultural production (Meadows et al., 1972; Mesarovic and Pestel, 1974; Tinbergen, 1976). Based on the Malthusian perspective, most of the early simulation models had assumptions built into them which resulted in the pessimistic prediction of a global "crash" sometime in the twenty-second century. More importantly, the models suggested the futility of concentrating on any one component of the global system. Instead, they concluded that *everything* had to be considered simultaneously.

Chapters 13 and 14 present the results of projections based on models which incorporate different assumptions about the relationship between population and resources, technology, pollution, and the production of agricultural and industrial products. The Global 2000 report (Chapter 13) continues the mainstream pessimistic perspective. Simon's superoptimist model (Chapter 14), by contrast, assumes that as population increases, so will technology and the standard of living. Although others (Boserup, 1981; Clark, 1967) have pointed out the benefits of population growth for sparsely populated areas and suggested that population growth acts as as an incentive to innovation, they have not carried the argument as far as Simon (1976; 1981) or his colleague Herman Kahn (1982; Simon and Kahn, 1984), or extended it to more developed countries.

Some demographers believe Simon is correct in attacking the "big lie" of the "population establishment" (concerning which see Demerath, 1976; Mass, 1976; Simon, 1981). At the same time, they are critical of his failure to recognize the high levels of poverty and environmental degradation that exist today, and they point out numerous failings in method and logic. First, Simon uses output per worker rather than output per person as his measure of well-being. This is an accurate measure of productivity, but it ignores the problem—indeed, the existence—of nonproducing consumers (the unemployed, the very young, and the very old). Second, Simon assumes that population growth stimulates creativity, invention, and the development of technology that enables the world to overcome environmental constraints and accommodate more and more people, by increasing the odds that a "genius"—an Einstein, a Henry Ford—will be born. A larger population does not necessarily mean more new discoveries in science and technology; it may instead mean more people discovering about the same thing at the same time, a point concerning which Merton's (1961) work on the sociology of science may be instructive. As Merton suggests, the dominant pattern of scientific discovery may be that of several researchers coming to the same discovery at about the same time. That we associate a particular innovation with a particular individual may reflect nothing more than priority of publication. Third, Simon's model has a positive outcome only in the long run, and this depends on the assumption that as the labor force grows, the capital for the necessary demographic investment will grow automatically. In the short run, 30 to 80 years, even moderate rates of population growth are detrimental to levels of well-being. Fourth, Simon's predictions raise but do not answer the question of causal direction: Does larger population lead to progress, or does progress lead to a larger population? Finally, Simon's predictions are for such long periods of time that they, like the earlier Club of Rome models, cannot possibly take into account some of the far-reaching changes that are likely to occur in the next 200 or more years—even as Malthus and Marx could not predict, respectively, the development of mechanized agriculture or the dependency of the LDCs on the MDCs for food in the twentieth century. Simon's "anti-Malthusian" view, as it is called by his supporters, has gained considerable popularity among those who oppose abortion or oppose public funding of family planning programs domestically and abroad (Population Reference Bureau, 1984c, especially p. 10).

Since, as Meadows (1985) and Hughes (1984) have observed, simulation and forecasting models can be constructed to generate any outcome, they can be misused. On the other hand, when used appropriately, they do expand our ability to explore alternative futures and to make conscious, informed policy choices.

POPULATION THEORY AND POLICY

As we discussed in Part I, many nations now believe their rates of growth are too high, and some believe they are too low. For the reduction of population growth, mass emigration is no longer an option for any nation, and explicit intentions to allow or create higher death rates are not morally or culturally acceptable. To increase population growth, few nations are willing to invite large numbers of permanent immigrants (Australia being an exception in recent history), although some do invite temporary "guest workers" to augment the labor force. Trying to increase population growth by reducing the death rate would be acceptable, but many nations that want a higher growth rate already have very low death rates (e.g., East and West Germany). Thus, with the exception of high mortality nations that want a higher rate of growth, adjustments in fertility are seen as the primary way to regulate national population growth rates. Teitelbaum (1974) has outlined sixteen contemporary positions regarding the need for special population programs and fertility policy. These can be subsumed under two major positions, Developmentalist and Family Planning.

Developmentalist

The developmentalist perspective comes primarily from the theory of demographic transition (see Part I) in which it is hypothesized that modernization, urbanization, and industrialization will lead to reduced mortality which, in turn, will lead to reduced fertility. This was the position of many of the LDCs at the 1974 United Nations World Population Conference. Those nations spoke of a "natural decline in fertility as if economic development itself has contraceptive properties (Stycos, 1974). The Marxist variation of this theme is that only economic development that eliminates class inequalities will also eliminate so-called overpopulation. According to the Developmentalist perspective, family planning programs divert funds away from development efforts and may be little more than a disguised scheme to eliminate the poor rather than reform the system that created poverty (Mass, 1976; Michaelson, 1981; Kleinman, 1980; Gordon, 1976). United States blacks have made similar arguments about family planning programs in the United States, going so far as to call them genocidal (Weisbord, 1973).

Some developmentalists have argued along the lines of Simon (1976) that since the MDCs became wealthy while they were growing rapidly, the LDCs do not need to reduce their birth rates. However, this view ignores the large differences in the situations of these two groups of nations. When the now-MDCs were undergoing economic development, they had smaller populations, lower fertility and growth rates than today's LDCs, and they could rely on emigration to relieve population burdens. They also had considerable support from the now-LDCs in the form of plunder of riches, colonies, slaves—in short, cheap raw materials and cheap labor. Moreover, there were not more powerful nations to compete with in the international economy.

Family Planning

Those who strongly adhere to the neo-Malthusian perspective believe that parents in high fertility nations do not act in their own best interests when they have large numbers of children. Furthermore, since Family Planning advocates believe that most higher-order births (fifth, sixth, etc., children) are unplanned and often unwanted, it is believed that that fertility will decline substantially once family planning education and services are made widely available. Economic development without family planning is seen as a detour, if not a wrong turn, on the road to reduced fertility (Mamdani, 1972; Tsui and Bogue, 1978; Simon, 1981; Demerath, 1976).

The U.S. Position

At the 1974 World Population Conference the United States expressed great concern about "overpopulation" and was a strong advocate of the Family Planning position. It acknowledged that economic development is necessary for fertility to decline, but secondary in importance to family planning. The LDCs at the conference, by contrast, advocated a largely developmentalist position (Mauldin et al., 1974).

At the 1984 World Population Conference, with Julian Simon as a major influence, the United States did an about-face, declaring that population growth is a "neutral phenomenon" and putting forth the idea that if government intervention in development were abandoned to the invisible hand of the capitalistic free market, population growth would not be problematic and would decline. Family planning programs would then be a necessary but secondary concern. Ignoring the counterexample of China and illustrating its case with Singapore, Hong Kong, South Korea, and Taiwan, the U.S. delegation did not acknowledge that the governments they used as examples exert considerable intervention and influence on economic development and reproductive behavior (Brown, 1984; Wulf and Willson, 1984). Singapore, for example, was then offering $10,000 (Singapore currency) to uneducated women with a household income of less than $1,500 if they agree to sterilization no later than after the second birth (Population Reference Bureau, 1985a).

At the conference, the United States announced that it would no longer contribute to nongovernmental organizations that perform or actively promote abortion in other nations. Subsequently, the United States canceled its $17 million grant to the International Planned Parenthood Federation, a major provider of family planning education and services in LDCs. Less than 1 percent of IPPF's proposed 1985 total budget was abortion related, none of it providing abortion services; 30 percent of its funds come from the United States. It is estimated that the $5 million worth of contraceptives that will not be distributed free in LDCs because of the budget cut could have prevented as many as 776,000 unwanted pregnancies, which could lead in turn to over 100,000 abortions (Peterson, 1985; Population Reference Bureau, 1985b).

The Emerging Consensus[1]

From the extremes of Malthus, Marx, and Simon, a consensus is taking shape regarding the relationships among population growth, economic development, the necessity for social and economic change, and the importance of family planning programs (Teitelbaum, 1974; Brown, 1974; World Bank, 1984; Freedman, 1979; World Resources Institute, 1984; Birdsall, 1980). First, following the Malthusian perspective, there is agreement that there are real population problems which tend to retard economic development and exacerbate poverty and environmental degradation. They include:

Continuous growth

In order just to maintain its present standard of living, a society must continuously expand in all areas because each year the number of children born is larger than in the previous year. As each birth cohort ages, the society needs to provide more health care, food, schools, housing, jobs, etc. In most LDCs, where fertility is high and the standard of living is low, continuous growth makes it even harder to raise the standard of living or to prevent or redress environmental damage which is often necessitated by poverty (e.g., depletion of soils because dung must be used for fuel instead of fertilizer). Although wealthier nations and families may be able to afford to make the "demographic investment" necessary to accommodate a growing population and even raise the standard of living, population growth also means growth in already high levels of resource depletion, pollution, and other environmental degradation (Brown, 1981).

High fertility

High fertility not only contributes to rapid population growth but also creates a young age distribution (see Chapter 39). For instance in Kenya, where the birth rate remains

1. The consensus position described here was reflected in the statement of Rafael Salas, executive director of the United Nations Fund for Population Activity (UNFPA) to the 1974 World Population Conference. Acknowledging the negative economic effects of rapid population growth and the limits of the biosphere to sustain life, he also noted the failure of development programs in the LDCs and linked this failure to still-high birth rates: "[D]evelopment must be diffused socially and geographically throughout all levels and throughout all areas. A society of sufficiency for all, replacing the distortions of both excess and deprivation must be our aim. . . . Family size is affected not only by income level, but by a complex of social and economic factors as well. The existence of adequate housing, education and health services, improvement in the status of women, and the redistribution of income may be of crucial importance" (1974:2–3). Ten years later, at the next World Population Conference, Salas reported that neither the distortions of excess and deprivation nor fertility had been reduced. From 1974 to 1984 the global birth rate declined from about 33 to about 28, mostly as a result of declining fertility in China, and the global population increased by 770 million (Brown, 1984). Salas expects LDC fertility to decline at an even slower rate in the future (Salas, 1984).

very high, half the population is under 15, whereas in Belgium, where fertility has been low for many years, only 20 percent of the population is under 15 (Population Reference Bureau, 1984a). Poor countries and families with high fertility may not only have a hard time making an adequate demographic investment in their children, but also usually must call on their children to become paid or, more often, unpaid workers at an early age, thus perpetuating a low-skilled, uneducated labor force.

Momentum of population growth

Because the age distribution of a growing population is like a triangle with the children at the fat base, the parents in the thinner middle, and the grandparents at the skinny peak (see Part VI, particularly Chapter 41 and the insert preceding Chapter 41), it takes a long time for population growth to slow down or cease. For zero population growth (ZPG), births must equal deaths. The most likely way for that to happen is if replacement fertility is achieved by an average family size of two. But for births to equal deaths, the age "triangle" must look more like a rectangle, and this will not occur in most LDCs for about 60 to 70 years, when the first generation of replacement-fertility children have become the grandparents, and their children, the second generation of replacement-fertility children, have given birth to the third generation of replacement-fertility children. Only then will the numbers of birth and deaths be approximately equal. But during that time, most LDCs are expected to at least double in size (World Bank, 1984). This built-in inertia in combination with exponential growth (Part I) is what makes population growth seem so dangerous—a population bomb (Ehrlich, 1968; Piotrow, 1980; Hardin, 1974; Mumford, 1984)—and its control so urgent.

On the other hand, according to the consensus view, while high birth rates may retard economic development contribute to national and household poverty, population growth is not considered to be the only or even the main cause of poverty, environmental degradation, illiteracy, hunger, etc. "The ultimate solution to such problems depends on the true social and economic development of the poor countries and regions of the world. Such development cannot be 'bought cheaply' by concentrating on population as the major problem" (Teitelbaum, 1974:754). The consensus position also contradicts the neo-Malthusian perspective that children in large families are not especially wanted but just happen as a result of unrestrained sex. Instead, it is believed that fertility is rational and people try to have about as many children as they believe they need (Mamdani, 1972; Faaland, 1982; Goliber, 1985). Children may perform many valuable economic and noneconomic services for their parents (see Part IV). Beyond that and especially in the LDCs, many cultural, legal, and religious incentives for high fertility are still in force from the not very distant past when high death rates made high birth rates essential for survival. Consequently, the consensus position argues that while family planning education and services should be available to all, fertility will not decline until infant mortality is low enough that "spare" children are not wanted and parents can afford or are provided with substitutes for child labor and services such as economic security in old age. Furthermore, since children do provide emotional as well as economic benefits, fertility will not decline until men and women have socially acceptable and personally satisfying alternatives to parenthood.

FOR FURTHER READING

1. Philip Appleman, ed. 1976. *Thomas Robert Malthus: An Essay on the Principle of Population* (New York: W. W. Norton). The full text of Malthus' original essay, excerpts from the second edition, and commentaries from supporters and detractors of Malthusian theory. Successfully places Malthus' work in historical context.

2. For the advanced student who wants a first-hand exposition of Marxist population theory, D. I. Valentey, ed. 1978. *The Theory of Population: Essays in Marxist Research* (Moscow: Progress Publishers) is available in English translation and includes articles at varying levels of technical sophistication.

3. U.S. Council on Environmental Quality and the Department of State. 1978. *The Global 2000 Report to the President,* volumes 1 and 2 (Washington, DC: U.S. Government Printing Office). A detailed, exhaustive presentation of projections for the population, resources, and the environment for the United States and the world as we enter the twenty-first century. A great deal of reading, but nontechnical enough for the beginning student.

4. Julian Simon and Herman Kahn. 1984. *The Resourceful Earth: A Response to Global 2000* (New York: Basil Blackwell). The debate continues in this detailed response to the Global 2000 report. Julian Simon's books (*The Economics of Population Growth* and *The Ultimate Resource,* both by Princeton University Press) also deserve mention here.

5. Barry Hughes. 1985. *World Futures* (Baltimore: Johns Hopkins). This is an analysis of global systems models and research from the super-optimistic to the super-pessimistic, including some covered in this book (Chapters 13 and 14). Hughes compares and critiques world views or paradigms, values, assumptions, data, and methods. For the advanced reader.

6. Norman Myers. 1984. *GAIA: An Atlas of Planet Management* (Garden City, New York: Anchor/Doubleday). A sumptuously illustrated, well-documented, balanced study of the global interrelationships among population, environment, technology, and socioeconomic organization. Human ecology at its best.

9

An Essay on the Principle of Population

THOMAS ROBERT MALTHUS[1]

THE BASIC ARGUMENT

I think I may fairly make two postulata.

First, That food is necessary to the existence of man.

Secondly, That the passion between the sexes is necessary and will remain nearly in its present state.

These two laws, ever since we have had any knowledge of mankind, appear to have been fixed laws of our nature, and, as we have not hitherto seen any alteration in them, we have no right to conclude that they will ever cease to be what they now are, without an immediate act of power in that Being who first arranged the system of the universe, and for the advantage of his creatures, still executes, according to fixed laws, all its various operations.

Assuming my postulata as granted, I say, that the power of population is indefinitely greater than the power in the earth to produce subsistence for man.

Population, when unchecked, increases in a geometrical ratio. Subsistence increases only in an arithmetical ratio. A slight acquaintance with numbers will shew the immensity of the first power in comparison of the second.

By that law of our nature which makes food necessary to the life of man, the effects of these two unequal powers must be kept equal.

This implies a strong and constantly operating check on population from the difficulty of subsistence. This difficulty must fall some where and must necessarily be severely felt by a large portion of mankind.

Through the animal and vegetable kingdoms, nature has scattered the seeds of life abroad with the most profuse and liberal hand. She has been comparatively sparing in the room and the nourishment necessary to rear them. The germs of existence contained in this spot of earth, with ample food, and ample room to expand in, would fill millions of worlds in the course of a few thousand years. Necessity, that imperious all pervading law of nature, restrains them within the prescribed bounds. The race of plants, and the race of animals shrink under this great restrictive law. And the race of man cannot, by any efforts of reason, escape from it. Among plants and animals its effects are waste of seed, sickness, and premature death. Among mankind, misery and vice. The former, misery, is an absolutely necessary consequence of it. Vice is a highly probable consequence, and we therefore see it abundantly prevail, but it ought not, perhaps, to be called an absolutely necessary consequence. The ordeal of virtue is to resist all temptation to evil.

This natural inequality of the two powers of population and of production in the earth and that great law of our nature which must constantly keep their effects equal form the great difficulty that to me appears insurmountable in the way to the perfectibility of society. All other arguments are of slight and subordinate consideration in comparison of this. I see no way by which man can escape from the weight of this law which pervades all animated nature. No fancied equality, no agrarian regulations in their utmost extent, could remove the pressure of it even for a single century. And it appears, therefore, to be decisive against the possible existence of a society, all the members of which should live in ease, happiness, and comparative leisure; and feel no anxiety about providing the means of subsistence for themselves and families.

Consequently, if the premises are just, the argument is conclusive against the perfectibility of the mass of mankind.

I have thus sketched the general outline of the argument, but I will examine it more particularly, and I think it will be found that experience, the true source and foundation of all knowledge, invariably confirms its truth.

POPULATION AND THE EARLY STAGES OF CIVILIZATION

In the rudest state of mankind, in which hunting is the principal occupation, and the only mode of acquiring food, the means of subsistence being scattered over a large extent of territory, the comparative population must necessarily be thin. It is said that the passion between the sexes is less ardent among the North American Indians than among any other race of men. Yet notwithstanding this apathy, the effort towards population, even in this people, seems to be always greater than the means to support it. This appears from the comparatively rapid population growth that takes place whenever any of the tribes happen to settle in some fertile spot and to draw nourishment from more fruitful sources than that of hunting, and it has been frequently remarked that when an Indian family has taken up its abode near any European settlement and adopted a more easy and civilized mode of life, that one woman has reared five or six, or more children, though in the savage state it rarely happens, that above one or two in a family grow up to maturity. The same observation has been made with regard to the Hottentots near the Cape. These facts prove the superior power of population to the means of subsistence in nations of hunters, and that this power always shews itself the moment it is left to act with freedom.

It remains to inquire whether this power can be checked, and its effects kept equal to the means of subsistence, without vice or misery.

The North American Indians, considered as a people, cannot justly be called free and equal. In all the accounts we have of them, and, indeed, of most other savage nations, the women are represented as much more completely in a state of slavery to the men than the poor are to the rich in civilized countries. One half the nation appears to act as Helots to the other half, and the misery that checks population falls chiefly, as it always must do, upon that part whose condition is lowest in the scale of society. The infancy of man in the simplest state requires considerable attention, but this necessary attention the women cannot give, condemned as they are to the inconveniences and hardships of frequent change of place and to the constant and unremitting drudgery of preparing every thing for the reception of their tyrannic lords. These exertions, sometimes during pregnancy or with children at their backs, must occasion frequent miscarriages, and prevent any but the most robust infants from growing to maturity. Add to these hardships of the women, the constant war that prevails among savages, and the necessity which they frequently labour under of exposing their aged and helpless parents, and of thus violating the first feelings of nature, and the picture will not appear very free from the blot of misery.

Of the manners and habits that prevail among nations of shepherds, the next state of mankind, we are even more ignorant than of the savage state. But that these nations could not escape the general lot of misery arising from the want of subsistence, Europe, and all the fairest countries in the world, bear ample testimony. Want was the goad that drove the Scythian shepherds from their native haunts, like so many famished wolves in search of prey. Set in motion by this all powerful cause, clouds of Barbarians seemed to collect from all points of the northern hemisphere. Gathering fresh darkness and terror as they rolled on, the congregated bodies at length obscured the sun of Italy and sunk the whole world in universal night. These tremendous effects, so long and so deeply felt throughout the fairest portions of the earth, may be traced to the simple cause of the superior power of population, to the means of subsistence.

In these savage contests many tribes must have been utterly exterminated. Some, probably, perished by hardship and famine. Others, whose leading star had given them a happier direction, became great and powerful tribes, and, in their turns, sent off fresh adventurers in search of still more fertile seats. The prodigious waste of human life occasioned by this perpetual struggle for room and food was more than supplied by the mighty power of population, acting, in some degree, unshackled from the constant habit of emigration. The tribes that migrated towards the South, though they won these more fruitful regions by continual battles, rapidly increased in number and power, from the increased means of subsistence. Till at length, the whole territory, from the confines of China to the shores of the Baltic was peopled by a various race of Barbarians, brave, robust, and enterprising, inured to hardship, and delighting in war. Some tribes maintained their independence. Others ranged themselves under the standard of some barbaric chieftain who led them to victory after victory, and what was of more importance, to regions abounding in corn, wine, and oil, the long wished for consummation, and great reward of their labours. An Alaric, an Attila, or a Zingis Khan, and the chiefs around them, might fight for glory, for the fame of extensive conquests, but the true cause that set in motion the great tide of northern emigration, and that continued to propel it till it rolled at different periods, against China, Persia, Italy, and even Egypt, was a scarcity of food, a population extended beyond the means of supporting it.

THE POWER OF POPULATION

I think it will be allowed, that no state has hitherto existed (at least that we have any account of) where the manners were so pure and simple, and the means of subsistence so abundant, that no check whatever has existed to early marriages, among the lower classes, from a fear of not providing well for their families, or among the higher classes, from a fear of lowering their condition in life. Consequently in no state that we have yet known has the power of population been left to exert itself with perfect freedom.

Whether the law of marriage be instituted or not, the dictate of nature and virtue seems to be an early attachment to one woman. Supposing a liberty of changing in the case of an unfortunate choice, this liberty would not affect population till it arose to a height greatly vicious; and we are now supposing the existence of a society where vice is scarcely known.

In a state therefore of great equality and virtue, where pure and simple manners prevailed, and where the means of subsistence were so abundant that no part of the society could have any fears about providing amply for a family, the power of population being left to exert itself unchecked, the increase of the human species would evidently be much greater than any increase that has been hitherto known.

In the United States of America, where the means of subsistence have been more ample, the manners of the people more pure, and consequently the checks to early marriages fewer than in any of the modern states of Europe, the population has been found to double itself in twenty-five years.

This ratio of increase, though short of the utmost power of population, yet as the result of actual experience, we will take as our rule, and say, that population, when unchecked, goes on doubling itself every twenty-five years or increases in a geometrical ratio.

Let us now take any spot of earth, this Island for instance, and see in what ratio the subsistence it affords can be supposed to increase. We will begin with it under its present state of cultivation.

If I allow that by the best possible policy, by breaking up more land and by great encouragements to agriculture, the produce of this Island may be doubled in the first twenty-five years, I think it will be allowing as much as any person can well demand.

In the next twenty-five years, it is impossible to suppose that the produce could be quadrupled. It would be contrary to all our knowledge of the qualities of land. The very utmost that we can conceive, is, that the increase in the second twenty-five years might equal the present produce. Let us then take this for our rule, though certainly far beyond the truth, and allow that by great exertion, the whole produce of the Island might be increased every twenty-five years, by a quantity of subsistence equal to what it at present produces. The most enthusiastic speculator cannot suppose a greater increase than this. In a few centuries it would make every acre of land in the Island like a garden.

Yet this ratio of increase is evidently arithmetical.

It may be fairly said, therefore, that the means of subsistence increase in an arithmetical ratio. Let us now bring the effects of these two ratios together.

The population of the Island is computed to be about seven millions, and we will suppose the present produce equal to the support of such a number. In the first twenty-five years the population would be fourteen millions, and the food being also doubled, the means of subsistence would be equal to this increase. In the next twenty-five years the population would be twenty-eight millions, and the means of subsistence only equal to the support of twenty-one millions. In the next period, the population would be fifty-six millions, and the means of subsistence just sufficient for half that number. And at the conclusion of the first century the population would be one hundred and twelve millions and the means of subsistence only equal to the support of thirty-five millions, which would leave a population of seventy-seven millions totally unprovided for.

A great emigration necessarily implies unhappiness of some kind or other in the country that is deserted. For few persons will leave their families, connections, friends, and native land, to seek a settlement in untried foreign climes, without some strong subsisting causes of uneasiness where they are, or the hope of some great advantages in the place to which they are going.

But to make the argument more general and less interrupted by the partial views of emigration, let us take the whole earth, instead of one spot, and suppose that the restraints to population were universally removed. If the subsistence for man that the earth affords was to be increased every twenty-five years by a quantity equal to what the whole world at present produces, this would allow the power of production in the earth to be absolutely unlimited, and its ratio of increase much greater than we can conceive that any possible exertions of mankind could make it.

Taking the population of the world at any number, a thousand millions, for instance, the human species would increase in the ratio of—1, 2, 4, 8, 16, 32, 64, 128, 256, 512, &c. and subsistence as—1, 2, 3, 4, 5, 6, 7, 8, 9, 10, &c. In two centuries and a quarter, the population would be to the means of subsistence as 512 to 10: in three centuries as 4096 to 13, and in two thousand years the difference would be almost incalculable, though the produce in that time would have increased to an immense extent.

No limits whatever are placed to the productions of the earth; they may increase for ever and be greater than any assignable quantity; yet still the power of population being a power of a superior order, the increase of the human species can only be kept commensurate to the increase of the means of subsistence, by the constant operation of the strong law of necessity acting as a check upon the greater power.

The effects of this check remain now to be considered.

Among plants and animals the view of the subject is simple. They are all impelled by a powerful instinct to the increase of their species, and this instinct is interrupted by no reasoning or doubts about providing for their offspring. Wherever therefore there is liberty, the power of increase is exerted, and the superabundant effects are repressed afterwards by want of room and nourishment, which is common to animals and plants, and among animals, by becoming the prey of others.

The effects of this check on man are more complicated. Impelled to the increase of his species by an equally powerful instinct, reason interrupts his career and asks him whether he may not bring beings into the world, for whom he cannot provide the means of subsistence. In a state of equality, this would be the simple question. In the present state of society, other considerations occur. Will he not lower his rank in life? Will he not subject himself to greater difficulties than he at present feels? Will he not be obliged to labour harder? and if he has a large family, will his utmost exertions enable him to support them? May he not see his offspring in rags and misery, and clamouring for bread that he cannot give them? And may he not be reduced to the grating necessity of forfeiting his independence, and of being obliged to the sparing hand of charity for support?

These considerations are calculated to prevent, and certainly do prevent, a very great number in all civilized nations from pursuing the dictate of nature in an early attachment to one woman. And this restraint almost necessarily, though not absolutely so, produces vice. Yet in all societies, even those that are most vicious, the tendency to a virtuous attachment is so strong that there is a constant effort towards an increase of population. This constant effort as constantly tends to subject the lower classes of the society to distress and to prevent any great permanent amelioration of their condition.

The way in which these effects are produced seems to be this.

We will suppose the means of subsistence in any country just equal to the easy support of its inhabitants. The constant effort towards population, which is found to act even in the most vicious societies, increases the number of people before the means of subsistence are increased. The food therefore which before supported seven millions must not be divided among seven millions and a half or eight millions. The poor consequently must live much worse, and many of them be reduced to severe distress. The number of labourers also being above the proportion of the work in the market, the price of labour must tend toward a decrease, while the price of provisions would at the same time tend to rise. The labourer therefore must work harder to earn the same as he did before. During this season of distress, the discouragements to marriage, and the difficulty of rearing a family are so great that population is at a stand. In the mean time the cheapness of labour, the plenty of labourers, and the necessity of an increased industry amongst them, encourage cultivators to employ more labour upon their land, to turn up fresh soil, and to manure and improve more completely what is already in tillage, till ultimately the means of subsistence become in the same proportion to the population as at the period from which we set out. The situation of the labourer being then again tolerably comfortable, the restraints to population are in some degree loosened, and the same retrograde and progressive movements with respect to happiness are repeated.

This sort of oscillation will not be remarked by superficial observers, and it may be difficult even for the most penetrating mind to calculate its periods. Yet that in all old states some such vibration does exist, though from various transverse causes, in a much less marked, and in a much more irregular manner than I have described it, no reflecting man who considers the subject deeply can well doubt.

POPULATION, POVERTY, AND WELFARE

The positive check to population by which I mean the check that represses an increase which is already begun, is confined chiefly, though not perhaps solely, to the lowest orders of society. This check is not so obvious to common view as the other[2] I have mentioned, and, to prove distinctly the force and extent of its operations would require, perhaps, more data than we are in possession of. But I believe it has been very generally remarked by those who have attended to bills of mortality that of the number of children who die annually, much too great a proportion belongs to those who may be supposed unable to give their offspring proper food and attention, exposed as they are occasionally to severe distress and confined, perhaps, to unwholesome habitations and hard labour. This mortality among the children of the poor has been constantly taken notice of in all towns. It certainly does not prevail in an equal degree in the country, but the subject has not hitherto received sufficient attention to enable any one to say that there are not more deaths in proportion among the children of the poor, even in the country, than among those of the middling and higher classes. Indeed, it seems difficult to suppose that a labourer's wife who has six children, and who is sometimes in absolute want of bread, should be able always to give them the food and attention necessary to support life. The sons and daughters of peasants will not be found such rosy cherubs in real life as they are described to be in romances. It cannot fail to be remarked by those who live much in the country that the sons of labourers are very apt to be stunted in their growth, and are a long while arriving at maturity. Boys that you would guess to be fourteen or fifteen, are upon inquiry, frequently found to be eighteen or nineteen. And the lads who drive plough, which must certainly be a healthy exercise, are very rarely seen with any appearance of calves to their legs; a circumstance, which can only be attributed to a want either of proper or of sufficient nourishment.

To remedy the frequent distresses of the common people, the poor laws of England have been instituted; but it is to be feared, that though they may have alleviated a little the intensity of individual misfortune, they have spread the general evil over a much larger surface. It is a subject often started in conversation and mentioned always as a matter of great surprise that notwithstanding the immense sum that is annually collected for the poor in England, there is still so much distress among them. Some think that the money must be embezzled, others that the church-wardens and overseers consume the greater part of it in dinners. All agree that some how or other it must be very ill-managed. In short the fact that nearly three millions are collected annually for the poor and yet that their distresses are not removed is the subject of continual astonishment. But a man who sees a little below the surface of things would be very much more astonished if the fact were otherwise than it is observed to be, or even if a collection universally of eighteen shillings in the pound instead of four, were materially to alter it.

The poor-laws of England tend to depress the general condition of the poor in two ways. Their first obvious tendency is to increase population without increasing the food for its support. A poor man may marry with little or no prospect of being able to support a family in independence. They may be said therefore in some measure to create the poor which they maintain, and as the provisions of the country must, in consequence of the increased population, be distributed to every man in smaller proportions, it is evident that the labour of those who are not supported by parish assistance will purchase a smaller quantity of provisions than before and consequently more of them must be driven to ask for support.

Secondly, the quantity of provisions consumed in workhouses upon a part of the society that cannot in general be considered as the most valuable part diminishes the shares that would otherwise belong to more industrious and more worthy members, and thus in the same manner forces more to become dependent. If the poor in the workhouses were to live better than they now do, this new distribution of the money of the society would tend more conspicuously to depress the condition of those out of the workhouses by occasioning a rise in the price of provisions.

I feel no doubt whatever that the parish laws of England have contributed to raise the price of provisions and to lower the real price of labour. They have therefore contributed to impoverish that class of people whose only possession is their labour. It is also difficult to suppose that they have not powerfully contributed to generate that carelessness and want of frugality observable among the poor, so contrary to the disposition frequently to be remarked among petty tradesmen and small farmers. The labouring poor, to use a vulgar expression, seem always to live from hand to mouth. Their present wants employ their whole attention, and they seldom think of the future. Even when they have an opportunity of saving they seldom exercise it, but all that is beyond their present necessities goes, generally speaking, to the ale-house. The poor-laws of England may therefore be said to diminish both the power and the will to save among the common people, and thus to weaken one of the strongest incentives to sobriety and industry, and consequently to happiness.

The mass of happiness among the common people cannot but be diminished, when one of the strongest checks to idleness and dissipation is thus removed, and when men are thus allured to marry with little or no prospect of being able to maintain a family in independence. Every obstacle in the way of marriage must undoubtedly be considered as a species of unhappiness. But as from the laws of our nature some check to population must exist, it is better that it should be checked from a foresight of the difficulties attending a family and the fear of dependent poverty than it should be encouraged, only to be repressed afterwards by want and sickness.

The evils attendant on the poor-laws are in some degree irremediable. If assistance be to be distributed to a certain class of people, a power must be given somewhere of discriminating the proper objects and of managing the concerns of the institutions that are necessary, but any great interference with the affairs of other people, is a species of tyranny, and in the common course of things the exercise of this power may be expected to become grating to those who are driven to ask for support. The tyranny of Justices, Churchwardens, and Overseers, is a common complaint among the poor, but the fault does not lie so much in these persons, who probably before they were in power, were not worse than other people, but in the nature of all such institutions.

The evil is perhaps gone too far to be remedied, but I feel little doubt in my own mind that if the poor-laws had never existed, though there might have been a few more instances of very severe distress, yet that the aggregate mass of happiness among the common people would have been much greater than it is at present.

PROPOSED REMEDIES

By encouraging the industry of the towns more than the industry of the country, Europe may be said, perhaps, to have brought on a premature old age. A different policy in this respect, would infuse fresh life and vigour into every state. While from the law of primogeniture, and other European customs, land bears a monopoly price, a capital can never be employed in it with much advantage to the individual; and, therefore, it is not probable that the soil should be properly cultivated. And, though in every civilized state, a class of proprietors and a class of labourers must exist; yet one permanent advantage would always result from a nearer equalization of property. The greater the number of proprietors, the smaller must be the number of labourers: a greater part of society would be in the happy state of possessing property; and a smaller part in the unhappy state of possessing no other property than their labour.

To remove the wants of the lower classes of society is indeed an arduous task. The truth is that the pressure of distress on this part of a community is an evil so deeply seated that no human ingenuity can reach it. Were I to propose a palliative, and palliatives are all that the nature of the case will admit, it should be, in the first place, the total abolition of all the present parish-laws. This would at any rate give liberty and freedom of action to the peasantry of England, which they can hardly be said to possess at present. They would then be able to settle without interruption, wherever there was a prospect of a greater plenty of work and a higher price for labour. The market of labour would then be free, and those obstacles removed, which as things are now, often for a considerable time prevent the price from rising according to the demand.

Secondly, Premiums might be given for turning up fresh land, and all possible encouragements held out to agriculture above manufactures, and to tillage above grazing. Every endeavour should be used to weaken and destroy all those institutions relating to corporations, apprenticeships, &c, which cause the labours of agriculture to be worse paid than the labours of trade and manufactures. For a country can never produce its proper quantity of food while these distinctions remain in favour of artizans. Such encouragements to agriculture would tend to furnish the market with an increasing quantity of healthy work, and at the same time, by augmenting the produce of the country, would raise the comparative price of labour and ameliorate the condition of the labourer. Being now in better circumstances, and seeing no prospect of parish assistance, he would be more able, as well as more inclined, to enter into associations for providing against the sickness of himself or family.

Lastly, for cases of extreme distress, county workhouses might be established, supported by rates upon the whole kingdom, and free for persons of all counties, and indeed of all nations. The fare should be hard, and those that were able obliged to work. It would be desirable that they should not be considered as comfortable asylums in all difficulties, but merely as places where severe distress might find some alleviation. A part of these houses might be separated, or others built for a most beneficial purpose, that of providing a place where any person, whether native or foreigner, might do a day's work at all times and receive the market price for it. Many cases would undoubtedly be left for the exertion of individual benevolence.

A plan of this kind, the preliminary of which should be an abolition of all the present parish laws, seems to be the best calculated to increase the mass of happiness among the common people of England. To prevent the recurrence of misery, is, alas! beyond the power of man. In the vain endeavour to attain what in the nature of things is impossible, we now sacrifice not only possible but certain benefits. We tell the common people that if they will submit to a code of tyrannical regulations, they shall never be in want. They do submit to these regulations. They perform their part of the contract, but we do not, nay cannot, perform ours, and thus the poor sacrifice the valuable blessing of liberty and receive nothing that can be called an equivalent in return.

It is undoubtedly a most disheartening reflection that the great obstacle in the way to any extraordinary improvement in society is of a nature that we can never hope to overcome. The perpetual tendency in the race of man to increase beyond the means of subsistence is one of the general laws of animated nature which we can have no reason to expect will change. Yet, discouraging as the contemplation of this difficulty must be to those whose exertions are laudably directed to the improvement of the human species, it is evident that no possible good can arise from any endeavours to slur it over or keep it in the back ground. On the contrary, the most baleful mischiefs may be expected from the unmanly conduct of not daring to face truth because it is unpleasing. Independently of what relates to this great obstacle, sufficient yet remains to be done for mankind to animate us to the most unremitted exertion. But if we proceed without a thorough knowledge and accurate comprehension of the nature, extent, and magnitude of the difficulties we have to encounter, or if we unwisely direct our efforts towards an object, in which we cannot hope for success, we shall not only exhaust our strength in fruitless exertions and remain at as great a distance as ever from the summit of our wishes, but we shall be perpetually crushed by the recoil of this rock of Sisyphus.

NOTES

1. From Thomas Robert Malthus, "An Essay on the Principle of Population," first (1798) edition, edited for this collection by Scott Menard. The order of presentation has been slightly altered for this collection, some phrases have been deleted, and some punctuation has been altered.
2. The preventive check of discouraging early marriage, discussed briefly at the beginning of the previous section ("The Power of Population"). Malthus provides more detail on this in his second or revised (1803) edition of the essay.

10
Outlines of a Critique of Political Economy (1844)

FRIEDRICH ENGELS

Malthus . . . asserts that population constantly exerts pressure on the means of subsistence; that as production is increased, population increases in the same proportion; and that the inherent tendency of population to multiply beyond the available means of subsistence is the cause of all poverty and all vice. For if there are too many people, then in one way or another they must be eliminated; they must die, either by violence or through starvation. When this has happened, however, a gap appears once more, and this is immediately filled by other propagators of population, so that the old poverty begins anew. Moreover, this is the case under all conditions—not only in the civilized but also in the natural state of man. The savages of New Holland, who live *one* to the square mile, suffer just as much from overpopulation as England. In short, if we want to be logical, we have to recognize *that the earth was already overpopulated when only one man existed.* Now the consequence of this theory is that since it is precisely the poor who constitute this surplus population, nothing ought to be done for them, except to make it as easy as possible for them to starve to death; to convince them that this state of affairs cannot be altered and that there is no salvation for their entire class other than that they should propagate as little as possible . . . .

Is it necessary for me to give any more details of this vile and infamous doctrine, this repulsive blasphemy against man and nature, or to follow up its consequences any further? Here, brought before us at last, is the immorality of the economists in its highest form. What were all the wars and horrors of the monopoly system when compared with this theory? And it is precisely this theory which is the cornerstone of the liberal system of free trade, whose fall will bring the whole edifice down with it. For once competition has here been proved to be the cause of misery, poverty and crime, who will still dare to say a word in its defense?

. . . If, however, it is a fact that every adult produces more than he can himself consume, that children are like trees, returning abundantly the expenditure laid out on them—and surely these are facts?—one would imagine that every worker ought to be able to produce far more than he needs, and that the community ought therefore to be glad to furnish him with everything that he requires; one would imagine that a large family would be a most desirable gift to the community. But the economists, with their crude outlook, know no other equivalent apart from that which is paid over to them in tangible hard cash. They are so firmly entangled in their contradictions that they are just as little concerned with the most striking facts as they are with the most scientific principles.

We shall destroy the contradiction simply by resolving it. With the fusion of those interests which now conflict with one another, there will disappear the antithesis between surplus population in one place and surplus wealth in another, and also the wonderful phenomenon—more wonderful than all the wonders of all the religions put together—that a nation must starve to death from sheer wealth and abundance; and there will disappear too the crazy assertion that the earth does not possess the power to feed mankind. . . .

The Malthusian theory, however, was an absolutely necessary transitional stage, which has taken us infinitely further forward. Thanks to this theory, as also thanks to economics in general, our attention has been drawn to the productive power of the soil and of humanity, so that now, having triumphed over this economic despair, we are forever secure from the fear of overpopulation. From this theory we derive the most powerful economic arguments in favor of a social reorganization; for even if Malthus were altogether right, it would still be necessary to carry out this reorganization immediately, since only this reorganization, only the enlightenment of the masses which it can bring with it, can make possible that moral restraint upon the instinct for reproduction which Malthus himself puts forward as the easiest and most effective countermeasure against overpopulation. Thanks to this theory we have come to recognize the dependence of man upon competitive conditions his most complete degradation. It has shown us that in the last analysis private property has turned man into a commodity, whose production and consumption also depend only on demand; that the system of competition has thereby slaughtered, and is still slaughtering today, millions of people—all this we have seen, and all this impels us to do away with this degradation of humanity by doing away with private property, competition and conflicting interests.

However, in order to deprive the general fear of overpopulation of all foundation, let us return once again to the question of the relation of productive power to population. Malthus puts forward a calculation upon which his whole system is based. Population increases in geometrical progression—1 + 2 + 8 + 16 + 32, etc. The productive power of the land increases in arithmetical progression—1 + 2 + 3 + 4 + 5 + 6. The difference is obvious and horrifying—but is it correct? Where has it been proved that the productivity of the land increases in arithmetical progression? The area of land is limited—that is perfectly true. But the labor power to be employed on this area increases together with the population; and even if we assume that the increase of output associated with this increase of labor is not always proportionate to the latter, there still remains a third element—which the economists, however, never consider as important—namely, science, the progress of which is just as limitless and at least as rapid as that of population. For what great advances is the agriculture of this century obliged to chemistry alone—and indeed to two men alone, Sir Humphry Davy and Justus Liebig? But science increases at least as fast as population; the latter increases in proportion to the size of the previous generation, and science advances in proportion to the body of knowledge passed down to it by the previous generation, that is, in the most normal conditions it also grows in geometrical progression—and what is impossible for science? But it is ridiculous to speak of overpopulation while "the valley of the Mississippi alone contains enough waste land to accommodate the whole population of Europe," while altogether only one-third of the earth can be described as cultivated, and while the productivity of this third could be increased sixfold and more merely by applying improvements which are already known.

11

The Tragedy of the Commons

GARRETT HARDIN

The population problem has no technical solution; it requires a fundamental extension in morality.

At the end of a thoughtful article on the future of nuclear war, Wiesner and York[1] concluded that: "Both sides in the arms race are . . . confronted by the dilemma of a steadily increasing military power and steadily decreasing national security. *It is our considered professional judgment that this dilemma has no technical solution.* If the great powers continue to look for solutions in the area of science and technology only, the result will be to worsen the situation."

I would like to focus your attention not on the subject of the article (national security in a nuclear world) but on the kind of conclusion they reached, namely that there is no technical solution to the problem. An implicit and almost universal assumption of discussions published in professional and semipopular scientific journals is that the problem under discussion has a technical solution. A technical solution may be defined as one that requires a change only in the techniques of the natural sciences, demanding little or nothing in the way of change in human values or ideas of morality.

In our day (though not in earlier times) technical solutions are always welcome. Because of previous failures in prophecy, it takes courage to assert that a desired technical solution is not possible. Wiesner and York exhibited this courage; publishing in a science journal, they insisted that the solution to the problem was not to be found in the natural sciences. They cautiously qualified their statement with the phrase, "It is our considered professional judgment. . . ." Whether they were right or not is not the concern of the present article. Rather, the concern here is with the important concept of a class of human problems which can be called "no technical solution problems," and, more specifically, with the identification and discussion of one of these.

It is easy to show that the class is not a null class. Recall the game of tick-tack-toe. Consider the problem, "How can I win the game of tick-tack-toe?" It is well known that I cannot, if I assume (in keeping with the conventions of game theory) that my opponent understands the game perfectly. Put another way, there is no "technical solution" to the problem. I can win only by giving a radical meaning to the word "win." I can hit my opponent over the head; or I can drug him; or I can falsify the records. Every way in which I "win" involves, in some sense, an abandonment of the game, as we intuitively understand it. (I can also, of course, openly abandon the game—refuse to play it. This is what most adults do.)

The class of "No technical solution problems" has members. My thesis is that the "population problem," as conventionally conceived, is a member of this class. How it is conventionally conceived needs some comment. It is fair to say that most people who anguish over the population problem are trying to find a way to avoid the evils of overpopulation without relinquishing any of the privileges they now enjoy. They think that farming the seas or developing new strains of wheat will solve the problem—technologically. I try to show here that the solution they seek cannot be found. The population problem cannot be solved in a technical way, any more than can the problem of winning the game of tick-tack-toe.

WHAT SHALL WE MAXIMIZE?

Population, as Malthus said, naturally tends to grow "geometrically," or, as we would now say, exponentially. In a finite world this means that the per capita share of the world's goods must steadily decrease. Is ours a finite world?

A fair defense can be put forward for the view that the world is infinite; or that we do not know that it is not. But, in terms of the practical problems that we must face in the next few generations with the foreseeable technology, it is clear that we will greatly increase human misery if we do not, during the immediate future, assume that the world available to terrestrial human population is finite. "Space" is no escape.[2]

A finite world can support only a finite population; therefore, population growth must eventually equal zero. (The case of perpetual wide fluctuations above and below zero is a trivial variant that need not be discussed.) When this condition is met, what will be the situation of mankind? Specifically, can Bentham's goal of "the greatest good for the greatest number" be realized?

No—for two reasons, each sufficient by itself. The first is a theoretical one. It is not mathematically possible to maximize for two (or more) variables at the same time. This was clearly stated by von Neumann and Morgenstern,[3] but the principle is implicit in the theory of partial differential equations, dating back at least to D'Alembert (1717–1783).

The second reason springs directly from biological facts. To live, any organism must have a source of energy (for example, food). This energy is utilized for two purposes: mere maintenance and work. For man, maintenance of life requires about 1600 kilocalories a day ("maintenance calories"). Anything that he does over and above merely staying alive will be defined as work, and is supported by "work calories" which he takes in. Work calories are used not only for what we call work in common speech; they are also required for all forms of enjoyment, from swimming and automobile racing to playing music and writing poetry. If our goal is to maximize population it is obvious what we must do: We must make the work calories per person approach as close to zero as possible. No gourmet meals, no vacations, no sports, no music, no literature, no art. . . . I think that everyone will grant, without argument or proof, that maximizing population does not maximize goods. Bentham's goal is impossible.

In reaching this conclusion I have made the usual assumption that it is the acquisition of energy that is the problem. The appearance of atomic energy has led some to question this assumption. However, given an infinite source of energy, population growth still produces an inescapable problem. The problem of the acquisition of energy is replaced by the problem of its dissipation, as J. H. Fremlin has so wittily shown.[4] The arithmetic signs in the analysis are, as it were, reversed; but Bentham's goal is still unobtainable.

The optimum population is, then, less than the maximum. The difficulty of defining the optimum is enormous; so far as I know, no one has seriously tackled this problem. Reaching an acceptable and stable solution will surely require more than one generation of hard analytical work—and much persuasion.

We want the maximum good per person; but what is good? To one person it is wilderness, to another it is ski lodges for thousands. To one it is estuaries to nourish ducks for hunters to shoot; to another it is factory land. Comparing one good with another is, we usually say, impossible because goods are incommensurable. Incommensurables cannot be compared.

Theoretically this may be true; but in real life incommensurables *are* commensurable. Only a criterion of judgment and a system of weighting are needed. In nature the criterion is survival. Is it better for a species to be small and hideable, or large and powerful? Natural selection commensurates the incommensurables. The compromise achieved depends on a natural weighting of the values of the variables.

Man must imitate this process. There is no doubt that in fact he already does, but unconsciously. It is when the hidden decisions are made explicit that the arguments begin. The problem for the years ahead is to work out an acceptable theory of weighting. Synergistic effects, nonlinear variation, and difficulties in discounting the future make the intellectual problem difficult, but not (in principle) insoluble.

Has any cultural group solved this practical problem at the present time, even on an intuitive level? One simple fact proves that none has: there is no prosperous population in the world today that has, and has had for some time, a growth rate of zero. Any people that has intuitively identified its optimum point will soon reach it, after which its growth rate becomes and remains zero.

Of course, a positive growth rate might be taken as evidence that a population is below its optimum. However, by any reasonable standards, the most rapidly growing populations on earth today are (in general) the most miserable. This association (which need not be invariable) casts doubt on the optimistic assumption that the positive growth rate of a population is evidence that it has yet to reach its optimum.

We can make little progress in working toward optimum population size until we explicitly exorcise the spirit of Adam Smith in the field of practical demography. In economic affairs, *The Wealth of Nations* (1776) popularized the "invisible hand," the idea that an individual who "intends only his own gain," is, as it were, "led by an invisible hand to promote . . . the public interest."[5] Adam Smith did not assert that this was invariably true, and perhaps neither did any of his followers. But he contributed to a dominant tendency of thought that has ever since interfered with positive action based on rational analysis, namely, the tendency to assume that decisions reached individually will, in fact, be the best decisions for an entire society. If this assumption is correct it justifies the continuance of our present policy of laissez-faire in reproduction. If it is correct we can assume that men will control their individual fecundity so as to produce the optimum population. If the assumption is not correct, we need to reexamine our individual freedoms to see which ones are defensible.

TRAGEDY OF FREEDOM IN A COMMONS

The rebuttal to the invisible hand in population control is to be found in a scenario first sketched in a little-known pamphlet[6] in 1833 by a mathematical amateur named William Forster Lloyd (1794–1852). We may well call it "the tragedy of the commons," using the word "tragedy" as the philosopher Whitehead used it[7]: "The essence of dramatic tragedy is not unhappiness. It resides in the solemnity of the remorseless working of things." He then goes on to say, "This inevitableness of destiny can only be illustrated in terms of human life by incidents which in fact involve unhappiness. For it is only by them that the futility of escape can be made evident in the drama."

The tragedy of the commons develops in this way. Picture a pasture open to all. It is to be expected that each herdsman will try to keep as many cattle as possible on the commons. Such an arrangement may work reasonably satisfactorily for centuries because tribal wars, poaching, and disease keep the numbers of both man and beast well below the carrying capacity of the land. Finally, however, comes the day of reckoning, that is, the day when the long-desired goal of social stability becomes a reality. At this point, the inherent logic of the commons remorselessly generates tragedy.

As a rational being, each herdsman seeks to maximize his gain. Explicitly or implicitly, more or less consciously, he asks, "What is the utility to *me* of adding one more animal to my herd?" This utility has one negative and one positive component.

1. The positive component is a function of the increment of one animal. Since the herdsman receives all the proceeds from the sale of the additional animal, the positive utility is nearly +1.
2. The negative component is a function of the additional overgrazing created by one more animal. Since, however, the effects of overgrazing are shared by all the herdsmen, the negative utility for any particular decision-making herdsman is only a fraction of −1.

Adding together the component partial utilities, the rational herdsman concludes that the only sensible course for him to pursue is to add another animal to his herd. And another; and another. . . . But this is the conclusion reached by each and every rational herdsman sharing a commons. Therein is the tragedy. Each man is locked into a system that compels him to increase his herd without limit—in a world that is limited. Ruin is the destination toward which all men rush, each pursuing his own best interest in a society that believes in the freedom of the commons. Freedom in a commons brings ruin to all.

In an approximate way, the logic of the commons has been understood for a long time, perhaps since the discovery of agriculture or the invention of private property in real estate. But it is understood mostly only in special cases which are not sufficiently generalized. Even at this late date, cattlemen leasing national land on the western ranges demonstrate no more than an ambivalent understanding, in constantly pressuring federal authorities to increase the head count to the point where overgrazing produces erosion and weed-dominance. Likewise, the oceans of the world continue to suffer from the survival of the philosophy of the commons. Maritime nations still respond automatically to the shibboleth of the "freedom of the seas." Professing to believe in the "inexhaustible resources of the oceans," they bring species after species of fish and whales closer to extinction.[8]

The National Parks present another instance of the working out of the tragedy of the commons. At present, they are open to all, without limit. The parks themselves are limited in extent—there is only one Yosemite Valley—whereas population seems to grow without limit. The values that visitors seek in the parks are steadily eroded. Plainly, we must soon cease to treat the parks as commons or they will be of no value to anyone.

What shall we do? We have several options. We might sell them off as private property. We might keep them as public property, but allocate the right to enter them. The allocation might be on the basis of wealth, by the use of an auction system. It might be on the basis of merit, as defined by some agreed-upon standards. It might be by lottery. Or it might be on a first-come, first-served basis, administered to long queues. These, I think, are all the reasonable possibilities. They are all objectionable. But we must choose—or acquiesce in the destruction of the commons that we call our National Parks.

POLLUTION

In a reverse way, the tragedy of the commons reappears in problems of pollution. Here it is not a question of taking something out of the commons, but of putting something in—sewage, or chemical, radioactive, and heat wastes into water; noxious and dangerous fumes into the air; and distracting and unpleasant advertising signs into the line of sight. The calculations of utility are much the same as before. The rational man finds that his share of the cost of the wastes he discharges into the commons is less than the cost of purifying his wastes before releasing them. Since this is true for everyone, we are locked into a system of "fouling our own nest," so long as we behave only as independent, rational, free-enterprisers.

The tragedy of the commons as a food basket is averted by private property, or something formally like it. But the air and waters surrounding us cannot readily be fenced, and so the tragedy of the commons as a cesspool must be prevented by different means, by coercive laws or taxing devices that make it cheaper for the polluter to treat his pollutants than to discharge them untreated. We have not progressed as far with the solution of this problem as we have with the first. Indeed, our particular concept of private property, which deters us from exhausting the positive resources of the earth, favors pollution. The owner of a factory on the bank of a stream—whose property extends to the middle of the stream—often has difficulty seeing why it is not his natural right to muddy the waters flowing past his door. The law, always behind the times, requires elaborate stitching and fitting to adapt it to this newly perceived aspect of the commons.

The pollution problem is a consequence of population. It did not much matter how a lonely American frontiersman disposed of his waste. "Flowing water purifies itself every 10 miles," my grandfather used to say, and the myth was near enough to the truth when he was a boy, for there were not too many people. But as population became denser, the natural chemical and biological recycling processes became overloaded, calling for a redefinition of property rights.

FREEDOM TO BREED IS INTOLERABLE

In a world governed solely by the principle of "dog eat dog"—if indeed there ever was such a world—how many children a family had would not be a matter of public concern. Parents who bred too exuberantly would leave fewer descendants, not more, because they would be unable to care adequately for their children. David Lack and others have found that such a negative feedback demonstrably controls the fecundity of birds.[9] But men are not birds, and have not acted like them for millenniums, at least.

If each human family were dependent only on its own resources; *if* the children of improvident parents starved to death; *if,* thus, overbreeding brought its own "punishment" to the germ line—*then* there would be no public interest in controlling the breeding of families. But our society is deeply committed to the welfare state,[10] and hence is confronted with another aspect of the tragedy of the commons.

In a welfare state, how shall we deal with the family, the religion, the race, or the class (or indeed any distinguishable and cohesive group) that adopts overbreeding as a policy to secure its own aggrandizement?[11] To couple the concept of freedom to breed with the belief that everyone born has an equal right to the commons is to lock the world into a tragic course of action.

Unfortunately this is just the course of action that is being pursued by the United Nations. In late 1967, some 30 nations agreed to the following[12]:

> The Universal Declaration of Human Rights describes the family as the natural and fundamental unit of society. It follows that any choice and decision with regard to the size of the family must irrevocably rest with the family itself, and cannot be made by anyone else.

It is painful to have to deny categorically the validity of this right: Denying it, one feels as uncomfortable as a resident of Salem, Massachusetts, who denied the reality of witches in the 17th century. At the present time, in liberal quarters, something like a taboo acts to inhibit criticism of the United Nations. There is a feeling that the United Nations is "our last and best hope," that we shouldn't find fault with it: we shouldn't play into the hands of the archconservatives. However, let us not forget what Robert Louis Stevenson said: "The truth that is suppressed by friends is the readiest weapon of the enemy." If we love the truth we must openly deny the validity of the Universal Declaration of Human Rights, even though it is promoted by the United Nations. We should also join with Kingsley Davis[13] in attempting to get Planned Parenthood-World Population to see the error of its ways in embracing the same tragic ideal.

CONSCIENCE IS SELF-ELIMINATING

It is a mistake to think that we can control the breeding of mankind in the long run by an appeal to conscience. Charles Galton Darwin made this point when he spoke on the centennial of the publication of his grandfather's great book. The argument is straightforward and Darwinian.

People vary. Confronted with appeals to limit breeding, some people will undoubtedly respond to the plea more than others. Those who have more children will produce a larger fraction of the next generation than those with more susceptible consciences. The difference will be accentuated, generation by generation.

In C. G. Darwin's words: "It may well be that it would take hundreds of generations for the progenitive instinct to develop in this way, but if it should do so, nature would have taken her revenge, and the variety *Homo contracipiens* would become extinct and would be replaced by the variety *Homo progenitivus*."[14]

The argument assumes that conscience or the desire for children (no matter which) is hereditary—but hereditary only in the most general formal sense. The result will be the same whether the attitude is transmitted through germ cells, or exosomatically, to use A. J. Lotka's term. (If one denies the latter possibility as well as the former, then what's the point of education?) The argument has here been stated in the context of the population problem, but it applies equally well to any instance in which society appeals to an individual exploiting a commons to restrain himself for the general good—by means of his conscience. To make such an appeal is to set up a selective system that works toward the elimination of conscience from the race.

MUTUAL COERCION MUTUALLY AGREED UPON

The social arrangements that produce responsibility are arrangements that create coercion, of some sort. Consider bank-robbing. The man who takes money from a bank acts as if the bank were a commons. How do we prevent such action? Certainly not by trying to control his behavior solely by a verbal appeal to his sense of responsibility. Rather than rely on propaganda we follow Frankel's[15] lead and insist that a bank is not a commons; we seek the definite social arrangements that will keep it from becoming a commons. That we thereby infringe on the freedom of would-be robbers we neither deny nor regret.

The morality of bank-robbing is particularly easy to understand because we accept complete prohibition of this activity. We are willing to say "Thou shalt not rob banks," without providing for exceptions. But temperance also can be created by coercion. Taxing is a good coercive device. To keep downtown shoppers temperate in their use of parking space we introduce parking meters for short periods, and traffic fines for longer ones. We need not actually forbid a citizen to park as long as he wants to; we need merely make it increasingly expensive for him to do so. Not prohibition, but carefully biased options are what we offer him. A Madison Avenue man might call this persuasion: I prefer the greater candor of the word coercion.

Coercion is a dirty word to most liberals now, but it need not forever be so. As with the four-letter words, its dirtiness can be cleansed away by exposure to the light, by saying it over and over without apology or embarrassment. To many, the word coercion implies arbitrary decisions of distant and irresponsible bureaucrats; but this is not a necessary part of its meaning. The only kind of coercion I recommend is mutual coercion, mutually agreed upon by the majority of the people affected.

To say that we mutually agree to coercion is not to say that we are required to enjoy it, or even to pretend we enjoy it. Who enjoys taxes? We all grumble about them. But we accept compulsory taxes because we recognize that voluntary taxes would favor the conscienceless. We institute and (grumblingly) support taxes and other coercive devices to escape the horror of the commons.

An alternative to the commons need not be perfectly just to be preferable. With real estate and other material goods, the alternative we have chosen is the institution of private property coupled with legal inheritance. Is this system perfectly just? As a genetically trained biologist I deny that it is. It seems to me that, if there are to be differences in individual inheritance, legal possession should be perfectly correlated with biological inheritance—that those who are biologically more fit to be the custodians of property and power should legally inherit more. But genetic recombination continually makes a mockery of the doctrine of "like father, like son" implicit in our laws of legal inheritance. An idiot can inherit millions, and a trust fund can keep his estate intact. We must admit that our legal system of private property plus inheritance is unjust—but we put up with it because we are not convinced, at the moment, that anyone has invented a better system. The alternative of the commons is too horrifying to contemplate. Injustice is preferable to total ruin.

It is one of the peculiarities of the warfare between reform and the status quo that it is thoughtlessly governed by a double standard. Whenever a reform measure is proposed it is often defeated when its opponents triumphantly discover a flaw in it. As Kingsley Davis has pointed out,[16] worshippers of the status quo sometimes imply that no reform is possible without unanimous agreement, an implication contrary to historical fact. As nearly as I can make out, automatic rejection of proposed reforms is based on one of two unconscious assumptions: (i) that the status quo is perfect; or (ii) that the choice we face is between reform and no action; if the proposed reform is imperfect, we presumably should take no action at all, while we wait for a perfect proposal.

But we can never do nothing. That which we have done for thousands of years is also action. It also produces evils. Once we are aware that the status quo is action, we can then compare its discoverable advantages and disadvantages with the predicted advantages and disadvantages of the proposed reform, discounting as best we can for our lack of experience. On the basis of such a comparison, we can make a rational decision which will not involve the unworkable assumption that only perfect systems are tolerable.

RECOGNITION OF NECESSITY

Perhaps the simplest summary of this analysis of man's population problems is this: the commons, if justifiable at all, is justifiable only under conditions of low-population density. As the human population has increased, the commons has had to be abandoned in one aspect after another.

First we abandoned the commons in food gathering, enclosing farm land and restricting pastures and hunting and fishing areas. These restrictions are still not complete throughout the world.

Somewhat later we saw that the commons as a place for waste disposal would also have to be abandoned. Restrictions on the disposal of domestic sewage are widely accepted in the Western world; we are still struggling to close the commons to pollution by automobiles, factories, insecticide sprayers, fertilizing operations, and atomic energy installations.

In a still more embryonic state is our recognition of the evils of the commons in matters of pleasure. There is almost no restriction on the propagation of sound waves in the public medium. The shopping public is assaulted with mindless music, without its consent. Our government is paying out billions of dollars to create supersonic transport which will disturb 50,000 people for every one person who is whisked from coast to coast 3 hours faster. Advertisers muddy the airwaves of radio and television and pollute the view of travelers. We are a long way from outlawing the commons in matters of pleasure. Is this because our Puritan inheritance makes us view pleasure as something of a sin, and pain (that is, the pollution of advertising) as the sign of virtue?

Every new enclosure of the commons involves the infringement of somebody's personal liberty. Infringements made in the distant past are accepted because no contemporary complains of a loss. It is the newly proposed infringements that we vigorously oppose: Cries of "rights" and "freedom" fill the air. But what does "freedom" mean? When men mutually agreed to pass laws against robbing, mankind became more free, not less so. Individuals locked into the logic of the commons are free only to bring on universal ruin: once they see the necessity of mutual coercion, they become free to pursue other goals. I believe it was Hegel who said, "Freedom is the recognition of necessity."

The most important aspect of necessity that we must now recognize, is the necessity of abandoning the commons in breeding. No technical solution can rescue us from the misery of overpopulation. Freedom to breed will bring ruin to all. At the moment, to avoid hard decisions many of us are tempted to propagandize for conscience and responsible parenthood. The temptation must be resisted, because an appeal to independently acting consciences selects for the disappearance of all conscience in the long run, and an increase in anxiety in the short.

The only way we can preserve and nurture other and more precious freedoms is by relinquishing the freedom to breed, and that very soon. "Freedom is the recognition of necessity"—and it is the role of education to reveal to all the necessity of abandoning the freedom to breed. Only so, can we put an end to this aspect of the tragedy of the commons.

REFERENCES

1. J. B. Wiesner and H. F. York. *Sci. Amer.* 211 (No. 4), 27 (1964).
2. G. Hardin. *J. Hered.* 50, 68 (1959); S. von Hoernor. *Science* 137, 18 (1962).
3. J. von Neumann and O. Morgenstern, *Theory of Games and Economic Behavior* (Princeton, NJ: Princeton Univ. Press, 1947), p. 11.
4. J. H. Fremlin, *New Sci.*, No. 415 (1964), p. 285.
5. A. Smith, *The Wealth of Nations* (NY: Modern Library, 1937), p. 423.
6. W. F. Lloyd, *Two Lectures on the Checks to Population* (Oxford: Oxford University Press, 1833), reprinted (in part) in *Population, Evolution, and Birth Control,* G. Hardin, ed. (San Francisco: Freeman, 1964), p. 37.
7. A. N. Whitehead, *Science and the Modern World* (NY: Mentor 1948), p. 17.
8. S. McVay, *Sci Amer.* 216 (No. 8), 13 (1966).
9. D. Lack, *The Natural Regulation of Animal Numbers* (Oxford: Clarendon Press, 1954).
10. H. Girvetz, *From Wealth to Welfare* (Stanford CA: Stanford Univ. Press, 1950).
11. G. Hardin, *Perspec. Biol. Med.* 6, 366 (1963).
12. U Thant, *Int. Planned Parenthood News,* No. 168 (February 1968), p. 3.
13. K. Davis, *Science* 158, 730 (1967).
14. S. Tax, ed., *Evolution After Darwin* (Chicago: Univ. of Chicago Press, 1960), vol. 2, p. 469.
15. C. Frankel, *The Case for Modern Man* (NY: Harper, 1955), p. 203.
16. J. D. Roslansky, *Genetics and the Future of Man* (NY: Appleton-Century-Crofts, 1966), p. 177.

12
Food First

FRANCES MOORE LAPPE
JOE COLLINS

FOOD FACTS

How many people are badly nourished?
Two thousand million people—about half the world's population.

How many are actually starving?
The U.N. Food and Agriculture Organization estimates that 462 million are "actually starving" and about half of them are children under five.

Where are they?
Twenty-eight million in the developed countries, 36 million in Latin America, 30 million in the Near East, 67 million in Africa, and 301 million in the Far East.

What is the average required number of calories per day for a person to stay healthy?
It varies a lot, but 1,900 calories per day is the recommended minimum.

Is enough food being grown to provide everybody in the world with this recommended minimum?
Yes. In fact, enough is being grown to provide every person in the world with 3,000 to 4,000 calories per day.

But is there enough land and water in the world to grow food for a population which will be doubled in 30 years?
Easily. There are many estimates of the world's food potential and almost all of them see no difficulty in doubling world food production. For example, W. H. Pawley of FAO estimates that the earth's resources could feed 36 billion people (present population about 4 billion).

If enough food to feed everybody is being grown now, and even more could be grown, why are people starving and what needs to be done so that their basic need for food can be met?
That is a matter for much debate. Some say the problem is too many people and that the answer is birth control or even more famine deaths to reduce population. Some say the problem is not enough food and that improved production and new technology is the answer. Some say the problem is that existing food is wrongly distributed and that the answer is for the rich to eat less and for more food and agricultural aid to be given to the poor. The New Internationalist believes in the analysis of the problem and its outline solution put forward in these pages—that the problem is the present ownership of the land and the means for making it productive and that the solution lies in redistributing that power to the poor and the hungry in order that they may use the land and its necessary inputs, first and foremost for meeting their basic need for food.

For the last several years we have struggled to answer the question "why hunger?" Analyses that call for more aid or for reducing our consumption so that the hungry might eat left us with growing doubts.

Here we want to share the six myths that kept us locked into a misunderstanding of the problem as well as the alternative view that emerged once we began to grasp the issues. Our hope is to help anchor the hunger movement with an unequivocal and cogent analysis. Only then will our collective potential no longer be dissipated.

Myth One: People are hungry because of scarcity—both of food and agricultural land.

Can scarcity seriously be considered the cause of hunger when even in the worst years of famine in the early 1970s there was plenty to go around—enough in grain alone to provide everyone in the world with 3,000 to 4,000 calories a day, not counting all the beans, root crops, fruits, nuts, vegetables, and non-grain-fed meat:

And what of land scarcity?

We looked at the most crowded countries in the world to see if we could find a correlation between land density and hunger. We could not. Bangladesh, for example, has just half the people per cultivated acre that Taiwan has. Yet Taiwan has no starvation while Bangladesh is thought of as the world's worst basket case. China has twice as many people for each cultivated acre as India. Yet in China people are not hungry.

Finally when the pattern of *what* is grown sank in, we simply could no longer subscribe to a "scarcity" diagnosis of hunger. In Central America and in the Caribbean, where as much as 70 percent of the children are undernourished, at least half of the agricultural land, and the best land at that, grows crops for export, not food for the local people. In the Sahelian countries of Sub-Saharan Africa, exports of cotton and peanuts in the early 1970s actually *increased* as drought and hunger loomed.

Next we asked: What solution emerges when the problem of hunger is defined as scarcity?

Most commonly, people see greater production as the answer. So techniques to increase production become the central focus: supplying the "modern" inputs—large scale irrigation, chemical fertilization, pesticides, machinery, and the seeds dependent on these other inputs. All of this is designed to make the land produce more. But when a new agricultural technology enters a system shot through with power inequalities, it brings greater profit only to those who already have some combination of land, money, credit "worthiness," and political influence. This alone has barred most of the world's rural population and all the world's hungry from the benefits of "producing more."

MORE PRODUCTION, MORE HUNGER

Once agriculture is viewed as a growth industry in which the control of the basic inputs guarantees big money, a catastrophic chain of events is set into motion. Competition for land sends land values soaring (land values have jumped three to five times in the "Green Revolution" areas of India). Higher rents force tenants and sharecroppers into the ranks of the landless. With the new profits the powerful buy out small farmers who have gone bankrupt (in part through having been forced to double or triple their indebtedness trying to partake of the new technology). Moreover, faced with a short planting and harvest time for vast acreages planted uniformly with the most profitable crop, large commercial growers mechanize to avoid the troublesome mobilization of human labor. Those made landless by the production focus, finding ever fewer agricultural jobs, join an equally hopeless search for work in urban slums.

Fewer and fewer people gain control over more and more land. In Sonora, Mexico, the average farm before the Green Revolution was 400 acres. After 20 years of publicly funded modernization, the average has climbed to 2,000 acres with some holdings running as large as 25,000 acres.

The poor pay the price. Total production per capita may be up yet so are the numbers who face hunger. A strategy to solve hunger has led directly to increased inequality, in fact, to the absolute decline in the welfare of the majority. A study now being completed by the ILO shows that in the very South Asian countries—Pakistan, India, Thailand, Malaysia, Philippines, and Indonesia—where the focus has been on production and where the GNP has risen, the majority of the rural population are worse off than before.

But if the scarcity diagnosis, with the implied solution of increasing production, by technical inputs, has taken us not forward but backward, what is the right diagnosis?

We could answer the question only after our research at IFDP led us to conclude that there is *no* country without sufficient agricultural resources for the people to feed themselves and then some. And if they are not doing so, you can be sure there are powerful obstacles in the way. The prime obstacle is not, however, inadequate production to be overcome by technical inputs. The obstacle is that the people do not control the productive resources. When control is in the hands of the producers, people will no longer appear as liabilities—as a drain on resources. People are potentially a country's most underutilized resource and most valuable capital. People who know they are working for themselves will not only make the land produce but through their labor make it even more productive.

Myth Two: A hungry world simply cannot afford the luxury of justice for the small farmer.

We are made to believe that, if we want to eat, we had better rely on the large landowners. Thus governments, international lending agencies, and foreign assistance programs have passed over the small producers, believing that concentrating on the large holders was the quickest road to production gains. A study of

83 countries, revealing that just over 3 percent of the landholders control about 80 percent of the farmland, gave us some idea of how many of the world's farmers would be excluded by such a concentration.

Yet a study of Argentina, Brazil, Chile, Colombia, Ecuador, and Guatemala found the small farmer to be 3 to 14 times more productive per acre than the larger farmer. In Thailand plots of 2 to 4 acres yield almost 60 percent more rice per acre than farms of 140 acres or more. Other proof that justice for the small farmer increases production comes from the experience of countries in which the redistribution of land and other basic agricultural resources like water has resulted in rapid growth in agricultural production: Japan, Taiwan, and China stand out.

But where has the grip of this myth led? As the large holders are reinforced, often with public subsidies, the small holders and laborers have been cut out of production through the twin process of increasing land concentration and mechanization. *To be cut out of production is to be cut out of consumption.*

FLOWERS NOT FOOD

As fewer and fewer have the wherewithal either to grow food or to buy food, the internal market for food stagnates or even shrinks. But large commercial farmers have not worried. They orient their production to high-paying markets of a few strata of urban dwellers and foreign consumers. Farmers in Sinaloa, Mexico, find they can make 20 times more growing tomatoes for Americans than corn for Mexicans. Development funds have irrigated the desert in Senegal so that multinational firms can grow eggplant and mangoes for air freighting to Europe's best tables. Colombian landholders shift from wheat to carnations that bring 80 times greater return per acre. In Costa Rica the lucrative export beef business expands as the local consumption of meat and dairy products declines. Throughout the nonsocialist countries we find a consistent pattern. Agriculture, once the livelihood for millions of self-provisioning farmers, is being turned into the production site of high-value nonessentials for the minority who can pay.

Moreover, entrusting agricultural production to the large farmers means invariably the loss of productive reinvestment in agriculture. Commonly profits of the large holders that might have gone to improve the land are spent instead on conspicuous consumption, investment in urban consumer industries or job-destroying mechanization. The control of the land by large holders for whom the land is not the basis of daily sustenance often means its underutilization. In Colombia, for example, the largest land owners control 70 percent of all agricultural land but actually cultivate only 6 percent.

It is not enough simply to deflate the myth that justice and production are incompatible. We must come to see clearly that the only solution to hunger is a conscious plan to reduce inequality at every level. The reality is that not only will the redistribution of control of agricultural resources boost production but it is the only guarantee that today's hungry—the rural poor and the urban refugees—will eat.

Myth Three: We are now faced with a sad trade-off. A needed increase in food production can come only at the expense of the ecological integrity of our food base. Farming must be pushed onto marginal lands at the risk of irreparable erosion. And the use of pesticides will have to be increased even if the risk is great.

Is the need for food for a growing population the real pressure forcing people to farm lands that are easily destroyed?

Haiti offers a shocking picture of environmental destruction. The majority of the utterly impoverished peasants ravage the once-green mountain slopes in near-futile efforts to grow food to survive. Has food production for Haitians used up every easily cultivated acre so that only the mountain slopes are left? No. These mountain peasants must be seen as exiles from their birthright—some of the world's richest agricultural land. The rich valley lands belong to a handful of elites, who seek dollars in order to live an imported lifestyle, and to their American partners. These lands are thus made to produce largely low-nutrition and feed crops (sugar, coffee, cocoa, alfalfa for cattle) and exclusively for export. Grazing land is export-oriented, too. Recently U.S. firms began to fly Texas cattle into Haiti for grazing and reexport to American franchised hamburger restaurants.

A World Bank study of Colombia states that "large numbers of farm families try to eke out an existence on too little land, often on slopes of 45 degrees or more. As a result, they exploit the land very severely, adding to erosion and other problems, and even so are not able to make a decent living." Overpopulation? No.

Colombia's good level land is in the hands of absentee landlords who use it to graze cattle, raise animal feed and even flowers for export to the United States ($18 million worth in 1975).

During the Sahelian drought media coverage highlighted over-grazing as a cause of the encroachment of the desert. Too much demand for meat? No. Suppressed FAO reports show that, while more than enough grain for everyone in the Sahel was produced during the drought, much of it was hoarded for speculation. Nomads found that one month they could exchange one head of cattle for four bags of millet while the next month one head was "worth" only a single bag of millet. One reason, therefore, the pastoralists tried to increase their herds was to survive in a food speculation economy. The tragedy was that everyone trying to have a herd large enough to survive resulted in the destruction of the means by which anyone could have any herd at all.

The Amazon is being rapidly deforested. Is it the pressure of Brazil's exploding population? Brazil's ratio of cultivatable land to people (and that excludes the Amazon Forest) is slightly better than that of the United States. The Amazon forest is being destroyed not because of a shortage of farmland but because the military government refuses to break up the large estates that take up over 43 percent of the country's farmland. Instead the landless are offered the promise of future new frontiers in the Amazon basin even though most experts feel the tropic is not suited to permanent cropping. In addition, multinational corporations like Anderson Clayton, Goodyear, Volkswagen, Nestle, Liquigas, Borden, Mitsubishi, and multibillionaire Daniel Ludwig's Universe Tank Ship Co. can get massive government subsidies to turn the Amazon into a major supplier of beef to Europe, the United States and Japan.

It is not, then, people's food needs that threaten to destroy the environment but other forces: land monopolizers who export nonfood and luxury crops, forcing the rural majority to abuse marginal lands; colonial patterns of cash cropping that continue today; hoarding and speculation on food; and irresponsible profit-seeking by both local and foreign elites. Cutting the number of the hungry in half tomorrow would not stop any of these forces.

THE REAL PESTS

Still we found ourselves wondering whether people's legitimate need to grow food might not require injecting even more pesticides into our environment. In the emergency push to grow more food, won't we have to accept some level of damage from deadly chemicals?

First, just how pesticide-dependent is the world's current food production? In the United States about 1.2 billion pounds, a whopping 6 pounds for every American and 30 percent of the world's total, are dumped into the environment every year. Surely, we thought, such a staggering figure means that practically every acre of the nation's farmland is dosed with deadly poisons. United States food abundance, therefore, appeared to us as the plus that comes from such a big minus. The facts, however, proved us wrong.

Fact one: Nearly half the pesticides are used not by farmland but by golf courses, parks, and lawns.

Fact two: Only about 10 percent of the nation's cropland is treated with insecticides, 30 percent with weedkillers, and less than 1 percent with fungicides (the figures are halved if pastureland is included).

Fact three: Nonfood crops account for over half of all insecticides used in U.S. agriculture. (Cotton alone received almost half of all insecticides used. Yet half of the total cotton acreage receives no insecticides at all.)

Fact four: The U.S. Department of Agriculture estimates that, even if all pesticides were eliminated, crop loss due to pests (insects, pathogens, weeds, mammals and birds) would rise only about seven percentage points, from 33.6 percent to 40.7 percent.

Fact five: Numerous studies show that where pesticides are used with every greater intensity crop losses due to pests are frequently *increasing.*

What about underdeveloped countries? Do pesticides there help produce food for hungry people?

In underdeveloped countries most pesticides are used for export crops, principally cotton, and to a lesser extent fruits and vegetables grown under plantation conditions for export. In effect, then, these enclaves of pesticide use in the underdeveloped world function as mere extensions of the agricultural systems of the industrialized countries. The quantities of pesticides injected into the world's environment have very little to do with the hungry's food needs.

The alternatives to chemical pesticides—crop rotation, mixed cropping, mulching, hand weeding, hoeing, collection of pest eggs, manipulation of natural predators, and so on, are numerous and proven effective. In China, for example, pesticide use can be minimized because of a nationwide early warning system. In Shao-tung county in Honan Province, 10,000 youths make up watch teams that patrol the fields and report any sign of pathogenic change. Appropriately called the "barefoot doctors of agriculture," they have succeeded in reducing the damage of wheat rust and rice borer to less than 1 percent and have the locust invasions under control. But none of these safe techniques for pest control will be explored as long as the problem is in the hands of profit-oriented corporations. The alternatives require human involvement and the motivation of farmers who have the security of individual or collective tenure over the land they work.

Myth Four: Hunger is a Contest between the Rich World and the Poor World.

Rather than seeing vertical stratified societies with hunger at the lower rungs in both so-called developed and underdeveloped countries, terms like "hungry world" and "poor world' make us think of uniformly hungry masses. Hunger becomes a place—and usually a place over there. Rather than being the result of a social process, hunger becomes a static fact, a geographic given.

Worse still, the all-inclusiveness of these labels leads us to assume that everyone living in a "hungry country" has a common interest in eliminating hunger. Thus we look at an underdeveloped country and assume its government officials represent the hungry majority. Well-meaning sympathizers in the industrialized countries then believe that concessions to those governments (e.g., preference schemes or increased foreign investment) represent progress for the hungry when in fact the "progress" may be only for the elites and their partners—the multinational corporations.

Moreover, the "rich world" versus "poor world" scenario makes the hungry appear as a threat to the material well-being of the majority in the metropolitan countries. To average Americans or Europeans the hungry become the enemy who, in the words of Lyndon Johnson, "want what we got." In truth, however, hunger will never be addressed until the average citizen in the metropolitan countries can see that the hungry abroad are their allies, not their enemies.

THE GRIP OF AGRIBUSINESS

What are the links between the plight of the average citizen in the metropolitan countries and the poor majority in the underdeveloped countries? There are many. One example is multinational agribusiness shifting production of luxury items—fresh vegetables, fruits, flowers, and meat—out of the industrial countries in search of cheap land and labor in the underdeveloped countries. The result? Farmers and workers in the metropolitan countries lose their jobs while agricultural resources in the underdeveloped countries are increasingly diverted away from food for local people. The food supply of those in the metropolitan countries is being made dependent on the active maintenance of political and economic structures that block hungry people from growing food for themselves.

Nor should we conclude that consumers in the metropolitan countries at least get cheaper food. Are Ralston Purina's and Green Giant's mushrooms grown in Korea and Taiwan cheaper than those produced stateside? Not one cent, according to a U.S. government study. Del Monte and Dole Philippine pineapples actually cost the U.S. consumers more than those produced by a small company in Hawaii.

The common threat is the worldwide tightening control of wealth and power over the most basic human need, food. Multinational agribusiness firms right now are creating a single world agricultural system in which they exercise integrated control over all stages of production from farm to consumer. Once achieved, they will be able to effectively manipulate supply and prices for the first time on a world wide basis through well-established monopoly practices. As farmers, workers and consumers, people everywhere already are beginning to experience the cost in terms of food availability, prices and quality.

Myth Five: An underdeveloped country's best hope for development is to export those crops in which it has a natural advantage and use the earnings to import food and industrial goods.

There is nothing "natural" about the underdeveloped countries' concentration on a few, largely low-nutrition crops. The same land that grows cocoa, coffee, rubber, tea, and sugar could grow an incredible diversity of nutritious crops—grains, high-protein legumes, vegetables, and fruits.

Nor is there any advantage. Reliance on a limited number of crops generates economic as well as political vulnerability. Extreme price fluctuations associated with tropical crops combine with the slow-maturing nature of plants themselves (many, for example, take two to ten years before the first harvest) to make development planning impossible.

Often-quoted illustrations showing how much more coffee or bananas it takes to buy one tractor today than 20 years ago have indeed helped us appreciate that the values of agricultural exports have simply not kept pace with the inflating price of imported manufactured goods. But even if one considers only agricultural trade, the underdeveloped countries still come out the clear losers. Between 1961 and 1972 half of the industrialized countries increased their earnings from agricultural exports by 10 percent each year. By contrast, at least 18 underdeveloped countries are earning *less* from their agricultural exports than they did in 1961.

Another catch in the natural advantage theory is that the people who need food are not the same people who benefit from foreign exchange earned by agricultural exports. Even when part of the foreign earnings is used to import food, the food is not basic staples but items geared toward the eating habits of the better-off urban classes. In Senegal the choice land is used to grow peanuts and vegetables for export to Europe. Much of the foreign exchange earned is spent to import wheat for foreign-owned bakeries that turn out European-style bread for the urban dwellers. The country's rural majority goes hungry, deprived of land they need to grow millet and other traditional grains for themselves and local markets.

The very success of export agriculture can further undermine the position of the poor. When commodity prices go up, small self-provisioning farmers may be pushed off the land by cash crop producers seeking to profit on the higher commodity prices. Moreover, governments in underdeveloped countries, opting for a development track dependent on promoting agricultural exports, may actively suppress social reform. Minimum wage laws for agricultural laborers are not enacted, for example, because they might make the country's exports "uncompetitive." Governments have been only too willing to exempt plantations from land reform in order to encourage their export production.

Finally, export-oriented agricultural operations invariably import capital-intensive technologies to maximize yields as well as to meet product and processing specifications. Relying on imported technologies then makes it likely that the production will be used to pay the bill—a vicious circle of dependency.

LAND FOR FOOD

Just as export-oriented agriculture spells the divorce of agriculture and nutrition, food first policies would make the central question: How can this land best feed people? As obvious as it may seem, this policy of basing land use on nutritional output is practiced in only a few countries today; more commonly, commercial farmers and national planners make hit-and-miss calculations of which crop might have a few cents edge on the world market months or even years hence. With food first policies industrial crops (like cotton and rubber) and feed crops would be planted only after the people meet their basic needs. Livestock would not compete with people but graze on marginal lands or, like China's 240 million pigs, recycle farm and household wastes while producing fertilizer at the same time.

In most underdeveloped countries the rural population contributes much more to the national income than it receives. With food first policies agricultural development would be measured in the welfare of the people, not in export income. Priority would go to decentralized industry at the service of labor-intensive agriculture. A commitment to food self-reliance would close the gap between rural and urban well-being, making the countryside a good place to live. Urban dwellers, too, like those volunteering to grow vegetables in Cuba's urban "green belts," would move toward self-reliance.

Food self-reliance is not isolationist. But trade would be seen, not as the one desperate hinge on which survival hangs, but as a way to widen choices once the basic needs have been met.

Myth Six: Hunger should be overcome by redistributing food.

Over and over again we hear that North America is the world's last remaining breadbasket. Food security is invariably measured in terms of reserves held by the metropolitan countries. We are made to feel the burden of feeding the world is squarely on us. Our over-consumption is tirelessly contrasted with the deprivation elsewhere with the implicit message being that we cause their hunger. No wonder that North Americans and Europeans feel burdened and thus resentful. "What did we do to cause their hunger?" they rightfully ask.

The problem lies in seeing redistribution as the solution to hunger. We have come to a different understanding. Distribution of food is but a reflection of the control of the resources that produce food. Who controls the land determines who can grow food, what is grown, and where it goes. Who can grow: a few or all who need to? What is grown: luxury nonfood or basic staples? Where does it go: to the hungry or to the world's well-fed?

Thus redistribution programs like food aid or food stamps will never solve the problem of hunger. Instead we must face up to the real question: How can people everywhere begin to democratize the control of food resources?

SIX FOOD FIRST PRINCIPLES

We can now counter these six myths with six positive principles that could ground a coherent and vital movement:

1. There is no country in the world in which the people could not feed themselves from their own resources. But hunger can only be overcome by the transformation of social relationships and is only made worse by the narrow focus on technical inputs to increase production.
2. Inequality is the greatest stumbling block to development.
3. Safeguarding the world's agricultural environment and people feeding themselves are complementary goals.
4. Our food security is not threatened by the hungry masses but by elites that span all capitalist economies profiting by the concentration and internationalization of control of food resources.
5. Agriculture must not be used as the means to export income but as the way for people to produce food first for themselves.
6. Escape from hunger comes not through the redistribution of food but through the redistribution of control over food-producing resources.

What would an international campaign look like that took these truths to be self-evident?

If we begin with the knowledge that people can and will feed themselves if allowed to do so, the question for all of us living in the metropolitan countries is not "What can we do for them?" but "How can we remove the obstacles in the way of people taking control of the production process and feeding themselves?"

Since some of the key obstacles are being built with our taxes, in our name, and by corporations based in our economies, our task is very clear:

Stop any economic aid—government, multilateral, or voluntary—that reinforces the use of land for export crops. Stop support for agribusiness penetration into food economies abroad through tax incentives and from governments and multilateral lending agencies. Stop military and counter-insurgency assistance to any underdeveloped country; more often than not it goes to oppose the changes necessary for food self-reliance.

Work to build a more self-reliant food economy at home so that we become even less dependent on importing food from hungry people. Work for land reform at home. Support worker-managed producers and distributors to counter the increasing concentration of control over our food resources.

Educate, showing the connections between the way government and corporate power works against the hungry abroad and the way it works against the food interests of the vast majority of people in the industrial countries.

Counter despair. Publicize the fact that 40 percent of all people living in underdeveloped countries live where hunger has been eliminated through common struggle. Learn and communicate the efforts of newly liberated countries in Africa and Asia to reconstruct their agriculture along the principles of food first self-reliance.

Most fundamentally, we all must recognize that we are not a "hunger" movement. Rather we all can become moulders of the future who have chosen to seize this historical moment. We have chosen to use the visible tragedy of hunger to reveal the utter failure of our current economic system to meet human needs.

13

The Global 2000 Report to the President

MAJOR FINDINGS AND CONCLUSIONS

If present trends continue, the world in 2000 will be more crowded, more polluted, less stable ecologically, and more vulnerable to disruption than the world we live in now. Serious stresses involving population, resources, and environment are clearly visible ahead. Despite greater material output, the world's people will be poorer in many ways than they are today.

For hundreds of millions of the desperately poor, the outlook for food and other necessities of life will be no better. For many it will be worse. Barring revolutionary advances in technology, life for most people on earth will be more precarious in 2000 than it is now—unless the nations of the world act decisively to alter current trends.

This, in essence, is the picture emerging from the U.S. government's projections of probable changes in world population, resources, and environment by the end of the century, as presented in the Global 2000 Study. They do not predict what will occur. Rather, they depict conditions that are likely to develop if there are no changes in public policies, institutions, or rates of technological advance, and if there are no wars or other major disruptions. A keener awareness of the nature of the current trends, however, may induce changes that will alter these trends and the projected outcome.

Principal Findings

Rapid growth in world population will hardly have altered by 2000. The world's population will grow from 4 billion in 1975 to 6.35 billion in 2000, an increase of more than 50 percent. The rate of growth will slow only marginally, from 1.8 percent a year to 1.7 percent. In terms of sheer numbers, population will be growing faster in 2000 than it is today, with 100 million people added each year compared with 75 million in 1975. Ninety percent of this growth will occur in the poorest countries.

While the economies of the less developed countries (LDCs) are expected to grow at faster rates than those of the industrialized nations, the gross national product per capita in most LDCs remains low. The average gross national product per capita is projected to rise substantially in some LDCs (especially in Latin America), but in the great populous nations of South Asia it remains below $200 a year (in 1975 dollars). The large existing gap between the rich and poor nations widens.

World food production is projected to increase 90 percent over the 30 years from 1970 to 2000. This translates into a global per capita increase of less than 15 percent over the same period. The bulk of that increase goes to countries that already have relatively high per capita food consumption. Meanwhile per capita consumption in South Asia, the Middle East, and the LDCs of Africa will scarcely improve or will actually decline below present inadequate levels. At the same time, real prices for food are expected to double.

Arable land will increase only 4 percent by 2000, so that most of the increased output of food will have to come from higher yields. Most of the elements that now contribute to higher yields—fertilizer, pesticides, power for irrigation, and fuel for machinery—depend heavily on oil and gas.

During the 1990s world oil production will approach geological estimates of maximum production capacity, even with rapidly increasing petroleum prices. The study projects that the richer industrialized nations will be able to command enough oil and other commercial energy supplies to meet rising demands through 1990. With the expected price increases, many less developed countries will have increasing difficulties meeting energy needs. For the one-quarter of humankind that depends primarily on wood for fuel, the outlook is bleak. Needs for fuelwood will exceed available supplies by about 25 percent before the turn of the century.

While the world's finite fuel resources—coal, oil, gas, oil shale, tar sands, and uranium—are theoretically sufficient for centuries, they are not evenly distributed; they pose difficult economic and environmental problems; and they vary greatly in their amenability to exploitation and use.

Nonfuel mineral resources generally appear sufficient to meet projected demands through 2000, but further discoveries and investments will be needed to maintain reserves. In addition, production costs will increase with energy prices and may make some nonfuel mineral resources uneconomic. The quarter of the world's population that inhabits industrial countries will continue to absorb three-fourths of the world's mineral production.

Regional water shortages will become more severe. In the 1970 to 2000 period population growth alone will cause requirements for water to double in nearly half the world. Still greater increases would be needed to improve standards of living. In many LDCs, water supplies will become increasingly erratic by 2000 as a result of extensive deforestation. Development of new water supplies will become more costly virtually everywhere.

Significant losses of world forests will continue over the next 20 years as demand for forest products and fuelwood increases. Growing stocks of commercial-size timber are projected to decline 50 percent per capita. The world's forests are now disappearing at the rate of 18 to 20 million hectares a year (an area half the size of California), with most of the loss occurring in the humid tropical forests of Africa, Asia, and South America. The projections indicate that by 2000 some 40 percent of the remaining forest cover in LDCs will be gone.

Serious deterioration of agricultural soils will occur worldwide, due to erosion, loss of organic matter, desertification, salinization, alkalinization, and waterlogging. Already, an area of cropland and grassland approximately the size of Maine is becoming barren wasteland each year, and the spread of desert-like conditions is likely to accelerate.

Atmospheric concentrations of carbon dioxide and ozone-depleting chemicals are expected to increase at rates that could alter the world's climate and upper atmosphere significantly by 2050. Acid rain from increased combustion of fossil fuels (especially coal) threatens damage to lakes, soils, and crops. Radioactive and other hazardous materials present health and safety problems in increasing numbers of countries.

Extinctions of plant and animal species will increase dramatically. Hundreds of thousands of species—perhaps as many as 20 percent of all species on earth—will be irretrievably lost as their habitats vanish, especially in tropical forests.

The future depicted by the U.S. government projections, briefly outlined above, may actually understate the impending problems. The methods available for carrying out the study led to certain gaps and inconsistencies that tend to impart an optimistic bias. For example, most of the individual projections for the various sectors studied—food, minerals, energy, and so on—assume that sufficient capital, energy, water, and land will be available in each of these sectors to meet their needs, regardless of the competing needs of the other sectors. More consistent, better-integrated projections would produce a still more emphatic picture of intensifying stresses, as the world enters the twenty-first century.

Conclusions

At present and projected growth rates, the world's population would reach 10 billion by 2030 and would approach 30 billion by the end of the twenty-first century. These levels correspond closely to estimates by the U.S. National Academy of Sciences of the maximum carrying capacity of the entire earth. Already the populations in sub-Saharan Africa and in the Himalayan hills of Asia have exceeded the carrying capacity of the immediate area, triggering an erosion of the land's capacity to support life. The resulting poverty and ill health have further complicated efforts to reduce fertility. Unless this circle of interlinked problems is broken soon, population growth in such areas will unfortunately be slowed for reasons other than declining birth rates. Hunger and disease will claim more babies and young children, and more of those surviving will be mentally and physically handicapped by childhood malnutrition.

Indeed, the problems of preserving the carrying capacity of the earth and sustaining the possibility of a decent life for the human beings that inhabit it are enormous and close upon us. Yet there is reason for hope. It must be emphasized that the Global 2000 Study's projections are based on the assumption that national policies regarding population stabilization, resource conservation, and environmental protection will remain essentially unchanged through the end of the century. But in fact, policies are beginning to change. In some areas, forests are being replanted after cutting. Some nations are taking steps to reduce soil losses and desertification. Interest in energy conservation is growing, and large sums are being invested in exploring alternatives to petroleum dependence. The need for family planning is slowly becoming better understood. Water supplies are being improved and waste treatment systems built. High-yield seeds are widely available and seed banks are being expanded. Some wildlands with their genetic resources are being protected. Natural predators and selective pesticides are being substituted for persistent and destructive pesticides.

Encouraging as these developments are, they are far from adequate to meet the global challenges projected in this study. Vigorous, determined new initiatives are needed if worsening poverty and human suffering, environmental degradation, and international tension and conflicts are to be prevented. There are no quick fixes. The only solutions to the problems of population, resources, and environment are complex and long-term. These problems are inextricably linked to some of the most perplexing and persistent problems in the world—poverty, injustice, and social conflict. New and imaginative ideas—and a willingness to act on them—are essential.

The needed changes go far beyond the capability and responsibility of this or any other single nation. An era of unprecedented cooperation and commitment is essential. Yet there are opportunities—and a strong rationale—for the United States to provide leadership among nations. A high priority for this nation must be a thorough assessment of its foreign and domestic policies relating to population, resources, and environment. The United States, possessing the world's largest economy, can expect its policies to have a significant influence on global trends. An equally important priority for the United States is to cooperate generously and justly with other nations—particularly in the areas of trade, investment, and assistance—in seeking solutions to the many problems that extend beyond our national boundaries. There are many unfulfilled opportunities to cooperate with other nations in efforts to relieve poverty and hunger, stabilize population, and enhance economic and environmental productivity. Further cooperation among nations is also needed to strengthen international mechanisms for protecting and utilizing the "global commons"—the oceans and atmosphere.

To meet the challenges described in this study, the United States must improve its ability to identify emerging problems and assess alternative responses. In using and evaluating the government's present capability for long-term global analysis, the study found serious inconsistencies in the methods and assumptions employed by the various agencies in making their projections. The study itself made a start toward resolving these inadequacies. It represents the government's first attempt to produce an interrelated set of population, resource, and environmental projections, and it has brought forth the most consistent set of global projections yet achieved by U.S. agencies. Nevertheless, the projections still contain serious gaps and contradictions that must be corrected if the government's analytic capability is to be improved. It must be acknowledged that at present the federal agencies are not always capable of providing projections of the quality needed for long-term policy decisions.

While limited resources may be a contributing factor in some instances, the primary problem is lack of coordination. The U.S. government needs a mechanism for continuous review of the assumptions and methods the federal agencies use in their projection models and for assurance that the agencies' models are sound, consistent, and well documented. The improved analysis that could result would provide not only a clearer sense of emerging problems and opportunities, but also a better means for evaluating alternative responses, and a better basis for decisions of worldwide significance that the President, the Congress, and the federal government as a whole must make.

With its limitations and rough approximations, the Global 2000 Study may be seen as no more than a reconnaissance of the future; nonetheless its conclusions are reinforced by similar findings of other recent global studies that were examined in the course of the Global 2000 Study. All these studies are in general agreement on the nature of the problems and on the threats they pose to the future welfare of humankind. The available evidence leaves no doubt that the world—including this nation—faces enormous, urgent, and complex problems in the decades immediately ahead. Prompt and vigorous changes in public policy around the world are needed to avoid or minimize these problems before they become unmanageable. Long lead times are required for effective action. If decisions are delayed until the problems become worse, options for effective action will be severely reduced.

14
World Population Growth: An Anti-Doomsday View

JULIAN L. SIMON

Every schoolchild seems to "know" that the natural environment is deteriorating and that food is in increasingly short supply. The children's books leave no doubt that population size and growth are the villains. In the *Golden Stamp Book of Earth and Ecology* we read: "If the population continues to explode, many people will starve. About half of the world's population is underfed now, with many approaching starvation. . . . All of the major environmental problems can be traced to people—more specifically, to too many people." But these facts, which are reported to children with so much assurance, are either unproven or wrong.

The demographic facts, to the extent that they are known, are indeed frightening, at first glance. The human population appears to be expanding with self-generated natural force at an exponential rate, restrained only by starvation and disease. It seems that, without some drastic intervention to check this geometric growth, there will soon be "standing room only."

Worry about population growth is not new. Euripides, Polybius, Plato, and Tertullian are on record as citizens who feared that population growth would cause food shortages and environmental degradation. Malthus did "standing room only" arithmetic. In 1802, a Dutch colonial official wrote that Java, which had a population of 4 million, was "overcrowded with unemployed." Now most of Indonesia's 125 million people live in Java, and again the country is said to be overcrowded.

The common view of population growth—especially of population growth in poor countries—is that people breed "naturally." That is, poor people are assumed to have sexual intercourse without concern for the possible consequences. In the words of the environmentalist William Vogt, whose book *Road to Survival* (1948) sold millions of copies, population growth in Asia is the result of "untrammeled copulation" by Moslems, Sikhs, Hindus, and the rest of "the backward billion." A. J. Carlson, a physician, wrote in a 1955 issue of the *Journal of the American Medical Association,* "If we breed like rabbits, in the long run we have to live and die like rabbits." This idea goes hand in hand with the view that population growth will increase geometrically until starvation or disease halts it.

The idea of "natural breeding," "natural fertility," or "untrammeled copulation" has been buttressed by experiments in animal ecology, which some biologists say can serve as models of human population growth. The analogies that have been proposed include John B. Calhoun's famous observations of Norwegian rats in a pen, the putative behavior of flies in a bottle or of germs in a bucket, and the proclivities of meadow mice and cotton rats—creatures that keep multiplying until they die for lack of sustenance. But as Malthus himself acknowledged in the revised edition of his *Essay on Population,* human beings are very different from flies or rats. When faced with a bottle-like situation, people are capable of foresight and may abstain from having children for "fear of misery." That is, people can choose a level of fertility to fit the resources that will be available. Malthus wrote, "Impelled to the increase of his species by an equally powerful instinct, reason interrupts his career, and asks him whether he may not bring beings into the world, for whom he cannot provide the means of support."

Demographic history offers evidence that people can also alter the limit—expand the bottle. That is, they can increase resources when they need to. Population growth seems not to have been at all constant or steady over the long sweep of time. The broadest picture of the past million years shows three momentous and sudden changes, according to the paleoecologist Edward Deevey. The first such change, a rapid increase in population around

1 million B.C., followed the innovations of tool-using and tool-making. Deevery speculates that the aid of various tools "gave the food gatherer and hunter access to the widest range of environments." But when the new power from the use of primitive tools had been exploited, the rate of population growth fell and population size became almost stable.

The next rapid jump in population started perhaps 10,000 years ago, when men began to keep herds and to plow and plant the earth, rather than simply foraging for the plants and game that grew naturally. Once again, the rate of population growth abated after the initial productivity gains from the new technology had been exploited, and again population size became nearly stable in comparison with the rapid growth previously experienced.

These two episodes of a sharp rise and a subsequent fall in the rate of population growth suggest that the present rapid growth—which began in the West between 250 and 350 years ago—may also slow down when, or if, the new industrial and agricultural knowledge that followed the Industrial Revolution begins to yield fewer innovations. Of course, the current knowledge revolution may continue without foreseeable end. Either way, over the long term, population size can be seen to adjust to productive conditions, contrary to the popular belief in constant geometric growth. In this view, population growth represents economic success and human triumph, rather than social failure.

Deevey's account of population history still leaves us with the impression that population growth has an irresistible, self-reinforcing logic of its own. That perspective is so broad, however, that it can be misleading. For example, the demographers Colin Clark and Margaret Haswell have shown in their book *The Economics of Subsistence Agriculture* that even in as large an area as Europe, where local ups and downs might be expected to cancel each other out, population from 14 A.D. to 1800 did not grow at a constant rate, nor did it always grow. Instead, there were advances and reverses, provoked by a variety of forces; famine and epidemic were not the only checks.

Income has a decisive effect on population. Along with a temporary jump in fertility as income rises in poor countries comes a fall in child mortality, because of better nutrition, better sanitation, and better health care (though in the twentieth century mortality has declined in some poor countries without a rise in income). As people see that fewer births are necessary to achieve a given family size, they adjust fertility downward. Increased income also brings education and contraception within reach of more people, makes children more expensive to raise, and perhaps influences the desire to have children. It usually initiates a trend toward city living; in the city, children cost more and produce less income for the family than they do in the country.

The process by which these effects of economic development reduce fertility in the long run is called the "demographic transition." We see clearly in the excellent historical data for Sweden that the deathrate began to fall *before* the birthrate fell. We can see the same relationship between income and birthrate in many other countries. At present, the birthrate is far below replacement—that is, below zero population growth—for a number of the largest countries in Europe. Fertility has been falling in many developing countries as well. For example, the birthrate per thousand people declined in Cuba and Singapore from 1965 to 1975 by 40 percent; in Hong Kong by 36 percent; in South Korea by 32 percent; in Costa Rica by 29 percent; in Taiwan by 20 percent; in China by 24 percent; in India by 16 percent. I think we can be reasonably sure that the European pattern of demographic transition is being repeated now in other parts of the world as mortality falls and income rises.

When looking at the demographic facts with an eye to judging what ought to be done about population, we want to know what the future holds, how great the "pressures" of population size and growth will be. However, the history of demographic predictions gives us reason to be humble about turning forecasts into policy. In the 1930s, most Western countries expected and feared a decline in their populations. The most extensive investigation of the matter was undertaken in Sweden, in 1935, by some of the world's best social scientists. All four of their projections predicted that the number of Swedes would decline by as much as 2 million by 1985. But all of their hypotheses about the future—intended to bracket all of the conceivable possibilities—turned out to be far below the actual course of population, which has instead grown by about 2 million. That is, the future turned out far better, from the point of view of those scientists, than any of them guessed it might. If the Swedes had introduced fertility-increasing programs, as the demographers advised, the results would have been contrary to what they *now* want.

The Swedes were not alone in making inaccurate, pessimistic forecasts. A research committee of eminent scientists appointed by Herbert Hoover in 1933 reported that "we shall probably attain a population between 145 and 150 million during the present century." None of a variety of forecasts made in the 1930s and 1940s by America's greatest demographic experts predicted a population as large as 200 million people even for the year 2000, but the United States reached a population of 200 million sometime around the year 1969, and is far beyond that now. A good many of the forecasters actually predicted a decline in population before the year 2000, which at the present time we know is impossible unless there is a holocaust.

There is no reason to believe that contemporary forecasting methods are better than older ones. We have seen great variety in forecasts of world population through the 1970s. For example, in 1976, "the best demographic estimates" of world population for the year 2000 set it at "nearly 7 billion," according to the executive director of the United States Fund for Population Activities (UNFPA), Raphael Salas. By 1979, Mr. Salas spoke of nearly 6 billion people by 2000. Thus, in three years, Mr. Salas's figures declined by almost a billion people, or nearly one seventh.

In the United States, as recently as 1972, the President's Commission on Population Growth forecast that "even if the family size drops gradually—to the two-child average—there will be no year in the next two decades in which the absolute number of births will be less than in 1970." How did it turn out? In 1971—the year *before* this forecast was transmitted to the President and then published—the absolute number of births (not the birthrate) was already less than in 1970. By 1975, the absolute number of births was barely higher than in 1920, and the number of white births was actually lower than in most years between 1914 and 1924. In this case, the commission did not even backcast correctly, let alone forecast well. Embarrassing mistakes like this ought to make us think twice before we take demographic predictions to heart.

Making forecasts of population size requires making assumptions about people's choices; such assumptions have proven wrong in the past, as we have seen. We can expect that income will continue to rise, but how much of it will people expect a child to cost them? What other activities will compete with child-rearing for parents' interest and time? Such hard-to-predict judgments are likely to be the main determinants of population growth. We can at least say confidently, however, that the growth of population during the past few centuries is no proof that population will continue to grow straight upward toward infinity and doom.

Although no one knows what population size or rate of growth the future holds in store, one often hears that zero population growth, or ZPG, is the only tolerable state. Classical economic theory bolsters this conviction. It purports to show that population growth inevitably reduces the standard of living. The heart of all economic theory of population, from Malthus to *The Limits of Growth,* can be stated in a single sentence: The more people using a stock of resources, the lower the income per person, if all else remains equal. This proposition derives from what economists have called the law of diminishing returns. Two men cannot use the same tool, or farm the same piece of land, without producing less than they would if they did not have to share. A related idea is that two people cannot nourish themselves as well as one person can from a given stock of food. The age distribution that results from a high birthrate reinforces this effect: the number of children in proportion to workers will be larger. Also, the more children women have, the less chance they have to work outside the home, so the work force is diminished further.

According to this reasoning, both sheer numbers of people and the age distribution that occurs in the process of getting to the higher numbers ought to have the effect of a smaller per capita product. But the evidence does not confirm the conventional theory. It suggests that population growth almost certainly does not hinder, and perhaps even helps, economic growth.

One piece of historical evidence is the concurrent explosion of population and economic development in Europe from 1650 onward. Further evidence comes from a comparison of the rates of population growth and output per capita in those developed countries for which data are available for the past century. No strong relationship between the two variables appears. For example, population has grown six times faster in the United States than in France, but the rate of increase in output per capita has been about the same. The populations of Great Britain and Norway grew at the same pace for the past century, but the rate of Norway's output per capita was about a third faster. Australia, on the other hand, had a very fast rate of population growth, but its rate of increase in output per capita was quite slow.

Studies of recent rates of population growth and economic growth are another source of evidence. In less-developed countries, per capita income has been growing as fast as or faster than in the developed countries, according to a World Bank survey for the years 1950 to 1975, despite the fact that population has grown faster in developing countries than in developed countries.

Such evidence does not show that fast population growth in developed countries *increases* per capita income. But it does contradict the belief that population growth inevitably *decreases* economic growth. The lack of a cause-and-effect relationship between population and economic growth has a number of explanations, as follows:

- People make special efforts when they perceive a special need. For example, American fathers work extra, the equivalent of two to five weeks a year, for each additional child. In the long run, this yearly 4 to 10 percent increase in work may fully (or more than fully) balance the temporary loss of labor by the mother. (The other side of this coin is that people may slack off when population growth slows and demand lessens.)
- The larger proportion of young people in the labor force which results from population growth has advantages. Young workers produce more in relation to what they consume than older workers, largely because the older workers receive increases in pay with seniority, regardless of productivity. And because each generation enters the labor force with more education than the previous generation, the average worker becomes more and more knowledgeable.
- Population growth creates business opportunities and facilitates change. It makes expansion investment and new ventures more attractive, by reducing risk and by increasing total demand. For example, if housing is overbuilt or excess capacity is created in an industry, a growing population can take up the slack and remedy the error.
- More job opportunities and more young people working mean that there will be more mobility within the labor force. And mobility greatly enhances the efficient allocation of resources: the best matching of people to jobs.
- Population growth promotes "economies of scale": the greater efficiency of larger-scale production. Through this mechanism, the more people, the larger the market, and therefore the greater the need for bigger and more efficient machinery, division of labor, and improved transportation and communication. Hollis B. Chenery, an economist, compared manufacturing in less-developed countries and found that, all else being equal, if one country is twice as populous as another, output per worker is 20 percent larger. It is an established economic truth that the faster an industry grows, the faster its efficiency improves. One study, which compared the output of selected industries in the United States with the output of those same industries in the United Kingdom and Canada, showed that if you quadruple the size of an industry, you may expect to double the output per worker and per unit of capital employed. This should hold true for the developed world in general.

A larger population also provides economies of scale for many expensive social investments that would not be profitable otherwise—for example, railroads, irrigation systems, and ports. And public services, such as fire protection, can also be provided at lower cost per person when the population is larger.

All of the explanations just summarized have economic force, but the most important benefit that population growth confers on an economy is that people increase the stock of useful knowledge. It is your mind that matters economically, as much as or more than your mouth or hands. In the long run, the contributions people make to knowledge are great enough to overcome all the costs of population growth. This is a strong statement, but the evidence for it seems strong as well.

The importance of technological knowledge has clearly emerged in two famous studies, by Robert Solow in 1957 and by Edward Denison in 1962. Using different methods, both calculated the extent to which the growth of physical capital and of the labor force could account for economic growth in the United States. Denison made the same calculations for Europe. They found that even after capital and labor are allowed for, much of the economic growth cannot be explained by any factor other than improvement in technological practice (including improved organization). Economies of scale as a result of larger factories do not appear to be very important from this point of view, though technology improves more rapidly in large, fast-growing industries than in small, slow-growing ones. This improvement in productivity doesn't come for free; much of it is bought with investments in research and development. But that does not alter its importance.

What is the connection between innovation and population size and growth? Since ideas come from people, it seems reasonable that the number of improvements depends on the number of people using their heads. This is not a new idea. William Petty wrote in 1683 that "it is more likely that one ingenious curious man may rather be found out amongst 4 millions than 400 persons." Hans Bethe, who won the Nobel Prize for physics in 1967, has said that the prospects for nuclear fusion would be rosier if the population of scientists were larger. Bethe said, "Money is not the limiting factor. . . . Progress is limited rather by the availability of highly trained workers."

Even a casual consideration of history shows that as population has grown in the last century, there have been many more discoveries and a faster rate of growth in productivity than in previous centuries. In prehistoric times, progress was agonizingly slow. For example, whereas routinely we develop new materials—say, plastics and metals—millennia passed between the invention of copper metallurgy and of iron metallurgy. If population had been larger, technological discoveries would surely have come along faster. Ancient Greece and Rome have often been suggested as examples contrary to this line of reasoning. Therefore, I plotted the numbers of great discoveries, as recorded by historians of science who have made such lists, against Greek and Roman populations in various centuries. This comparison showed that an increase in population or its rate of growth (or both) was associated with an increase in scientific activity, and population decline with a decrease.

In modern times, there is some fairly strong evidence to confirm the positive effect of population growth on science and technology: in countries at the same level of income, scientific output is proportional to population size. For example, the standard of living in the United States and in Sweden is roughly the same, but the United States is much larger than Sweden and it produces much more scientific knowledge. A consideration of the references used in Swedish and United States scientific papers and of the number of patented processes that Sweden licenses from the United States bears this out.

Why isn't populous India a prosperous and advanced country? I have not argued that a large population will by itself overcome all the other variables in a society—its climate, culture, history, political structure. I have said only that there is no evidence to prove that a large population *creates* poverty and underdevelopment. India is poor and underdeveloped for many reasons, and it might be even more so if it had a smaller population. The proper comparison is not India and the United States but India and other poor countries, and the fact is that India has one of the largest scientific establishments in the Third World—perhaps in part because of its large population.

It cannot be emphasized too strongly that "technological and scientific advance" does not mean only sophisticated research, and geniuses are not the only source of knowledge. Much technological advance comes from people who are neither well-educated nor well-paid: the dispatcher who develops a slightly better way of deploying the taxis in his ten-taxi fleet, the shipper who discovers that garbage cans make excellent cheap containers, the supermarket manager who finds a way to display more merchandise in a given space, the clerk who finds a quicker way to stamp prices on cans, and so on.

Population growth spurs the adoption of existing technology as well as the invention of new technology. This has been well documented in agriculture, where people turn to successively more "advanced" but more laborious methods of getting good as population density increases—methods that may have been known but were ignored because they weren't needed. For example, hunting and gathering—which require very few hours of work a week to provide a full diet—give way to migratory slash-and-burn agriculture, and that yields to settled, long-fallow agriculture, and that to short-fallow agriculture. Eventually fertilizer, irrigation, and multiple cropping are adopted. Though each stage initially requires more labor than the one before, the end point is a more efficient and productive system.

This phenomenon also explains why the advance of civilization is not a race between technology and population, each progressing independently of the other. Contrary to the Malthusian view, there is no direct link between each food-increasing invention and increased production of food. Some inventions, such as a better calendar for planting, may be adopted as soon as they prove successful, because they will increase production with no more labor. Others, such as settled agriculture or irrigated multicropping, require more labor, and thus will not be adopted until there is demand.

The fact that people learn by doing is a key to the improvement of productivity in particular industries, and in the economies of nations. The idea is simple: the bigger the population, the more of everything that is produced. With a greater volume come more chances for people to improve their skills and to devise better methods. Industrial engineers have understood this process for many decades, but economists first grasped its importance when they examined the production of airplanes during World War II. They discovered that when twice as many airplanes are produced, the labor required per plane is reduced by 20 percent. That is, if the first airplane requires 1,000 units of labor, the second will require 800 units, and so on, though after some time the gains from increased efficiency level off. Similar "progress ratios" describe the production of lathes, machine tools, textile machines, and ships. The effect of learning by doing can also be seen in the progressive reduction in price of new consumer devices in the years following their introduction to the market—room air-conditioners and color television sets, for example.

In the short run, all resources are limited: the pulp-wood that went into making this book, the pages the book will allow me, and the attention the reader will devote to what I say. The longer run, however, is a different story. The standard of living has risen along with the size of the world's population since the beginning of recorded time. There is no convincing economic reason why these trends toward a better life should not continue indefinitely. Adding more people causes problems, but people are also the means to solve these problems. The main fuel to speed the world's progress is our stock of knowledge, and the brake is our lack of imagination. The ultimate resource is people—skilled, spirited, and hopeful people—who will exert their wills and imaginations for their own benefit, and so, inevitably, for the benefit of us all.

PART III

MORTALITY

The historical transition from high to low mortality, and the extraordinary circumstances of high mortality that result in depopulation, are discussed in Part I. Here in Part III we examine contemporary patterns and causes of death.

CAUSES OF DEATH

When we hear of someone dying at a young age we may call that person unlucky, and if we learn of someone who has lived for a very long time we may say that person is lucky. As Eckholm (1977) suggests in a discussion of health, illness, and death in the less developed and more developed countries (LDCs and MDCs), death has very little to do with luck. On the Titanic, first class passengers had greatest access to the lifeboats; on spaceship earth, the same seems to be the case (Antonovsky and Berstein, 1977; Eckholm, 1979; Newland, 1981).

Although the predisposition to good health or certain illnesses plays some part, the major determinant of how and when you will die is your place in the global social structure: the circumstances of your birth and childhood, your gender, the places where you have lived, your social status (age, race, income, education, occupation, marital status) as an adult, and within the contest of these opportunities, constraints, and influences, the choices you make about your own life-style.

An interesting way to think about death is as an avoidable and unavoidable event. With the passing of time, many of the major causes of death that were once considered unavoidable—infectious diseases, parasites, infections, famine—are today easily and inexpensively avoidable, and yet they are still the causes of illness and death for most of the people of the world (Chandler, 1984; Omran, 1977). In the MDCs, where the majority of the population need not worry about these problems, it has been thought that death was primarily caused by "degenerative diseases" and other unavoidable conditions either associated with aging or genetic in origin. Now, however, we are learning that most of the major causes of "premature" death, or death before reaching the known maximum human lifespan, are avoidable (Prescott and Flexer, 1982; Chandler, 1984; Bourgeois-Pichat, 1983). As we have become more "civilized," we also seem to have become more suicidal, as individuals and as a society.

From studies of leading causes of death we can discern four major categories of currently avoidable contributors to serious illness and death:

1. Environmental. This includes the use of some herbicides and pesticides; disposal of toxic wastes in land, air, and water; inadequate protection from hazardous substances, conditions, and machinery in the workplace; and toxic building materials.

2. Harmful products and services. This includes some chemical additives in foods, beverages, and cosmetics; some prescription and nonprescription drugs; and certain health care and contraceptive practices.
3. Voluntary high-risk choices. This includes inadequate exercise or rest; excessive stress or risk taking; unhealthy diet (high in saturated fat, sugar, or calories and low in fiber or nutrients); high alcohol consumption; and especially cigarette smoking.
4. Involuntary high-risk choices. This includes inadequacy or unaffordability of preventive or curative health care; unaffordability of adequate nutrition; impure drinking water; inadequate drainage or sewage systems; excessive exposure to the elements due to inadequate shelter, fuel, or clothing; overwork or excessive stress; and inadequate education, which perpetuates ignorance concerning practices that can increase—or decrease—one's chances of survival.

In the more developed countries, the two leading causes of death are cancer and cardiovascular diseases (United Nations and World Health Organization, 1982). As seen in Table III.1, in 1980, they accounted for about 70 percent of the deaths in the United States. Researchers estimate that about 90 percent of these cases are preventable; that is, they are related to the four types of causes listed above, especially the first three (Prescott et al., 1982). Five of the remaining top ten causes of death in the United States (accidents, chronic obstructive pulmonary diseases, pneumonia and influenza, chronic liver diseases and cirrhosis, and suicide) are also substantially related to these four factors. Diabetes mellitus, conditions originating in the perinatal period, and perhaps homicide/legal intervention are largely unavoidable by the victims. We see, then, that in the MDCs, chronic illness, prolonged suffering, premature death, and large expenditures on health care are often a matter of personal (though sometimes uninformed and highly pressured) choice and, arguably, personal and collective social irresponsibility. In the LDCs, by contrast, much of the death that occurs can be attributed to category four—death because of poverty and inequality. Here too, however, the effects of categories one to three, especially environmental factors and smoking, are becoming more important. A recent example is the 1984 disaster in Bhopal, India, where thousands were killed and many thousands more injured by a leak from a Union Carbide chemical factory. According to one report, "A silent killer left a nation in agony. It also served notice of the hazards brought by industrial growth" (Lang and Mukherjee, 1984:25). Even more recently, a fire at the Chernobyl nuclear power facility in the Soviet Union released radio-

Table III.1. Leading Causes of Death in the United States, 1980

Rank	Cause	Percent of Deaths	
1	Major cardiovascular disease	49.6	}70.5
2	Malignancy	20.9	
3	Accidents and adverse effects	5.3	
4	Chronic obstructive and pulmonary disease	2.8	
5	Pneumonia and influenza	2.7	
6	Diabetes mellitus	1.7	
7	Chronic liver disease and cirrhosis	1.5	
8	Suicide	1.3	
9	Homicide and legal intervention	1.2	
10	Conditions originating in the perinatal period	1.1	

Source: U.S. Department of Commerce, *Statistical Abstracts of the U.S., 1984*, table 109.

active material into the atmosphere. Several people were killed immediately following the accident, and the long-term impact on health has yet to be determined.

In a sense, Eckholm suggests in *The Picture of Health* (from which Chapter 15 is an excerpt) that the more developed countries may be exporting mortality. As smoking in MDCs declines, the MDC cigarette manufacturers have been heavily promoting cigarettes in LDCs (many of which have their own tobacco industries). Moreover, as MDCs have strengthened pollution laws and banned some of the most harmful pesticides, herbicides, drugs, and chemical additives, highly polluting factories have been moving to the LDCs, and banned harmful substances are being sent there. Some of these return to us via imported food, coffee, and tea (Weir and Shapiro, 1982).

MORTALITY DIFFERENTIALS

From the foregoing discussion, it is not difficult to understand that we may expect major differences in mortality by age, occupation, income, location, and socioeconomic system. Yet there is one marked differential—gender—which is not readily understood. At birth, the *sex ratio* is about 104, that is, there are about 104 males per 100 females. Today in the United States this gap is closed by age 20, and by old age females considerably outnumber males. In fact, the sex ratio for those aged 65 and over has declined from 102 in 1900 to 68 in 1980. The exception to this general pattern of lower age-specific death rates for females is that females may have higher ASDRs during the childbearing years in areas with high mortality and high fertility rates, and a lifelong disadvantage in societies that heavily discriminate against females (Morgan, 1984; Preston, 1982). India is perhaps the leading example of such a society (Miller, 1981).

The female advantage has been attributed to sex role socialization, where men are taught to take more risks (drinking, smoking, driving fast), to hide weakness (for example, by not admitting being sick or by trying to ignore the illness), and to involve themselves in fast-paced, highly stressful occupations. As a result, although women are "sick" more often than men (i.e., they are more likely to seek health care), they are less likely to be involved in serious accidents or to develop chronic and terminal illnesses (Verbrugge, 1976; Nathanson, 1977). However, cigarette smoking appears to be the primary cause of adult male–female mortality differentials (Retherford, 1975; American Association for the Advancement of Science, 1983). Statistics from the American Cancer Society show that as smoking has increased among women, so has lung cancer, so that in 1984 it reached 18 percent, the same proportion of cancer deaths in women as breast cancer. Lung cancer accounted for 35 percent of cancer deaths among U.S. males (New Directions for Women, 1985). However females may still have a biological advantage. Women who have chronic, life-threatening diseases are less likely to die than men with comparable diseases (Verbrugge, 1976). Also, in most nations with high infant mortality rates—even where there is a preference for male children—infant mortality is lower for females than for males (Morgan, 1984).

In Chapter 16, Gove explains not only the male–female mortality differential but also the married–unmarried differential among males and females, and obtains some surprising results. It appears that marriage is "healthier" for males, because married males are less likely to engage in voluntary, health-threatening behavior. The same advantage is not found for females. It may be that in marriage, sex role socialization works against women by creating an unequal partnership in which the wife does most of the child care, housework, and emotional support, often in addition to employment outside the home. Although this article was first published in 1973, it still stands out for its thoroughness in dealing with alternative hypotheses that attempt to explain the difference between male and female mortality. While the results reported in Chapter 16 do not completely resolve the issue of whether the male–female differential is biological or social in nature, they do make it clear that death is not just a matter of biology.

MEASURES OF MORTALITY AND SOCIAL INDICATORS

The most commonly used measure of mortality is the crude death rate (CDR), the number of deaths in a year per 1,000 members of the midyear population (which is assumed to reflect the average population size for the year), or

$$\text{CDR} = 1{,}000 \times \text{deaths/midyear population}$$

Since the crude death rate is strongly influenced by the age distribution of a population (the proportion of older or younger people in the population), a more accurate measure of the risk of dying is the age-specific death rate (ASDR), the number of deaths among those of a specific age or age range. The infant mortality rate (IMR) is a special age-specific death rate, which strongly reflects socioeconomic conditions such as sanitation, nutrition, and quality of medical care. The IMR is the number of deaths among those between birth and one year old, per 1,000 births for the year under consideration, or

$$\text{IMR} = 1{,}000 \times \text{deaths to infants (age 0 to 1)/total births for a given year}$$

Life expectancy at birth is sort of a summary of ASDRs; it tells how long a person would live if (1) that person were born this year, and if (2) the current ASDRs remained the same throughout that person's life. As seen in the top part of Table III.2, the risk of dying is, on the average, much higher in LDCs than in MDCs. In East Timor, at one extreme, where the IMR is 211, a newborn is over 30 times as likely to die before its

Table III.2. Death Rates for MDCs and LDCs circa 1984

Location	CDR (per 1000)	IMR (per 1000 born)	Life Expectancy at Birth (years)	GNP per Capita (dollars)	Percent Under 15/ Over 64
MDCs	9	19	73	9190	23/12
LDCs	11	94	58	750	38/4
Sri Lanka	6	38	66	320	35/4
Saudi Arabia	12	110	55	16000	32/2
China	8	35	65	310	34/5
India	14	125	50	260	39/3
United States	9	11	74	13160	22/12
Italy	11	13	73	6840	20/14

first birthday than in Finland, where the IMR is 6.5 (Population Reference Bureau, 1984a).

Death rates or life expectancy are frequently used as "social indicators," indicators of the quality of health care, nutrition, or general level of well-being in a nation. Table III.2 shows that such interpretations of demographic data must be made with great care. Although infant mortality is lower and life expectancy is higher in MDCs than in LDCs, the crude death rates are almost the same. This apparent inconsistency can be explained by differences in the age distribution of the population and the very consistent relationship between age and the risk of dying. In LDCs the risk of dying at any age is higher than in the MDCs; however the pattern of age-specific death rates is very similar. In most nations the risk of dying is moderate to high from birth to age one or two, then it drops quite low before rising sharply again around age 60 in the MDCs and somewhat earlier in the LDCs. Thus the LDCs with an average of 12 percent of their population over age 64 have a much larger proportion of their population at the greatest risk of dying than the LDCs, with only 4 percent of their population over age 64. If the LDCs had the same age distribution as the MDCs, the CDR of the LDCs would be much higher. When comparing the relative risk of dying or level of well-being among nations with different age distributions, therefore, it is better to use age-specific death rates such as IMR or life expectancy than crude death rates.

Contrary to what we might expect, differences in the economic status of nations (as indicated by GNP per capita) are not always good predictors of differences in the risk of dying. In Table III.2, two small and two very large Asian countries and two MDCs with a wide spread in GNP per capita are compared. Here, incongruencies in the CDR cannot be accounted for by differences in age distribution. Saudi Arabia and India, with the youngest populations, have the highest CDRs. They also have the highest infant mortality and the lowest life expectancy. India is the poorest of these nations with a GNP per capita of $260, but Saudi Arabia is the richest with a GNP per capita of $16,000. Comparison of India and China, both large countries with low GNP and similar age distributions, reveals that a baby born in India has almost four times the risk of a baby born in China of dying before its first birthday. The differences between the two smaller Asian nations, one very rich and one very poor, are equally striking. Like China, residents of economically poor Sri Lanka have a very low risk of death, while those of wealthy Saudi Arabia, like India, have a very high chance of death. In a similar comparison, Italy, with half the GNP per capita of the United States, has similar levels of mortality. For less developed countries generally, the correlation between infant mortality and per capita GNP ranges from −0.27 (using data from Mauldin and Berelson, 1978) to −0.55 (using data from Tsui and Bogue, 1978, for slightly different years). These correlations are lower than those for education or literacy, for example, which range from −0.77 to −0.83 for the same data, again suggesting that aspects of social development other than general economic prosperity may be more important in reducing mortality. (Reliable correlations between mortality and income inequality are not available at the cross-national level; see Menard, 1986.) Chandler (1985b) argues that education, particularly female education and education which includes instruction on nutrition, may be crucial elements in decreasing infant mortality in less developed countries.

These data suggest that a nation's economic status alone does not have as much to do with the well-being or life chances of its citizens as does public and private policy regarding public health and the distribution of a nation's wealth, employment opportunities, land, and basic necessities such as safe water, sanitary facilities, food, shelter, education, and medical care. These are much more important than GNP per capita alone. Sri Lanka and China have emphasized efforts to distribute the opportunity to lead a healthy life more than have India and Saudi Arabia. The United States-Italy comparison may in part result from the fact that the United States is the only MDC without some form of universal national health insurance; as a result, low-income people in the United States may both live in an unhealthy environment and be unable to afford adequate health care. In addition, the infant mortality rate for American blacks, the largest of the U.S. minorities, has consistently been twice that of whites (see Chapter 17). A high per capita GNP does not guarantee a healthy or long life unless a conscious effort is made so that all citizens benefit.

INFANT MORTALITY RATES

Chapters 17 and 18 include consideration of infant mortality differentials, but they also illustrate problems and issues common to all demographic data. (A thorough discussion of infant mortality is found in Newland, 1981.) The quality of data is highly uneven, definitions are not consistent, and counting may be incomplete (people and events are not represented). In the many LDCs which have not had a recent census or which do not have reliable registration systems for births and deaths, birth and death rates may be little more than crude estimates (United Nations and World Health Organization, 1982). In addition, as noted above, demographic data, even that of known low quality, may be used as social indicators to draw conclusions about a society far beyond that which is warranted.

Chapter 17 is concerned with the measurement of IMR and the reasons for the relatively high IMR in the United States. Hartford discusses changes in the way in which infant mortality statistics are tabulated and factors which may affect infant mortality rates independent of the quality of health care. Chapter 18 is concerned with a recent rise reported in the mortality rates of the Soviet Union. A report in from the U.S. Census Bureau (Davis and Feshbach, 1980) on recent apparent increases in Soviet infant mortality rates became the center of a sharp, political debate, with some concluding that there is a health crisis in the Soviet Union and others declaring that the interpretation of the data was politically biased (Eberstadt, 1981 and 1984; Kutzik, 1981; Szymanski, 1982; Jones and Grupp, 1983 and 1984; Feshbach, 1984). Chapter 18, written by S. Maksudov, is one of the most balanced and thorough discussions of the issue. Maksudov points out that there were many factors contributing to the increased reported infant and adult mortality—social, biological, and methodological. Maksudov suggests that the real surprise should not be that the mortality in the Soviet Union is so high, but rather that it is so low in what is essentially a poor developing nation. He also points out that the gap between the Soviet Union and the United States is comparable to that between the United States and Sweden.

The Soviet Union is not alone in controversy over changes in infant mortality rates. Miller (1985) suggests that infant mortality rates in the United States may have been adversely affected by cutbacks in federal programs for mothers and children. Miller's analysis of U.S. infant mortality is strikingly similar to that of Soviet mortality by authors who suggest a health crisis in that country. There is, however, a major difference between the Soviet and American cases. In the Soviet Union, for reasons suggested by Maksudov in Chapter 18, mortality statistics indicate an increase in actual rates of mortality. In the United States, as described by Miller, the *rate of decline* in infant mortality has slowed down (that is, we are not making as much progress as before in reducing infant mortality), but infant mortality has not actually increased. Perhaps the overall lesson to be learned from Chapters 17 and 18 (and from related material published elsewhere) is the willingness of some authors to use mortality statistics to make political points, and the danger of accepting uncritically the data upon which such political statements are based. It may be that government policies in both the United States and the Soviet Union have led to higher than necessary levels of mortality (and data on countries with lower infant mortality rates, as presented by Hartford in Chapter 17 certainly support this view), but short-term changes in the data may reflect a number of influences (most notably, completeness of registration) besides government policy.

FOR FURTHER READING

1. William H. McNeill. 1976. *Plagues and Peoples* (New York: Anchor/Doubleday). Interesting and extremely well-written history of epidemic disease. McNeill (excerpted in the first part of this reader) argues that disease may have had enormous political and social consequences in the past.
2. William U. Chandler. 1985. "Investing in Children," Worldwatch Paper number 64 (Washington, DC: Worldwatch Institute). Brief overview of mortality and its causes in the present-day less developed countries.
3. Christopher Davis and Murray Feshbach. 1980. Rising Infant Mortality in the U.S.S.R. in the 1970s. Series P-95, Number 74. (Washington, DC: U.S. Bureau of the Census). For the more advanced student, this is worth reading both to know what all the fuss is about (see the reading by S. Maksudov) and as a study in the analysis of mortality from limited data.
4. United Nations and World Health Organization. 1980. *Levels and Trends in Mortality since 1950* (New York: United Nations). Review of the quality of data and analysis of causes of death, mortality differentials, and historical trends in mortality for the nations of the world. Very dry, but very informative.

15
Ways of Life, Ways of Death

ERIK P. ECKHOLM

The day before her forty-fifth birthday, a New Jersey woman learns that she is dying. The lining of her chest cavity has been invaded by cancer. Her doctor is puzzled: he has seen this rare malignancy only in asbestos workers, and this patient is a lawyer. But as he sifts through the records of her past, the origins of her tragedy became clear. The patient's father had spent 1947 working in an asbestos-insulation factory. His clothes and hair had been covered with whitish fibers when he came home from work each evening, and his daughter had frequently laundered his work clothes. The father, like tens of thousands of former asbestos workers around the world, died of cancer two decades after his stint in the factory. Now, still another decade later, the daughter discovers that her own fate was sealed thirty years ago.

The parents of a three-year-old Ecuadorian girl watch helplessly as chronic diarrhea takes her life. They are unaware that in lands where everyone has access to clean water and where children are well nourished, diarrhea seldom takes lives. Nor do they know that their daughter is but one of thirty-five thousand small children who die every day, in many cases because undernutrition has sapped the victims' ability to survive simple infectious diseases. As the parents compare the straggly crops on their eroded patch of hillside with the lush hacienda fields below, they do realize that, unlike the family of the hacienda owner, their remaining five children will be kept from sleep by hunger.

Widowed at age forty-two by her husband's heart attack, an Englishwoman doubles her devotion to her eighteen-year-old son. More than devotion will be necessary, however, if a similar catastrophe is not to strike the son when he reaches middle age; the family's rich diet is promoting deadly arterial degeneration. The son, who smokes as much as his father did, has a vague fear of developing lung cancer in old age. He does not suspect that cigarettes, like fatty foods, contributed to his father's sudden demise—and are helping to lay the groundwork for his own heart attack. Both mother and son would be surprised to learn that one in three of their acquaintances—indeed, one in three people in North America and Europe—will succumb to heart disease.

Alongside the River Nile, a *fellah,* or peasant farmer, plants his second cotton crop of the year. His government has dammed the river upstream and now the irrigation canals carry water year-round. As he stoops to pull a weed, he is wrenched by pains in his lower abdomen and he feels unusually tired; once again he will be unable to finish his day's work. As he relieves himself on the canal bank, he unwittingly returns to the water thousands of parasite eggs in his urine, which has turned blood-red. The fellah's plight is not his alone. While year-round irrigation has boosted incomes in his village, half the villagers now complain of internal pains and fatigue. Three have died of inexplicable causes. Like 200 million others who live near slow-moving tropical waters and lack safe sewage facilities, he is infected with schistosomiasis.

Individuals who enjoy good health rightly think of themselves as fortunate. But luck has little to do with the broad patterns of disease and mortality that prevail in each society. The striking variations in health conditions among countries and cultural groups reflect differences in social and physical environments. And increasingly, the forces that shape health patterns are set in motion by human activities and decisions. Indeed, in creating its way of life, each society creates its way of death.

The "environment" that influences health involves much more than the esthetic state of our natural surroundings with which many associate the terms. Social and economic policies that leave people too poor to purchase adequate diets, without access to safe water, or ignorant of the rudiments of sanitation all affect health. So do production processes and political decisions that permit the pollution of workplaces or neighborhoods with dangerous substances. Individuals' eating, drinking, smoking, and exercise habits form the roots of many major diseases; and these habits are in turn influenced by cultural traditions, economic institutions, and governmental policies.

Given particular environmental conditions, health patterns within societies can thus be predicted. Where undernutrition and filth reign, infectious diseases and childhood deaths are commonplace. Overeating, sedentary living, and smoking take their toll among the middle-aged in the forms of cardiovascular diseases and cancer. Where industry is not closely regulated, workers in mines, factories, and fields often pay, through job-induced disease and death, an extraordinary price that never figures into production costs.

The ideal of a disease-free existence for all may never be realized. Humans are evolving, disease agents are evolving, and the biological, geological, and chemical features of the environment are changing faster than ever as humans lend an unskilled hand. Still, by making effective use of what we know about the sources of ill health, we could vastly reduce unnecessary suffering and the frequency of premature deaths.

Major improvements in health will not be achieved, however, by pouring more and more funds into costly curative measures. Changes in the social structures and personal behavior patterns that promote diseases will do far more than doctors and drugs can to minimize the burden of disease and the tragedy of early death. Better health may require, for instance, land reforms in El Salvador, the control of air pollution in Japan, and well-digging programs in rural India; dietary changes in the United States, a cut in cigarette smoking in Scotland, and the control of cotton dusts in an Egyptian textile factory.

Identifying environmental threats to health is, of course, far easier than overcoming them. Unlike advanced medical technologies, the social changes essential to better health cannot usually be purchased, lent, or donated. An inquiry into environmental influences on health involves delving into economics, politics, personal lifestyles, and humans' relationships with their natural surroundings. The picture of health is, ultimately, a reflected image of society.

16
Sex, Marital Status, and Mortality

WALTER R. GOVE

In the final analysis, mortality is due to a physical phenomenon. However, social processes play a role in the etiology of many disorders that lead to death and frequently determine how promptly and persistently one seeks treatment. And, of course, with some types of mortality, such as suicide, the role of social factors is obvious. This chapter will explore the possibility that the psychological states and life-styles associated with the different marital roles in our society affect life chances with regard to selected types of mortality.

The data on psychological well-being (Gurin, Veroff, and Feld, 1960; Bradburn and Caplovitz, 1965; Bradburn, 1969) uniformly indicate that the married, at least with regard to psychological variables, are better situated than the unmarried. As Gurin et al. (1960:232) state, "The most striking finding is that married respondents report feeling happier than those that are unmarried, and the difference is a sharp one for both men and women." The studies of mental illness likewise almost invariably show that the unmarried, whether single, widowed, or divorced, have higher rates of mental illness than the married (e.g., Gove 1972a). Probably, as Gurin et al. (1960:230–231) indicate, the key difference between the roles of the married and the unmarried (whether single, widowed, or divorced) is that the unmarried live a relatively isolated existence which lacks the close interpersonal ties that the data suggest are a key factor in maintaining a sense of well-being.

Another very consistent finding, at least in recent years, is that married women are more likely to be emotionally disturbed than are married men. In a recent paper (Gove, 1972a) I show that every study in Western industrial countries conducted after World War II has found that married women have higher rates of mental illness than married men. These results are supported by the studies on psychological well-being (Gurin et al., 1960; Bradburn and Caplovitz; 1965; Bradburn, 1969) which indicate that married women, compared with married men, find their roles constricted and frustrating. For example, Gurin et al. (1960) found that women are less happy in their marriages and report more marital problems than men. Furthermore, they found that women are more negative about parenthood than men, reporting less satisfaction with being a parent and more problems of adjustment.

The situation is quite different when we compare single men and women, for in this category it is the women who appear to be better situated. The pioneering study by Gurin et al. (1960:233) found that "single women apparently experience less discomfort than do single men; they report greater happiness, are more active in their working through of the problems they face, and appear in most ways stronger in meeting the challenges of their positions than men." This finding is supported by the subsequent work on psychological well-being (Bradburn and Caplovitz, 1965; Bradburn, 1969), and a large majority of the studies of mental illness indicate that single men have higher rates of mental illness than single women (Gove, 1972a). Probably a major difference between single men and women is that single women are apt to have stronger ties to family and friends (e.g., Gurin et al., 1960:232–235).

There is much less data on the other unmarried statuses. However, Gurin et al. (1960:236–238) did find that widowers are more poorly situated than widows, a finding substantiated by the fact that most of the studies on mental illness which provide a sex breakdown of widowed persons find that widowed men have higher rates than widowed women (Gove, 1972a). Comparing the divorced on mental illness produces similar results, that is, the substantial majority of the studies indicate that divorced men have higher rates of mental illness than divorced women. However, the pattern for the divorced is not as clear as for the widowed, since the limited data on the psychological well-being of the divorced (Gurin et al., 1960:235–236) are not consistent with the data on mental illness.

To summarize, the data on psychological well-being and mental illness suggest that the married are in a more advantageous position than the never married, the widowed, and the divorced. There are, however, important sex differences. Being married appears to be more advantageous to males than females, while being single, widowed, and probably divorced is more disadvantageous to males. These results allow us to construct some testable hypotheses regarding the relationship between marital status and mortality—if we assume that one's emotional state affects one's life chances with regard to at least certain types of mortality. First, if being married is more advantageous than not being married, the coefficient formed by the ratios (single mortality rate)/(married mortality rate), (widowed mortality rate)/(married mortality rate), and (divorced mortality rate)/(married mortality rate) should be larger than one. Second, if the analysis of the sex differences is correct, then the coefficients for men should be consistently larger than the coefficients for women.[1]

This chapter focuses on the size of these coefficients across selected types of mortality, paying particular attention to variations between the sexes.[2] It should be noted at this point that Durkheim (1951) used this same coefficient in his classic work on suicide, referring to it as the coefficient of preservation. Implicit in this term, and explicit in his analysis is the assumption that marriage, through its strong social ties, provides a person with a sense of meaning and importance, thereby serving to inhibit the destructive impulses associated with suicide. Durkheim is able to support this assertion with empirical evidence. First, he demonstrates that the large value of the coefficient of preservation is not primarily due to the selective processes associated with marriage, that is, it is not primarily due to stable persons being more likely to marry than unstable persons (Durkheim, 1951:182–193). Durkheim (1951:185–202) then demonstrates that the size of the coefficient of preservation varies directly with the presence of children.[3] Finally, he finds that as one moves from country to country, the sex that has the higher coefficient of preservation appears to be a response to the nature of marital roles in a society and the sex that is favored will vary from society to society. In a recent paper (Gove, 1972b) I looked at three forms of suicidal behavior (threats, attempts, and completions) and showed that for such behaviors men tend to have larger coefficients of preservation in both the United States and Western Europe.

For the analysis of the relationship between sex, marital status, and mortality, I will rely primarily on a recent publication of the National Center for Health Statistics (1970) that provides age-specific mortality rates for selected causes by race, sex, and marital status for the years of 1959 to 1961. Because the death rates of whites and nonwhites are quite different and because much less is known about the nature of the marital roles of nonwhites, I will deal only with the mortality of whites. Furthermore, for a number of reasons, I will be primarily concerned with the ages 25 through 64. First, this is the age span with which the role explanation is most concerned, for it is during this time of the life cycle that people are involved in their full range of adult roles. Second, before the age of 25, mortality rates from many causes tend to be unreliable simply because there are very few cases of mortality. The lack of reliability is particularly a problem in the widowed and divorced categories. Third, before this age the patterns of mortality are more complex and less easily interpreted,[4] perhaps because many persons are not yet established in their adult roles. Therefore, for reasons of accuracy, space, and coherence I will not, in this chapter, deal with mortality for persons under the age of 25. By the age of 65 the role configuration of most people has shrunk, and we might expect the differences in mortality between the married and the unmarried to have also diminished. Furthermore, the older age groups have high rates of mortality, which, to some extent may override and thus mask the influence of social factors. For these reasons the differences between the marital groups in the older categories are perhaps less relevant to my role analysis. However, given their high mortality, their rates should be reliable, so the relevant coefficient will be presented.

One last note before turning to the data. With the exception of work on suicide (e.g., Durkheim, 1951; Gove, 1972b), I have been unable to locate any studies in the sociological literature dealing with how the mortality of men and women differs between the various marital states. There are, however, a few studies in the medical literature (e.g., Shurtleff, 1956; Kraus and Lilienfeld, 1959) and the public health literature (e.g., Berkson, 1962; Sheps, 1961; Carter and Glick, 1970) that do make such a comparison. With the exception of Carter and Glick (1970), who use 1959 to 1961 data, all of these studies use 1949 to 1951 data. Although some of the studies are very concerned with establishing the validity of the statistics, they present little in the way of either a medical or sociological framework for interpreting their data. I would note that data for the two time periods 1949 to 1951 and 1959 to 1961 are in general similar.

MORTALITY DUE TO OVERT SOCIAL ACTS

In this section I will look at the relationship between sex and marital status, and mortality due to suicide, homicide, and various types of accidents. In all instances I assume that there will be an inverse relationship between close, meaningful social ties and mortality. Following the research on psychological well-being and mental illness, I presume that such ties are more characteristic of the married than the unmarried and that the differences between the married and unmarried statuses are greater for men than for women.

The assumption that suicide is inversely related to close interpersonal ties is, of course, a standard one in the sociological literature. Regarding accidental death, I postulate that a lack of close interpersonal ties frequently results in carelessness and even recklessness which may lead to death.[5] In the case of homicide I assume that in many instances persons who are murdered have to some degree precipitated the act by their behavior and that this behavior frequently reflects frustration and dissatisfaction with life. Just as with accidental death, it is probably also the case that recklessness increases the likelihood of being murdered. It should be noted that, with regard to some accidental deaths, and probably with some homicides, the person killed may be in no way responsible. This is particularly clear in some motor accidents, where the person killed may be simply a passenger, a situation that is probably very common among married women. There is, in some cases, also the issue of differential exposure to risk; thus, it is possible, for example, that at younger ages single persons drive more than married persons and thus experience a greater risk.

The data on suicide, homicide, and accidental death are presented in Tables 16.1 through 16.5. Each table presents the ratios produced by dividing the mortality rate of the unmarried (single, widowed, or divorced) by the mortality rate of the married, with each sex taken separately. In the first section of the table the age-specific ratios are presented, while in the second section the averages of these ratios are presented. The first average in this latter section deals with all ages 25 and over, and the second average deals with ages 25 through 64. This last figure deals with the age span with which we are primarily concerned, for it is during this time in the life cycle that persons are involved in the full range of their adult roles. I would call the reader's attention to the fact that the time span is not constant in the age-specific categories and that in calculating the average of these ratios each age-specific ratio was weighed according to the time span covered. If the reader wishes, he may view the average ratios as being based on age-standardized rates which are calculated using a theoretical population in which each year is equally weighed.[6]

The suicide data are presented in Table 16.1.

Table 16.1. Suicide: Ratios Produced by Dividing the Suicide Rate of the Unmarried by the Rate of the Married, Whites, United States, 1959 to 1961[a]

Unmarried Category (ratio)	Age								Average Ratio	
	25–34	35–44	45–54	55–59	60–64	65–69	70–74	75+	25+	25–64
Single:										
Male	2.47	2.07	1.74	1.68	1.75	1.92	2.22	2.11	2.01	2.00
Female	2.13	1.63	1.16	1.09	1.12	1.10	1.61	0.90	1.42	1.51
Widowed:										
Male	8.15	5.79	3.52	2.65	2.51	2.28	2.38	2.05	4.25	5.01
Female	3.32	0.94	1.87	1.82	1.64	1.39	1.79	1.49	2.04	2.21
Divorced:										
Male	6.08	5.38	3.95	3.54	3.61	2.88	3.24	3.03	4.28	4.75
Female	5.36	3.74	2.33	2.05	2.52	2.68	2.36	4.25	3.34	3.43

[a]Ratios calculated by the author from the mortality rates presented by the National Center for Health Statistics (1970).

Table 16.2. Homicide: Ratios Produced by Dividing the Homicide Rate of the Unmarried by the Rate of the Married, Whites, United States, 1959 to 1961[a]

Unmarried Category (ratio)	Age 25–34	35–44	45–54	55–59	60–64	65–69	70–74	75+	Average Ratio 25+	25–64
Single:										
Male	2.02	2.31	1.95	1.70	2.69	2.00	3.05	2.79	2.25	2.12
Female	0.90	0.68	0.35	0.42	0.55	1.13	0.73	0.94	0.69	0.60
Widowed:										
Male	5.09	3.17	2.69	3.49	3.69	2.42	2.81	1.90	3.29	3.64
Female	4.21	3.42	1.59	1.42	1.18	1.25	0.87	0.82	2.18	2.63
Divorced:										
Male	8.48	8.10	7.21	6.27	6.73	3.85	10.05	5.79	7.30	7.57
Female	6.26	4.95	3.94	3.42	2.64	0.50	0.93	3.71	3.77	4.54

[a]Ratios calculated by the author from the mortality rates presented by the National Center for Health Statistics (1970).

As can be seen from the last column, for ages 25 through 64 single men are, controlling for age, exactly twice as likely to commit suicide as married men. In contrast, comparable single women are 51 percent more likely than married women to commit suicide. Turning to the widowed, we see that between these ages, widowed men commit suicide five times more frequently than married men, while widowed women commit suicide 2.2 times more frequently than married women. The divorced show a similar pattern.

The data on homicide are generally similar to the data on suicide, except that single women have a lower mortality than married women (see Table 16.2). Thus, for women the shift from being single to being married increases the likelihood of being murdered, while for men the shift decreases their chances. For both men and women, the shift from being married to being widowed markedly increases their likelihood of being murdered, with the difference noticeably greater for men than women. The data indicate that the divorced, particularly divorced men, are especially likely to be murdered.

Accidental deaths show a pattern similar to deaths due to suicide and homicide. Looking at mortality due to motor accidents (excluding pedestrian mortality), we find again that the single statuses appear to be worse for men than for women. As with homicide, single women are less likely to be killed than married females, while with all other comparisons the married have lower mortality rates than the unmarried (see Table 16.3). Pedestrian deaths are much more likely to occur among the unmarried than the married, and again the differences between the marital statuses are significantly greater for men than for women (see Table 16.4). Accidental deaths due to all other causes have exactly the same pattern as pedes-

Table 16.3. Motor Accident Deaths (Excluding Pedestrian Deaths): Ratios Produced by Dividing the Mortality Rate of the Unmarried by the Rate of the Married, Whites, United States, 1959 to 1961[a]

Unmarried Category (ratio)	Age 25–34	35–44	45–54	55–59	60–64	65–69	70–74	75+	Average Ratio 25+	25–64
Single:										
Male	1.79	1.49	1.20	1.00	1.02	0.97	0.89	0.84	1.24	1.36
Female	1.28	0.82	0.54	0.63	0.63	0.60	0.57	0.49	0.74	0.82
Widowed:										
Male	5.37	3.68	2.73	2.36	2.06	1.94	1.72	1.21	2.99	3.50
Female	5.80	3.15	1.66	1.15	0.91	0.85	0.69	0.65	2.32	2.91
Divorced:										
Male	4.58	4.26	3.28	2.34	2.43	2.23	2.15	1.59	3.18	3.63
Female	4.38	3.04	1.60	1.08	0.99	0.59	0.81	0.73	2.02	2.51

[a]Ratios calculated by the author from the mortality rates presented by the National Center for Health Statistics (1970).

Table 16.4. Pedestrian Deaths: Ratios Produced by Dividing the Mortality Rate of the Unmarried by the Rate of the Married, Whites, United States, 1959 to 1961[a]

Unmarried Category (ratio)	Age								Average Ratio	
	25–34	35–44	45–54	55–59	60–64	65–69	70–74	75+	25+	25–64
Single:										
Male	2.86	4.94	4.89	4.30	4.07	3.89	3.78	2.87	4.03	4.22
Female	2.50	1.83	1.50	1.77	2.10	2.41	2.46	2.43	2.08	1.94
Widowed:										
Male	3.71	6.77	4.65	4.81	2.82	3.01	2.73	2.16	4.16	4.74
Female	3.25	2.50	2.50	2.06	2.50	2.31	2.17	1.67	2.47	2.63
Divorced:										
Male	5.79	8.29	9.62	8.19	5.77	4.41	4.65	3.51	6.72	7.67
Female	6.50	3.67	3.17	4.59	2.50	1.69	2.51	2.38	3.67	4.22

[a]Ratios calculated by the author from the mortality rates presented by the National Center for Health Statistics (1970).

trian deaths, although the differences between the marital statuses, and to some extent the differences between the sexes, are not as great (see Table 16.5).

Taken together, these data show a pattern that very closely parallels the data on psychological well-being and mental illness. In all cases, the shift from being single to being married appears, from the mortality rates, to have a more favorable effect on men than on women, while the shift from the married to an unmarried state appears to have a more unfavorable effect on men than on women. For men, being unmarried is uniformly associated with mortality rates that are higher than those of the married, with the widowed and divorced having especially high rates. The data for women are generally similar, although the relationships are neither as strong nor as consistent.

Another pattern worth noting is that in most instances the disparity between being married and unmarried diminishes with age. The drop in the size of the ratio usually starts by the age of 44 and frequently by the age of 34. The younger ages are, of course, the time young children are in the home, and it is possible, as Durkheim noted, that having young children provides a form of protection. It is perhaps worth emphasizing that at the relatively early ages, the differences between the married and unmarried rates are often very large. For example, between the ages of 25 and 34, widowed men are 8.2 times more likely to commit suicide than married men, and in the same age bracket divorced men are 8.5 times more likely than married men to be murdered.

MORTALITY ASSOCIATED WITH THE USE OF SOCIALLY APPROVED "NARCOTICS"

In this section I will look at two types of mortality associated with the use of socially ap-

Table 16.5. All Other Accidental Deaths: Ratios Produced by Dividing the Mortality Rate of the Unmarried by the Rate of the Married, Whites, United States, 1959 to 1961[a]

Unmarried Category (ratio)	Age								Average Ratio	
	25–34	35–44	45–54	55–59	60–64	65–69	70–74	75+	25+	25–64
Single:										
Male	1.68	2.56	2.53	2.41	2.41	3.00	2.97	2.27	2.42	2.30
Female	2.44	2.06	1.56	1.53	2.06	1.60	1.67	2.17	1.92	1.96
Widowed:										
Male	3.43	3.19	2.99	2.51	2.42	2.37	2.14	2.22	2.81	3.02
Female	3.54	2.78	2.31	1.69	1.69	1.44	1.42	1.94	2.31	2.58
Divorced:										
Male	3.18	5.08	5.40	4.70	4.44	4.25	3.79	2.49	4.27	4.56
Female	3.51	3.37	2.73	2.66	2.21	1.86	2.08	1.74	2.71	3.02

[a]Ratios calculated by the author from the mortality rates presented by the National Center for Health Statistics (1970).

Table 16.6. Cirrhosis of the Liver: Ratios Produced by Dividing the Mortality Rate of the Unmarried by the Mortality Rate of the Married, Whites, United States, 1959 to 1961[a]

Unmarried Category (ratio)	Age								Average Ratio	
	25–34	35–44	45–54	55–59	60–64	65–69	70–74	75+	25+	25–64
Single:										
Male	4.07	3.85	2.76	2.37	2.58	2.39	2.00	1.50	2.93	3.29
Female	2.15	1.06	0.78	0.74	0.76	0.76	0.76	0.74	1.07	1.19
Widowed:										
Male	2.50	7.23	5.08	3.85	3.39	3.09	2.15	1.40	3.95	4.61
Female	6.54	3.81	2.05	1.54	1.30	1.28	1.15	1.04	2.83	3.45
Divorced:										
Male	11.29	10.61	7.84	6.16	5.10	4.16	2.99	2.06	7.27	8.84
Female	8.54	4.71	2.55	2.01	1.82	1.56	1.38	1.30	3.61	4.43

[a]Ratios calculated by the author from the mortality rates presented by the National Center for Health Statistics (1970).

proved "narcotics," namely, cirrhosis of the liver and lung cancer.

In a recent article Terris (1967) presents convincing evidence that a very major determinant of death due to cirrhosis of the liver is the consumption of alcohol. Alcohol use is, of course, in part regulated by social norms. However, heavy users of alcohol frequently appear to be trying to "drown" their troubles. If this is the case, then it would seem to follow that the mortality rates for cirrhosis of the liver should conform to the pattern associated with deaths due to overt social acts.

The data on mortality due to cirrhosis of the liver are presented in Table 16.6. As can be seen in the last column, for the ages 25 through 64 single men are, controlling for age, 3.3 times more likely to die of cirrhosis of the liver than married men. In contrast, single women are only slightly more likely than married women to die of cirrhosis of the liver, and in fact, in the older ages, single women have noticeably lower mortality rates than married women. Widowed men and women are both more likely to die from cirrhosis of the liver than their married counterparts, with the difference being greater among men. The divorced have the same pattern as the widowed, but their mortality rates are markedly higher, especially for males. In fact, in the 25 to 34 age bracket, divorced men are 11.3 times more likely to die than married men from cirrhosis of the liver.

There is quite strong evidence that smoking is causally related to lung cancer (Public Health Service, 1964a). People smoke, of course, for a wide variety of reasons. One of these reasons, although perhaps not a major one, is to relax. If we assume that relaxation as a reason for smoking is important enough to affect overall patterns of use, it seems plausible that mortality due to lung cancer would show, in a moderate form, the pattern found with cirrhosis of the liver. The data on mortality due to lung cancer are presented in Table 16.7, and

Table 16.7. Lung Cancer: Ratios Produced by Dividing the Mortality Rate of the Unmarried by the Mortality Rate of the Married, Whites, United States, 1959 to 1961[a]

Unmarried Category (ratio)	Age								Average Ratio	
	25–34	35–44	45–54	55–59	60–64	65–69	70–74	75+	25+	25–64
Single:										
Male	1.07	1.24	1.14	1.84	2.88	1.17	1.11	1.06	1.36	1.45
Female	1.33	1.09	0.97	1.06	1.02	1.16	1.06	1.01	1.01	1.11
Widowed:										
Male	2.33	1.92	1.74	2.49	3.46	1.39	1.26	1.15	1.98	2.24
Female	0.67	1.53	1.40	1.35	1.09	1.22	1.14	1.17	1.20	1.20
Divorced:										
Male	2.73	2.78	2.63	3.34	4.96	1.88	1.80	1.68	2.72	3.07
Female	1.67	2.00	1.59	1.71	1.43	1.25	1.75	1.24	1.63	1.71

[a]Ratios calculated by the author from the mortality rates presented by the National Center for Health Statistics (1970).

they do in fact show the same pattern, although the differences between the marital statuses are not nearly as great.

I might note that these mortality data do not completely correspond to the available information on smoking patterns in the United States. The surveys by Hammond and Garfinkel (1961) and Haenszel, Skinkin, and Miller (1956) indicate, as do the mortality data, that the widowed and especially the divorced, of both sexes, are more likely to smoke than married individuals. However, both of these studies suggest that single men and women are somewhat less likely to smoke than their married counterparts, while the mortality data would suggest a lower rate among the married. It is possible that the lower rates of mortality caused by lung cancer among the married are not due to higher rates of lung cancer but instead of how promptly and diligently people seek treatment.

MORTALITY ASSOCIATED WITH DISEASES REQUIRING PROLONGED AND METHODICAL CARE

It seems logical that one's willingness to undertake the very prolonged and methodical care required in the treatment of certain diseases would be related to one's emotional state, willingness to take risks, etc. If the unmarried find their roles less satisfying than the married, and this is more true for men than for women, then we might expect this fact to be reflected in the mortality statistics of diseases requiring prolonged, attentive care. In this section I will look at the mortality statistics of two such diseases, tuberculosis and diabetes.

Tuberculosis is an infectious disease whose effective treatment requires the careful scheduling of one's life. Effectively treated tuberculosis will usually move into a latent phase; however, it is apt to become activated again if one becomes physically dissipated due to poor diet, lack of rest, etc. Furthermore, it appears to be the case that psychological stress and physical dissipation are related to initial infection (Derner, 1953; Wolff, 1953:27–32).

The data on tuberculosis are presented in Table 16.8. As can be seen in the last column, between the ages 25 and 64 single men are, controlling for age, 5.4 times more likely than married men to die from tuberculosis, while the comparable figure for women is 3.3. Widowed and divorced men are even more likely than single men to die of tuberculosis. For the widowed, the differences reach 11.5 times the married rate between the ages 25 and 34, and reach a similar value among the divorced during the ages 35 through 44. For widowed and divorced women we find a different pattern, namely, that they are somewhat less likely than single women to die from tuberculosis. This, of course, means that when we compare the coefficients of preservation for men and women across the widowed and divorced categories, the differences are especially large.

In contrast, to tuberculosis, the likelihood that one will become diabetic is determined largely by one's genetic inheritance (Duncan, 1964; Knowles, 1965). However, at least among those who have a propensity for diabetes, social factors such as diet, and possibly such factors as stress, affect one's chances of becoming diabetic. It is necessary for most diabetics to carefully schedule major aspects of

Table 16.8. Tuberculosis: Ratios Produced by Dividing the Mortality Rate of the Unmarried by the Mortality Rate of the Married, Whites, United States, 1959 to 1961[a]

Unmarried Category (ratio)	Age								Average Ratio	
	25–34	35–44	45–54	55–59	60–64	65–69	70–74	75+	25+	25–64
Single:										
Male	5.67	6.64	5.20	4.30	3.87	3.47	3.12	2.57	4.74	5.37
Female	4.50	3.29	3.04	2.23	2.58	2.09	1.70	1.75	2.91	3.31
Widowed:										
Male	11.50	8.82	6.69	4.22	3.33	2.71	2.08	1.62	6.18	7.70
Female	3.88	2.62	2.11	1.47	1.94	1.51	1.39	1.29	2.26	2.58
Divorced:										
Male	7.67	11.45	10.63	7.79	6.87	4.77	4.57	2.77	7.84	9.27
Female	4.00	3.38	2.78	2.30	2.21	1.35	1.76	1.16	2.65	3.10

[a]Ratios calculated by the author from the mortality rates presented by the National Center for Health Statistics (1970).

Table 16.9. Diabetes: Ratios Produced by Dividing the Mortality Rate of the Unmarried by the Mortality Rate of the Married, Whites, United States, 1959 to 1961[a]

Unmarried Category (ratio)	Age								Average Ratio	
	25–34	35–44	45–54	55–59	60–64	65–69	70–74	75+	25+	25–64
Single:										
Male	3.56	3.37	2.21	1.70	1.52	1.29	1.07	0.93	2.25	2.69
Female	3.19	3.13	1.10	0.76	0.63	0.53	0.54	0.54	1.62	2.03
Widowed:										
Male	3.83	2.26	1.88	1.86	1.85	1.49	1.47	1.32	2.18	2.46
Female	1.69	2.29	1.59	1.37	1.13	1.14	1.09	1.08	1.54	1.71
Divorced:										
Male	6.78	5.66	2.98	2.05	1.71	1.66	1.31	1.19	3.52	4.32
Female	2.50	2.21	1.11	0.87	0.83	0.85	0.77	0.71	1.42	1.67

[a]Ratios calculated by the author from the mortality rates presented by the National Center for Health Statistics (1970).

their life. They must be especially careful about what they eat and when they eat, as well as remember to take medications, etc.

The mortality data on diabetes are presented in Table 16.9. Again, the unmarried have higher rates of mortality than the married, and the differences are noticeably greater for males than for females. As with tuberculosis, widowed and divorced women have a somewhat lower mortality rate than single women. Among the males, the mortality rate of the widowed is relatively similar to the rate of those who are single, while the divorced have a noticeably higher mortality rate.

MORTALITY LARGELY UNAFFECTED BY SOCIAL FACTORS

Assuming that one's marital status is related to how promptly and diligently he seeks treatment, one would expect some relationship between almost any cause of mortality and marital status. However, in cases where one's emotional state is unrelated to the etiology of a disorder and interacts minimally with the potential effectiveness of treatment, we would, following a role analysis, expect the relationship between mortality and marital status to be slight. Two such disorders are leukemia and aleukemia.

The relationship between deaths due to leukemia and aleukemia and marital status, by sex, are presented in Table 16.10. These data indicate that there is in fact very little relationship between marital status and mortality caused by leukemia and aleukemia. Note also that in the case of the single and the widowed, it is the women and not the men who tend to have the larger coefficient of preservation—a finding that runs counter to the other types of mortality presented. I would also note that an analysis of the relationship between marital

Table 16.10. Leukemia and Aleukemia: Ratios Produced by Dividing the Mortality Rate of the Unmarried by the Mortality Rate of the Married, Whites, United States, 1959 to 1961[a]

Unmarried Category (Ratio)	Age								Average Ratio	
	25–34	35–44	45–54	55–59	60–64	65–69	70–74	75+	25+	25–64
Single:										
Males	1.25	1.08	1.07	0.84	0.94	0.91	1.01	0.84	1.03	1.07
Females	1.26	1.27	1.08	1.01	1.16	0.78	0.92	0.93	1.09	1.17
Widowed:										
Males	0.71	0.81	1.01	1.10	1.12	1.10	1.06	1.08	0.96	0.91
Females	0.95	1.27	1.10	1.05	1.10	0.99	1.04	1.10	1.08	1.10
Divorced:										
Males	1.38	1.08	1.29	1.38	1.36	1.08	1.21	1.10	1.24	1.28
Females	1.47	0.89	0.90	1.24	1.01	1.19	0.83	1.34	1.10	1.10

[a]Ratios calculated by the author from the mortality rates presented by the National Center for Health Statistics (1970).

status and mortality caused by cancer of the digestive organs shows only slightly larger relationships than those found for leukemia and aleukemia (data not shown; see National Center for Health Statistics, 1970).

The data on leukemia and aleukemia bear on a possibility raised by Sheps (1961), who suggested that a major reason the unmarried groups appear to have higher rates of mortality than the married is that unmarried, particularly the widowed and divorced, are underenumerated in the census. Furthermore, he suggests that this underenumeration is greater for males than for females, which would account for the generally larger coefficients of preservation among males. However, if this were true, then the effects of underenumeration should be constant for all causes of mortality. If Sheps's proposal were valid, then with regard to leukemia and aleukemia, the data would show the unmarried to have markedly higher rates of mortality than the married, and these differences would be greater for men than for women. However, for the widowed, particularly widowed males, the data clearly indicate that underenumeration is not an important issue. Among the divorced the data are consistent with the possibility that divorced males may be slightly underenumerated; however, the differences between the statuses are quite small. In short, it is clear that the relationships presented above could, at most, have been only marginally affected by underenumeration (also see Kraus and Lilienfeld, 1959).

MORTALITY—ALL CAUSES

The relationships between status and mortality due to all causes are presented in Table 16.11. The unmarried have, controlling for age, noticeably higher mortality rates than the married, with the differences being significantly greater for men than for women. As one would expect, these differences, although substantial, are generally not as great as the differences associated with those types of mortality where social factors would appear to be especially important. In general, the more detailed differences shown by these data closely parallel the patterns associated with the specific causes of mortality previously presented, and this is a good place to summarize these patterns.

From the last column in Table 16.11 it is obvious that for men there are marked differences in mortality associated with the three unmarried statuses. Divorced men have, controlling for age, a much higher mortality rate than widowed men, who in turn have a much higher mortality rate than single men. In contrast, mortality rates for women across these three marital statuses are quite similar. From these data it appears that when women shift from a married to an unmarried state, their life chances simply revert to those associated with the single status. However, this is not the case for men, for here the formerly married have higher mortality rates than the never married. It may be that, as men (apparently) benefit more from marriage than do women, they also experience more of a "shock" on reverting to an unmarried state, a shock which has the effect of decreasing their life chances.

Previously, I noted, when discussing mortality associated with overt social acts, that the coefficient of preservation is largest during the early ages and drops off rapidly thereafter. This pattern also occurs with most of the other types of mortality where the social element ap-

Table 16.11. Mortality, All Causes: Ratios Produced by Dividing the Mortality Rate of the Unmarried by the Mortality Rate of the Married, Whites, United States, 1960[a]

Unmarried Category (ratio)	Age								Average Ratio	
	25–34	35–44	45–54	55–59	60–64	65–69	70–74	75+	25+	25–64
Single:										
Male	2.23	2.25	1.83	1.49	1.50	1.46	1.43	1.38	1.81	1.95
Female	2.29	1.88	1.42	1.16	1.11	1.04	1.05	1.49	1.55	1.68
Widowed:										
Male	3.85	2.86	2.16	1.83	1.56	1.49	1.42	1.56	2.33	2.64
Female	2.43	1.82	1.54	1.29	1.26	1.22	1.18	1.45	1.64	1.77
Divorced:										
Male	3.92	4.07	3.14	2.58	2.27	1.99	1.83	1.59	2.96	3.39
Female	2.86	2.00	1.56	1.41	1.31	1.28	1.26	1.38	1.77	1.95

[a]Ratios calculated by the author from mortality rates presented by Grove and Hetzel (1968, p. 335).

Table 16.12. Presence of Children in Husband-and-Wife Families, 1959, by Percent[a]

Presence and Age of Own Children	Age of Husband			
	25–34	35–44	45–64	65+
With own children under 18 and at least some under 6	74.6	42.9	8.1	0.1
With own children under 18 but none under 6	11.2	42.9	34.9	3.2
Without own children under 18	14.2	14.2	57.0	96.7

[a]Data taken from Bureau of the Census (1960, table a).

pears to be particularly important, and can be seen in Table 16.11, where all types of mortality are grouped together. As is shown in this table, for women the disparity between the three unmarried statuses and the married status is in each case greatest between the ages 25 through 34. For men the disparity between being married and being single or divorced is greatest between the ages 35 and 44 (although it is almost as large between 25 and 34), while the disparity between being married and widowed is greatest between the ages 25 and 34. These ages correspond closely to the time most families have young children in the home (see Table 16.12), and it may be, as Durkheim indicated, that children provide a form of "protection" (through their effect on the concerns and behavior of parents).

I would note also that between the ages 25 and 34 the disparity between being married and being single is actually slightly larger for women than for men. Furthermore, as one moves to the older ages, where children tend not to be present in the home, the relative drop in the size of the coefficient of preservation tends to be larger for women than for men. It may be that young children provide more "protection" for women than for men. This is what Durkheim (1951:189, n.27) concluded from his analysis of suicide. Furthermore, the data of psychological well-being suggest that this is a plausible possibility. For example, Gurin et al. (1960:130) found that women "view children as more essential to their growth as a person, to their stability and maturity, and to the focusing of their life, giving such responses as: 'children provide a goal in life,' 'they are a fulfillment,' . . ."

DISCUSSION

This chapter analyzes the relationship between sex, marital status, and mortality. Previous research on psychological well-being and mental illness indicates that the married of both sexes find life more satisfying than the unmarried. This research, however, suggests that there are important differences between the sexes, namely, that males find being married more advantageous than do females and being single, widowed, or divorced more disadvantageous. This chapter is based on the premise that if the research on psychological well-being and mental illness is valid, then similar relationships should appear in the data on mortality, particularly among those types of mortality which are clearly affected by such things as one's emotional stability and willingness to take risks.

As we have seen, the mortality rates of the unmarried statuses are, controlling for age, higher than those of the married, and the differences between the married and unmarried statuses are much greater for men than for women. The evidence from specific types of mortality suggests that these differences can be largely attributed to characteristics associated with one's psychological state. More precisely, the variations in the mortality rates are particularly large where one's psychological state (1) appears to play a direct role in death, as with suicide, homicide, and accidents, (2) is directly related to acts such as alcoholism that frequently lead to death, and (3) would appear to affect one's willingness and ability to undergo the drawn-out and careful treatment required for diseases such as tuberculosis. In contrast, there is little difference between the marital statuses in the mortality rates for diseases such as leukemia and aleukemia, where one's psychological state has little effect on either the etiology of the disease or treatment.

Further support for attributing the variation in mortality rates to variations in psychological factors related to the marital roles is provided by patterns in the way the rates vary. For both men and women the coefficients of preservation are large during the time children tend to be at home and then drop markedly thereafter. Furthermore, children appear to "protect" women more than men, a result previously noted by Durkheim and one that is suggested by the data on psychological well-being.

The pattern of mortality that is found between the marital statuses of the sexes is one that would be predicted by a role framework. However, other authors have suggested an alternative explanation, namely, that most of the observed differences are due to selective processes associated with marriage (e.g., Zalokar, 1960; Sheps, 1961; and to some extent Carter and Glick, 1970:324–357, although see 341–342). The selective argument is essentially as follows. Marriage is a selective process, and persons who are emotionally unstable and/or physically handicapped are much less likely to get married than those who are emotionally and physically healthy. Furthermore, the selective processes are such that the man (because he plays the dominant role in courtship) finds it more difficult to get married if he is handicapped than does a woman.[7] The first part of the argument seems quite reasonable, and I would assume that handicapped persons do find it difficult to marry. The question in my view is how much of the variation in the mortality rates between the marital states can be attributed to selective processes. The second part of the argument I find less convincing, although plausible. I would think that neither a man nor a woman would want a spouse who was emotionally unstable or about to die, and that there would be little difference between the sexes in this desire. Unfortunately, with the available evidence it is impossible to evaluate either of these selective arguments in a definitive fashion. However, it is possible to begin such an evaluation.

If, as the selective argument holds, more unstable women than men marry, this means that among persons who become either widowed or divorced, a higher proportion of women, as compared with men, would be emotionally unstable. A similar analysis can, of course, be made with regard to physical disability. This being the case, we would not expect, at least on the first analysis, the coefficients of preservation to be smaller for divorced and widowed women than for comparable men. In fact, at least with those coefficients relating to instability, we might expect them to be larger for women. It seems reasonable to assume that instability contributes to the likelihood of divorce, and this, in concordance with the selective hypothesis, suggests that a particularly large number of divorced women would be unstable (while a large number of divorced men would not be unstable but would simply have been formerly married to unstable women).

Proponents of the selective hypothesis would reply to this argument that, although the unstable and physically disabled would be more frequent among divorced and widowed women than among divorced and widowed men, the divorced and widowed frequently remarry and this screening process may result in the residual divorced and widowed population having proportionately more disabled and unstable men than women. It is, of course, true that many widowed and divorced persons remarry. I would note, however, that both the widowed and divorced have successfully passed through one selective process, and one would not expect a second, fairly comparable screening to produce greater differences than the initial screening. (In fact, I would expect it to produce a smaller difference.) This seems particularly obvious with regard to the widowed. However, the divorced and widowed, particularly males, have, controlling for age, higher mortality rates than the never married. Furthermore, as can be seen from Table 16.11, the differences between the sexes tend to be greater among the widowed and divorced than among the never married.

In this classic work on suicide, Durkheim (1951:182–183) attempted to evaluate the relative validity of the selective and role explanations of the high rates of suicide among the never married. He argued that if the reason single persons have higher rates of suicide than the married is because stable persons tend to marry and unstable persons tend not to, then we would expect the differences between the single and married to be greater in the later years after virtually everyone who is going to marry has married, and smaller in the earlier years when the single category still contains a sizable number of stable persons who will eventually marry. As we have seen, not only with suicide but also with most forms of mortality, the difference between the never married and the married is greater during the early years and undergoes a marked decline over time. However, although these data are consistent with the role explanation, at our present state of knowledge they could also plausibly be explained by a selective explanation. For example, from a selective perspective it could be argued that (1) as it is "misfits" who die early there would be fewer misfits at risk in later years regardless of marital status and (2) the relative importance of selective processes may diminish with increasing age as mortality rates from most causes increase. It is going to take considerable work, with better data, before the relative importance of these explanations can be adequately assessed.[8]

Further evidence that the differences in mortality between the various marital statuses is not due primarily to selective processes associated with marriage is provided by Kraus and Lilienfeld (1959). Noting that the 1949 to 1951 U.S. data on mortality indicated that the young widowed group had very high rates of mortality from certain causes, they attempted to see whether these differences could be attributed to the remarriage of healthy widows, which had left a residual "ill" widowed population. To do this they made very generous estimates of the characteristics of the widowed population that had remarried (i.e., they overestimated the number of widows who had remarried and assumed that none of the remarried widows had died), added the "remarried" widows to the residual widow population, and calculated the mortality rate of all widows (whether remarried or not). Although this reduced the difference between the widowed and married somewhat, most of the difference remained, and they were forced to conclude that at least for the young widowed group, the selective hypothesis could, at best, explain only a slight part of the differences in the mortality rates of the unmarried and married.

Another piece of evidence that strongly suggests that, at least for our purposes, the selective processes are not of major importance are the mortality patterns associated with diseases where the role explanation suggests little variation in mortality across the marital statuses but where the selective explanation suggests there should be marked variations. The mortality rates associated with leukemia and aleukemia provide an excellent example. These diseases are almost inevitably fatal, but persons who have been stricken with them may live for a long time, time for the selective processes, if they are important, to produce marked variations in the mortality rates associated with the different marital statuses. However, as is shown in Table 16.10, for these diseases there is very little variation in the mortality rate between the marital statuses. Furthermore, the mortality rates associated with these diseases may be interpreted as indicating that it is disabled women and not disabled men who are the least likely to get married.

In this chapter I have suggested that the different mortality patterns for men and women across the married and unmarried statuses can be largely explained by the nature of the marital roles. Although we have looked at selective processes as an alternative explanation of the data, we have, to this point, ignored the traditional independent variable of sociology—social class. As one's socioeconomic position in society has a strong inverse relationship to both mortality (e.g., Antonovsky, 1972) and mental illness (e.g., Hollingshead and Redlich, 1958; Rushing, 1969; Kohn, 1968), a few words are in order. Unfortunately, the national data used in this study do not allow for economic controls. Nevertheless, on the basis of national data for 1960 it is possible to show that it is very unlikely that the particular pattern of mortality dealt with in this chapter is a product of economic factors. First, the average economic position of married men and women can, almost by definition, be taken as comparable. Second, the economic position of never-married white men and women is quite comparable, with women slightly better off (e.g., Carter and Glick, 1970:318). Third, white widowed women and white divorced women have much less income than their male counterparts (e.g., Carter and Glick, 1970:266, 295). Thus, if it were the economic situation of men and women that determined the mortality pattern across the marital statuses, we would expect very little differences between men and women in the size of the never married/married ratio (the women's ratio might be slightly smaller), while we would expect the ratios of divorced/married and widowed/married to be much larger for women than for men. However, as we have seen for two out of the three marital categories, the ratios are the reverse of what the economic perspective would suggest.

In conclusion, with regard to the relationship between marital status and mortality for men and women, the married have lower mortality rates than the unmarried and the differences between being married and being single, widowed, or divorced are greater for men than for women. These differences are particularly marked among those types of mortality where one's psychological state would appear to affect one's life chances. It would seem that these results can be tentatively attributed to the nature of marital roles in our society—in part, because the data on psychological well-being and mental illness indicate the same pattern of relationships; in part, because the "protective" aspects of marriage appear to be greatest at the time the role explanation would predict; and, in part, because the alternative explanation, namely, that the differences are due primarily to selective processes associated with marriage, tends not to be supported by the available data. I would note, however, that we know very little about how such variables as emotional instability and physical disability affect the likelihood of marriage. This is particularly true with regard to possible sex differences. Until such information is available, the precise weighing of the relative importance of the role explanation and the selective explanation of the mortality data must, in my view, remain tentative.

NOTES

I would like to note that in writing this chapter I have benefited from conversations with Omer Galle, and I would like to thank Antonina Gove and William Parish for their comments on an earlier draft. The research for this chapter was supported by the Vanderbilt University Research Council.

1. In some cases, death among the widowed is probably related to the death of the widowed's spouse. For example, if the spouse of a widowed person had died of an infectious disease, the widowed person is probably more likely than the average person to have been infected and is thus also more likely to die. This means that to some extent the size of the widowed/married ratio is affected by processes we are not considering. However, unless one assumes that such effects are sex specific (e.g., that a husband of a sick wife is more likely to get infected than the wife of a sick husband), such effects should have only minimal impact on the sex differences in the size of the ratios. I would note that if there is a sex difference in the likelihood of infection from one's spouse, I suspect it would be wives who would be more likely to become infected because of their presumed greater tendency to care for others. This, of course, would tend to increase the size of the woman's ratio, producing an effect counter to the predicted one.
2. Since men and women have different mortality rates, the use of these coefficients allows us to avoid many of the problems involved in comparing the mortality of men and women. Some of the factors creating different life chances for men and women are noted below. First, there is considerable evidence that women have a longer life-span than men (e.g., Madigan, 1957). Second, the life chances of men and women are differentially affected by social norms; it has, for example, been socially more appropriate for men to smoke and drink, which increases the likelihood that men will die because of lung cancer and cirrhosis of the liver. Third, men and women characteristically have quite different life styles, which may affect their life chances due to different rates of exposure to disease and to the possibility of accidents. Fourth, men and women appear to have different ways of behaving, which would affect their life chances. For example, men in general appear to be more aggressive and willing to take risks. Such ways of behaving would not only increase the death rate of men due to accidents but might also mean that men would be less apt to enter treatment early and be less likely to persist in the prolonged and careful treatment that is necessary for many disorders such as tuberculosis and diabetes. I would note that the different behavioral patterns of the sexes have long been recognized in the study of suicide, where investigators do not simply compare the rates of men and women but instead look for patterned variations (e.g., Durkheim, 1951; Gove, 1972b).
3. Parish and Schwartz (1972), like Durkheim, show that the size of the household was inversely correlated in France during the latter part of the 19th century. Their analysis, however, suggests that it is the number of adults in the household and not the number of children that is responsible for variations in the suicide rate. Their conclusions are, in my view, open to question, in part because they are based on ecological data. However, even if they are valid they do not challenge Durkheim's contention that the presence of children has a "protective" effect on the married. For example, Durkheim (1951:186) demonstrated (in a section not discussed by Parish and Schwartz) that in France in 1889 to 1891 the "protective" effect of marriage among married men with children was almost four times as great as it was for married men without children. Similarly, he showed that married women without children had a significantly higher rate of suicide than unmarried women, while married women with children experienced considerable protection (Durkheim, 1955:188–189). Furthermore, the protective effect of children persisted into widowhood. It may be that beyond the first child the number of additional children made little difference (which might explain the Parish and Schwartz results), but there can be little question that the presence or absence of children was of major importance.
4. For example, as had been noted by Durkheim (1951) and others (e.g., Maris, 1969), in the very young age groups married persons frequently have higher suicide rates than single persons. A similar pattern occurs with some but not most other forms of mortality. I hope in a later paper to deal with the issue of marital status and mortality in the younger age groups.
5. For a recent discussion of the relationship between social control, deviance, and accidents see Suchman (1970).
6. The typical way of calculating age-standardized rates would be to standardize on the U.S. population. How-

ever, for our purposes such a procedure is likely to produce misleading results. In the United States we have more young people than old people, which means the young age groups will contribute more heavily to the age-standardized rate. However, in the present instance the younger ages are not, a priori, more important, and I see no theoretical reason why they should be weighed more heavily. Perhaps even more important is the fact we have subpopulations with very different age structures. The typical form of standardization would mean, for example, that in developing the age-standardized rates for the widowed, one would find that the rates of young widows play a much greater role than the rates of older widows. This would obviously be a questionable procedure, in part because widowed persons in the younger age groups are very rare and their rates thus unreliable, but also because they are a very atypical segment of the widowed population.

7. Carter and Glick (1970:258, 337) posit a third explanation with regard to the divorced. They suggest that divorced women, because of their status (presence of children, etc.), find it more difficult to remarry than divorced men. On the basis of this assumption they suggest that because more divorced men than divorced women remarry, and as it is the healthy who remarry, the residual divorced population will contain few healthy males (and thus the mortality rate of divorced males will be high) and many healthy females (and thus the mortality rate of divorced females will be low). However, their basic assumption is incorrect, for slightly more divorced women than divorced men remarry (Public Health Service, 1964b, table 2-22). I would note that the remarriage rate among the living divorced population is higher for males than females. This is true because even after controlling for age and sex differences divorced men have a higher mortality rate than divorced women. From a selective perspective, this means that among the persons who get divorced, approximately an equal number of (healthy) males and females remarry, but that more *unhealthy* divorced males than females are selected out (i.e., die early), which hypothetically would mean that at any given time the remaining population of divorced males should be healthier than the remaining population of divorced females.
8. I would note that Bradburn (1969:152–156) performed an analysis similar to that of Durkheim's on single males to see whether his results could be explained by selective processes and concluded that the "unhappy" state of single males was largely due to their reaction to their roles. Because of the nature of this data, it is very unlikely that his results could be attributed to the selective mortality of "misfits."

REFERENCES

Antonovsky, Aaron. 1972. "Social Class, Life Expectancy and Overall Mortality." In *Patients, Physicians and Illness,* edited by E. Gertly Jaco. New York: Free Press.

Berkson, Joseph. 1962. "Mortality and Marital Status." *American Journal of Public Health* 52 (August): 1318–29.

Bradburn, Norman. 1969. *The Structure of Psychological Well-Being.* Chicago: Aldine.

Bradburn, Norman, and David Caplovitz. 1965. *Reports on Happiness.* Chicago: Aldine.

Bureau of the Census. 1960. "Household and Family Characteristics." *Current Population Reports,* ser. P-20, no. 100 (March 1959). Washington, DC: Government Printing Office.

Carter, Hugh, and Paul Glick. 1970. *Marriage and Divorce: A Social and Economic Study.* Cambridge, MA: Harvard University Press.

Derner, Gordon. 1953. *Aspects of the Psychology of the Tuberculous.* New York: Hoeber.

Duncan, G. C. 1964. *Diseases of Metabolism.* Philadelphia: Saunders.

Durkheim, Émile. 1951. *Suicide: A Study in Sociology.* New York: Free Press.

Gove, Walter R. 1972a. "The Relationship between Sex Roles, Marital Roles and Mental Illness." *Social Forces* 51 (September): 34–44.

———. 1972b. "Sex, Marital Status and Suicide." *Journal of Health and Social Behavior* (in press).

Grove, Robert, and Alice Hetzel. 1968. *Vital Statistics Rates in the United States 1940–1960* (National Center for Health Statistics). Washington, DC: Government Printing Office.

Gurin, Gerald, Joseph Veroff, and Sheila Feld. 1960. *Americans View Their Mental Health.* New York: Basic Books.

Haenszel, W., M. Skinkin, and H. Miller. 1956. *Tobacco Smoking Patterns in the United States.* Public Health, Monograph no. 45 (Public Health Service Publication no. 463). Washington, DC: Government Printing Office.

Hammond, E. Cuyler, and Lawrence Garfinkel. 1961. "Smoking Habits of Men and Women." *Journal of the National Cancer Institute* 27 (August): 419–42.

Hollingshead, August, and Fredrick Redlich. 1958. *Social Class and Mental Illness.* New York: Wiley.

Knowles, H. C. 1965. "The Incidence and Development of Diabetes Mellitus." In *Diabetes,* edited by R. H. Williams. New York: Harper & Row.

Kohn, Melvin. 1968. "Social Class and Schizophrenia: A Critical Review." In *The Transmission of Schizophrenia,* edited by David Rosenthal and Seymour Kety. New York: Pergamon.

Kraus, Arthur, and Abraham Lilienfeld, 1959. "Some Epidemiologic Aspects of the High Mortality Rate in the Young Widowed Group." *Journal of Chronic Diseases* 10 (September): 207–17.

Madigan, Francis. 1957. "Are Sex Mortality Differences Biologically Caused?" *Milbank Memorial Fund Quarterly* 21 (January): 145–55.

Maris, Ronald. 1969. *Social Forces in Urban Suicide.* Homewood, IL: Dorsey.

National Center for Health Statistics. 1970. *Mortality from Selected Causes by Marital Status,* ser. 20, no. 8. Washington, DC: Government Printing Office.

Parish, William, and Moshe Schwartz. 1972. "Household Complexity in Nineteenth Century France." *American Sociological Review* 37 (April): 154–73.

Public Health Service. 1964a. *Smoking and Health: Report of the Advisory Committee to the Surgeon General of the Public Health Service.* Public Health Service Publication no. 1103. Washington, DC: Government Printing Office.

———. 1964b. *Vital Statistics of the United States 1960.* Vol. 3. *Marriage and Divorce.* Washington, DC: Government Printing Office.

Rushing, William. 1969. "Two Patterns in the Relationship between Social Class and Mental Illness Hospitalization." *American Sociological Review* 34 (August): 533–41.

Sheps, Mindel. 1961. "Marriage and Mortality." *American Journal of Public Health* 51 (April): 547–55.

Shurtleff, David. 1956. "Mortality among the Married." *Journal of the American Geriatrics Society* 4 (July): 654–66.

Suchman, Edward. 1970. "Accidents and Social Deviance." *Journal of Health and Social Behavior* 11 (March): 4–15.

Terris, Milton. 1967. "Epidemiology of Cirrhosis of the Liver." *American Journal of Public Health* 57 (December): 2076–88.

Wolff, Harold. 1953. *Stress and Disease.* Springfield, IL: Thomas.

Zalokar, Julia. 1960. "Marital Status and Major Causes of Death in Women." *Journal of Chronic Diseases* 11 (January): 50–60.

17

The Case of the Elusive Infant Mortality Rate

ROBERT B. HARTFORD

A year ago, *Intercom* published Carl Haub's article "Where Does the U.S. Stand in Infant Mortality?" in which the United States was compared with 30 other countries,[1] and ultimately ranked nineteenth. Nevertheless, the underline in Haub's title illustrated a nagging doubt shared by many that such comparisons may not be valid.

For example, we sometimes hear statements like, "You can't compare the United States with its large mixed population with small European countries"; "They (the other countries) must be counting a different way."

These statements voice the layperson's concern with four criteria for comparability of data: (a) *appropriateness of unit of analysis,* whether or not the population measured is a certain minimum size or conforms to some social or demographic standard; (b) *completeness*—the extent to which all relevant events are counted; (c) *coverage*—the extent to which all population segments or subgroups are included in the registration system within a country; and (d) *uniformity of measurement*—use of standard definitions and measurement procedures.

The appropriateness criterion meant that (following U.N. practice) Haub excluded countries reporting less than 50 infant deaths, whose rates might be easily skewed. (In addition, the "city-states" of Hong Kong and Singapore are candidates for exclusion, as they lack the urban/rural diversity of the other countries on the list.) Completeness of registration was not a problem in highly industrialized countries with highly developed medical care and statistics-recording systems, and in recent years, coverage has been essentially comprehensive.

It is with the uniformity of measurement that complications arise—in discriminating between a fetal death and an infant death. The U.N. standard lists four life signs for an infant (heart beat, breath, pulsation of umbilical cord, voluntary muscle movement) any one of which constitutes a live birth.[2] Other countries have had a shorter list of admissible signs, or have not specified them. For example, the East German criteria are "action of heart *and* lungs." In Yugoslavia either breathing *or* pulsation of the heart, but *not* voluntary muscle action or pulsation of the umbilical cord, constitute "life."[3]

Still other countries have excluded infants dying within twenty-four hours of birth (e.g., Spain prior to 1975) or prior to birth registration (e.g., France), or set viability criteria (minimum body weight, length, etc.) for including newly born in the infant category.

But the statistics in many cases have become more standardized. Sweden, which once used a nonstandard definition, adopted the U.N. definition in 1960.[4] While Japan officially recognized the U.N. standards, in past practice other standards were apparently used until sometime in the 1970s. But analysis of the age components of Japan's infant mortality suggests that this problem was eliminated by about 1979. In France the true rate still appears to be well below the United States in 1980—approximately 10.8 in France and 12.5 in the United States.

The biased rates of the remaining deviant cases are higher than the United States rates. A better comparison between East Germany and the United States is possible by examining infant mortality after the first day, which is relatively unaffected by the nonstandard definition. In 1979 (the latest year for which the appropriate East German data were available to this writer), infant mortality after the first day was 10.0 as compared to 8.3 in the United States, strongly suggesting that the overall East German rate in 1980 was higher, and we should move the United States from sixteenth to fifteenth place. The East German rate is

Table 17.1. Countries of the World Ranked by 1980 Infant Mortality

Country	Infant Mortality Rate		
	1980	1981	1982
1. Sweden	6.9*	6.9*	6.8
2. Japan	7.5*	7.1	6.6
3. Finland	6.7	6.5	
4. Norway	8.1	7.5	
5. Denmark	8.5*	7.9	8.4(p)
6. Netherlands	8.6	8.2	8.3
7. Switzerland	9.1	7.6	
8. France[a]	10.1*	9.7*	9.3
9. Canada	10.4	9.6	9.1
10. Australia	11.0	10.0	10.3
11. Belgium	11.0	11.7	11.7(p)
12. Spain	11.1	10.3	
13. Ireland	11.2	10.6	
14. United Kingdom	12.1	11.0(p)	
15. East Germany[b]	12.1	12.3	
16. United States	12.5	11.7	11.2(p)
17. West Germany	12.6	11.6	10.9
18. New Zealand	13.0*	11.8*	
19. Austria	14.3*	12.6	12.8
20. Italy	14.3	14.1	12.7(p)
21. Israel	15.1	14.6	13.9
22. Malta	15.5	13.1	13.9(p)
23. Brunei	17.5		12.8
24. Greece	17.9	14.3(p)	
25. Puerto Rico	18.5	18.6	
26. Czechoslovakia	18.5*	16.9	16.1(p)
27. Costa Rica	19.1	18.0	
28. Cuba	19.6	18.5	17.3(p)
29. Bulgaria	20.2	19.5	
30. Poland	21.2	20.6	20.2(p)
31. Hungary	23.2*	20.8*	19.7(p)

* = updated

(p) = provisional

[a]Because of slight undercounting of first day mortality, the French rates are probably low by about 0.6 to 0.8, which would place France after Canada in the list.

[b]The nonstandard definitions in use in East Germany probably reduce the rates by 2.0 to 2.5, which means that East Germany should rank somewhere between New Zealand and Israel.

probably on the order of 14.2 to 14.5 which would place it somewhere between New Zealand and Israel.

Now let us return to the first objection raised in this article: "You can't compare the United States with its large mixed population with small European countries."

This objection is rather puzzling; presumably it is based either on the notion that health is easier to improve in a small country than in a large one, or that ethnically homogeneous populations are healthier or are more amenable than large or heterogeneous populations to improvements in health.

Without questioning the rationale of the objection, let us examine 10 states of the United States with the lowest infant mortality rates in 1980. They are: New Hampshire (9.2), Wyoming (9.8), Vermont (9.9), Minnesota (10.0), Colorado (10.1), Wisconsin (10.3), Hawaii (10.3), Kansas (10.4), Utah (10.4), and Massachusetts (10.5).

The populations of most of these states are small and homogeneous. If we were to insert these states into Haub's list, we would find that all 10 fell between eighth and tenth place. Even excluding the nonwhite infant mortality from the 10 states would not improve their ranking. In fact, on a national level, the infant mortality of whites in the United States (11.0) would only qualify for a tenth place.

The performance of Japan would seem to deal a final blow to this objection; with a population about half that of the United States, it nevertheless attained an infant mortality rate of 6.6 in 1982, placing it slightly lower than Sweden (6.8), which has traditionally had the lowest infant mortality in the world.

In the final analysis, only three modifications are suggested to Haub's ranking: (a) Remove the city-states, Hong Kong and Singapore, from the list; (b) move East Germany to a higher ranking—probably somewhere between New Zealand and Israel; (c) update provisional to final data and shift ranking as necessary. (Updated data are indicated by an *.)

We then conclude that instead of ranking 19 out of 33, the United States ranks 15 out of 31. While it is clear that the United States still lags behind many industrialized countries, we must recognize that even our best efforts may not materially affect our ranking in the immediate future. What we do need to recognize is that there is solid evidence that we can achieve much lower rates than we have now and that we must carefully monitor our progress to ensure that infant mortality declines are sustained by all segments of the population, not just by the national total.

REFERENCES

1. Haub, Carl, "Where Does the U.S. Stand on Infant Mortality?," *Intercom*, March/April, 1983.
2. "A WHO Report on Social and Biological Effects on Perinatal Mortality," Volume 1, p. 33. World Health Organization.

3. Klinger, A., *Infant Mortality in Eastern Europe 1950–1980,* pp 58–61. Statistical Publishing House, Budapest, Hungary, 1982.
4. Chase, Helen C., "International Comparison of Perinatal and Infant Mortality," National Center for Health Statistics, Series 3, Number 6, pp. 9–10, 1967.

18

Some Causes of Rising Mortality in the U.S.S.R.

S. MAKSUDOV

Recently the American press has given much attention to a heated discussion of demographic problems in the Soviet Union. Of special interest is the rise in mortality rates over the last decade.[1] The discussion begun after Christopher Davis and Murray Feshbach published their "detective" work (as one of the participants, Nick Eberstadt, rightly called it)[2] on the trends in Soviet infant mortality in the 1970s.[3] Unfortunately the authors could investigate only the first half of the decade (1970 to 1975), but this was hardly their fault. After 1975, Soviet demographic statistics avoid mention of infant mortality, or for that matter mortality in any age groups.[4] This silence itself speaks volumes.[5]

This discussion has revealed a great deal. For one thing it became obvious that life expectancy and low mortality are two of the most important criteria for measuring the quality of life of the population. Secondly, these criteria aid Western scholars who attempt to study the character of socialist society. As Eberstadt has stated, a boy in Delhi can expect to live longer than the boy of the same age in the U.S.S.R.[6] Not long ago drops in mortality rates and rises in life expectancy served Soviet propaganda as convincing evidence of the superiority of the socialist system. Now the situation has changed, but the politicization of the problem remains and this makes it more difficult to examine the problem. The debate is making it possible for the first time to answer some of the questions involving the life and death of Soviet man. It reveals some disturbing facts: mortality for almost all age groups continues to rise—infant mortality by up to 40 percent—while life expectancy is falling.

The question, however, still begs an answer: How can it be that a backward society emerging from the Stalinist era just twenty years ago could have overtaken many more developed countries in life expectancy by the 1960s?

First we should try to determine how the country could have attained such a demographic pinnacle. I will try to show that the high life expectancy among the Soviet population in the fifties and sixties was a coincidental result, not of medical or social improvements, but of historical circumstances. The population was subject to rigorous natural selection whereby the weak and the sick died off, leaving the strong to carry on.

The first stage of selection takes place at birth. Infant mortality prior to the revolution reached 30 percent of live births, up to 50 percent before age five. Doubtless generally only the healthiest and most vigorous survived.

The second major element in the selection process was the period of the civil war. Starvation and disease carried off many millions; the end of the war not by accident coincides with a sharp decline in mortality.

A third factor was the Second World War which brought with it new terrors of illness and malnutrition—and a higher death rate among all age groups. Once again the end of the war saw a rise in life expectancy.

All of these circumstances were of a temporary nature. The influence of selection gradually diminished and death rates in all groups began to rise in the sixties. It was not a true rise but a return to the "natural" level that had been artificially restrained.

RUSSIA AND THE U.S.S.R.

Before turning to the more alarming situation of today, let us look back, first to Russia at the time of the first census of 1897, and then to the Soviet Union of the 1970s.

In Russia, birth control was practically unknown. A family with five children was small, while ten children in a family was not considered particularly unusual; infant mortality was incredibly high.

The birth rate in Russia at that time was close to the physiological limit.[7] The demographic behavior of the Russian *muzhik* at the turn of the century was marked by early marriage and lack of means of birth control. This behavior was dictated by a socio-psychological pattern that had developed in the rural countryside over the course of centuries and depended little on the desires or personal characteristics of individuals.[8] Tradition demanded marriage as early as possible, boys at 18 to 20 years of age, girls at age 16 to 18. Differences in age between spouses were small (in rural communities it was considered disgraceful for a woman to marry an "old" man more than 2 to 3 years her senior). To remain unmarried was a disgrace (35 percent of women in the 20–24 year age group were ummarried, but only 5 percent in the 45–49 age bracket). Divorce was a grave sin; adultery and illegitimate children were serious crimes. Interfering with conception was not only a sin but a criminal offence.[9]

Nevertheless, the stereotype did not extend to child care in the modern sense. The well-known writer D. V. Grigorovich wrote, "The most affectionate father, the most caring mother will leave their child in the hands of fate with almost unconscionable carelessness, and not a thought even for the child's physical development, despite the fact that it is their single most important concern, simply because nothing better ever occurred to them. No sooner is the child out of diapers than he is handed over to his sister, herself no more than 4 or 5 years of age."[10] Average births for a woman at that time was 10 or 11, according to some researchers. The woman was turned into a baby-making machine.[11] The tremendous physiological stress of giving birth was added to the already enormous physical burden of housekeeping and agricultural labor. "The sickly, undernourished, crippled and prematurely wizened and aged figure of the rural woman, with obtuse, depressed and mournful expression. . . ."[12] It is no coincidence that the mortality of middle-aged women in 1897 outstripped that of men. Overall, life expectancy among men and women was about equal and generally low. (See Table 18.1) The percentage of men over age 60 was about 6.9, about the same as for women, 7. The corresponding figures for 1979 (8.7% and 16.7%)[13] differ almost by a factor of 2. The population was surprisingly young. Children and adolescents (up to age 19) accounted for almost half of the population (in 1979, one-third), while the same group accounted for two-thirds of the deaths (in 1970, 7 percent).[14]

Table 18.1. Probability of Death within a Year (per 1,000)

	1896–1897		1968–1971	
Age	M	F	M	F
0	298	259	27.8	21.8
5	20.4	20.2	0.94	0.69
10	6.84	6.48	0.67	0.45
15	4.57	5.29	0.97	0.47
20	6.63	6.7	2.08	0.75
25	7.47	7.91	2.91	0.91
30	7.89	8.62	3.89	1.19
35	9.31	9.94	4.91	1.67
40	11.2	11.2	6.36	2.18
45	14.8	13.4	8.42	3.26
50	18.8	16.5	11.3	4.76
55	25.4	23.9	16.2	6.79
60	32.6	33.1	23.2	9.81
65	48.7	50.3	34.9	26.7
70	67.7	66.6	48.6	50.4
75	87.9	85.2	73.6	82.7
80	112	112	107	124
Life Expectancy (in years)	31	33	64	74

Sources: Tsentral'noe Statisticheskoe Upravlenie Pri Sovete Ministrov S.S.S.R., *Itogy vsesoyuznoi perepisi naseleniia 1959 goda (Results of the U.S.S.R. Population Census of 1959)*, Moscow, 1962, p. 258.

Ts.S.U. S.S.S.R., *Naseleniye S.S.S.R. 1973; Statisticheskii sbornik (Population of the U.S.S.R. in 1973; A Statistical Compilation)*. Moscow, Statistika, 1975, p. 139.

Vestnik Statistiki (Herald of Statistics), Moscow, 1974, No. 2, p. 95.

Most of the demographic characteristics above were not peculiar to Russia. A well-known demographer wrote, "Russian mortality was generally typical for an agricultural economy lagging behind in hygiene and cultural development. But for its extraordinary high death rate in the lower age groups and its extremely low death rate among the aged, Russia occupies a special place among analogous states."[15]

Another peculiarity in the Russian mortality figures was her greater mortality levels in the cities than in the countryside. Except for children, the rural population (particularly men) lived significantly longer than the urban. The coefficient of mortality between the ages of 40 and 44 for male dwellers in 1897 was 18.7, for males in rural areas, 11.2; for women living in cities the figure was 12.9, while for rural women it was 11.1. Corresponding figures for the 50–54 age group were 28.8, 19, 17.5, and 16.9. And for ages 60–64 they were 47.6, 33.4, 32.1, and 34.1.[16]

Of special interest is the proximity of the indexes for rural men and for rural women (slightly higher for women) as well as the minor difference between the mortality figures for rural as opposed to urban women. Only men going to the cities to work in factories were in a worse position demographically.

Demographically, the U.S.S.R. today differs greatly from old Russia. People, their relationships, and the demographic stereotype of behavior have changed. Women now have not ten, but one, two, or at most three children (with the exception of Muslim groups) and their children are 10 times less likely to die in infancy.

Later marriages, large gaps between the ages of spouses, large numbers of unmarrieds, divorces, and births out of wedlock—all these have become commonplace occurrences. Birth control, only squeamishly approached by the progressive writers at the turn of the century and which they attributed to the wealthier classes,[17] is now so widely practiced that the U.S.S.R. has easily held the world record for some time now in absolute and relative numbers of abortions.

Removing from women such overwhelming physical and physiological burdens, plus other social and medical developments, have led to a complete reversal in the mortality figures for men and women. Death rates among women in practically all age groups are lower than for men. Women live longer and outnumber men in the middle ages.[18]

Significant shifts have also occurred in comparisons of mortality between urban and rural populations. Today deaths in almost all age groups are higher in the countryside than in the cities.

The age structure of the population has also changed. The population is older and the number in their working years has increased. The distribution of deaths by age group today is completely different. Almost 90 percent of the population lives to age 30 (3 times greater than in old Russia) and 40 percent live past age 70 (6 times greater than before).[19]

But the primary socio-psychological outcome might be considered to be the change in attitude toward children, toward their upbringing, and a sharp decline in infant mortality, which in any case, remains very high in comparison with other countries.

INFANT MORTALITY IN THE U.S.S.R.

Let us now briefly consider the study which has laid the groundwork for general discussion of the problem and, not surprisingly, generated a lot of interest. Davis and Feshbach painstakingly compiled data from widely scattered sources. Together with some peripheral data and additional suppositions, they were able to calculate a coefficient for infant mortality in the U.S.S.R. for 1975 and 1976. Davis and Feshbach, moreover, examined differences in methodology for determining infant mortality in the Soviet Union and the United States and then recalculated the Soviet statistics using the Western methodology.[20] This allowed them to compare data on infant deaths in the U.S.S.R. with worldwide statistics.

In considering the reasons for increases in infant mortality in the U.S.S.R., the authors considered the following:

1. Changes in numbers of children born in cities and in the countryside occurred in favor of the cities where death rates are lower and therefore could not depress the overall coefficient of infant deaths.
2. Rises in birth rates in the "Muslim" republics with higher infant mortality rates amounted to 1.6 percent for the period 1970 to 1976 and could only in small measure be due to the general rise in the rate of deaths among children.
3. The increase in the birth rate from 1.7 percent in 1969 to 1.84 percent in 1976 was too small to influence the rise in deaths.
4. The age of motherhood during the period under review dropped somewhat, which, however, could not have played a significant role.
5. Changes in order of births. It is known that deaths are more frequent among first-born than among second births, and higher among second children than among third-born. Over the given period the share of first- and second-born children in the total number of births grew, which would imply a general rise in death rates. Referring to American statistics, Davis and Feshbach demonstrate that this factor also played little part in the rise of U.S.S.R. mortality rates.

The major reasons for the growth in infant mortality according to Davis and Feshbach are not demographic but social, economic, and medical: more mothers who smoke and drink, more working women, poor health among mothers (according to Davis and Feshbach, serious illness in the mother can increase the probability of death for a newborn child by a factor of ten), more abortions,[21] inadequate medical care during pregnancy, poor nutrition among mothers and their infants, poor housing conditions, more children with genetic defects, a decline in the level of child care at home due to disintegration of families of multiple generations, poor quality of training among medical personnel, epidemics of flu and pneumonia.

A number of other factors could be added here. For example, deterioration of the "quality of the birthing population"—the appearance among mothers of individuals who, weak in childhood, nevertheless survived thanks to modern medicine; decreasing effectiveness of antibiotics in mothers and as passed from mother to child; appearance of new strains of viruses and bacterias; extreme lags in the availability of new, relatively expensive drugs (some, such as rondomycin, sigmamycin, ceparin, etc., have been around for more than ten years, but physicians are forbidden to prescribe them since they can be obtained only in clinics for the elite).

Another serious problem is the contamination of maternity centers and children's health clinics, in particular, with staphylococci. In the opinion of a number of physicians this has become a growing concern in recent years and affects the health of mothers as well as children. The health of children is also adversely affected by the employment of women in hazardous industries. (Research in the U.S.S.R. has shown that among women working on tractors the probability of their having children with birth defects rises by orders of magnitude.)

Thus, the rise in infant mortality in the U.S.S.R. is defined by social and medical factors. But the distribution of the increase geographically and by nationality plays a very important role.

From Table 18.2 it is not difficult to see that overall mortality in the Soviet Union is rising faster than the R.S.F.S.R. [Russian Soviet Federated Socialist Republic], the Ukraine, or the Baltic region. It follows then that the rise in the overall coefficient is due primarily to increases in infant mortality in the republics of Central Asia and the Caucasus, whose data is not published. Given the fact that these regions ac-

Table 18.2. Infant Mortality Rate, U.S.S.R. and by Republic: 1968 to 1976 (number of deaths per 1,000 live births)

Republics	1968	1969	1970	1971	1972	1973	1974	1975	1976
U.S.S.R. official data	26.4	25.8	24.7	22.9	24.7	26.4	27.9	29.4[a]	31.1[a]
acc. to Western method.	30.2	29.5	28.3	26.2	28.3	30.2	31.9	33.6	35.6
Slavic Republics									
R.S.F.S.R.	25.0	25.0	23.0	21.0	22.0	22.0	23.0	24.0	NA
Ukraine	18.6	18.4	17.3	16.2	17.4	17.4	NA	NA	NA
Belorussia	20.0	19.0	19.0	16.0	16.0	17.0	17.0	NA	NA
Baltic Republics									
Estonia	18.3	16.9	17.8	17.6	15.8	15.8	17.6	NA	NA
Latvia	19.0	18.0	18.0	16.0	16.0	16.0	19.0	NA	NA
Lithuania	19.9	20.7	19.3	14.8	17.4	18.1	19.4	NA	NA
Transcaucasian Republics									
Armenia	26.0	NA	NA	NA	NA	NA	NA	NA	NA
Azerbaydzhan	38.0	NA	NA	NA	NA	NA	NA	NA	NA
Georgia	28.7	NA	NA	NA	NA	NA	NA	NA	NA
Central Asian Republics and Kazakhstan									
Kazakhstan	26.5	NA	NA	NA	NA	NA	NA	NA	NA
Kirgiziya	NA	NA	NA	NA	NA	NA	NA	NA	NA
Tadzhikistan	NA	NA	NA	NA	NA	NA	NA	NA	NA
Uzbekistan	NA	NA	NA	NA	NA	NA	NA	NA	NA
Non-Reported Republics									
Turkmenistan	NA	NA	NA	NA	NA	NA	NA	NA	NA
Moldavia	NA	NA	NA	NA	NA	NA	NA	NA	NA

NA — not available.

[a]Estimated.

[b]Infant mortality rates for Turkmenistan and Moldavia have never been published. Rates for all other 13 republics are available for only 2 years during the period 1958 to 1976. For these 2 years, 1960 and 1967, an estimate for the two republics, in combined form, was made by a residual method.

This table does not include indirect data from the literature. It is known, for example, that infant mortality among Uzbeks in 1973 to 1975 was 2½ times higher than among Ukrainians.[22]

Table 18.3. Computation of Infant Mortality Rates in the U.S.S.R.

	Share of the Newborn Children, Percent				Infant Mortality Rates			
Year	U.S.S.R.	R.S.F.S.R.	West	East	U.S.S.R.	R.S.F.S.R.	West	East
1959	100	53	27	20	40.6	41	36	46
1960	100	52	26	22	35.3	37	31	36
1965	100	47	26	27	27.2	27	21	34
1970	100	45	27	28	24.7	23	18	34
1971	100	45	27	28	22.9	21	16	33
1972	100	45	27	28	24.7	23	17	35
1973	100	45	26	29	26.4	22	17	42
1974	100	45	26	29	27.9	23	18	44
1975	100	45	26	29	29.4	24	18	48
1976	100	45	25	30	31.1	24	18	53

West—includes the Ukraine, Belorussia, the Baltic republics, Moldavia, and Georgia. East—includes Central Asia, Kazakhstan, Armenia, and Azerbaydzhan. This division follows that of Davis and Feshbach. In addition to materials cited by these authors, I have used Ts.S.U. S.S.S.R., *Naseleniye S.S.S.R. 1973: Statisticheky sbornik (Population of the U.S.S.R. in 1973: A Statistical Compilation).* Moscow, Statistika, 1975, pp. 69–83 on birth rates in different regions.

counted for nearly a third of the births in 1976, one can reconstruct their average coefficient of infant mortality (see Table 18.3).

The results appear somewhat strange. Death rates in the Asian territories of the U.S.S.R. (the East) dropped sharply in 1960 (by more than 20 percent), and it remained stable at a low level for 12 years, after which it rose again over a four-year period by 50 percent. Both the dramatic rise between 1973 and 1976 and the stable low level between 1960 and 1972 appear suspicious. One could be led to believe that mortality rates in the sixties were underestimated. And in fact, such was the proposition of Gosplan official A. Smirnov in an interview with Western correspondents.[23] Let us assume that these assertions are legitimate, and that the rise in the death rate in the seventies in the Asian areas of the country followed the trends in the Russian republic and the Ukraine (about 10 percent). This would mean that in 1970 to 72, infant deaths in these regions amounted to approximately 45 per thousand births, and that the underestimation was about 30 percent. A derivation of the infant mortality rate using such assumptions is illustrated in Table 18.4.

Table 18.4. An Evaluation of Death Rates among Newborns in the U.S.S.R. with Adjustments

	Infant Mortality Rate				
	According to Soviet Methodology				According to Western Methodology
			With Corrections for Incompleteness of data		
Year	U.S.S.R. (official)	East (est.)	East	U.S.S.R.	U.S.S.R.
1	2	3	4	5	6
1959	40.6	46	61	44	48
1960	35.3	36	48	38	42
1965	27.2	34	45	30	34
1970	24.7	34	45	28	32
1971	22.9	33	44	26	30
1972	24.7	35	46	28	32
1973	26.4	42	47	28	32
1974	27.9	44	48	29	33
1975	29.4	48	49	30	34
1976	31.1	53	53	31	35

The result seems fairly convincing. The drastic rise and close correspondence in rates to the figures of Western areas in some years—an artifact unsupported from the medical and social point of view—has disappeared.

A recomputation of the rates for the country as a whole, adjusted for missing data and using the Western methodology, shows that the level of infant mortality in the nation in the sixties and seventies was noticeably higher than has been generally accepted. It never dropped below 30 per thousand. The rise in infant mortality in the seventies was not as sharp as it appeared—amounting to 10 to 15 percent. Over the last 10 to 15 years we can see not so much a growth in the rate of infant mortality, but a stabilization, or lack of decline. this is a rather unusual phenomenon, putting the Soviet Union in a special position, since virtually all countries (at least those which keep track of infant death rates) have cut mortality rates among newborns significantly.

LIFE EXPECTANCY IN THE U.S.S.R. AND ELSEWHERE

The reconstruction of infant mortality rates in the U.S.S.R. on the Western model conducted by Davis and Feshbach has clarified many issues. From Table 18.5 it is evident that infant deaths in the Soviet Union during the sixties and seventies was noticeably higher than in the developed West. This gap has since widened, not as a consequence of any catastrophic rise in mortality in the U.S.S.R., but as a result of dramatic decreases in mortality in the West. The explanation therefore, lies less in any mysterious changes in the Soviet Union, but, on the contrary, in the very lack of any substantial change. Maintenance of health care and a level economic situation should cause a rise in the death rate due to deterioration in the effectiveness of available drugs, changes in the ethnic composition (a more rapid rate of growth in the Muslim populations), as well as a number of other factors.[24]

This is in fact what has occurred. Over the past 20 years, the death rate for the country has not dropped, and not surprisingly. Indeed it would be amazing for a nation with the biggest military industry to allocate enough additional resources for health care and social welfare in order to overtake more industrially developed countries not burdened with such enormous unproductive expenses.[25]

The Soviet Union's position in Table 18.5 is fairly well defined. Based on the two fundamental demographic indicators of infant mor-

Table 18.5. Infant Mortality and Life Expectancy

	Infant Deaths per 1000 Births (numbers are rounded)			Life Expectancy (years)		
Country	1960	1970	1977	1960	1970	1977
Industrial countries,	28	17	12	69	72	73
incl.: Sweden	17	11	8	72	74	75
U.S.	26	20	15	70	71	73
W. Germany	34	24	17	69	70	71
South Europe	56	37	32	65	69	70
incl.: Greece	40	30	23	68	71	73
Yugoslavia	88	56	35	62	68	69
Portugal	78	58	39	62	68	69
Socialist countries	47	31	23	67	70	70
Hungary	48	36	26	67	69	70
Rumania	76	49	31	64	69	70
U.S.S.R.	42	32	35	68	70	68
Latin America	95	71	58	56	61	64
Far East	60	50	41	53	58	61
Middle East				46	51	54
South Asia				43	47	49
Africa				40	44	47

This table has been compiled from *World Tables*, the second edition (1980). Published for the World Bank by the Johns Hopkins University Press. Some of the data cited is less than precise, but it gives rather accurate impressions of the global demographic situation. Only the data for the U.S.S.R. is adjusted.

tality and life expectancy, the U.S.S.R. should not belong in the ranks of developed nations—nor should it have claimed membership 20 years ago despite the arguments of the Soviet propagandists. The Soviet Union occupies a place among the countries of South and Eastern Europe, though she has lost her place as a leader in this group. But is the situation so bad as to give support to a notion of degeneration of the population and demographic catastrophe? The table does not bear this out.

The Soviet Union lags behind the United States by approximately 5 years in life expectancy, and leads the United States by a factor of more than 2 in infant deaths. But there is an almost identical gap between the United States and Sweden, and in favor of the latter. The gap between the Soviet Union and the developing world is much larger. In Latin America, for example, infant mortality on average is almost twice as high, and life expectancy lags behind the Soviet Union by nearly 4 years. Africa and Southern Asia, moreover, trail Latin America by more than ten years in expected lifespan, and infant death rates are 2 to 3 times higher. Compared against worldwide levels, then, the shifts in the demographic situation in the U.S.S.R. do not appear so calamitous; they represent a more or less traditional lag behind the industrialized world. The U.S.S.R.'s "catastrophic" levels will remain for decades only a distant dream for underdeveloped countries.

LIFE EXPECTANCY IN THE SOVIET UNION AND IN THE UNITED STATES IN THE TWENTIETH CENTURY

The Soviet lag appears even less threatening when life expectancy among other age groups is examined. Table 18.6 shows that Americans between the ages of 10 and 30 can expect to live 3 years longer than their counterparts in the U.S.S.R. This would be 5 to 7 percent of their expected life spans. For a 40-year-old, the gap narrows to 2 years, and by age 50 to only 1 year. Twenty years ago the comparison would have been similar, but in favor of the U.S.S.R.

Curiously, life expectancy for most age groups in the United States in 1978 coincides with figures for the Soviet Union in 1958. Over the 20-year period America has risen to the level of the Soviet Union, while the U.S.S.R. has fallen to the previous U.S. position. There is nothing especially uncommon about the simple fact of a narrowing of life expectancy by 1½ to 2 years. American census statistics covering the twentieth century show 21 occurrences of shortened life expectancy over a 78-year period, from relatively small changes on the order of 0.2 to 0.3 in 1963 and 1968, to very large (3.6 in 1928, 3.2 in 1936), not to mention the extraordinary drop of 11.8 years in 1918. An overall rise in life expectancy in the United States was punctuated by periods of

Table 18.6. Average Additional Life Expectancy for Various Age Groups

Age	1897 Russia	1900 USA	1927 USSR	1929 USA	1939 USSR	1939 USA	1958 USSR	1958 USA	1971 USSR	1971 USA	1975 USSR	1978 USA
0	32	49	44	61	47	64	69	69	70	71	68	73
10	49	51	54	56	56	59	63	62	62	63	61	65
20	41	43	45	47	47	49	54	52	53	54	52	55
30	34	35	38	39	39	41	45	43	44	44	43	46
40	27	28	30	30	31	32	36	34	35	35	34	36
50	20	21	23	23	24	24	27	25	26	26	26	28
60	14	15	16	16	17	16	19	17	19	19	18	19
70	10	7	10	10	11[a]	10	13[a]	11	12	12	12	13
80	7	5	6	6	7	6	8	7	7	7	7	8
85	6	4	5	4	5	4	6	5	5	5	5	6

Sources: Ts.S.u. S.S.S.R., *Naseleniye S.S.S.R. 1973; Statistichesky sbornik (Population of the U.S.S.R. in 1973; A Statistical Compilation),* Moscow, Statistika, 1975, p. 139. *Vital Statistics of the United States,* Vol. II, Section 5, "Life Tables," U.S. Department of Health and Human Services, Public Health Service. Data rounded to whole numbers. Data cited are for the given years, and for the surrounding period (e.g., 1976 to 1978, 1969 to 1971).

[a] *Narodonaselenie stran mira (Population of the World),* Moscow, 1978, p. 178. The figures are lower: 10 years in 1939, 11 in 1958. Apparently the author (M. S. Bedny) considers the mortality tables for 1939 and 1959 insufficiently precise in the higher age groups.

stagnation and even decreases in expected lifespan (1921–1931, 1933–1943, 1961–1968). The later period is somewhat reminiscent of the situation in the seventies in the U.S.S.R. Life expectancy settled at about 70.2 years in the United States as a result of a rise in death rates among males in a number of age groups. The life expectancy of males reached 66.8 years in 1959 and hovered about this figure through 1969. Only in 1970 did it begin rising once again. It is worth noting that, as differs from the Soviet Union where the drop in life expectancy was determined in part by a rise in infant mortality, in the United States the deterioration in the position of the male population occurred against the backdrop of an improvement in infant death rates (i.e., at the expense of other age groups). Non-white males appeared to be in an especially poor position. Life expectancy among non-white males reaching age 5 in 1959 to 1961 was 1½ years higher than in 1969 to 1971. The same applies to 10- to 15- and 20-year-olds. In the 25–40 year group, the gap narrows to one year, or a half year, and only among men aged 75 years do we notice some progress in life expectancy over the 10-year period.

Neither the lag of several years behind the United States, nor the decreases in life expectancy is therefore particularly surprising. Such a situation might be expected in a country that puts all of its resources into the development of heavy industry and the arms race. Such was the case before the revolution and prior to the Second World War. Strange were the shifts in relative rates of mortality between the two great powers, in particular the unexpected zigzag during the 1950s. At the turn of the century the advantageous position of the United States as regards life expectancy is noted in all age groups under 70, while Russian elderly lived longer. By the end of the twenties to forties differences in mortality in the middle age groups evened out (the United States is ahead in ages 40 and above). By the end of the fifties we see the U.S.S.R. with a clearly dominant position, which then began to quickly erode (Table 18.6).

We must note that over the entire period under consideration the Soviet Union maintains an even or better position in life expectancy in the older age groups. The primary reason for this phenomenon is evident.

DEPENDENCE OF MIDDLE AGE MORTALITY ON LEVELS OF INFANT MORTALITY

The extraordinary longevity of older people in Russia at the turn of the century drew the attention of contemporary researchers who pointed to the quiet life of the Russian peasant.[26] But yet another factor played a substantial role—high infant mortality. Nearly half of all babies born died before age five. This severe selection process carried off the weaker segments of the population. The survivors lived longer but made up a smaller share of the total population than in countries with lower rates of infant deaths. We observe a similar phenomenon when comparing white and nonwhite groups in the United States population (Table 18.7). The white population experiences lower infant mortality and dominates the middle age groups, but their life expectancy beyond 70 years of age is somewhat lower. We see a similar situation when comparing mortality of various groups in the U.S.S.R., as for example between Ukrainians and Uzbeks. Death rates in the higher age groups are less among populations with higher rates of infant mortality. In the 0–4 age group, Uzbeks expe-

Table 18.7. Life Expectancy of Americans (years)

	Whites				Nonwhites			
	Males		Females		Males		Females	
Age	1978	1900	1978	1900	1978	1900	1978	1900
0	70.2	48.2	77.8	51.1	65.0	32.5	73.6	35.0
40	33.6	27.7	39.9	29.2	30.4	23.1	37.0	24.4
70	11.1	9.0	14.8	9.6	11.6	9.3	14.8	9.6
85	5.3	3.8	6.7	4.1	7.8	4.0	9.9	5.1

Vital Statistics of the United States, Vol. II, Section 5, "Life Tables," U.S. Department of Health and Human Services, Public Health Service, 1978, pp. 5–13.

rience death rates 2½ times as high as Ukrainians (13 and 5.1 per thousand); by age 40 the relative mortality rates even out (4.4 per thousand); for groups over 70 years of age, mortality among Uzbeks is noticeably lower at 45.6 per thousand as opposed to 77.5 per thousand for Ukrainians.[27]

An analagous picture is presented when comparing urban and rural populations in the U.S.S.R. Up to ages 40 to 45, mortality is noticeably higher in the countryside than in the cities; but after age 50 the reverse is true. Among those aged 65 to 69 deaths amounted to 29.1 per thousand in urban areas and 24.5 per thousand in rural areas.[28]

So it becomes apparent that the most diverse ethnic and social groups experience an inverse relationship between deaths among infants and among older people. High infant mortality serves as a severe selector, ensuring somewhat higher survivability in older generations. This, in part, helps to confirm the somewhat higher levels of life expectancy in older age groups in the U.S.S.R. when compared with the United States, which we noted earlier. Infant mortality in Russia/the U.S.S.R.—up until the 1950s—was significantly higher than in America and it is exactly this which in large part helped to assure longevity in the older population.

With the sharp decline in infant mortality in the 1950s, this "advantage" began to disappear, to the point where today the situation is about the same for cohorts up to 25 years of age in both the United States and the Soviet Union. But not quite, since the West at the time began an intensive assault on infant mortality.

ON THE THRESHOLD OF A SECOND DEMOGRAPHIC REVOLUTION

As in the past, so today, infant mortality is due to the three primary factors: disease contracted by a child from the environment (infection, colds, intestinal ailments, etc.), traumas arising from the birth process (prematurity, asphyxiation, dislocations), and birth defects, mainly genetic deficiencies. Under conditions of high infant mortality and when numbers of deaths among infants approximate deaths in the older age groups, the primary cause of death among newborns was infection. The assault on infant mortality, begun in the developed countries in the nineteenth century—and in the underdeveloped countries in the middle of the twentieth century—led to a sharp drop in deaths among children from causes of the first group. Where the curve describing general mortality once had the shape of a "U," it has more recently taken on the shape of a "J"—mortality among infants is now considerably lower than among the oldest generations. A demographic explosion occurred—the first demographic revolution.[29]

It is worth noting the differences between reasons for the drop in infant mortality in the U.S.S.R. and in the West.[30] In the developed countries it happened gradually; as the culture developed, more attention was paid to the needs of the child and his environment improved. Medical discoveries and general social advancement supported this tendency which then was adopted by the family. In the U.S.S.R. and in the underdeveloped countries the drop in infant mortality was a result primarily of measures introduced by the state and society (the creation of a health care system, new medications, long maternity leave and the like). Family life, the care of the child and for his environment, changed gradually, and with a substantial lag. Government health care programs (women's clinics, childbirth centers, polyclinics and hospitals) were intended primarily to preserve the health of the child.[31] Thus, advances against the second and third groups of primary causes of deaths among infants overtook efforts of the first. Today the structure of infant mortality in the U.S.S.R. differs from Western experience in a higher proportion of illnesses of the first category. In the West such diseases as pneumonia seldom lead to death, while in the Soviet Union they account for a significant share of infant deaths.[32]

This discrepancy grows still larger as a result of efforts against early childhood diseases in recent decades in the West. Whereas in 1950 about 1.1 percent of newborns died in the first day of birth defects, underdevelopment and other prenatal causes in the United States, in 1981 a similar share (1.2 percent) died during the course of the first year. There was a sharp drop in the mortality of infants from all types of birth defects and genetic illnesses.[33] In Sweden, where mortality today is two times lower than in the United States, the decline in deaths from birth defects has been greater still.[34]

Unfortunately, in the majority of instances, preserving the lives of infants suffering from the effects of genetic defect and childbirth trauma does not always result in total cure, and only a fraction are assured a normal future life. Society, therefore, supports a growing number of mentally and physically handicapped individuals.[35] This situation can gradually lead to a decline in the general vitality of the population. The threat of genetic disease is especially serious.

There are more than a thousand known genetic defects which can be transmitted by either father, mother, or both. A number of these conditions have been passed down through many previous generations; others have appeared relatively recently, as a result of mutual alterations caused by unfavorable environmental circumstances, radiation, chemical mutagens, etc.[36] These diseases can be divided into three primary groups: chromosomal deficiencies, genetic blood defects, and metabolic disorders. Some types of genetic illness appear during pregnancy and can lead to spontaneous abortion[37] while others appear as abnormal development of the organism after birth, sometimes well into maturity. According to available data, genetic deficiencies affect no less than 5 percent of newborns, and the number is growing.[38]

By mentioning all these examples I do not pretend to discovery of, or even research into, a complex modern phenomenon. I merely note its existence. By analogy with the struggle against exogenous disease, we could call this process the second demographic revolution. It presents mankind with complex moral problems which I will not argue here: human life is precious and the saving of an individual child is a blessing. Eugenic selection practiced by the ancient Greeks is not only impossible but is, by outward appearances, beyond the comprehension of our civilization. We must find other means of resolving this issue which comes ever closer to modern man, first in the developed countries, later in the developing world and the U.S.S.R.

The problem appears less serious in the Soviet Union than in the West because of higher levels of infant mortality (two times higher than in America, four times higher than in Sweden). But, as noted above, the U.S.S.R. is undertaking serious efforts to decrease mortality due to birth defects and early childhood diseases.

Thus, the determined assault on infant mortality in the Western countries developed over recent decades has cut mortality primarily from genetic deficiency. It is possible that this process could lead to some decline in the overall vitality of each succeeding generation. Some deterioration in the genetic fund of the population could also result. The Soviet Union must also confront these issues, albeit with a lag.

TRENDS IN MORTALITY FOLLOWING THE REVOLUTION

As we have already seen, mortality in Russia remained at a very high level. The drop at the turn of the century was slight and affected primarily infants and the younger age groups (Table 18.8). In several age categories for males there was even some growth in death rates.

The First World War similarly had little effect. Mortality over the period 1914 to 1917 remained at the pre-war level, falling only slightly as a result of a decline in the birth rate. (Remember that childhood mortality at the time comprised a high proportion of population losses.)

The civil war that followed changed completely the demographic situation in the country. Famine, typhus epidemics, and Spanish influenza[39] carried off many millions.[40] The country emerged from the war exhausted, depleted, weakened, and (paradoxically) having a sharply reduced death rate. This surprising fact is demonstrated in Table 18.8. Virtually all age groups in 1926 to 1927 demonstrated greater robustness (by 20 to 30 percent). How could this happen?

For Soviet authors there is nothing strange here: brilliant successes in medicine and social

Table 18.8. Mortality by Age Cohorts (per thousand)

Age	1896–1897	1907–1908	1926–1927	1938–1939	1958–1959
0–1	375	290	174	167	41
0–4	133	119	78.9	75.8	11.9
5–9	12.9	10.7	7.3	5.5	1.1
10–14	5.4	5.4	3.1	2.6	0.8
15–19	5.8	5.7	3.7	3.4	1.3
20–24	7.6	7.6	5.5	4.4	1.8
25–29	8.2	8.3	6.1	4.7	2.2
30–34	8.7	8.6	6.3	5.4	2.6
35–39	10.3	10.3	7.5	6.8	3.1
40–44	11.8	11.7	9.0	8.1	4.0
45–49	15.7	15.6	10.9	10.2	5.4
50–54	18.5	18.3	14.0	13.8	7.9
55–59	29.5	29.0	18.1	17.1	11.2
60–64	34.5	34.0	24.7	24.5	17.1
65–69	61.6	62.0	36.5	35.0	25.2
Over 70	89.0	90.0	79.5	78.9	63.8
All population	32.4	28.4	20.3	17.4	7.4

Sources: *Narodonaseleniye Stran Mira (Population of the World)*, Moscow, 1978, p. 176. *Smertnost' i Prodolzhitel'nost' Zhizni Naseleniya S.S.S.R., 1926–1927, Tablitsy Smertnosti (Mortality and Longevity of the Population of the U.S.S.R., Life Tables, 1926 to 1927)*, Moscow, 1930.

welfare on the part of the Soviet state. This conclusion, however, does not hold up under scrutiny. All the fundamental measures undertaken (training thousands of doctors, creation of a network of medical and childcare facilities, mass innoculations hospital expansions and the like) were carried out between 1926 and 1939. A glance at Table 18.8 leaves one with a feeling of bewilderment of how little effect all these efforts had (mortality rates in 1926 and 1939 were virtually identical). The drop in mortality occurred all at once and not in 1926, but somewhat earlier. The urban census of 1923 showed an improvement in life expectancy. For example, in Leningrad, of 100,000 males, 55,091 had reached age 20 in 1910 to 1911, 69,673 had reached age 20 in 1923, and 69,770 in 1926 to 1927. For females the corresponding figures are 59,926, 73,033, and 72,973.[41]

Denying the miraculous effects of the newly organized Soviet institutions, we are forced to search for other explanations for the vitality of the Soviet population in 1923 and succeeding years. Out of demographic cataclysm the population emerged renewed, and this is no metaphor. The sharp decline in mortality in 1923 to 1926 is more readily explained by the preceding catastrophe. Naturally, the popular notion that mass epidemics and famine weakens a population is legitimate. But it should be added that, statistically, disease carried off the weaker population, or those "who should have died" during the post-war years, but because of a deterioration in the living conditions, they perished prematurely. In addition, heightened immunity generally follows massive epidemics—most significant with many childhood diseases.

Finally, it should not be forgotten that a complete restructuring of the system for compiling mortality rates took place during this period. Civil registration replaced parish records. It is not impossible that a discrepancy could arise between church records and those of a state official concerning the birth of a living or stillborn infant. Moreover, the population did not immediately adapt itself to the civil procedures for recording deaths, seeing nothing particularly significant in the requirement. Death rates from a variety of social causes also dropped (such as alcoholism and venereal disease).[42]

All of these factors (greater losses among a weakened population, greater immunity, poor registration) were temporary in nature and should have gradually disappeared. Mortality should have begun to increase somewhat. This was not the case (Table 18.8), apparently due to the broad health and social measures undertaken in the 1930s, due to population movements to the cities where death rates were substantially lower than in the countryside at the time. The famine of 1932 to 1933 and the losses of rural population during deportations, for some areas could have accounted for a greater "natural" selection. Considering all these factors, variations between morality tables for 1939 and 1926 appear small.[43]

Thus, the mortality rate before the revolution was significant and was declining, except infant mortality, very slowly. During the civil war many millions of people perished, first of all the weak and ill. This increased the statistical viability of those who survived. As a result, mortality rates in all age cohorts dropped greatly in 1923 to 1926.

During the succeeding pre-war years, shifts in mortality were insignificant despite sweeping health care and social programs. It is possible that the stability was due to the effect of two conflicting trends: a return of the death rate to previous "normal" levels, and a decline in mortality as a result of better medical care.

Prior to the Second World War, life expectancy in age groups over 40 was close to the level in the West.

Almost immediately after the war, in 1946 to 1950, the mortality rate reached the level of that of the developed nations and further decline in the rate during subsequent years took place mainly because of a decrease in infant mortality. The rate of the latter was 80 per thousand in 1950, and became only 41 in 1958.

Unfortunately, there are no reliable data on infant mortality in 1946. It is known that as a result of sulfa drugs, it decreased somewhat in 1944 to 45 compared to 1943,[44] which was 80 percent higher than in the last pre-war year, 1940. But new drugs and medical care at the end of the war were mostly for the urban population. Therefore, it might be assumed that actual infant mortality in 1946 was close to the pre-war rate. This is supported by the data on infant mortality in Leningrad: it was 119 per thousand in 1946, in contrast to 144 per thousand in 1939.[45] One should not think that high infant mortality in 1946 was a consequence of the weakening of the Leningrad population during the blockade. The autnor from whom our data is obtained emphasizes that all basic measurements of newborn in 1946 were of prewar proportions.[46] Because of the central position of Leningrad, and the blockade in the immediate past, it received a larger share of the new drugs in comparison with rural areas. Therefore, applying the decline in infant mortality in Leningrad in 1939 to 1946 to the whole country, we would not exaggerate the result. From what has been said, it follows that the infant mortality rate in 1946 was approximately 140 per thousand.

Hence, although the overall mortality rate for the whole population was relatively low in 1946, infant mortality remained rather high. Let us try to eliminate infant mortality from the computation (Table 18.9). We observe that the mortality rate of those 1 year old and older in 1946 was virtually stable and in 1958 was insignificantly lower—17 percent. Apparently this decline was distributed unevenly among age cohorts, and the biggest drop was in the 1 to 5 year age group. (A process analogous to infant mortality should have taken place within this group.) Taking this fact into account, one may assert that mortality by age groups in 1958 to 1959 reflects the level of mortality achieved in 1946, except for those 0 to 4 years old. The level is shown in Table 18.8. Compared with that of 1938 to 1939, infant mortality was 5 to 7 percent lower in 1958 to 1959; mortality of middle-aged cohorts was half the previous level; and that of the elderly (over 50 years old) was two-thirds the previous level.

This huge jump was the second, and for the most of the age cohorts, the last significant decline in mortality of the Soviet population.[47]

Thus, in the middle of the century, the Soviet mortality rate declined sharply. For the elderly cohorts, it was caused by brutal selection during the war, and therefore coincides with its ending. For children, the decline in mortality had been taking place gradually from the end of the 1940s till the beginning of the 1960s, and followed the introduction of sulfa drugs and antibiotics.

TENDENCIES OF CHANGE IN MORTALITY OF THE SOVIET POPULATION IN THE 1960S AND 1970S

Changes in mortality have been already considered in the literature. Up to the middle of the 1960s, mortality continued to decline (Table 18.10), and then mortality of the senior cohorts grows slowly. The changes in mortality of males and females are substantially different. For males under 30, the tendency is down; for those over 30, the growth is stabilized with small fluctuations.[48] Mortality of those 45 to 49 years old, that is, born during the civil war, has increased considerably. Mortality of females continued to decline (Table 18.10).

A noticeable rise in mortality of those over 30 began in the middle of the 1960s. People of these cohorts were born before 1928 and more or less sustained the selection of high infant mortality, of the last war, and, some of them, of the civil war. But during the following 15 years, the machinery of this selection began to weaken. The "normal," natural level of mortality, which would have existed if these cohorts had not endured the catastrophes of the previous period, started to restore itself. Soviet medicine in the 1960s and 1970s did not have enough revolutionary developments (something comparable to the introduction of antibiotics) which could make us for this restoration of mortality. Various measures merely smoothed this growth.[49]

Growth in male and female mortality is tak-

Table 18.9. Mortality Rate of Those 1 Year and Older (millions)

Year	Population Average for the Year Except Newborns	Born	Died, Total of Those	Younger Than 1 Year	Older Than 1 Year	Mortality Rate of Those 1 Year Old and Older, %
1958	201	5.240	1.490	0.212	1.278	0.64
1950	175	4.805	1.745	0.395	1.350	0.77
1946	166[a]	4.022	1.836	0.563	1.273	0.77
1940	189	6.096	3.520	1.148	2.372	1.26

Source: *Naseleniye S.S.S.R. 1973 (Population of the U.S.S.R. in 1973)*, Moscow, 1975, pp. 7, 69, 141.

[a]Calculated from 1950 using birthrates for 1946 to 1949 (published in *Zhenshchiny v S.S.S.R.* [*Women in the U.S.S.R.*], Moscow, 1975, p. 101) and with average mortality during 1946–50 of 1 percent.

Table 18.10. Change in Mortality Rate, 1960 to 1980

Age	1958–1959		1964–1965		1971–1972		1974		1979[a]	
	Males	Fem.	Males	Fem.	Males	Fem.	Males	Fem.	Males	Fem.
0–4	12.6	10.8	7.7	6.5	7.5	6.0	8.5	6.8	8.7	7.0
5–9	1.3	0.9	0.9	0.7	0.8	0.5	0.8	0.5	0.8	0.5
10–14	1.0	0.7	0.5	0.5	0.6	0.4	0.6	0.4	0.7	0.4
15–19	1.7	1.0	1.3	.06	1.4	0.6	1.4	0.6	1.5	0.6
20–24	2.4	1.3	2.1	1.0	2.5	0.8	2.5	0.8	2.7	0.8
25–29	3.0	1.5	2.8	1.1	3.3	1.0	3.1	0.9	3.7	1.0
30–34	3.6	1.7	3.7	1.4	4.3	1.3	4.4	1.4	4.6	1.4
35–39	4.5	2.2	4.6	1.9	5.6	1.9	5.4	1.8	6.7	2.0
40–44	6.0	3.0	5.7	2.5	7.3	2.6	7.4	2.6	8.4	2.7
45–49	8.1	3.9	7.5	3.5	9.6	3.7	9.7	3.7	11.8	4.2
50–54	12.2	5.6	11.9	5.4	13.6	5.8	13.9	5.8	15.6	6.1
55–59	18.2	8.3	16.5	7.4	19.2	7.9	19.5	8.2	22.3	8.9
60–64	26.1	12.8	26.2	12.6	28.3	12.6	28.7	12.6	32.1	13.8
65–69	36.2	21.3	36.0	18.9	40.5	20.2	40.9	20.2	45.2	21.6
CT.70	77.6	60.5	—	—	—	—	90.5	66.7	91.8	79.4
	8.0	7.0	7.6	6.7	9.0	7.8	9.3	8.2	10.1	8.9

Sources: *Narodonaseleniye Stran Mira (Population of the World)*, Moscow, 1978, p. 172. *Vestnik Statistiki (Herald of Statistics)*, Moscow, 1975, No. 12; 1976, No. 11.
All numbers above the double line pertain to those born after the revolution. all numbers above the single line pertain to those born after World War II.

[a]Estimate.

ing place with different intensities, but one should not forget that male and female losses were also very different during the previous period. The difference in male and female mortality became bigger throughout the twentieth century and by the end of the 1970s was of huge magnitude. Today, the difference in age at death is almost 11 years. In most of the developed countries, the gap is 6 to 7 years, and in the developing countries, it is 2 to 3 years. In the U.S.S.R. the inequality of the sexes in life expectancy is to a large extent social in character. For example, in cohorts of 20 to 40 year-olds, where mortality is relatively low, it is determined by social, rather than medical, factors (occupational injuries, alcoholism, crime); thus, male and female mortality rates have opposite tendencies. The former is growing, the latter is falling or is stable. This, without doubt, indicates that certain social conditions in the country are unfavorable.

That growth in mortality of these age cohorts has, to a significant extent, a social character is supported also by the fact that this tendency is more evident in rural rather than urban areas. In the countryside, mortality of all age cohorts of 50 and under is higher than in cities, and is growing faster. Many authors think that the introduction of modern techniques, and especially chemicals (fertilizers), into rural life plays a substantial role. It leads to growth of occupational hazards and gradual poisoning of the human organism throughout the environment.[50]

Children and youth—up to 20 years of age—have not passed through the catastrophic war period, and the tendency of their mortality reflects real medical and social conditions of the Soviet populace. During the last two decades, mortality of this generation declined noticeably (for females more, males less). A large part of the decline corresponds to the first half of the 1960s when medicines came into widespread use. The consequent period is characterized by a highly stable mortality rate, with small fluctuations (Table 18.10).

High infant mortality gives heightened viability for a certain period to children of subsequent cohorts. Therefore, child mortality (1 to 9 years) in the U.S.S.R. is not high compared with that of other countries.

Thus, during the 1970s, there was smooth growth of mortality in all those age cohorts which had passed through the severe selection of the catastrophic years. The normal level was restored, and this coincides with given medical and social conditions. Child mortality declined or stayed at a stable level. Infant mortality has increased somewhat recently.

CONCLUSIONS

1. Infant mortality in the U.S.S.R. has always been at a rather high level—not less than 3 percent of newborns. During the last 15 years, stabilization of infant mortality, and even some growth—especially in Asian—is observed. Probably in part this can be explained by improvements in recording mortality. The lack of reduction in infant mortality over the long term is a specific peculiarity of the U.S.S.R. in contrast to other countries. Another world record of the U.S.S.R. is its number of abortions—about 5 million a year. The Third World's achievement in demography is, indisputably, the gap in life expectancy of females and males (the lifespan of males is 62 years, and of females, 73 years).
2. In life expectancy and infant mortality, the Soviet Union has never been among developed countries, but was between them and the underdeveloped countries. Nowadays, the lag behind the industrial world has increased somewhat, but it is not catastrophic—about 10 percent of newborns' life expectancy, and 1 to 2 percent of that of the elder cohorts.
3. The specific peculiarity of the country has always been the high life expectancy of the oldest cohorts. It is explained by high infant mortality, which serves as a cruel selector of the viable individuals. An analogous picture can be observed when comparing different ethnic and social populations in various countries.
4. High infant mortality does not serve as a guarantee against the growth of inherited diseases and genetic defects. These phenomena are threatening the U.S.S.R., but possibly less so than the West.
5. Changes in the basic tendencies of mortality of the Soviet populace in the century were determined by powerful, non-accidental selection, when the country was passing through terrible social and military catastrophe. Life expectancy increased by quantum jumps immediately after the civil war in 1923 to 26, and after World War II in 1946.

   Hunger and disease carried off many millions in the civil war, and made the generations which underwent these terrible experiences more viable. The situation repeated itself during World War II.

   The generations sifted by these catastrophes were smaller numerically, but were distinguished by the middle of the 1950s by their greater viability. This temporary and peculiar situation gave the impression, in the U.S.S.R. and in the West, of high life expectancy of the Soviet populace, in comparison with that of the Western countries.
6. Gradual removal of the "margin of safety," which sprang up during the catastrophes, led to the growth of mortality in the 1960s and 1970s. More precisely, it led to the restoration of the "natural" level of mortality. This process is going on unevenly in rural and urban areas, with males and females, and among different ethnic groups in the Soviet Union. It is going on under complex, contradictory conditions, so that side by side with various measures of the health care system, social and living conditions of Soviet citizens are worsening.

MORTALITY IN THE U.S.S.R. IN THE YEAR 2000

The mortality rate of elderly people during the rest of this century and part of the next will grow. This is mainly because the normal level of mortality, which was artificially reduced by catastrophes, will be restored. Another even more lasting tendency will be the gradual replacement of the generations which went through the severe selection of infant mortality by the generations which did not endure it in their childhood. This process will lead to the leveling off of low mortality of the elder cohorts in rural areas, and of Muslims, to the level of mortality of city dwellers and of Slavs. (Actually, in more remote territories, the present rate will rise above that of those who have better medical and social conditions.)

This apparently is already going on, or is just about to start, and will continue for 30 to 40 years until the "selected" generations give way to the younger ones, born after World War II under conditions of generally sharply reduced child mortality. It seems that the country's present infant mortality rate, 3 to 4 percent of newborns, is not such a powerful selection factor of more viable infants, and its impact will not affect the general mortality rate for many decades.

The middle-aged cohorts' mortality, which is determined to a great extent by social reasons, will emerge from the press of selection earlier than the elder cohorts. For them, this process will be completed, seemingly, during the next decade. After this, the life expectancy of these cohorts will be determined by economic and political conditions. I would like to hope that these conditions will be favorable. Most likely, the mortality of these groups will stabilize at a somewhat higher level than now, and at the beginning of the next century will start to decline little by little. Gradual change in the ethnic structure of these cohorts—the growth of the numbers of Muslims—will be an unfavorable circumstance in this regard.

Infant mortality, to all appearances, has stopped growing and will soon stabilize, then will start to decrease. The ground for such an assertion is a world-wide tendency—and the U.S.S.R., so far, has rather steadily repeated, although with a lag, all the basic movements of the West. No substantial medical discoveries or measures will be needed to reduce the impact of mortality from external causes (such as influenza-pneumonia). This will happen step by step because of the general rise in the culture of the population, and raising of the more remote territories to a level existing already in some regions. In the same direction, reduction of the birthrate in the country as a whole and in its various parts will work, also. An infant mortality rate of about 15 per thousand seems probable to the end of the century.

On the whole, life expectancy of the population will increase a little (to 70 to 71 years), and for a long time will be at the same level. That of the West, meanwhile, will cross the threshold of 75 to 76 years, and life expectancy of some countries of Asia and South America will come close to the Soviet level.

The latter will be, at the same time, at the threshold of the new century and of the second demographic revolution.

At approximately the same time, by the very end of this millennium will occur another important demographic event—stabilization of world population. Birth and death rates will level off, then the number of people will gradually decrease. Probably this will be of great interest: newspapers will print articles about a demographic catastrophe; but maybe this problem will not be considered of serious interest.

NOTES

1. I consider here only one aspect of the issue: the general trends in mortality in the U.S.S.R. in peacetime. The cataclysms of 1918 to 1922, 1932 to 1938, and 1939 to 1953 which resulted in massive losses of population deserve independent study, to which I expect to return at another time.
2. Nick Eberstadt, "The Health Crisis in the U.S.S.R.," *The New York Review of Books,* February 19, 1981.
3. Christopher Davis and Murray Feshbach, *Rising Infant Mortality in the U.S.S.R. in the 1970s,* The U.S. Bureau of Census, Series P-95, No. 74, Sept. 1980.
4. In the Comecon handbook, the figure for infant mortality in the U.S.S.R. was originally displaced at first by an elipsis. In later years the entry for the Soviet Union was omitted altogether. (See *Statisticheskiy Ezhegodnik Stran-Chlenov Soveta Ekonomicheskoi Vzaimopomoshchi* for 1975 to 1980, sections "Infant mortality" and "Average life expectancy.") (Statistics Yearbook Comecon 1975–80)
5. The lack of data appears still more threatening because of the history of such grave silences in the U.S.S.R. Demographic statistics (in particular, data on births, deaths, and population) disappeared from print at the start of the thirties. The Soviet Union is certainly not alone among the Socialist countries in discontinuing publication when the data begins to look unpleasant. The Comecon yearbooks present a rather curious picture. Bulgaria provides life expectancy figures for three-year intervals but updates the information only when it demonstrates progress. The 1977 issue presents data for 1969 to 1971. Cuba has not altered its data since 1970. Soviet data were frozen in 1971 to 1972. But the record belongs to Mongolia. Having achieved a life expectancy of 65 years in 1964 to 1965, they have not seen fit to part company with good news and so have simply repeated the figure in all successive yearbooks.
6. Eberstadt, Nick, "Replies," *The New York Review of Books,* Nov. 5, 1981.
7. Rashin, A. G., *Naselenie Rossii za sto let 1811–1913 (The Population of Russia from 1811 to 1913),* Moscow, 1956, p. 32.
8. Mironov, B. N., in *Brachnost', Rozhdaemost', Smertnost', v Rossii i S.S.S.R. (Marriage, Birth, and Death in Russia and the U.S.S.R.),* Moscow, 1977, pp. 83–104.
9. "Under our criminal code, persons found guilty of criminal abortion are subject to loss of all civil rights, and exile to the remotest regions of Siberia." *Entsiklopedicheskii slovar' Brokgauza i Efrona (Encyclopaedia),* under 'Vykidysh" (miscarriage), vol. VIIa, 1892, p. 511.
10. Grigorovich, D. V., *Izbrannye Proizvedeniia (Selected Writings),* Moscow, 1959, p. 87.
11. Zhbankov, D. N., in *Vrach,* 1889, No. 13, p. 309.

12. Shingarev, A. I., in *Meditsinskaia Beseda,* 1889, No. 9, p. 25.
13. *Pervaia Vseobshchaia Perepis' Naseleniia Rossiskoi Imperii 1897 (First General Census of Population of the Russian Empire in 1897),* 89 vols (1899–1905).
14, Compiled from census data.
15. Novosel'skii, S. A., *Smertnost' i prodolzhitel'nost' zhizni v Rossii (Mortality and Expectation of Life in Russia),* Petrograd, 1916, p. 179.
16. Bednyi, M. S., *Prodolzhitel'nost' zhizni v Gorodakh i Selakh (Life Expectancy in Cities and the Countryside),* Moscow Statistika, 1976, pp. 40–41. The recording of deaths in the countryside was not good, which could distort the data.
17. "Science has provided the wealthier classes with dozens of means of aborting a fetus . . . The evil is already widespread, spreads daily even more widely, and soon will encompass all women in the upper classes." Tolstoy, L. N., *Collected Works,* Moscow, vol. 25, 1937, p. 408.
18. The differences between numbers of males and females first appeared during the cataclysms of revolution, war, and Stalinism when males perished in greater numbers.
19. Compiled from census data.
20. Soviet medical statistics do not include births earlier than 28 weeks following conception, less than 1 kilogram in weight or 35 centimeters in length, if the newborn dies within 7 days of birth. Davis and Feshbach studied data of the U.S. National Institutes of Health for 1960 (when infant mortality stood at 25.1 per 1,000 and births numbered 4.258 million, approximating the levels in the U.S.S.R. in 1968) and determined that the group excluded from Soviet statistics on live births amounted to 14.4 percent of infant deaths in the United States (0.36 percent of newborns). Davis and Feshbach adjusted data for 1959 to 1976 proportional to the infant mortality rate.

    The number of such births is presumably more closely related to birth rates than to infant death rates. In this case the adjustment to the Soviet figures would be 0.36 percent per year which would produce a variance from Davis and Feshbach of 10 to 20 percent.

    Adjusting Soviet data on numbers of deaths among premature newborns from U.S. statistics (due to a lack of such statistics from the U.S.S.R.) can be somewhat risky. There are significant differences between the two countries in the composition of infant mortality rates and abortion rates; relationships among first, second, and third births for individual mothers; maternal health; and obstetrical science. The discrepancies can have a substantial effect on differences in pre-term birth rates.
21. Davis and Feshbach cite Western research on abortions in the U.S.S.R. According to these data, 16.5 million abortions were performed in 1966, or 6 abortions per woman. The data appear to be weakly supported and somewhat inflated. Abortion statistics in the U.S.S.R. are kept secret, but among informed medical specialists in Moscow, abortion in recent times have stabilized at about 5 million annually. A. Smirnov, in an interview with Western journalists stated that the number of abortions closely approximates the number of births, which corresponds to our own data. (*Christian Science Monitor,* June 4, 1981).

    It should be kept in mind that 5 million would be a record in both absolute and relative terms, a record held for many years now by the Soviet Union. (By comparison, the United States recorded 1.157 million abortions in 1978.) The World Almanac and Book of Facts 1982, N.Y., 1982, p. 961.
22. Tsentral'noe Statisticheskoe Upravlenie (Ts.S.U.) pri Sovete Ministrov Uzbekskoi S.S.R. *Narodnoye Khoziaistvo Uzbekskoi SSR v 1974 godu; statisticheskii ezhegodnik (The National Economy of the Uzbekistan S.S.R. in 1974; A Statistical Yearbook).* Tashkent, 1975, p. 12.
23. *The Christian Science Monitor,* June 4, 1981.
24. The population's standard of living cannot be considered particularly stable. Some factors have evidently taken a turn for the worse, affecting the rise in mortality in the process. Among them are changes in working and living conditions; a lowering of physical demands and the consequent weakening of the human organism; changes in nutrition (increasing use of preservatives and food additives, deterioration of variety and quality of food products, occasional overeating); environmental pollution (air, soil, water); increasing use of chemicals in agriculture; more intense working conditions (automation, exposure to harmful chemicals, greater psychological stress, injuries on the job); increasing numbers of women in the industrial labor force; degradation in health among older generations as a result of higher survival rates in prior years among weaker children; weakening of social structures (alcoholism, crime).

    Some researchers have pointed to the growth in the incidence of diseases and cancer as current trends. (S. Kazenov in *Prodolzhitel'nost' Zhizni* [*Expectation of Life*], Moscow, 1974, p. 34.) Without doubt such diseases contribute to a growing number of deaths. Whereas in 1960 they accounted for 51 percent of all deaths, in 1970 they contributed 62 percent. (Yu. P. Lisitsyn, *Sotsial'naia Gigiena i Organizatsiia Zdravookhraneniia* [*Social Hygiene and Organization of Health Services*], Moscow, 1973, p. 182.) The spread of such diseases is apparently related primarily to changes in population structure as well as improved diagnosis. M. V. Kurman (*Aktual'nye voprosy demografii* [*Actual Questions of Demography*] Moscow, 1976, p. 74.) believes that mortality increases in the older age groups are due to just these factors, while the rise among males generally is due primarily to social factors.
25. It appears that the state as a totalitarian machine has little interest in significantly prolonging the lives of

its subjects, particularly the chronically ill and the elderly. Naturally no one would publicly support such an inhuman proposition. Nevertheless, the country's health care system is oriented more toward the working population. Pensioners as a rule are unwelcome in hospitals, they have difficulty obtaining scarce drugs or admission to sanatoria. Upon retirement, middle-ranking officials lose their health care privileges, including access to specialized clinics hospitals.

26. Mendeleev, D. K., *K poznaniiu Rossii (Toward the Understanding of Russia),* St. Petersburg, 1906. Novosel'sky, S. A., *Smertnost' i Prodolzhitelnost' Zhizni v Rossii (Mortality and Expectation of Life in Russia),* Petrograd, 1916. A large number of those who lived longer—and subsequently the low mortality rate of elderly people—can be explained in part by illiteracy of the population, which often rounded ages upward.

    The fact that those in the elder cohorts exaggerate their ages is evidenced by inaccurate unreliable correlations within these cohorts. For example, in England in 1901 there were 9,538 people over 90 years old, or 3.96 percent of the number of those over 60. Those 100 years old and older were 0.06 percent of all those over 60. For Russia, these numbers were 15.16 percent and 1.82 percent. *Smertnost' i Prodolzhitelnost' Zhizni Naseleniia SSSR, 1926–1927, Tablitsy Smertnosti (Mortality and Longevity of the Population of the USSR, Life Tables, 1926–1927),* Moscow, 1930.
27. Footnote 22, op. cit.
28. *Vestnik statistiki (Herald of Statistics),* Moscow, 1973, No. 12, p. 79.
29. In the U.S.S.R. mortality rates still have a U-form. Infant mortality is more or less equal to the mortality of those 65 to 70 years old (in the United States, 40 to 45 years old). All consequences of the first demographic revolution, achieved by modern medicine, developed in the West and spread around the world, are not quite clear today. The social structure of mankind turned out to be unprepared for the tempestuous growth of the population. Lack of energy, food, and other resources, adequate living space, and many other problems, became obvious. And while the rich West has gotten out of these difficulties (actually it was not into them because the birthrate was reduced in time), the East and the South have a long, difficult path to travel.
30. Differences in matrimony in Eastern and Western Europe had a great impact on birth rate and infant mortality. In the eighteenth and nineteenth centuries, late marriages were characteristic in the West, and there were relatively fewer of them. But the psychological pattern of Eastern Europe demanded early marriages. England is an example of the Western pattern. The proportion of unmarried women in 1900 was: 20 to 24 years old: 73 percent; 25 to 29 years old: 42 percent; 45 to 49 years old: 15 percent. (Hajnal, John in Glass, D. V., and Everslay, D. E. C. *Population in History,* London, 1965.) In the European part of Russia, according to the census of 1897, the proportion of unmarried women was: 20 to 29: 23 percent; 40 to 49 years old: 5 percent.

    It should also be said that the Western European pattern included a noticeable reduction in the birth rate as a result of some measures in the family (Coale, Ansley J. in *Fertility and Family Planning,* Ann Arbor, 1969.) In Russia, at the beginning of the century, the birthrate was close to the biological limits.
31. Workers in and the administrators of maternity hospitals are interested in reducing indicators of stillbirths. Therefore they try to restore the breathing of a newborn, if necessary, for a long time. If it is not done during the first five minutes, brain damage is highly likely. I am not going to judge what doctors should do in such cases; I do not know what is being done in the West. But I simply notice that in the U.S.S.R., despite rather high infant mortality, the number of traumas in infants who survive is rather high.
32. A third of infant mortality in the Soviet Union is due to pneumonia, but in the United States it is only 4 percent (Davis and Feshbach, *Rising Infant . . .,* Sept. 1980.)
33. The correction suggested by Davis and Feshbach demonstrates how substantially infant mortality went down and what it consists of. Almost 15 percent of all newborns who died during their first year were underdeveloped, were born prematurely, or were of low birth weight (three times less than normal). After 1960 infant mortality in the United States was halved; it seems that the proportion of insufficiently developed infants is now higher among both those who die during their first year and those who live.
34. Inherited defects and infant disease took, in 1920, 2.92 percent of all newborns in Sweden; today mortality from all causes is 0.8 percent (Preston, S., Keyfitz, N., Schoen, R., *Causes of Death. Life Tables for Nation Populations,* New York, 1972, pp. 652–58). Certainly a number of diseases of various types (for example, septic diseases) decreased, but on the other hand, analysts note that the pathology of pregnancy and labor is increasing. This seemingly is linked to the growth of the proportion of first children among newborns and with the growth and intensity of pathogenic factors. These, in turn, are determined by the development of modern technology, changes in the professional stature of working women, expanding overuse of strong medicines (antibiotics, soporifics, smoking, narcotics, alcoholism, pollution, radioactivity, age of mothers, etc. (Shaburov, K. Yu. in *Prodolzhitel'nost' Zhizni: Analiz i Modelirovaniye,* Moscow, 1979, p. 36.)
35. In the course of this discussion one strange misconception appeared. Davis and Feshbach and, after them, Eberstadt, wrote about the growth in inherited diseases in the U.S.S.R., quoting a samizdat book by B. Komarov (Komarov, Boris (pseud.), *Unichtozheniye prirody: obostryeniye ekologicheskogo krizisa v*

S.S.S.R. [*The Destruction of Nature: The Intensification of the Ecological Crisis in the U.S.S.R.*] Posev-Verlag, Frankfurt/Main, 1978.)

Komarov took these data from a well-known Soviet genetic specialist academician Dubinin. He had no Soviet data (there was almost no such research in the U.S.S.R., and if there was any, the results are kept secret). Dubinin writes that according to the information of Western scientists, the number of children affected by this problem was published in the scientific magazine *Protection of Nature.* On this magazine is stamped "For office use only." The fact of the restriction says a lot by itself.

36. Nowadays there are not only negative, but also positive tendencies in the spread of inherited diseases. In particular, higher migration decreased the number of marriages among relatives, which had led to more genetic diseases. Still, researchers note that the decline in the birth rate has cancelled the positive effect of migration, and in a number of rural localities, the proportion of marriages among cousins is high. (Sutler, J. in *Fertility and Family Planning,* Ann Arbor, 1969, p. 293.)
37. The frequency of recorded spontaneous abortions is, on the average, 15 to 20 percent of the number of pregnancies diagnosed. Moreover, some of these abortions go unnoticed during the earliest stage (*Lektsii po Meditsinskoi Genetike* [*Lectures on Medical Genetics*], Moscow, 1974, p. 160.)
38. *Narodonaseleniye Stran Mira (Population of the World),* Moscow, 1978, p. 184; Friedland, I. G., *Gigiena Zhenskogo Truda (Hygiene of Women's Labor),* Leningrad, 1975, p. 16.
39. Spanish flu led to a jump in the mortality rate in the world: for example, to a record decline in life expectancy in the United States for 12 years in 1918. But, certainly, in the hungry countryside, without a health care system, its effect was much more terrible.
40. Population losses in catastrophic periods deserve serious independent consideration. By moving the 1926 census results back to 1913, one can estimate the losses to be about 10 million. Heavy losses of females of various ages prove that it was mainly sanitary losses.
41. Kaminskii, L. S., *Meditsinskaia i Demograficheskaia Statistika (Medical and Demographic Statistics),* Moscow, 1974, p. 128. The number of Petrograd-Leningrad inhabitants per doctor was as follows: in 1911, 700; in 1923, 875; in 1926, 400. The professional skills of pre-revolutionary doctors and those who were taught during the civil war were, of course, rather different. By 1926, a lot of hospitals, other health centers, day nurseries and kindergartens were created, but they could not provide a significant curative effect.
42. In 1922–13, 35 people in Petrograd per 100,000 population died from alcoholism, but in 1923, it was 1.6; in 1926, 10.9; and in 1928, 25.9 (Kaminskii, cited above, p. 134). Losses from other social causes such as gangsterism increased (Novoselskii, S. A., *Demografiia i Statistika (Demography and Statistics),* Moscow, 1978, p. 113).
43. Many authors note that the tables of 1939 pertain to the whole country (and tables of 1926 to the European part), and are more precise, and see in this the reason for a small difference. They suggest that the decline in mortality in the European areas was offset by addition of the data from the Asian territories where mortality was higher. One should take into account that outside European Russia, recording of deaths was done very badly. This is still true. There is considerable underrecording of mortality in Asian territories, which could lead to some understating of the rates for 1939.
44. *Yestestvennoye Dvizheniye Naseleniya Sovremennogo Mira (Natural Movement of the Population of the Contemporary World),* Moscow, 1974.
45. Sifman, R. I. in *Prodolzhitel'nost' Zhizni: Analiz i Modelirovaniye (Life Expectancy: Analysis and Simulation),* Moscow, 1979, pp. 50–59.
46. Ibid., p. 251.
47. In 1946, life expectancy of those 5 years and older was about 67 years in the Soviet Union. It was higher than in the United States at that time.
48. The fluctuations in mortality rate are determined partially by a noticeable heterogeneity of life of various age cohorts. For example, the group of 20 to 24-year-olds in 1958 to 1959 consists of those born before the war, when infant mortality was significant; in 1964 to 1965, it consisted of the scanty generation born during the war; in 1971 to 1972, it consisted of the first postwar generation, when infant mortality was rather high; in 1979, it consisted of the relatively populous post-Stalin generation, with relatively low infant mortality (having been cured by antibiotics). No doubt the differences of "life experience" should affect the mortality of these cohorts.
49. One can get the impression from what has been said that the introduction of modern medical care complexes in the 1950s and 1960s played no role in the U.S.S.R. This is not so. It is precisely because of medical achievements that the manifold reduction of child mortality (0 to 9 years) should be explained. Medical achievements played a very important role for other age groups as well, however—it led not to a reduction of the mortality rate, but it prevents its increase. Mortality would have grown, gradually returning to the 1939 level, without the artificial reduction in it brought about by modern medical care. Medicine also reduced the mortality rate of some age cohorts in 1958 to 1965.
50. Bednyi, M. S., *Prodolzhitel'nost' Zhizni v Gorodakh i Poselkakh (Life Expectancy in Cities and the Countryside),* Moscow, 1976, p. 49.

PART IV

FERTILITY

MEASURES OF FERTILITY

The most widely used measure of *fertility*—the number of children born—is the crude birth rate (CBR). The CBR is the number of births per 1,000 population during a given year.

$$\text{CBR} = 1000 \times \text{births/midyear population}$$

Since only women from about age 15 to age 49 bear children, there are fertility rates which refer more closely to the population "at risk" of childbearing and which allows a more meaningful comparison among groups or within the same group across time. These rates may be calculated for married women only, unmarried women, or both.

The gross reproduction rate (GRR) is the number of births in a particular year per 1,000 *women* of reproductive age. As with mortality, fertility can be studied in more detail through age-specific fertility rates (ASFRs), the number of children born per 1,000 women of a specific age (e.g., women aged 25 or women aged 25 to 29). There are two ways to measure total fertility rates (TFR), or average number of births per woman. The *period* total fertility rate is based on the age-specific fertility rates of women of all ages during a specific year. It is a good predictor of actual total fertility only to the extent that the age-specific fertility rates have been and will remain fairly constant. In this regard, it is similar to life expectancy at birth, which is a period measure of mortality. The *cohort* total fertility rate is based upon the age-specific fertility rates of a single age group (cohort) of women as they pass through their reproductive lifetime. Although it is very accurate, it has no predictive value because it cannot be calculated until after the cohort has finished childbearing. The cohort total fertility rate is most useful for examining long-term historical trends in fertility, while the period total fertility rate is more useful for looking at present-day patterns of fertility.

Under usual circumstances, when ASFRs are stable or gradually declining, there is a fairly close relationship among CBR, GRR, and TFR. If ASFRs should change considerably, then the CBR and the GRR will not be as good as predictors of the TFR. A change in ASFRs may reflect an actual change in the cohort TFR or it may reflect a change in the timing of births. There are times when there may be a dramatic but temporary change in ASFRs which result in a baby bust (as births are postponed) or a baby boom (when births that may have been delayed are no longer postponed). This is part of what happened in the United States during the period of the Great Depression and World War II, when marriages and births were postponed, and then during the postwar prosperity, when couples could afford to make up for lost reproductive time.

Worldwide, crude birth rates range from 10 to 55, and period TFR from 0.5 to 8.0 (World Bank, 1984). Within nations, however, there may be more variation, with some regions having higher or lower CBR or TFR than the national totals.

DETERMINANTS OF FERTILITY

We tend to think of childbearing as a very personal, private affair. The most recent United Nations world population conferences have affirmed the right of couples (1974) and individuals (1984) to determine the number and spacing of their children. Considerable research has been done at the individual and couple level on the psychological determinants of fertility. When the individual is placed in social context and when biological factors over which there may be little control are taken into account, however, there may not be very much room for choice.

Imagine an individual or a couple at the center of a series of concentric circles, representing the family, the social-economic-political system, the physical environment, and history. Although there is interaction among the rings and the center, there is certainly a strong cumulative flow of influences from the outer rings to the center. Cutting across all of the rings with its own influence is biology. There may be external or internal biological factors which aid or hinder reproduction: famine, leading to malnutrition and temporary female infertility; exposure to mumps leading to male sterility; or genetic hormone deficiency leading to low sperm production in the male.

As indicated in Chapters 26 to 29, nations may consider their rate of growth too high or too low, and may try to influence fertility either directly or indirectly. According to the Population Reference Bureau (1984a), none of the high-income industrial or oil-producing countries consider their population growth rate to be too high, despite a range of growth rates from less than 1 to more than 3 percent. Fewer than 20 percent of the industrial nations with planned economies consider their growth rate too low. In contrast, with even less variation in rates of growth, fewer than half of the low to moderate income countries are satisfied with population growth rates. About 12 percent believe that their population growth rates are too *low* and desire more rapid population growth; just over 40 percent consider their growth rate too high, and many of these have implemented policies designed to reduce growth rates by reducing fertility.

Whether changes in the birth rate are voluntary or involuntary depends on the particular circumstances of the individual or couple, and on the nature of population policies. As we discuss in Chapter 16, fertility declines are not always the consequence of conscious, voluntary efforts to prevent unwanted births. For example, reduced *fecundity*—the biological ability to have children—may lead to an involuntary decline in fertility. If food is scarce, there may be both involuntary declines in fertility, as a result of reduced fecundity, and voluntary declines in fertility, as people choose to forego wanted children, or postpone childbearing until circumstances improve.

BIOLOGICAL FACTORS

We have all heard of women who have borne 15 or 20 single births. In fact, it would seem likely that with a reproductive lifetime of over 30 years, a healthy population that does not practice birth control (or where it is unreliable or used by only a small proportion of those at risk of childbearing) would have a TFR of well over 20; yet this is not the case. As the World Bank (1984) indicates, even the highest TFRs are well under 10.

In Chapter 19, Bongaarts examines the biological components of birth intervals to show why in a noncontracepting population, high birthrates are necessarily much lower than the theoretical biological maximum of one birth every nine months.

In Chapter 20, McFalls looks at the variety of problems that may lead to lower than desired fertility. In less developed countries (LDCs), malnutrition, venereal, infectious and parasitic diseases, and wars influence fecundity to make natural fertility lower and to prevent many people from having as many children as they would like. Even in the low-fertility MDCs, many people are not able to have the few children they would like (Sherris and Fox, 1983). McFalls, in the more detailed work from which Chapter 20 is taken, considers the diversity of possible causes of infecundity in more developed countries, including exposure to nuclear radiation, toxic wastes, smoking, and unintended long-term side effects of abortion and some methods of contraception.

HISTORICAL AND ECOLOGICAL FACTORS

To understand contemporary fertility, we need to be aware not only of past history (a war will have reproductive consequences for many years), but also the peculiar historical circumstances of the moment. Reproductive choice and control were very different before the introduction of the birth control pill, or before the legalization of sterilization and abortion. Events such as business cycles, epidemics, famines, massive emigration, and the "echoes" of previous baby booms or busts are likely to affect the period TFR, and sometimes the cohort TFR as well. In addition, technology, transportation, and widespread trade have substantially reduced the dependency of populations on local environments. Nevertheless, the climate, the quantity and quality of farm lands, grasslands, forests, fisheries, and the capacity of the natural environment to absorb and purify wastes, all affect the economy, health, and mortality, which in turn influence fertility.

SOCIAL, POLITICAL, AND ECONOMIC SYSTEMS

Society can have enormous influence on fertility. It may operate, for instance through population-related policies, programs, and laws, through its influence on the factors that determine the costs and benefits of children, and through norms regarding appropriate family size and reproductive behavior. As discussed in Part II, the level of economic development and the distribution of its benefits are also important. The more coercive or totalitarian a government, the more it can regulate fertility independently of other influences.

CULTURE

The traditions, values, and norms of a society may exert a very powerful influence over our behavior, and yet they may be so ingrained, so taken for granted, that we do not even notice their importance. In many nations, a man's status may be measured in considerable part by the number of children—especially sons—he has fathered. In addition to the dominant culture, there may be important subcultures based on race, ethnicity, religion, age, and social class distinctions. These, along with gender, may provide the basis for additional or different traditions, norms, and values, as well as discrimination by the dominant society against these subgroups. Consequently, these factors must be taken into consideration when analyzing fertility.

FAMILY STRUCTURE

The amount of influence the family may have over reproduction is related to proximity and the degree of interdependence of the individual and the family system. When an extended family or kinship group functions as a unit, then its political, social, and economic strength may depend on numbers, and therefore on fertility (Yu and Liu, 1980). This is the main point of Mamdani's (1972) book, *The Myth of Population Control.* The more isolated nuclear family, especially one that lives some distance from its families of origin, is freer in its reproductive decisions, although even modern urban couples may under great pressure to make their parents grandparents or to "preserve the family name."

INDIVIDUAL-LEVEL INFLUENCES ON FERTILITY

Within the historical, environmental, biological, and social constraints discussed above, people are free to choose the number and spacing of children. Not that much is known about the effects of individual psychological variables or the dynamics of these intrapersonal and interpersonal decisions. In Chapter 21, Beckman develops a social-psychological model of how couples make fertility decisions. She assumes that there are underlying psychological variables which act independently and in combination with the broader contextual setting to create individual preferences and motivations regarding fertility and fertility-related behavior. Exchange theory is used to link external influences to the internal psychic structure. According to this perspective, each person considers the subjective costs and benefits of a first or additional child, and balances these against other options and the status quo. If the two individual decisions are not in agreement, the final decision becomes a matter of negotiation, bargaining, and conflict resolution, with relative power an important factor.

In Chapter 22, Bongaarts outlines the most common reasons why even the most conscious and well-planned reproductive decisions may be thwarted: contraceptive failure, permanent infertility, conception delay, intrauterine death, congenital defects in the newborn, unwanted gender composition of offspring, divorce, and death of a spouse or child. Bongaarts concludes that very few people are actually able to fulfill their reproductive plans.

EXPLAINING FERTILITY: PREDOMINANT THEMES

There are numerous influences on fertility and wide contemporary and historical variations among these influences among nations and subgroups within nations. There may also be idiosyncratic variation among individuals that may affect fertility independently of membership in some social category. It is therefore not too surprising that we are not able to accurately explain or predict fertility. Enough is known, however, to be able to sketch out a general though incomplete understanding of why total fertility is high or low, and why the transition from high to low occurs. Research and theory are concentrated in three areas. The microlevel determinants of fertility are influences which operate at the individual, couple, or household level. The macrolevel determinants of fertility operate in the broader social and historical context, and act indirectly through the microlevel determinants. The third area of research and theory is the link between the macrolevel and microlevel influences. Here we can only mention some of the major themes from these areas and give a few examples. Note that in most work on the determinants of fertility, subfecundity (the reduced biological ability to have children) and infecundity (the biological inability to have children) are not considered.

MICROLEVEL INFLUENCES

When extended beyond purely economic costs and benefits, cost-benefits analysis has been a more useful tool for understanding fertility (Becker, 1981; Bulatao, 1979; Espenshade, 1977; Bulatao and Fawcett, 1983; Cain, 1978; Yu and Liu, 1980). Costs and benefits may be categorized as economic, psychological, physical, and time. There are direct costs and opportunity costs, the latter being potential benefits that are foregone in order to have children. Examples of direct costs are the price of food, clothing, and education, (economic) and the mental and physical demands of raising children or the stress associated with having an unwanted child (psychological and physical). Opportunity costs include activities or purchases foregone because of money, energy, and time devoted to having children (e.g., extensive travel or additional education). Benefits may include household labor (time), support in old age (economic), and the satisfaction and pleasure of raising children (psychic). Seldom discussed in the cost-benefit approach, but also important, are the costs of *not* having children. These may be substantial, especially for women in a society where male dominance and pronatalism are strongly institutionalized. There may be no place, no security or even means of survival for women who are not married or who do not bear children (Morgan, 1984).

One of the earlier versions of this perspective was a purely economic cost-benefit analysis which predicted that if the ability to control fertility were equal among all social groups, fertility would be positively associated with income. It was assumed that decision regarding childbearing and regarding the purchase of consumer durables are made in the same way, so that the more money that is available, the more consumer goods or children will be purchased (Becker, 1960). Since fertility is so consistently lower among higher income families, and since these families tend to buy higher quality rather than greater quantities of a consumer durable, this view has been modified with the idea that as incomes change, tastes and preferences regarding consumer goods and children also change. Consequently, according to this perspective, MDC fertility is low because affluence generates tastes and preferences for more costly consumer goods and leisure time as well as for "high quality" children who are expensive to raise (Easterlin, 1969).

This perspective has been criticized as being class biased. It is pointed out that the poor of the world do prefer better housing and other consumer durables, as well as "high quality" children, but in the absence of any opportunity for social mobility for themselves or their children, they may perceive no alternative to having large families or they may see little purpose or benefit in having smaller ones (Michaelson, 1981; Gimenez, 1980; Mamdani, 1972). In LDCs such families will make adjustments in fertility when it is perceived that in doing so they can take advantage of an opportunity to improve the well-being of the family, for instance through education (Caldwell et al., 1985; Knodel et al., 1984).

Nevertheless the idea that tastes and preferences influence fertility helps us to understand the low, late-transition fertility of MDCs in terms of choices between life-styles which emphasize consumption and leisure, and childbearing—choices that are essentially unavailable to the vast majority of people in LDCs (Bulatao and Fawcett, 1983).

A sociological variant of cost-benefit analysis especially popular at the World Population Conference of 1974 focuses on the opportunity costs of childbearing and suggests an inverse relationship between fertility and *female* employment. It is suggested that the employee role is in conflict with the childcare role, especially when childcare is unavailable or expensive, when children cannot be at the workplace, when work requires travel, and when the mother has sole responsibility for childcare. Weaknesses in this perspective include the fact that many women want both children and work outside the home, that others bear children and also seek employment out of financial necessity, and that women may choose or be forced to sacrifice sleep, leisure, or time needed for personal advancement rather than employment or childbearing (Moen, 1977). As others explain, it is not an extra work role for women that will lead to a reduction in fertility, but rather sources of status and security that are not tied to being a wife and mother (Goliber, 1985; Morgan, 1984).

MACROLEVEL ANALYSIS

The purpose of macrolevel analysis is to uncover the social, ecological, and historical contexts which are most conducive to high or low fertility. As discussed in the introduction to Part II, the predominant theme of this work is the relationship among fertility, economic development, and national efforts to promote family planning. Consensus seems to be developing regarding the social context most conducive to voluntary low fertility. A high level of economic development is not necessary for fertility to decline but, instead, a pattern of development that reduces the need for children by reducing infant and child mortality and provides access to substitutes for children as a source of income and social status.

Family planning programs, according to the consensus perspective, can make an independent contribution to fertility declines by raising the level of awareness about the possibility, means, and appropriateness of spacing and limiting births through effective methods of birth control. Also, regulating fertility so that births are adequately spaced and occur during the healthiest reproductive years contributes to lower infant and child mortality and thereby could contribute to subsequent lower fertility. Still, family planning programs will not have a major impact until macro- and microlevel development processes stimulate a demand for these services as something other than substitution for more traditional means of birth control.

Caldwell's theory (summarized by Stark in Chapter 23) regarding intergenerational flows of wealth (which are determined to a considerable extent by the macrosocial context) is a useful way to understand birthrates at a particular time as well as transitions in fertility over time. Although Caldwell refers to economic costs and benefits, noneconomic factors, especially social norms regarding childbearing, must also be considered. In LDCs, if changes in norms (such as the preference for sons) and other social "props" for high fertility have lagged behind a change in the economic value of children, families may have fewer children, but still more than are economically rational (Freedman, 1963; Morgan, 1984; Williamson, 1977; see also Chapter 6).

Fertility declines and intergenerational transfers may be initiated by interclass transfers brought about by macrosocial change. As Banks and Banks (1969) found in their study of England's demographic transition, social and economic reforms led to lower fertility among the poor because the new possibilities to improve their standard of living and rise in the class structure could be most successfully realized with smaller families and educated children. Conversely, since these reforms came at the expense of the upper class, these families had to choose between maintaining their sumptuous life-style and having many children. England's demographic transition thus began within the upper class and was completed by upwardly mobile workers. Similarly, more equitable distributions of income and land are seen as important, although controversial, macrolevel stimulants of LDC fertility declines (Repetto, 1979; Kocher, 1973; Ben-Porath, 1982).

As far as current and future world population growth is concerned,the most important countries are China and India. With similar per capita gross national products (GNP), these two of the world's poorest countries account for nearly 40 percent of its population. Having very different development and population policies, China's adult literacy rate is nearly double that of India (66 percent vs. 36 percent according to the World Bank, 1982); life expectancy at birth in China is 67, compared to India's 55; and the infant mortality rates for China and India are 67 and 97, respectively. In addition, employment and the relative status of women are considerably higher in China than in India. Excluding China and India, the average crude birth rate for low income nations is 44; for lower-middle income countries it is 37. China's crude birth rate is 19; India's is 34. China's period total fertility rate is 2.0, one third to one half that of most low and lower-middle income countries; India's PTFR is 2.9 (World Bank, 1984). Globally, literacy and infant mortality rates, which reflect the distribution of at least the most basic benefits of development, are more closely linked to fertility than is per capita GNP (Menard, 1983).

Chapters 24 and 25 are recent examples of macrolevel analysis of fertility. Tsui and Bogue present a position that emphasizes the importance of family planning programs in reducing fertility. They show that, even controlling for development, family planning program efforts may be the most important influence on levels of fertility in less developed countries. In Chapter 25 Menard and Moen attempt to pick up where Tsui and Bogue (and others) have left off, by looking at those cases which the family planning perspective has the most difficulty explaining. Bear in mind that more developed countries are excluded from this analysis. Because of this, the range of variation in mortality is more limited than it would be in a more representative sample of nations. Including the more developed countries in the analysis changes the outcome of the analysis and points to mortality rather than family planning as the most important influence on fertility (Menard, 1983). Moreover, none of these analyses include *indirect* influences on fertility; this also leaves questions about the relative importance of the various influences on national level fertility.

LINKING MACROLEVEL AND MICROLEVEL ANALYSES

To fully understand fertility we need to understand the links between social structure and social psychology. Society can affect individuals' and couples' reproductive behavior in two ways: directly, through influences on reproductive behavior, and indirectly, through influences on microlevel factors which, in turn, influence fertility behavior directly. The link between microlevel and macrolevel influences on fertility was first clearly detailed by Davis and Blake (1956). They indicated that social structure influences fertility by acting through 11 intermediate variables, or proximate determinants (Bongaarts and Potter, 1983) which, in turn, influence one of the three biological events necessary for a birth to occur:

A. Factors affecting exposure to intercourse
   1. age of entry into sexual unions (married or unmarried; when do people begin having sexual intercourse? This may be affected by, for example, legal age of marriage)
   2. extent of permanent celibacy (affected by, e.g., monasticism)
   3. amount of reproductive period spent outside of sexual unions (affected, for example, by taboos on postpartum intercourse, divorce laws)
   4. extent of voluntary abstinence (for example, temporary avoidance of intercourse in order to space children)
   5. frequency of intercourse within a sexual union (affected, for example, by cultural norms regarding sexual behavior)
   6. frequency of involuntary abstinence (for example, temporary impotence, or separation because of employment or war)

B. Factors affecting exposure to conception
   7. fecundity affected by involuntary causes (for example, low sperm count, or infecundity resulting from malnutrition)
   8. fecundity affected by voluntary causes (for example, voluntary sterilization)
   9. use of contraceptives (for example, the diaphragm or condom)

C. Factors affecting gestation and successful birth
   10. fetal mortality from involuntary causes (spontaneous abortion or miscarriage)
   11. fetal mortality from voluntary causes (induced abortion)

As the list indicates, both microlevel and macrolevel phenomena can influence fertility. Personal preferences or microlevel economic concerns may influence the use of contraceptives (9); these microlevel preferences and concerns may, in turn, be influenced by the social and economic structure of the society, as well as by organizational efforts to promote birth control. War may result in involuntary separation of husbands and wives (6), impotence (6 or 7), and widowhood (3).

In LDCs and especially where contraception is not widespread, factors which affect exposure to intercourse are very important, especially those which influence age at entry into sexual unions (particularly marriage), and the proportion married (factors 1 and 2, respectively). Also important is voluntary abstinence (factor 4) and temporary infecundity (8) associated with breastfeeding. Efforts to raise the age of marriage and create alternatives to marriage and childbearing thus could play a substantial role in LDC fertility reduction. In MDCs, factors affecting exposure to conception are most important, especially contraception and sterilization (factors 8 and 9). Spontaneous and induced abortion (10 and 11) are also important (Bongaarts and Potter, 1983; Bongaarts et al., 1984).

FERTILITY POLICY

The design and implementation of fertility policy is not a simple matter because there is little agreement among or within nations on a desirable rate of growth or level of fertility. Moreover, although a nation may have very explicit policies to directly influence fertility or even to coercively enforce compliance, there are also public and private policies which, while not directly aimed at affecting fertility, may reinforce or work against the explicit fertility policy.

This only serves to underscore one of the themes that recurs in the readings in this collection: that theory and policy concerning population have important political components. What a country says about demographic processes may be incongruent with what it practices. At the 1974 World Population Conference, China strongly promoted the idea that rapid population growth is good and family planning programs are "unnatural and unnecessary." Even then, China had one of the world's most effective fertility reduction programs. India was one of a group of countries that was emphatic about the impropriety of coercion as an element of fertility reduction programs; yet after the conference, India introduced a highly coercive sterilization program which contributed to the fall of the government (Moen, 1977).

Every aspect of society influences reproductive behavior, and birth rates, in turn, affect every aspect of society. Despite the rhetoric about freedom to determine the number and timing of births, many believe that society does have a legitimate concern and a right to intervene when birth rates are deemed detrimental to the society as a whole.

This is the point of Hardin's argument in Chapter 11. Still, as critics of Hardin have been quick to point out, great care must be taken to determine which problems are "population problems" and who is to bear the brunt of their solutions. These critics warn that it is not only gross injustice but sheer folly to expect to solve the problems of resource shortages, pollution, and underdevelopment simply through a reduction of fertility among the world's poorest people.

Chapters 26 to 30 are concerned with some of the major issues and controversies regarding fertility policy. Most nations which have achieved low fertility have done so in the absence of national family planning programs and, for the most part, in the absence of the modern birth control methods that are today considered essential for effective fertility limitation. Nevertheless, national fertility policy has focused almost entirely on the provision of modern family planning services.

Perhaps no issue is as emotionally charged in the area of fertility control as that of the voluntary termination of a pregnancy. Those who are most opposed to this kind of abortion argue that the fetus is a living human being from the moment of conception, and regard their antiabortion activity as a matter of conscience, akin to protecting any child from a would-be murderer. Those who strongly advocate individual privacy and choice maintain that since the lives of women are greatly affected by pregnancy and birth, and there is neither religious nor scientific agreement regarding when an embryo or a fetus becomes a person, the decision to have an abortion should be strictly a matter of individual conscience for pregnant women. In Chapter 26, Donovan discusses the consequences and implications of a "Holy War" against abortion which, among other things, has led to a wave of bombings of abortion facilities in the United States.

Chapter 27 is concerned with pronatalist policies in low-fertility nations. Although it focuses on Eastern Europe, Western European nations, including France and West Germany, are also trying to encourage higher fertility, though with little success. In 1984, the European Parliament (Western Europe) adopted a resolution encouraging the ten-member European Economic Community to promote population growth in (West) Europe in order to maintain its "standing and influence" in the world (European Parliament, 1984). Pronatalist measures in Eastern Europe have focused on cash and other incentives to promote childbearing and restriction of access to legal abortion. It appears that these policies have had short-term successes, but that long-term fertility increases have remained elusive.

Fertility policies in China and India are discussed in Chapters 28 and 29. Although Demerath (1976) calls India's family planning efforts a total failure, fertility has declined and an estimated one fourth of married couples of reproductive age use modern contraceptive methods (Soni, 1983). On the negative side, India's limited success has required considerable coercion (incentives and force) and has relied heavily on sterilization. Also, poor health and nutrition may have contributed to reduced fecundity. One study of ten Indian states has concluded that improved child survival is the main reason for the voluntary adoption of modern birth control methods. However, increased use of these methods is not likely to significantly lower the cohort total fertility rate because these families want as many children as those whose child survival rate is lower and who, consequently, are not regulating their fertility (Jejeebhoy, 1984). India's fertility policy is discussed further in Chapter 28.

China's fertility reduction policies, which were seriously undertaken in 1962, can be divided into two broad phases. The first phase cannot be separated from an overall development policy that led to increased literacy, decreased morbidity and mortality, and increased availability of child substitutes. The latter included employment coupled with wages and prices that enabled two adults to support a small family, small-scale technology, the provision of health care, welfare for those unable to work, greater access to water and fuel, "homes of respect" for elders with no family, and adequate pensions for urban workers. The costs of having children were not raised; in fact, China made it easier to have children. Health care for mother and child, increased food rations, free childcare and education, the reduction of heavy workloads for pregnant women, long paid maternity leaves, and work breaks for breastfeeding all kept the cost of childbearing low. On the other hand, the cost of not having children was reduced. Major reforms in the marriage and divorce laws, property rights, marriage age, and slogans such as "women hold up half the sky" were all parts of a not-entirely-successful effort to raise the status of women, provide legitimate options to childbearing, and to reduce the long-held preference for sons.

These steps, along with concerted education and exhortation regarding population growth and family planning, brought about a significant decline in the birth rate. However, it was soon realized that the enormous number of young people, the legacy of previous high fertility, even with as yet unrealized cohort fertility rates of two, would cause future population growth of such magnitude that it could only bring disaster to such a large, poor nation. Thus began the second phase of China's population policy, never before tried or even suggested by other nations: to bring about a drastic decline in the birth rate via the one-child family. This is the subject of Chapter 29.

If China's one-child family program is successful for the years deemed necessary (it seems to be being relaxed), the implications fall nothing short of major social transformation. Consider first of all the practical implications: younger generations substantially smaller than the generations preceding them, resulting in a heavy burden of old-age dependency which may be only partially alleviated by decreases in dependency of the young. In this respect, China would find itself in a position similar to, but more pronounced than, that which is common to many of the present-day more developed countries (see Part VI). Beyond this, consider a nation in which, almost none of the affected cohorts has cousins, aunts, uncles, brothers, or sisters. To the extent that the one-child policy succeeds in the long run, familial relationships will be lineal or intergenerational, involving only one's parents and offspring, until one marries. Marriage, in which kinship is achieved by choice rather than ascribed by birth, will be the only collateral or intragenerational kinship relationship; one's spouse will be the only member of one's own generation to which one is related. The impact of such a change is difficult to imagine, especially in a society in which the family has traditionally played such a central role (Quale, 1966:257–259).

There is little agreement on optimum levels of population growth or on the design of policies to regulate them. One reason is lack of knowledge; another equally important though less often discussed reason is that individuals, nations, and subgroups have different perceptions of the consequences and meaning of population growth and control of reproductive behavior. In Chapter 30, Moen examines the public consequences of childbearing, a seemingly private act, and concludes that one reason societies attempt to control women is because of the power inherent in the control over fertility. She then considers this conclusion in light of the feminist demand for "control over our bodies." If Moen's analysis is correct, then are international declarations that individuals and couples should be free to determine the number and spacing of their children merely camouflage for battles over the control of reproduction? With this in mind, it may not be unreasonable to wonder about the ultimate purpose of reproductive technologies, such as *in vitro* fertilization, that are now being developed.

FOR FURTHER READING

1. Mahmood Mamdani. 1972. *The Myth of Population Control* (New York: Monthly Review Press). Short, readable, controversial, devastating critique of the methods and evaluation of family planning programs in India. Recommended as much for what it says about the quality of family planning program data as for its relevance to fertility.
2. Amy Ong Tsui and Donald J. Bogue. 1978. "Declining World Fertility: Causes, Trends, and Implications," *Population Bulletin* volume 33, number 4 (Washington, DC: Population Reference Bureau). For the more advanced student, the best of a series of studies suggesting that family planning program effort is critical (and probably more important than development) for the reduction of fertility in less developed countries.
3. Scott Menard. 1983. "Fertility, Development, and Family Planning." *Studies in Comparative International Development* XVIII (3): 75–100. A response to Tsui and Bogue (and to other, similar studies) that suggests that development, particularly education, is more important for fertility reduction than family planning effort if we consider the number of people, rather than the number of countries, affected.
4. Kristin Luker. 1975. *Taking Chances: Abortion and the Decision Not to Contracept;* 1984. *Abortion and the Politics of Motherhood* (both Berkeley, CA: University of California Press). Two important, readable, thought-provoking books on the subject of contraception and abortion in California.
5. John C. Caldwell. 1982. *Theory of Fertility Decline* (New York: Academic Press). One of the more promising theoretical approaches to the understanding of high and low fertility and transitions. Includes reports from the village-level research from which the theory was developed and refined. For the more advanced reader.
6. John Bongaarts and Susan Greenhalgh. 1985. "An Alternative to the One-Child Policy in China," *Population and Development Review,* volume 11 (December), pp. 585–617. An excellent example of demographic methods in the design and analysis of population policy. The authors conclude that China could accomplish its growth rate goals without resorting to the one-child policy.

19

Why High Birth Rates Are So Low

JOHN BONGAARTS

The highest fertility ever recorded reliably in a society is found among the Hutterites, a religious sect living in small communities near the United States-Canadian border. In 1950 Hutterite women who had reached the end of their reproductive years had given birth to an average of 8.9 children. With mortality near national U.S. levels, this high rate of childbearing has resulted in the unprecedented growth of the Hutterite population, which increased nearly 20-fold between 1870 and 1950.

Although Hutterite fertility is very high compared with that of many other human populations, it is surprisingly low from the point of view of biological reproductive efficiency. Clearly, a woman is able to bear more than about nine children during her 30 years or so of reproductive life (ages 15 to 45 approximately), as is evident from the numerous examples of women who have given birth more than 15 times.[1] A theoretical upper limit would be around 40 births per woman during 30 reproductive years, since an interval between two successive births cannot be shorter than about nine months required for a complete pregnancy.

Why then are women in societies such as the Hutterites, where deliberate birth control is absent, reproducing at rates substantially below biological limits? Before discussing the demographic and biological factors responsible for this finding, some aspects of the measurement of fertility and the values of fertility indices in various countries around the world will be presented.

MEASURING FERTILITY

The most widely used measure of fertility is the birth rate, that is, the annual number of births per one thousand persons. The usefulness of this rate stems from the fact that the required data are easily obtained and generally available, so that birth rates for almost all of the world's countries can be estimated. In addition, the difference between a country's birth rate and death rate (the annual number of deaths per one thousand persons) yields the annual rate of natural increase, which is one of the most important demographic indices.

Birth, death, and growth rates vary substantially among countries. Figure 19.1 plots these rates for 82 countries with populations over 5 million, covering 97 percent of the world's population.[2] Despite the large variations, countries tend to fall into two clusters: one with high birth and growth rates, the other with low birth and growth rates. The former includes most less developed countries, the latter contains most of the industrialized nations. Differences between the birth rates in the two areas are largely the consequence of differences in the degree of birth control practice.

In the countries with the highest levels of fertility, birth rates range from 40 to 50. From numerous intensive studies it has become clear that in populations with birth rates around 50 the use of deliberate fertility control measures such as contraception and induced abortion is almost completely absent. In the cases where birth rates are near 40, some birth control is

Figure 19.1. Estimated birth and death rates (1970–1975) of 85 countries with over 5 million population.

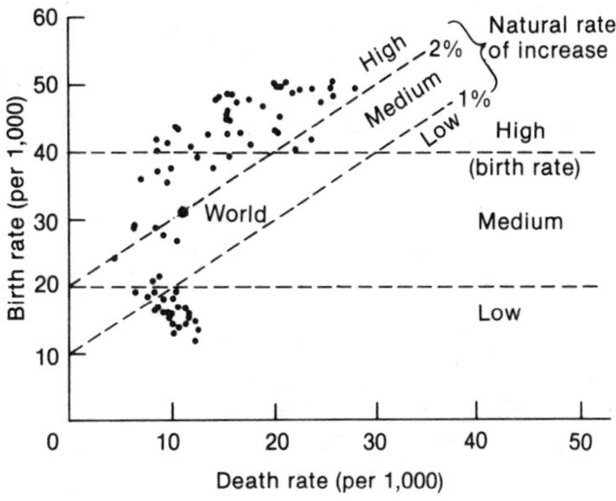

usually being applied, mainly among well-educated city dwellers. The term "natural fertility" is used for societies in which no deliberate effort is made to avoid having children. Fertility practices in today's high birth rate countries are close to natural, as they have been historically.

At the other extreme one finds birth rates of around 15 in countries with controlled fertility. This implies that most couples are able to limit the number of their offspring to an average of about two per family.

Although the birth rate has proven to be a valuable indicator of fertility, it has one major drawback: it is influenced by the age composition of the population. For example, the birth rates in two societies where women are bearing the same number of children would differ if the proportions of women in the childbearing ages were not identical. To avoid this problem, demographers now use the "total fertility rate" as a purer measure of fertility. The total fertility rate is equal to the average number of births a woman would have by the end of her reproductive years, if fertility levels at each age during her childbearing period remained constant at the levels prevailing at a given time. The relations between the birth rate, the total fertility rate, and the age composition have been studied extensively with the assistance of mathematical models. It has been demonstrated that the proportions of males and females at different ages are roughly constant over time in populations where, except for minor fluctuations, the birth rate is constant and where the death rate is either constant or declining steadily. Furthermore, one finds that in such populations the relation between the birth rate and the total fertility rate is nearly fixed at levels shown in Figure 19.2.[3] The rates observed in the high birth rate countries, also plotted, are in close conformity with the values predicted by the mathematical models, because the age structure in each of these populations has been rather stable. We can conclude from Figure 19.2 that current populations with fertility at or near natural levels typically have birth rates around 50 and total fertility rates near 7.

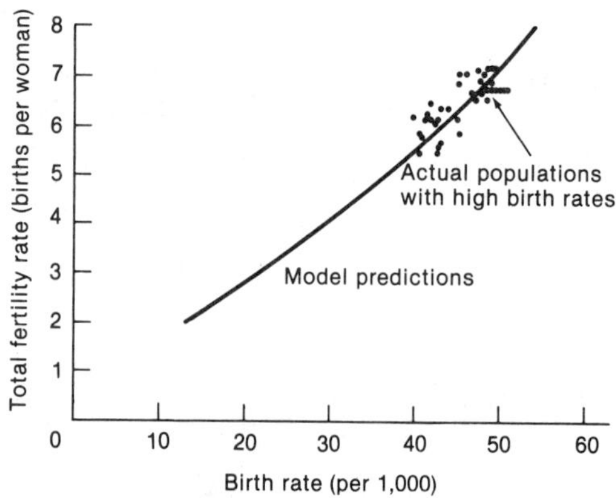

Figure 19.2. Relationship between the total fertility rate and the birth rate (1970–1975) in actual and model populations.

DEMOGRAPHIC FACTORS AND NATURAL FERTILITY

Marriage is the principal demographic factor affecting the birth rate in populations with natural fertility. For simplicity we will assume that marriage is the starting point of a woman's reproductive career, although this is not the case in every society. For example, in India young brides often stay with their parents for some time after marriage, and in parts of Latin America childbearing is legitimate in consensual unions before the official marriage ceremony. Among younger women the proportions married in different age groups depend mainly on the average age at first marriage, while over age 30 the incidence of celibacy, widowhood, divorce, and remarriage is the chief determinant. In a comprehensive study of nuptiality around the world in the 1950s, Bourgeois-Pichat found that one could distinguish major geographic areas within which marriage patterns were similar, despite some substantial differences among individual countries in each area. At the extremes were the patterns of Africa and of Europe, with averages of, respectively, 10 and 40 percent[4] of potential marital life remaining unused between the ages of 15 and 45. Among high fertility countries, values for lost reproductive years of about 25 percent were common, so that of the 30 years of potential reproductive life, only 22.5 years were spent in the married state. This implies that, if the total fertility rate equals 7 births per woman, the rate of childbearing is 0.31 births (7/22.5) per married woman per year.

It should be emphasized that a marital fertility rate of 0.31 is an average; higher values prevail in age groups below age 30, whereas near the end of the reproductive period fertility is much lower. One of the first analyses of age patterns in natural marital fertility rates was made by Louis Henry,[5] who collected data from 13 societies with widely varying cultural characteristics in which deliberate birth control could be assumed absent. Averaging the fertility rates in these 13 populations resulted in the following values: 0.42 for women aged 20 to 30 years, 0.33 for those aged 30 to 40, and 0.15 for those women aged 40 to 45. There is a clear age pattern, but the value of 0.31 for all ages, arrived at by the above crude calculations, appears to be a representative average of observed natural age specific marital fertility rates.

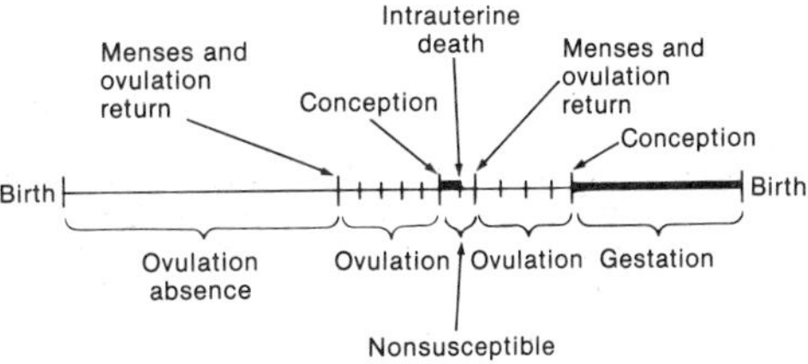

Figure 19.3. Components of a typical birth interval.

BIOLOGICAL FACTORS AND NATURAL FERTILITY

Sterility is the biological factor primarily responsible for the age pattern in natural marital fertility. A distinction is usually made among the following three types: (1) adolescent sterility, present among teenagers who have not yet reached menarche (start of menstruation) or who ovulate irregularly after menarche; (2) primary sterility, among women who are never able to reproduce; and (3) secondary sterility, which sets in after having been fertile. Little is known about the determinants of the prevalence of each of the forms of sterility, but presumably health and nutrition are important. From the few available measurements, it is estimated that in healthy populations the loss of fertile years among all women between the ages of 15 and 45 is probably less than 20 percent,[6] but in areas where malnutrition and poor health conditions are common, a higher sterility incidence may be observed. One could, therefore, find that in a natural fertility population only 17 or 18 out of the 22.5 years of married life are nonsterile and thus available for reproduction. If the total fertility rate is 7 births per woman, this would mean a rate of 0.4 births (7/17.5) per nonsterile married woman per year and an average interval between births of about 2.5 years (17.5/7). Obviously, the majority of birth intervals exceed by a large margin the theoretical minimum duration of nine months required for a full-term pregnancy.

Figure 19.3 outlines how the time between two successive births may be divided into subintervals. Immediately following a birth, women experience "postpartum amenorrhea," a period during which the normal cyclical pattern of menstruation and ovulation is absent. Observed average durations of this interval range from a few months to more than 1.5 years. There is now excellent evidence that the duration and intensity of breastfeeding are the principal determinants of the length of postpartum amenorrhea, but prolonged breastfeeding cannot be regarded as a reliable contraceptive because menstruation and ovulation usually return months before breastfeeding is terminated.

After the regular ovulatory function is restored (at approximately the same time as the first postpartum menses), married women are subject to the risk of conception.[7] Conception rates have proven difficult to measure, particularly because many conceptions that abort spontaneously shortly after fertilization remain unrecognized. Tentative estimates for the value of the monthly probability of a fertilization range from 0.15 to 0.50 among ovulating women who have intercourse regularly.[8] The reason why this probability is substantially less than 1.0 is that conception is possible only during a very brief period, probably only two days, in the middle of a woman's cycle. As a consequence, the average waiting time to conception, which is inversely related to the probability of conception, may be several months. The wide range of conception probabilities is largely due to their dependency on the coital frequency, which is affected in turn by various cultural customs.

Once an ovum has been fertilized, it has about a 50 percent chance to survive nine months and yield a live birth, with approximately one-third of the fertilized ova being rejected during the first two weeks after conception.[9] This high rate of reproductive failure appears to be the result of an effective natural mechanism for eliminating defective embryos, since a high incidence of genetic and other abnormalities has been observed in spontaneously aborted embryos. On average, about two fertilizations are needed to yield one live birth. The implication for the duration of the birth interval is that for every intra-uterine death a brief nonsusceptible period (duration of aborted pregnancy and postabortum anovulation) an a conception waiting time are added.

Given the above rough estimates of the segments of an interval between two births, a typical thirty-month birth interval in a natural fertility population may be divided as follows: twelve months postpartum amenorrhea, four months waiting time to conception before an intrauterine death, a one-month nonsusceptible period associated with the intrauterine death, another four months' conception waiting time before a live birth, and finally a nine-month full-term pregnancy.

In summary, the highest observed birth rates are much lower than is biologically possible because women in natural fertility societies are pregnant during only about one-sixth of their reproductive years. The remainder of these potential childbearing years is spent in the unmarried, sterile,[10] postpartum anovulatory, nonsusceptible, or ovulatory states (Figure 19.4). As a result, birth rates rarely exceed 50 in populations in which no deliberate actions are taken to affect the biological process of reproduction. Voluntary fertility control efforts by couples during the childbearing years are required to reduced birth rates below this natural level.

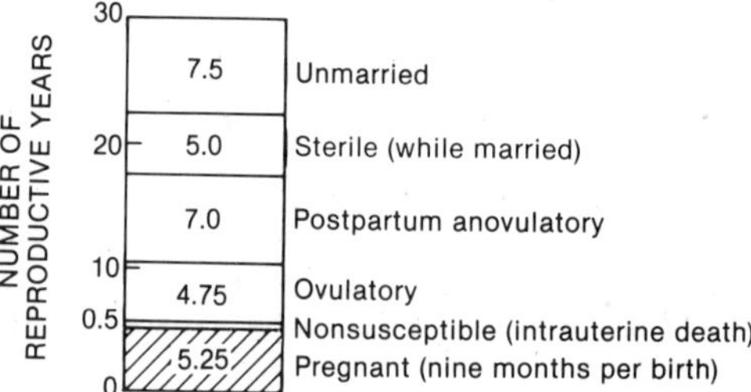

Figure 19.4. Example of the numbers of childbearing years spent in various reproductive states in a population with a total fertility rate of 7.

NOTES

1. For simplicity, twins, triplets, etc. are counted as one birth.
2. Data for Figures 19.1 and 19.2 are taken from United Nations, Department of Economics and Social Affairs, Population Division, Working Paper No. 55, May 1975.
3. The actual total fertility rates are found by multiplying the available gross reproduction rates by 2.05. The model relationship between the total fertility rate and the birth rate in a stable population varies slightly with the level of mortality. The curve presented in Figure 19.2 is plotted from data for the female "West" population at mortality level 11 presented in Ansley J. Coale and Paul Demeny in *Regional Model Life Tables and Stable Populations* (Princeton University Press, 1966).
4. These percentages are taken from Colin Clark, *Population Growth and Land Use* (London: McMillan, 1964). Clark simply takes the unweighted average of the percentages of women not married in each five-year age group between 15 and 45, using data originally presented by Jean Bourgeois-Pichat in "Les facteurs de la fécondité non dirigée," *Population* 20, no. 3 (1956): 383–424. A different and more accurate approach to estimating the impact of marriage on fertility is taken by A. Coale in "Factors associated with the development of low fertility: an historic summary," *Proceedings of the World Population Conference, Belgrade, 1965* Vol. 2 (New York: United Nations, 1967), pp. 205–209. Coale calculates an index of the proportion by which fertility is reduced due to years spent outside marriage by weighing each five-year age group differently, the largest weights being given to women in the most fertile years. This method correctly takes into account the fact that a year of reproductive life lost when a woman is near menopause obviously has a lesser effect on fertility than a year lost when fecundity is at a maximum.
5. Louis Henry, "Some data on natural fertility," *Eugenics Quarterly 8* (1961):81–96.
6. This percentage is calculated from estimates of the incidence of sterility by age, as given by Louis Henry in "Some data on natural fertility."
7. Following standard medical definitions, the terms "fertilization" and "conception" are used synonymously.
8. Demographers often define a conception as a fertilization that results in a delayed or missed menstruation, that is, fertilized ova are ignored if they fail to implant or are rejected within the first two weeks after fertilization. The monthly probability of such a conception is called "fecundability." Typical fecundability estimates range from 0.1 to 0.3 in different populations.
9. W. James, "The incidence of spontaneous abortions," *Population Studies,* 24, (1970):241–248.
10. As plotted in Figure 19.4, the sterile state includes only women who are both sterile and married; nonmarried sterile women are included in the unmarried state.

20

Frustrated Fertility: A Population Paradox

JOSEPH A. MCFALLS, JR.

On July 25, 1978, in Oldham, England, a baby girl, Louise, was born to Gilbert and Lesley Brown. The birth was announced in headlines throughout the world and reporters pressed in on the small hospital to get pictures of Louise and statements from her parents. The reason for this extraordinary interest in the birth of one child was that Louise Brown was the first baby in history to be conceived outside her mother's body. Lesley Brown, unable to conceive because her fallopian tubes are missing, underwent a simple operation to remove several ripened eggs from her ovary. These eggs were fertilized in a laboratory dish with a preparation of her husband's sperm and, after several stages of cell division, a suitable embryo was implanted in Mrs. Brown's uterus. Louise was born by Cesarean section thirty-seven weeks later, premature but evidently healthy and normal.

For this brief period the world's attention was diverted from the more familiar demographic topic of runaway population growth to a rarely discussed problem which nonetheless affects a sizable minority of the world's population—subfecundity. Subfecundity is any level of reproductive ability which is less than maximum. For the Browns and millions of other couples it is a curse that prevents them from having a child or the number of children they desire. But for a substantial minority of the world's population it is a blessing in that it limits the number of unwanted births. Thus subfecundity has a significant impact on the fertility of many individuals, and hence on population fertility.

This chapter considers the effect of population subfecundity on the fertility of present and historical societies and examines some of its more important causes. But first it is necessary to clarify important terminology and expand on what is meant by subfecundity.

DEFINING SUBFECUNDITY

Fecundity is used here to mean reproductive ability as opposed to *fertility* which denotes actual childbearing. *Subfecundity* refers to the diminished capacity to reproduce. The most severe form of subfecundity is *infecundity,* the total inability to reproduce both presently and in the future. Infecundity may develop in an individual who in the past was fecund and perhaps even had children. A *subfecundity factor* refers to a cause of subfecundity such as disease or psychic stress.

Subfecundity results from impairment of any of the biological aspects of reproduction—coitus, conception, and the ability to carry a conceptus to a live birth. *Coital inability* is defined as the inability to perform normal heterosexual intercourse. It afflicts both men and women, especially the former, and can be chronic or temporary. *Infertility* is defined as the diminished ability to conceive or to bring about conception. Thus infertility refers here only to conceptive difficulties, although the term has been used elsewhere to cover pregnancy loss and even coital problems as well. *Sterility* is the *complete* inability to conceive or bring about conception. It is simply the lowest point on the infertility continuum. Infertility is an important cause of subfecundity in both men and women, and like coital inability, can be chronic or temporary. Finally, *pregnancy loss* refers to the involuntary termination of a pregnancy before a live birth. It includes spontaneous abortion (miscarriage), late fetal death, and still-birth, but not induced abortion or neonatal mortality (death in the first four weeks of life). While primarily a form of female subfecundity, pregnancy loss is partly due to defective sperm and thus is also a form of male subfecundity. *Perinatal mortality,* a joint term for late fetal mortality and neonatal mortality, is also discussed with respect to the findings of studies which do not differentiate between these two components.

Although both men and women can be subfecund, most specialists in this field prefer to focus on the couple because the couple's subfecundity is frequently the result of several defects, often minor, in both partners. Also, two otherwise fecund individuals may form a subfecund couple due to various biological incompatibilities. A woman, for instance, may produce antibodies against her partner's sperm. Napoleon and Josephine were a classic case of such "situational subfecundity"; both were fertile with another mate but were unable to have children together.

A population's fecundity is the average fecundity of its individual members. Individual fecundity varies widely. Some individuals are unable to have children throughout their lives. Others are superfecund, the world record for fecundity (and fertility) being held by a nineteenth century Russian woman who reputedly produced 69 children in 27 pregnancies. Although this claim is suspect, there is no doubt that some women have given birth to more than 30 children. Raymond Pearl, for instance, mentions one woman who had 32 children by age 40.[1] Thus individual fecundity varies from zero to more than 30 children. Maximum population fecundity falls somewhere between these extremes. It is impossible to calculate actual population fecundity, but by splicing together the highest age-specific fertility rates on record and considering other hypothetical models, most authorities estimate maximum population fecundity to be about 15 children per woman.[2] In other words, a population of women who engaged in regular sexual intercourse from menarche to menopause without using any form of birth control would, under the most favorable reproductive circumstances, average about 15 children per woman. A population is subfecund to the extent that it is biologically incapable of achieving this roughly estimated average. Since no population enjoys completely favorable reproductive circumstances, some causes of subfecundity are present in all real populations, and hence all are subfecund according to this definition. It is their relative ability to achieve this standard, however, that is pertinent here and of demographic significance.

The actual fertility of almost all populations ranges from one to eight children per woman, with about four being the worldwide average in 1978. Of course, subfecundity accounts for only some of the difference between this performance and the 15-child estimate of maximum fecundity. As demographers Kingsley Davis and Judith Blake pointed out in a classic article,[3] besides subfecundity, a society's fertility level is also determined by various forms of birth control and by the fact that much of individuals' reproductive period is spent without regular coital activity. One of the basic tasks of fertility studies is to determine the relative impact of these subfecundity, birth control, and "mate exposure" factors which Davis and Blake characterize as "intermediate variables."

Population subfecundity varies widely between populations due to substantial differences in rates of coital inability, conceptive failure, and pregnancy loss, and the length of time between puberty and the climacteric in men and between menarche and menopause in women. The average length of the reproductive period, for instance, is greater in developed than in developing societies. Subfecundity also varies over time for a given population. German women at the turn of the century, for example had a reproductive span 10 years shorter than today's. On the average, they now reach childbearing age (menarche) at 12 and leave with menopause at age 52; 75 years ago, their reproductive lifetime stretched only from ages 15 to 45.

The relative contribution of male and female disorders to subfecundity differences between populations and over time is also highly variable. This is difficult to pinpoint because men's reluctance to admit responsibility for a couple's subfecundity, particularly in developing societies, means less is known about the prevalence of male subfecundity. However, experts estimate that male subfecundity accounts in whole or in part for from 20 to 60 percent of the subfecundity in various populations. In the United States, the consensus is that men contribute to subfecundity in 30 to 40 percent of cases and women, in 60 to 70 percent.

CAUSES OF POPULATION SUBFECUNDITY

Population students know very little about the fundamental causes of subfecundity and tend to prefer concentrating on how to measure its effects. Demographers have made advances in understanding how subfecundity is evident in longer intervals between births, but there is not much research that goes beyond this to identify its fundamental causes and quantify their impact on fertility. One authority, Hansluwka, concludes:

> The gaps in our knowledge are too large to permit the construction of a reasonably plausible model of the effects of health on fertility via fecundity.[4]

What knowledge does exist permits the causes of population subfecundity to be separated into five categories: genetic factors, psychopathology, disease, nutritional deficiencies, and environmental factors. To be included in one of these categories, a subfecundity factor must fulfill two criteria: it must be capable of depressing individual fecundity and it must be able to affect a substantial proportion of a population's potentially fecund members.

EFFECT OF SUBFECUNDITY ON FERTILITY

That subfecundity is one of the major determinants of population fertility is not just deduction. Statistics reveal that it is true of all populations, even of the group thought to be reproducing closest to the maximum rate—the Hutterites, a small religious sect scattered through the Dakotas and Montana in the United States and the prairie provinces of Canada. Their increasing fertility from generation to generation during the first half of this century was partly due to concomitant improvements in health conditions which affect fecundity. The power of subfecundity to affect fertility is most vividly seen in essentially noncontracepting societies with unexpectedly low fertility. These populations frequently reveal extraordinarily high rates of subfecundity. Africa presents a flagrant example of this today. In parts of Gabon, Cameroon, Zaire, the Central African Empire, the Sudan, and elsewhere across Central Africa, 20 to 50 percent of women aged 50 and older have never borne children, and subfecundity is recognized as an acute problem.

Importance in Historical Societies

Subfecundity has doubtless depressed fertility since the human race began about one million years ago. During most of this time, the rate of population growth was scarcely above zero. For such a low growth rate to be sustained, fertility and mortality had to be roughly the same. Experts conclude that for much of world history, average life expectancy was about 20 years. To offset this mortality, women would have had to average six to seven children, that is, substantially less than the biological maximum. Birth control and "mate exposure" variables probably accounted for much of this "fertility deficit," but subfecundity undoubtedly also played an important role in curtailing fertility and holding down population growth. Indeed, Rose Frisch suggests that subfecundity may be even more important in pre-modern societies than is usually assumed, for it could also be responsible for some of the shortfall usually credited to the other factors, especially traditional forms of birth control such as abstinence and prolonged breastfeeding.[5]

Population history prior to the 18th century can be divided into two periods, one extending back to about 8000 B.C. when agriculture was introduced and the other from 8000 B.C. to the beginning of mankind. Subfecundity influenced fertility in both periods although the leading causes were probably different. Subfecundity in historical preagricultural societies may have been similar to that observed among some contemporary hunting and gathering societies. The Kung tribe of Africa's Kalahari Desert, for instance, has moderate fertility with relatively long intervals between births. This may be partly due to poor nutrition and low body weight which reduce fecundity, conditions that may have also been common in historical preagricultural societies. The village life of the agriculturalists, on the other hand, brought comparatively many individuals close together, facilitating the spread of many diseases which cause subfecundity. Also, by relying more on crops for survival, agriculturalists became more vulnerable to crop failure which led to unpredictable and catastrophic famines and the gross malnutrition that is a potent cause of subfecundity. Thus, chronic undernutrition may have been a relatively more important cause of subfecundity in the preagricultural period, and disease and starvation may have been relatively more potent in the agricultural period.[6]

This capsule description of population history glosses over the short-term variations that occurred in growth, death, and birth rates in many societies. Subfecundity also fluctuated with the ups and downs of food supply and disease.

One disease that may have had a significant impact on the fecundity and fertility of numerous historical populations in tuberculosis. Evidences of this venerable disease have been found in the skeletons of prehistoric men. It is probable that in Eurasia after 500 A.D. tuberculosis affected mortality, fecundity, and fertility as much as or more than smallpox or plague. Tuberculosis was very prevalent in Europe prior to the twentieth century and may have been a significant cause of subfecundity there.[7] It has also been suggested as a prime cause of subfecundity among U.S. blacks during the latter half of the nineteenth and early twentieth centuries.[8] Smallpox is another disease that may have considerably reduced fecundity and thus fertility, as Peter Razzell feels it did in Britain before 1850.[9] Sudden declines in the prevalence of such subfecundity-producing diseases as tuberculosis and smallpox are often accompanied by a rise in fertility as happened in Europe during the nineteenth century or more recently in parts of the Third World.[10]

Importance in Developing Societies Today

Today subfecundity affects fertility more in developing than in developed societies. This is primarily due to two situations. First, in developing societies there are fewer social checks on fertility such as effective contraception and thus more fertility potential for subfecundity to negate. Second, these societies are far more exposed to powerful causes of subfecundity, particularly disease and malnutrition. This situation is compounded (and perpetuated) by the relative absence of quality health care and facilities.

Just how poor health care is in parts of many developing nations is graphically summarized in the following description written in 1974 of a health facility near Lagos, Nigeria, where one of the few known Americans to contract Lassa fever laid over while awaiting travel accommodations to the United States:

> The Pest House was a crumbling building set aside for contagious diseases, with rough plaster walls and the inevitable corrugated tin roof. . . . There were no fans or screens. . . . The room was dimly lit and suffocatingly hot. . . . Within minutes she became aware of the mosquitoes; hoards of them coming in through the open windows. The small sink was black with them, and with flies. There were no nets on the beds. . . . As she got into bed . . . she saw the bedbugs, wingless blood-sucking insects with a faint acrid odor. . . . A rat scurried across the floor, darted erratically back and forth, then disappeared. . . .[11]

Bad as these conditions are, almost one billion of the earth's inhabitants, most of whom live in developing societies, still have no access to any health care at all. Rampant, untreated disease is probably the most important reason for the subfecundity which afflicts such developing societies as the band of Central African countries with unexpectedly low fertility and high proportions of childless women.

Subfecundity can have a significant effect even on the fertility of developing societies thought to have excessively high fertility. For instance, the married Yoruba women in Ibadan City, Nigeria, average about six children per woman. Yet, by age 45, 8 percent are involuntarily childless and another 25 percent have had less than four live births in a society where four or more living children is considered the ideal.[12] If this apparent subfecundity were not present, the already high fertility of the whole population would rise materially.

Importance in Developed Societies Today

Although not as virulent or as prevalent as in developing societies, subfecundity factors are still demographically important in developed societies. Indeed, despite the fact that the major U.S. fertility surveys of the last several decades have tended to omit subfecund women, they still found extraordinarily higher rates of subfecundity among their respondents. About one-third of the married white couples of reproductive age surveyed in the 1941 Indianapolis Study[13] and in the 1955 and 1960 Growth of American Families Studies[14] were considered subfecund. Sociologist Carl Harter also classified 33 percent of a New Orleans sample as subfecund.[15] Coital inability is particularly rife in developed societies. Sex researchers Masters and Johnson estimate—conservatively, they say—that half of U.S. couples experience sexual dysfunction sometime during their lives.[16] This seems confirmed by a recent study among white, well-educated, and happily married U. S. couples, in which a startling 40 percent of the men reported difficulties with erection or ejaculation and 63 percent of the women admitted some form of sexual dysfunction.[17]

There is reason to believe that subfecundity is on the rise in developed societies. One factor is the dramatic increase in venereal disease which can seriously damage reproductive potential. Another is the widespread use of the pill and the IUD which can also cause problems for a few women who later hope to bear children. But since the majority of couples choose low fertility and are able to attain it through birth control, the impact of subfecundity on fertility is not as substantial as it is in developing societies. However, it is still important.

If subfecundity were to be eliminated in developed societies, fertility would certainly rise. Involuntarily childless couples or those who have fewer children than desired due to subfecundity would increase their fertility. Since it is now estimated that 15 percent of U.S. couples are involuntarily childless and another 10 percent have fewer children than they want,[18] such an eventuality would have a substantial impact on U.S. fertility—without even considering increases in fertility among those other subfecund couples who do not want more children and for whom subfecundity is a blessing.

Moreover, within contracepting developed societies, there are often significant subgroups not practicing effective birth control whose fertility would rise if subfecundity were not present. In the United States such subgroups would include lower income whites and blacks as well as teenagers. Indeed, it could be that many subfecundity factors are disproportionately prevalent among such groups. As demographer Ronald Freedman notes:

> Health conditions and poor nutrition may affect the fecundity of the whole society or may affect the lowest stratum with special force as a result of the operation of the economic distribution system.[19]

As in the developing societies, lack of medical care is also an important cause of subfecundity among the underprivileged in developed societies. Even in the United States with its relative abundance of medical professionals, medical care is spotty; it is unavailable on a regular basis, for instance, to 10 million underprivileged children.

Subfecundity can also affect the fertility of high-natality subgroups in developed societies. Take the Older Order Amish, for example, another high-fertility religious group in the United States. Recent cohorts have completed childbearing with a mean family size of 7 compared to 2.7 for comparable national cohorts. The fertility of the Amish has been increasing over the last 100 years, and childlessness has been declining. In a fascinating forthcoming article, Julia Ericksen and her associates argue that this is chiefly due to reductions in subfecundity, noting the group's willingness to take advantage of modern medical technology as soon as it appears.[20] They also observe that while the Amish have 7 children on average, the number varies greatly between families, probably due mostly to subfecundity. Even in one sample of particularly high-fertility Amish women which happened to include no childless women they were able to classify 10 percent of the women as significantly subfecund using infertility criteria alone. These women finished childbearing with only 4.6 children on average compared to 9.4 for the sample as a whole. In short, the authors conclude that the extraordinarily high fertility of the Amish would have been still higher had subfecundity not existed.

Some might argue that most subfecund women in developed societies still have the number of children they want; it just takes them longer. In other words, subfecundity would not affect completed fertility. This position denies the reality that substantial fractions of ever-married women in developed societies are involuntarily and permanently childless and that large numbers with children can have no more. It also ignores the effect of the timing of fertility on completed family size. For example, many women in the United States are now postponing childbearing until their late twenties and early thirties. This gives them fewer years to achieve their desired fertility and also requires that they do so in the face of the lower fecundity characteristic of these years due to aging and accumulated subfecundity from causes such as disease. About the much-speculated-upon possibility that many U.S. women are about to try to have their quota of two children late in their reproductive careers, demographer Conrad Taeuber has commented:

> It's a pretty cloudy crystal ball. If women have these two children, we're bound to see the number of births go up. . . . But there is some reason to believe that some women will be disappointed and find they can't have these children.[21]

Subfecundity can also have important *indirect* effects on population fertility. It may influence fertility behaviorally through others of the Davis-Blake intermediate variables, reducing, for instance, the chances of marrying or maintaining a stable sexual union.[22]

It can also indirectly affect population fertility by influencing the timing of early fertility. Most women are relatively subfecund until about age 17 and delays in early childbearing which sexually active adolescents might experience because of this could provide women with the opportunity to develop a lifestyle other than that of becoming the mother of a large family. Also, the presence of subfecundity during the early reproductive years can allow progress to be made toward learning effective birth control which would reduce unwanted fertility or give a woman time to consider what her reproductive goals really are and then attempt to stick by them.[23] The subfecundity produced by syphilis, for instance, can provide such a delay. Usually contracted early in reproductive life, syphilis causes high rates of pregnancy loss during the two years after first infection. However, even untreated syphilis has little effect on pregnancy outcome after this period so that a direct effect on completed fertility would be unlikely for couples with low or moderate family size desires. But the two-year respite during the peak reproductive years provided by the subfecundity gives a woman the opportunity to revise her reproductive goals.

Although not so important demographically, it is worth noting that subfecundity can also affect fertility indirectly by influencing the timing of late fertility. Delays in second or later children can result in lower lifetime fertility. Subfecundity used to be responsible for a considerable proportion of two-family women—those who had children early, stopped childbearing for many years due to a variety of reasons including subfecundity, and then had other children who were far younger than the first group. Today, with the increased availability of induced abortion and better contraceptives, women more often forego the second family in favor of other life-styles. If it were not for subfecundity in the middle years, many of these women, especially those who had not yet achieved their desired family size, might well have had additional children spaced close to the first set. Thus subfecundity, by altering when women are able to have their higher-order children, may alter completed family size as well.

These indirect effects of subfecundity on fertility may now make the most difference in developed societies. But they were doubtless also important in historical societies and remain so in developing societies. For example, the subfecund wife cast out by a disappointed husband has been a familiar tragedy throughout history and still is in many developing societies today.

In sum, subfecundity can affect fertility directly and may also affect fertility indirectly by altering the timing of births or by acting through one of the other Davis-Blake "intermediate variables." Conversely, these intermediate variables, which have to do mostly with birth control and mate exposure, may themselves cause subfecundity and thus affect fertility in this way also. For example, Winifred Cutler and her associates have uncovered evidence that later and less frequent intercourse is associated with subfecundity.[24] Understanding population fertility fully may take more knowledge about the complex interrelationships between subfecundity, birth control, and mate exposure. But it cannot be denied that subfecundity is a major determinant of population fertility in developed, developing, and historical societies.

NOTES

1. Pearl, Raymond, *The Natural History of Population* (New York: Oxford University Press, 1939) p. 36.
2. See, e.g., H. Hansluwka, "Health, Population, and Socio-economic Development," in Leon Tabah (ed.), *Population Growth and Economic Development in the Third World* (Belgium: Ordina, 1975) p. 203; and William Petersen, *Population,* 3rd edition (New York: Macmillan, 1975) p. 199.
3. Davis, Kingsley and Judith Blake, "Social Structure and Fertility: An Analytic Framework," *Economic Development and Cultural Change,* Vol. 4 (1956) pp. 211–235.
4. Hansluwka, op. cit., p. 205.
5. Frisch, Rose, "Demographic Implications of the Biological Determinants of Female Fecundity," *Social Biology,* Vol. 22 (1975) p. 21.
6. For a fuller discussion of the historical information in this and the preceding paragraph, see Ansley Coale, "The History of the Human Population," *Scientific American,* Vol. 231, No. 3 (1974) pp. 40–51.
7. Gray, Ronald, "Biological Factors Other than Nutrition and Lactation which May Influence Natural Fertility: A Review," paper presented at the IUSSP Seminar on Natural Fertility, Paris, 1977, p. 29.
8. For a discussion of the impact of tuberculosis on the fertility of the U.S. black population and other populations, see Joseph McFalls, *Disease and Fertility* (New York: Academic Press, forthcoming).
9. Razzell, Peter, *The Conquest of Smallpox: The Impact of Inoculation on Smallpox Mortality in Eighteenth Century Britain* (Sussex: Caliban, 1977) p. vi.
10. Tabah, Leon, "World Population Growth at the Turning Point," *Intercom,* Vol. 5, No. 12 (December 1977) p. 7.
11. Fuller, John, *Fever: The Hunt for a New Killer Virus* (New York: Ballantine, 1974) pp. 59–61.
12. Arowolo, Oladele, "A Demographic Note on Relative Infertility in Nigeria," forthcoming report derived from Segment 1 of the Changing African Family Project in Nigeria, 1978, p. 13.
13. Whelpton, Pascal and Clyde Kiser, *Social and Psychological Factors Affecting Fertility* (New York: Milbank Memorial Fund, 1946–1958).
14. Freedman, Ronald, Pascal Whelpton, and Arthur Campbell, *Family Planning, Sterility and Population*

Growth (Princeton: Princeton University Press, 1959); and Pascal Whelpton, Arthur Campbell, and John Patterson, *Fertility and Family Planning in the United States* (Princeton: Princeton University Press, 1966).

15. Harter, Carl, "The Fertility of Sterile and Subfecund Women in New Orleans," *Social Biology,* Vol. 17 (1970) pp. 195–206.
16. Masters, William and Virginia Johnson, *Human Sexual Inadequacy* (Boston: Little Brown, 1970) p. 369.
17. Frank, Ellen, Carol Anderson, and Debra Rubinstein, "Frequency of Sexual Dysfunction in Normal Couples," *The New England Journal of Medicine,* Vol. 299 (1978) pp. 111–115.
18. These figures come from the deliberations of The Scientific Group on Basic, Clinical, and Public Health Aspects of Subfecundity and Sterility convened by the World Health Organization in Geneva, September-October, 1969. The proceedings were not subsequently published but these figures are cited often: see, e.g., Richard Amelar, Lawrence Dubin, and Patrick Walsh, *Male Infertility* (Philadelphia: Saunders, 1977) p. ix.
19. Freedman, Ronald, *The Sociology of Fertility* (Oxford: Basil Blackwell, 1963) p. 51.
20. Ericksen, Julia, Eugene Ericksen, John Hostetler, and Gertrude Huntington, "Fertility Patterns and Trends among the Old Order Amish," *Population Studies,* forthcoming 1979.
21. Cited in Ann Blackman, "Baby Boom Not Likely Now," *Philadelphia Inquirer,* November 2, 1975, WA, p. 1.
22. The factors which *can* cause subfecundity—genetics, psychopathology, disease, nutritional deficiencies, and environment—need not actually do so in order to register an impact on fertility, since they are also able to influence fertility behaviorally through others of the Davis-Blake "Intermediate variables," such as contraceptive use, coital frequency, sterilization, and voluntary abortion. For example, the identification of diseases harmful to the fetus and better detection of these diseases in pregnant women, together with readily available abortion, have undoubtedly raised rates of fetal wastage. Pregnant women who contact German measles (rubella) face increased risks of spontaneous abortion, but the induced abortions obtained by infected women who fear their offspring might be malformed by this virus account for far greater amounts of "pregnancy wastage." Even inadvertent vaccination of pregnant women with the attenuated virus of German measles, though not conclusively known to cause malformations in the fetus, is a frequent cause of induced abortion. In one series, 50 percent of vaccinated women sought abortions, yet not one of the continued pregnancies ended in congenital rubella. Syphillis is also a good example of a subfecundity factor that can indirectly affect fertility through other intermediate variables. Infected persons, as well as those trying to avoid the disease, often use prophylactic procedures during coitus (most commonly, condoms) that are secondarily contraceptive. The discovery of syphilis during the frequently mandatory premarital blood test may force postponement or even cancellation of marriage. And before antibiotics, the prospect of giving birth to a child with congenital syphilis was probably a reason for voluntary abortion. Syphilis is also almost certain proof of one partner's infidelity and undoubtedly increases the frequency of separation and divorce.
23. For a discussion of these ideas, see George Masnick and Joseph McFalls, "A New perspective on the Twentieth-Century American Fertility Swing," *Journal of Family History,* Vol. 1 (1976) p. 224, and "Those Perplexing U.S. Fertility Swings: A New Perspective on a 20th Century Puzzle," *PRB Report,* November 1978, p. 5.
24. Cutler, Winnifred, Celso Ramon Garcia, and Abba Krieger, "Infertility and Age at First Coitus," *Journal of Biosocial Science,* forthcoming 1979, and "Sexual Behavior Frequency and Fertility are Associated in Gynecologically Mature Premenopausal Women," presently under review by *Psychoneuroendocrinology.*

21
Couples' Decision-Making Processes Regarding Fertility

LINDA J. BECKMAN

The major objective of this chapter is to elucidate a social-psychological model of fertility decision making in order to call increased attention to the role of psychological and motivational variables in the determination of fertility. Social-psychological theory and research that pertain to how individuals and marital dyads form preferences and make choices regarding childbearing will be reviewed. The focus will be on these processes as they occur in the United States and other developed countries, for one likely concomitant of modernization is increased importance of decision making in the determination of fertility.

Women in developed countries use contraception to reduce their fertility far below their biological ability. Many couples (or individuals) are making choices regarding the use of contraception and the limitation of fertility. The questions to be considered are *how* they "decide" to limit fertility and *what* determines their decisions.

Fertility-related decision processes recently have attracted the interest of psychologists and social psychologists for the following reasons. First, with increasing utilization of the more effective means of fertility regulation, it seems likely that fertility "decision" processes are becoming more salient, and preferences regarding fertility may be increasingly in accord with actual fertility. Second, as sociodemographic differentials in fertility decrease (Ryder and Westoff, 1972; Turchi, 1975; U.S. Bureau of the Census, 1973, 1974; Westoff and Ryder, 1969), individual factors in decision making attain increasing explanatory power. While the decline of sociodemographic differentials in fertility may be a reflection of declining variance in desired and actual fertility in the United States, an alternative assumption is that subgroup normative influences have become less salient while individual instrumental values and preferences regarding fertility have gained in predictive power. Motivational preferences are less likely merely to reflect sociodemographic differences and may operate independently to influence fertility behavior.

DEMOGRAPHY'S IMPLICIT RECOGNITION OF MOTIVATIONAL INFLUENCES

Demographers have postulated implicitly that fertility decision making occurs, but, because of their emphasis on aggregate data, have generally not explicitly examined or defined decision-making processes. Psychologists (Edwards, 1954; Fishbein, 1967; Janis and Mann, 1977; Jones and Gerard, 1967; Lee, 1974) have examined the decision-making process extensively, but in the past have rarely applied it to the area of fertility.

Most demographers postulate underlying subjective psychological variables, as in use of the concept *value of children,* to explain transitions from high fertility to low fertility during economic development. But in their reliance on data from censuses and large-scale national sample surveys, demographers largely have avoided problems of reliability and validity that plague researchers dealing with these "softer" variables. Even when they have used motivational variables, these have tended to be unidimensional variables such as desired, expected, or ideal family size. Thus although implicitly recognizing that some type of decision making or preference-crystallization process occurs, demographers have left the area of choices, preferences, and decisions regarding fertility to two divergent groups: economists and psychologists.

Despite demographers' reluctance to examine these microlevel variables, I believe that our models must be reductionistic and must attempt to examine individual preferences and decisions. If contraceptive use depends on a process of individual and family decision making, macromodels of sociological or demographic variables are not sufficient. Attention must be given to the correspondence or interaction between sociodemographic and motivational variables, that is, how macrovariables are translated into microvariables. Even more important is the possibility that motivational variables can explain differences in fertility not accounted for by demographic differentials (Beckman, 1974, 1976). Such an approach has been criticized severely (Hauser and Duncan, 1959; 96–102) for the psychological reductionism or rationalization inherent in such accounts, lack of representativeness, reliability and validity, and inability to deal with fertility in the aggregate or to measure trends over time. However, none of these difficulties, except for reductionism, is inherent in psychological variables, and the alternative is to postulate (implicitly if not explicitly) intervening processes or variables while refusing to examine them.

SOCIAL-PSYCHOLOGICAL APPROACHES TO FERTILITY DECISION MAKING

There are several possible existing paradigms or theoretical orientations to a social-psychological approach to fertility decision making (Davidson and Jaccard, 1975; Fishbein, 1972; Fishbein and Jaccard, 1973; Hass, 1974; Terhune, 1973; Terhune and Kaufman, 1973; Townes et al., 1974). Most social-psychological theories of fertility decision making owe much to the economists, but consider psychological as well as economic costs and benefits of parenthood. They begin with the premise that behavior is motivated and that motivation is governed by positive and negative incentives (Smith, 1973). Usually the assumption is made that if costs of an additional child outweigh the benefits, the person will choose not to have an additional child. If benefits outweigh costs, the person will desire an additional child (Beckman, 1974; Hass, 1974). These models are defined as "rational" because, in effect, it is assumed that the individual makes a choice, based on perceived benefits and costs, which maximizes his or her psychic (that is, subjective expected) utility.

Almost all theorists and researchers of fertility decision making (with notable exceptions, for example, Hass, 1974; Mellinger, 1974) have looked at individual preferences and decisions rather than couples' decision processes regarding fertility. In so doing, they have inadvertently eliminated one extremely important stage of the fertility decision process, that is, how individual preferences or choices are combined to reach a joint decision regarding fertility. The assessment of the impact of the decision process itself on fertility levels is of importance. Although it is true that either member of a couple may alone make a decision to control fertility, in 1975 81 percent of married women in Los Angeles County reported that both spouses shared equally in the decision of how many children to have (unpublished data from a study conducted among a representative sample of 583 married women aged 18 to 49; see Beckman, 1976).

A SOCIAL-PSYCHOLOGICAL MODEL OF COUPLES' FERTILITY DECISION-MAKING PROCESSES

In societies where knowledge and practice of contraception are wide-spread, the assumption is often made (Thompson, 1974) that rational-instrumental models of individual decision making (such as the Fishbein model) are most appropriate. The conceptualization that I shall develop is perhaps best characterized as a rational-type model of fertility, although it does not ignore normative influences. The model assumes that a continuum exists from preference to individual decision to joint decision. A decision indicates a conscious choice whereas a preference indicates a subjective favorability or affect. In this conceptualization it is assumed that individuals and couples, in varying degrees, make decisions or choices regarding fertility, based at least partially on personal tastes or preferences, for varying long- or short-term time spans.

Motivation for A/Another Child

Before discussing couples' decision making, it is desirable to consider individual decision making. This necessitates explication of a hypothetical construct called *motivation for parenthood.* This construct can be defined as the general strength of the tendency to have a first or an additional child. It represents a predisposition to act and serves to arouse, maintain, and direct behaviors toward or away from the goal of having a first or an additional child. The strength of motivation for or against a/another child depends on the perceived satisfactions and costs of having an *n*th child (the marginal utility of an *n*th child), as compared to various alternatives to children. Rewards and costs can be defined as *perceived* positive outcome (satisfactions or benefits) and negative outcomes (costs) associated with having and interacting with an *n*th child.

For women, the perceived rewards and costs of parenthood and the perceived rewards and costs of major alternative sources of psychic satisfaction (such as employment or leisure) affect decisions whether and when to have an additional child, and therefore, affect fertility variables such as use of contraception and length of time between marriage and first birth (see Figure 21.1). Fertility decision making is conceptualized as a sequential process (Hass, 1974) in which the key decision probably is whether to have another child, rather than how many children to have.

The preference structures of individuals (that is, the perceived satisfactions and costs) may have built into them some preconscious satisfactions (i.e., desiring a child because of an unconscious need to mother or an unconscious need to prove one's virility) or costs that are not easily measured and that may cause discrepancies between predicted motivation for parenthood and actual choices. Also it is possible that some satisfactions or preferences serve as lexicographic events (Pope and Namboodiri, 1968), that is, they constitute normative or moral acts that, as ends in themselves, are not weighed against other alternatives as suggested in the general model. A normative or moral act (for instance, having at least two children) may be chosen automatically, whatever the disutility or opportunity costs involved; it is not bound by rational considerations. In such cases it is expected that situational and individual factors gain importance once minimal cultural norms have been met. For instance, the weighing of the salience of perceived advantages and disadvantages of parenthood for married couples may become more evident after the second child is born (Hass, 1974; Kammeyer, 1971). Before that point, for most people the weighing of positive and negative factors could determine the timing of the birth, but not the probability of occurrence of the birth. (Of course, the timing of early births is related to the probability of occurrence of later births.)

Proposed Causal Relationships of the Model

Figure 21.1 shows the critical variables of interest in the present formulation. Underlying personality characteristics, sociodemographic characteristics, and situational determinants are thought to affect perceived satisfactions and costs, and thus motivation for parenthood. Sociodemographic variables may affect personality variables as well as directly influence the satisfactions and costs of a/another child. For instance, persons of lower socioeconomic status may evidence higher sex-role traditionalism than do persons of higher SES, and sex-role traditionalism may be one of several

Figure 21.1. A model of fertility decision making (at one point in time).

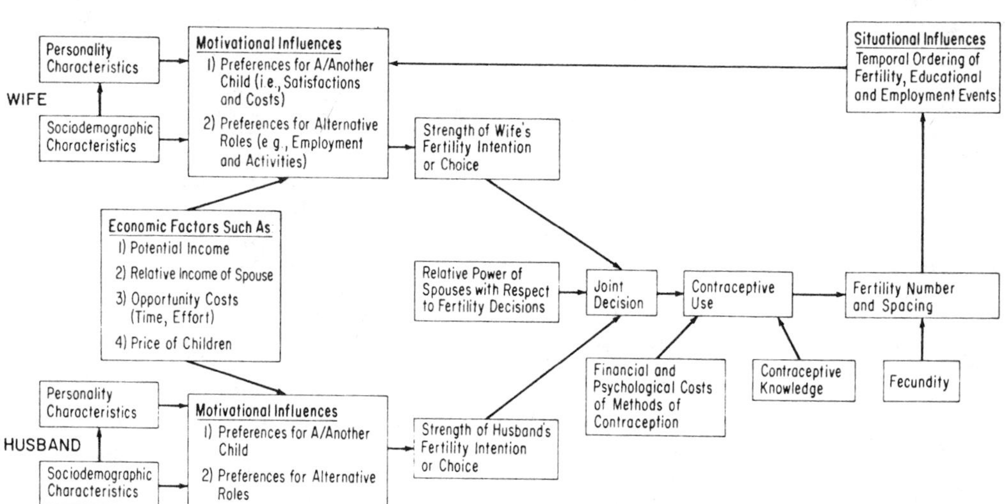

personality variables that mediate the association between demographic variables and preferences for children.

Factors such as race, urban-rural residence, education, or father's socioeconomic status may help to explain why, although two persons may have similar objective circumstances (for example, income, employment, standard of living), the *subjective* perceptions of the rewards and costs of having a child may greatly vary. However, it is not assumed that perceived satisfactions and costs of children are entirely dependent on such factors. When sociodemographic variables are controlled, it is predicted that some variation in preferences (arising from differences in other personality or situational characteristics) will remain. Data from both the Los Angeles County sample of married women (Beckman, 1976) and from a smaller pilot study of employed married women in the later years of childbearing (Beckman, 1974) strongly support this contention.

In a similar way, normative influences that differ among demographic groups interact with situational determinants and personality factors to influence motivations for various alternatives to an additional child. The most prominent of these alternative roles for women is employment, and it is the alternative emphasized here. However, other socially acceptable alternatives, such as education, leisure activities, and volunteer work, are also relevant. Volunteer activities on a part-time basis may give women some of the same satisfactions (for example, self-esteem, a sense of making a social contribution) as does employment without many of the high costs involved (for instance, lack of time for children or housework).

The choice of additional motherhood or an alternative role does not represent an either-or decision for a woman. Allocation of time, energy, and money demands that a woman choose a certain amount of participation in each role (Turchi, 1975), and given limited resources (the economic factors in Figure 21.1), she will seek by her choice regarding amount of participation to maximize psychic utility, her sense of satisfaction. One manifestation of sex differences in factors affecting motivation for childbearing is that the issue of employment and parenthood as alternative roles rarely arises for men. Although it is possible that men may weigh parenthood against alternative material goods (a more expensive car) or alternative activities (foreign travel), it is assumed and accepted that a man will fulfill both roles. Even if the perceived positive benefits of children are identical for men and women, their respective desired and expected fertility may vary because women must make a tradeoff between the two roles.

Contraceptive practices are directly affected by decision processes, contraceptive knowledge (including beliefs about susceptibility to conception), and perceived financial and psychological costs of use of various methods of contraception (Easterlin, 1969). In my model, an intention reflects an individual choice, while a joint decision implies couple communication. Obviously one member of a couple can make a unilateral decision regarding parenthood, but fertility regulation usually does not represent a unilateral choice. Individual intentions or choices lead to joint decisions, which in turn lead to the actual behavior of couples concerning birth planning practices. The decision outcome chosen in cases of disagreement depends on the relative power of the spouses, the relative ability of each person to influence the other. Contraceptive practices affect fertility outcomes such as number of children, interval between marriage and first birth, and other birth intervals.

Other Characteristics of Fertility Decisions

For decision making to take place, certain preconditions are necessary (Back, 1967). The person must be aware that a choice (in this case, the choice to limit conception) can be made, and he/she must have the means to implement it. The person must be motivated (and have the values) to make a definite choice. The person must have the environment that makes it possible to act on an intention, and the psychological makeup to act on it.

The fertility decision is important, irreversible after late pregnancy, and yet involves uncertain outcomes A decision with these characteristics is likely to be delayed as long as possible (Janis and Mann, 1977). Individuals may actively avoid a fertility decision unless some action is forced on them. Whether this means delaying a decision to use contraception (that is, a decision to stop having children) or delaying a decision to discontinue the use of contraception (a decision to have child) may depend on the personal dispositions and cultural norms of the individual decision maker or the couple.

Fertility decisions may follow various patterns. Many individuals cannot pinpoint a particular instance of having made a choice (for example, a definite decision to have an *n*th child). In some cases a series of minor choices leads to a slow drift into parenthood. Others may choose not to make a decision, which ultimately is itself a decision not to control one's fate. A decision to stop use of a contraceptive may be different than a decision for a nonuser to begin usage. The latter requires not only a choice to use fertility regulation but also a decision regarding what kind of contraception to use.

Fertility decisions may involve a long- or short-term time perspective. While some couples may plan their children several years in advance, many childless couples remain undecided about whether to have children and only gradually come to the realization that the wife is too old or they are too settled in a lifestyle to desire children. Some persons may only make a decision not to have a child now, while others may decide that they want no more children. These different patterns of decision making are worthy of examination, because the fertility decision-making process may help to predict future fertility behavior.

Because of the emphasis of the present chapter on decision processes, two components of Figure 21.1, motivational influences and the relative power of spouses in the joint decision, will be more extensively discussed.

INDIVIDUAL PREFERENCES REGARDING CHILDREN

My discussion of preference (motivation) for a/another child is primarily based on social exchange theory (Homans, 1961; Thibaut and Kelley, 1959). Social behavior may be explained in terms of the rewards and costs incurred in social interaction. The attractiveness of a present or future relationship (for example, a parent-child relationship) is a function of the reward-cost outcomes that persons experience or think they will experience in relation to some minimal level of expectation of what these outcomes should be. This minimal level is called the *comparison level* (CL) and is influenced by a person's past experience in the relationship, his past experience in comparable relationships (for example, with other children), his perception of what others like himself (for example, his sociodemographic group) are receiving, and his perception of the outcomes available in alternative relationships.

The comparison level is a standard against which a person evaluates the rewards and costs of a relationship in terms of what is felt to be deserved, that is, the minimum that a person thinks ought to be gained from the interaction. Usually it is not directly measured, but rather inferred from the level of a person's perceived satisfaction or dissatisfaction with the relationship. Thus the CL serves as a psychologically meaningful neutral point on a scale of outcomes (that is, satisfaction versus dissatisfaction). The value that a person places on an outcome or choice is not determined by the absolute amount of gain or loss that a person expects, but rather by the amount expected relative to a comparison level. A person receiving outcomes at comparison level would be neither satisfied nor dissatisfied with a relationship. To the degree that outcomes are above CL, the person would be attracted to and satisfied with a relationship. On the other hand, relationships entailing outcomes falling below CL would be relatively unattractive and unsatisfying (Thibaut and Kelley, 1959).

Individuals may remain in a relationship even though the outcomes they receive are below comparison level, because they perceive that in the alternatives available the costs are greater or the rewards are less. For example, in a loveless marriage the couple may stay together even if they are both unhappy. The wife may stay because she sees no chance for getting a better husband and no prospect for adequate support for her and her children except through her current marriage. A parent-child relationship also can become nonvoluntary, that is, the person is constrained in the relationship despite the fact that outcomes are below CL and better outcomes are available from other relationships, activities, or roles. Because of normative constraints the parent usually cannot or will not leave the relationship.

In my past research I have used an exchange theory approach to examine motivation for a first or an additional child versus motivation for the alternative role of employment. According to the theory, a person should want or intend to have a child (have high motivation for parenthood) when the rewards or advantages strongly outweigh the disadvantages. He or she should not want to have a child (have low motivation for parenthood) when the costs or disadvantages of parenthood outweigh the rewards. To determine if a person wants to have another child, it is necessary to delineate the perceived rewards and costs of an additional child and the salience of each. There should be a high correlation between a summary measure of rewards and costs and desires or behavioral intentions (Fishbein, 1967, 1972) regarding additional parenthood. Application of the theory requires specification of the type of cognitive algebra or psycho-logic to be used in deriving a summary index that combines the relative strength of these incentives. Many theorists have used a decision theory or subjective expected utility approach that assumes that likelihood of an outcome as well as its evaluative component must be taken into account. In most such formulations the value of an outcome is multiplied by its expectancy of occurrence, and then scores are summed (Davidson and Jaccard, 1975; Fishbein, 1967, 1972). A simpler additive approach that utilizes importance ratings may be just as effective. Salience or importance ratings may already include a person's internal assessment of likelihood (that is, an outcome would not be rated as important if the expectation that it would occur was very low). Because of measurement problems (that Townes et al., 1974, may have adequately solved), I initially chose this simpler model.

Because an economic approach requires that the strength of preference for a child must be compared to the strength of preferences for possible alternatives, motivation for a/another child was compared to motivation for the alternative of employment or a career. Those women with greater preferences for the alternative of employment should have lower fertility and fertility intentions. It was predicted that women would choose their amount of interaction within each of these social situations (parenthood and employment) depending on the reward-cost outcomes (that is, ΣRewards $-$ ΣCosts) of additional participation in each situation and their combined outcomes. For instance, a woman would choose (or desire) to have a child or an additional child (and not to work) when the net reward-cost outcome of the motherhood role was considerably greater than the net reward-cost outcome of the work role, and the satisfactions of additional parenthood clearly outweighed the costs. Similarly, she would choose both roles if the rewards of both roles were high and the costs low.

Empirical Evidence Regarding Individual Preferences for Children

In my study of the motivation for parenthood of approximately 600 married women from Los Angeles County, respondents assessed the salience of a series of satisfactions and costs of an additional child and satisfactions and costs of employment on 7-point rating scales. Motivation for parenthood was defined as the sum of the importance ratings of the rewards of a/another child minus the sum of the importance ratings of the costs of a/another child. Motivation for employment was defined in an analogous manner. Then the relationship between these summary measures and desires regarding children and employment was examined. Respondents were divided into groups based on their scores (high or low) on motivation for a/another child and their scores (high or low) on motivation for employment. Of those with high motivation for a/another child, 83 percent wanted at least one additional child, while of those low in motivation, 10 percent wanted a child. Similarly, 85 percent of those with high motivation for employment intended to work in the next year, while only 27 percent of those with low motivation for employment intended to work.

As in other studies, employment appeared to influence fertility. Women with greater employment experience had produced fewer children, and currently employed women had lower motivation for a/another child than did unemployed women.

The Bidirectionality of the Employment—Fertility Relationship

My data suggest that one of the opportunity costs of a/another child that is more important to women who are currently employed is limitation of employment or a career. The perceived limitation of employment, that is, the degree of perceived role incompatability between parenthood and employment, appeared to be influencing employed women to have fewer children than women who were not employed. Causality also can operate in the reverse direction; women with smaller families have more time to work (Sweet, 1970). The existence of an inverse relationship between female employment and fertility is well documented (Blake, 1965; Hoffman, 1974; Nye and Hoffman, 1963; Siegel and Haas, 1963). Studies explicating the relationship have examined both the effects of work activity on fertility (Fortney, 1972; Freedman and Coombs, 1966; Groat et al., 1976) and the effects of fertility events (number of children, birth intervals, desired number of children) on female labor force participation (Stycos and Weller, 1967; Sweet, 1970; Weller, 1971; Whelpton et al., 1966). The best that can be said about the employment-fertility relationship at this point is that causality is most probably bidirectional, and the multiple causal paths involved are not clearly understood (Terry, 1975).

Stability of Rewards and Costs of Parenthood

The manner in which rewards an costs of parenthood change over time and the relationship between changes in rewards, costs, and changes in preferences for children have not been adequately examined. It may well be that some perceived satisfactions and costs of children (for example, motherhood as "woman's role") are established early in adolescence or even in childhood. These stable motives for or against having children may have been incorporated by the child during the process of identification with the same-sex parent. However, it can be argued that other satisfactions and costs of children are unstable and change systematically. If, as cognitive psychologists have postulated, thinking and reasoning precede decision and action, changes in desired or actual family size may be preceded or accompanied by changes in perceptions regarding the value of parenthood. Also, "naive" psychology tells us that the birth of a child (especially a first child) affects motivation for future childbearing. The process by which this occurs may be conceptualized as follows:

Change in perceived reward or cost → Change in total motivation for (additional) parenthood →

Change in decision regarding future children → Change in fertility regulation

Before the child's birth, the parent may perceive the costs of parent-child interaction as relatively low and the rewards as great. Later on, for some parents the rewards may remain constant or become even greater, but the costs (changes in the form of husband-wife relations, anxiety over the child's development) also may rise drastically. Other persons may perceive the costs of children but not the high rewards of children until they are able to watch their own children grow and develop. For them, having children raises the level of satisfaction with the parenthood role and may increase their motivation for additional children. Cross-sectional studies that have compared the preference structures of persons of differing fertility have revealed some differences in the salience of various satisfactions or costs (Beckman, 1976; Townes et al., 1974; Vinokur-Kaplan, 1976). Although changes in rewards and costs as a result of a child's birth have been inferred from such cross-sectional research, adequate examination of these hypotheses awaits further results of longitudinal studies of family decision making, some of which are currently in progress.

RELATIVE POWER AND JOINT DECISION MAKING OF COUPLES

Social-psychological theories are most important when the members of the marital dyad initially do not have similar preferences or behavioral intentions regarding children. In such cases they do not agree about the importance of the perceived satisfactions and costs of children and as a consequence do not always concur about having a/another child, desired number of children, or spacing of children. In a pilot study of North Carolina couples married from 10 to 12 years, Mason (1974) observed that 28 percent disagreed as to the total number of children desired. Among newly married couples who have not yet settled initial disagreements, differences in fertility intentions might be even more evident.

The process by which couples decide whether or not to have an *n*th child or decide on an acceptable family size is incompletely understood. The manner in which such decisions are translated into fertility regulation has been relatively unexplored. Two streams of research bear on these processes, those of family sociology and social psychology. In comparison to social psychology, the family sociology literature has a large amount of empirical information available but is often weak on theory. The great advantage of the social psychology research is its base in several sophisticated social psychology theories. One of the common areas of application of these theories is the family or marital dyad. Particularly applicable to fertility decision making are studies of social power and influence (French and Raven, 1959; Raven and Kruglanski, 1970), conflict resolution (Deutsch, 1969; Rausch et al., 1974), social exchange, and bargaining processes (Schelling, 1960; Siegel and Fouraker, 1960; Shubik, 1964; Thibaut and Kelley, 1959).

Conflict Resolution

A theoretical model developed by Jourard (1971a, 1971b), Rausch et al., (1974), and others is concerned with the constructive resolution of conflict in intimate relationships. It is assumed that hostilities and conflicting needs, desires, and preferences are inevitable in any close relationship. It is proposed that conflicts cannot be resolved adequately unless they are expressed openly and managed constructively. Couples in our society often try to suppress hostile feelings and avoid overt conflicts that lead to resentment and dissatisfaction.

The model identifies three essential requirements in order to resolve conflict constructively:

1. Open communication.
2. Accurate perceptions regarding the degree and nature of conflict.
3. Constructive efforts to resolve conflict, which at minimum include each partner being willing to consider the other's point of view and alternative solutions, and to be willing to compromise if necessary.

Breakdown of communication at any level can lead to defensiveness, self-doubt, confusion, and behavior perceived as inappropriate.

Mellinger (1974) has applied this theory to fertility decision making by suggesting that unsuccessful resolution of conflict may be an important factor in unwanted fertility. As long as overt decision making does not occur, conflict appears to be avoided, but covert decisions may be made to "take a chance" or to be careless in use of contraception. Such covert decisions may end the stress of internal conflict or avoid overt conflict with one's spouse.

Exchange and Bargaining

Social exchange theory, which originated in economic analysis and game theory, already has been discussed in relation to individual preferences. Originally it was applied to social interaction in two-person groups and can be used to represent an exchange relationship between husband and wife under conditions of divergent interests. Game theory is a method for the study of decision making in situations of conflict. When two persons (in this case, the marital dyad) have different goals or objectives but their fates are intertwined, each person must consider how to achieve the most favorable outcome for self while taking into account the desires and strategies of the other person (Shubik, 1964). *Bargaining* typically refers to the processes by which parties attempt to reach a joint decision regarding what each shall obtain in some transaction between them (Raven and Rubin, 1976). Although generally applied to tangible outcomes such as a buyer and seller attempting to reach agreement on the price of a used car, it also could be applied to areas of family decision making such as where to go on vacation or when to have a next child. Although bargaining generally assumes that parties interact through a series of offers and counteroffers, it is possible to conceive of a bargaining process taking place in the marital dyad.

Types of Social Power

Once spouses realize that they hold divergent positions, each may attempt to convert the other to his/her own viewpoint. The outcome will depend upon several factors, two of the most important being the type of influence employed and the relative power of each spouse. The most well-known bases of power (that is, ability to influence) are reward power and coercive power. At least four additional bases of social influence can be defined: legitimacy (norms or accepted behavioral rules); reference (the desire to be similar to another person or group); expertness (superior knowledge); and informational (influence based on information communicated).

Among couples one or more of these forms of power may be operative in any situation. Measurement is complicated because the power sources operate in a somewhat nonadditive fashion and because of structural dissimilarities between some of the power bases and individual differences in susceptibility to the various power bases.

Various power bases may be negatively related to each other. For instance, if expertness is high, referent power may be reduced; by definition a person is dissimilar to another who has a different level of knowledge. If reference is high, expertness may be diminished.

A person susceptible to one power base may be relatively invulnerable to another. Persons who are highly authoritarian or sex-role traditional may be much more susceptible to legitimate or expert influence than to the other power bases. While in certain situations use of several power bases might be more effective than use of any one power base, in other situations the spouse's concomitant use of several power bases may be interpreted as "manipulation" and may increase the partner's resistance to influence attempts. Often a person has a choice regarding which power base to use. The husband may give rewards like affection to his wife for doing as he wants, or he may state that his demands are a legitimate part of his marital relationship. He may emphasize his greater experience in the world in certain areas, or he may try to move his wife to his point of view with more facts and new information. Which approach is more effective depends on the situation and the goals to be accomplished. If it were possible to determine which source of power would be more effective in different types of families with regard to fertility decision making (for example, sex-role traditional couples may be more susceptible to legitimate or expert influence) and which spouse tended to utilize each power base, predictions could be made regarding spouses' relative power when a discrepancy existed in a couple's preferences for children.

Reference, expert, and informational influence from sources external to the marital dyad may be of prime importance in determining what kind of contraception is used. Although my previous research (Beckman, 1974) suggests that on a conscious level the expectations of friends and relatives have little influence on decisions to use or not use contraception, friends (referent power) or the woman's physician (expert power) may have primary influence over the *method* of fertility control used. Because methods differ greatly in effectiveness, friends or physicians indirectly influence the rate at which unwanted pregnancies are likely to occur. In addition, since there may be a method-person interaction (that is, some type of persons have more success than others with certain methods), the judgment of the physician or friend regarding ability of a person to use a method becomes important.

Other Social-Psychological Factors Affecting Couples' Fertility Decisions

Other social-psychological factors such as openness of communication also are related to the success of fertility regulation. Many studies have found a relationship between aspects of marital interaction and contraceptive effectiveness (in the United States, Rainwater, 1960, 1965; in France, Michel, 1967; and in Puerto Rico, Hill et al., 1959). Michel showed that in a French urban sample the amount of communication in the couple was more closely related to contraceptive success than was education or income. Thus it would appear that unwanted pregnancies were more characteristic of those who, because of lack of communication, did not coordinate fertility control efforts.

The resolution of discrepancies between marital partners with respect to strength of preferences or intentions for roles or material goods that compete with childbearing may indirectly affect fertility. We know that even when demographic factors such as education are controlled, women with full-time labor force participation have lower fertility rates than other women in the United States (Fortney, 1972; Ridley, 1969). If a wife desires to work full-time and the husband does not want her to work, does the woman acquiesce to her husband's wishes or assert her own will? Assuming employment affects fertility, the resolution of this disagreement may have indirect implications for that woman's completed fertility. To give another example, if a husband desires a lavish life-style (a new car every year, a boat, an expensive vacation) that keeps him in debt and a wife prefers to save money, the resolution of these differences should have implications for fertility; couples have only so much money to allocate between children and alternative goods. The higher the couple's life-style, given a constant amount of money, the lower the desire for children.

Measurement of Relative Power in the Marital Dyad

A conflict or disagreement regarding fertility intentions or other factors affecting or interacting with fertility desires may be resolved in various ways. The key variable appears to be the relative *power,* that is, ability to influence, of each member of the couple. Power in the marital dyad is rarely equal. Changes in behaviors, values, or attitudes regarding fertility that occur through interaction or communication are more likely to converge on the high power person. Thus if a couple has divergent perceptions of children and motivation for an additional child, the less powerful member of the dyad may tend to adopt or at least behaviorally comply with the attitudes and values of the more powerful member. This formulation suggests that the more powerful person in the marital dyad will have more stable preferences regarding parenthood.

One problem that has plagued both the family sociology and social psychology literature is how best to measure power in the marital dyad. Although power is a multidimensional concept, too often decision making (which is assumed to be a measure of power) is defined only in terms of who "wins" or makes the final decision without regard to the process of decision making. We need to know not only who makes a decision, but who has the authority to make the decision and who controls who makes the decision (Safilios-Rothschild, 1970). Resistance to influence is also a variable. For example, the more publicly committed a person is to a belief, the more resistant it is to change (Deutsch and Gerard, 1955; Kiesler and Kiesler, 1969).

Unfortunately, in the subtle complex area of family interaction indirect nonobservable methods of influence between husband and wife abound. Some authors (Safilios-Rothschild, 1970) have attempted to describe these influence patterns and suggest nonobtrusive ways of measuring them. Survey questions, for example, can elicit reports of activities that cannot be recorded using observational techniques (Safilios-Rothschild, 1969, 1970), because of their intimate nature, because of the optimal timing required for their application (e.g., "when he is in a good mood"), because influence is exercised through application of highly personal techniques ("cooking something he likes" or "buying the wife a gift I know she will like" as a use of reward power), or because it takes a long time (e.g., "nagging" as a case of coercive power).

Blood and Wolfe's (1960) resource theory view of marital power suggests that each individual's relative power is determined by the relative resources each spouse brings to the marriage (in terms of education, occupation, income, and so on). The spouse with the greater amount of resources should be the most powerful. Safilios-Rothschild (1975) suggests expanding the acknowledged resources brought into the marriage to include the entire range of resources exchanged between spouses, such as love, sex, and companionship. These intrinsic resources can be extremely effective instruments of power manipulation. The most crucial hypothesis of her interpretation of marital power is the contention that the relative degree to which one spouse loves and needs the other spouse determines who can most effectively influence family decision making. This same principle was expounded by Waller and Hill (1951) as the "principle of least interest."

Recent formulations of equity theory (Walster, 1973) offer similar concepts, although here outcomes as well as inputs are considered. Heer's (1963) exchange theory also incorporates these outcomes by introducing the concept of marital alternatives. His assumption is that the person who has greater alternatives outside the marriage, for example, the person who could more easily find a spouse as desirable or more desirable than the one he/she currently has, also is more powerful. One problem with these formulations is that no one has adequately measured all important resources. How, for example, does one measure housekeeping ability or affection of each spouse? What these relative resource theories do suggest, which may be of importance, is the need for and some approaches to measuring relative power independent of decision-making outcomes. Relative power, if measured, could then be used as a proxy for ability to influence.

A methodological controversy in the study of family decision making is that between use of survey, in-depth interviewing, and observational techniques (Bahr, 1972; Olsen, 1969; Safilios-Rothschild, 1970; Turk and Bell, 1972). Because I doubt that social demographers are likely to begin using observational techniques or in-depth interviewing, my general approach here has been to discuss fertility decision making with the implicit assumption that any data collected will be survey data. Although a few brave souls (Lee, 1974) have tried, it is unlikely that fertility decision making can be effectively studied in the field or in the laboratory using observational techniques. It is possible, however, that researchers can observe couples' power, decision making, or communication style in general and that a variable identifying general style could be applied to specific decision-making situations.

The relationship between general measures of power and decision making and measures of decision making in a specific decision area such as fertility rarely has been addressed. The assumption is often made that there is a strong relationship between general and specific decision making. (I have assumed this myself in my earlier discussion.) However, attempts to relate global measures of power or decision making to decision making in specific areas where power may be completely delegated to one spouse may have questionable validity. In computation of indices of overall decision making, the total decision-making score depends on the particular decisions sampled (Centers et al., 1971; Safilios-Rothschild, 1970). The relationship between general decision making and behavior specific decision making must be empirically studied, for it cannot safely be assumed.

Given that power can be operationalized and its relationship to fertility decision-making outcomes hypothesized, the picture still is cloudy. It can be predicted that, in general, the more powerful or dominant the husband is in the family, the more control he has over decisions regarding childbearing. However, the wife might bear primary responsibility for seeing that such decisions are effectively carried out through use of contraception. Findings regarding the specificity of dominance within task and decision domains (Blood and Wolfe, 1960; Centers et al., 1971) suggest that "fertility control and regulation" is a domain that is traditionally considered feminine. Decisions or behaviors relating to fertility regulation (especially among lower SES groups) may be considered women's work. The husband's use of coercive or reward bases of social influence may not be effective in this situation, because the wife has the means to subvert his wishes through her effective or ineffective use of contraception, and her behavior may not be easily observable by the husband.

Theory and research on joint decision making in the marital dyad in cases of disagreement between spouses are sketchy and unclear. Much of the past research on family decision making can be faulted on methodological or conceptual grounds (Bahr, 1972; Olsen and Rabunsky, 1972; Safilios-Rothschild, 1970; Turk and Bell, 1972). Nevertheless, I believe there are a few general areas of social-psychological explanation—influence processes, bargaining processes, conflict resolution, and so on—that can usefully be applied to couples' decision making regarding fertility and that have the potential of helping us to make sense of this muddied area.

CONCLUSION

This chapter has been concerned primarily with explicating rather than with testing a model of fertility decision making. Because several other social-psychological models of fertility decision making also exist, more empirical evidence to distinguish between alternative models seems essential. A review of those aspects of the social-psychological approach outlined in this chapter that have been inadequately examined suggests future directions for our empirical efforts and for conceptual development.

Attention should be devoted both to individual preferences and to couples' joint decision-making processes. Although conceptualizations and research on individual intentions and decisions are fairly extensive, the value of this line of research is still questioned by many demographers. However, researchers have found relationships of significant magnitude between the various components of their models and fertility intentions, decisions, or behaviors. In general, these relationships have been with fertility intentions or past fertility rather than with actual future fertility. Especially in research on psychological variables that are subject to rationalization and distortion, this is an obvious weakness, but it is a weakness that future longitudinal designs can correct.

Research on individual intentions or choices may follow several directions. Primary are studies of how persons make fertility decisions, including examination of the formation of preferences and their changes over time. Second, the issue of whether or not people make conscious fertility decisions, that is, the rationality of fertility decision making, should be examined. From the first two areas it follows that research is needed on individual characteristics or personality traits that are related to whether people make conscious decisions regarding fertility and how they make these decisions. Such characteristics could include rationality, locus of control, modernity, and competence. Finally, it is important that innovative, reliable, and valid instruments be developed to measure individual preferences and desires and that these be tested on national representative samples to determine the distribution of each psychological characteristic.

Studies of joint decision making regarding fertility are in one sense less important than studies of individual decision making, for if initial intentions are congruent, a joint decision making or influence process is not important. However, there are a large number of marriages or relationships in which couples do not agree regarding fertility desires. One method of studying such couples is to select a sample in which we would expect a high proportion of couples to have discrepant views because of different cultural backgrounds, demographic characteristics, personality characteristics, or situational contexts. While we would not have a representative sample of all disagreeing couples, any common features of the decision-making process regarding fertility should be revealed.

In this chapter the importance of social-psychological theory in explanation of couples' decision making has been suggested. While primary concentration has been on social power and influence and the relative power of the spouses, conflict resolution and bargaining and exchange processes also have been noted. The difficulties in measuring some of these variables as they occur in the marital dyad are enormous, and the question of the relationship between general decision making and fertility-specific decision making remains to be answered. While survey data have the potential of providing valuable information on couples' decision-making processes, diverse question formats and other methodologies must be developed and tested. Methodologies such as in-depth interviewing and laboratory observation probably will have to be utilized in order to provide a fuller multidimensional picture of couples' decision-making processes. While social demographers may not always feel comfortable with these techniques, I do hope they will recognize their potential value in explaining fertility decision making, and that future research on fertility will incorporate the concepts and methodologies of a number of disciplines.

ACKNOWLEDGMENTS

Preparation of this chapter was supported, in part, by grant HD-52807 from Center for Population Research NICHD and by Career Development Award AA-00002 to the author.

I am grateful for the comments and suggestions of Larry Bumpass, Edward Conolley, and Betsy Bosak Houser.

REFERENCES

Beck, K. W. 1967. "New frontiers in demography and social psychology." *Demography* 4:90–97.

Bahr, S. J. 1972. "Comment on the study of family power structure: A review 1960–1969." *Journal of Marriage and the Family* 34:239–243.

Beckman, L. J. 1974. "Relative costs and benefits of work and children to professional and non-professional women." Paper presented at the American Psychological Association meetings, New Orleans.

———. 1976. "Motivations, roles and family planning of women." Final report prepared for Center for Population Research, NIH, Grant HD-07323.

Blake, J. 1965. "Demographic science and the redirection of population policy." *Journal of Chronic Diseases* 18:1181–1200.

Blood, R. O., and D. M. Wolfe. 1960. *Husbands and Wives.* New York: Free Press.

Centers, R., B. H. Raven, and A. Rodrigues. 1971. "Conjugal power structure: A reexamination." *American Sociological Review* 36:264–278.

Davidson, A., and J. Jaccard. 1975. "Population psychology: A new look at an old problem." *Journal of Personality and Social Psychology* 31:1073–1082.

Deutsch, M. 1969. "Socially relevant science: Reflections on some studies of interpersonal conflict." *American Psychologist* 24:1076–1092.

Deutsch, M., and H. G. Gerard. 1955. "A study of normative and informational social influence upon individual judgment." *Journal of Abnormal and Social Psychology* 51:629–636.

Easterlin, R. A. 1969. "Towards a socioeconomic theory of fertility: A survey of research on economic factors in American fertility." Pp. 127–156 in S. J. Behrman, L. Corsa, and R. Freedman (eds.), *Fertility and Family Planning: A World View,* Ann Arbor: University of Michigan Press.

Edwards, W. 1954. "The theory of decision making." *Psychological Bulletin* 51:380–417.

Fishbein, M. 1967. "Attitude and prediction of behavior." Pp. 477–492 in M. Fishbein (ed.), *Readings in Attitude Theory and Measurement.* New York: John Wiley and Sons.

———. 1972. "Toward an understanding of family planning behaviors." *Journal of Applied Social Psychology* 2:214–227.

Fishbein, M., and J. Jaccard. 1973. "Theoretical and methodological considerations in the prediction of family planning intention and behavior." *Representative Research in Social Psychology* 4:37–51.

Fortney, J. A. 1972. "Achievement as an alternate source of emotional gratification to childbearing." Paper presented at the annual meeting of the Population Association of America, Toronto.

Freedman, R., and L. Coombs. 1966. "Economic consideration in family growth decisions." *Population Studies* 20:217–221.

French, J. R. P., Jr., and B. H. Raven. 1959. "The bases of social power." Pp. 150–167 in D. Cartwright (ed.), *Studies in Social Power.* Ann Arbor: University of Michigan Press.

Groat, H. T., R. L. Workman, and A. G. Neal. 1976. "Labor force participation and family formation: A study of working mothers." *Demography* 13:115–125.

Hass, P. H. 1974. "Wanted and unwanted pregnancies: A fertility decision-making model." *Journal of Social Issues* 30:125–165.

Hauser, P. M., and C. D. Duncan. 1959. "Demography as a body of knowledge." Pp. 76–105 in P. M. Hauser and C. D. Duncan (eds.), *The Study of Population.* Chicago: University of Chicago Press.

Heer, D. M. 1963. "The measurement and bases of family power: An overview." *Marriage and Family Living* 25:133–139.

Hill, R., J. M. Stycos, and K. W. Back. 1959. *The Family and Population Control: A Puerto Rican Experiment in Social Change.* Chapel Hill, NC: University of North Carolina Press.

Hoffman, L. W. 1974. "The employment of women, education, and fertility." *Merrill-Palmer Quarterly* 20:99–119.

Homans, G. C. 1961. *Social Behavior: Its Elementary Forms.* New York: Harcourt, Brace.

Janis, I. L., and L. Mann. 1977. *Decision-Making: A Psychological Analysis of Conflict, Choice, and Commitment.* New York: Free Press.

Jones, E. E., and H. B. Gerard. 1967. *Foundations of Social Psychology.* New York: John Wiley and Sons.

Jourard, S. M. 1971a. *The Transparent Self.* New York: Van Nostrand.

———. 1971b. *Self-Disclosure: An Experimental Analysis of the Transparent Self.* New York: John Wiley and Sons.

Kammeyer, K. C. W. 1971. *An Introduction to Population.* San Francisco: Chandler.

Kiesler, C. A., and S. B. Kiesler. 1969. *Conformity.* Reading, MA: Addison-Wesley.

Lee, J. 1974. "Spousal decision making process: A study of families, planned and unplanned." Paper presented to NICHD Conference on Fertility Related Decision Making, Belmont, MD.

Mason, K. 1974. "Women's labor force participation and fertility." Final Report to National Institutes of Health.

Mellinger, G. D. 1974. "Individual and couple fertility decisions as related to parity, marital stage, and education: A pilot study." Proposal submitted in response to RFPNICHD-BS-75-2.

Michel, A. 1967. "Interaction and family planning in the French urban family." *Demography* 4:615–625.

Nye, F. I., and L. W. Hoffman, eds. 1963. *The Employed Mother in America.* Chicago: Rand McNally.

Olsen, D. H. 1969. "The measurement of family power by self-report and behavioral methods." *Journal of Marriage and the Family* 31:545–550.

Olsen, D. H., and C. Rabunsky. 1972. "Validity of four measures of family power." *Journal of Marriage and the Family* 34:224–234.

Pope, H., and N. K. Namboodiri. 1968. "Decisions regarding family size: Moral norms and utility model of social choice." *Research Previews* 15:6–17.

Rainwater, L. 1960. *And the Poor Get Children.* Chicago: Quadrangle.

———. 1965. *Family Design: Marital Sexuality, Family Planning, and Family Limitations.* Chicago: Aldine Publishing Co.

Rausch, H. L., W. A. Barry, R. K. Hertel, and M. A. Swain. 1974. *Communication Conflict and Marriage.* San Francisco: Jossey-Bass.

Raven, B. H., and A. W. Kruglanski. 1970. "Conflict and power." Pp. 69–109 in P. G. Swingle (ed.), *The Structure of Conflict.* New York: Academic Press.

Raven, B. H., and J. Z. Rubin. 1976. *Social Psychology: People in Groups.* New York: John Wiley and Sons.

Ridley, J. C. 1969. "The changing position of American women: Education, labor force participation, and fertility." Pp. 199–250 in *The Family in Transition.* Fogarty International Proceedings, Washington, DC: U.S. Government Printing Office.

Ryder, N. B., and C. F. Westoff. 1972. "Wanted and unwanted fertility in the United States: 1965 and 1970." Pp. 467–487 in C. F. Westoff and R. Parke, Jr. (eds.), *Demographic and Social Aspects of Population Growth,* vol. 1. (The Commission of Population Growth and The American Future Research Reports) Washington, DC: U.S. Government Printing Office.

Safilios-Rothschild, C. 1969. "Family sociology or wives' family sociology? A cross-cultural examination of decision-making." *Journal of Marriage and the Family* 31:290–301.

———. 1970. "A study of family power structure: A review 1960–1969." *Journal of Marriage and the Family* 32:539–552.

———. 1975. "A macro- and micro-examination of family power and love: An exchange model." Paper presented at "Dynamics of Family Ecology" session of the ISS BD symposium, Surrey, England.

Schelling, T. C. 1960. *The Strategy of Conflict.* Cambridge, MA: Harvard University Press.

Shubik, M. 1964. "Game theory and the study of social behavior: An introductory exposition." Pp. 3–77 in M. Shubik (ed.), *Game and Theory and Related Approaches to Social Behavior.* New York: John Wiley and Sons.

Siegel, S., and L. E. Fouraker. 1960. *Bargaining and Group Decision Making.* New York: McGraw-Hill.

Siegel, A. E., and M. B. Haas. 1963. "The working mother: A review of research." *Child Development* 34:513–542.

Smith, M. B. 1973. "A social-psychological view of fertility." Pp. 3–18 in J. T. Fawcett (ed.), *Psychological Perspectives on Population.* New York: Basic Books.

Stycos, J. M., and R. H. Weller. 1967. "Female working roles and fertility." *Demography* 4:210–217.

Sweet, J. A. 1970. "Family composition and the labor force activity of American wives." *Demography* 7:195–209.

Terhune, K. W. 1973. "Fertility values: why people have children." Paper presented at American Psychological Association convention, Montreal, Canada.
Terhune, K. W., and Kaufman, S. 1973. "The family size utility function." *Demography* 10:599–618.
Terry, G. B. 1975. "Rival explanations in the work-fertility relationship." *Population Studies* 29:191–205.
Thibaut, J. W., and H. H. Kelley. 1959. *The Social Psychology of Groups.* New York: John Wiley and Sons.
Thompson, V. 1974. "Family size: Implicity policies and assumed psychological outcomes." *Journal of Social Issues* 30:93–124.
Townes, B. D., F. L. Campbell, L. R. Beach, and D. C. Martin. 1974. "An application of decision theory to the study of birth planning." Paper presented at the American Psychological Association convention, New Orleans.
Turchi, B. 1975. *The Demand for Children: The Economics of Fertility in the U.S.* Cambridge, MA: Ballinger.
Turk, J. T., and N. W. Bell. 1972. "Measuring power in families." *Journal of Marriage and the Family* 34:215–222.
U.S. Bureau of the Census. 1973. Birth Expectations of American Wives: June, 1973. Current Population Reports. Series P-20, No. 254. Washington, DC: U.S. Government Printing Office.
———. 1974. *Statistical Abstract of the United States: 1974* (95th ed.). Washington, DC: U.S. Government Printing Office.
Vinokur-Kaplan, D. 1976. "Family planning decision making: A comparison and analysis of parents' consideration." Unpublished manuscript.
Waller, W., and Hill, R. 1951. *The Family.* New York: Dryden Press.
Walster, E. 1973. "New directions in equity research." *Journal of Personality and Social Psychology* 25:151–176.
Weller, R. H. 1971. "The impact of employment upon fertility." Pp. 154–166 in A. Michel (ed.), *Family Issues of Employed Women in Europe and America.* Leiden: E. J. Brill.
Westoff, C. F., and N. B. Ryder. 1969. "Recent trends in attitudes toward fertility control and in the practice of contraception in the United States." Pp. 388–412 in S. J. Behrman, L. Corsa, and R. Freedman (eds.), *Fertility and Family Planning: A World View.* Ann Arbor: University of Michigan Press.
Whelpton, P. K., A. A. Campbell, and J. E. Patterson. 1966. *Fertility and Family Planning in the United States.* Princeton, NJ: Princeton University Press.

22

Building a Family: Unplanned Events

JOHN BONGAARTS

In contemporary developed societies most newlyweds have a fairly clear set of preferences regarding the size and composition of their future family. The degree of specificity of these preferences varies considerably among couples. Some would be happy if the number of children were to fall within a rather wide range, while others are aiming to have a precise number of offspring. Similarly, desires regarding the spacing and the sex combination of children vary. To achieve their reproductive goals, virtually all couples now practice contraception for at least part of their reproductive years and a growing minority also resort to induced abortion. Despite the widespread use of modern birth control technology, family building plans are often frustrated. Eventual family size may be larger or smaller than desired and spacing and sex composition goals are frequently not reached. It is the objective of this paper to quantify the frequency with which different unwanted outcomes or events occur.

For newlyweds to be completely successful in achieving precise family building goals would require that they do not experience one or more of the following events:

- Contraceptive failure in delaying a desired pregnancy
- Involuntary childlessness (permanent infertility)
- Prolonged conception delay once conception is desired
- Intrauterine death (miscarriage or stillbirth)
- Congenital defect in newborn
- Unwanted sex combination of offspring
- Unwanted birth after the last desired birth
- Divorce
- Death of a spouse or child during the early phases of the family life cycle

Needless to say, the degree to which these different outcomes frustrate reproductive intentions varies enormously. For example, the death of a family member is incomparably more serious than a very prolonged conception delay. Nevertheless, these events can all be considered unplanned.

The probability of occurrence of each of these unplanned events will now be reviewed briefly using U.S. data. Findings related to the biological aspects of the family building process (involuntary childlessness, intrauterine death, congenital defect, and unwanted sex combination) would, with minor variations, also apply in most other societies.

CONTRACEPTIVE FAILURE IN DELAYING A DESIRED PREGNANCY

The chance of an unplanned pregnancy depends on the type of contraception used and on the care with which it is practiced. Figure 22.1, using U.S. data for 1970 to 1973, presents cumulative proportions of couples who wish to delay their next wanted pregnancy but fail to do so for different methods of contraception.[1] The percentage failing after two years ranges from 3.8 for the pill to 32.4 for foam/cream/jelly. It should be emphasized that these method-specific failure rates are averages for groups of couples with greatly differing individual risks. The most careful contraceptors will approach theoretical failure rates that are much lower than the average use-failure rates in Figure 22.1. On the other hand, careless users will fail more often than average. The degree of carelessness is presumably closely related to the strength of the desire to delay conception. The average failure rate for all methods combined was 7.3 percent after one year and 12.1 percent after two years.

These findings suggest that a couple desiring a three-year interval between marriage and first birth, on average, would have about a 13 percent chance of a premature conception because contraception would be required for two years and three months (allowing nine months for a full-term gestation). Similar average risks would prevail before higher order births if three-year birth intervals are desired. The

Figure 22.1. Cumulative percentage of couples that fail to delay their next wanted pregnancy, by method and duration of use.

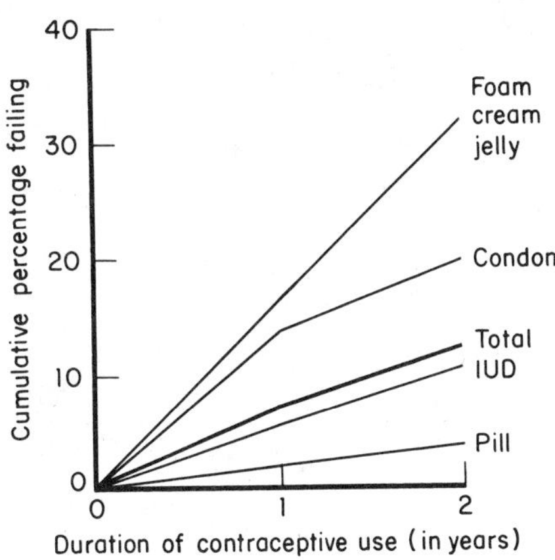

above estimates are all based on the implicit assumption that contraception is practiced continuously throughout the desired spacing interval. Since in reality contraception is not infrequently interrupted for significant periods of time, for example when switching methods, unprotected intercourse sometimes takes place. As a consequence, the actual average incidence of premature conceptions, including unwanted pregnancies during periods of nonuse, may be even higher than the use-failure rates estimated in Figure 22.1.

INVOLUNTARY CHILDLESSNESS

Some couples who try to have a child are unable to do so because either the husband or the wife is sterile. In discussions of this topic a distinction is often made between primary sterility, which is measured among couples who have never had a child, and secondary sterility, which occurs among previously fertile couples. Figure 22.2 plots approximate levels of involuntary infertility by age of the women.[2] Infertility is measured as the proportion of couples who remain childless after a given age of the woman, despite continuous efforts to conceive. It is assumed that there is a negligible incidence of pathological sterility caused by widespread untreated venereal disease. The risk of experiencing primary infertility ranges from a few percent in the early twenties to about 20 percent between ages 35 and 40. By age 50 all couples may be considered unable to reproduce. The proportion of couples experiencing secondary sterility is lower at all ages because the sterility risk that would have accumulated before the time of the last birth is eliminated. Secondary infertility has only accumulated since the last birth and it therefore varies not only with age but also with duration since last birth. A couple wanting a first birth when the wife is 28 years old would run a 6 percent risk of primary involuntary infertility; but with a three-year birth interval to the next birth, the risk of secondary infertility would only be about 2 percent.

PROLONGED CONCEPTION DELAY

Once conception is desired, many fecund couples experience an unexpected conception delay. The probability of conceiving in a month is about 20 percent for noncontracepting fecund couples engaging in intercourse at a fairly typical rate of twice a week. If this conception risk is maintained in successive months, the average waiting time to conception would be five months. This monthly probability of conceiving is perhaps lower than might have been expected a priori. There are three explanations for this finding.[3]

1. The fertile period (the days in the middle of the cycle during which fertilization can occur) lasts on average only about two days. If intercourse takes place only twice a week, a substantial proportion of cycles would have no insemination during the fertile period.

Figure 22.2. Percentage of couples experiencing primary and secondary involuntary infertility, by age of the woman and duration since last birth.

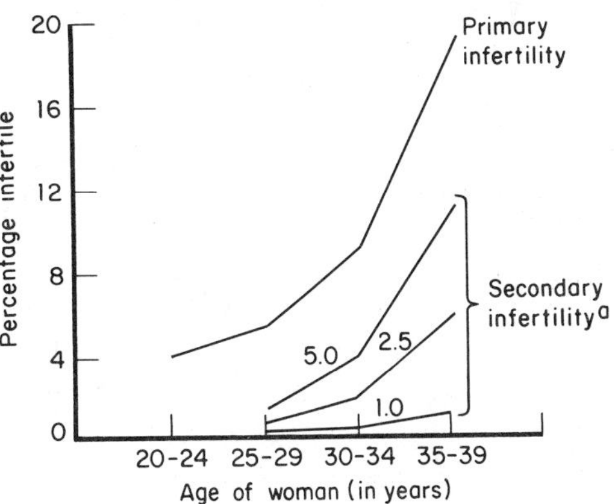

[a]Numbers refer to years since last birth.

2. In a significant proportion of cycles ovulation does not occur or else ova are defective or are lost in transit to the oviduct.
3. Even when fertilization does take place, a large proportion (probably about half) of all fertilized ova do not yield a recognizable conception because of high embryonic mortality in the first two weeks after fertilization.

The simplest way for couples to raise their chances of conception is by increasing their frequency of intercourse. The proportion conceiving in a month would be around 40 percent if coitus takes place daily or at least every other day around the time of ovulation.[4] If this conception probability of 0.4 were maintained in successive months, the average waiting time would only be 2.5 months. In practice, however, the probability of conception declines in successive months. This decline is due in part to a reduction in the frequency of intercourse and in part to the increasing selection of the subfecund among couples who have not yet conceived. Figure 22.3 gives the observed proportions of fecund couples without a conception by duration of exposure,[5] and it compares these observations with model estimates of conception delays for different frequencies of intercourse.[6] As expected, couples can raise or lower their conception chances substantially by varying their frequency of intercourse. Unless a high coital frequency is maintained, a significant percentage of fecund couples will fail to conceive within a year. The observed incidence of a delay of a year or more is 9 percent among couples who plan their pregnancies.[7] Of course, very few of these couples expect such a prolonged conception delay.

Figure 22.3. Observed and model estimates of percentage of fecund women without a conception, by duration of exposure to conception risk and frequency of intercourse.

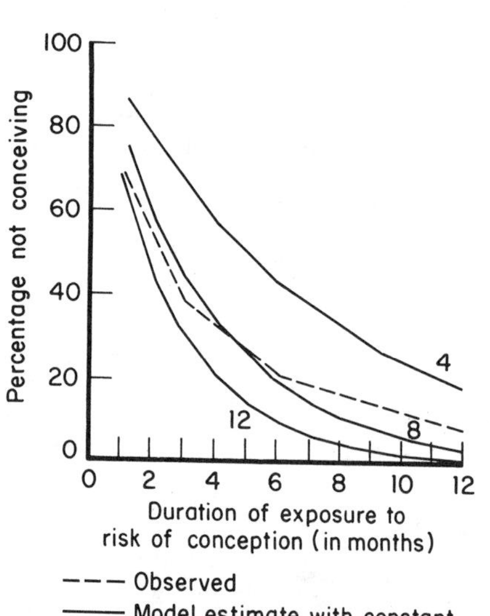

INTRAUTERINE DEATH

Approximately one in five conceptions (recognized by the delay of menstruation after fertilization) fails to end in a live birth.[8] Most of the miscarriages occur in the early months of gestation. Although the cause of an intrauterine death can often not be determined, it is known that genetic and chromosomal abnormalities play a major role because a large proportion of aborted fetuses suffer from these defects. The risk of an intrauterine death varies significantly with the age of the mother; it rises slowly from the early twenties to the mid-thirties and increases rapidly thereafter.[9]

CONGENITAL DEFECTS

Congenital malformations range widely in severity from trivial to incompatible with life. Excluding the inconsequential, approximately 2 percent of newborns have defects that either result in an early death or are clinically significant because they require intensive or prolonged medical treatment.[10] The risk of a congenital defect rises slightly with the age of the mother. This increase is almost entirely due to the association between age and the incidence of abnormalities.[11] Since amniocentesis can detect these chromosomal defects, they can be eliminated by parents who are willing to use induced abortion for this purpose.

SEX COMPOSITION

On average, about 51 of every 100 live births are male and 49 are female. The probability of having a specific sex combination in a two-child family is therefore as follows: Two boys, 26 percent; two girls, 24 percent; boy, first birth, girl, second birth, 25 percent; and girl, first birth, boy, second birth, 25 percent. Only 50 percent of parents who want one boy and one girl will achieve their desired sex combination with two births. The other couples will have to continue childbearing if they want at least one child of each sex: 25 percent will require three births, 12.5 percent four births, and the remaining 12.5 percent five or more children before achieving the objective of at least one boy and one girl.

UNWANTED BIRTHS

Once a couple has reached its desired family size, it faces a prolonged period (often exceeding ten years) during which further births are to be avoided. Many couples practice contraception for this purpose, but sterilization and induced abortion are increasingly used. The cumulative proportion of U.S. couples with an unwanted birth by duration since last wanted birth are plotted in Figure 22.4 for two recent periods (these are life-table estimates for synthetic cohorts based on the reported incidence of unwanted births during the two periods).[12] The projected proportion of couples with an unwanted birth 15 years after the last wanted birth has declined from 21 percent in 1971 to 1973 to 11 percent in 1973 to 1976. Three factors have contributed to this decline: (1) an increase in the use of the more effective contraceptives; (2) a rise in the proportion of sterilized couples; and (3) more frequent use of induced abortion. The use of sterilization and induced abortion has seen especially rapid change during the early 1970s. The proportion of couples with a contraceptive sterilization rose from 10.6 to 19.3 percent between 1970 and 1976.[13] Over the same period the annual number of abortions per 1,000 married women aged 15 to 44 nearly quadrupled—from 1.3 to 5.1—largely due to the legalization of abortion on demand in the early 1970s.[14] It is not possible to accurately estimate what the eventual cumulative probabilities of an unwanted birth in Figure 22.4 would have been in the absence of sterilization and induced abortion. It would certainly exceed the 21 percent after 15 years since last wanted birth estimated for 1971 to 1973, and perhaps would be as high as 30 percent.

Figure 22.4. Cumulative percentages of couples with at least one unwanted birth, by duration since last wanted birth, United States, 1971–1973 and 1974–1976.

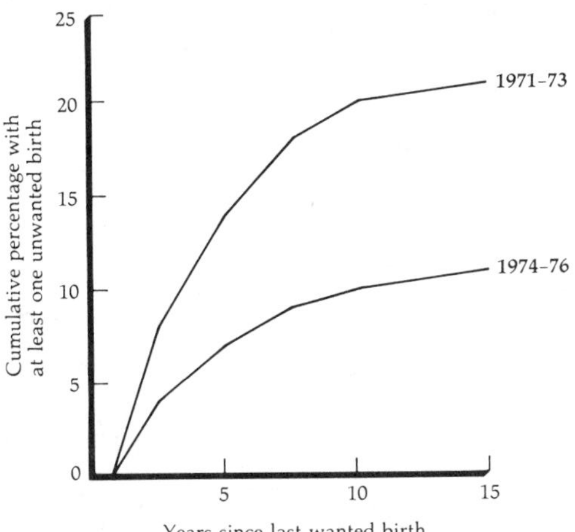

DIVORCE

The U.S. rates of divorce and separation have been rising steadily over the past several decades. This increase has been very substantial, as is evident from the cumulative probability of separation after first marriage given in Figure 22.5.[15] (The usual delay between separation and divorce makes the former a slightly better indicator of marital disruption.) Among women born from 1920 to 1924, 15 percent experienced a separation in the first 20 years of marriage. In contrast, the cohort born in the early 1950s exceeded this level of separation after only five years of marriage. A recent analysis of U.S. divorce statistics estimates that approximately half of all first marriages will end in divorce if these marriages experience the U.S. divorce rates measured in 1975.[16] After the first 20 years of marriage 42.8 percent of newlyweds will have had a divorce. Unless past trends are reversed these already high probabilities of marital disruption may increase further in the future.

DEATH OF A SPOUSE OR CHILD

In 1975 the life expectancy of the U.S. population reached 68.7 years for males and 76.5 years for females.[17] These estimates imply a low risk of mortality in the early decades of life. Indeed, the annual probability of dying at any age up to age 50 is only a fraction of a percent, except in the first years after birth when 1.6 percent of newborns die. Females have consistently lower levels of mortality than males. While these mortality risks are impressively small, they do add up to significant cumulative levels over one or more decades of family life. For example, 8.8 percent of newlyweds will experience the death of one of the spouses in the first 20 years of marriage.[18] The chance that at least one child dies before age 20 is 5 percent in a two-child family.

Figure 22.5. Cumulative probability of separating after first marriage, by years since marriage and birth cohort, United States, Caucasians.

Table 22.1. Probability of Experiencing and Avoiding Unplanned Events During the First Two Decades of Marriage Among Couples That Marry at Age 25 of the Wife and Want Two Children, One of Each Sex, at Three-Year Intervals After Marriage

Events	Probability of Experiencing Event	Probability of Avoiding Event
Contraceptive failure before		
First birth	0.13	0.87
Second birth	0.13	0.87
Involuntary childlessness		
Primary	0.06	0.94
Secondary	0.02	0.98
Conception delay over one year before		
First conception	0.09	0.91
Second conception	0.09	0.91
Intrauterine death after		
First conception	0.20	0.80
Second conception	0.20	0.80
Congenital malformation		
First birth	0.02	0.98
Second birth	0.02	0.98
Undesired sex combination (bb or gg)	0.50	0.50
Unwanted birth (at least one)	0.30	0.70
Divorce	0.43	0.57
Death of		
Parent	0.09	0.91
Child	0.04	0.96
Probability of avoiding all unplanned events		0.062

CONCLUSION

The foregoing discussion has indicated the general order of magnitude of the risks of experiencing various unplanned events. These risks often depend on the specific family building plans, including the desired number, spacing, and sex combination of children. The estimation of the probability of encountering at least one of the unplanned events over the course of the family life cycle requires more specific assumptions about the desired family building pattern. By way of illustration, let us take a not atypical couple that marries when the wife is age 25 and wants two children, one of each sex. Let us further assume that the couple uses contraception with average effectiveness to space children at three-year intervals after marriage. After the last birth contraception is used, but sterilization and induced abortion are assumed to be not acceptable. The probabilities of experiencing each of the nine unplanned events during the first 20 years of marriage of this hypothetical couple are presented in Table 22.1. The estimates in this table are based on the earlier discussion of the different topics and should be considered rough approximations. To find the probability of avoiding all of these events, one can simply multiply the probabilities of not experiencing each event in the last column of Table 22.1. The result is surprising: only 6.2 percent of couples subjected to the risks will manage to be completely successful in achieving their exact family building goals. The remaining 93.8 percent will experience at least one unplanned event.

Varying the assumptions that underlie the calculations in Table 22.1 would of course have an impact on the results. For example, if only one child of a given sex is desired, then the percentage with at least one unplanned event declines slightly from 93.8 to 89.6. A lower age at marriage would not necessarily have an important effect because the declining risk of some events such as spontaneous intrauterine death or childlessness is at least in part compensated for by a rising risk of divorce. Resorting to sterilization or induced abortion after the last wanted birth would eliminate unwanted births, but for the large majority of couples it would still be difficult to avoid at least one other unplanned event. Clearly, achieving a desired family composition is not a simple matter, and most couples will have to accept modified versions of their ideal family.

NOTES AND REFERENCES

1. J. Trussell and J. Menken, "Life Table Analysis of Contraceptive Failure," in *The Role of Surveys in the Analysis of Family Planning Programs,* eds. A. Hermalin and B. Entwisle (Liege: Ordina, 1982).
2. J. Bongaarts, "Infertility after 30: A False Alarm." *Family Planning Perspectives* 14, no. 2 (March/April 1982):75–78. It is assumed here that a couple's risk of becoming sterile is only a function of the age of the wife. If $S(a)$ denotes the proportion sterile at age a of the wife, then this function also equals the probability of experiencing primary sterility at age a. The proportion experiencing secondary sterility at age a among those who had a birth at age a' of the wife equal $1 - (1 - S(a))/(1 - S(a'))$.
3. J. Bongaarts and R. Potter, *Fertility, Biology and Behavior: An Analysis of the Proximate Determinants* (New York: Academic Press, 1983).
4. Bongaarts and Potter, cited in note 3.
5. C. Tietze, "Time required for conception in 1727 planned pregnancies," *Fertility and Sterility* 1, no. 4 (1950):338–346.
6. The estimated conception rates for different coital frequencies are based on a model described in Bongaarts and Potter, cited in note 3.
7. Tietze, cited in note 5.
8. H. Leridon, *Human Fertility: The Basic Components* (Chicago: University of Chicago Press, 1977).
9. Leridon, cited in note 8; and D. Nortman, "Parental age as a factor in pregnancy outcome and child development," *Reports on Population/Family Planning,* no. 16 (August 1974).
10. L. M. Hellman and J. A. Pritchard, *Williams Obstetrics,* 14th edition (New York: Appleton-Century-Crofts, 1970).
11. Nortman, cited in note 9.
12. C. Westoff, "The decline in unwanted fertility, 1971–1976," *Family Planning Perspectives* 13, no. 2 (1981):70–77.
13. Menken, J. Trussell, K. Ford, and W. Pratt, "Experience with contraceptive methods in developed countries," in *Contraception, Science, Technology and Application* (Washington: National Academy of Sciences, 1979).
14. Tietze, cited in note 5.

15. J. McCarthy, A. Cherlin, and A. Pendleton, "Marriage paths of cohorts of American women," paper presented at the General Conference of the IUSSP, Manila, 1981 (mimeo).
16. J. Weed, "National estimates of marriage dissolution and survivorship: United States," *Vital and Health Statistics Analytical Studies,* Series 3, no. 19 (1980). Estimates are taken from duration of marriage tables with divorce or death as the only form of marital disruption.
17. U.S. Bureau of the Census, *Statistical Abstract of the United States: 1977* (Washington, DC, 1977).
18. Weed, cited in note 16.

23
The Asset Demand for Children During Agricultural Modernization

ODED STARK

In developing societies, grown children as rural to urban migrants may assume the unique role of financial intermediaries in an economy in which the introduction of modern agricultural methods is constrained by inadequate institutional (as well as noninstitutional) sources of credit and a high aversion to risk. This role of the migrant may be an element conducive to an increase in the value of and the demand for children in the early stages of economic development. This chapter discusses the implications of this hypothesis for John Caldwell's intergenerational wealth flows theory and suggests some of the more general implications of the role of children as migrants for farm households.

In a series of thoughtful contributions John Caldwell has meticulously advanced and carefully examined the "wealth flow theory" of fertility transition, relating a decline in fertility to a change in the direction of the intergenerational, intrafamilial transfers.[1] He points out that: "In terms of its ultimate impact on fertility, the significant aspect of the economy is whether production is based on the familial organization of labor or whether there is a free and monetized labor market (i.e., capitalist production). A declining chance of an economic return from children in later life, together with the fact that their productive usefulness when young has crumbled, turned the wealth flow downward and made low fertility inevitable." Education (or mass education) is cited as having assumed a crucial role here since "invariably educated children cost more and give less."[2]

The picture that emerges is that *in the transformation* from "familial production" to "capitalist production" children (and educated children in particular), hence fertility, become "less economic," or "contrary to the family's economic interest." This tallies well with other views. For example, Eva Mueller argues that the advent of high-yielding varieties of grains has enhanced the need for purchased modern inputs rather than for the kinds of human capital that are embodied in household labor.[3] Consequently, it is probably more important for farmers to economize on family expenditures than to have extra working hands. The opportunity cost of supporting children, who compete with the externally produced input, is thus raised, exerting downward pressure on fertility.

The hypothesis advanced here is that the same "situational variables" pointed out by Caldwell may have exactly the opposite effect. Since "familial production" and "capitalist production" are imperfect substitutes, grown children *as migrants* may assume a specific positive role in an economy where the range of financial and insurance markets is less than full. In many cases this may account for the considerable variability ("lags" as Caldwell puts it) around the secular change so forcefully described in Caldwell's paper. The hypothesis has added appeal in that it responds to one of Caldwell's main criticisms of recent research on the economics of fertility: namely, that analysts have given relatively little attention to the importance of other demographic variables in explaining fertility change. The hypothesis focuses on rural-to-urban migration and its likely repercussions for desired fertility and fertility behavior.

Consider a modal agricultural family, assumed to be the decision-making entity[4] that attempts to transform its "familial production" into "capitalist production." It usually faces two major constraints. First, there is the "investment capital" constraint; the transformation (e.g., to high-yielding varieties of grains) requires investment funds that a small farmer family with its existing resource endowment and a "precapitalist" mode of production is unlikely to possess or generate. It is both relevant and interesting to note that most of the recent "relevant technological transformations" depend crucially on new factors and inputs—elements in which the very transformation, the new technology, is embodied. This in itself (apart from the component-complementarity that characterizes these technologies) creates strong discrete needs for investment capital and produces a new pattern of technological change, different from traditional technological progress, which involves gradual increments to the quantities of *existing* factors, facilitated, in turn, by a continuous accumulation of savings.

The second constraint is that of risk. The transformation to a new technology magnifies the subjective risks involved in agricultural production, and the family unit is assumed to be risk-averse. Thus, the major obstacles encountered are bridging the gap between the family's desired investment capital and its necessary cash outlays (including existing savings) and, once this is accomplished, resolving the conflict between the family's aversion to risk and the increased risk element in its portfolio.

In the absence of smoothly functioning credit markets or appropriate institutional facilities, and when insurance markets either do not exist or charge prohibitive premiums, the family must reorganize the utilization of its *own* resources. It is here that rural-to-urban migration by the most suitable family member—a mature son or daughter (especially if educated)—comes into the picture. In bypassing the credit and insurance markets (with their bias against small farmers), migration facilitates the transformation; it succeeds in doing this via its dual role in the accumulation of investment capital (acting as an intermediate investment, between technological investments, which have a certain lumpiness, and investment in financial assets, which—if feasible—have a low, or even negative return), usually generating significant urban-to-rural flows of remittances,[5] and through diversification of income sources, in controlling the level of risk. This "portfolio investment" in urban earning activity (migration by a maturing family member) as a risk-alleviating device assumes, in particular, that the urban sector is statistically independent of agricultural production.[6]

In an economy in which the transformation of production cannot be performed directly, grown children *as migrants* thus assume the unique rôle of financial intermediaries. From a private, parental point of view, and considering lifetime utility, children are generally seen to yield various direct and indirect utilities that may be conveniently designated "consumption utility" (children are a source of personal pleasure and satisfaction), "income utility" (children directly contribute to the family's income by working), and "status, security, and insurance utility" (status, e.g., when position and power are established through children-generated familial ties; security—especially old-age security; insurance—an extra child can generate various utilities if other children fail to do so mainly because of early mortality). The alleged role of children as migrants implies that a new element is added to the utilities-from-children vector, namely, facilitating the transformation of production. This element is distinct from the others, especially from the income utility element, in that children's primary role as migrants is not to generate an income stream per se, but to act as catalysts for the generation of such a stream by precipitating an income-increasing technological change on the family farm.[7]

The hypothesis is enriched by allowing for education. Take, for example, the credit crunch. Whereas the small farmer has no effective (or sufficient) access to institutional or other credit—nor can he expect this situation to change[8]—his children usually do have access to some sort of state education, which is often a pure public good, one largely financed by government subsidies and not (directly) by the pupil's parents. Thus, a small farmer's vicarious entrance into a less discriminating market can be viewed as a surrogate for participation in one into which his entrance is effectively barred. Banking on the expectation of a high cross return to the joint decision of educating a child and then "expelling" him or her to the urban sector, migration (and the education preceding it) thus remedy the credit deficiency whose alleviation is mandatory in facilitating technological change on the family farm. Farmers therefore deliberately use the educational system to prepare for their children's migration.[9]

This extension of the hypothesis reinforces its profertility implications. As indicated, children can be a source of several different benefits. But not all children—or any particular child—can efficiently provide *all* utilities, especially in a less developed economy. Specialization by children in the production of different utilities increases total utility from children; and specialization *and* indivisibility often imply that the same child cannot provide "supply side" competing utilities. Children's capacity to generate different utilities becomes a planning variable, and children are prepared differentially to perform competing tasks. Thus, one child may be singled out for preparation for eventual migration (possibly with other children contributing to this preparation). The potential migrant will receive more (or better) urban-oriented education whereas his or her siblings are likely to be intensively engaged in farm production.[10] Finally, a high degree of specialization by children in the provision of different utilities sharply reduces the possibility of cross-substitution among children; this, in turn, increases the risk involved in losing a particular child. In these circumstances, the number of children becomes crucial to the risk-averse household. This once again favors a high level of fertility. Thus, although the effects of economic development eventually lead to a decrease in the demand for children, the very generation of economic development may initially increase the asset demand for children.

Although the hypothesis set forth here requires thorough testing and verification before introduction into the policy arena, and although the policy implications are beyond the direct concern of this note, it is tempting to speculate on the possible repercussions of the hypothesis for induced fertility reduction efforts. It seems that policies directed at reducing the incentives for greater reproduction would have to take into consideration the prevalence of an additional pronatalist factor. Children are seen to yield a specific new benefit—removal of some of the risk and credit constraints inhibiting the transformation of production in the agricultural sector. Thus, just as a social security tax (on workers) and transfer (to the retired) system, which socializes the within-family, young-to-old, intergenerational transfers, is an essential device in depressing the "provision for old-age security" motive for having children, so may an institutional arrangement catering to the effective supply of credit and hedging against risk be required to defuse the "migration motive" for bearing and rearing children.

There is also an interesting social-welfare implication. If the modernization of agricultural production is deemed socially desirable, then there are *social* (not only private) returns to the bearing and rearing of children; the necessary expenditures can thus be regarded as a social investment, and the family as an effective social institution. Given the institutional structure of the economy, it may prove to be a very efficient one, too; privately (familial) optimal behavior may therefore not diverge from socially optimal behavior.

NOTES

I am grateful to John Caldwell, Ansley Coale, Nathan Keyfitz, and Frank Notestein for comments on an early draft of this chapter.

1. Most recently, John C. Caldwell, "The Mechanisms of Demographic Change in Historical Perspective," *Population Studies,* 35 (March 1981): 5–27; but see also "Toward a Restatement of Demographic Transition Theory." *Population and Development Review* 1, no. 3–4 (September /December 1976): 321–366; "A Theory of Fertility: From High Plateau to Destabilization," *Population and Development Review* 4, no. 4 (December 1978): 553–577.
2. The quotes are from Caldwell, "Mechanisms," cited in note 1, pp. 8, 13, 21.
3. Eva Mueller, "The Economic Value of Children in Peasant Agriculture," in *Population and Development,* ed. Ronald G. Ridker (Baltimore: Johns Hopkins University Press, 1976).
4. I have detailed empirical and theoretical reasons for this assumption elsewhere. See Oded Stark, *Economic-Demographic Interactions in Agricultural Development: The Case of Rural-to-Urban Migration* (Rome: Food and Agriculture Organization of the United Nations, 1978); "Rural-Urban Migration and Surplus Labour," *Oxford Economic Papers* (forthcoming); and "Game theory, migration theory and the family" (mimeo., 1981).
5. Significant urban-to-rural transfer of remittances is one of the most important observed regularities of rural-to-urban migration in developing countries. See Oded Stark," On the Role of Urban-to-Rural Remittances in Rural Development," *The Journal of Development Studies.* 16 (April 1980). 369–374.
6. For formal and fuller treatments see, Stark. *Interactions.* Appendix II, and Oded Stark and David Levhari, "On Migration and Risk in LDCs." *Economic Development and Cultural Change* (forthcoming).
7. In a lifetime utility-maximization exercise, where discounted stream of benefits and costs associated with bearing and rearing children are considered, a lower net price (cost minus benefit) of children implies that more of them will be desired (through the positive impacts of both the substitution and the income effects, assuming that children are a normal good).

8. Credit markets are imperfect, not fully formed, and highly fragmented; the quantity of marketable assets as collaterals for credit possessed by the small farmer is very limited, and so forth.
9. Nathan Keyfitz has pointed out to me that "to the motivation of parents to have children and then educate them one could add the notion of upward mobility; quite aside from the financial benefit, there is a basic aspiration common to all instances of industrialization [and economic transformation] that is satisfied by children rising to a higher social status."
10. Preferences are generated for children of specific characteristics that are assumed to be positively and closely associated with their urban-market productivity and likelihood of success as migrants. If the possession of these characteristics is (at least to some extent) exogenously determined, and if the probability of a given birth having these traits is independent of that of an earlier birth having them, desired fertility will tend to increase as will family size and population growth. (Note, though, that if through learning, experience, and technological progress the possession and production of these characteristics gradually become endogenized, the alleged effect on fertility will be weaker.)

24

Declining World Fertility: Trends, Causes, Implications

AMY ONG TSUI
DONALD J. BOGUE

No social problem, other than war, has attracted greater and more sustained public concern during the decades since World War II than the "population explosion." As every reader of newspapers and news magazines has been frequently and accurately instructed, this phenomenon was caused by a sudden and rapid reduction in the human death rates of less developed countries while their high birth rates remained comparatively unchanged. Almost every nation of Asia, Latin America, and Africa has been growing at rates in excess of 2 percent per year as a result of "natural increase" alone (births minus deaths)—rates at which populations double in less than 35 years. In contrast, none of the nations of Northwestern Europe or their colonial offspring ever grew this rapidly simply as a consequence of high birth and low death rates. (Instances of such high growth usually had a large migration component.) This was due to the fact that in Europe and America, birth rates began a downward trend within a reasonably short time lag after death rates and were never so high as in most of today's less developed countries (LDCs). Also, death rates declined more slowly so that the "demographic gap" between fertility and mortality never became so huge as it has recently been in most LDCs.

Following World War II, successful reduction of mortality from the major infectious diseases—malaria, cholera, typhoid fever, yellow fever, smallpox, tuberculosis, and complications resulting from respiratory diseases (in large part due to advances in medical treatment and epidemiological control)—led to the sudden and unprecedented rapid decline in death rates of LDCs. Meanwhile, fertility rates, buttressed by tradition, culture, religion, and public opinion, continued on a high plateau. The resulting growth was so rapid that mass starvation, political and social disorder, and even major world wars were predicted for the latter decades of this century and throughout the next—as a result of a social disorder called "population pressure."

Contrary to demographic predictions and official population forecasts, growth rates in the less developed countries appear to have begun a decline in recent years, considerably sooner than expected. The turning point seems to have occurred between 1970 and 1975, and appears to be progressing at an accelerating pace. Two factors combine to cause this result:

1. Death rates have sunk to such a low level in many developing areas that further decline can only come from slower and gradual improvement in nutrition and environmental conditions and treatment of chronic and degenerative diseases.
2. Birth rates in the LDCs have begun to decline and may be declining more universally and more rapidly than had been anticipated.

As a consequence of these two developments, the "demographic gap" now seems to be narrowing in many countries.

It had been expected for several years that death rates would go into a phase of much slower decline as the easiest-to-control diseases became less important causes of death. However, the decline in birth rates has come earlier than predicted just a few years ago. This development is so new that many demographers still do not believe it has occurred, or think that it is a comparatively minor exception to a general worldwide picture of continuing high fertility.

The purpose of this chapter is to assemble much of the data available for estimating the recent trends and present level of fertility for each nation of the world. On the basis of this evidence, the authors arrive at an estimate of fertility levels in 1968 and 1975 and the implied change in the seven-year period 1968 to 1975. According to these estimates, the world's total fertility rate had dropped from 4.6 to 4.1 births per woman in these seven years. By 1975, less than 20 percent of the world's population was to be found in nations which were failing to show evidence of distinct fertility decline. And many of the most populous LDCs formerly viewed as potential seedbeds for population-related catastrophes, such as China, India, Indonesia, and Egypt, were showing evidence of major and continuing fertility declines.

A study is made of the factors that appear to have accounted for this change. Here we address an issue that has been of particular importance since the 1974 World Population Conference in Bucharest with its slogan, "Development is the best contraceptive." To induce fertility decline, what set of factors is of most importance? There are two competing propositions. One is that it is "development" or "modernization" which arouses the motivation to control fertility. The other argues that it is the organized provision of family planning services which encourages the limitation of family size. Certainly a third tenable proposition is that when both factors are present they may be simultaneously responsible. Only a few studies have attempted to answer these questions comprehensively, most notably a 1974 study of the World Bank and a recently published study by W. Parker Mauldin and Bernard Berelson of the Population Council.[1] This chapter confirms their findings and considers further the implications for future population growth.

We have assembled data for 113 LDCs—virtually all of the Third World's population—focused as closely as possible on our reference period, 1968 to 1975, on eight socioeconomic indicators which represent factors in development that can be presumed to be among the most important in affecting fertility motivations: per capita gross national product (GNP), percent urban of the population, the infant mortality rate, life expectancy at birth, percent of the employed female population working in agriculture, percent of the population which is literate, and the percent of males and females aged 6 to 23 years enrolled in school. The available data are too unreliable (or missing) to measure socioeconomic change with complete accuracy, especially in this short time period. However, they are the best available and can be assumed to reflect valid orders of magnitude. They suggest that the social progress made in developing countries by the early 1970s was less than had been hoped for. It is possible that the absolute gains that were made were largely consumed by population growth and the remainder absorbed by a small slice of upper and middle classes, with comparatively little "trickling down" to the great masses.

Yet these "great masses" have reduced their fertility during this period. What is the explanation? To measure the family planning component of fertility change we adopted a "family planning effort scale" used by Mauldin and Berelson which assesses the situation in 94 developing countries about 1972. These scores were entered into our statistical analysis of the 1968 to 1975 change in the total fertility rates of LDCs along with the values for our chosen socioeconomic indicators. The results suggest that organized family planning efforts have been a major contributing factor in the fertility decline now evident in much of the developing world. Begun in the early 1960s, these efforts have developed into a major campaign, involving international agencies, many national governments (in both developed and developing nations) and many foundations and private organizations. The conclusion is almost inescapable that this campaign has been a major force for social change and has been successful in averting a major world catastrophe.

This leads to the prediction that the future course of world fertility may be determined in large part by the size, quality, and spread of the family planning campaign. Family planning has not yet been admitted to those few countries that still have near-maximal and unchanging fertility. It is assumed that at least a moderate effort in this direction will be made in the coming decade.

What implications and consequences does this situation have for the future? The authors make the assumption that the world movement toward family planning will continue at its present level of intensity or increase somewhat, and will gradually spread to all nations. On this basis, we have prepared projections of total fertility rates and population growth rates to the end of the century. These are compared with similar projections from the World Bank, the United Nations, and the U.S. Bureau of the Census. As of the year 2000, according to our estimates, less than a fifth of the world's population will be in the "red danger" circle of explosive population growth—2.1 percent or more annually. Most LDCs will be in a phase of fertility decline, with growth rates steadily sinking. About that time, a large number of countries, many of them now underdeveloped, will be at or near the replacement level of fertility. As a result, we predict that the total population of the world will be 5.8 billion at the turn of the century, in contrast to the World Bank's projection of 6 billion and the United Nations projection of 6.3 billion.

Our optimistic prediction is premised upon a big "IF"—*if family planning continues.* It remains imperative that all of the developed nations of the world continue their contribution to this program undiminished, and that their professional resources be dedicated to collaborating with the professional resources of the developing nations in a team effort to make the demographic transition take place as quickly as possible with the least possible economic and social disruption.

REGRESSION ANALYSIS

A third mode of analysis is multivariate regression that relates the 1975 TFR estimates to the 1968 TFR estimates, the 1968 level of development according to five socioeconomic indicators, and the 1972 family planning program effort score. This approach explores the "lagged" effects of the factors on fertility levels.

The analysis of the average amount of fertility change related to various levels of development in 1975 and of the correlations between these variables has upheld the important effects of social and economic development. However, relative to the effect of family planning effort, the role of development in affecting fertility decline is lessened. The correlations demonstrate that the frequently postulated socioeconomic correlates of declining fertility are somewhat but not intensely related with fertility change from 1968 to 1975. In a combined manner, the socioeconomic factors might possibly have a more significant impact.

The multivariate regression performed assesses the combined effects of socioeconomic development and family planning effort on fertility levels. A more statistically efficient means for analyzing the TFR change for 1968 to 1975 requires expressing the variable in different terms. This calls for placing the 1975 TFR in the "predicted" position and including the 1968 TFR as one of the "predictors." Thus, to illustrate, if the desired regression is

$$(1975\ \text{TFR} - 1968\ \text{TFR}) = a + bX$$

where a is the constant and b the slope or regression coefficient associated with the predictor variable X, then the following rearrangement

$$1975\ \text{TFR} = a + bX + c(1968\ \text{TFR})$$

yields a "lagged" regression. This form is preferred because it reduces the amount of prediction error and locates the 1975 TFR relative to its 1968 value. If the predicted 1975 TFR is 4000, the amount of TFR change depends on the 1968 value, whether it be 2500 or 3800. Change in fertility can then be obtained after the fitted regression line is estimated, by substituting values for X and the 1968 TFR.

In looking at the combined effect of socioeconomic development on fertility, we have adopted the following model: the 1975 TFR is being "predicted" by the 1968 TFR and 1968 values for selected socioeconomic indicators. For the latter set of variables, 1968 levels are used, instead of 1975 as discussed in earlier tables, because the impact of development is not instantaneous. (In general the correlations are higher between 1968 indicators and the 1968 to 1975 TFR *change* rather than 1975 TFR *level,* although not reported here.) Out of the eight indicators, five were suitable to be included in the regression. Literacy, male school enrollment, and life expectancy measures were excluded because they correlated highly with several of the other five indicators.

The regression analysis results are given in Table 24.1 for the three regions and for the developing world as a whole. Panel 1 is based on the socioeconomic factors alone. The standardized coefficients, ranging from 0 to 1, positive or negative, can be compared in order to identify the stronger determinants of 1975 fertility levels. The best predictor of the TFR in 1975 is, of course, its value in 1968, particularly in Asia (coefficient of .771). But among the socioeconomic indicators, the largest contribution comes from the infant mortality rate and per capita GNP. For the developing area as a whole, the six predictors were able to account for just over 81 percent of the variation in 1975 TFRs (R^2 = .813; see bottom row of panel 1). The 1968 TFR alone accounted for almost 76 percent (75.8 percent) and almost 1 percent each was accounted for by the infant mortality rate and per capita GNP. (These R^2s are not shown.) The five socioeconomic indicators combined accounted for only an additional 5.5 percent of the total variation in 1975 total fertility rates, a result which does not strongly support social and economic development as the primary causal factor of 1975 fertility levels.

Table 24.1. Standardized Regression Coefficients for 1975 TFR Regressed on 1968 TFR, Five 1968 Socioeconomic Indicators, and 1972 Family Planning Effort Score

Variable	Africa	Asia	Latin America	Total LDCs
Panel 1				
TFR 1968	.705	.771	.752	.742
Per capita GNP 1968	.066	.164	−.108	.125
Percent urban 1968	−.093	.181	−.169	−.017
Infant mortality rate 1968	.300	.152	.134	.165
Percent of employed females in agriculture 1968	.176	.203	.029	.074
Female school enrollment ratio 1968	.016	−.132	−.052	−.100
R^2	.731	.841	.767	.813
Panel 2				
TFR 1968	.671	.575	.580	.626
Per capita GNP 1968	−.014	.086	−.122	.067
Percent urban 1968	−.055	.028	−.193	−.017
Infant mortality rate 1968	.210	.207	.013	.070
Percent of employed females in agriculture 1968	.078	−.048	−.082	−.003
Female school enrollment ration 1968	−.030	−.016	−.046	−.089
Family planning effort score 1972	−.187	−.370	−.360	−.308
R^2	.745	.912	.836	.860
Number of countries	39	30	20	89

In panel 2 of Table 24.1, the 1972 family planning effort score is introduced as an additional predictor of 1975 fertility. Here we see that the level of family planning effort expended by any developing country is the *second* best predictor (after TFR 1968) of the fertility achieved in 1975. Its explanatory value surpasses that of all social and economic indicators. The standardized coefficients show that, with family planning effort included, the effect of the 1968 TFR decreases (by comparing the coefficients for TFR 1968 in panels 1 and 2). The substantial negative impact (−.308) of family planning effort on 1975 fertility levels in the regression for developing countries as a whole has the effect of reducing the magnitude of the coefficients associated with the other factors. For individual regions, the inclusion of family planning effort enhances the effects of some of the socioeconomic indicators. In Asia the effect of infant mortality increases as does percent urban in Latin America.

One can think of the regression model for the developing countries as a whole in the following terms: 100 percent of the variation in 1975 TFRs is to be explained, 75.8 percent of which can be accounted for by the 1968 TFR and whatever other factors it represents. This leaves 24.2 percent of the variance to be explained by hypothesized factors such as socioeconomic development and family planning effort. Our analysis shows that 5.5 percent can be accounted for by five socioeconomic factors combined and the one family planning effort measure accounts for 4.7 percent of the variance. (R^2 is now .860; see bottom row of panel 2.) There still remains 14 percent unexplained variance. From an analytical point of view, the model's performance is good, but the important implication is not the amount of total explanation rendered by the model but the verification of family planning's independent effect on birth rates. Having allowed other factors to reign freely in explaining 1975 fertility levels, we find that, by including family planning effort last, it is able to make an independent and significant impact on 1975 fertility levels.[2]

Regionally, the performance of family planning effort is weaker in Africa, which is not unexpected since the family planning movement there was barely underway by 1972. Here it explains an additional 1.4 percent of the unexplained variance of 5.2 percent of the remaining variance. In Latin America, family planning effort increases the explained variance by 6.9 percent, or 23.3 percent of the remaining unexplained variance. In Asia, it adds 7.1 percent to the explained variance, or 44.7 percent of the remaining variance to be explained. Across all regions, the family planning coefficients rank second to those for the 1968 TFR in relative effects on the 1975 TFR.

The measurement of the impact of a service program, such as family planning, is not, therefore, impossible but it has not been applied to the developing world's population growth context until recently. In part, this is because widespread fertility reduction in LDCs has only just been acknowledged as a real phenomenon. Secondly, comparable family planning data have been elusive, and, with the exception of a few notable publications, it is difficult to assemble performance measures for all countries with or without formal policies. The main task ahead, in addition to a major upgrading of internal service statistics reporting, is to accumulate standardized measures of program effort so that analyses over time can be made. The intensity with which a family planning program is administered will not remain constant hereafter, and monitoring programmatic changes precisely is a critical objective for improving evaluation research.

This discussion and analysis have attempted to validate the stronger role which family planning programs are assuming and their relative impact on recent fertility declines in the developing world. As additional sources of data on current fertility levels and family planning practice become available, particularly from the World Fertility Survey, it will be easier to assess national patterns in the relationship.

IMPLICATIONS OF DECLINING WORLD FERTILITY

The evidence seems clear. Separate and independently prepared estimates of total fertility rates for developing countries show fertility declining at present. Although most are still at high fertility levels, a sizable number of these countries have experienced at least some drop from their 1968 fertility levels. We have investigated several factors associated with the decline and confirmed the negative impact of socioeconomic development on recent fertility. However, in addition and more importantly, family planning program effort depresses birth rates in its own fashion. Given these results, the prediction of future fertility levels will clearly have to take these two forces behind fertility change into account.

But it is necessary to ask first whether a long-term fertility decline is in store for the developing world, enabling it to surmount slowly the barriers to rapid economic development. Or is the recent decline just a brief respite and will the population explosion return to undermine the gains made in the economic sector and by family planning organizations? The authors feel that the decline is not a temporary development, but rather that it can evolve into a major process of social change under certain conditions.

Two policy implications of overpowering significance emerge from this review of the trends and causes of fertility decline:

1. If recent trends continue, the world population crisis appears resolvable. Only ten years ago, doomsday prophesizing called for mass starvation, world chaos, and possible world war by the year 2000. The Malthusian orientation of those forecasts resolutely conjured up a dire future created by the teeming billions. Today the future seems definitely more optimistic and demographic forecasts no longer call for uncontrollable growth rates. Future trends in fertility in the eleven most populated developing countries in 1975 will have a major impact on the level of population growth in the year 2000 and beyond. As we have seen, fertility rates declined by 10 percent or more between 1968 and 1975 in six of these eleven countries: the People's Republic of China, Indonesia, Bangladesh, Mexico, Vietnam, and Thailand. Family planning is provided as part of official policies to reduce population growth rates in nine of the eleven and in the remaining two—Nigeria and Brazil—is now supported by the government on the grounds of health and human rights. Thus, the present behavior of these eleven crucial LDCs indicates that the population crisis is manageable and that their growing population size no longer threatens the social order of the future. Likewise as fertility rates decline, other things being equal, the opportunities for economic growth increase so that it is not inconceivable, and certainly seems desirable, that in the next 50 years the developing world can approach the standard of living presently enjoyed by the developed world. Even if they fall short of that goal, it seems likely that they will nevertheless have near-replacement fertility.

2. Because fertility rates do appear to be responsive to the strength of family planning efforts, the solution of the population problem is in the hands of world leaders. These include government and civic leaders, heads of international agencies, and professional groups within each country. Their course of action, hopefully in a united and coordinated direction, will profoundly affect the quantity and quality of national investment in the organized provision of family planning services. This does not preclude an equal if not greater investment in human capital development. In the past, many political and civic leaders have encouraged the multipronged approach to reducing fertility. The interaction between the two causal processes should only enhance the

rates of fertility decline. On the other hand, one concern of this report is that the efficacy of service programs not be underestimated.

Needless to say, the continued success of the family planning movement requires the education and motivation of country leaders to intensify their support for family planning policies. It also requires continued financial and technical support on the part of international funding and development agencies. It stands to reason that, with the growing interest in the administration, training, communication, and service components of programs, these units will improve their efficiency and effectiveness, thereby upgrading the overall quality of the program.

In total, the amount of planned human effort and investment of resources will determine whether the world has a population explosion or not. With intensive action, disorder can be averted everywhere, but with inaction, it can happen in every developing country.

NOTES AND REFERENCES

1. "The Relationship between Program Inputs, Socioeconomic Levels, and Family Planning Performance," Appendix B, in Timothy King (coordinating author), World Bank, *Population Policies and Economic Development,* A World Bank Staff Report (Baltimore: Johns Hopkins University Press, 1974); and W. Parker Mauldin and Bernard Berelson, "Conditions of Fertility Decline in Developing Countries," *Studies in Family Planning,* Vol. 9, No. 5 (New York: The Population Council, May 1978). See also, Bernard Berelson, "An Evaluation of the Effects of Population Control Programmes," in H. B. Parry (ed.), *Population and Its Problems: A Plain Man's Guide* (Oxford: Clarendon Press, 1974), pp. 133–168; K. S. Srikantan, *The Family Planning Program in the Socioeconomic Context* (New York: The Population Council, 1977); and, Ronald Freedman and Bernard Berelson, "The Record of Family Planning Programs," *Studies in Family Planning,* Vol. 7, No. 1 (New York: The Population Council, 1976).
2. In a related analysis (see Amy Ong Tsui, Jay D. Teachman, and Donald J. Bogue, "Predicting Fertility Trends in LDCs over the Next Century," paper presented at the Annual Meeting of the Population Association of America, Atlanta, Georgia, April 13–15, 1978), the dynamic model proposed examines the effects of socioeconomic development indicators and family planning effort on the *rate* of fertility change between 1968 and 1975. Similar results were obtained as in the analysis reported here in that neither the level of development held in 1968 *nor* the amount of social and economic development between 1968 and 1975 had a large effect on the rate of fertility change.

25

The Relative Importance of Family Planning and Development for Fertility Reduction: Critique of Research and Development of Theory

SCOTT MENARD
ELIZABETH W. MOEN

The contemporary debate concerning population and development reaches back to the late eighteenth century and involves such writers as David Hume, Robert Wallace, Adam Smith, the Marquis de Condorcet, William Godwin, and of course T. R. Malthus (Appleman, 1976). Although in the past there was little agreement regarding whether population growth was encouraging or detrimental to national prosperity, all seemed to agree that prosperity encouraged the growth of population. Now the experience of the Western nations suggests that national prosperity actually leads to decreased population growth (Rich, 1973), and some authors argue that population has little or no effect on national prosperity (Meek , 1971).

The "either/or" nature of the debate regarding family planning and development has retarded the development of theory and policy regarding the relationship between fertility and development. On one hand there are statements that the mere availability of family planning programs causes fertility declines independent of cultural, political, or socioeconomic influences. On the other hand there are statements that development will bring about a "natural" decline in fertility that is presumably independent of contraception.[1]

For less-developed countries (LDCs) the population/development issue is a crucial one. If population growth hinders economic progress and social development, then it is futile to pour funds into development projects without also taking steps to reduce population growth. If population growth responds to economic and social development, then it may be possible to concentrate on development in order to reduce the need for large families and create a demand for family planning services.

In this chapter we review three recent studies about the relative effects of family planning and development in an attempt to point out their shortcomings and to augment them. We first present a tentative theoretical framework from which the problem of fertility reduction may be viewed. Then, in response to critiques of these studies and in line with our own theoretical framework, we present an analysis of the "outliers" in one of the three studies. This analysis involves consideration of macrosocial and contextual aspects of different nations as a supplement to other analyses.

THREE RECENT STUDIES

Recent studies by Mauldin and Berelson (1978) and Tsui and Bogue (1978) used indicators of social setting[2] and family planning effort[3] to explain declines in, respectively, crude birth rate between 1965 and 1975, and total fertility rate between 1968 and 1975. As Table 25.1 indicates, the two studies used nearly identical sets of explanatory variables. With both studies using the same indicators, except for "labor force" (in which Mauldin and Berelson concentrate on males while Tsui and Bogue concentrate on females), it is hardly surprising that they arrived at the same results. These results, moreover, were previously obtained by Freedman and Berelson (1976), who also used the Lapham-Mauldin index of family planning effort along with similar, though fewer, indicators of social setting.

Freedman and Berelson found that birth rate declines could be explained better by program

Table 25.1. Variables Used in Mauldin and Berelson (1978) and Tsui and Bogue (1978)

Variable	Mauldin and Berelson	Tsui and Bogue
1. Literacy	Yes	Yes
2. Primary and secondary school enrollment	Male and female Combined	Male and female Separately
3. Life expectancy	Yes	Yes
4. Infant mortality	Yes	Yes
5. Per capita GNP	Yes	Yes
6. Urbanization	Percent in cities of 100,000 or more	Percent in urban locations
7. Labor force	*Males,* age 15–64 nonagricultural	Employed *females* in agriculture
8. Family planning effort Lapham-Mauldin index	Yes	Yes
9. Fertility	Crude birth rate (CBR)	Total fertility rate (TFR)

effort [which independently explained 17 percent of the variance in crude birth rate (CBR) declines] than by social setting (which independently accounted for 7 percent of that variance), and that the 1972 birth rate itself was similarly explained (15 percent of the variance attributed to program effort alone, 5 percent to social setting alone). Mauldin and Berelson obtained nearly identical results: program effort explained 17 percent of the decline in CBR, while social setting explained only 5 percent. These results were further supported by the exploratory data analysis done by Sykes who concluded that "program effort was associated with three or four times the amount of CBR decline associated with social setting" (in Mauldin and Berelson, 1978: 120).

In the Tsui and Bogue study, the contribution of the 1968 level of fertility was clearly the dominant influence on the 1975 total fertility rate. The standardized regression coefficient indicated that previous fertility explained 50 to 60 percent of subsequent fertility by direct relationship, a figure comparable to the social setting-family planning interaction effects (44 to 58 percent) in the two other studies. Their socioeconomic indicators explain about 5.5 percent of the variance in 1975 fertility, while family planning effort explains about 9 percent. Overall, the results are substantially the same as those obtained by Freedman and Berelson and by Mauldin and Berelson. Insofar as it is possible to separate the effects of previous fertility from socioeconomic development, and to compare development with family planning effort, family planning effort appears to explain independently about two to four times the variance in fertility than that is independently explained by socioeconomic variables.

The similarities in the analyses and the data used for these studies have also generated a certain similarity in the criticisms they have received from Demeny (1979) and Dixon (1978). To summarize these critiques, four major problems emerge from these studies:

1. The analyses are not grounded in theory or even on the existing empirical evidence regarding the interrelationships among socioeconomic development, the desire to control or limit fertility, the existence and character of national family planning programs and policies, and changes in the birth rate. Unless one subscribes to the theory of unmet need or to the "Mount Everest Theory" (people use contraceptives because they are there), such an analytical framework is essential.
2. There is too heavy a reliance on data which are available for a large number of countries, rather than allowing the theory to specify the variables to be used; this suggests that convenience is more important than theory.
3. Specific country differences, for example coercion, preclude a highly generalized approach to the study of the determinants of fertility reduction due to the adoption of contraception or for other reasons. The studies cited all ignore these differences.
4. Because of the use of composite indices and the *ad hoc* nature of the selection of variables, the analyses provide no real policy guidelines and do not contribute to a resolution of the family planning/development debate.

Consequently, according to both Dixon and Demeny, an understanding of the effects of family planning programs and socioeconomic development is first to be found in in-depth, country-by-country analyses based on an explicit analytical framework. Given the current state of the discipline, however, the framework would be subject to ongoing testing and revision.

THEORETICAL FRAMEWORK

While it is not the purpose of this paper to develop fully a theory of the interrelationships among fertility, development, and family planning, we do wish to outline some of the more important factors which should have been included or which were inappropriately operationalized in the studies just mentioned. We assume that fertility behavior is generally rational and intended to benefit the immediate family. Although this assumption may not hold for certain individuals, there is evidence that it accurately characterizes larger aggregations of people (Mamdani, 1972; Mueller, 1976). We develop our framework around three questions:

1. Under what circumstances does fertility decline occur—with or without the use of birth control (a) for voluntary versus involuntary reasons or (b) for positive (unwanted children are foregone) versus negative reasons (wanted children are foregone)?
2. What, if anything, about the cultural, political, and geographic setting (the context of development) encourages or discourages fertility limitation?
3. What, if anything, about social and economic development creates a desire for smaller families or brings about the postponement of reproduction?

Reasons for Fertility Decline

Although it is generally assumed that fertility declines are the result of a conscious effort to limit unwanted births and that acceptance of family planning is voluntary, there is good reason to believe that part of the decline in fertility in the LDCs is involuntary and attributable to coercion or to reduced fecundity resulting from poor health and nutrition. For instance, according to McFalls (1979), involuntarily childless women in African countries may constitute between 20 and 50 percent of all childless women. The extreme example of coercion is India, where force was used to secure "acceptors" for birth control programs. To the extent that malnutrition, disease, and coercion prevent wanted births they are negative, as well as involuntary, reasons for a decline in birth rates.

Fertility may be voluntarily limited (i.e., limited as a result of personal choice) for negative reasons as well. A wanted third child, for example, may be foregone because of a scarcity of food or resources, or because the mother is overburdened with the multiple roles of mother, housekeeper, and employee. Migration may also affect fertility, as men and women move to obtain employment, either postponing marriage or leaving spouses behind (Boserup, 1970; Boulding, 1977; United Nations, 1979). Although the migration may be voluntary, the resulting infertility may not be.

Examples of involuntary but positive reasons for infertility include natural infecundity, coercion, or involuntary separation among couples who no longer want additional children. These are positive in the sense of implementing the couple's wishes, but involuntary in the sense that the couple has not chosen this method to avoid having children. To round out the typology, an example of voluntary and positive family limitation would be the voluntary use of contraceptives to space wanted children or to stop childbearing after the desired number of children have been born.

From a humanistic perspective, it is essential to distinguish between voluntary/involuntary and positive/negative reasons for childbearing for the analysis of birth rates and especially for the analysis and design of policy. These dimensions of fertility behavior should be considered continuous rather than discrete categories, and they can be applied to high or increasing birth rates as well as to low or declining birth rates. The important point is that the reasons for childbearing or for fertility reduction may or may not be desirable and acceptable to individuals or to society.

Mauldin and Berelson (1978:111) themselves discuss several characteristics of a society that could lead to fertility rates other than those which would be predicted from social setting (development) or family planning scores. Included in the contextual variables are the "cultural props" for high (or low) fertility discussed by Bulatao (1979: 75) such as religious and social obligations, or the definition of adult status and "normal" or "natural" behavior. Political props for highly coercive pronatalist or antinatalist policies could also be considered as contextual variables. The contextual variables specifically discussed by

Mauldin and Berelson are ethnicity, religion, residence on an island, and rapid social change.

As Mauldin and Berelson note, black African and Chinese ethnics generally tend to have higher and lower fertility, respectively. It seems likely that ethnicity is a proxy for cultural characteristics. Religion, on the other hand, may directly affect fertility. Roman Catholic orthodoxy prohibits most modern contraceptive measures and abortion, and like Islamic orthodoxy encourages large families. Residence on an island or "quasi-island" is also associated with reduced fertility. Bairoch (1975: 9) suggests that fertility declines in LDCs most often take place in

> small countries . . . which have already benefited from some economic and social development and have received a large volume of aid. They have also undertaken birth control campaigns of a thoroughness which would be out of the question in the larger countries.

If, as Mauldin and Berelson suggest, low fertility is also a function of overcrowding or feelings that there is just "no place to go," small size or island status may interact with family planning effort and social and economic development to amplify their influence on fertility. The citation from Bairoch also suggests a point made by Taeuber and cited in Mauldin and Berelson (1978:111) that rapid social change such as swift modernization, rapid economic growth, revolution or war are also " . . . more conducive to family restriction than social adjustments that preserve continuities."

Briefly then, contextual variables may influence fertility in two ways. First, they may influence fertility independently of social setting, family planning effort, or both. Second, they may amplify the effects on fertility of social setting, family planning, or both. The former circumstance would call for the inclusion of contextual variables in the analysis; the latter would call for analyses of interaction terms or separate analyses of, for example, Catholic or ethnically Chinese countries.

Development and Desired Family Size

According to Coale (1973) "there are three preconditions for a substantial fertility decline: (1) the acceptance of calculated choice as a valid element in marital fertility, (2) the perception of advantages from reduced fertility, and (3) knowledge and mastery of effective techniques of control."[4] The first two points will be dealt with subsequently, but the third deserves comment before we proceed. It would be wrong to equate "effective techniques of control" with "modern" contraception. Historical evidence indicates that societies have been able to exercise fairly effective family size limitation long before modern contraceptive technology was available (Dumond, 1975; Wrigley, 1969). Although we agree that family planning programs may trigger thinking about family planning and increase its convenience and effectiveness, such programs are neither sufficient nor necessary conditions for fertility declines.

On Coale's second point, what would lead to perceived advantages from reduced fertility? While there are a number of answers to this question, they all converge upon a central theme, the value and cost of children. If, as we assume, most fertility decisions are rational, then voluntary use of family planning services would be expected when economic and social development bring about changes that make children less valuable or more costly in social, economic, or psychic terms. Explanations of declining fertility based on the value and cost of children may take three basic forms: children as productive assets, children as a form of social security, and children as consumer goods for which substitutions are possible—at least when fertility is high.[5]

On the positive side, development may reduce the desired number of children by reducing the need to have many children just to enlarge the family labor force (children might be replaced by machinery or hired labor); to insure assistance for parents in sickness and old age (children might be replaced by higher income, health insurance, or old age benefits); or as a source of status or emotional gratification (children might be replaced by education or consumer goods and the maternal role may be at least partially replaced by other roles). On the negative side, economic development and concomitant rural to urban migration may make a desired large family too difficult to manage (by loss of childcare provided through an extended family); or too expensive (through factors such as child labor laws, decreased value of children's work or opportunities to work, or increased costs of housing, food, clothing, and education).[6]

Implications for Analysis

Measures of class and gender stratification are either missing or inappropriately operationalized in Freedman and Berelson, Mauldin and Berelson, and in Tsui and Bogue. Such measures would be indicative of the psychic, economic, or social need for children and the substitutes for the benefits of children available to potential parents. If fertility reductions associated with development are associated with changes in individual access to alternatives to childbearing, a large decline in fertility should not be expected unless development affects a large proportion of the population—especially the poorest—through an equitable distribution of opportunity, income, and services by class and gender. A redistribution of opportunity, income, and services also contributes to a reduction in fertility among the well-to-do and upwardly mobile by raising the costs of children or reducing the parents' ability to pay the costs.

As Goran Ohlin stated in his keynote address for the 1977 meeting of the International Union for the Scientific Study of Population, "societies with more equal income distributions and better provisions of social amenities have faster fertility decline than more inegalitarian countries, even though their average per capita income is lower" (quoted by van der Tak, 1977: 7). These conclusions were restated recently by the President of the World Bank, Robert McNamara: "if the growth in national income does not result in improvements in the living conditions of the lower income group it will not help to reduce fertility throughout the society" (quoted by Nagel, 1978; also see Rich, 1973; Simon, 1976; Repetto, 1979).[7]

Among the indicators of social setting used by Freedman and Berelson, Mauldin and Berelson, and Tsui and Bogue, four—literacy, per capita school enrollment, life expectancy, and infant mortality—may be correlated with the distribution of income and opportunity. Literacy and enrollment are themselves distributional variables, and it is reasonable to expect at least modest correlation among measures of distribution (e.g., .35 between land and income distribution).[8] Growth in per capita GNP is at best weakly correlated with income distribution; the type of economy (socialist or capitalist) is probably much more important (Ahluwalia, 1974; see also data in Jain, 1975).

The percentage of males in the non-agricultural labor force and the percentage of females in the agricultural labor force are probably not good indicators of income inequality. What they do indicate is industrialization, which tends to be associated with per capita GNP. Moreover, the percentage of females in agricultural work is not an indication of the absolute or relative status of women because it does not tell what proportion of all women are employed or what their employment status is relative to men. Furthermore, employment in agriculture may increase the need for women to bear children in order to have help with the farm labor (Boulding, 1977). The level of urbanization is questionable as an indicator of development or of inequality because residence in an urban area no longer necessarily represents an entry into the modern sectors of society or a sharing of the benefits of development (Tabah, 1975; Abu-Lughod and Hay, 1977). Omran's conclusions regarding urbanization in Arab countries can be generalized to many developing nations: "[U]rbanization is often mistaken as a sign of modernization . . . in fact it is creating as many problems as it solves—over-concentrating people with inadequate facilities and services to meet their basic needs . . . Also lacking is the expected correspondence between urbanization and two other measures of development, industrialization and modernization" (1979: 13).

In addition to the foregoing considerations concerning development and fertility, it is also important to clarify the role of contextual variables and of reasons (positive or negative, voluntary or involuntary) for fertility reductions before forcing the data into additive, simple linear models involving only family planning programs and development as independent variables. Finally, it would be appropriate to specify what kinds of family planning programs were used in which countries in order to identify which appear to be most effective.

As an illustration of the potential usefulness of our theoretical framework for increasing both the substantive and statistical explanations of fertility we shall briefly examine the case of India. Because India's very low per capita GNP and food resources are inequitably distributed, and because India has suffered droughts and food shortages during the time under consideration, some of the decline in the crude birth rate in India may be attributed to reduced fecundity associated with malnutrition and to a deliberate reduction in fertility for negative reasons among those who were so lacking in resources and opportunity that they realized additional children could not possibly benefit the family. For these reasons alone, it is not surprising that India's fertility decline was greater than predicted by its fairly low social setting score in the Mauldin and Berelson study. India also has had a coercive birth control program, first offering rewards that very poor people have found hard to resist and later moving to social pressure, negative incentives, and physical force. The most coercive phase occurred after 1975, but the massive number of sterilizations which took place during the late 1960s and early 1970s occurred under less-than voluntary conditions.

Even with coercion and subfecundity, India's fertility decline was less than Mauldin and Berelson predicted from the program effort score. Since India has the world's oldest and largest family planning program (Ratcliffe, 1978), it is important to try to understand why the results have been so disappointing—why more people have not limited fertility to a greater degree on a voluntary basis. We believe the answer may lie in those aspects of the social setting ignored by Mauldin and Berelson, class and sex inequality. First of all, the status and condition of women has "deteriorated alarmingly" during the last 20 years. Differentials which favor men have increased for mortality, health care, literacy, education, vocational training, and employment, and there is also increased prostitution, traffic in women, and the use of women to display wealth and promote business (Mazumdar, 1979). Under such circumstances and especially in a Hindu society, women have few options for survival other than establishing security through childbearing. Second, Mamdani (1972) has provided very convincing evidence that fertility decisions are generally rational in India and that people have large families because they believe (though it is not always true) this is the only way to improve their standard of living, and they have smaller families when substitutes for children such as technology and social welfare programs are available.

This does not mean that India must achieve rapid economic growth or a very high per capita GNP in order to see a reduction in fertility; instead India may need a pattern of development more like that which was proposed by Gandhi (i.e., a pattern of development which both reduces the need for children and provides women alternatives to marriage and childbearing). Evidence of this point is found in Kerala, a state in India with a per capita income of only $80 (U.S., 1978). According to Ratcliffe (1978), Kerala has received little attention from Indian development planners, yet it has managed to surpass all Indian states in literacy, life expectancy at birth, reduced infant mortality, reduced crude death rate, and reduced crude birth rate which in 1978 was below 23 as compared to 35 for all of India. Moreover, none of the studies of Kerala's impressive decline in fertility—from 39 in 1961—has "... been able to demonstrate that family planning program efforts have even marginally influenced fertility declines" (Ratcliffe, 1978: 13). Instead, the decline appears to be associated with a development program that included deliberate steps to reduce long-standing wealth and income inequalities, educational reform, and efforts to improve the status of women. Kerala has the highest age of marriage of any Indian state and many women are able to choose when to marry or to choose not to marry at all. There is also widespread political participation.

Although these reforms were initiated during the late 1950s when Kerala had a Communist government, they have been perpetuated by successive governments. Ratcliffe concludes:

> The Indian failure to resolve its national population problem is commonly blamed on the irrational breeding habits of its impoverished and illiterate peasantry. The Kerala experience suggests that neither birth rates nor the impoverishment and illiteracy of the peasantry are independent of the unjust organization of Indian institutions and the unfair distribution of economic resources, social services and political power.... The implications of the Kerala experience for other Third World nations, as well as for the western population control movement, seem clear and straightforward. *If* the reduction of population growth rates is indeed a priority and *if* an improved quality of life for all members of society is more than merely a rhetorical goal of development strategies, then institutional change is an essential strategy (1978: 15).

OUTLIER ANALYSIS

The remainder of this chapter will be devoted to an analysis of the "outliers" (or extreme cases) in the exploratory data analysis done by Sykes for Mauldin and Berelson (1978: 115–120). Examination of the outliers is intended primarily to indicate the extent to which the model used by Mauldin and Berelson and in the other studies can be extended to explain those cases which are currently not well explained, and perhaps to provide a more valid understanding of what the model does explain statistically if not really substantively. In addition, the narrower focus allows us to bring to bear a more qualitative, and perhaps more enlightening, approach to the analysis.

For these purposes, we have divided the outliers in Sykes' exploratory data analysis along two dimensions. The first involves the relationship between predicted and actual reductions in fertility. *Positive outliers* are the countries with fertility declines larger than predicted, while *negative outliers* are the countries with fertility declines smaller than expected. The second dimension refers to the independent variables used to predict the fertility declines. The largest group of outliers are those with fertility declines not well predicted by social setting only. The remaining outliers are those with fertility declines which could not be predicted well with program effort, either alone or in combination with social setting. The analysis will be divided into two parts: an analysis of contextual variables and an analysis of distributional variables.

Contextual Variables

Table 25.2 presents the set of contextual variables described previously: ethnicity, religion, island status, pace of change.

Table 25.2. Contextual Variables

Country	Ethnic (a)	Religion (b)	Island Status (c)	Pace of Change (d)
Positive outliers				
(Social setting only)				
Singapore*	1	0	yes	fast
Cuba*	0	1	yes	fast
India	0	3	no	—
Dominican Republic	0	1	quasi	—
Hong Kong	1	0	yes	fast
Thailand	1	0	no	fast
China	1	0	no	fast
Tunisia	0	2	no	fast
Malaysia	1	2**	quasi	—
North Vietnam	1	0	no	fast
(All other)				
Egypt	0	2	no	fast
Turkey	0	2	no	—
Singapore*	1	0	yes	fast
Cuba*	0	1	yes	fast
Mongolia	1	0	no	—
Negative outliers				
(Social setting only)				
Brazil	0	1	no	fast
Mexico	0	1	no	—
Paraguay	0	1	no	—
Kuwait	0	2	no	—
North Korea	1	0	quasi	—
Peru	0	1	no	—
Lebanon	0	2**	no	—
Jordan	0	2	no	—
Libya	0	2	no	—
(All other)				
Iran	0	2	no	—
El Salvador	0	1	quasi	—
Indonesia	0	2	yes	fast
Jamaica	0	0	yes	fast
Fiji	0	0	yes	fast
Panama	0	1	quasi	fast

(a) 1 = Chinese or other Oriental, 0 = other (from Mauldin and Berelson, 1978).
(b) 3 = Hindu, 2 = Muslim, 1 = Catholic, 0 = other (from Taylor and Hudson, 1972).
(c)(d) (from Mauldin and Berelson, 1978).

*Cuba and Singapore are positive outliers for both social setting and all other. No other country is an outlier in both categories.

**Islam is predominant but not a majority religion in Lebanon and Malaysia, encompassing 42 and 44 percent of the population, respectively. Lebanon has a 43 percent Christian minority, 36 of the 43 percent of whom are Catholic.

1. Ethnicity. One of the 15 negative outliers and seven of the 13 positive outliers are ethnically Chinese or Chinese-related populations. With the exception of North Korea, the only negative outlier, all have experienced rapid social change between 1965 and 1975, the period in question. Is it possible, then, that Chinese ethnicity or culture may predispose a nation to respond to rapid social change by a pragmatic adoption of lower fertility rates?

2. Religion. Of the 15 negative outliers, six are predominantly Catholic and six predominantly Muslim. Of the 13 positive outliers, four are Muslim, two Catholic, and one Hindu. (The remaining positive outliers are all ethnically Chinese, predominantly Buddhist.) Religion, however, is confounded with region: the Catholic countries here are all Latin American countries and the Muslim countries, except Malaysia and Indonesia, are in the Middle East.

The Catholic religion has traditionally contributed to high fertility in these countries by supporting partriarchal *mores* and institutions and offering solace rather then reform to the poor. The importance of the Muslim tradition in maintaining high fertility and limited options for women has been highlighted by recent events in Iran and Pakistan. In Iran, the Ayatollah Khomeini has attempted to reinstate the *chador,* has forbidden coeducation, reduced the civil rights of women, severely curtailed contraceptive and abortion services, and outlawed sterilization. In Pakistan, " . . . the movement towards greater conformity with Islamic law has reportedly resulted in the complete suspension of family planning promotional efforts, and a national press ban on publicity related to population issues" (Lippman, 79: 14). Although it appears to be weaker than the relationship between ethnicity and fertility, the relationship between religion and fertility may add to our understanding of differences infertility declines. A problem with both ethnicity and religion as variables is the fact that they overlap with one another and with geographic region: Catholicism with South America and southern Europe, Islam with North Africa and West Asia, Buddhism with East Asia, etc. The effects of religion, ethnicity, culture, and geography become virtually impossible to separate in macroscocial analysis.

3. Island status. The lack of a relationship between the outliers and island status casts doubt on the island hypothesis raised by Mauldin and Berelson. It is worth noting, however, that the positive and negative outliers which are islands or quasi-islands cluster into separate categories along the social setting/program effort dimension. Of the six islands which are social setting outliers, five are positive. Of the five other island outliers, all are negative. This suggests that island status may strengthen the effect of social setting relative to that of family planning effort on fertility. In other words, for islands or quasi-islands, social setting is relatively more important and family planning effort relatively less important than for non-island nations.[9]

4. Pace of social change. There is no distinct pattern for the relationship between rapid social change and fertility for the outliers except in relation to social setting. Taking social setting outliers alone, seven of ten positive outliers but only one of nine negative outliers experienced rapid social change between 1965 and 1975. Of the other outliers, three of five positive and four of six negative outliers experienced rapid social change. The implication is that rapid social change and family planning programming are closely associated, and that neither will explain a great deal when the other is controlled.

Another notable aspect of social change is that all of the negative outliers except North Korea have experienced rapid social change in the form of development without explicit concern for distribution while four of the positive outliers (China, Cuba, North Vietnam, and Mongolia) have become socialist and at least one other positive outlier, Singapore, is experiencing development with explicit concern for distribution. These findings suggest that it is the nature of social change rather than rapid social change per se that is important.

To summarize, the contextual variables may add a substantial amount to the explanation of the outliers, but they do not all operate in the same way. Chinese ethnicity in the presence of rapid social change appears to have some promise as an independent variable, but pace of change or ethnicity alone otherwise add nothing to the explanation beyond social setting and program effort. Island status does not appear to affect fertility directly, but instead magnifies the effect of social setting relative to program effort. Religion may have too complicated a relationship to fertility to be of general use in explaining differences in its rates of decline, but it may be very important in specific cases. In general, the issue of contextual variables deserves more attention.

Distributional Variables

Table 25.3 presents a set of measures dealing with stratification: the distribution of wealth, income, and social services; and the status of women relative to men.

1. *Income and land distribution.* The data on land distribution are obtained from Taylor and Hudson (1972), and the data on income distribution from Jain (1975).[10] The land and household Gini coefficients support the argument that distribution operates independently of both program effort and other measures of social setting to promote lower fertility. The coefficient for distribution of land is, for those countries for which data are available, .675 or higher for all but one of the negative outliers and .674 or lower for all but one of the positive outliers. The mean land Gini coefficient is .587 for the positive outliers and .766 for the negative outliers. This difference is significant (t = 3.01, df = 12) at the .01 level for a one-tailed test.

These results are paralleled by the Gini coefficients for household income distribution. The 1960 Gini best discriminates between pos-

Table 25.3. Distributional Variables

Country	Land Gini	Mean Income Gini		Distribution of Social Services			Status of Women		
		1960	1970	(a)	(b)	(c)	(d)	(f)	(e)
Positive outliers									
(Social setting only)									
Singapore*	NA	NA	NA	3	−1	−1	.18	.65	—
Cuba*	NA	NA	NA	3	1	1	.13	.44	1934
India	.522	.47	.48	3	−2	−2	.32	.58	1949
Dominican Republic	.803	NA	.49	3	−4	−2	.11	.53	1942
Hong Kong	NA	NA	.43	NA	NA	NA	.33	.81	—
Thailand	.460	.45	.42	1	−5	−4	.49	.68	1932
China	NA	NA	NA	4	3	3	NA	NA	1947
Tunisia	NA	.47	.46	4	−2	−1	.06	.60	1959
Malaysia	.473	.57	.52	3	−3	−2	.27	NA	1957
North Vietnam	NA	NA	NA	3	−1	−1	NA	NA	—
(All others)									
Egypt	.674	.43	NA	4	−1	−1	.06	.60	1956
Turkey	.592	NA	.57	3	−5	−2	.40	.67	1934
Singapore*	NA	NA	NA	3	−1	−1	.18	.65	—
Cuba*	NA	NA	NA	3	1	1	.13	.44	1934
Mongolia	NA	NA	NA	NA	NA	NA	NA	NA	1924
Negative outliers									
(Social setting only)									
Brazil	.845	.55	.60	5	0	1	NA	.55	1932
Mexico	.694	.56	.58	3	−2	−2	.18	.58	1953
Paraguay	NA	NA	NA	3	1	−2	.23	.65	1961
Kuwait	NA	NA	NA	2	−1	−3	.07	.43	—
North Korea	NA	NA	NA	NA	NA	NS	NA	NA	—
Peru	.933	.57	.55	3	−1	−2	.19	.69	1955
Lebanon	NA	.54	NA	4	0	0	NA	NA	1957
Jordan	NA	NA	NA	1	−5	−4	.06	.64	—
Libya	.700	NA	NA	4	−1	−1	.05	.58	1963
(All others)									
Iran	.625	.54	.50	4	−3	0	.13	.55	1963
El Salvador	.827	.51	.43	3	−5	−2	.18	.57	1950
Indonesia	NA	NA	.43	3	−3	−3	.33	.63	1945
Jamaica	.770	.58	NA	2	−2	−3	.37	.45	1953
Fiji	NA	NA	.43	2	−2	−3	.06	.56	—
Panama	.735	.50	.45	3	−4	−2	.20	.50	1946

(a) coded for simple presence or absence of five social services (see text) 1 = present, 0 = absent.
(b) Agricultural population: 1 = present, 0 = restricted or limited, −1 = absent.
(c) Total population: 1 = present, 0 = restricted or limited, −1 = absent.
(d) Index of femaleness for economic acticity.
(f) Index of femaleness for illiteracy.
(e) Year that female suffrage was granted.

itive and negative outliers. For 1960, the mean Gini is .480 for positive outliers and .540 for negative outliers. The difference is statistically significant (t = 2.80, df = 11) at the .01 level for a one-tailed test. Of the negative outliers in 1960, all eight have Gini coefficients larger than .500; of the positive outliers, one of the five (Malaysia) has a Gini coefficient larger than .500. The pattern is similar but less clear-cut for the 1970 Gini coefficients. The difference in the means of the positive and negative outliers (.480 and .500, respectively) is smaller and it is not statistically significant. There is no clear pattern between change in distribution and fertility decline, and there are too few cases with available data to permit a comparison between social setting outliers and other outliers.

2. Social services. A third aspect of distribution is the distribution of social services. Data are taken from the U.S. Department of Health, Education, and Welfare (1977). The five social services examined in that report were work injury; old age, invalidity, and death; sickness and maternity; unemployment; and family allowances. Coding for just the presence or absence of these services, there is no association with social setting outliers but a weak positive association with other outliers, indicating that Mauldin and Berelson's measure of social setting probably accounts for simple presence or absence of social services. Coding for inclusion of agricultural workers, the social setting outliers indicate that provision of services is associated with *higher* than expected fertility, while for the other outliers it is associated with lower than average fertility. The differences are small but, as others have found, the initial improvements in social setting may actually increase fertility for agricultural populations (e.g., see Simon, 1976). Finally, *equality* of distribution of social services is examined for the entire population. Each country was coded 1 for each service universally provided, 0 for each service provided to a limited or restricted group, and −1 for each service not provided at all. Based on this coding (summing the scores on the five services—see Table 25.3), distribution of services is uniformly associated with lower fertility.

3. The status of women. Three indices of the relative status of women were taken from Boulding, et al. (1976). Those countries in which female participation in the labor force is high relative to that of males, and in which suffrage was granted earlier rather than later, tend to be countries with higher than expected declines in fertility. Contrary to expectations, the index of female illiteracy compared to male illiteracy indicates that countries with higher female illiteracy relative to males have larger declines in fertility than expected from social setting and family planning effort. The difference between the positive and negative outliers, however, is entirely attributable to Thailand's inclusion among the positive outliers—with a female illiteracy ratio of .81, considerably larger than any other among the outliers. Even with Thailand included, the relationship is weak.

There is, however, a reasonable explanation for a positive relationship between female literacy and fertility. Cochrane (1979: 7) notes that uniformly inverse relations between fertility and education, as measured by literacy, are more likely in countries with high levels of female literacy. In fact, of all the outliers for which literacy data were available, only Cuba and Jamaica have over 70 percent female literacy, and the positive outliers tend to have lower levels of female literacy than the negative outliers. Both of these facts would lead us to expect a weakening or slight reversal of the expected relationship.

CONCLUSION

Freedman and Berelson (1976), Mauldin and Berelson (1978), and Tsui and Bogue (1978) have presented analyses of fertility decline which statistically explain a sizable proportion of the variance in fertility and fertility change, but do not substantively explain this variance because they fail to include variables which are (1) theoretically important, (2) empirically important, and (3) important to policy makers.

While our analysis is limited by missing data, theirs is plagued by missing variables: contextual variables, distributional variables, and unique national, regional, or local circumstances. These can only be adequately revealed by case studies and may be important influences on fertility behavior. Effects of family planning and social setting may be conditioned by contextual variables (e.g., island status as in Taiwan), or unique circumstances (e.g., coercion as in India), and distribution appears to have a direct effect of its own.

We have tried to give some indication of the importance of these other variables and of the ways in which they may affect the results obtained by the aforementioned studies. These studies in their present stage are probably inappropriate guides to policy, but augmented with careful consideration of information which may be less convenient to obtain (but more enlightening for policy decisions) they may prove more valuable in the future. In emphasizing the need for micro-level case studies, we merely echo much that has been said before (Dixon, 1978; Demeny, 1979). Macrolevel cross-country analysis is important; it allows us to make broad scientific generalizations, to project the future with some accuracy, and to provide a broad framework within which micro-level studies may be better understood. But it is not sufficient as a guide to policy.

NOTES

Authorship of this chapter is shared equally by Menard and Moen.

1. Variations on these themes are described by Teitelbaum (1975) and are discussed in the context of the 1974 World Population Conference by Mauldin, et al. (1974).
2. The index of social setting, which Mauldin and Berelson use as an indicator of *demand* for fertility reduction in the regression equation, was constructed from measures of (1) adult literacy, (2) primary and secondary school enrollment, (3) life expectancy, (4) infant mortality, (5) males aged 15 to 64 in the nonagricultural labor force, (6) per capita GNP, and (7) population in cities of 100,000 or more. The measure was constructed by adding the ranks of the countries included in the study on the seven variables (or those for which data were available), dividing by the number of variables, and multiplying by 100.
3. The index of family planning was developed by Lapham and Mauldin (1972) and codes "2" for presence, "1" for limited presence, and "0" for absence of the following: (1) family reduction included in official policy, (2) favorable statements by public leaders, (3) contraception readily and easily available, (4) importation of contraceptives allowed by law and custom, (5) vigorous effort to provide contraceptives to married women of reproductive age, (6) adequate family planning administrative structure, (7) training facilities available and utilized, (8) full-time home-visiting field workers, (9) availability of postpartum counseling services, (10) abortion legal and available, (11) sterilization legal and available, (12) mass media used to promote family size reduction, (13) government provides substantial part of family planning funds, (14) adequate record-keeping system, and (15) serious and continuous evaluation effort. Mauldin and Berelson modified the scale slightly.
4. These are actually preconditions for voluntary reduction in marital fertility associated with the use of birth control. Substantial fertility declines may also be brought about through increased age of marriage and sanctions against premarital sex and pregnancy such as have been instituted in China, or through coercion.
5. The literature on the value and cost of children is extensive and growing. See, for example, Arnold et al. (1975), Cain (1977), Espenshade (1977), Mamdani (1972), Mueller (1976), and Reining et al. (1977).
6. Another factor related to the value of children is infant mortality. High infant mortality may reduce the value of the individual child and, paradoxically, raise fertility at the same time. With a lower probability of any one child surviving, the level of investment in any one child may be low (in both financial and emotional terms), while the level of investment in all of one's children collectively may be high. By contrast, where the death rate is low for children, parents may invest the same amount in their children, but may do so more intensively in each child, therefore reducing the total number of children as the cost of each increases (Schultz, 1976).
7. Fertility decline might occur if *all* income levels were raised significantly, but considering mounting evidence, that under capitalist development strategies increases in aggregate income tend to accrue disproportionately to the upper classes and thus increase inequality, this seems most unlikely (Kocher, 1973; ul Haq, 1976; Adelman, 1975). Whether or not the level of income or income distribution per se is an important prerequisite for fertility reduction is a debatable issue (see e.g., Birdsall, 1977; Repetto, 1977).
8. Based on Gini coefficients for land distribution (Taylor and Hudson, 1972) and household income distribution (Jain, 1975) for the 25 nations, c. 1960, for which information is available.
9. Rich (1973) and others have already observed that island nations which have had a rapid decline in birth rates had more equitable distributions of income than most developing nations. We take up the issue of inequality in the section on distributional variables.
10. A word is in order about the Gini coefficients obtained from Jain. In order to examine both levels of income before and during the period in question (1965 to 1975) and to examine, where possible, the changes in distribution, we decided to obtain Gini coefficients for both c. 1960 and c. 1970. The data in Jain involved income distribution measured in several ways, most notably for households and for persons. While the Gini coefficients do show considerable change over time, household and personal income distributions are highly correlated for the same year. Choosing Gini coefficients to minimize this effect, the correlation is about .82; taking a more reasonable set of Gini coefficients for Japan, the correlation

is at least .95, and may be greater if Gini coefficients for other countries are selected to maximize the correlation. Given these results, a bivariate regression equation was used to calculate household income distribution from personal income distribution. The equation, using the more favorable results for Japan, was:

Household Gini = [.95 Personal Income Gini] – .0132.

One set of Gini coefficients for Japan involves estimates by Wada (1974); the other set comes from Japan's Bureau of Statistics and from articles by Ishizaki (1967) and Oshima (1963), which are consistent with one another and with figures from Schnitzer (1974). It should be noted that the two sets of Gini coefficients yield opposite trends. Wada's data indicating increased inequality and the other sources indicating both lower levels of inequality and a trend toward reduced inequality. Preference was given to published, official sources rather than to the data presented by Wada.

REFERENCES

Abu-Lughod, J., and R. Hay, Jr. 1977. *Third World Urbanization.* Chicago: Maaroufa.

Adelman, I. 1975. "Development Economics—A Reassessment of Goals." *American Economic Review* (May):302–309.

Ahluwalia, M.S. 1974. "Income Inequality: Some Dimensions of the Problem." In H. Chenery, M. S. Ahluwalia, C. L. G. Bell, J. H. Duloy, and R. Jolly (eds.), *Redistribution with Growth.* London: Oxford University.

Appleman, Philip (ed.). 1976. *Thomas Robert Malthus: An Essay on the Principle of Population.* New York: Norton.

Arnold, F., R. A. Bulatao, C. Buripakdi, B. J. Chang, J. T. Fawcett, T. Iritani, S. J. Lee, and T. Wu, with S. C. Albores. 1975. *The Value of Children: A Cross-National Study. Volume 1: Introduction and Comparative Analysis.* Honolulu: East-West Population Institute, East-West Center.

Bairoch, P. 1975. *The Economic Development of the Third World Since 1900.* Berkeley: University of California.

Birdsall, N. 1977. "Reply to Robert Repetto." *Population and Development Review* 3: 489–492.

Boserup, Ester. 1970. *Woman's Role in Economic Development.* New York; St. Martin's.

Boulding, E. M. 1977. *Women in the Twentieth Century World.* New York: Wiley.

Boulding, E. M., S. Nuss, D. Carson, and M. Greenstein. 1976. *Handbook of International Data on Women.* New York: Sage.

Bulatao, R. A. 1979. *On the Nature of the Transition in the Value of Children.* Honolulu: East-West Center.

Cain, M. T. 1977. "The Economic Activities of Children in a Village in Bangladesh." *Population and Development Review* 3:201–228.

Coale, A. 1973. "The Demographic Transition." *Proceedings of the International Population Conference.* Liege, Volume 1:52–72.

Cochrane, S. H. 1979. Fertility and Education: What Do We Really Know? *World Bank Staff Occasional Paper* Number 26. Baltimore: Johns Hopkins.

Demeny, P. 1979. "On the End of the Population Explosion." *Population and Development Review* 5:141–162.

Dixon, R. B. 1978. "On Drawing Policy Conclusions from Multiple Regressions. Some Queries and Dilemmas." *Studies in Family Planning* 9:286–287.

Dumond, D. E. 1975. "The Limitations of Human Population: A Natural History." *Science* 187:713–721.

Espenshade, T. J. 1977. "The Value and Cost of Children," *Population Bulletin* 32(1). Washington: Population Reference Bureau.

Freedman, R., and B. Berelson. 1976. "The Record of Family Planning Programs." *Studies in Family Planning* 7:1–40.

Haq, M. ul. 1976. *The Poverty Curtain.* New York: Columbia University.

Ishizaki, T. 1967. "The Income Distribution in Japan." *The Developing Economies* 5:356.

Jain, S. 1975. *Size Distribution of Income: A Compilation of Data.* Washington: World Bank.

Kocher, J. E. 1973. *Rural Development, Income Distribution, and Fertility Decline.* New York: Population Council.

Lapham, R. J., and P. Mauldin. 1972. "National Family Planning Programs: Review and Evaluation." *Studies in Family Planning* 3:31–34.

Lippman, L. 1979. "Iran's Family Planning Future in Doubt." *Intercom* 7:13–14.

Mamdani, M. 1972. *The Myth of Population Control.* New York: Monthly Review.

Mauldin, W. P., N. Chourcri, F. Notestein, and M. Teitelbaum. 1974. "A Report on Bucharest." *Studies in Family Planning* 5:357–395.

Mauldin, W. P., and B. Berelson, with Z. Sykes. 1978. "Conditions of Fertility Decline in Developing Countries, 1965–1975." *Studies in Family Planning* 9:89–147.

Mazumdar, V. 1979. "Fertility Policy in India." In J. Lipman-Blumen and J. Bernard (eds.), *Sex Roles and Social Policy.* Beverly Hills, CA: Sage.
McFalls, J. A., Jr. 1979. "Frustrated Fertility: A Population Paradox." *Population Bulletin* 34(2). Washington: Population Reference Bureau.
Meek, R. L. (ed.). 1971. *Marx and Engels on the Population Bomb.* Berkeley: Ramparts Press.
Menken, J. 1979. "Seasonal Migration and Seasonal Variations in Fecundability." *Demography* 16:103–120.
Mueller, E. 1976. "The Economic Value of Children in Peasant Agriculture." In R. G. Ridker (ed.), *Population and Development: The Search for Selective Interventions.* Baltimore: Johns Hopkins.
Nagel, J. S. 1978. "Mexico's Population Policy Turnaround." *Population Bulletin* 33:1–40.
Omran, A. 1979. "Urbanization in the Arab World." *Populi* 6:13–18.
Oshima, H. T. 1970. "Income Inequality and Economic Growth: The Postwar Experiences of Asian Countries." *Malayan Economic Review* 5:13.
Ratcliffe, J. 1978. "Kerala: Testbed for Transition Theory." *Populi* 5:11–6.
Reining, P., C. Fernando, B. Chinas, R. Fanole, S. Gojam de Millan, B. Lenkard, I. Shinohara, and I. Tinker. 1977. *Village Women: Their Changing Lives and Fertility.* Washington: American Association for the Advancement of Science.
Repetto, Robert. 1979. *Economic Equality and Fertility in Developing Countries.* Baltimore: Johns Hopkins.
———. 1977. "Income Distribution and Fertility Change: A Comment." *Population and Development Review* 3:486–489.
Rich, W. 1973. *Smaller Families through Social and Economic Progress.* Washington: Overseas Development Council.
Schnitzer, M. 1974. *Income Distribution.* New York: Praeger.
Schultz, T. P. 1976. "Interrelationships between Mortality and Fertility." In Ronald G. Ridker (ed.), *Population and Development: The Search for Selective Interventions.* Baltimore: Johns Hopkins.
Simon, Julian. 1976. "Income, Wealth and Their Distribution as Policy Tools in Fertility Control." In Ronald G. Ridker (ed.), *Population and Development.* Baltimore: Johns Hopkins.
Tabah, L. (ed.). 1975. *Population Growth and Economic Development in the Third World.* Dolhain, Belgium: Ordina.
Taylor, C. L., and M. C. Hudson. 1972. *World Handbook of Political and Social Indicators.* Second edition. New Haven, CT: Yale University.
Teitelbaum, M. S. 1975. "Relevance of Demographic Transition Theory for Developing Countries." *Science* 188:420–425.
Tsui, A. O., and D. J. Bogue. 1978. "Declining World Fertility: Trends, Causes, Implications." *Population Bulletin* 33(4). Washington: Population Reference Bureau.
United Nations. 1979. *The World Population Situation in 1977.* New York: United Nations.
U.S. Department of Health, Education and Welfare. 1977. *Social Security Programs throughout the World.* Washington: U.S. Government Printing Office.
Van der Tak, J. 1977. "World's Population Experts Meet in Mexico City." *Intercom* 5:7.
Wada, R. O. 1974. "Impact of Economic Growth on the Size Distribution of Income: The Postwar Experience of Japan." Paper delivered to the Joint JERC-CAMS Seminar on Income Distribution, Employment, and Economic Development in Southeast and East Asia, Tokyo.
Wrigley, E. A. 1969. *Population History.* New York: McGraw-Hill.

26
The Holy War

PATRICIA DONOVAN

DIRECT ACTION

Direct action simply recognizes what in fact is taking place, that innocent human lives are being destroyed, and that the only appropriate response is one that stops this killing.

Curtis Beseda, convicted of four counts of bombing and arson of abortion clinics, in "It's Not Terrorism to Stop the Slaughter," in *USA Today,* Nov. 23, 1984.

By day, antiabortion demonstrators who describe themselves as "sidewalk counselors" scream epithets and wave posters of bloody fetuses in the faces of abortion clinic patients and staff; by night, inflamed zealots are using bombs, torches and sledgehammers to bring their holy war against abortion to the facilities where abortion is performed.

The new year had barely begun when a Washington, D.C., women's clinic that performs abortions was severely damaged by an explosive device. A man telephoned *The Washington Times* later in the day to claim credit for the bombing on behalf of the Army of God, East Coast Division, pledging that the bombings would continue—the next one in Ohio.

Early on Christmas morning, bombs exploded at three medical facilities providing abortions in Pensacola, Florida; one facility was destroyed, the others suffered extensive damage. One of the targets had been forced to relocate last summer after an earlier bomb demolished the clinic. Four suspects have been arrested and charged with the bombings, which closed out a year that had seen a large increase in violent acts directed at abortion facilities.

Among other major incidents during the year was one that occurred shortly before dawn on November 19, when a bomb exploded at the Metropolitan Medical and Women's Center in Wheaton, Maryland, setting off a two-alarm fire that destroyed the 11-year-old abortion clinic. Minutes later, another blast rocked a Planned Parenthood family planning clinic in nearby Rockville, causing an estimated $50,000 in damage. As of the end of 1984, no suspects had been arrested.

On August 20, Cypress-Fairbanks Family Planning, an abortion clinic in Houston, was destroyed by a bomb, and it remains closed. Over the next two and a half weeks, three other abortion facilities in and around Houston were seriously damaged by bombs and fires. No one has been arrested in connection with any of the incidents.

In April, the Feminist Women's Health Center in Everett, Washington, was completely destroyed by its third fire in less than a year of operation. Curtis A. Beseda, an unemployed roofer who had been active in antiabortion causes, was convicted of setting the fires and also of firebombing an abortion clinic in Bellingham, Washington. He has been sentenced to 20 years in prison and ordered to pay almost $300,000 in restitution.

Beverly Whipple, executive director of the Everett clinic, says she hopes to reopen the facility, but she faces three serious obstacles that many of the other targets of violence also face—the loss of the clinic's lease, the cancellation of its fire insurance and a severe shortage of funds.

The Hillcrest Clinic in Norfolk, Virginia, suffered $140,000 in damage as a result of a fire in May 1983. The abortion clinic closed for three weeks to make repairs. Then, in February 1984, it was the target of a bomb that damaged a bank in the same building instead.

Like many clinics, the Hillcrest Clinic has had to take elaborate and expensive measures to protect itself and its patients from the threat of violence. In addition to spending $5,000 for a security system, Hillcrest has retained a 24-hour security guard at a cost of $4,000 a month, has installed double glass doors and a security wall in the corridor outside the clinic's suite and has hired a full-time employee, at a cost of $11,000 a year, to monitor traffic into the clinic.

As these examples and their consequences illustrate, the controversy over abortion has taken a destructive turn. The National Abortion Federation (NAF) reports that in 1984, there were 24 incidents of arson and bombing of abortion facilities[1] in seven states[2] and the District of Columbia (Table 26.1). Six abortion clinics were totally destroyed, and others suffered extensive damage. An additional six clinics were the targets of unsuccessful attacks, and at least 38 others received bomb threats. In comparison, three incidents of bombing or arson occurred in 1983, eight in 1982 and one in 1981.

Since 1982, damage from bombings and fires has cost well over $2 million, and that does not include the damage resulting from vandalism. According to the NAF, acts of vandalism have more than tripled in the last two years, from eight reported incidents in 1982 to 31 in 1984. During the same period, the number of invasions of clinics by antiabortion protesters more than doubled from 14 to 31. Moreover, in 1982, no death threats to clinic personnel were reported; in 1984, 21 death threats were reported.

Although no one has yet been injured or killed, two physicians have had terrifying encounters with the extremist fringe of the antiabortion movement. In 1981, a Florida physician was accosted by a man who held a gun to his head and demanded to know if he was "the baby-killer." The assailant eventually fled without harming the doctor, but two of the doctor's clinics were completely destroyed by fires six months later. In August 1982, Hector Zevallos, medical director of the Hope Clinic for Women in Granite City, Illinois, and his wife were kidnapped and held hostage for eight days. The Hope Clinic had suffered $250,000 in damage from a bombing earlier in the year.

Table 26.1. Violent Acts Directed at Abortion Clinics, 1981–1984

Type of Violence	1981	1982	1983	1984
Total	**9**	**45**	**53**	**161**
Invasion	3	14	16	31
Vandalism	2	8	19	31
Death threat	2	0	1	21
Assault and battery	0	3	3	7
Burglary	0	3	0	2
Arson	1	4	0	6
Bomb	0	4	3	18
Bomb threat	0	7	9	38
Kidnapping/hostage-taking	0	1	1	0
Attempted arson/bombing	1	1	1	6

Source: National Abortion Federation.

Clinic bombings have become so frequent that President Reagan, who is strongly antiabortion and who had remained silent in the face of the growing violence in 1984, issued a statement on January 3 condemning "in the strongest terms those individuals who perpetrate these and all such violent, anarchist activities." The President said he "will do all in my power to assure that the guilty are brought to justice," and he asked the Attorney General to see that "all federal agencies with jurisdiction pursue the investigation vigorously."[3]

The White House indicated that this does not mean that the Federal Bureau of Investigation (FBI) will assume major responsibility for the investigation. Currently, the Bureau of Alcohol, Tobacco and Firearms, which has primary jurisdiction over federal gun control, explosives control and antiarson laws, is in charge of the investigations of the clinic bombings, and the FBI provides laboratory tests and other assistance. As the violence has escalated, however, legal abortion advocates have pressed for the FBI to head up that effort. The FBI has refused to do so because it contends that the clinic bombings and fires are not terrorist acts, thus ruling out a special FBI counterterrorism investigation. (Terrorism is one of the FBI's four highest priorities.)

FBI Director William H. Webster told a group of reporters recently that antiabortion violence does not constitute terrorism because the incidents were not attacks on the government and were not caused by a "definable group or activity."[4] For the last two years, however, the FBI's annual reports have defined terrorism as "the unlawful use of force or violence against persons or property to intimidate or coerce a government, the civilian population or any segment thereof, in furtherance of political or social objectives."[5]

Webster's comments have been widely criticized. An aide to Sen. Jeremiah Denton (R.-Ala.), chairman of the Senate Subcommittee on Security and Terrorism and an opponent of abortion, questions Webster's position. The antiabortion bombings and fires, says Joel Lisker, chief counsel of the subcommittee, were "violent acts designed to intimidate a section of the community on a contentious social issue, and if that's not terrorism, I don't know what is."[6]

The investigatory agencies say that there is currently no evidence pointing to a national conspiracy directing the violence, even though there have been some instances of multiple bombings on the same day (including targets as far apart as San Diego and Atlanta). Individuals purporting to be members of a small radical antiabortion group known as the Army of God have claimed responsibility for some of the attacks, and Don Benny Anderson, a member of that group, is currently serving a prison sentence for setting fires in 1982 that destroyed two clinics in Florida and for the kidnapping of Zevallos and his wife. Law enforcement officials believe that Anderson and two other men imprisoned for the 1982 fires are the only members of the Army of God and that individual radicals or local groups are simply using the name without coordinating their activities.

CLINIC CONFRONTATIONS

Just as the violence has escalated, so have picketing and harassment of abortion clinics and patients. According to the NAF, 157 clinics reported being targets of antiabortion demonstrations in 1984, compared with 61 in 1983. These figures are thought to be understated, since they represent only clinics that have contacted the NAF.

Although clinics have been picketed ever since the Supreme Court legalized abortion in 1973, the nature of the protests has changed dramatically. Earlier antiabortion demonstrations were, for the most part, peaceful and quiet; protesters were content to pray the rosary, hand out literature and carry picket signs. Now, demonstrators commonly block entrances to clinics, bang on clinic windows, invade waiting rooms and harass staff members at their homes and private offices.

In addition, many protesters engage in tactics they refer to as "sidewalk counseling." Catholics United for Life (CUL), which developed the technique, sponsors instructional seminars and workshops around the country. Its literature often describes sidewalk counseling as a peaceful, sensitive effort to persuade women to rethink their decision by providing them with information and with offers of help. In reality, sidewalk counseling often fits another description provided by its originators, which says that it is "a last-minute confrontation" with a woman who is about to enter an abortion clinic.[7]

On Saturday mornings, for example, patients at the Planned Parenthood clinic in Baltimore are often unable to get out of their cars before they are surrounded by sidewalk counselors who display color photographs of dismembered fetuses and who scream at the women not to "murder" their "babies." At the Women's Health Services clinic in Pittsburgh, patients are often greeted by gruesome placards covered with dolls' arms, legs and torsos splattered with red paint and labeled "Pro-Choice Meats." At the Fort Wayne, Indiana, Women's Health Organization, demonstrators hand out two-inch pink plastic models of a 12-week-old male fetus, complete with facial features and limbs. In Charleston, West Virginia, right-to-life protesters photograph patients as they enter the Women's Health Center, causing them to worry that their picture may appear in the local newspaper.

Clinics frequently use escorts to shield their patients from sidewalk counselors, and they warn women who call for an appointment that they are likely to encounter the demonstrators. It is impossible, however, to spare patients entirely from these encounters.

Antiabortion groups insist that tactics such as these are necessary because abortion providers fail to give women complete information about abortion. "It is an outrage that a woman is not given details of fetal development, the hazards of the abortion procedure and the different options or alternatives available to her," declares John Willke, president of the National Right to Life Committee (NRLC). "It is rare that such information, particularly on fetal development, is given, and it is not done in any . . . meaningful fashion. . . . The vast number of women have no idea what they carry; when they know, some change their mind. Those operating the abortion facilities don't give them that opportunity."[8]

"That is simply propaganda. Women coming here receive a tremendous amount of therapy, probably more than for any other procedure," responds Bonita Collins, executive director of the Hillcrest Clinic. Collins says that on the day of the scheduled abortion, each patient at her clinic attends two counseling sessions so that clinic staff can ensure that she understands the procedure and the options available to her. In addition, the staff wants to be sure that she is comfortable with her decision to have the abortion and that the decision has not been forced on her by others.[9]

Dee Duemling of the Fort Wayne Women's Health Organization says that her clinic also requires attendance at two counseling sessions, and that she personally explores the decision-making process with each patient until she is satisfied that the abortion decision is the woman's alone. Neither of the clinics volunteers information about fetal development, although they provide it if a woman asks. "We don't impose guilt in an effort to influence her decision," explains Collins.[10]

According to a recent national poll, 72 percent of Americans think antiabortion demonstrators should not stand in front of clinics to interfere with women who enter and try to get them to change their minds about having an abortion. Fifty-one percent say that they are strongly opposed to such tactics.[11]

Nevertheless, CUL maintains that sidewalk counseling "can win public opinoin almost overnight by saving . . . little innocent babies."[12] Charles E. Rice, a constitutional law professor at the University of Notre Dame, asserts that sidewalk counseling "is a tactic that can bring down the whole structure of legalized abortion."[13] Rice is cochairman of Free Speech Advocates, an arm of CUL that was established to provide volunteer legal aid "for pro-life activists engaged in peaceful and lawful counseling on public property" and to train lawyers to "work to see the civil rights of sidewalk counselors redressed, restored and respected."[14] (Other conservative and religious organizations, including the Catholic League for Religious and Civil Rights in Milwaukee and the Rutherford Institute in Manassas, Virginia, also provide legal assistance to abortion protesters, particularly those charged with trespassing.)

COURT ACTIONS

Freedom of speech provisions in the First Amendment give protesters the right to picket and conduct peaceful demonstrations on public property. However, in at least 13 states,[15] clinics have gone to court and obtained injunctions that prohibit antiabortion protesters from engaging in activities that the judges have determined are not protected by the Constitution. These include blocking the entrances to clinics or clinic parking lots; threatening, harassing, intimidating, insulting, molesting, pushing, elbowing or shouldering patients or staff; peering into or shouting through clinic windows; trespassing on private property; invading clinics; shouting abusive epithets or obscenities at patients; photographing or videotaping patients; engaging in face-to-face harassment; using any means of voice amplification; interfering with or harassing patients or clinic staff at their homes; making phone calls intended to disrupt clinic operations; and making false appointments.

Some courts have also limited the number of protesters that can demonstrate at any given time; barred picketers from carrying signs with such messages as "baby-killer," "murderer" or other slogans "intended to induce emotional distress";[16] specified the distance the picketers must remain from the clinic entrance; and ordered demonstrators not to park their cars in front of a clinic in an effort to deprive patients of convenient parking spaces.

Court orders restricting the activities of demonstrators are based on the recognition that the right of free speech sometimes conflicts with patients' rights to privacy and providers' rights to conduct their business without undue interference. As one court pointed out, "The First Amendment does not guarantee the right to communicate one's views at all times and places or in any manner that may be desired."[17]

The Supreme Court has held that the test of whether restrictions on the time, place and manner of protests are reasonable "is whether the manner of expression is basically incompatible with the normal activity of a particular place at a particular time."[18] Under this standard, according to the American Civil Liberties Union (ACLU), noisy demonstrations that disrupt normal activities of the clinic by intruding upon patient counseling may be prohibited because "medical facilities and their patients, whether hospitals or clinics, are entitled to protection from the kind of boisterous and threatening conduct that can disturb the tranquility necessary to carry out [their] functions."[19]

Similarly, the ACLU contends, obstruction of a clinic entrance, physical or verbal threats to patients or staff, activities that violate patient confidentiality (such as photographing or videotaping patients or taking down their license numbers), and picketing that is physically intimidating may be restricted. A court in Washington, for example, recently barred picketers from forming a gauntlet in front of a clinic because, the court said, it was "not for the purpose of speech . . . but primarily for the purpose of intimidation and coercion."[20]

At the same time, the court refused to restrict the messages carried on antiabortion signs, even though it acknowledged that they could be offensive, distasteful and upsetting to patients. "Any restriction on a message must not be based on whether one disagrees with the message or finds [it] offensive or upsetting," the court noted, "but must be based on other grounds," such as whether the message creates a "clear and present danger," uses "fighting words" or defames.[21] The court determined that signs referring to patients and staff as baby-killers and murderers were not fighting words and did not create a clear and present danger.

A NEW STRATEGY

Harassment and violence are part of a new strategy by some elements of the right-to-life movement that have become frustrated by their failure after 12 years to reverse *Roe* v. *Wade* and to prohibit abortion. That frustration was fueled in the summer of 1983 by two events. First, the Supreme Court forcefully reaffirmed a woman's constitutional right to terminate an unwanted pregnancy and, in the process, struck down a variety of restrictions, such as waiting periods and consent requirements, that the antiabortion community had hoped would at least limit access to abortion.[22] Second, the Senate rejected a constitutional amendment to allow the states and the federal government to prohibit abortion.[23] In addition, the Senate had earlier tabled consideration of the human life statute, which would have circumvented the amendment process by allowing a simple majority in Congress to outlaw abortion merely by declaring the fetus to be a human being from the moment of conception.[24]

These setbacks were particularly bitter given the earlier optimism within the antiabortion community that the 1980 election of Ronald Reagan and the elevation of antiabortion senators to key committee chairmanships would produce some congressional action to overturn *Roe* v. *Wade*. The defeats left the movement fractured, and they convinced its more radical elements that the legislative and judicial strategy for outlawing abortion was ineffective. These radicals began exhorting their followers to take to the streets to "shut down the abortion industry"[25] through continuous harassment of clinics and patients.

Led by such groups as the Pro-Life Action League, CUL, Women Exploited by Abortion and People Expressing a Concern for Everyone, and joined by a growing number of fundamentalist churches and state affiliates of the NRLC, this activist wing has become an increasingly powerful voice within the antiabortion movement. In the process, it has changed both the strategy and the tone of the opposition to abortion.

"The more extremist elements of the so-called prolife community were better controlled when the more moderate factions could say that the situation would be remedied in the courts and in Congress," observes Daniel Pellegrom, executive director of Planned Parenthood of Maryland, whose Baltimore clinic has been picketed regularly for more than 10 years. "They are harder to control now because they feel led astray. The demonstrators have become much more vituperative to patients and more hostile and nasty to staff."[26]

Jeri Rasmussen, public affairs director of Planned Parenthood of Minnesota, which is picketed daily, agrees. "The saner heads have moved on, leaving protesters who are more extreme."[27]

For their part, the radical groups are often openly critical of the moderates, and particularly of the NRLC, which is the largest antiabortion organization and has led the long, unsuccessful fight for a constitutional amendment. Alluding to the failure of the moderates' strategy to outlaw abortion, Joseph Scheidler, director of the Pro-Life Action League, told a gathering of antiabortion activists, "We're in control of the movement now and we're not going to blow it."[28] (Scheidler claims to have organized the nationwide antiabortion picketing of Democratic vice presidential candidate Geraldine Ferraro during the recent campaign.)

Elasah Drogin, president of CUL, is also disenchanted with the moderates' efforts to end abortion through legislative action. "After 10 years of nonreligious, politically oriented prolife work, we have more abortions than ever," notes Drogin, who converted to Catholicism following her own abortion. "When certain 'prolife' politicians were elected into high positions, the prolife movement stopped. Everyone ignored the babies who were scheduled to be murdered . . . and began to hope . . . that . . . a law might be passed outlawing abortion."[29]

Patti McKinny, vice president of Women Exploited by Abortion, says, "Getting out in front of those abortion facilities and freeing those women to choose life is . . . very important work that has been ignored for too long in too many places."[30] Her organization is composed of women who have had an abortion, but regret their decision. These women blame their decision on their doctor's or clinic's failure to provide information on the physical and, particularly, the psychological risks of abortion, which, they say, would have persuaded them to continue the pregnancy.

Last May, more than 600 right-to-life activists from around the country gathered in Fort Lauderdale, Florida, for a three-day conference on how to close abortion clinics and discourage women from seeking the procedure. The attendees heard representatives from several militant groups declare that from now on the right-to-life movement, or at least their wing of it, would eschew a legislative strategy in favor of direct action.

"We in the prolife community are now beyond the point of talking," asserted Woody Cumbie, pastor of the First Baptist Church in Fort Lauderdale. "We're putting our time, . . . our energy, . . . our prayers . . . and our money where our mouths have been. We're at the point of action, and our unified action is going to shut down the abortion industry in America."

Disillusionment with their supporters in Congress was evident in the remarks of several speakers, including Nancy Hackle of the Cleveland chapter of People Expressing a Concern for Everyone, who criticized Rep. Henry Hyde (R.-Ill.), one of the movement's strongest advocates in Congress, for his failure to appear on picket lines. Stephen Settle of the Catholic League for Religious and Civil Rights, declared, "What is going to be demanded is . . . sacrificial action on behalf of the individual prolifer. We cannot depend on the occasional statement from national leaders and politicians to do this job for us."

Also appearing as speakers at the conference were Phyllis Schlafly, Cal Thomas of the Moral Majority and Jean Doyle, then president of the NRLC. None of these speakers discussed the shift to direct action. Doyle, for example, merely urged the audience not to become discouraged over the continuing failure to outlaw abortion. However, their presence was an indication of the growing strength within the antiabortion movement of the action-oriented militant wing.

A RELIGIOUS CRUSADE

Although opposition to abortion has always had a strong religious foundation, antiabortion groups portray themselves more and more as the forces of good, who have a mandate from God to stamp out the evil perpetrated at abortion clinics. Scheidler exhorted the activists in Fort Lauderdale, "I challenge every person who is not a cloistered nun or doing time in a federal penitentiary to come out in the streets at least two hours a month. Don't let a month pass when you haven't been there as a foot soldier. Almighty God wants to use you!"

The struggle over abortion is frequently referred to as a war, and even moderate right-to-life leaders have accepted this characterization. "This is a basic struggle between good and evil," asserts former NRLC president Doyle. "This is a war we're engaged in."[31]

To reinforce this sense of evil, abortion is often compared to Hitler's extermination of more than six million Jews during World War II. Clinics are labeled "aboratoriums," clinic employees are denounced as Nazis, swatiskas appear on protest signs and speakers often refer to Dachau and Auschwitz in their condemnation of abortion.

Scheidler says that he advocates only nonviolent protests, but adds that he feels justified in breaking trespass laws to serve a higher law: "When the law sanctions the killing of innocent people, maybe you have to break a law to save lives. That means that we will have more sit-ins."[32]

Other activist leaders say that they have a religious duty to disobey the laws of man when they conflict with the laws of God. It is not an argument the courts are likely to accept, however. As a Florida court observed in restricting the activities of demonstrators at a Ford Lauderdale clinic, "the religious motives of the [demonstrators], no matter how well intended, do not as a matter of law give [them] the right to violate the [clinic's] rights to do legal business in a lawful manner." To rule otherwise, the court said, would result in "anarchy" and "a totally unacceptable chaos."[33]

Scheidler and others often leave the impression that while they may not engage in bombings and arson, they approve of the results of those who do. "I have yet to shed my first tear when I see a charred abortion clinic," Scheidler remarked.[34] Jean Emond, president of the Debate Foundation, which sponsored the Fort Lauderdale conference and which describes itself as a nonprofit corporation "founded on the premise that all life is sacred," goes even further. He told activists in attendance, "We would all rejoice . . . if tomorrow morning we picked up our newspapers and read that every butchery mill, every abortion clinic, in the United States were burnt to the bottom."

More than any other individual, Scheidler epitomizes the aggressive character of the antiabortion activists. Sometimes referred to by his admirers as the "green beret" of the movement, Scheidler travels around the country exhorting antiabortion demonstrators and leading protesters in front of, and sometimes into, clinics. He is the idea man for activists, suggesting to his audiences a wide array of tactics that he says will force clinics to close their doors for lack of patients. He says he will soon publish a book on his methods entitled *Closed: 99 Ways to Close the Abortion Clinics.*

A former Catholic seminarian and journalism instructor, Scheidler has been in the antiabortion movement for years, but until recently was considered too radical to be taken seriously. In January 1984, however, he was among the antiabortion leaders invited by President Reagan to the White House on the 11th anniversary of *Roe* v. *Wade.*

Scheidler has become famous for the bullhorn he uses at demonstrations to denounce clinics as "death chambers" and to tell women entering clinics that God will punish them. He also tries to frighten patients with false claims that 10 percent of women become sterile after an abortion and that an abortion significantly increases the risk of tubal pregnancies, miscarriages, premature births and deformed babies in the future.

Sometimes, Scheidler says, the best tactic is "to scare the hell out of" patients by making up stories that "girls have been brought out of [the clinic] on a stretcher"[35] and that the clinic's doctors are being sued for practicing medicine without a license. Scheidler contends, with apparent satisfaction, that the complication rate for abortions increases by four to five percent when demonstrations are going on outside the clinic.

MUTED CRITICISM

Despite such inflammatory tactics, moderate antiabortion leaders have failed to criticize or disassociate themselves from Scheidler and other militant groups. NRLC president Willke, for example, says that he has nothing negative or positive to say about Scheidler, adding only that "Scheidler is doing something a lot of people feel is very important, although some feel there are better ways."[36]

Willke asserts that the militants' protests "supplement" rather than detract from the legislative strategy of the NRLC. At the same time, he tries to downplay the influence of the radical groups, contending that the increase in antiabortion demonstrations over the last year or so has less to do with the organizational efforts of national antiabortion groups than with the "influx into the movement of a large number of evangelical Christians who have elected to witness publicly." These people, Willke said in an interview, "believe they have a Christian duty to . . . do something [to stop] what is seen by them as deeply offensive to the laws of God as they know them."[37]

Most right-to-life leaders either remained silent about violence against clinics until the bombings became highly publicized late in the year, issued weak criticisms or attempted to rationalize it by saying that the violence that occurs during an abortion is as bad as or worse than the bombing or arson that destroys a clinic. "We abhor violence," says Willke. But, he maintains, "the way to stop the violence outside [of the clinic] is to stop the violence inside."[38]

Similarly, Cal Thomas of the Moral Majority recently wrote an article in which he said that "tactically, as well as politically, the bombing of abortion clinics is *probably* not a good idea" (emphasis added).[39] Later, on ABC-TV's "Night Line," he added that the bombings will have served a useful purpose if they result in a national debate on the abortion issue, which he says has not taken place so far. (In early January, after President Reagan issued his statement, Jerry Falwell, leader of the Moral Majority, told reporters that the bombings of abortion clinics are being carried out by "deranged" people who are diverting attention from the "real atrocity.")

The Catholic bishops, who sought to make abortion a major issue in the recent election, also failed to condemn the violence.

Barbara Radford, executive director of the NAF, believes that out of frustration over the continuing failure to outlaw abortion, all elements of the antiabortion movement "are increasingly resorting to tactics and rhetoric that stir passions and hatred and surely incite the most radical among them to violence. When activists are told by their leaders that they have a mandate from God to get rid of abortion clinics and that the struggle over abortion is a war between good and evil, some extremists must certainly believe that they are justified in destroying or vandalizing a clinic," she says.[40]

NOTES AND REFERENCES

1. Two of the targets—Planned Parenthood of Cobb County, Georgia, and the Planned Parenthood clinic in Rockville, Maryland—do not perform abortions, but do provide abortion referrals. A third victim, the National Abortion Federation, a professional organization of abortion providers, offers no medical or referral services.

2. California, Delaware, Florida, Georgia, Maryland, Texas, and Washington.
3. Office of the Press Secretary, The White House, Washington, DC, Jan. 3, 1985.
4. "Terrorist Bombings Decline; Abortion Attacks Excluded," *Washington Times,* Dec. 5, 1984, p. A4.
5. S. Taylor, Jr., "When Is a Terrorist Not Necessarily a Terrorist," *New York Times,* Dec. 12, 1984, p. A28.
6. Ibid.
7. Catholics United for Life (CUL), *The Best Way to Save Babies,* pamphlet, p. 2.
8. J. Willke, personal communication, Sept. 20, 1984.
9. B. Collins, personal communication, Oct. 19, 1984.
10. Ibid.
11. Poll of 1,200 people aged 18 or older by Harrison and Goldberg, Boston, conducted Mar. 19–25, 1984.
12. E. Drogin, "CUL's Answer to the Violence of Abortion," *Catholics United for Life,* May 1984, p. 3.
13. CUL, op. cit. (see reference 5).
14. C. E. Rice, fundraising letter for Free Speech Advocates, undated.
15. Arizona, California, Florida, Indiana, Kentucky, Michigan, Mississippi, Missouri, New Jersey, New York, Ohio, Virginia, and Washington.
16. Birth Control Institute, Inc. v. Bible Missionary Fellowship, Case No. 523248, Calif. Super. Ct. (San Diego County), July 9, 1984.
17. Feminist Women's Health Center v. Women Exploited by Abortion, No. 83-2-04152-8, Wash. Super. Ct. (Snohomish County) May 18, 1984.
18. Grayned v. City of Rockford, 408 U.S. 104 (1972).
19. Cleveland Facilities Co. v. Life Services Foundation, Case No. 7199, Ohio Ct. of Common Pleas (Cuyahoga County). Amicus curiae brief filed Oct. 3, 1984.
20. Feminist Women's Health Center v. Women Exploited by Abortion, 1984, op. cit. (see reference 14).
21. Ibid.
22. City of Akron v. Akron Center for Reproductive Health, 103 S. Ct. 2481 (1983).
23. S. J. Res. 3.
24. S. 2148.
25. W. Cumbie, National Conference on Pro-Life Activism, Fort Lauderdale, Fla., May 11, 1984.
26. D. Pellegrom, personal communication, Sept. 4, 1984.
27. J. Rasmussen, personal communication, Sept. 4, 1984.
28. J. Scheidler, National Conference on Pro-Life Activism, Fort Lauderdale, Fla., May 12, 1984.
29. "CUL President Featured at Roman Catholics Obedient to Pope John Paul Rally on January 22," *Catholics United for Life,* Easter 1983, p. 1.
30. P. McKinny, "The Sidewalk Counselor: Saving Babies and the Women They Live Within," National Conference on Pro-Life Activism, Fort Lauderdale, Fla., May 10, 1984.
31. J. Doyle, National Conference on Pro-Life Activism, Fort Lauderdale, Fla., May 11, 1984.
32. T. F. Roeser, "The Prolife Movement's Holy Terror," *Reader,* Aug. 5, 1983, p. 15.
33. Summit Women's Center, Inc. v. Hairston, Case No. 82-25608 CN, Fla., Cir. Ct., 17th Judicial Circuit (Broward County), Apr. 12, 1983.
34. J. Scheidler, 1984, op. cit. (see reference 28).
35. Ibid.
36. J. Willke, personal communication, Sept. 20, 1984.
37. Ibid.
38. Ibid.
39. C. Thomas, "Bombing Abortion Clinics: It's Violent but Why Not?" *Los Angeles Times,* Nov. 27, 1984.
40. B. Radford, personal communication, July 24, 1984.

27

Eastern Europe: Pronatalist Policies and Private Behavior

HENRY P. DAVID

In the mid-1970s while fertility was plummeting below replacement level in most other industrialized countries, birth rates were stable or rising in several of the nine socialist countries of Central and Eastern Europe—the Soviet Union, Poland, Yugoslavia, Romania, the German Democratic Republic, Czechoslovakia, Hungary, Bulgaria, and Albania. Satisfied policymakers believed this trend to be the result of the successful application of pronatalist policies involving cash benefits to encourage couples to have children and restrictions on access to legal abortion. Thus, for other developed nations concerned about low birth rates, it is said, Eastern European experience could be a guide to how public policies might influence private reproductive behavior.

Some 15 years earlier, in the early 1960s, the European fertility picture had been the reverse. While much of Northwestern Europe was experiencing a mild baby boom, fertility was falling rapidly in several of the socialist countries, though not to levels as low as they now are in North and West Europe and in the United States. The fertility decline coincided with a wave of abortion liberalization. Ahead of most Western nations and following the lead of the Soviet Union where abortion was reliberalized in 1955, all the socialist countries except Albania passed laws permitting abortion on broad social grounds or on request, although full liberalization was delayed to 1972 in the German Democratic Republic. The subsequent surge in legal abortions was perceived as a direct, powerful cause of the unintended and unwelcomed fertility decline. Fearful of future labor shortages, aging populations, and even "national demographic suicide," policymakers responded with active pronatalist measures in most of the socialist countries. Abortion was again restricted in four countries—drastically in Romania in 1966 and mildly in Czechoslovakia, Hungary, and Bulgaria at various times during the 1960s and early 1970s. Most of the nine countries introduced or stepped up pronatalist cash incentives such as lump-sum birth grants, paid maternity leave, monthly family and child-care allowances, and even low-interest loans for newlyweds which are progressively written off with the birth of each child.

By the early 1970s in Czechoslovakia, for example, 10 percent of the government's annual budget was being spent on direct payments to parents or potential parents plus indirect pronatalist incentives such as subsidies for nurseries, kindergartens, school meals, and children's transportation, and rent reductions for families in government housing. Official population policy is currently explicitly pronatalist to varying degrees in all of the socialist countries except for heterogeneous Yugoslavia—the first country in the world to incorporate into its federal constitution (in 1974) that "it is a human right to decide freely on childbirth."

Although these pronatalist policies are credited with producing the higher birth rates of at least several of the socialist countries during the 1970s, the latest data suggest that their impact may be short-lived. Fertility had turned down again by 1980 in Hungary, Bulgaria, and Czechoslovakia, and already in the late 1960s in Romania. Some observers suggest that the main impact of cash benefits paid to parents or prospective parents has been to encourage couples to have first and second births sooner than they otherwise would, without stimulating the resurgence in third and higher order births that would be necessary to ensure a marked upturn in population growth. Surveys shows that, for the past decade and more, two children has been considered the ideal family size by the overwhelming majority of couples in most socialist countries, as is now true in almost all developed countries. Unless pronatalist incentives are progressively increased to keep pace with rising living costs and rising expectations for more income to improve living standards, desired family size is not likely to increase beyond two children, and the actual achieved family size is likely to average out at less than two children per woman, that is, below the level necessary to ensure replacement of the population in the long run.

Counteracting the potential impact of pronatalist measures are many factors which tend to discourage couples from having more than one or two children. In line with socialist ideology which stresses the equality of women and men and the need for women's labor to boost economic grwoth, women's labor force participation is higher in most of these socialist countries than anywhere else in the developed world. But the equality which women have largely achieved in the job market and in education has not extended to domestic duties: women are still primarily responsible for child care, shopping, and all other household tasks. Their double burden is complicated by continuing shortages in child-care facilities, in services, and in consumer goods, as well as men's reluctance to share what are perceived as women's roles. Further deterrents to childbearing are the continuing shortage of adequate housing, the rising cost of such consumer goods as there are, and—in at least the Soviet Union and Poland in recent years—deteriorating living standards. Divorce rates have risen in all countries, except for Catholic-dominated Poland (and presumably in maverick, Muslim Albania). Sex education has increased in some of the countries, but in some—particularly in the USSR—attitudes toward sex remain prudish.

This chapter reviews recent trends in the nine countries of Central and Eastern Europe in fertility, abortion and contraception, pronatalist economic incentives, women's roles, and in marriage, divorce, and attitudes toward sex. It is based, with permission, on the volume prepared by the *Bulletin's* author jointly with Robert J. McIntyre, *Reproductive Behavior: Central and Eastern European Experience,* published by Springer Publishing Company, in October 1981. To set these issues in context, we begin with brief descriptions of each of the countries.

SIMILARITIES AND DIFFERENCES: THE BACKGROUND

The nine countries generally have in common the goals of a centrally managed economy (except for Yugoslavia), a one-party political system, and the sometimes submerged but seldom forgotten socialist ideal of the social and political equality of women and men. Beyond that, while heavily influenced by the Soviet Union and its political, social, and population policy history, they are not a monolith. On the contrary, each has its own historical, cultural, and religious traditions, its own personality, and its own political and demographic experience. Even today, there are considerable variations among the nine countries in social and economic development, urbanization, and even in fertility rates, as well as between them and Western European countries and the United States, as seen in Table 27.1.

In 1980, natural increase (births minus deaths) ranged from a high of 2.5 percent in Albania to a low of 0.03 percent in Hungary, but annual births were not actually lower than deaths in any of the nine socialist countries as they were in the Federal Republic of Germany (West Germany). The total fertility rate around 1980 was above the replacement level of 2.1 births per woman in Poland (2.3), Romania (2.5), the Soviet Union (2.3) and especially in Albania (4.2), while the rate was at or just below replacement level in the other five socialist countries, compared to consistently below-replacement-level fertility in the six nonsocialist developed countries listed in Table 27.1. In Gross National Product (GNP) per capita in 1979, the socialist countries ranged from a low of $840 in Albania to a high of $6,430 in the German Democratic Republic (GDR), compared to a range in the other countries from $6,320 (United Kingdom) to $11,930 (Sweden). The GDR also stands out among the socialist countries with its low infant mortality rate in 1980 (12.1 deaths per 1,000 live births) and high rate of urbanization (77 percent of the population), both on a par with rates for the six nonsocialist developed countries shown in Table 27.1. Other similarities and differences among the nine socialist countries are noted in the following vignettes.

U.S.S.R.

As the first to establish a socialist society based on Marxist principles, the Union of the Soviet Socialist Republics holds a preeminent position among the nations of Central and Eastern Europe. It is the third most populous nation in the world (after China and India), with an estimated 268 million people in mid-1981. Over 100 ethnic groups are represented in its 15 union republics and 28 autonomous republics.

The USSR pioneered in the liberalization of

Table 27.1. Population Statistics: East and West Europe and United States, 1980, 1981

Country	Population, Mid-1981 (Millions)	Birth Rate, 1980	Death Rate, 1980	Natural Increase, 1980 (%)	Total Fertility Rate, 1980	Urban Population (%)	Infant Mortality Rate, 1980	GNP per Capita, 1979 (U.S.$)
Albania	2.8	27.4[a]	6.4[a]	2.1[a]	4.2[a]	37	40[a]	840
Bulgaria	8.9	14.3	10.7	0.4	2.2[b]	64	19.9	3,690
Czechoslovakia	15.4	16.2	12.1	0.4	2.1	67	16.6	5,290
German Democratic Republic (East)	16.7	14.6	14.2	0.04	1.9	77	12.1	6,430
Hungary	10.7	13.9	13.6	0.03	1.9	54	23.1	3,850
Poland	36.0	19.5	9.8	1.0	2.3	57	21.2	3,830
Romania	22.4	18.6[b]	9.9[b]	0.9	2.5[b]	48	31.6[b]	1,900
U.S.S.R.	268.0	18.3	10.4	0.8	2.3[b]	65	36[c]	4,110
Yugoslavia	22.5	17.0	9.0	0.8	2.0	42	32.8	2,430
Federal Republic of Germany (West)	61.3	10.0	11.5	0.2	1.5	92	12.6	11,730
France	53.9	14.8	10.1	0.5	2.0	78	10.0	9,950
Netherlands	14.2	12.8	8.1	0.5	1.6	88	8.6	10,230
Sweden	8.3	11.7	11.0	0.1	1.7	83	6.7	11,930
United Kingdom	55.9	13.5	11.8	0.2	1.9	76	11.9	6,320
United States	229.8	15.8	8.7	0.7	1.8	74	12.5	10,630

Sources: Population mid-1981 and urban population: Population Reference Bureau, *1981 World Population Data Sheet;* GNP per capita 1979: World Bank, *World Development Report, 1981;* birth and death rate (per 1,000 population), total fertility rate (birth rate per woman aged 15–49), and infant mortality rate (deaths under age one per 1,000 live births); Alain Monnier, "Europe and Overseas Developed Countries: Statistical Data" (in French), *Population,* Vol. 36, No. 4–5 (July–October 1981) Tables 2 and 3, pp. 888, 889.

[a]1978 or 1979. Source: Dudley Kirk, "Albania," in Henry P. David and Robert J. McIntyre, *Reproductive Behavior: Central and Eastern European Experience* (New York, Springer, 1981) pp. 300–304.

[b]1979.

[c]Estimate for 1976 in Christopher Davis and Murray Feshbach, "Rising Soviet Infant Mortality," *Intercom,* July 1980, p. 12.

abortion legislation in 1920, restricted abortion again in 1936, and then reliberalized it in 1955, an action eventually followed by all its neighboring socialist countries except Albania. Despite evidence that its abortion rate may be the highest in the world—well above the birth rate in most cities at least—the liberal law of 1955 has remained in force.

The country's overall fertility rate has been more stable than that of any of its neighbors over the past quarter century, declining only from 2.8 births per woman in 1957 to 2.3 in 1979. That it has not fallen lower is attributed to very high fertility in the Muslim, little urbanized Central Asian Republics—up to more than 6 births per woman in the Tadzhik SSR, for example, compared to 1.9 in the Russian Republic in 1978 to 1979.[1]

Along with the implication of low fertility for the future supply of labor, this fertility differential worries Soviet officials, who foresee a decline in the purely Russian ethnic proportion of the total population to under half by the 1990s. (This proportion declined from 53.4 percent to 52.4 percent between the censuses of 1970 and 1979.) Stimulating fertility among ethnic Russians is increasingly debated, although the USSR claims to have no official pronatalist policy. Until recently, at least, it has been insisted that "the state must not interfere in the free exercise of the will of families with respect to childbearing."[2] However, at the Twenty-sixth Party Congress in February 1981, President Brezhnev and Premier Tikhonov endorsed new measures to stimulate fertility, which are written into the Eleventh Five Year Plan (1981 to 1985) and are to be introduced first in the low-fertility, predominantly Slavic European, Siberian, and Pacific regions of the country.[3]

Always short of consumer goods and housing, the USSR currently faces a new round of austerity as a result of 1981's crop failure—the third in a row—due to drought and inefficiencies in the Soviet collectivized agricultural system, and a slowdown in the production of such commodities as oil, coal, and steel.[4] The 1981 grain harvest of 190 million tons was 46 million tons short of the 1978 harvest, similar to the shortfalls in 1980 and 1979. Industrial production grew by only 3.4 percent in 1979, the slowest gain since such statistics became available in 1950. In September 1981, the price of gasoline was doubled and raised up to 40 percent on vodka, tobacco, and many other consumer items. Although the prices of meat and dairy products remain at their 1962 levels, the *Washington Post* Moscow correspondent reports, that "the government has reinstated a system of informal rationing as a precaution against food shortages expected as a result of this year's poor harvest."[5]

Deteriorating health conditions are also evident in the rise of death rates at all ages during the 1970s and especially of infants. Deaths among infants under age one rose from 22.9 per 1,000 live births in 1971 to 27.9 in 1974 when publication of official infant mortality data ceased. Murray Feshbach and Christopher Davis, experts on the Soviet Union, estimate that, by 1979, the infant mortality rate may have been more than three times the 12.9 rate recorded in the United States in that year.[6] They attribute the rise, among other factors, to poor quality formula milk fed to infants, "an inability to cope with influenza which leads to pneumonia that kills infants," "long waits and short hours combined with haphazard diagnostic work in polyclinics," more single-parent families due to rising divorce, and women's multiple abortions using the now-outmoded sharp curettage method which increase the likelihood of later premature infants among whom the mortality rate is "many times higher" than for full-term infants. Feshbach points out that the share of the Soviet budget spent on health care dropped from about 6.6 percent in 1965 to 5.2 percent in the mid-1970s.[7]

Poland

Poland is second in area and population (36 million in 1981) to the Soviet Union among Eastern European countries. Its experience over the past century has diverged significantly from that of most of its socialist neighbors. The country suffered vast devastation and loss of life during World War II, but acquired industrialized Silesia from Germany following the war, giving up agricultural land in the east to the USSR. However, Poland has industrialized only slowly. In 1970, a third of the labor force was still engaged in agriculture and small-scale private agriculture remains important. Two-thirds of agricultural land remains in private lands. The population is ethnically almost entirely Polish and the overwhelming majority of Poles are Roman Catholic. The Catholic Church plays a strong role in national life.

Poland's postwar history has been marked by a series of workers' strikes to protest living and working conditions: in 1956, 1970, 1976, 1980, and 1981. Most have been followed by a change of government and efforts to improve economic conditions, with varying results. In the early 1970s, under Gierek, who succeeded Gomulka as First Secretary of the controlling Polish Communist Party in 1970, Poland briefly enjoyed one of the highest economic growth rates in the world. But this was soon dampened by inflation, recession in the West, and domestic market problems, compounded by agricultural shortfalls. Consumer goods shortages, which worsened steadily during the late 1970s, reached crisis proportions following the birth of the independent Solidarity trade union movement in August 1980.[8] The shortages have seriously affected efforts to reform the poor health care system which was a major impetus for the 1980 worker revolution.[9] Although millions of low-rent apartments have been built in Poland's war-damaged cities, waiting times for the two- to three-room apartments, usually shared by more than one family, are now ten years long.

Polish population policy was pronatalist in the first post-World War II years. However, as economic conditions deteriorated during the 1950s and annual population growth reached nearly 2 percent, a campaign was launched to encourage couples to have smaller families. The approach was again reversed with a series of pronatalist measures after the birth rate plummeted to 16.2 per 1,000 population in 1968. By 1980, Poland's birth rate of 19.5 per 1,000 population was the highest among the Eastern European countries (except for Albania). Despite increasing condemnation by the Roman Catholic Church, the country's liberal abortion law of 1956—further liberalized in 1959—was still in force in early 1982. At the time abortion was liberalized, the government also backed the formation in 1957 of the Polish Family Planning Association (then called the Association for Conscious Motherhood). The Association was allowed to affiliate with the International Planned Parenthood Federation and took a leading role in providing family planning services throughout the country. In early 1980, the Association was renamed the Family Development Association and declared eligible for government subsidies to encourage adoption of more efficient contraception as an alternative to reliance on abortion. However, government support appeared to weaken during the turmoil beginning with the strikes of summer 1980. In late 1981, it was reported that two bodies, Gaudium Vita and the Association for the Protection of the Unborn

Child, now had Ministry of Health backing for their aggressive campaign aimed at eliminating all mechanical methods of contraception as well as restricting the liberal abortion legislation.[10]

Yugoslavia

Yugoslavia is a Socialist Federal Republic, composed of six constituent republics (Bosnia-Herzogovina, Croatia, Macedonia, Montenegro, Serbia, and Slovenia) and two autonomous provinces within Serbia (Kosovo-Metohija and Vojvodina). Its population of about 23 million in 1981 is the most heterogeneous in Eastern Europe, with five official nationalities and twelve ethnic minorities, added to the influences of three major religions (Orthodox, Roman Catholic, and Muslim) and three cultural heritages (Central European, Ottoman, and Veneto-Mediterranean). Socioeconomic development, as well as the quality and availability of health care, family planning, and social services, also varies considerably with the result that population growth rates vary regionally from very low to among the highest in Europe. The 1980 national rate of natural increase (0.8 percent) was tied with that of the USSR in fourth place among the nine socialist countries in that year and just ahead of the 0.7 percent natural increase rate of the United States (see Table 27.1).

After Albania, Yugoslavia is the least urbanized of the socialist countries (42 percent of the population: Table 27.1). Agricultural collectivization was abandoned in the early 1950s and 85 percent of arable land is owned and worked privately. A limit of 10 hectares (26 acres) on land that can be held by a single person helps counteract the influence that the large rural proportion of the population might have on increasing average family size; many heirs would mean splintering of already small land holdings.[11]

Following its political rupture with the Soviet Union in 1948, Yugoslavia gradually decentralized economic planning into a "socialist market economy" guided by workers' "self-management" and market forces. Its population has enjoyed a considerably higher consumer welfare than other socialist countries and much more personal freedom, including the freedom to travel. The latter has resulted in the temporary migration of as many as a million Yugoslavs to North and West Europe, mainly male "guestworkers." Frequent returns home mitigate the effect such family separations might have on the birth rate.

Decentralization extends to population policymaking, uniquely in Eastern Europe. National policy, embodied in a 1969 federal assembly "Resolution on The Family" and in the 1974 federal constitution, espouses individual freedom of choice in reproductive matters rather than demographic objectives. Specific measures to disseminate contraceptive information and supplies and to encourage less reliance—although no limitations—on abortion are left to constituent republics, provinces, and communes.

Romania

Romania's population of close to 22.5 million in 1981 is homogeneous. Some 88 percent of its people are ethnically Romanian and 80 percent belong nominally to the Romanian Orthodox Church.

Although still one of the least developed countries of Europe with over half the population in rural areas and an important collectivized agricultural sector, Romania has aimed for—and achieved—rapid industrial development. According to World Bank estimates, it has sustained one of the world's highest growth rates in GNP per capita since World War II—9.2 percent a year from 1960 to 1979—which places it just below Japan (9.4 percent) and far ahead of the United States (2.4 percent).[12] However, the level of GNP per capita head reached only $1,900 by 1979 (Table 27.1).

Romania's response to plunging fertility after abortion was liberalized in 1956 was the most dramatic of any in Eastern Europe. When the birth rate dropped to 14.3 births per 1,000 population in 1966 from 25.6 in 1955, abortion availability was curtailed drastically, with a month's warning, in order to "eliminate abortion as a form of birth control," and "stimulate the natality [to] reach 18 to 19 per 1,000, which should assure Romania a population of about 24 to 25 million inhabitants by 1990."[13] The birth rate rose abruptly to 27.4 in 1967, and although it has since drifted downward, it was still 18.6 per 1,000 in 1979. The use of "positive" pronatalist cash incentives has been less than in several other of the socialist countries.

German Democratic Republic

The GDR was established in 1949, following the collapse of reunification negotiations among the powers occupying Germany. With 17 million people in 1981, it is the most urbanized and industrialized of the Central and Eastern European socialist countries and enjoys the highest GNP per capita of the region. As in West Germany, with whom it still shares many characteristics, population growth trends have long been a major concern of state policy. Conditions were ripe for low fertility in the postwar decades with rapid economic growth, high educational levels, and heavy pressures on women to work outside the home to compensate for population losses during and after the war until the Berlin Wall was erected in 1961. Birth rates were also low and death rates relatively inflated because of a deficit of males in the reproductive ages and the relatively high proportion of elderly persons. The birth rate dropped below the death rate in 1969, but turned upward again in 1975 and exceeded the death rate by 1979. In West Germany, by contrast, the birth rate dropped below the death rate in 1972 and was still lower than the death rate in 1980 (see Table 27.1).

Probably because of low fertility, full legalization of abortion was delayed to 1972 in the GDR, longer than elsewhere in Eastern Europe. For the next two years, the birth rate dropped lower—as also happened in those years, however, in West Germany where abortion was still restricted. The upturn in the GDR's birth rate since 1976 coincides with a strengthening of pronatalist cash incentives that are currently among the most generous to be found anywhere.

Czechoslovakia

Czechoslovakia was established in 1918 as one of the successor states of the Austro-Hungarian empire. It is a federation of two republics—the Czech Socialist Republic, which includes Bohemia and Moravia, and the Slovak Socialist Republic. The population of 15.4 million in 1981 is about 65 percent Czech and 30 percent Slovak. Differences in language and culture are not large, especially compared to other European multinational states. While the northern Czech areas are somewhat more economically advanced, the entire country has long been among the most advanced and industrialized of European countries.

With the emergence of a socialist government in the late 1940s, Czechoslovakia began to stress heavy industry over agriculture and consumer goods and services and adopted a strict form of central planning. Adaptation of Soviet-type centralized planning to the complex industrial sector proved difficult; productivity and quality deteriorated and economic growth was irregular and slow by comparison to other Eastern European countries.[14] Efforts begun in the early 1960s to reform the economy, as well as to improve social and political conditions, flagged with the Soviet intervention of 1968. Although the economy was recentralized in the 1970s, subsequent reforms resulted in improved economic performance and a rise in living standards.

With the emphasis on industrialization over consumer goods, the need for women in the labor force, and liberalization of abortion in 1957, Czechoslovakia's birth rate dropped to a low of under 15 births per 1,000 population in 1968, down from more than 20 in 1955. In an effort to stem the fertility decline, the government expanded what was already a broad package of special welfare measures aimed at lessening the economic burden of childbearing. Abortion was also restricted mildly in 1973 as it had been in 1963 and 1964. By the end of the 1970s, as demographer Tomas Frejka observes:

> . . . young people in Czechoslovakia live under what is probably the most extensive, comprehensive, and costly fertility-related population policy regime in the developed world. The system has evolved over the past 30 years and includes efforts to inculcate fertility-supporting values through education in the schools and through the media; an effective maternal and child health-care system; liberal availability of contraceptives and induced abortion; and a diversified and costly system of pronatalist economic incentives.[15]

Although both the total fertility rate and the birth rate peaked in 1974 after rising from the lows of 1968, Frejka observes that "the total fertility rate in 1977 was still almost 20 percent higher than it had been in 1968, and the crude birth rate in 1978 was 15 to 45 percent higher than it might have been." He suggests that there is "reasonably solid ground" for the inference that this higher fertility was in part brought about by the pronatalist policy measures. As already noted, however, data for 1980 show a continuing fertility decline in Czechoslovakia.

Hungary

Left a remnant of its former self with the defeat of the Austro-Hungarian empire in World War I, Hungary has traditionally considered itself the Eastern outpost of Western civilization in Europe. Three-quarters of the population, which totaled just under 11 million in 1981, are Roman Catholic. The economy was predominantly agricultural before World War II, but with the emphasis on industry since then, the proportion of the labor force working in agriculture is now under 30 percent. Postwar economic growth was uneven until the adoption of the New Economic Mechanism in 1968. Under this system, the state retains ownership of the means of production and provides overall planning, but, within limits, enterprises (including collective farms) are allowed to direct their own activities and encouraged to show a profit. The result has been a modest improvement in living standards and improved economic growth until the disruptive effects of the world oil crisis in the late 1970s.

Hungary's population policy has been explicitly pronatalist since the late 1950s when fertility fell sharply following legalization of abortion in 1956. By 1962, the birth rate was 12.9 per 1,000 population—the lowest in the world at that time—and the total fertility rate was 1.8 births per woman. The decline halted with increases in family allowances and paid maternity leave during the 1960s and early 1970s. However, fertility remained below replacement level until 1974 when abortion was somewhat restricted for married women with less than three children. The October 1973 decision of the Council of Ministers announcing these restrictions also introduced new measures aimed at raising family size to about 2.4 children and promoting more effective contraceptive practice. As described by Hungarian demographers Klinger and Szabady, "The present aim of Hungarian population policy is to gradually increase the number of births, at least to ensure replacement of the population, which would otherwise become skewed toward the old."[16] After a brief spurt, however, fertility again turned down. By 1980, Hungary's birth rate was 13.9 per 1,000 population (compared with 15.8 in the United States) and the rate of natural increase, at 0.03 percent, was the lowest in Eastern Europe and among the lowest in the world.

Bulgaria

Bulgaria, with just under 9 million people in 1981, lies at the edge of Europe, heavily influenced by Turkish and Eastern Orthodox cultures. Of all the socialist countries of Eastern Europe, it is closest to the Soviet Union in language, culture, and history. At the end of World War II, it was one of the least industrailized countries in Europe, with more than 80 percent of the work force employed in agriculture. That proportion is today under 40 percent as the country has industrialized rapidly. Although still one of the lowest income countries of Europe, the country has developed rapidly, with much assistance from the Soviet Union and following the Soviet pattern of a centrally planned economy.

Bulgarian population policy has been described as "one that consistently promotes childbirth while preserving individual freedom to determine the number of children and the time of their birth."[17] The total fertility rate was already a low 2.4 births per woman when abortion was liberalized in 1956—the first country to follow the Soviet example—and continued to decline at the same pace to a low of just under 2 births per woman in 1966. Marked increases in pronatalist cash incentives and moderate restrictions in abortion availability in 1968 and again in 1973 prompted only brief spurts in fertility. By 1980 Bulgaria's birth rate of 14.3 per 1,000 population was the lowest in the country's history.

Albania

Albania is the maverick of Europe. Its GNP per capita is lowest ($840); its language has no close relatives; and—unique in Europe—some 70 percent of its population (estimated at 2.8 million in 1981) is of Moslem tradition, although Albania prides itself on being the first truly "atheist" state. Politically, it has retained a strong independent Stalinist ideology. It has long been at odds with the Soviet Union and with neighboring Yugoslavia, and, since the death of Mao, is no longer allied to China.

Demographically, Albania belongs among the world's less developed countries, with a rate of natural increase estimated at 2.1 percent for 1978 (Table 27.1). However, the birth rate declined from 44.5 per 1,000 population in 1955 to 27.4 in 1978. According to Stanford University demographer Dudley Kirk, "the specific causation of the fertility reduction is obscure," although "there is evidence of significant socioeconomic development."[18] The average age at marriage is relatively high (22.1 for women and 22.6 for men); 46 percent of women work outside the home; the urban proportion of the population rose from under one-fourth (21.3 percent) in 1945 to about 38 percent in 1979; and infant mortality fell from 121 per 1,000 live births in 1950 to "about 40 at present."

The fertility decline has occurred despite the officially stated policy that Albania can support (and needs) millions more inhabitants—

"a readily understandable position in view of the country's small size and acutely perceived political isolation," Kirk remarks. This pronatalism is supported by legal barriers to abortion and modern contraception. Abortion remains illegal except when pregnancy threatens a woman's life. Legally, contraceptives are neither produced nor imported and only condoms can be sold—in pharmacies for prophylactic purposes. Withdrawal is evidently the most widespread means of contraception backed up by illegal abortion.

Official pronatalism has not extended to positive incentive measures. Kirk observes:

> Apparently, there are no family allowances payments or tax reductions for children. The official position is that Albania has no taxes, making it the first country in the world to be completely free of imposed taxes and levies. Resources required to support public activities are provided through state management of the economy and are not available for private use.

CONCLUSIONS AND PROSPECTS

Eastern European policymakers can take satisfaction in the effect of pronatalist measures instituted in several of the nine socialist countries of the region during the late 1960s and early 1970s. Birth rates did indeed rise where access to legal abortion was restricted and/or young couples were offered substantial cash incentives to have more children. However, the subsequent downturn in fertility in Bulgaria, Czechoslovakia, Hungary, and Romania suggests that policy-induced upturns in fertility are temporary.

Demographic factors alone are likely to keep birth rates low in several of these countries during the 1980s and 1990s. Because of low birth rates in the 1960s, there will be fewer women in the prime childbearing ages of 20 to 29 in at least Poland, Czechoslovakia, Bulgaria, and Hungary. Also, in countries which still have a large rural population, such as Bulgaria, Hungary, Poland, Romania, and Yugoslavia, continuing urbanization is likely to mean lower national birth rates, because urban fertility is generally lower than in rural areas.

The experience of Bulgaria, Czechoslovakia, Hungary, and especially Romania suggests that the effect of restrictions on access to legal abortion is particularly short-lived. Couples quickly adjust their private behavior, practicing more efficient contraception or resorting to illegal abortion when necessary. Although restrictions on abortion have been publicly debated in recent years, particularly in Poland, no other Central or Eastern European socialist country has followed the 1966 Romanian example of sudden and severe restriction of access to legal abortion. (Theoretically, legal abortion in Romania is not now freely available to women under age 40 and those with less than four children; however, increasing numbers of abortions have been permitted on grounds of "mental health" in recent years.) While availability of modern contraceptives appears to have been manipulated from time to time in some countries, the German Democratic Republic and Hungary have succeeded in popularizing modern contraceptive methods (particularly the pill) as effective alternatives for reliance on abortion.

With pronatalist cash incentives, the main effect appears to have been to advance the timing of first and second births, without substantially increasing the number of third births—the birth that is crucial if national fertility is to remain above the average of 2.1 births per woman needed to replace the population over the long term. In several countries, however, these incentives may have prevented a further decline in the ultimate average family size. But this has been at a high budgetary cost—up to 10 percent of the annual government budget in at least Czechoslovakia. Moreover, to remain effective as pronatalist incentives, the size of the cash benefits must evidently be increased regularly to keep pace with rises in wages and prices and to counteract people's tendency to begin to take them for granted as social welfare benefits. Eastern European governments are also faced with the dilemma of how much women should be encouraged to stay at home to bear and rear future workers when the same women are currently so much needed in the workforce to help meet economic goals.

In sum, the experience of Eastern Europe suggests that policy efforts to influence private reproductive behavior can only be moderately successful so long as living conditions are such that women are determined not to have more than one or two children. It is uncertain if this would also apply in Western Europe where fertility in several countries has now fallen lower than it ever has in most Eastern European countries. While living conditions there may be more conducive to fertility than they are in Eastern Europe, women have come to share the goals of their sisters in Eastern Europe for full emancipation, including fulltime careers away from the home. There is also growing awareness everywhere that the psychological satisfactions of parenthood can be enjoyed by having only one or two children while also attaining a better life style.

The pronatalist economic measures of the socialist countries are fully justified on humanitarian grounds. As Czech demographer Zdenek Pavlik puts it:

> They help to increase the standard of living in specific social groups where it is the most desirable—among young cuples with small children, who bear the heavy financial burden. The measures help to compensate for this disadvantage and equalize this group with other social groups.[19]

However, their demographic effect appears to be limited.

REFERENCES

1. Haub, Carl, "The Population of the Soviet Union," *Population Profiles,* Second Series (Washington, Conn.: Center for Information on America, 1981).
2. Urlanis, B. Ts., "Demographic Policies in the Contemporary World" (in Russian). *The World Economy and International Relations,* May 1975, p. 111.
3. Weber, C. and A. Goodman, "The Demographic Policy Debate in the USSR," *Population and Development Review,* Vol. 7, No. 2 (June 1981) pp. 279–295.
4. Klose, Kevin, "Soviet Breadbasket Languishes Under Stalinist Legacy of Waste," *The Washington Post,* June 28, 1981, p. A20; Terri Minsky, "Soviets' Drought-Plagued Grain Harvest May Be Worst of 3 Bad Years, Analysts Say," *New York Times,* February 26, 1980.
5. Doder, Dusko, "Soviets Increase Prices of Fuel, Consumer Items," *The Washington Post,* September 15, 1981.
6. Davis, Christopher and Murray Feshbach, "Rising Soviet Infant Mortality," *Intercom,* July 1980, pp. 12–14.
7. Quoted in Spencer Rich, "Infant Mortality Soars in Russia, U.S. Study Finds," *The Washington Post,* June 26, 1980.
8. Darnton, John, "Lack of Essential Goods in Poland Is Making Life Almost Unbearable," *New York Times,* September 20, 1981.
9. Spivak, Jonathan, "Polish Health-Care System Is Beset by Shortages: Crisis is Major Social Problem Facing Solidarity," *Wall Street Journal,* October 16, 1981.
10. International Planned Parenthood Federation, *Open File,* October 10, 1981, p. 12.
11. Rusinow, D. I., "Yugoslavia," in H. Brown and A. Sweezy (eds.), *Population: Perspective, 1971* (San Francisco: Freeman, Cooper, 1972) pp. 269–288.
12. World Bank, *World Development Report 1981* (Washington, DC: 1981) Table 1.
13. Muresan, P. and I. M. Copil, "Romania," in B. Berelson (ed.), *Population Policy in Developed Countries* (New York: McGraw-Hill, 1974) pp. 367–68.
14. Zauberman, A., *Industrial Progress in Poland, Czechoslovakia, and East Germany, 1937–1962* (London: Oxford, 1964).
15. Frejka, Tomas, "Fertility Trends and Policies: Czechoslovakia in the 1970s," *Population and Development Review,* Vol. 6, No. 1 (March 1980) p. 89.
16. Klinger, A. and E. Szabady, "Patterns of Abortion and Contraceptive Practice in Hungary," in H. P. David et al. (eds.), *Abortion in Psychosocial Perspective: Trends in Transnational Research* (New York: Springer, 1978) pp. 168–198.
17. Stefanov, I. et al., *Demography in Bulgaria* (in Bulgarian) (Sofia: Nauka, Izkustvo, 1974).
18. Kirk, Dudley, "Albania," in Henry P. David and Robert J. McIntyre, *Reproductive Behavior: Central and Eastern Experience* (New York: Springer, 1981) p. 301.
19. Pavlik, Zdenek, "Baby Boom in Czechoslovakia?" *Intercom,* October 1978, pp. 8–9.

28
Fertility Policy in India

VINA MAZUMDAR

I

Social policy in modern India has been influenced by many visible and invisible, internal and external, complementary and contradictory ideas and forces. Two typical representatives of the last type are policies for women's development and policies for population control or population change.

It is easy to find reasons for such contradictions in the heterogeneous character of Indian society, with its multiplicity of linguistic, regional and religious cultures, social inequalities, and wide range of peoples in different stages of historical and economic development. These differences and disparities have often been hidden by assumptions and images of traditional society which were generally the result of inadequate knowledge and reflected certain class biases. The problem becomes even more complex with the influence of differing (sometimes warring) ideologies of social and economic development, the constraints provided by a democratic federal polity, and the compulsions and dependence that result from poverty and underdevelopment in a world economy characterized by gross inequalities. To add to this, there are many institutional biases—some traditional, some carried over from the days of colonial dependency and some originating from contemporary forces outside the country—that influence attitudes within organized establishments which determine social policies. The bureaucracy, the learned professions, political parties, social workers, the media, the designers, builders and evaluators of development in its multiple forms, all are prisoners, to a certain extent, of institutional structures that were fairly effective for a society which changed very little for centuries, but which have become dysfunctional in times of rapid socio-economic and political transformation.

II

The policies for women's welfare and development, and the constitutional pledge of "equality of status and opportunities" and non-discrimination on grounds of sex in law and public office were direct outcomes of the socio-political movements that convulsed Indian society during the hundred years before independence. They also represent a consensus among the elite, of non-opposition to women playing increasing, if not equal, roles in the process of national development.[1] Differences have, however, been sharp in the understanding of these roles or their implications, or the rationale for supportive measures to enable women to perform them adequately and effectively. Conservatives argue that children need healthier, better equipped, more conscious mothers to enable them to develop into conscientious, patriotic, constructive persons, and hence, women need greater attention from nation builders than they have received before. Progressives adopt a more direct position; they argue for equality of opportunity, dignity and social justice for women as well as men on grounds of human rights. Radicals go a step further, and demand removal of all discrimination against women and equal rights and obligations, irrespective of sex, in social economic and political spheres. All groups agree on the basic instruments for development of the human resources of any modern society—education, protection of individual rights by law, and support of essential social services, namely, health, education and welfare, by the State. Women as the "weaker sex" are generally regarded as standing in greater need of such services, not only for themselves, but also to ensure health and minimum living conditions for the future population. Even policies of population control have been justified as necessary to ensure better health, longer life, and better care for mothers and their children. This agreement between otherwise conflicting groups is a legacy of the movements that preceded independence.

The process of modernization begun during the colonial period developed both an inward and an outward thrust. The questioning of weaknesses within Indian society resulted in a movement for social reform in the Indian sub-continent, preceding the political movement for freedom from colonial rule. Improving the status of women was, from the beginning, a major objective of this movement. Historians generally have seen its origin in the influence of Western education and liberal ideas, the pressure of Christian missionary influence and the demonstration effect of the women's movement in Western countries. It is now possible to trace its indigenous roots also—in the pressure of urbanization on social institutions like the family, in the increasing communication gap between men and women in the urban families, in the slackening hold of traditional familial authority on the younger generation, and in the increasing threat of urban prostitution and criminal activities which represented threats to the traditional social structure.

The urban bias of the social reform movement has been evident to scholars for some time. What was not understood for a long time were the middle class bias and wrong assumptions about traditional roles of women latent in the movement to improve their status in society. This becomes clear if we analyze the reform movement by its perception of women's problems and the instruments chosen for intervention. The main enemy was identified as obscurantist customs and traditional attitudes. Women were seen mainly as victims of "purdah" or seclusion within the home, ignorance and oppressive marriage and property laws. Polygamy, child marriage, the oppressed condition of widows, denial of the right of remarriage and divorce, and inadequate rights to property were particularly singled out for attack.[2] The instruments for change were education, reform of marriage and property laws, elimination of purdah and, above all, the combating of traditional attitudes which regarded women as inferior beings.

The reformers believed that education and the removal of these oppressive customs would enable women to develop into better wives and mothers. They did not question the validity of women's traditional role as the homemaker with tasks confined to the care of the family. On the other hand, reform was defended as necessary to strengthen the hold of traditional values in society. Since women were the custodians of traditional culture, greater efficiency on their part would strengthen the family as the basic unit of social organization and insulate the younger generation from the destructive influences let loose by westernization.[3]

Even a cursory knowledge of the lives of the masses of women, particularly in the rural areas, would have demonstrated that these problems were unreal and irrelevant in their lives. A computation based on the 1931 Census reveals that less than 10 percent of the population of the Indian sub-continent at that time were affected by these oppressive marriage laws. The rest had always been permitted considerable freedom and flexibility in marriage, divorce and remarriage by the customs of their communities. Denial of education could hardly be regarded as sex discriminatory among the vast masses of illiterates. The same could be said about property laws for the vast millions who could claim little outside their name as property. Purdah was practised only in upper and middle class society, cutting across all communities. Among the working population, social norms were dictated by the necessities of economic survival. Women were men's partners as producers and sellers in agriculture, industry and traditional service. There was division of labour between the sexes, but the line of differentiation was not between work and home, between bread-winning and home-management, between harder and lighter tasks. The unit of labour was not the individual, but the family, or the household, with men, women and children sharing most tasks. This pattern continues wherever traditional forms of economic organization still prevail.

> Regional differences in the type and quantum of work expected of women expose the hollowness of the myths attached to these sex-linked roles. In the North-Eastern region, weaving is the monopoly of women but there are parts of India where a women may not touch the loom. Embroidery work is a male activity in Kashmir and a female one in the Punjab and elsewhere. In agriculture the variations in women's tasks in different regions prove the invalidity of the assumption that men are supposed to do the heavier work. In the Northern hill regions, women carry heavy logs weighing 200 to 300 lbs., slice the timber and help in wood chopping. What is important is that the tasks assigned to men are considered more prestigious in most communities and regions. Women are generally the unpaid family workers.[4]

The major role of women in certain types of economic activity can be realized from the fact that, until 1921, women outnumbered men in agricultural labour and formed about one third of the labour force in mining, quarrying, livestock, fishing and other occupations in the primary sector, in manufacturing industry, construction and trade and commerce.[5]

These traditional economic roles certainly did not relieve women from their housekeeping or child-nurturing roles, or did they guarantee for them equal status with men. There was not much option in the choice of occupation or life-styles, as the majority were expected to follow family trades. At the most, a women could migrate, along with the family, from starvation in village agriculture or industry, to tea, coffee, rubber or indigo plantations, coal or mica mines, or the new jute and textile industries in the town. But the substantial value of their contribution to the family economy enabled them to enjoy, relatively, a far higher degree of freedom in social relations, particularly vis-à-vis men, than their counterparts in upper and middle class society. Their basic problems lay in poverty, excessive workload, insecurity and exploitation by their wealthy employers, and not in oppressive customs. Except for child marriage (which was prevalent among the majority of the population, except the tribal groups), the social reformers failed to perceive the needs of this majority.

The second factor that affected policies for women was their spontaneous and massive participation in the struggle for freedom from the colonial rule. When women joined the political struggle in large numbers, the quality of their participation surprised even progressive leaders.[6] Equality between the sexes—at least in civil and political life—emerged as one of the goals of the freedom movement. The demand for equal franchise, which had been voiced by the nascent women's movement only in 1917 came to be accepted as a national objective by the majority of leaders by the 1930s and was incorporated in the political system after independence.

There is ample evidence that the movement for women's rights, particularly for the vote, in its earlier years was considerably influenced by its counterpart in Britain. The initial leadership of the women's organizations invariably came from upper class, educated families, and had extensive contacts with suffragist groups in the West. Their male supporters were close to the progressive liberal groups in Western countries and saw the women's desire to play some role in public life as a logical extension of the modernization process, and of education for women which was being advocated by all "modernizers."

The discordant, and perhaps unexpected, element in this picture of a gradual, smooth process—of improving women's position by some concessions to their aspirations, provided they qualified for the privilege by birth, education and social status[7]—was introduced by Mahatma Gandhi, who brought a completely new dimension to the debate on the women's question. Beginning from the basic premise that the subjugation and exploitation of women were the product of "man's interested teachings, and women's acceptance of them," he broke away from the reform tradition. He preached a different philosophy—not only of absolute equality of rights between the sexes, but of the pragmatic necessity of enrolling women's support—to transform the nationalist struggle for the transfer of political power from British to Indian hands into a social revolution. This revolution would abolish illiterate, high castes and the untouchables, workers and nonworkers, the industrial capitalist and the rural peasant, an authoritarian, oppressive alien government and the masses of the people of the country.

The non-exploitative social order that Gandhi visualized had to be achieved by the participation of the mass of the people and the resolution of social conflicts by non-violent protests. Women, he claimed, were better than men in waging non-violent protests because they had greater capacity for sacrifice and endurance, were less self-seeking, and had more moral courage. They must, therefore, become conscious of their historic role, reject the disgraceful role of being 'man's plaything', and extend their capacity for love and sacrifice beyond their families to "embrace the whole of humanity." Equality of legal and political rights, freedom from any coercion from the family or the society, and autonomy to choose their own way of moral and self-development were only basic conditions to enable women to play their destined role.[8]

One of the justifications for Gandhi's economic policy of reviving the village economy and cottage industry was to restore to women their lost economic strength. The decline of village industry because of increasing competition from mass-produced goods of modern technology and capitalist modes of production had eroded considerably women's productive roles and increased their burden and problems. This process had to be arrested through the revival of village industries and the restoration of women's economic base. Excessive burden of labour for no return and discrimination in wages demonstrated their exploited position.

Today the sole occupation of a woman amongst us is supposed to be to bear children, to look after her husband and otherwise to drudge for the household . . . not only is the woman condemned to domestic slavery, but when she goes out as a labourer to earn wages, though she works harder than man, she is paid less.[9]

The radical note struck by Gandhi found a close parallel in the ideas of Karl Marx which influenced socialists of different shades in India:

The emancipation of women and their equality with men are impossible and must remain so as long as women are excluded from socially productive work and restricted to housework, which is private.[10]

These two strains of social ideas, from different sources, were fused in the mind of Jawaharlal Nehru, who played a dominant role in the shaping of social policy in the first decade after independence. As President of the Indian National Congress in 1931, he steered the resolution that pledged the nation to a policy of sex-equality in law, and political and economic life after independence. As a leading member of the Constituent Assembly, he incorporated the pledge into specific articles in the Constitution of the Indian Republic. As Prime Minister, he steered the laws improving the rights of Hindu women in marriage, guardianship and inheritance, and special labour laws for the protection of women workers in factories, mines and plantations, making the passage of these laws a prestige issue for his government. A new agency, the Central Social Welfare Board, was created to organize special measures to assist women, particularly in the rural areas, in their problems:

We talk about a welfare state and direct our energies towards its realization. That welfare must be the common property of everyone in India and not the monopoly of the privileged groups as it is today. If I may be allowed to lay greater stress on some, they would be the welfare of children, the status of women and the welfare of the tribal and hilly people in our country. Women in India have a background of history and tradition behind them, which is inspiring. It is true, however, that they have suffered much from various kinds of suppression and all these have to go so that they can play their full part in the life of the nation.[11]

The First Five Year Plan admitted the significance of the new rights conferred on women, and held that they called for adequate provision of education and health services, including family planning. The implications of equality were clearly stated in the objectives for women's education:

The general purpose and objectives of women's education cannot, of course, be different from the purpose and objectives of men's education. At the secondary and even at the university stage women's education should have a vocational or occupational bias.[12]

The early fifties thus came to be regarded as the period of women's triumph, with middle class women—from a background of restricted lives, confined to the roles of wives and mothers—entering administrative, professional and political employment as the equals of men. Institutions of professional education in law and technology which had until then barred women's entry, were compelled to admit them. Women entered new occupations in the modern sector in increasing numbers. Women from aristocratic families, both Hindu and Muslim, began to abandon purdah and sought public offices. Women were elected to Parliament and the State Legislatures, became Cabinet ministers, governors of States, ambassadors, vice-chancellors of universities and judges, and exercised their vote in increasing numbers in successive general elections. Local self-governing bodies, both in urban and rural areas, were asked to include a few women on their panels by nomination, if they did not come through election channels.

All these could suggest, as they did to most people concerned with social policy in India, that "the revolution in the status of women," and the extension of their roles in society were well on the way. But the review undertaken in the early seventies by the Committee on the Status of Women in India reached a very different conclusion: "Though women do not constitute a minority numerically, they are acquiring the features of one by the inequality of class, status and political power."[13]

Three years after the Committee's Report, a group of social scientists have drawn attention in an even sharper manner to what they call "the national neglect of women."[14] The alarming deterioration in women's status, their research proves, began several decades ago, but has accelerated in the last three decades. Demographic trends, with growing differential between men and women in mortality, access to health care and medical services, literacy, education and vocational training, and accelerated decline in employment provide, in their view, "indisputable evidence of steady decline in the value of women in society." The best indicator of this trend is the persistent decline in the sex-ratio in the population:

> Unless the economic and social utility of women is enhanced in the eyes of their families and the nation by opportunities to take part in socially and economically productive roles, the national neglect of women will continue. Erosion of productive roles emphasizes women's position as consumers and bearers of children, makes their lives cheap and easily expendable through increasing malnutrition and mortality, reduces employability through inadequate training opportunities and increases economic discrimination and exploitation.[15]

Development plans and supportive services have tended to view women only as target groups for social services, ignoring their productive roles. In consequence, development itself has contributed to the massive displacement of women from agricultural, industrial and trading occupations. The marginal increase in the number of women in the service sector cannot offset this trend, but the visibility of middle-class women in white-collar occupations has helped to build an illusion of progress, hiding the stark reality of the shrinking roles of the majority. Even in the service sector, much of the increased employment is in poverty-oriented occupations, that is, personal and domestic services generated by population increase, especially in urban areas. Prostitution and traffic in women, the commercial use of females for career and business promotion, and illegal activities all point to growing use of women as commodities. The sex-specific roles prescribed by traditional society, even though limited, guaranteed greater dignity to the majority than its modern counterpart.

One traditional role that has expanded is the use of women as vehicles for display of wealth and status. Previously restricted to the feudal aristocracy, whose status required keeping their women idle and bejewelled, this practice is now imitated by new or aspiring entrants to the middle class. The payment of dowry to obtain a husband for a young woman, which had become difficult during the thirties because of opposition from the Gandhian women's movement, has, in spite of a prohibitory law, increased in volume and incidence, affecting even communities which had followed the opposite practice of paying brideprice until a few years ago.[16] There are many such examples of "regression from the norms developed during the freedom struggle." In politics, the emergence and fall of a woman Prime Minister has not succeeded in arresting the steady decline in the number of women in the legislative bodies, and in the parties' sponsorship of women for such positions. Gandhi's dream seems indeed to have receded very far from the social horizon of contemporary India.

III

The only explanations now available for these developments are still hypothetical, lacking empirical evidence. The patriarchal ideology inherent in the capitalist path of development; the choice of technology and forms of economic organization imposed by international capital; blind imitation of Western materialist values, life and consumption styles to the detriment of indigenous cultural values; urban middle-class and westernized bias in planning; over-concentration on economic growth and neglect of social development; increasing population and income disparity; or differential spread of the fruits of development among different classes of the population—one may select one or more of these explanations according to one's own ideological inclinations. Whether a substantial link exists between population growth, policies for its control, and the trends in roles and status of women remains to be investigated.

Looking at the evolution of the population question in India, one can note certain significant trends. At a time when apprehensive and critical views of India's population growth were limited to members of the British administration, and sparked off indignant protests from nationalist leaders who regarded it as an imperialist conspiracy to explain away the failure to solve India economic problems, the women's organizations were the first to demand the provision of birth control services. When questioned about this "dangerous trend" by some orthodox persons, Gandhi replied that women should have the right not to have children or to limit the number of children, though he would prefer sexual abstinence to contraceptive methods for this purpose. In his appeals to young people of both sexes to contribute a part, if not all, of their lives to the cause of national freedom and reconstruction, he exhorted them to forego or postpone having children, as this would interfere with their commitment to the national cause. Family planning services were developed only by some voluntary women's organizations in some of the metropolitan cities and were used only by educated families.

In the post-independence period, with a government committed to rapid economic development, the population question gradually emerged as a critical issue. During the First and Second Five Year Plans, the problem of population growth and the need for family planning were viewed as a long term objective, depending essentially on "improvement in living standards and more widespread education, especially among women." The Planning Commission, however, admitted the need for positive measures to spread family planning education and techniques among the people. Efforts to restrain population growth were seen only as a complement to a massive development effort.

From the Third Plan, however, the control of population growth, with time-bound targets for reducing the birth rate, heavy investment in the administrative network to mount the family planning programmes on the lines of a military operation, and the adoption of financial incentives to make sterilization acceptable to the poor, emerged as crucial features of government policy. Abortion in cases of contraceptive failure was legalized and some State Governments began to initiate systems of disincentives, such as denial of maternity benefits to women after the birth of a third child. This change in emphasis relied heavily on the clinical, rather than the welfare, approach to family planning. The general health and welfare services suffered relatively as resources were diverted for family planning services. The administration of this programme became a parallel empire within the Ministry of Health in all the States, competing successfully for allocation of both funds and personnel.

In the case of women, maternity and child health services, adult education and family welfare—all of which had been identified as essential to improve their status in the earlier plans—suffered from lack of resources, and family planning began to be propagated as the most important developmental programme for women. Research sponsored both by government and external agencies which offered aid to India to control her population growth sought to emphasize improvement in the status of women as a *direct* consequence of acceptance of family planning. Unfortunately for such propagandists, most quality research in this field invariably indicated that the relationship was far more complex, viz. that improved status of women, with rise in the age of marriage, education, employment, better living conditions and general awareness in concert have a direct impact on the adoption of family planning methods. Evaluating the role of family planning in changing women's status in India, the Committee on the Status of Women observed:

> If the sexual role were the main determinant of male dominance and authority in a society, there would have been no communities in the world where the women are dominant, or equal, members. The status of women in any society depends on a complex set of social, economic, demographic and political variables, among which the woman's ability to control the size of her family could be a contributory factor. But in our view, emphasizing it as a direct cause of improvement of women's status is somewhat exaggerated, and ignores the evolution of women's status in different societies. The matriarch of many ancient civilizations and primitive communities certainly enjoyed a much higher status than the women with complete control on the size of their families in the developed, modern societies of the West today. Knowledge of family planning techniques may have liberated Western women from excessive pregnancies, but it has not basically changed their status in these societies either economically or politically. Even in the sphere of social attitudes, with all the progress in education, and different types of social freedoms and changing roles, their image as sex-symbols has been intensified, not eliminated.[17]

The draft Fifth Plan sought to correct the perspective, in view of the growing realization of the unpopularity and failure of the programme among many sections, and evaluation reports that coercive methods could not overcome the socio-economic and psychological resistance to population control. Official statements in 1973 to 1974 indicated the Government of India's return to the original philosophy—that "development was the best contraceptive." The draft Fifth Five-Year Plan called for a minimum needs programme for the poverty-stricken masses. Extension of health services, integrated with family planning, particularly for the vulnerable groups—children, pregnant women and nursing mothers—was an important feature of the proposed programme.

Unfortunately this wisdom was abandoned during the recent period of national emergency, when the draconian powers assumed by the Government were used to revive the policy of reducing the birth-rate rapidly by all kinds of questionable methods. "Sterilization became the symbol of tyrannical denial of all that one was entitled to expect from one's government."[18]

The minimum needs and employment programmes which were the central theme of the draft Fifth Plan were whittled down to unimportant adjuncts in the final Plan, with no integral relationship to the design of long-term economic growth. The national population policy announced in April 1976 stated clearly that it was "not a practical solution" to wait for education and economic development to bring about a drop in fertility. The results of the national elections of February 1977 have demonstrated clearly that population control divested of other developmental measures can bring about the fall of even the most powerful government.

One consequence of the heavy investment in family planning was the proliferation of research. This is the one sector of social research which has received maximum encouragement, from both government and other funding agencies, national, international and foreign (i.e., donor agencies from rich countries). Such research has progressively revealed that fertility is influenced by a complex of many factors, social, economic, cultural and political[19], in which the individual's choice may play a minor role. "Birth control and the small family norm have to find social acceptance before finding individual acceptance."[20]

While many of these studies admit that the status of women plays a critical role in acceptance of family planning, they do not display any clear understanding of variations in women's roles and statuses in different classes and fail to see their influence on fertility choices. In assuming traditional values to be the source of resistance, and depending on propaganda regarding the advantages of the small family for the future, the propagators of this policy display biases similar to those that have influenced policies for women.

The logic and the rationale for the small family rest on the experience of the established middle class, which seeks to ensure its future by investment in income-generating property, and the education of children. Since the majority of this class comes from high caste Hindus or the aristocracy of other communities, their current aspiration harmonizes with their traditional cultural values, which attach higher status to non-manual occupations and emphasize careful nurturing of children. As the extended family begins to crack under the pressure of new socio-economic demands, and occupations shift outside the home, the emphasis on the nurturing[21] of children, and "extended infantilism" puts increasing pressure on women, particularly in nuclear families. The breakdown of the extended family reduced the family pressure on young women to have more children. Since young women in this class also enjoy relatively easy access to education, better nutrition and modern health services, they are able to ensure far better chances of survival for their children. The care of children is socially accepted as a full-time occupation despite the inroads made on the mother's role by the educational system, peer-groups and other extra-familial institutions.

At the other end of the social structure, the family's subsistence depends on the household economy,

> Where little—be it agriculture, household industry, fishing, lumbering, forest-produce gathering, livestock and poultry keeping, the informal sector in urban livelihoods, construction, petty trade or commerce, or non-powered transportation, or the whole range of unorganized services—is possible without substantial contribution of unpaid family work, mainly for keeps, by all members of the household. . . . This is necessary to enable the head of the household to extract the economic surplus from the pool of unrecompensed family labour. Such a process of extraction of surplus is made possible by the semblance of democratic sharing of whatever is available—food or starvation—within the household. . . . So long as unpaid family labour remains the mainstay of the great bulk of economic activity in the country, the one-or-two child family will remain a far cry. . . .[22]

Future is a meaningless concept when your entire effort is concentrated on daily survival. Malnutrition and high infant mortality, lack of access to education and health services, and the low cost of child-rearing when the children join the labour force from the age of five or six, make a large family a rational choice. At least that way one can ensure that one or two may survive to maturity.

Between these two comes a third group—the new entrants to, or the aspirants to the middle class, risen through education or some increase in prosperity or security from a job of supposedly higher status than traditionally enjoyed by the group. For this group, too, the small family appears unnatural. The slight improvement in economic or social prospects "expands the horizon of expectations—children are seen as investments, who can receive these benefits and yield highest over-life-time" returns. "Enterprise being seen by an Indian as centered on the household, anything that goes to enhance the wealth of the household is well worth investing in."[23]

A typical characteristic of these mobile groups from the bottom of the pyramid is the sharp change in women's roles. The prosperous farmer, the industrial worker receiving higher wages or a first generation white-collar worker react uniformly in this matter. Their women are withdrawn from economic activity outside the home as this is believed essential to improving the family's social status.[24]

High fertility among these women is certainly not only from economic considerations, nor is it due to high infant mortality, because the access of this class to modern health services is far better now than that previously enjoyed. The explanation, it appears to me, has to be sought in other factors. If women cease to be economic assets to the family and become liabilities instead (as manifested in the increasing incidence and volume of dowry), and at the same time are not social assets through education and adaptive ability to their new social circumstances, the only way to maintain their value within the family would appear to be through bearing more children. This problem seems to call for much greater investigation than it has so far received.

The class variable in fertility research has tended to be over-simplified, using income as the indicator of class status. In societies like India's, however, the generational position is often a more important indicator of acceptance in a new class, rather than income or even education. The *Bhadralog*[25] find it much harder to assimilate the lower orders, whatever their income position. Their attitude to new entrants retains a social distance at least for one generation. Education is regarded as the great leveller of such class distinctions, but since education is not widespread among adult women of this class, its effect remains limited.

In regarding fertility as the result of individual choice by couples, the authors of the policy of population control ignore all these variables, as well as the inter-relationship among the class-structure, the roles of women and children and the manner in which these are being affected by the process of economic change. Increasing disparity in income and growing unemployment and underemployment among both men and women indicate a failure to develop a substitute for the household economy, or to improve the demographic quality of the population. In the Indian context, the latter depends on reduction of infant mortality and malnutrition, elimination of illiteracy, and minimum health services. These, in turn, depend on universal employment and raising the economic value of women "by cutting down on unpaid family labour and introducing a system of social accounting where appropriate money-value is imputed to the work of women."[26]

Such a change would threaten the present power-structure, which rests on inequalities and links among property, political power, ownership of land, and lineage systems—all of which seem to have an indirect influence on fertility, and on women's status and roles. The evidence of an inter-relationship between the pattern of development and these aspects of population change can be inferred from a simple periodization of development and population trends. The Indian economy experienced its first major growth during the first world war, slumped during the depression, but started growing again during the thirties. The second world war provided a further spurt, which continued well into the fifties, after which it began to slow down, except for a short period of buoyancy during 1973 to 1974. The decline in women's work participation began around 1920, and accelerated after 1951. The sex-ratio in the population remained constant between 1921 and 1931, but dropped sharply after that. Regions which had a high sex-ratio and considerably higher work-participation of women changed character during the twenties, and began a declining trend in both the sex-ratio and the work-participation of women. The Scheduled Castes and tribal communities, which traditionally have maintained very high work-participation of women, and a relatively higher sex-ratio (particularly among the tribes), appear now to be joining the mainstream trend. Some ongoing studies indicate that in many of these areas, large-scale development and commercialization precipitate these changes even if they do not initiate them. The first sharp increase in the Indian population also took place in the twenties, and was accelerated during the fifties. Hitherto this increase has been attributed only to control of epidemics. While it is not suggested that public health measures played no role in this growth, recent investigations indicate sharp differentials in access to health services, between urban and rural areas, between rich and the poor, between men and women. It is necessary to investigate now whether other factors, like the changing roles and status of women and the nature of the development process itself also contributed to this growth.

A population policy, to be effective, will have to take this range of factors and variations into consideration. Just as compulsory schooling, or restrictions on the age of marriage become impossible to enforce where economic and social necessities go against them, the small family can only be acceptable when the family's situation makes it appear reasonable and attractive. The critical issues in bringing about this transformation lie in the family's economic position, the value of the woman, which depends on the roles that she performs for the family and the community, and the structure of social inequalities.

The unconscious middle-class bias in the population control policy has failed to understand the basic contradiction between the household economy of the poor and the individualist economy of the capitalist modern sector. The percolation of middle-class norms of behaviour to lower levels of society may create greater demand for social services, but they also increase the proportion of dependents in the population. The impact of this on sex-roles is disastrous—both for women's status and the population growth.

NOTES

1. The terms of reference of the Committee on the Status of Women in India appointed by the Union Government in 1971 included a review of legal and administrative provisions which sought to improve women's status, and suggestion of measures "which would enable women to play their full and proper role in building up the nation."
2. While these problems were more acute for Hindu women, it was admitted by Muslim, Parsee and other reformers that similar evils had also crept into their communities under Hindu influence.
3. For a more elaborate discussion of these ideas see Vina Mazumdar, "The Social Reform Movement from Ranade to Nehru" in B. R. Nanda (ed.), *Indian Women from Purdah to Modernity,* Delhi: Vikas, 1976. Also *Towards Equality*—Report of the Committee on the Status of Women in India, Government of India, 1974, Chapter 3.
4. *Status of Women in India:* synopsis of the Report of the National Committee, Indian Council of Social Science Research & Allied Publishers, 1975 pp. 28–29.
5. Advisory Committee on Women's Studies, Indian Council of Social Science Research, *Critical Issues on the Status of Women: Employment, Health, Education: Suggested Priorities for Action* 1977, p. 25.
6. Jawaharlal Nehru, *Discovery of India.* Bombay: Asia, 1972, p. 27.
7. The Constitutional Reforms of 1919 authorized the elected legislatures in the provinces to concede votes to women if they so desired. The Reforms Act of 1921 enfranchised a very small fraction of the Indian population, including women, if they possessed qualifications of wifehood, property and education. The Government of India Act of 1935 increased the number of enfranchised Indians and relaxed some of the previous qualifications. Women over 21 could vote provided they fulfilled the conditions of property and education.
8. M. K. Gandhi, *Young India,* 15 December 1921, 8 October 1921, 21 March 1927, *Harijan* 4 August 1940. See also Vina Mazumdar, op. cit.
9. M. K. Gandhi, *Young India,* 26 February 1918; quoted in *Towards Equality,* op. cit., p. 148.
10. Karl Marx and Friedrich Engels, *Selected Works,* Vol. 2, Moscow: Progress, 1972, p. 310.
11. Jawaharlal Nehru: foreword to *Social Welfare in India,* The Planning Commission, 1955.
12. Government of India, *First Five-Year Plan,* New Delhi, 1952, Chapter 33.
13. *Towards Equality,* op. cit., p. 372.
14. Indian Council of Social Science Research: Advisory Committee on Women's Studies, op. cit., p. 1.
15. Ibid, p. 2.
16. T. Scarlett Epstein: *South India Yesterday, Today & Tomorrow,* London: Macmillan, 1973: also M. N. Srinivas: *Changing Position of Indian Women:* Thomas Huxley Memorial Lecture: Royal Anthropological Society, London: 1976. Published in *Man* (new series), 12, 12 August 1977.
17. *Towards Equality,* op. cit., p. 232.
18. Asok Mitra: "National Population Policy in Relation to National Planning." *Population and Development Review,* New York, 3, 3 September 1977.
19. For a brief review of sociological studies on Indian fertility behaviour, see M. N. Srinivas and E. A. Ramaswamy: *Culture and Human Fertility in India,* New Delhi: Oxford University Press, 1977.
20. Ibid, p. 29.
21. J. Bernard, *The Future of Motherhood,* New York: Dial, 1974.
22. Asok Mitra, op. cit., pp. 18–19.
23. Ibid, p. 12.

24. T. Scarlett Epstein, op. cit.: M. N. Srinivas *Changing Position of Indian Women, Man* (new series). Vol. 12 (2), August 1977 also D.R. Gadgil: *Women in the Working Force in India,* Bombay: Asia, 1965.
25. Literally meaning the "respectable classes" or the gentry, distinguished from *Chotolog,* meaning "small people" or the unrefined masses.
26. Asok Mitra, op. cit., p. 33.

29
Resistance to the One-Child Family

JEFFREY WASSERSTROM

B: *Without a baby boy, it will be hard to get things done in the future!*
A: *But this kind of thinking doesn't make any sense! Chairman Mao said: "The times have changed; men and women are the same. The things which male comrades can do can also be done by female comrades." Don't attach more importance to boys and less to girls.*

excerpt from "Changing Customs and Habits," a family planning propaganda skit; Orleans, 1979:52.

In the first quarter of 1982, in Meizhuang Brigade, Junqang Commune, eight babies were born, with the three male babies doing well, but three of the female babies were drowned and two other females were abandoned.

Findings of an investigation carried out by the Anhui Provincial Women's Federation; *Renmin ribao,* April 7, 1983.

The Chinese leadership has decided that China's future well-being depends on the government's ability to limit population growth. This decision has led it to launch an ambitious and problematic drive to reduce the size of Chinese families through a "planned birth" campaign. Its approach is ambitious in that it calls for demographic changes that are both drastic and swift. It is problematic because in order to accomplish these changes, policies that rip at the heart of traditional Chinese values must be adopted.

Population policy was changeable during the early years of the People's Republic. Throughout the 1950s and 1960s population control was alternately embraced as a practical necessity and viewed as theoretically suspect because classical Marxism holds that Malthusian constraints only operate within capitalist states. Policy oscillations were frequent during these period as leadership groups more sensitive to theoretical purity gave way to more "pragmatic" ones, and as demographic realities changed.[1]

In recent years, however, the situation has stabilized considerably. The practical necessity of limiting population growth has become increasingly accepted, as has the legitimacy of non-Malthusian theories of population control (for a full elaboration of these theories, see Tien, 1980). As a result, official support for family planning has become more unequivocal, and population control has assumed an ever higher national priority. This evolutionary process begun in the 1970s reached two important watersheds in 1978. First, in that year family planning became enshrined in the reformulated national constitution: "The state advocates and encourages family planning" (quoted in Orleans, 1979:3). Second, in the same year the boldest population control campaign ever attempted in China was launched: the one-child family campaign. The campaign was based on the controversial premise that couples should stop procreating after the birth of their first child, whether that child be male or female.

As radical as this notion is in China, the one-child family campaign has met with much success. The authorities have tried to sweeten the prospect of having only a single child with a combination of remunerative and normative rewards. (Coercive measures, though always officially condemned, have also doubtless played a part in the success, at least in some locales.)

Despite its successes, the one-child family policy has certainly not gone unopposed. This is not surprising because a nation of one-child families naturally means that about half the couples will have no sons, a fact that is bound to lead to difficulties given the immense symbolic and practical importance of male offspring within Chinese society. The number of articles that have recently appeared in the Chinese press criticizing the continuing desire, particularly among peasants, to have at least one son suggests that opposition to current population policy may be great indeed.[2] Reports of female infanticide, abuse of women who give birth to daughters, and other manifestations of this continuing preference for sons show clearly that such opposition is often translated into active forms of resistance.

This resistance is highly significant, not only because of the human misery involved but also because the continuing preference for sons, which is its root cause, calls into question many common assumptions regarding male-female equality in contemporary China. It also brings into focus in yet another context the more general question of the level of success of the party's attempts to reshape the traditional attitudes and beliefs of the Chinese peasantry. This chapter will attempt to give an overview of the problem of resistance to the one-child family by examining the forms this resistance is taking, the ways the Chinese authorities are trying to curtail it, and certain problematic features of the interpretation of the situation that underlie the measures the government is taking. Before starting this general task, though, some prefatory remarks concerning the most disturbing and tragic form of resistance—female infanticide—are in order.

The recent reappearance of female infanticide in rural China is a complex phenomenon, one that must be understood on its own terms, as the result of specific cultural, historical and—above all—economic factors. If these factors are not taken into account, it can all too easily be misunderstood, or even used as ammunition by those wishing to convince us of the "barbarity" of the Chinese people, or the CCP, or both.[3] The reality surrounding female infanticide is this:

First, female infanticide is *not* a coercive measure used by the authorities to limit population growth. This fact should be obvious. However, because a number of Western articles speak of infanticide and forced abortions in the same breath (see *Far Eastern Economic Review,* April 28, 1983: 50–53), the two have regrettably become linked in some people's minds. Actually, female infanticide is a negative reaction to population directives, not a coercive means of enforcement. It is thus more similar analytically to wife-beating associated with the birth of daughters, refusal of couples with one or more children to stop procreating, and other such phenomena than it is to forced abortion. Furthermore, whereas the CCP may or may not condone forced abortions (an issue that lies outside the scope of this chapter), it has always opposed female infanticide and the abuse of women who bear daughters, and during the past two years it has taken important steps to try to end the resurgence of such acts of defiance.

Second, the PRC's demographic situation is critical: China has a huge population, an ever increasing number of youths reaching childbearing age, and limited arable land and other natural resources. The government's ability to keep the nation's more than one billion people from starving has amazed demographers for years. There is little chance of it continuing to be able to do so, with roughly 20 million youths a year reaching marriageable age (*Beijing Review,* 1983, No. 7: 21), without taking steps very different from those taken in the past to limit population growth. Thus its decision to try to create a nation of one-child families—to which female infanticide is an extreme negative reaction—is understandable if not reasonable.

Third, female infanticide is seldom, if ever, simply an expression of senseless cruelty. Though undeniably cruel, it is usually committed only by people faced with desperate circumstances who see no other way to ensure their survival. Traditionally, female infanticide was a last resort of peasant families threatened by starvation. When parents were driven to kill their own children, it was a sign of how dire their poverty was; that those they killed were daughters was a reflection of the antifemale bias embedded in traditional Chinese culture, Confucian and folk alike, and the fact that sons had much greater potential for benefiting the family economically. Female infanticide was virtually never practiced by the gentry, who held their daughters in at least as low regard as did the peasants; this suggests how great was the causal role of poverty. Given that the Chinese kinship system is both patrilineal and patrilocal, only sons were full and permanent members of, and contributors of labor power to, their parents' family. To have at least one and preferably many sons was therefore seen as one of life's most basic necessities. Only a son could guarantee that the family name would survive and the parents would be succored in their old age. A man had not done his duty to his ancestors—in the Chinese system of ancestor worship male offspring played the crucial role—or secured his own economic and spiritual well-being until he had a son. A woman, on the other hand, was expected to bear her husband an heir and was not fully accepted into his family or village until she did so. In short, traditionally sons fulfilled vital symbolic and economic functions, whereas daughters were seen as merely temporary members of the household at best and extra mouths to feed at worst.

Contemporary female infanticide is, like that of earlier times, the result of a combination of ideological and material factors. Some peasants are no doubt still influenced by traditional ideas concerning ancestor worship and keeping the family line alive. And the frustration such people feel if their first child is female (given that under current policy they will be denied further chances to fulfill their filial obligations) contributes to the present problem. Nevertheless, as in traditional China, in precipitating infanticide structural factors that make sons more advantageous than daughters play an even greater role than such super-structural ones. Of the several "structural factors" discussed in this article (below), it is the implementation of the "rural responsibility system," under which the household displaces the commune, brigade, or team as the main productive and distributive unit, that has made having at least one son a practical necessity again for many Chinese peasants. In the absence of a developed rural social welfare system, the only way peasants can feel secure about their old age is by knowing they will have a son to take care of them later on. Responsibility for caring for parents still tends to rest primarily with male offspring, and almost invariably daughters still move to their husband's village. Female infanticide is thus a last resort of those hoping to ensure their survival. As in the past, it is proof of desperation, not a sign that the Chinese are inherently cruel. Infanticide has been practiced for similar reasons in many other times and places, and members of virtually every culture have been known to commit comparably heinous acts with faced with survival-threatening circumstances.

The current resurgence of female infanticide should therefore be interpreted as unintended consequence of steps taken by the Chinese government to solve the population problem, steps that although undeniably radical, clearly seem to it to be necessary. The fundamental contradiction between limiting births and the culturally embedded preference for and practical necessity of sons is at the heart of the resurgence. The continuing influence of traditional ideas and the lack of a developed rural social welfare program both contribute to the current problem. These factors, rather than an inherent lack of human feeling among the people of China or malevolence on the part of their government, are the cause of female infanticide.

ACTS OF RESISTANCE

For the good of the country, the good of the collective, and the good of our families we must all have only one child.

From a *Zhongguo Funü* article entitled "For the Sake of the Four Modernizations Glorify Only Giving Birth to One Child"; 1979, No. 8:24.

But whatever it takes, even at the cost of our lives, we women still want to have sons. . . . Why would we risk our lives to do this bitter thing which endangers the nation and ourselves? Because in our village, if a woman does not have a son, she suffers from discrimination and mistreatment which is even greater in its bitterness than this risking of our lives!

From a letter to the editor in *Renmin ribao* jointly written by fifteen women who had given birth to daughters; February 23, 1983.

For all its apparent novelty, the one-child family policy is in essence less a departure from than a radical intensification of earlier birth control programs. Many of its components, such as the way it links family planning with broader health care issues and uses peer group pressure to encourage birth limitation, are easily recognizable features of the general Chinese population control model (as described in Chen, 1976; Orleans, 1972; and Aird, 1972). But the model has been modified in certain important ways to fit current needs.

The most significant way in which the model has been modified is that its guiding principle—that a small family norm should replace the traditional large family ideal—has been taken to a new extreme. Current policy is based on the notion that each couple should have only "one child if possible, two at the most, with a period of three years between them" (quoted in Goodstadt, 1982: 37). Some allowance was originally made in 1979—to a lesser degree is still being made—for regional differences. For instance, it is stated that although urban couples *must* limit themselves to one child, rural couples *should* do likewise and in any event not have a third child. Some lessening of birth control strictures also applied at first to minority regions (see *Beijing Review*, 1983, No. 7). But the overall intent of the policy from the start was and continues to be simply to keep as many couples as possible from having more than a single offspring.

The style of current birth control-related propaganda is also different from that used in the past. Chinese population control campaigns have always relied heavily upon ideological efforts to gain acceptance for birth control methods and to popularize new family size norms (see Orleans, 1978, for translations of a variety of songs and plays used for these purposes). The one-child family drive is no exception in this regard; nevertheless the propaganda that accompanies it is distinctive in that it puts much more emphasis on planning births in order to benefit the nation's and one's own economic self-interest and a good deal less on the "redness" of following party directives. Thus, for example, articles expressly linking population control to the achievement of the Four Modernizations have appeared in popular magazines (see *Zhongguo funü,* 1979, No. 8:24); journalists have extolled the good sense shown by those who enthusiastically comply with population control directives, such as the couple praised in *Zhongguo funü* for competing with each other over who would be allowed to be sterilized (1979, No. 4:45); and billboards showing happy couples with single children—usually daughters—and carrying captions dealing with the joys and economic advantages of small families. In a word, propaganda seems to have become more compatible with Deng Xiaoping's pragmatic style.

In addition to changes in the style of propaganda, the kinds of incentives offered to promote the one-child family are different from those employed in past family planning campaigns. Incentives under the post-1978 program are comparatively elaborate, as can be seen in the various sets of local regulations. (One such set of regulations is translated in full in FBIS, April 20, 1979: 01–03; see also *China News Analysis,* September 14, 1979: 5–7). Although these regulations vary from region to region, their most significant general feature is the use of "planned parenthood glory coupons." These coupons are awarded to couples who have agreed to practice a form of birth control aimed at ensuring that they will have no more than one child. (Most commonly this involves the wife having an IUD inserted, though there are other alternatives, including sterilization.) The coupons function as both a kind of ideological incentive, by being official commendations for good work, and as material ones as well, as they serve as the basis for the distribution of concrete forms of remuneration. For instance, cash bonuses in the form of monthly stipends ranging from 5 yuan in the cities to 40 yuan in the countryside, and extra ration allowances are given to all those who qualify for glory coupons. Only children are also given preferential health care and educational status. In addition, one-child (and in some cases also two-daughter) families are given special priority in the allocation of living space and/or land allotment. Along with these positive incentives, which one scholar estimates may end up accounting for a quarter to a third of a one-child household's total income (Saith, 1981: 492–496), come equivalent negative ones. For example, those who are awarded glory coupons and then bear a second child are required to make reparation for all the benefits they received. An "unplanned" birth can also lead to the parents having 10 percent of their monthly earnings withheld by the government. And third and fourth children may be denied rations for cloth and certain foodstuffs.

One final aspect of current incentive systems deserves mention: gender-based differentials. In some areas beginning in 1978–1979 a slightly higher remuneration was offered to those who had a single daughter as opposed to a single son. This difference was usually slight, but it shows that from the beginning it was realized that those without a son might need some kind of additional incentive to limit births. Giving couples with a single daughter 6 yuan a month when their counterparts with a single son received only 5 is a mild incentive. But the fact that any gender-based differential was offered shows that from the start at least an attempt was made to make some allowance for the Chinese people's continuing preference for sons. Further examples of this effort are evident in the tendency of propaganda to emphasize the joys of having a single daughter and in rules that stipulate that daughters as well as sons may inherit their fathers' jobs.

Despite these various kinds of incentives and disincentives, there has been resistance to the current family planning drive, most frequently by those who feel that none of the incentives makes up for not having a son. The main evidence of resistance comes from the Chinese press itself, which has not only reported on the successes of the one-child family policy but has also frankly treated the issues of female infanticide and wife-beating. Rarely has the Chinese press dealt so openly with deviant behavior and social unrest. The only plausible motive for this exposure of issues that are bound to reflect negatively on China is that the leadership considers the present problem to be of great importance.

Some of the most specific and heart-rending reports concerning resistance are contained in letters printed in *Zhongguo funü* ("Chinese Women") from women who have given birth to daughters and suffered because of it. The author of one such letter, entitled "What Crime Is There in Giving Birth to a Girl?" (1982, No. 10: 30), recounts that after the birth of a daughter her husband's attitude toward her changed completely. Her once happy marriage became a living hell, as her husband took to beating her because he blamed her alone for the fact that he had no heir. Her opposition to the steps he proposed to violate the planned birth program only added to his fury. Things got so bad, she reports, that she tried to commit suicide twice but was stopped both times by comrades. Her letter ends with an urgent plea to the readers of the magazine: "Please help me, help me!"

Two letters that appeared in the October 1981 edition (No. 10: 46) of the same magazine report similar examples of the lengths to which fear of having no sons leads some men. In the first of these a young worker recounts that she and her husband were happily married. But then, she writes, as soon as their daughter was born, "his attitude toward me went through a great change . . . When he wasn't hitting me, he was cursing me." Again the wife's desire to abide by the party's directive to "bear only one child" served as a further provocation to the enraged husband. The husband threatened to kill his wife in order to be free to have a son by another woman, brought over 20 men to his wife's natal home—to which she had fled to escape from his cruel treatment—for the purpose of making trouble, and then later dragged his wife to a divorce court. The wife ends her letter with the hope that the readers "will all harshly criticize the way of thinking that sees women as inferiors, for the sake of mothers who bear daughters and then receive cruel treatment."

The second letter that appeared in the same issue begins with praise for the many village youths who are "answering the Party's call and deciding to have only one child." The author is quick to point out, however, that there are still those who place less value on females than on males and thereby obstruct family planning work. She then mentions that in her own brigade a formerly happy marriage had recently soured. The sole reason for this: The couple's first child was a girl. The husband blamed his wife and took to beating her. Instead of abiding by the party's population directives, the husband now wanted to have a second or, if need be, even a third child.

A different perspective on this same phenomenon is provided by a man who wrote a letter that appeared a year later (1982, No. 10: 44). In this letter the author describes his own desire to have a son and its tragic consequences. Not satisfied with just a daughter, he and his wife went on to have two more children. After both of these turned out to be girls also, a "Population Control Propaganda Cadre" finally convinced them to stop trying for a son. The author's wife then had an IUD inserted. But although he had been convinced that population limitation was good and necessary at the time, the author's desire for a male child soon reasserted itself. He then took his wife to a man who made a practice of removing IUD's without letting family planning authorities know. The unfortunate result was that, due to the unskilled way in which the device was removed, the woman began to hemorrhage and eventually died. The letter ends with the writer's hope that men with similar ideas regarding the need for a son will learn from his sad experience.

A final, and perhaps even more poignant, is a letter from a mistreated mother that appeared in late 1982 (No. 12: 16–17). The author of this letter reports that her husband's attitude toward her changed even before she became pregnant, for her troubles began not with the birth of a daughter but with her husband entering into an affair. Though his cruelty began when she tried to interfere with his affair, it reached new lengths after their daughter was born. It is unclear at first whether the acts of which the author accuses her husband are related to the issue of birth control policy or simply the result of a bad marriage. But two things mentioned at the end of the letter show clearly that the author's plight has a great deal to do with the issue. First, her husband threatened to steal their daughter away from her and give the child to others in exchange for a baby boy. Second, after brutally abusing both mother and child the husband ended up drowning his own daughter.

Zhongguo funü is not the only journal that has reported female infanticide. Specific cases have been discussed in such widely disparate publications as *Zhongguo qingnian bao* (February 5, 1983) and *Beijing Review* (1983, No. 5: 4).

Although female infanticide and wife-beating are certainly the most reprehensible forms of resistance to the current population policy, other less dramatic forms are also discussed in the Chinese press. Some people, the press tells us, simply refuse to stop at one child. Furthermore, this particular type of resistance evidently extends even to those who are responsible for implementing national policy and who are to serve as models for the masses. A case in point is an article entitled "Leading Cadres Must Be the Vanguard in Planning Births" (*Zhongguo funü,* 1979, No. 10: 45). The article begins by noting that there are still cadres who oppose the ideal of male-female equality, and then goes on to discuss a certain cadre who "already had four daughters and one son" and yet wanted to have one more son for the sake of "protection." Similar accounts involving cadres and members of the PLA can be found sprinkled throughout the Chinese press (see, for instance *FBIS,* December 13, 1979: 6). Reports have particularly focused on Wenzhou district of Zhejiang province, which has become a sort of model in reverse. One Wenzhou official is even reported to have gone so far as the exclaim, "Each of my children is prettier than the last. The more children my wife has, the younger she looks!" (quoted in Goodstadt, 1983: 47).

Another variety of resistance to birth control is illicit removal of IUDs. Frequent criticisms of those who illegally remove these devices have appeared in the Chinese media during the last few years (for citation, see Aird, 1982). These indicate that this kind of resistance is a serious problem. The *Zhongguo funü* letter described earlier is illustrative of one kind of misfortune that can accompany illicit removal of IUDs. An even more tragic example is provided by a *Guangming ribao* article (March 16, 1983) that details the exploits of a criminal who made a practice of performing this service. This man's villainy lay not in the fact that he failed to inform the proper authorities when he removed a woman's IUD—though this in itself made him a criminal in the eyes of the authorities—but that he would use the opportunity of providing this service to rape the women who came to him. The report of his crimes includes the statements that he removed the IUDs of 83 young women, all of whom came from five Fujian communes; his actions resulted in 60 "unplanned births"; and he raped 16 women. This article is of particular interest in that (1) the main headline for it describes the criminal not as a rapist but as a "subverter of planned birth worth"; (2) it mentions that the criminal was sentenced to death for his acts; and (3) it gives an indication of how many people in a given area may wish to exceed the ordained birth quota.

One last kind of resistance deserves to be mentioned: sabotage of family planning work and personnel. The existence and seriousness of such sabotage can be inferred from new regulations prohibiting it. For instance, Article 12 in a list of rules regarding population control drawn up recently in Shanxi states that those "who attack or frame planned parenthood personnel should be strictly dealt with" (see the November 17, 1982 *Shanxi ribao* article translated in *JPRS,* May 20, 1982: 3: 59–66). Similarly, a Sichuan broadcast dealt with the need to investigate sabotage plots and the importance of "protection of family planning personnel" (BBC:SWB, January 22, 1983). Finally, at least one instance of sabotage (of the personal agricultural plots of family planning work personnel) has been reported (*Far Eastern Economic Review,* April 7, 1983: 7).

It is fairly easy to get an idea of the kinds of resistance taking place by surveying the Chinese press, but it is much harder to get an accurate picture of how common these various types of acts are. Occasionally, however, the press does provide clues as to the size and scope of the current problem. For instance, a letter coauthored by fifteen women, all of whom are mothers who gave birth to daughters and then suffered from mistreatment as a result, appeared in *Renmin ribao* on February 23, 1983. This letter—a quotation from which is given at the start of this section—indicates that in some areas it is not the exception but the rule for women who bear daughters to be abused. The authors write that in their village only women who have at least one son are considered "complete person" (*quanren*) and that all other women are viewed with contempt and discriminated against by the community as a whole. Their letter suggests that, far from being isolated sufferers, the women whose letters appeared in *Zhongguo funü* are simply the more verbal victims of a widespread, frighteningly commonplace phenomenon.

Indications of the possible scope of female infanticide are given by articles in the Chinese press dealing with male-female infant ratios. Typically, about 106 male babies are born for every 100 female ones (Petersen, 1961: 72). But according to the Xinhau News Agency (*Weekly Issue,* April 21, 1983: 9), in 1981 Anhui had over 111 surving male newborns for every 100 females. Even greater disproportions were found in some areas during a survey conducted by the Anhui Women's Federation. (Results of the survey were published in *Renmin ribao,* April 7, 1983, and translated in *FBIS* of the same date: K5–6.) According to this survey, in Huaiyuan county in 1981 there were more than 125 infant boys for every 100 infant girls, and in Longkang, a Huaiyuan commune, there were more than one and a half times as many male surviving newborns as there were females—145 baby boys but only 86 baby girls. The Women's Federation blamed these kinds of extreme, unnatural imbalances on "the malpractice of drowning and abandoning baby girls." Even if one allows for reporting errors and differential health care and nutrition, doubtless this assertion is at least partly valid: In a single Huaiyuan production brigade more than 40 instances of female infanticide reportedly occurred during 1980 and 1981 alone (*Renmin ribao,* April 7, 1983).

Of course, the goings on in Huaiyuan County are probably not at all typical (nor, unfortunately, are they totally unique). Yet, because female infanticide is a crime—and a dreadful one—it has undoubtedly received greater attention in the press (both Chinese and foreign) than much more prevalent forms of resistance. Certainly the most common form of resistance must simply be the simple bearing of more than one child, although with the data now available it is impossible to estimate how many couples oppose the policy this way. In any event, the evidence of various forms of resistance suggests that the current problem is significant and national in scope.

NOTES

I would like to thank Elizabeth Perry for her invaluable guidance and encouragement, and also the many other people who have read and made helpful suggestions regarding earlier drafts of this chapter.

1. As Orleans (1979) and others have noted, population policy oscillations in a general way have mirrored those of developmental policies as a whole. But whereas shifts in population policy have tended to conform to the "Maoist-Moderate" model, the actual situation is more complicated than the model suggests. First, although Maoist leadership groups may be *more* sensitive to the claims of Marxism and Moderate groups to those of pragmatism, neither group is oblivious to either type of claim. Second, by no means have demographic factors been static. The Moderates have taken pains to show that population control can be justified on Marxian grounds (see Tien, 1980). And the Maoist opposition to family planning weakened as pragmatic needs became more apparent after the early 1960s. (It is worth remembering that Mao himself both praised China's large population as its greatest strength and also exhorted the people to limit births—see Tien, 1980.)
2. A variety of such articles will be referred to as applicable. They have appeared in everything from *Renmin ribao* (April 7, 12, and 19, 1983) to *Zhongguo qingnian bao* (February 5, 1983) to *Beijing Review* (1983, Nos. 5 and 7). Articles appeared criticizing the continuing preference for sons as early as 1979 (see *Zhongguo funü,* No. 10: 45) and during the early months of 1983 seldom did a week pass without a published report of female infanticide or wife-beating.
3. A number of articles have appeared in Western periodicals during the last couple of years that use events relating to population control in the PRC in an attempt to establish the venality of the CCP or the Chinese people. Two of the more recent of these are "Infanticide in China" (a piece written by a pair of Chinese students studying in the United States, which appeared in the opinion section of the *New York Times* on April 11, 1983) and "The Slaughter of the Innocents Still Goes On" (*Far Eastern Economic Review,* April 28, 1983: 50–53). The latter—despite its title—is a good deal more subtle than the former and contains some valuable information. But both articles present the issue of resistance to the one-child family in a simplistic, distorted fashion, suggesting that female infanticide is either something that governmental policy encourages or at least something that does not disturb the authorities greatly. So little attention is paid to the material factors that precipitate infanticide, particularly in the former article, that one is left with the impression that infanticide is proof of the inherent barbarity of the Chinese and nothing else. Mosher's analysis of opposition to birth control policies (1983), although a good deal more comprehensive, also leaves one with a distorted view of the official attitude toward infanticide. He makes it clear that this act is a reaction to, rather than a means of enforcing, the one-child family policy (p. 252), but then he writes that the "state remains largely oblivious" to the social consequences of birth control policy (p. 254). No indication is given in any of these sources that the authorities are bitterly opposed to and trying urgently to curtail the continuing preference for sons and the brutal acts to which it leads.

REFERENCES

Aird, J. 1982. "Population policy and population studies in China." *Population and Development Review* 8, 2: 281–297.

———. 1972. "Population policy and demographic prospects of the People's Republic of China," pp. 220–231 in *The P.R.C.: An Economic Assessment*. Washington, DC: Government Printing Office.

BBC: SWB. British Broadcasting Co.: Survey of World Broadcasts, The Far East. London.

Chen Pi-Chao. 1976. *Population and Health Policy in the People's Republic of China*. Washington, DC: Smithsonian.

Croll, Elizabeth. 1983. "Production vs. reproduction: a threat to China's development strategy." *World Development* 11, 6: 467–481.

———. 1981. *The Politics of Marriage in Contemporary China*. Cambridge: Cambridge University Press.

Davis, K. 1967. "Population policy: will current programs succeed?" *Science* 158: 730–739.

Davis-Friedmann, D. 1981. "Chinese families and the four modernizations." pp. 67-78 in R. B. Oxnam and R. Bush (eds.) *China Briefing*. Boulder, CO: Westview.

Diamond, N. 1975. "Collectivization, kinship and the status of women in rural china." *Bulletin of Concerned Asian Scholars* 7, 1.

Far Eastern Economic Review, Hong Kong.

FBIS. Foreign Broadcast and Information Service. *Daily Report: China*. Washington, DC.

Goodstadt, L. 1982. "China's one-child family." *Population and Development Review* 8, 1: 37–58.

JPRS. Joint Publications Research Service. *China Report: Political, Sociological and Military Affairs*. Washington, DC.

Lewis, J. P. 1970. "Population control in India." *Population Bulletin* 26: 12–31.

Mamdani, Mahmood. 1972. *The Myth of Population Control*. New York: Monthly Review Press.

Mandelbaum, David Goodman. 1974. *Human Fertility in India*. Los Angeles: University of California Press.

Mosher, Stephen. 1983. *Broken Earth*. New York: Free Press.

Munro, Donald. 1969. *The Concept of Man in Early China*. Palo Alto: Stanford University Press.

O'Leary, G. and A. Watson. 1982. "The production responsibility system and the future of collective farming." *Australian Journal of Chinese Affairs* 8: 1–34.

Orleans, Leo, ed. 1979. *Chinese Approaches to Family Planning*. White Plains, NY: M. E. Sharp.

———. 1972. *Every Fifth Child*. Palo Alto: Stanford University Press.

Parish, William and Martin K. Whyte. 1978. *Village and Family in Contemporary China*. Chicago: University of Chicago Press.

Perry, E. 1983. "Rural violence in socialist China." (unpublished)

Petersen, William. 1961. *Population*. New York: Macmillan.

Saith. A. 1981. "Economic incentives for the one-child family." *China Q.* (September): 492–496.

Tien, H. Yuan, ed. 1980. *Population Theory in China*. London: Croom Helm.

Young, Marilyn, ed. 1973. *Women in China*. Ann Arbor: University of Michigan Press.

30
What Does "Control Over Our Bodies" Really Mean?

ELIZABETH W. MOEN

The sexual exploitation of women and their enforced submission within a society committed—when it feels like it—to the "naturalness" of their reproductive role, has caused the (women's) movement to develop the notion of the "control of one's body."

Juliet Mitchell

The most common meaning of "control over our bodies" is control of reproduction through knowledge of the process, and the financial and legal access to services and technology which enable women to have as many or as few children as they want, when they want. But as things stand now, reproduction is as much a social function as a biological function because the "natural" role of women in reproduction has been defined to include child care and socialization as well as childbearing and nursing.

Feminists generally agree that control over women is maintained through patriarchy (male dominance) which Kate Millet calls a "most ingenious form of interior colonization . . . sturdier than any form of segregation and more rigorous than class stratification." It is "the most pervasive ideology of our culture."[1] Patriarchy is institutionalized at every level of society, and is partially maintained through the socialization of children. As the primary socializers of children, women themselves are an integral part of the system, and they both teach and validate the behavior and attitudes necessary to perpetuate patriarchy (however unwittingly).

Although women are frequently aware that they are being controlled, and have some knowledge of how they are being controlled, they may not fully understand why. Millet has introduced the term "sexual politics" to broaden the meaning of politics (power structured relationships) and explain the *how* of male dominance. In this chapter the meaning of sex and reproduction will be broadened in an attempt to explain the why of male dominance. I will argue that reproduction is not just the private affair of women (or couples); it is a political and economic act with enormous public consequences, and this is the major reason for the control of women. Seen within this context, "control over our bodies" is a revolutionary concept. It means that in contemporary societies women must have full control over society, or an entirely new form of society which has no place for dominance must be developed.

FEMINISM AND REPRODUCTION

Pregnancy is barbaric . . .
And it isn't good for you.

Shulamith Firestone

Although feminists are a very diverse group of people with many different goals and as many different tactics for achieving them, they have been divided into three broad factions: the mainstream, the Marxists, and the radical (most of whom are socialist). Mainstream feminists, for example, The National Organization of Women (in the United States), are basically atheoretical, tending to see discrimination against women as an oversight which can be corrected by changing laws rather than changing society itself. Having seen that changes in laws such as those giving the vote to blacks and women have not dramatically affected the situation of either group, Marxists and radical feminists are more concerned with the development of theory which would both explain women's place in society and point to changes that must be made if women are to achieve equal opportunity. The main theoretical difference between the two is concern over what is the primary cause of the oppression of women: class, as proposed by the Marxist feminists, or gender as proposed by the radical feminists.[2]

Diverse as they are, the three feminist perspectives have some important features in common:

1. All see reproduction as a fundamental cause of women's disadvantaged situation.
2. All want control over reproduction so women can participate in society on an equal basis with men.[3]
3. There is a dearth of proposals for new forms of social organization beyond capitalism and socialism, which do not require the "liberated" women to adjust to a male ordered world. Scott has concluded that the world would be quite different if childbearing (or even childcare) were shared by men, "the wheels of progress long ago would have adjusted to the menstrual cycle and all other biological cycles that make women 'undependable' . . . and also, no doubt, to the demands of tiny infants and ill children."[4]
4. Most important, with only a rare exception, feminists do not fully recognize that, as will be explained below, control over reproduction is power, perhaps the ultimate power. This omission is a central weakness in feminist theories, perhaps the reason why none offers a satisfactory explanation of why women are dominated by men.

REPRODUCTION AS POLITICAL AND ECONOMIC POWER

A nation which is not increasing is committing suicide.

Theodore Roosevelt.

Marriage and procreation are fundamental to the very existence and survival of the race.

Luke T. Lee

Sociologist Norman Ryder, among others, has argued " . . . the simple but fundamental proposition that the replacement of a continually aging citizenry by new recruits is much too important to the entire body politic to tolerate untrammelled individual choice to hold sway. On this issue, as in so many others, the society intervenes, in obvious and in subtle ways."[5] The reasons why reproduction is too important to be left to individuals are to be found at every level of social organization from the global to the family.

Reproduction, Social Survival, and Political Power

The survival of any population depends upon births exceeding deaths. Until quite recently (the eighteenth century for the developed nations, and the mid-twentieth century for the developing nations), death rates have been so high that high birth rates were essential for survival. Today the opposite situation prevails. Death rates are much lower, the world's population is rapidly growing, and while technology and international trade have enabled some nations to maintain a high standard of living, ultimately there are limits to the number of people that can be supported at even a meagre standard of living. Thus, with low mortality, survival is threatened by high fertility.

The level of fertility is also important for international and subnational relationships. Even in this era of nuclear warfare population size is seen as a critical factor for military and political power. In *World Politics,* Organski has concluded that "Population size is the most important determinant of national power. With it, a lack of other determinants of power can be overcome, without it, great power status is impossible."[6] And according to the economist Neil Chamberlain:

> . . . when significant changes do occur in the numbers, composition and locations of a population, they are almost certain to have their impact on the distribution of the social advantage, the structure of authority which supports it, and the social organization from which these two follow.[7]

Calling the birth rate the "Dow Jones Index of elective politics" Littlewood has concluded that "all of the many facets of population politics, the most fundamental is concerned with the social institutions and public policies that regulate reproduction,"[8] *Consequently, it is in the best interest of both those desiring social change and those who wish to maintain the status quo to be in control of fertility.*

Below are just three examples of ways in which the control of fertility has recently been linked to political power.[9]

1. At the 1974 World Population Conference, China maintained that " . . . rapid population growth allows Third World countries to defend themselves against the attempted domination of the Super Powers."[10]
2. The government of Pakistan has a policy to reduce fertility in order to improve the economic condition of that country. The provinces, however, do not support the national family planning program because there are ethnic and provincial competitions for political representation

(based on the number of people) which make high fertility important.[11]

3. High fertility as a source of power for minorities is also an issue in the United States. Blacks and other minorities have interpreted free family planning and abortion services for the poor as attempts to eliminate minorities or poverty through genocide.[12] Many members of these groups believe their strength, for example, in elections, depends upon larger numbers and higher, not lower fertility. When black women have refused to support this position, militant blacks have attempted to wrest control of fertility from them by bombing and burning family planning clinics, and urging women to fight for civil rights "on their backs." "Our birth rate is the only thing we have. If we keep producing, they're either going to have to kill us or grant us full citizenship."[13] Even moderate black leaders and organizations such as the Urban League, NAACP and the National Medical Association have opposed or expressed suspicion of birth control programs in the U.S. And there is ample evidence to suggest they were at least partly correct.[14]

The "strength in numbers" philosophy is not peculiar to minorities in the United States; France, Germany, Italy, Israel, French Canada, the Roman Catholic Church, for example, have all engaged in such propaganda at one time or another. The most extreme policies were carried out in fascist Italy with the "battle for births," "baby marathon," and "demographic rejuvenation," and fascist Germany where Joseph Goebbels declared that the mission of women was to be beautiful and to bear children.[15]

In the United States the mid-nineteenth century eugenics movement arose out of feelings of need to protect the interests of white Anglo-Saxon protestant (WASP) stock from the threat of "inferior" stock which was both immigrating and reproducing at a faster rate. The eugenics movement resulted in the illegalization of contraception and abortion to encourage higher fertility among WASP women, and legalized forced sterilization to limit reproduction among "defectives." It also created a highly restrictive and racist immigration law which was modified only recently.[16] Conversely Socialists in the United States have also advocated a "strength in fewer numbers" policy. During the early part of this century Margaret Sanger and others encouraged working class women to limit their fertility so "the working class can use direct action by refusing to supply the market with children to be exploited, by refusing to populate the earth with slaves."[17]

Reproduction and the Economy

The rate of growth and size of a population also affects the economy of a society because the level of fertility is the main determinant of the age structure.[18] The age structure determines the relative sizes of the labor force and the dependent population, the number of older and younger as well as unemployed persons supported by the labor force, which, in turn, affects the standard of living. The proportion of the population available for military service is also determined by the age structure. The economy of a large or rapidly growing population may also suffer from "diminishing returns" to investment. On the other hand, if a population is too small or too sparsely settled, economic development may be retarded because the benefits of division of labor and economies of scale cannot be realized. Some economists also believe that population pressures stimulate innovation and the development of technology, thus hastening economic development.[19] Today there is a great deal of concern in the United States that the larger proportion of older people resulting from a declining birth rate will be too costly.

Reproduction and the Family

In addition to its national and international consequences, the level of fertility also has important consequences for the family or kin group. In *The Myth of Population Control,* Mamdani explains why large families are necessary for economic and physical security as well as social power and status in rural areas of developing nations. In many such societies a woman is expected to bear a large number of children for her husband and his family, and she is coerced into doing so even though high fertility may not be in the best interest of the woman or the nation as a whole.[20]

Reproduction as Volunteer Work

With just this brief discussion of the public, political and economic meaning of reproduction, it can be seen that whoever controls fertility does wield a great deal of real and imagined power. But another aspect of reproduction that is equally important to women, is their role of private producer of a public good. "Precisely because the production of children is so fundamental to the social order, an ideology exists which asserts that motherhood is natural, intrinsic, and most important, *voluntary*."[21]

By fostering the idea that childbearing and rearing is "natural" for women and a private act that people do for their own pleasure, every society has in effect created a slave class.[22] Women bear, nurse, and raise children as if these activities benefit no one except themselves or their family when, in fact, at a minimum they are serving society by reproducing and socializing the next generation and the labor force. They do this work essentially without remuneration and often with considerable physical and mental sacrifice. If they also work outside of the home (and the majority of working mothers are employed out of economic necessity) they are penalized in terms of pay and job advancement. What if women were to stop having babies? (Humanity would perish.) What if women were to be paid a salary, pension and fringe benefits for their labors? (The cost would be staggering.)[23] It is essential to realize that reproduction is not just a thing done for personal gratification. It is not a voluntary or private act;[24] society does intervene in obvious and subtle ways because reproduction is a vital industry, most important for national security, and it is almost wholly subsidized by the workers.[25] I believe the women's movement and feminist theory will not develop fully until the public significance of reproduction and the power implied by its control is taken into account.

WHAT DOES "CONTROL OVER OUR BODIES" REALLY MEAN?

When women can support themselves, have entry to all the trades and professions, with a house of their own over their heads and a bank account, they will own their bodies and be dictators in the social realm.

Elizabeth Cady Stanton

Clearly, control of reproduction means much more than being able to have as many or as few children as desired, but even within this narrower context, it is not just a simple matter of technology. In order to be in control of reproduction, women must be able to enhance or depress fertility, but they also must have the individual right to bear children, and they must have economic independence.

The Ability to Enhance or Depress Fertility

We often think of fertility control solely in terms of preventing or spacing births, but a sizeable number of women and men are not able to have any children or as many as they would like. It is questionable if enough research on infertility is being done, and infertility services are not nearly so available to the poor as are birth prevention services. And throughout the world it is much easier to obtain birth control devices than health or nutritional services which would enhance the prospects of fetal and infant survival. There is also the problem of forced, uninformed, or coerced sterilization, which have frequently been forced upon mentally retarded individuals, and also poor and minority women. In this country, one-fourth of all American Indian women are believe to have been pressured into sterilization by the U.S. Indian Health Service physicians.[26] On the other hand, women may be forced into childbearing because sex education is generally inadequate and comes too late, and a contraceptive that is both reliable and without side effects is not available to them.

For the moment, imagine things are different: all women understand reproductive processes; there are no legal or financial barriers to contraception, abortion and sterilization; a female contraceptive that is 100 percent effective, has no side effects and is pleasant to use is available to all; and there are remedies for all causes of infertility. Does this mean that women have control over reproducton? No.

Rumania, where abortion was the main form of birth control, is the classic example of how illusory such control is. In 1966 because the government was concerned about low birth rates, it abruptly reversed its very liberal abortion policy. The birth rate rose from 12.8 births per 1,000 population in December 1966 to 39.9 births per 1,000 population in September 1967.[27] Recently the governments of Saudi Arabia and Laos flatly banned the distribution and use of contraceptives. In the United States, one man, Califano of H.E.W., with the consent of the predominantly male Congress, has been able to deny federal funds for abortion to women receiving welfare payments; and five of the nine men on the Supreme Court can de-liberalize abortion and contraception laws as easily as they liberalized them. The point is, women cannot control their own reproduction unless they control the means of controlling reproduction: the research, the medical and contraceptive industries, education, and the law.

The Individual Right to Bear Children

The United Nations' declaration of human rights stating that all *couples* have the right to reproduce, was reaffirmed at the 1974 World Population Conference. Many of the patriarchal institutions which seem so natural and normal to us that we hardly even question them, are designed to ensure that children will only be born to women who are under the control of a man, for example, marriage (often arranged and forced upon young girls), the double sexual standards, laws that make divorce almost impossible for women, and the concept of illegitimacy. If women are to have control of their bodies, they must be free to marry when and whom they want and they must be free to have children whether married or not. Although the United Nations Declaration of the Rights of the Child refers to all children whatever the circumstances of their birth, only twenty-two countries do not distinguish between illegitimate and legitimate births.[28] Illegitimacy is a cruel social invention; it has pauperized, stigmatized and ostracized countless women and children. As Boulding concluded in a paper for the United Nations Year of the Child, "the cards are stacked against the unwed mother and the illegitimate child in every conceivable way."[29]

Economic Independence

One argument often used in support of the patriarchal system and against births outside of marriage is that women cannot afford to raise a family unless they are married. That is often true; in fact women's job opportunities and wages may be so low they cannot afford to support even themselves. On the other hand, many men do not earn enough to support a family either. It is a myth that most women and children are dependent upon the husband/father and a myth that most wives and mothers work for luxuries and pin money. Almost 50 percent of wives in the United States are employed today and most of them work out of economic necessity.[30]

But even when women work outside of the home to support or help support a family, they do not get fair treatment. According to Rowbotham, "our labor in the family goes unrecognized except as an excuse to keep us out of the better jobs in industry and accuse us of absenteeism and unreliability."[31] At home women are responsible for most of the house and child work, requiring time that could be used, as it is by men, for job advancement, and energy that could be saved, as it is by men, to do their work outside the home most effectively. At the same time, employed women are penalized for having children. They may be required to quit their job or take an unnecessarily long maternity leave without pay. Recently the U.S. Supreme Court ruled that private employers can exclude disability coverage for absence due to pregnancy.[32] Jobs may not be held for these women, and they lose seniority and pension time. Time out of work when children are young, sick, or out of school results in financial loss, loss of skills, and further retardation of job advancement. Equally important, this time out of work fortifies the stereotype that women aren't really interested in their work and, therefore, should not have positions of responsibility.

Among the more developed nations, the United States is quite behind regarding the treatment of employed mothers. Many nations provide a child allowance, a generous maternity leave (which Sweden extends to fathers) and guarantees that the job will be held with pension and seniority intact. The United States is also lagging behind in providing pre- and after-school care and on-the-job facilities for mothers who wish to nurse their babies.[33] Full time wives and mothers are in the most precarious position; they have little economic independence or security. Often they are are only marginally employable, and they are not able to support themselves or their children when their marriages are disrupted. High living on alimony and child support is also a myth.[34]

If women are to have control over reproduction, economic independence is essential. All people, regardless of sex or marital status should have the right to earn a decent income, and should have equal opportunities in employment. Despite all such legislation, women with children do not have either, and even women without children may be penalized because they might have them.

THE FEMINIST DILEMMA

Women's "biological" role, her function as the giver of life, has always been the one stubbornly changeless, limiting and determining factor in her . . . life and today still appears as the final insurmountable barrier to equality between the sexes. The problem now is not the demands of pregnancy and childbirth . . . but the fact that only women can do it.

Hilda Scott

"Control over our bodies" is more than a feminist slogan; it is a revolutionary concept. In order to be assured of control over reproduction, women, at a minimum, must have economic independence, they must have the freedom to bear or not to bear children regardless of their marital status, and they must be in control of much of society. And having gained control over reproduction, women will possess enormous political and economic power. This is a central dilemma of the feminist movement. On the one hand, the control of fertility by women as *individuals* is necessary for full and equal opportunity in society. On the other hand, the *aggregate* level of fertility is so important that no society can allow the individual full freedom of choice regarding reproduction. A woman's shackles are also her strength, and this is what makes the "woman problem" so intractable. Two major questions emerge from this dilemma. First, can birth control be separated from population control? And second, if not, how can women achieve maximum individual reproductive freedom?

Birth Control, Population Control and Feminist Theory

Woman's Body Woman's Rights by Linda Gordon is an important historical and political analysis of birth control in the United States. The lesson to be learned, according to Gordon, "is that reproductive freedom cannot be separated from the totality of women's freedom" because "there is a complex, mutual, causal relationship between birth control and women's overall power."[35] The implication of her conclusion is consistent with feminist theory: to be able to participate in society on an equal basis with men each woman must have full control over reproduction. This is contrary to my conclusion that women, as individuals, cannot have full reproductive freedom.

Gordon makes a distinction between birth control as a movement for reproductive self determination, and population control as a movement which puts birth rates before woman's rights. She defines population control as the programs and policies advanced primarily by the United States which "urge birth-rate reductions upon underdeveloped countries as a tool in economic development and upon poor people within the developed capitalist countries as a weapon against poverty."[36] I would say that this definition is too limited and that any attempt to manipulate birth, death, or migration rates is a form of population control. Moreover, the availability of birth control is never independent of a population policy.[37]

Even in the United States, the site of Gordon's case study, the correlation between the increased availability of birth control and the increased freedom of women was partially spurious because the contemporary feminist movement and the push for birth control occurred during a time when it had been determined that the United States would benefit from a slower rate of growth, when there was an expansion of female jobs in the economy, and when it was increasingly necessary for wives to enter the labor force because husband's salaries could not keep up with inflation. To take a more extreme example, Russia and the Eastern European socialist countries have at various times made birth control readily available (more often in the form of abortion than contraception) so that women could take jobs. Fertility did decline dramatically because the burdens of factory work, housework and child care were so great that women were foregoing wanted children.[38] These women cannot be considered emancipated.

On the other hand, with so much concern about over population in the world today it might be assumed that women will obtain reproductive freedom by default, if for not other reason. But some women want more than a few children and their reproductive freedom may be violated in the process because a low fertility policy can be just as coercive as a high fertility policy, as shown by the recent example of forced sterilization in India.[39] Furthermore, there is a bottom line to low fertility; at some point the policy and the trend will be reversed. Japan, Russia, and some of the Eastern European socialist countries are now concerned about the small size of the future labor force. The response of Rumania has already been cited; recently Czechoslovakia and East Germany have instituted policies to encourage reproduction which include shorter work hours for mothers with at least two children, the extension of pregnancy leave at full pay from 18 to 26 weeks, and generous financial support during a baby's first year, as well as interest-free loans and credits to buy houses and furniture.[40] For those who want more children these policies enhance reproductive freedom, but they also reduce the freedom of women and men by reinforcing the idea that house and child care are women's work, and reducing the opportunity and legitimacy of men's participation in the home. One also must wonder how long will it be before a policy to increase fertility, which is already called a "tailwind into marriage" by the East German media, will become highly coercive for women who do not want to bear children.

Explicitly coercive pronatalist and antinatalist policies are not restricted to socialist or to totalitarian countries. The West German city of Ellingen which is concerned about its low birth rate is expected to pass legislation that will provide direct financial aid and housing subsidies to women who decide to forego an abortion.[41] And a bill has recently been introduced in France that would give, in national elections, fathers one additional vote for each son and mothers one additional vote for each daughter until their children reach voting age. The sponsor of this bill, former Prime Minister Michel Debre, believes such a measure is necessary to combat the "peril of the declining birth rate."[42] Furthermore it would not be surprising if explicitly coercive pronatilism were to reemerge in the United States. Charles Westoff, a highly influential social demographer, has recently stated that if current fertility trends continue in the United States, " . . . there is little doubt that some types of financial incentives to encourage child bearing will have to be implemented as they already have been, in mild form, in many European countries."[43] Westoff is also well aware that these "mild forms" of birth incentives have been notoriously unsuccessful.

In sum, every country has a population policy. It may be explicit with highly coercive implementation, it may be a hidden agenda that can be achieved through existing trends, or it may be the sum of implicit and often conflicting policies such as the previously cited case of minority opposition to federally funded birth control clinics. Consequently, the availability of birth control in the form of contraceptives, abortion and sterilization, does not necessarily mean that women have reproductive freedom. Furthermore, since the availability of birth control technology and the encouragement or discouragement of its use always reflects some kind of population policy, birth control is not conceptually distinct from population control.[44]

Gordon herself points to the conclusions I have reached when she states, "There is of course, no hidden hand that guarantees that population size will be appropriately regulated by individual desires alone."[45] And she correctly states that population control alone cannot solve population problems. But when she concludes that "Reproductive freedom cannot be isolated from other human freedoms,"[46] that is, one cannot be free to reproduce unless one is free in every other way, I would have to add the following qualification: like all other freedoms there are limits to which freedom to reproduce, or not to reproduce, may be exercised. And these limits will be enforced because birth control is population control and the birth rate has political and economic consequences for every sector of society. It is especially tragic for women when one part of society believes a certain level of reproduction to be beneficial while another part of society believes it is harmful. It would be to all women's advantage if implicit policies and hidden agendas regarding fertility were made public because women's freedom is to be found more in their participation in decisions about aggregate reproductive goals than in access to birth control.

Feminist Futures

I have argued that men dominate and control women in order to control fertility. Most likely, as Marxist feminists contend, in capitalist societies it is really classes that control fertility,[47] but since this control is usually exerted through a patriarchal system, men are class agents. However, even in a socialist society, women, as individuals, cannot and do not have control over reproduction. Silveira has concluded, " . . . as long as women's bodies are means of reproduction, women's freedom means women's dominance, and men's freedom means men's dominance."[48] The analysis of this chapter leads to the same conclusion: in present societies, female control of reproduction means the replacement of a patriarchy with a matriarchy, a situation which is no more desirable than the *status quo*. Furthermore, even in a matriarchy individuals could not have full individual freedom in reproductive decisions.

Three questions facing the women's movement, then, are:

1. What kind of society will allow women as a group maximum participation in decisions regarding the aggregate level of fertility?

2. What kind of society will allow women as a group maximum participation in the design of policies that will provide women in every social category maximum individual freedom in reproductive decisions?
3. What kind of society will not penalize the women who bear and raise children and in fact, will recognize the public service they perform?

I do not know the answers to these questions, but it would seem that the first prerequisite for such a society would be that no group could control or dominate another group.

Feminist theorists have not fully faced the issue of how to achieve a truly egalitarian society, as well as a society which accords proper status and recognition to those who bear and rear children. Feminist visionaries have tackled the issue but not very successfully. Science fiction writer Joanna Russ believes it is "...very difficult to envision an egalitarian society ... attempts that are made are pretty much failures."[49] Pearson suggests that only women may know how to design societies without dominance because they have not had the experience of dominating.[50] But feminist science fiction generally pictures female dominated societies, all-female utopias, or people who experience life as a male and a female. In *Woman on the Edge of Time*, for example, Piercy is able to eliminate sexual dominance only by enabling men to bear children:

> It was part of women's long revolution. When we were breaking all the old hierarchies. *Finally there was one thing we had to give up too, the only power we ever had, in return for no more power for anyone. The original production: the power to give birth.* Cause as long as we were biologically enchained, we'd never be equal. ... So we all became mothers.[51]

The feminist political science fiction *Ecotopia*, written by a man, does offer a model. Ecotopia is a society that has eliminated class and sex discrimination without eliminating gender, sex, or biological reproduction. The women in Ecotopia do have economic independence and control over reproduction: "The fact that they have absolute control over their own bodies means that they openly exert a power which in other societies is covert or nonexistent: the right to select the father of their children. No Ecotopian woman ever bears a child by a man she has not freely chosen,"[52] and no Ecotopian mother is stigmatized if she is not married. Although Ecotopian women are in control of when and by whom they have children, they are not free to have as many children as they may want because Ecotopia has an explicit population policy to reduce the size of the population. But unlike a matriarchy, patriarchy, bureaucratic, or class society, the goals of the policy were reached through national debate by all of the people, and no particular group is disadvantaged by it.

Ecotopia is fiction, but it makes an important point. No matter what societies of the future may be like, reproduction will still be too important to be left in the hands of individuals; female control over reproduction will not mean that women can reproduce willy-nilly without regard to the overall social consequences.

CONCLUSIONS

A central feature of feminist theories and writings is the idea that to be equal with men, women must have control over reproduction. The purpose of this chapter has been to show first, that the political and economic power inherent in fertility control is a major reason for societal dominance and control over women, and second that the level of reproduction is so important to a society that individuals can never be totally free to reproduce, or not, as they please.

Control over reproduction involves much more than legal access to safe efficient contraceptives, abortion and sterilization. Such technology makes it easier to carry out reproductive decisions but it is not necessary as has been demonstrated, for example, by the dramatic decline in the birth rate of the United Sates during the depression, and the historically low birth rates in France when birth control technology was illegal. Fertility control really lies in control over the obvious and subtle ways society influences women's reproductive decisions and their ability to carry them out. At the crudest most coercive level it involves the concept of illegitimacy, or forced sterilization. But the black woman told to fight the revolution with "pussy power,"[53] or the Pakistani woman who dies giving birth to her sixth child to satisfy her in-law's need for sons, or the Chinese woman who must record her menstrual periods with her factory's women's committee, or the upwardly mobile white suburban housewife who learns that social status is to be found in fewer "high quality" children rather than the large family she might prefer,[54] are all being influenced or coerced to meet the reproductive goals of some level of society.

The only way women can have full control over reproduction is as a group which has full control over society. If such a reversal of dominance is not desired, then feminists need to consider alternative forms of social organization which would allow both men and women equal participation in decisions about a society's aggregate level of fertility, and in the design of policies which would provide maximum individual freedom in reproductive decisions as well as social and economic recognition of the work being done for society by those who bear and rear children. In "The Coming of the Gentle Society" feminist and futurist Elise Boulding reminds us of the need for new images: "Make no mistake about it: it was the utopian images of the seventeenth and eighteenth centuries that moved us to where we are today."[55] Boulding believes women will create the visions for our future and she believes these images will replace dominance with nurturance, elitism and bureaucratic hierarchies with decentralization.

Women are becoming more and more influential in contemporary society, and they will be shapers of the future, but they need new visions and new theories, lest the feminist revolution only result in a mirror image of patriarchy. This is why it is essential that women fully realize what they are asking when they demand control of their bodies.

NOTES

I would like to thank Elise Boulding, Eleanor Hull, Maria Krenz, Scott Menard, Joyce Nielson, and especially Martha Gimenez for very helpful comments on an earlier draft of this chapter.

1. Kate Millet, *Sexual Politics* (New York: Avon Books, 1971), p. 25.
2. For discussions of feminist viewpoints see Juliet Mitchell, *Woman's Estate* (New York: Vintage Books, 1971); Eli Zaretsky, *Capitalism, the Family and Personal Life* (Santa Cruz, CA: Loaded Press, 1973); and Charnie Guettell, *Marxism and Feminism* (Toronto: Women's Press, 1974).
3. While not contradicting feminists advocating for control of reproduction, Martha Gimenez, in a forthcoming manuscript "Feminism, Pronatalism and Motherhood," convincingly argues that feminism is basically pronatalist.
4. Hilda Scott, *Does Socialism Liberate Women?* (Boston: Beacon Press, 1974), p. 140.
5. Norman Ryder, "Comment," *Journal of Political Economy,* 18, 2 (1973), 565–569.
6. A. F. K. Organski, *World Politics* (New York: Knopf, 1968), pp. 203–209. Also see Philip M. Hauser, ed. *Population and World Politics* (Glencoe, IL: The Free Press, 1958). Recently U.S. Senator Goldwater attributed the recognition of the People's Republic of China and termination of diplomatic ties with The Republic of China (Taiwan) by the United States to the belief that "size and might make right."
7. Neil Chamberlain, *Beyond Malthus* (Englewood Cliffs, NJ: Prentice Hall, 1972), p. 44.
8. Thomas B. Littlewood, *The Politics of Population Control* (Notre Dame: University of Notre Dame Press, 1977), pp. 1–2.
9. I am not suggesting demographic determinism as the sole or even major explanation for social and political change, only that demographic changes may be *perceived* to be such. On the other hand, the 1975 Conference on Intergroup Relations which focused on increased concern in many nations about differential rates of population growth adds further emphasis to the *real* political importance of reproduction. A report on the conference is found in Milton Himmelfarb and Voctor Baras, eds. *Zero Population Growth—For Whom? Differential Fertility and Minority Group Survival* (Westport, CT: Greenwood Press, 1978).
10. Parker Maudlin et al., "Report on Bucharest," *Studies in Family Planning,* 5, 12 (1974), 363.
11. Lee L. Bean and A. D. Bhatt, "Pakistan's Population in the 1970's," *Journal of Asian and African Studies,* 8 (1973), 259–277.
12. William A. Dariety et al., "Race Consciousness and Fears of Black Genocide as Barriers to Family Planning," in Kenneth Kammeyer, ed. *Populations Studies* (Chicago: Rand McNally, 1975), p. 448; Robert G. Weisbord, "Birth Control and the Black American: A Matter of Genocide?" in Kammeyer, p. 448–473; Linda Gordon, *Woman's Body, Woman's Right* (New York: Grossman, 1976); Robert G. Weisbord, *Genocide?* (Westport, CT: Greenwood Press, 1973); and Littlewood.
13. Quoted in Weisbord, "Birth Control and the Black American, " p. 457.
14. Weisbord, *Genocide?,* see especially p. 124, "Reservations Among the Most Reasonable"; Littlewood; Gordon.
15. Weisbord, *Genocide?;* Gordon.
16. Weisbord, *Genocide?;* Littlewood; Gordon; Charles Keeley.

17. Quoted by Gordon, p. 233.
18. Ansley J. Coale, "How a Population Ages or Grows Younger," in Kammeyer, pp. 33–41.
19. For discussion of positive and negative aspects of population size and growth, see Judah Matras, *Introduction to Population* (Englewood Cliffs, NJ: Prentice Hall, 1977), pp. 3–14.
20. Mahmood Mamdani, *The Myth of Population Control* (New York: Monthly Review Press, 1972).
21. Kristen Luker, "Review, *Of Women Born,*" *American Journal of Sociology* 83, 6 (1978), 1561, Luker's emphasis.
22. According to David Reuben, M.D., author of *Any Woman Can,* "From the instant of conception onward, the primary thrust of every woman's being is to be fertilized, to conceive, and to reproduce." Quoted in Ellen Frankfort, *Vaginal Politics* (New York: Bantam Books, 1973), p. 177.
23. There is now a movement for pay for housework, but most proposed payment schemes, for example, from the Social Security Administration, are based on equivalent jobs in the labor market (domestic, cook) and the forty hour workweek, hardly a realistic view of the work done by wives and mothers. Guetell p. 61, argues that fair pay for housework could only be achieved under socialism. For analyses of the economic significance of housework, childbearing and child care see Zaretsky; Jeanette Silveira, *The Housewife and Marxist Class Analysis* (Pittsburgh: Know, 1975).
24. For a critique of "voluntaristic" theories of fertility, see Martha Giminez, "Do Parents Buy or Produce Children?" For further discussion of how motherhood is socially controlled see Adrienne Rich *Of Woman Born* (New York: W.W. Norton, 1976); Betty Friedan, *The Feminine Mystique* (New York: Norton, 1963).
25. Lest this statement sound too extreme it is important to note that during the 1978 Capon Springs Population and Food Conference, a resolution was introduced that the U.S. Department of Defense should be the executive agency for the management of world population problems in order to protect the national security of the United States.
26. Diana E. H. Russell and Nicole Van de Ven, *Crimes Against Women* (Millbrae, CA: Les Femmes, 1976); Weisbord, *Genocide?*; Littlewood; Gordon; Gene Marine, "Sterilization: Who Decides?" *Ramparts,* Sept. 1976.
27. Henry P. David and Nicholas H. Wright, "Abortion Legislation: The Rumanian Experience," *Studies in Family Planning* 2, 10 (1971), 207.
28. Elise Boulding, "Children's Rights and World Order," mimeo, Institute of Behavioral Science, University of Colorado, 1977.
29. Boulding, p. 24.
30. National Commission on the Observance of International Women's Year, *To Form a More Perfect Union* (Washington, DC: U.S.G.P.O., 1976); Jane R. Chapman, *Economic Independence for Women* (Beverly Hills, CA: Sage, 1976). In the developing nations today children may be an important part of the family labor force, and this was true of the more developed nations through the early part of this century.
31. Sheila Rowbotham, *Women's Consciousness, Man's World* (Baltimore: Penquin Books, 1975), p. 11.
32. Brenda Herbert, "Supreme Court Rules on Pregnancy Benefits," *Intercom* 5 (March 1977), 14.
33. Lynne B. Iglitzin and Ruth Ross, eds. *Women in the World* (Santa Barbara, CA: Clio Books, 1976); Janet Z. Giele, Audrey C. Smock, eds. *Women* (New York: John Wiley, 1977).
34. National Commission on the Observance of International Women's Year, p. 16.
35. Gordon, p. 418. Also see Russell and Van de Ven; Weisbord; Littlewood; James Reid, *The Birth Control Movement and American Society Since 1830* (New York: Basic Books, 1978); and James C. Mohr, *Abortion in America* (New York: Oxford University Press, 1978), who marshall overwhelming evidence that women are controlled in order to control fertility.
36. Gordon, p. 392.
37. Gordon has, however, pointed out another major instance of power inherent in the control of reproduction. With increasing dependence upon the labor, agricultural products, and natural resources of the developing nations, as well as increasing need to export to and invest capital in these nations, the more developed nations such as the United States find it in their best interest to try to influence the growth rates of the less developed nations of Africa, Asia, and Latin America. See, for instance, Mamdani; Population Crisis Comittee, "Third World Population Growth from a Business Perspective," *Population,* 8 (June, 1978); Bonnie Mass, *Population Target* (Brampton, Ontario: Charters Publishing, 1976).
38. Scott.
39. Lynn C. Landman, "Birth Control in India: The Carrot and the Rod?" *Family Planning Perspectives,* 9, 3 (1977), 101–110.
40. "East Germany Claims Baby Production Success," *Intercom,* 6,3 (March, 1978), 16; "Czech Mothers Get 'Paid' to Increase the Population," *Boulder Daily Camera* (August 10, 1977), p. 37.
41. "West Germany City Offers Marks for Motherhood," *Intercom,* 6 (July, 1978), 3.
42. " . . . and baby makes three (voters)," *Intercom,* 6 (August, 1978), 4.
43. Charles Westoff, "Some Speculations on the Future of Marriage and Fertility," *Family Planning Perspectives,* 10, 2 (1978), 82.

44. For further discussion of the inadequacies and sexual politics of theories and policies relating the status of women and birth control see Elizabeth Moen, "Third World Women, World Population Growth: A Case of Blaming the Victim?" *Journal of Sociology and Social Welfare,* 4, 8 (1977), 1186–1202.
45. Gordon, p. 394.
46. Ibid., p. 404.
47. Martha E. Gimenez, "Population and Capitalism," *Latin American Perspectives,* 15, 4 (Fall 1977), 5–40.
48. Silveira, p. 72.
49. See Ellen Morgan, "The Feminist Novel of Androgynous Fantasy," and Carol Pearson, "Women's Fantasies and Feminist Utopias," *Frontiers,* 2, 3 (1977). Joanna Russ, personal communication, May 1977.
50. Pearson.
51. Quoted by Pearson, p. 55. My emphasis.
52. Ernest Callenbach, *Ecotopia* (Berkeley, CA: Banyan Tree, 1975), p. 64.
53. Littlewood, p. 72.
54. Judith Blake, "Are Babies Consumer Durables?" *Population Studies,* 22 (March 1968), 5–25.
55. Elise Boulding, *Women in the Twentieth Century World* (Beverly Hills, CA: Sage, 1977), p. 281.

PART V

POPULATION LOCATION: MIGRATION, URBANIZATION, AND DENSITY

After mortality and fertility, migration is the third dynamic aspect of population change. Unlike mortality and fertility, migration does not affect how many people there are in the world; it just affects where in the world they are. To put it another way, migration affects the *distribution* of the world's population rather than its size. Since births and deaths are "vital" events, events involving a change in living-nonliving status, they are of great interest to medical practitioners, as well as social scientists. Migration, on the other hand, is almost entirely the province of the social sciences.

MEASURING MIGRATION

The definition of migration is more arbitrary than the definitions of mortality or fertility. Most of us would agree that moving from one nation to another is migration, but what about movement from one state or province to another, or from one city to another, or from one area of a city to another, or from one house to another house on the same street? The U.S. census asks a sample of the population questions about all of these types of migration or movement.

Before the world was carved up by nation-states and their political boundaries, migration would best have referred to the crossing of natural or geographic boundaries. At present, however, it is political rather than geographic boundaries which pose the greatest potential impediment to movement, so migration is generally defined in terms of the crossing of political boundaries. We commonly divide migration into internal migration, or movement within a given political boundary, and external migration (of which international migration is one example), which does involve the crossing of one or more specified political boundaries.

Migration can be viewed from two perspectives: that of the place where the migrants are arriving (the destination or receiving unit) and that of the place the migrants are leaving (the point of departure or sending unit). In international migration, those who leave a given country are (for that country) *emigrants,* while those who enter that same country are (for that country) *immigrants.* Of course, one country's immigrants are another country's emigrants. For migration that does not cross national boundaries, those who leave are *out-migrants,* and those who arrive are *in-migrants.* The difference between immigration (or in-migration) and emigration (or out-migration) is called *net migration.*

$$\text{Net migration} = \text{Immigration} - \text{Emigration}$$

The *rate* of immigration (or in-migration) is the number of immigrants (or in-migrants) divided by the midyear population of the *receiving* country (or area) and multiplied by 1,000; similarly, the rate of emigration (or out-migration) is the number of emigrants (or out-migrants) divided by the midyear population of the *sending* country (or area) and multiplied by 1,000.

$$\text{Immigration rate} = 1000 \times \text{immigrants/midyear population}$$
$$\text{Emigration rate} = 1000 \times \text{emigrants/midyear population}$$

The rate of net migration is equal to the rate of immigration (or in-migration) minus the rate of emigration (or out-migration).

Few countries have adequate data collection systems for measuring migration. Even for more developed countries (MDCs), data on migration include such varied sources as (1) statistics on immigrants and/or emigrants (not necessarily both) collected at border control points, (2) data from population registers or registers of aliens, (3) census data pertaining to the foreign-born population or population of foreign citizenship, (4) sometimes, mostly for MDCs, net migration computed from population census counts and the balance of births and deaths in the interval between censuses, and (5) most often, none of the above. Data obtained using methods 2 to 4 will generally underestimate the total number of immigrants and emigrants, because it will miss those who enter and then subsequently leave the country. Even the first method may underestimate the total migration *flow* (immigrants plus emigrants) if there is a substantial amount of illegal migration. Methods 1 and 4 may give fairly accurate estimates of net migration, *if* (for 1) statistics from border control points are accurate (i.e., no large one-way migration pattern that avoids border control points), and (for 4) if census and vital statistics records are accurate. The insert between Chapters 31 and 32 raises serious questions about the accuracy of such statistics for the United States.

HISTORICAL PATTERNS OF MIGRATION

The nature and causes of migration have shifted considerably over time. Initially, it seems likely that human migration was of two kinds. The first type, *cyclic* migration, was (and is) characteristic of hunting and gathering tribes and nomadic pastoralists, as well as seasonally migrant workers in contemporary societies. In cyclic migration, people move from place to place, but generally stay within a fairly clearly definable territory and return repeatedly to the same place. For nomadic hunter-gatherers, this usually means following herds of game animals and available water supplies as herds move to better pastures or as seasonal changes dry up waterholes. Over the course of a year, the migrants return to pretty much the same place from which they started. Migrant laborers picking fruit along the West Coast of the United States may show a similar pattern of cyclic migration, picking oranges in southern California, grapes in northern California, and apples in Washington over the course of the year.

A second form of migration involved the spread of large numbers of people from familiar territory to new, unfamiliar lands. This *exploratory* migration may have involved whole tribes following herds of game animals, or may have been preceded by the movement of individuals or small groups of people or families, as it sometimes was in the westward expansion of European settlers in North America. Archaeological evidence suggests that humans originated in eastern Africa, then spread throughout the African continent, eastward into Asia, and from there north and west into Europe, south and east into the Indian subcontinent, and north and east into Siberia and present-day China. From Siberia, people moved east across the Bering Strait, and from southern or southeast Asia they moved into Melanesia, Micronesia, Polynesia, Australia, and New Zealand. These primitive exploratory migrations took place over thousands and tens of thousands of years (millions, if one goes back past *homo sapiens* to the first hominids), and involved the migration of humans into areas which were previously uninhabited by humans (McEvedy and Jones, 1978).

By the year 5000 B.C., most of the known world was inhabited by humans, although a few outposts, such as New Zealand, remained free of human habitation as late as A.D. 750 (McEvedy and Jones, 1978). By the time of the great Middle Eastern civilizations, around 3000 B.C., primitive exploratory migration was largely ended. Nomadic hunter-gatherers and pastoral tribes still migrated in cyclic patterns and occasionally left their original homelands to settle elsewhere, but now their migration and resettlement involved the crossing of tribal or political boundaries and movement into lands already inhabited, however sparesely, by others. At this time, the distinction between *internal* migration, or migration within a political boundary, and *external* migration, or migration that crosses a political boundary, becomes relevant. *International* migration is the form of external migration most commonly studied, and "external" and "international" are sometimes used interchangeably to refer to international migration.

All migrations involve some combination of "pushes" from the old land and "pulls" to the new. In the migrations of early civilization, demographers tend to emphasize the push factors: war, famine, and slavery. Such migration is commonly referred to as *forced* migration. The Hebrew scriptures, for example, describe a series of forced migrations: fleeing from famine in Palestine, then from slavery and political oppression in Egypt (and incidentally generating some forced migration as they pushed out the indigenous inhabitants of Palestine on their way to establishing the kingdoms of Israel and Judea), and forced emigration first under the Babylonians and later the Romans. Although the written tradition is best known for the Hebrew migrations, they only mirror other such migrations that occurred during this same general period. Around 1500 B.C., the Aryans successfully invaded and settled in the northern part of the Indian subcontinent (Quale, 1966). Other great migrations included the invasions of Great Britain and Ireland by Celts, then Romans, then Germanic tribes; the expansion of the Mongols from Mongolia and the Huns and Magyars from central Asia; and the great German Volkerwanderung from northern Germany and Scandinavia south to the Mediterranean and east to the Urals (Greer, 1972). As with the later migrations from Europe to the Americas, these great migrations brought with them wars and plagues, and permanently altered the linguistic, political, and social characteristics of the areas they affected.

A second form of migration began with the rise of settled agricultural civilizations in the Middle East: *rural to urban* migration. Rural to urban migration may be dated as far back as the earliest permanent *settlements,* before 10,000 B.C., but the earliest true *cities* arose around 3000 B.C. in Mesopotamia, Egypt, and India. In early cities, death rates were often higher than those in the surrounding countryside, and at times they may have exceeded birth rates (Abrahamson, 1980). Early cities, consequently, depended on rural to urban migration for their growth. Even in modern societies, migration plays an important role in urban growth and decline.

Free individual migration, the migration of individuals independent of all but perhaps their immediate families, probably always existed to some extent, but difficulties in transportation prior to the use of roads, conveyances drawn by horses, mules, or oxen, and the advent of oceangoing sailing ships limited individual options. Cyclic, exploratory, and forced migrations were movements of whole tribes or peoples. Even slavery often involved the subjugation of entire peoples rather than isolated individuals, and the migration of European settlers to the Americas, while often involving the breaking of family as well as political and economic ties, was also similar in some respects to the earlier peregrinations of the Celts, Aryans, and Germans. Increasingly, however, migration *is* largely an individual or immediate family choice. In addition, geographic or technological barriers to migration have largely fallen and been replaced by financial and, often more importantly, political barriers. It is difficult for many who wish to enter the United States and other relatively prosperous, industrial nations. It is also difficult for many who wish to depart China, the Soviet Union, and other Eastern European nations. Internationally, the present era is a time of *politically* restricted migration.

CONTEMPORARY PATTERNS OF MIGRATION

Three patterns seem to dominate international migration in the world today: rural to urban migration, labor migration, and the migration of political and economic refugees. Labor migration refers to the permanent or temporary relocation of individuals or families seeking higher wages or better economic conditions, with emphasis on "pull" factors in the country of destination rather than "push" factors in the country of departure. Examples include Turkish "guest-workers" in Germany and workers from poorer Arab countries to the oil-rich countries of the Middle East. Labor migration is thus a type of free individual migration or politically restricted migration. This is not to say that there are no push elements in the migration; poor economic conditions in the country of departure (relative to those in the country of destination) play a role, and guest-workers who migrated from Turkey to Germany or from Ghana to Nigeria have been forcibly expelled in times of economic difficulty in their host countries.

In refugee migration, the emphasis is on push factors, such as war, political oppression, or famine. Examples include flight from drought-stricken areas in sub-Saharan Africa, the Jewish migration (especially from Europe) to Israel, the consequent Palestinian migration out of Israel into surrounding countries, and the flight of large numbers of people from war-torn southeast Asia and Central America. In addition to their impacts upon the receiving country, refugees and other displaced persons may, as a result of their migration, suffer severe emotional problems (Eitenger and Schwarz, 1981).

Cyclic migration continues in modern societies as we move toward the twenty-first century. The oldest form of migration is still with us in migrant agricultural labor, in the few remaining hunter-gatherers, and in industrial labor, which crosses international boundaries in times of industrial growth, then recrosses them as a result of either individuals' reuniting with their families, or as a result of expulsion by the country which received the migrants. With national boundaries encircling practically all of the inhabitable land on the earth, and with most of the inhabitable land populated, exploratory migration is largely ended.

The United Nations (1979) gives estimates of average annual net migration rates (per 1000 population) for 33 countries, only four of which are Asian and none of which are African or Latin American. These data, along with per capita gross national product (GNP) are presented in Table V.1. The data are presented for the years 1970 to 1974 where possible. Migrants, as the report notes, are predominantly young, aged 20 to 30.

Table V.1. Average Annual Net Migration per 1000 and per Capita GNP

Area	Average Annual Net Migration per 1000	Dates	Per Capita Gross National Product c. 1970
North America/Oceania			
Australia	+ 4.6	1970–74	5640
Canada	+ 4.4	1970–74	6650
New Zealand	+ 5.6	1970–74	4680
United States	+ 1.7	1970–74	7060
EUROPE			
Eastern Europe (average)	− 0.4		2800
Bulgaria	− 0.9	1970–74	2040
Czechoslovakia	− 0.2	1970–74	3710
German Democratic Republic	− 0.3	1970–74	4230
Hungary	+ 0.1	1960–70	2480
Poland	− 0.4	1970–74	2910
Romania	− 0.2	1970–74	1300
Northern Europe (average)	− 0.3		4590
Denmark	+ 1.1	1970–74	6920
Finland	+ 0.7	1970–74	5100
Ireland	− 1.0	1970–74	2420
Norway	+ 0.8	1970–74	6540
Sweden	+ 0.2	1970–74	7880
United Kingdom	− 0.6	1970–74	3840
Southern Europe (average)	− 2.1		2470
Greece	− 2.6	1970–74	2360
Italy	− 1.5	1960–70	2940
Malta	− 7.0	1970–74	1220
Portugal	− 7.8	1970–74	1610
Spain	− 2.3	1970–74	2700
Yugoslavia	− 4.3	1970–74	1480
Western Europe (average)	+ 3.7		6150
Austria	+ 2.2	1970–74	4720
Belgium	+ 1.7	1970–74	6070
Federal Republic of Germany	+ 5.9	1970–74	6610
France	+ 2.4	1970–74	5760
Luxembourg	+11.5	1970–74	6050
Netherlands	+ 2.0	1970–74	5590
Switzerland	+ 1.5	1970–74	8050
South and Southeast Asia			
Hong Kong	+ 3.2	1961–71	1720
Malaysia	− 5.4	1957–70	720
Singapore	+ 1.4	1957–70	2510
Sri Lanka	− 1.6	1963–71	150

Sources: United Nations (1979); United Nations (1977).

For overseas migration, they are more often families than single males, but intraregional and intracontinental migration more often involves only single males. For European countries, the data indicate a moderately strong correlation (about .66) between net migration rates and GNP. For the Asian countries, the two with GNPs over 1,000 have positive net migration, while the other two have negative net migration.

Two important points emerge from the data in the U.N. report, incomplete though these data are. First, most migration occurs within geographically contiguous areas; people are more likely to move from Malaysia to Hong Kong than from Malaysia to Sweden. Second, the tendency to move to more economically prosperous areas is limited by political and legal restrictions on international migration and by a variety of other social and political factors. Petras (1981) discusses the causes and consequences of international migration from a world-systems perspective. She suggests that the global division of labor and global inequality create pressures toward migration, and that those pressures are modified by national migration policies. In Europe, most of the net migration is attributable to labor migration; although there is some refugee migration, particularly from eastern to western Europe, this is effectively curtailed by the heavily militarized borders of eastern European nations.

According to the United Nations report, Latin America is generally characterized by negative net migration, mostly to the United States, but some also to the United Kingdom and Canada (from the former British West Indies) and the Netherlands (from Surinam). There is also considerable intracontinental migration from Paraguay, Chile, and Colombia to Argentina and Venezuela. These migration patterns are similar to those of Europe—poorer countries sending migrants to richer ones. The largest and most controversial source of migrants to the United States is, of course, Mexico. In Chapter 31, Portes explores the patterns of illegal migration to the United States by using data from *legal* Mexican immigrants to the United States. Much of the migration, Portes finds, is basically cyclic migration, with migrants crossing the border for some limited periods of time, then returning home. It is worth emphasizing that much of the illegal Hispanic migration to the United States is not Mexican, but comes from other Latin American countries. The U.S. Census Bureau, by comparing census data to immigration data on legal immigrants, estimated that about 2 million undocumented aliens were counted in the 1980 census. Mexicans accounted for 45 percent, other Latin Americans for 23 percent, Europeans and Asians 12 percent each, and 7 percent from other countries (Population Reference Bureau, 1984b).

African migration is largely intracontinental, much of it politically motived. The main currents are from northern Africa to Europe or Libya, within western Africa from the interior to the western coast and from north to south, and some migration from eastern Africa to the United Kingdom. Some of the migration reflects worsening conditions at the southern edge of the Sahara, as the desert, spurred by a combination of nature (weather) and human environmental destruction, spreads southward, pushing the people before it. Some migration reflects the arbitrary nature of the boundaries of African nations, set up by European colonial powers with little or no regard for existing tribal or linguistic boundaries.

In Asia, we find a mixture of labor migration in southwest Asia (from poorer Arab nations to wealthier, oil-producing nations) and refugee migration from southeast Asia. The end of American involvement in Vietnam brought with it a massive outpouring of Vietnamese and also Laotian and Kampuchean refugees who feared retaliation from their governments for their support of the Americans in southeast Asia. Principal recipients of Asian migration include West Germany (from Turkey), the United Kingdom (from its former colonies of India and Pakistan, and from Cyprus), and the United States (from China, Taiwan, Hong Kong, Japan, and the Philippines and, more recently, from southeast Asia). In Chapter 32, Newland describes the refugee situation in the early 1980s, including patterns of African, Asian, and Latin American refugee settlement, with particular attention to southeast Asian refugees. The two largest recipients of southeast Asian refugees are the United States with 44 percent (mostly U.S. allies in the Vietnam war) and, perhaps surprisingly, China with 30 percent, most of them Vietnamese of Chinese ethnicity. Newland also gives estimates of refugees who have been *internally displaced,* that is, have become refugees in their own countries.

U.S. MIGRATION POLICY

U.S. migration policy has a long history of controversy. Before, 1874, migration to the United States was largely unrestricted. From 1875 to 1920, a series of immigration laws were passed, most of which were aimed at excluding people with criminal records, diseases, unacceptable moral standards (e.g., prostitutes), and anarchists. In 1882, the first Chinese exclusion act was passed, prohibiting Chinese migration to the United States. In 1907, this was extended to include the Japanese, and, in 1917, all Asians. In the 1920s, national quotas were established which favored northern and western Europeans. This was an effort to maintain the racial and ethnic mixture prevalent in the United States at the time—an openly racist policy. (In 1943, the Chinese were granted a small quota in recognition of their alliance with the United States in World War II.) The quota system prevailed until 1965. In 1965, and subsequently to the present, immigration law has limited the number of immigrants to 20,000 per country and to 290,000 worldwide, and has favored relatives of U.S. citizens, certain occupational groups considered desirable or needed in the United States, and political refugees. There is considerable controversy regarding refugees, because the United States generally refuses to recognize as refugees and therefore deports people fleeing from political regimes friendly to the United States (Keely, 1979) such as Guatemala and El Salvador. In the case of Haiti, the United States allows some people in, but keeps most in refugee camps (Hutchinson, 1981).

Some of the results of U.S. immigration policy are reflected in Table V.2, which presents data from Gardner et al. (1985). Around the middle of the twentieth century, a majority of legal U.S. immigrants came from the European countries, and Europe remained the largest source of legal U.S. immigrants until the late 1960s. During the 1970s, Latin America became the largest source of legal immigrants to the United States. Asian immigration, once banned outright and later severely restricted by quotas based on national origin, also increased during this period, from about 5 percent of total legal U.S. immigration prior to 1965 to 14 percent from 1965 to 1969, and 29 percent in 1970 to

Table V.2. Legal Immigrants Admitted to the United States by Region of Birth, 1931–1984

	Percent of Total Legal Immigrants			
	1931–1960	1960–1969	1970–1979	1980–1984
Asia	5	12	34	48
Europe	58	39	19	12
Latin America	15	38	41	35
North America	21	10	3	2
Other	1	2	3	3

Source: Adapted from Gardner et al. (1985).

1974 (United Nations, 1979). By the early 1980s, Asians and not Latin Americans constituted the largest group of illegal immigrants, nearly half of the total (see Table V.2). This must be qualified, however, by noting that these figures do not include illegal immigration or migration from Puerto Rico, which is a U.S. Territory. Mexico remains the largest single country source of immigrants, followed by the Philippines. Despite the recent growth in immigration from Asia, some of which was fueled by refugees from southeast Asia, Asians still make up only about 2 percent of the U.S. population (Gardner et al., 1985).

The U.S. Congress has found it hard to develop a policy regarding immigration from Latin America or concerning those from Latin America who reside in the United States illegally. These issues have been documented and discussed by Crewdson (1983) and are complicated by the fact that "illegal immigration can be thought of as a well-established informal component of the U.S. immigration policy, equivalent to the mechanisms for securing a supply of temporary labor that have been at the heart of immigration policy in many other advanced societies of the capitalist world" (Zolberg, 1984:558). The Simpson-Mazzoli Bill, first introduced in 1982 and passed, highly modified, in 1986, created major changes in U.S. policy, regarding illegal immigration. The bill gives amnesty to those who can prove U.S. residence since 1982, imposes criminal and civil sanctions on those who hire illegal immigrants, and requires stronger border security. It is suggested that the lack of consensus on this bill reflects a fundamental national ambivalence about the control of immigration (Bean and Sullivan, 1985) as well as a fear of "Hispanization" (Zolberg, 1984). On the other hand efforts to keep Central American refugees are growing. These include the sanctuary movement, border witness programs, "Overland" and "Underground railways," and a variety of organizations that provide legal and material aid. This is clearly an important and divisive issue in U.S. policy (Ehrlich et al., 1979; Keely, 1982; Teitelbaum, 1980).

URBANIZATION

Unless it involves the crossing of national boundaries (which is not usually the case), rural to urban migration (or urban to rural, which is just *negative* rural to urban migration) is only a special type of internal migration, and there are no special measures associated with it. We do, however, measure levels and rates of urbanization. One measure used for level of urbanization is the percentage of people in cities. Although this may seem simple and direct, different countries have different definitions of what constitutes a city, and a population defined as urban in one country may not be defined as urban in another. A definition of urbanization that overcomes this problem is the percent of people in cities with some minimum population, for example, percent of population in cities with 50,000 or more. The advantage to this second definition is that the same population is treated the same way, regardless of the country in which it is found. Disadvantages are that the cutoff is arbitrary (why not 20,000 or 100,000?) and that places with similar populations (49,000 and 51,000) may be classified differently. In practice, however, the two measures of urbanization are highly correlated. Yet another method of measuring urbanization is measuring the population in metropolitan areas. In the United States, such areas are called Metropolitan Statistical Areas or MSAs (formerly Standard Metropolitan Statistical Areas, or SMSAs), and include not only the area within the politically defined central city but also adjacent communities which have a high degree of social and economic integration with that central city. Metropolitan populations are discussed in Chapters 33 and 35.

Urbanization is not only a structural condition; it is a process which has been going on for over 5,000 years. The rate of urbanization may be defined as the rate at which the population becomes increasingly concentrated in cities. Davis, in Chapter 33, however, makes a distinction between urbanization and the growth of cities, that is, between the population of cities and the *ratio* of the population of cities to the total population (the latter being the measure we use for level of urbanization). Using both the definitions of level of urbanization discussed above, Davis describes the historical process of urbanization until 1965, when this chapter was first published. Notice that his explanation for urbanization is largely economic, a fact consistent with explanations of international migration (as in Petras, 1981). Both Davis and Hardoy (Chapter 34) emphasize the importance of the difference between the historical urbanization of the more developed countries and the present urbanization of the less developed countries. During their demographic transition the nations of Europe had the option of sending "excess" (unemployed, poor, criminal) population to the Americas, Austrialia, etc. Today's developing nations do not have that choice except through illegal migration or the migration of temporary "guest workers" to the more developed countries, where they may experience discrimination and mistreatment on racial or religious grounds (e.g., Jones, 1984). Rural LDC families, however, *can* send children to the cities to find work. This solution to overpopulation or poverty on the local level does not alleviate national problems associated with high fertility, and as urban unemployment rises it is an increasingly risky choice for the family. Nevertheless, the strategy of sending children to cities is not only a household solution to fertility that may be too high for available resources, but also an incentive or justification to continue high fertility (see, e.g., Mamdani, 1972). Moreover, although "overpopulation" in rural areas has been a popular explanation for LDC urban growth, others argue that the real reasons are changes in the relative prices of urban based manufactures and rural based primary products (Kelley and Williamson, 1984).

Urbanization, Davis notes, has a beginning and an end. Morrison and Wheeler (1976) and Beale and Fuguitt (1978) describe a dramatic shift, a sort of "deurbanization," which became apparent in the United States in the 1970s, but which has now abated. The Migration Turnaround, as it was called, involved increased migration into nonmetropolitan areas and out of metropolitan areas, a reversal of a long-term trend which caught demographers by surprise (see the insert, "Six Demographic Surprises of the 1970s," which precedes Chapter 7 in this book). In Chapter 7, Beale's comments on internal migration suggested that the trend would abate but probably not reverse in the 1980s. Elsewhere, Beale and Fuguitt (1978:176) likened the Migration Turnaround to the Baby Boom in its impact on the thinking of demographers.

The Migration Turnaround, we now know, was like the baby boom in another respect as well: it was temporary, a brief interruption of a long-term trend. Agresta, in Chapter 35, describes the apparent end of that trend, the "turnaround of the turnaround." The reasons for the reversal are not yet altogether clear, and we do not know yet whether the more recent trends represent a short-term reversal in a new trend or a return to the previous pattern. What is clear is that with urbanization, as with fertility and mortality, it is dangerous to uncritically extrapolate past trends—or departures from past trends—into the future. More will be said about projections and forecasting in the last section of this book. Another important point to be made about the turnaround is that noneconomic reasons for migration played a more important role than they have for other types of migration (Morrison and Wheeler, 1976; see also Agresta, Chapter 35 of this book).

In addition to widespread nonmetropolitan growth which occurred especially within commuting distance of cities, the United States has also seen the reemergence of rural boom and bust towns, with their accompanying social problems, as a consequence of massive but unstable energy and mineral development (Moen et al., 1981; Covey and Menard, 1983, 1984; Menard and Covey, 1984; Gold, 1985). Haub, in Chapter 36, examines another striking aspect of U.S. internal migration, the movement away from the urban, industrial (and cold) northeastern and north central states to the "sunbelt" states of the south and west. Haub qualifies popular impressions of sunbelt migration and notes that fertility also plays an important part in sunbelt growth.

POPULATION DENSITY

The most straightforward measurement of those covered in this part is the measurement of population density, the number of people in a nation or other geographic or political unit divided by the land area of that nation or other unit. Cities are an example of high-density human settlements. Although the measurement of density may be straightforward, Day and Day explain in Chapter 37 why density in different areas may be as difficult and inappropriate to compare as urbanization in more and less developed countries. The urban density pattern is only one of several possible patterns of population distribution. As Day and Day note, some argue that density has negative social impacts, including psychopathology, crime, and violent or aggressive behavior. Others, they continue, see no threat in high density. Freedman, in Chapter 38, draws upon a series of experimental studies to develop a theory of crowding. Defining crowding as high population density, Freedman finds that high levels of denisty may have favorable or unfavorable effects on behavior, depending on the situation in which the crowding occurs. Crowding, he argues, can make a bad situation worse, but it can also enhance a pleasant situation (e.g., a party or an athletic event). Bear in mind that the experimental studies on which Freedman bases much of his argument involve small absolute numbers of people. Even so, Freedman makes a case for extending his analysis to larger populations, including cities, as well.

FOR FURTHER READING

1. Paul R. Ehrlich, Loy Bilderback, and Anne H. Ehrlich. 1979. *The Golden Door: International Migration, Mexico, and the United States* (Wideview Books). Good coverage of basic concepts of migration, the history of international migration, and an in-depth look at Mexican-American migration in the historical context of Mexican-American international political and economic relations.
2. Mary M. Kritz, Charles B. Keely, and Silvano M. Tomasi. 1981. *Global Trends in Migration: Theory and Research on International Population Movements* (Staten Island, NY: Center for Migration Studies). A collection of readings from different perspectives, including regional patterns and policy and the status of migrants in receiving countries. Appropriate for more advanced students.
3. Ralph Thomlinson, 1976. *Population Dynamics* (New York: Random House), Chapter 12: Measures and Theories of Migration (New York: Random House). Lucid, concise discussion of basic concepts and theories, including mathematical models of migration.
4. There are a number of good texts and readers on the subject of urban sociology and urban communities, but the best introduction to the urbanization process is still Noel P. Gist and Sylvia Fleis Fava. 1974. *Urban Society,* sixth edition (New York: Crowell/Harper & Row), Chapters 1 to 11 and 18.

31

Illegal Immigration and the International System, Lessons from Recent Legal Mexican Immigrants to the United States

ALEJANDRO PORTES

To assess the foreign policy implications of a new immigration policy, one must first understand its domestic implications for the countries involved. My purpose in this chapter is to examine the internal significance of illegal or undocumented immigration for the countries where it originates, as a necessary background against which to evaluate the Carter Administration's proposed policies. For this purpose, I will present data from an ongoing study of Mexican immigration, one addressing at least some of the questions generally asked about the nature of the movement. On the basis of these data and other recent studies, I will analyze (briefly) the Administration's policies for dealing with this illegal flow.

It is important to begin by clarifying what illegal immigration is *not*. It is not, first of all, a flow coming from a single country. The overwhelming representation of Mexico in apprehension statistics is, in part, a function of the development practices of the Border Patrol, which tends to concentrate its efforts along the southern border. Although Mexican immigrants are certainly a majority of the illegal or undocumented, the proportional representation of other countries—especially those from the Caribbean—is not insignificant (Office of the U.S. Attorney General, 1978). A relatively novel twist in Caribbean immigration is furnished by Dominican workers who are reported to enter the United States surreptitiously by crossing the Mona passage into Puerto Rico. Illegal immigration, then, should not be conceived simply as a process involving only Mexico and the United States, but as one originating in several peripheral societies.

Second, illegal immigration is not only caused by "push" forces in the original countries, but by the needs and demands of the receiving economy. The relative stability of the illegal flow, year after year, cannot be attributed to an impoverished alien population "overwhelming" the U.S. borders; it must be acknowledged that this flow of immigrants fulfills important needs for agricultural and urban industrial firms in the United States. Clearly, the persisting relationship illegal immigration creates is a symbiotic one, simultaneously fulfilling, concealed but nonetheless real economic needs—on both sides of the border (see Portes, 1977a,b; Bach 1978b).

Third, illegal immigration is not primarily a movement of economic "refugees" in search of welfare, but one of workers in search of job opportunities. The illegal flow is, above all, a displacement of labor. More specifically, it is a displacement of low-wage labor, advantageous for many enterprises.

Fourth, illegal immigration is not necessarily permanent. Available studies of Mexican immigration at its points of origin, as well as data from this study, suggest that there is a significant proportion of return migration. The dominant stereotype concerning illegal immigration still couples the image of "impoverished masses overwhelming the border" with the idea that those who cross the gates of the land-of-plenty do so never to return. But empirical research suggests that many illegal immigrants do return and that the process is a complex one often involving cyclical entries and departures from the United States (see Cornelius, 1978), Reasons for this pattern are not difficult to understand once one realizes that, although work-opportunities and wages are higher in the United States, the money saved from wages can be used for consumption or reinvestment at much higher rates in the country of origin.

The aspects of illegal immigration just reviewed are not, however, the only commonly held ideas about the nature of illegal immigration. They are merely the ones most convincingly clarified by past research. The following results begin to address a fifth and so far underresearched aspect—the socioeconomic backgrounds and present characteristics of the immigrants themselves.

THE STUDY

The data presented below come from a study of 822 documented Mexican immigrants interviewed at the point of arrival in the United States during 1972 to 1973. Interviews were conducted in Spanish immediately after the completion of immigration formalities. Interviews took place over a nine-month period at border check points in El Paso and Laredo. These are the two major ports of entry along the Texas border, and second and third, respectively, for Mexican immigrants in the nation.

Because of the exploratory nature of the study, the sample was limited to males in the economically productive ages, 18 to 60. Among Mexican immigrants, this group can be assumed to comprise the majority of family heads and self-supporting individuals. Immigrants were interviewed on a first-come basis during regular office hours. A few who crossed at night could not be interviewed. The refusal rate was less than 2 percent.

Statistical comparisons show that this sample is unbiased with respect to the universe of Mexican immigrants during fiscal year 1973 in such characteristics as average age, occupation, and education. Because of the geographic location of field sites, the sample does overestimate immigrants originating in central and eastern Mexico and destined for Texas, Arizona, New Mexico and Illinois, and underestimates those originating in western Mexico and destined for California. Except for the latter limitation, the sample appears generally representative of legal Mexican immigration.

The question then is, what relevance does this sample have for illegal immigration? Several past studies have noted the intimate relationship between undocumented Mexican immigration to the United States. The reason is that illegal immigrants can frequently manage to regularize their status through the "family reunification" provision of the 1965 Immigration Law. According to the previous studies, legal Mexican immigration differs from most immigrant flows in the past because most of the people involved are not first-comers, but already *de facto* residents of the United States (see Stoddard, 1976).

Results from the present study confirm this impression. Fully 43.7 percent of the sample came outside immigration quota limits as spouses of U.S. citizens (IR-1 visas). An additional 4.7 percent came as children of U.S. citizens (IR-2 visas). The Immigration and Naturalization Service does not break down figures on quota immigrants from the Western Hemisphere (SA-1 visas) by specific categories. Our belief is, however, that most of the 46.5 percent of quota immigrants in the sample received visas as spouses or immediate relatives of U.S. permanent residents.

When asked, 61.5 percent said they had resided previously in the United States. That figure is probably an underestimate, because some respondents might have been reluctant to report prior (illegal) entry: collating responses to a number of other relevant questions, we arrived at an estimate that 69.9 percent of the sample could be reliably regarded as having resided in the United States for extended periods prior to documented entry.

The point of these figures is that the study of legal Mexican immigration is, to a large extent, identical to that of *prior* illegal immigration. No claim is made that former illegal immigrants identified in this manner are representative of the total illegal population. They represent, however, an important and so far unresearched sector of that universe. Their characteristics ideally should be compared with those of illegals identified by other means, such as official apprehensions. Still, the present data offer an initial glimpse of those immigrants who have not only succeeded in remaining in the United States, but have consolidated their position through legal entry.

RESULTS

Everyone concerned with the process believes that illegal immigration occurs because of economic reasons: immigrants come to take advantage of the superior economic opportunities offered by a developed economy. The usual companion impression is that illegal immigrants must come from the most impoverished and backward sectors of their country of origin. In the specific case of Mexico, undocumented migration to the United States has, for decades, been associated with the plight of a largely illiterate and dispossessed rural population (Briggs, 1978; Santibañez, 1930). The dominant image held of surreptitious border crossers has been that they are peasants, frequently unemployed at home and coming to perform agricultural work in the United States.

Tables 31.1–31.7, drawn from the present sample, afford the opportunity to test these assertions. First, there is no doubt that immigration from Mexico occurs for economic reasons. Asked for their main reason for coming to the United States, 49.5 percent of immigrants in the sample responded in terms of work, wages and living conditions. This percentage equals those for all other response categories put together. Further, when asked what they considered was the major problem confronting Mexico, 61.1 percent mentioned poverty, unemployment, high prices and other economic difficulties (Table 31.1).

The hypothesis that immigrants come predominantly from rural communities is examined in Table 31.2 by comparing their community of origin (main locality of residence before age 16) with those of the overall population of Mexico. As seen in Table 31.2 the immigrant sample as a whole and immigrants with prior residence in the United States are more "urban" than the original population. In Mexico, 58 percent of the population lived in communities of less than 10,000 in 1970; so did 37.3 percent of all immigrants and 43.6 percent of immigrants with prior U.S. residence. Forty-eight percent of the formerly undocumented immigrants, however, came from urban communities of 20,000 or more; and the figure for the total Mexican population is only 35 percent.

A related notion is that illegal immigrants are destined primarily to small agricultural communities in the United States. This rural-to-rural migration pattern has figured prominently in most prior descriptions of the flow (Santibañez, 1930; Buroway, 1976). Table 31.3 presents the size-distribution of communities where immigrants intended to reside. Only 15.5 percent of the total sample and 16.4 percent of immigrants with prior U.S. residence planned to live in communities of 10,000 or less. At the other extreme, fully 73 percent of both formerly undocumented immigrants and of the total sample planned to reside in cities of 100,000 or more; of these, 54 and 46 percent, respectively, planned to live in cities of over half a million. Clearly, these immigrants not only come from cities in Mexico, far more than the majority intend to seek residence in metropolitan areas of the United States.

A third characteristic imputed to illegal

Table 31.1. Salience of Economic Problems for Recent Mexican Immigrants to the United States 1972–1973

Main Reason for Coming to the United States	%	Major Problem Confronting Mexico at Present	%
Reunite with family	28.3	No Major Problems	7.5
Work wages, better living conditions	49.5	*Economic Problems:* Poverty, unemployment, high prices, housing, etc.	61.1
Education for self and children	9.7		
Self-improvement in general, achieve independence	4.3	*Legal and Political Problems:* Corruption, inefficient bureaucracy, antiquated laws, lack of democracy, etc.	13.7
To learn more	1.7		
Likes the U.S.	2.9	*Class Inequality:* Indifference of the rich, exploitation of the people, control by those on top	1.8
Other reasons	3.7		
Total	100.0		
	(N = 818)[a]	*Educational Problems:* Lack of schools, teachers, illiteracy, etc.	7.0
		Crime Problems: Thieves, alcoholism, prostitution, drugs, etc.	6.3
		Other Problems	2.6
		Total	100.0

[a]Missing data = 4.

[b]Excludes 90 people who did not know or did not answer.

Table 31.2. Size-Class of Community of Origin of Mexican Immigrants and Distribution of Total Mexican Population

	Immigrant's Community of Origin, 1972–1973[1]		
Population	Prior Residence in the U.S. %	Total Sample %	Mexico—1970[2] %
9,999 or less	43.6	37.3	57.7
10,000–19,999	8.3	7.1	7.1
20,000–99,999	20.2	20.5	12.0
100,000 or more	27.9	35.1	23.2
Totals	100.0 (N = 564)	100.0 (N = 808)[3]	100.0 (N = 48,381,547)

[1]Source: Project data.

[2]Source: U.N., *Demographic Yearbook*, 1971—Table 10. Copyright United Nations, 1971. Reproduced by permission.

[3]Missing data = 14.

Mexican immigrants is that they are either illiterates or come from the least educated sectors of the source population. In one of the best available studies, Samora (1971) found that 28 percent of apprehended *mojados* had never attended school. Similarly, North and Houstoun (1976) reported that 43.5 percent of their sample of apprehended Mexican immigrants had received 4 years of education or less. These conclusions can again be examined on the basis of the present data. Figures in Table 31.4 compare various indicators of educational attainment for the immigrants studied and for the Mexican population. As seen in Table 31.4, the proportion of illiterates among such immigrants is much lower than for all adult Mexicans. Similarly, the percentages of immigrants (both the total set and those with prior U.S. residence) who completed primary education or had at least some secondary education is almost twice as high as the corresponding figure for the adult Mexican population. Clearly, while these immigrants by no means belong to the university-trained elite, they are from among those in the working class who have had at least some access to formal schooling and, in the process, acquired modest educational credentials.

Finally, there is the question of occupational background. Again, the stereotype is that illegal Mexican immigrants are predominantly landless peasants and agricultural workers. In 1970, close to 40 percent of Mexico's economically active population was employed in the agrarian sector, so the proportion among illegal immigrants should if anything, be higher. Table 31.5 presents data on occupational sector for our immigrant sample. (Last and next-to-last occupations are included because immigrants with prior residence in the United States probably were last employed in *this* country. By asking a question concerning em-

Table 31.3. Size-Class of Community of Destination of Mexican Immigrants, 1972–1973

Population of Intended U.S. Community of Residence	Immigrants with Prior U.S. Residence %	Total Sample %
9,999 or less	16.4	15.5
10,000–19,999	1.8	1.8
20,000–99,999	9.0	9.8
100,000–499,999	18.7	26.5
500,000 or more	54.1	46.4
Totals	100.0 (N = 567)	100.0 (N = 812)[b]

[b]Missing data = 10.

Table 31.4. Education of Mexican Immigrants and Comparative Figures for the Mexican Population

Education	Mexican Immigrants—1973		Mexican Population
	Prior Residence in the U.S. %	Total Sample %	15 years of age and older—1970 %
Percent illiterate (less than 2 years of formal schooling)	3.4	3.0	21.9[a]
Percent completing primary school or higher	58.7	65.4	31.0[a]
Percent with some secondary schooling	26.6	32.4	15.2
Percent completing secondary school or higher	5.3	5.5	4.7
	(N = 563)	(N = 806)[b]	

[a]Male population only.

[b]Missing data = 16.

ployment prior to the last one, we hoped to approximate their original occupation. Results are, however, similar in both cases.)

Only 12 percent (both of the total sample and of these immigrants with prior U.S. residence) were *last* employed in agriculture and other extractive activities. In contrast, a fourth of both samples were last employed in manufacturing, while transport, commerce and personal services had employed an additional two-fifths. *Next*-to-last employment was in agriculture and other extractive industries for nearly 20 percent of these formerly undocumented immigrants, but much higher percentages had been in manufacturing and service occupations instead; in fact the latter category was the next-to-last occupation of over a third of the total sample and of those with prior U.S. residence. It should also be noted that rates of reported *un*employment decreased significantly in the period from next-to-last to last occupation, and were especially low among former illegal immigrants (1.9 percent).

A related question is that of what occupations these immigrants originally had. The relevant data are presented in Table 31.6. Frequencies for main and next-to-last occupations are presented. (Main occupation refers to the job the immigrant declared he had mostly pursued as an adult.) Results for both variables are

Table 31.5. Last and Next-to-Last Sector of Employment of Mexican Immigrants, 1972–1973

Sector	Last Occupation		Next-to-Last Occupation	
	Immigrants with Prior U.S. Residence %	Total Sample %	Immigrants with Prior U.S. Residence %	Total Sample %
Out of labor market	1.9	6.1	6.7	15.2
Agriculture, fishing, mining	12.2	11.2	18.3	16.3
Manufacturing	29.3	24.0	22.7	17.9
Construction	17.3	15.1	15.5	13.0
Transport, commerce, and related services	15.4	18.4	18.2	18.7
Personal services	23.9	25.2	18.6	18.9
Totals	100.0 (N = 566)	100.0 (N = 808)[a]	100.0 (N = 555)	100.0 (N = 794)[b]

[a]Missing data = 14.

[b]Missing data = 28.

Table 31.6. Main and Next-to-Last Occupation of Mexican Immigrants, 1972–1973

	Main Occupation		Next-to-last Occupation	
Occupational Level	Immigrants with Prior U.S. Residence %	Total Sample %	Prior U.S. Residence %	Total Sample %
Out of labor market	2.5	6.5	6.5	15.1
Agricultural laborer	12.5	11.6	17.7	15.5
Minor urban service laborer and unskilled worker	24.7	21.4	29.6	25.0
Semiskilled and skilled urban worker	50.5	46.2	34.3	31.1
Intermediate urban service and white-collar worker	8.2	12.5	11.2	12.3
Manager and professional	1.6	1.8	0.7	1.0
Totals	100.0 (N = 556)	100.0[a] (N = 799)	100.0 (N = 554)	100.0[b] (N = 796)

[a]Missing data = 23.

[b]Missing data = 26.

again similar. Agricultural labor represents 12 percent of the distribution for main occupations and close to a fifth for next-to-last occupation. But the modal category in both cases is "skilled and semiskilled urban worker," followed by that of "unskilled worker and urban service laborer." Close to half of the immigrants declared skilled and semiskilled trades as their main occupation, and a third had such trades as their next-to-last occupation. Roughly a fourth of the sample, finally, reported unskilled and minor urban service occupations as main and next-to-last occupations.

These results contradict the common impression that illegal Mexican immigrants are mostly rural workers. Most men in the sample are manual workers, but in urban-based occupations. And most of these immigrants, whether formerly undocumented or new arrivals, do not intend to pursue farm occupations in the United States. Table 31.7 compares the occupational distribution for the total U.S. population with: (a) the universe of immigrants arriving in 1974; (b) the total legal Mexican immigration during that year; and (c) formerly undocumented immigrants in the sample.

Among all legal immigrants to the United States in recent years (i.e., those from all nations), the percentage of professionals and technicians has been higher than that among the total U.S. population. This has not been the case, however, for Mexican immigrants, among whom the proportion of highly trained occupations is insignificant. This trend again confirms the distinct character of Mexican immigration and its ability to bypass occupational certification requirements of the Immigration Law by taking advantage of family reunion provisions.

Farm work is not, however, the modal *intended* occupation for Mexican immigrants. For the total 1974 Mexican immigrant cohort, Table 31.7 shows that the proportion of farm laborers is 4 percent, essentially the same as for total immigration during the year. Among sample immigrants with prior U.S. residence, the proportion increases to 11 percent, but it is still a minority. The bulk of Mexican immigrants concentrates in the category of nonfarm laborer—unskilled and semiskilled urban workers. Other substantial percentages are found in the categories of service workers and of craftsmen and operatives, all urban-based occupations. This holds true both for the universe of legal Mexican immigrants and for our sample of formerly undocumented ones.

Several caveats are clearly in order at this point. First, these results refer only to Mexican immigration. As seen above, illegal immigration comes at present from several countries. Second, the data for illegal immigrants refer only to a sample of those who have regularized their situation in the United States. Such a group cannot be taken as representative of the total population of illegal Mexican immigrants. Studies based on interviews of appre-

Table 31.7. Occupational Distribution of Active U.S. Labor Force, Total Fiscal Year 1974 Immigrants, Total Mexican Immigrants, and Immigrants with Prior U.S. Residence

		Declared First Occupation in the United States		
Category	U.S.—1970[a]	FY 74[b] Immigrants	FY 74[b] Mexican Immigrants	Mexican Immigrants with Prior U.S. Residence 1972–1973[c]
Professional, technical, and kindred	14.1	23.5	2.2	0.8
Managers and proprietors	14.1	6.1	1.4	0.6
Farmers and farm managers	3.0	—	—	—
Clerical and sales	12.7	10.7	3.5	4.9
Craftsmen and kindred	20.9	13.2	7.7	18.5
Operatives	17.9	11.9	7.9	
Service workers including private household	8.2	17.8	27.5	11.9
Laborers, except farm	7.3	12.1	45.4	52.7
Farm laborers	1.8	4.7	4.4	10.6
Total	100.0	100.0	100.0	100.0

[a]As percentage of the occupationally active population. Source: *U.S. Census, Current Population Report—Persons of Spanish Origin in the U.S.-Series* P-20, No. 380, 1975.

[b]As percentage of occupationally active immigrants. Source: U.S. Immigration and Naturalization Service, *1975 Annual Report.*

[c]Recorded occupational category estimates for comparison with census classification Source: Project data.

hended illegals, such as those by Samora (1971) and North and Houstoun (1976), report findings in closer agreement with the generalized image of illegal immigration. The relative numerical significance of the different immigrant profiles emerging from alternative research and sampling strategies remains to be determined.

Nevertheless, it is still remarkable how systematically the present sample differs from the conventional image of illegal immigration. To summarize, most of these immigrants with prior residence in the United States came from cities in Mexico and were bound for metropolitan areas in the United States. Most were literate and, as a whole, exceeded the educational attainment of the source population. Only one-eighth had worked mostly as farm laborers or in related activities; the vast majority were concentrated in urban occupations—manufacturing and service. *Intended* first occupations in the United States were also overwhelmingly urban.

Given the probably importance of the universe represented by these immigrants, one must then ask why results are so different from conventional expectations. To answer, one must entertain a perspective contrasting markedly with that held by most scholars and by the general public.

IMMIGRATION AND DEVELOPMENT

Some reasons why the background of these undocumented immigrants differs from usual expectations can be found in a closer examination of Mexican society itself. Usual "economic dualist" views divide the country into a modern-urban Mexico and a rural-traditional Mexico, and assign illegal immigration to the latter. And the common corollary is that "as modernity overcomes tradition" the sources of the illegal flow will progressively be eliminated.

The above data suggest that a substantial proportion of illegal immigration comes from social groups already modernized, already living in cities and having above-average education. I will argue that the sources of this illegal immigration are not to be found in a backward and traditional rural economy but in the very contradictions accompanying Mexican *development.*

To summarize an argument made before, the process of capitalist industrialization in Mexico has been marked by four major contradictions. First, it mobilized a rural population, cutting traditional ties to the land without offering opportunities for alternative employment. The Mexican revolution, largely fought on the "agrarian question" (Womack, 1968), put many previously isolated peasants in contact with the benefits of modern urban civilization. Neither the triumph of the revolution nor the dominant economic strategy followed afterwards succeeded in responding to the new needs for mass employment.

In a country like Mexico, open and declared unemployment is a luxury; few really have access to the system of social security which might subsidize periods of enforced idleness. In 1969, only 20.9 percent of the economically active population (EAP) was covered by Mexican social security (Economic Commission for Latin America, 1974). Thus, it is not surprising that in the 1970 census declared unemployment amounted to only 3.8 percent of the EAP. Much more significant are the figures on disguised unemployment and on underemployment, representing people who must somehow survive with neither minimally remunerated nor stable employment. Twelve percent of the Mexican EAP was estimated to be in conditions of disguised unemployment and an additional 35 to 40 percent was underemployed in 1970. Together, they amount to almost half of the labor force (Urquidi, 1974; Alba, 1978).

Second, Mexico has experienced the contradiction of a sustained rate of economic growth coupled with an increasingly unequal distribution of national income. During the last three decades, the average annual rate of growth in national GNP has been 6 percent. During the same period, inequality in the distribution of income has not decreased, it has increased—substantially. By 1973, Mexico had a GNP per capita of (U.S.) $774. The top 5 percent of the population had 29 percent of the national income, and the top 20 percent received 57 percent of the national income. At the other extreme, the poorest 20 percent received an income share of only 4 percent (United Nations, 1974). Eighteen percent of the population had annual incomes of less than (U.S.) $75 (cf. Portes and Ferguson, 1977).

Third, Mexico has absorbed an increasingly modern culture and the modern cult of advanced consumption, while denying the mass of the population the means to participate even minimally in it. As in the advanced countries, the mass media have made sure that the attractions of modern consumerism reach the most remote corners of the country. Especially in urban areas, people are literally bombarded with advertising for new products and the presumed benefits that their acquisition would bring. But underemployment and a highly unequal income distribution actually deny access to these goods to the majority of the population (Eckstein, 1977; Alba, 1978).

This situation, which has been labeled the syndrome of "modernity-in-underdevelopment," provides an appropriate background for interpreting some of the findings in this study. It is not surprising that a sizable proportion of undocumented immigrants are neither rural nor illiterate, but come from cities and have above-average education and occupational training. These groups are most susceptible to the emigration alternative for they are most exposed to the contradictions between the desire to consume and the impossibility of doing so. The urban working class, especially its most literate groups, are more closely integrated into modern Mexican society than into the remaining enclaves of subsistence agriculture. For this reason, they are most subject to the contradictions of the system.

Fourth, Mexico faces the contradiction between a formally nationalistic government policy and an international reality of increasing dependence involving control of the Mexican economy by foreign sources. Approximately half of the 400 largest industries in Mexico are foreign-owned, predominantly by U.S. corporations. Over 25 percent of industrial production, especially in the most technologically advanced and dynamic branches, is generated by multinational companies. There are more subsidiaries of major U.S. multinationals in Mexico than in any other Latin American country and these foreign companies are buying up an increasing number of domestic firms (Vaupel and Curhan, 1977).

Mexican foreign trade is entirely dominated by the United States, which accounted, in 1976, for 62 percent of the imports and received 56 percent of the exports. Mexican external public debt, which in 1955 represented 54 percent of foreign exchange earnings, had surpassed 160 percent by 1970 (Bach, 1978a).

This extreme external dependence has two major effects on the process of labor emigration. First, Mexican industrialization, carried out under foreign auspices, has been based on importation of capital-intensive technology. The success in productivity of this strategy has been impressive. Manufacturing far outdistances agriculture at present as the most important and most dynamic sector of the economy. Practically all consumer goods now sold in Mexico are produced domestically and the share of manufactured products among total exports is the highest for Latin America. These successes have not been shared, however, by the mass of the population since so few are employed by the industries. Manufacturing absorbs approximately one-fifth of the economically active population, having increased its share by only 5 percent since the early days of the Revolution. The urban *service* sector, not manufacturing, is the one in which employment has increased most rapidly during the last three decades. (Cumberland, 1968). The increasing production of domestic goods, coupled with failure to widen the consumer market through employment in the industrial sector, has aggravated, in turn, the other contradictions of the system.

Second, the presence and influence of the United States have accelerated the modernization of Mexican culture and the spread of the cult of consumption. The North has come to appear to be the land where contradictions plaguing Mexico at present can be solved, at least for the individual. Massive emigration to the United States must be regarded as the natural response of part of the Mexican working class to conditions created *for them,* rather than *by them.* Efficient industry coupled with widespread underemployment, diffusion of modern styles of consumption coupled with high concentration of income in higher social class, both are processes which cannot be understood apart from recognition of the heavy presence in Mexico of foreign, mostly United States, capital and technology.

In the eyes of the Mexican worker, the United States stands as the place where the benefits of an advanced economy, promised but not delivered by the present national development strategy, can be turned into reality. It is only natural that many trek North in search of the means to acquire what transnational firms and the mass media have so insistently advertised for years. The individual immigrant data presented above and the analysis of the Mexican economic situation in this section have converged and show that illegal immigration has been propelled not by the failure of developement strategies, but by their success. The movement does not occur because Mexico is poor and stagnant, but precisely because it has developed rapidly—in one particular direction. The main implication is that we in the United States should not expect that illegal immigration will fade away as Mexico becomes less rural and more developed. Instead, if Mexican development proceeds along the lines it has followed in the past, we must expect more, not less, pressures at the southern border.

POLICY PROPOSALS

Mexican immigration is not only the most sizable component of the illegal flow, but the one for which more information is available. With necessary modifications, I believe that the essentials of the situation just described apply to other countries from which undocumented immigrants come. Caribbean nations, especially the Dominican Republic, have also begun a process of economic development based on import-substitution industrialization, importation of capital-intensive technology, and mobilization of the rural population into urban areas.

The Carter Administration's proposals to deal with illegal immigration consist in essence, of three measures: (1) amnesty for illegal aliens who can prove continuous residence in the United States since 1970; (2) five-year work permits without unemployment and social security benefits for those coming after that date; and (3) strict enforcement of the border to prevent continuation of illegal entries. A great deal of attention has been focused on the first two provisions (see Portes, 1978), but it is the third one that is most important to any analysis of the foreign policy implications of these proposals. I will not discuss here the means proposed to close the border, but rather, the purpose. Also, I will not advance an alternative policy, but will only comment on the implications of the existing border enforcement proposal.

There are two ways of looking at the actors or contenders involved in the Administration's proposed policies. The more apparent one is to conceive of two nation-states, the United States and Mexico (or other source country), which have opposite interests. The decision to enforce the border is then taken to defend the interest of one national community even at the expense of the other. A second way of considering the process is to view the different nation-states not as separate entities, but as integral components of the same overarching international system. This world system contains and indeed depends on the existence of national borders and national states, but both the nation-states and their borders function within the constraints imposed by the international totality.

In the specific case of international labor migration, the fundamental cleavage in the world-system is not between national states, but between social classes. Classes cut across national borders and may have interests contrary to those of the rest of the respective national populations. One could speak of capital and labor as the two relevant classes, but that is too general. Actually, there are four subclasses or class sectors primarily involved in the process: (a) foreign and domestic capital owners in Mexico (and the Mexican *state*); (b) competitive-sector enterprises in the United States; (c) unemployed and underemployed Mexican workers from rural and, as seen above, urban areas; and (d) workers in the United States who serve as an actual or potential labor force to competitive firms. Women and racial and ethnic minorities are disproportionately represented in this labor market.

Owners and managers in Mexico and the Mexican government are placed in the same category here because their interest in labor emigration is ultimately the same. Primarily, this is not an interest in would-be emigrants as an economic resource, but as a political threat. The contradictions of Mexican development and the mass of unemployed and underemployed are serious causes of concern for the future of the social order. This is especially true in a country which not so long ago witnessed popular revolutionary forces bring down an aristocratic regime. Emigration to the North functions in this situation as a welcome and important resource to maintain social peace and meliorate the tensions of economic growth without equality. For the Mexican state, the remittances (savings) sent by emigrants to the United States also represent an increasingly important means of counteracting balance-of-payments difficulties (Cornelius and Diez-Canedo, 1976).

Employers of illegal labor in the United States are not, by and large, major corporations but smaller competitive firms dependent for profits on holding down the costs of labor. In areas where illegals concentrate, many such firms have come to depend on this kind of labor for their very survival (North and Houstoun, 1976; Marshall, 1975). As stated above, illegal immigration thus establishes a symbiotic relationship among owners on both sides of the border, one in which the political legitimation needs of some and the economic labor-saving needs of others are served by the same process.

For the mass of Mexican workers, the best alternative in the long run is obviously a major transformation of the dominant economic order. No one lives in the long run, however, and in the here-and-now emigration to the United States offers many the best chance for fulfillment of their aspirations. As a respondent in Dinerman's recent study of emigrants from a village community in Lake Patzcuaro stated—he did not get too worried when money became scarce because "he could always go North" (Dinerman, 1978).

Illegal immigration does not pose an immediate threat to middle-class nonmanual workers to artisans and highly skilled workers, and in general to workers organized in strong unions in the United States. The reason is that illegal labor has neither sought nor gained entry into the mainstream of the American economy. No evidence exists that major corporations have knowingly hired a substantial number of undocumented immigrants. The class of workers in the United States most directly affected by illegal labor competition is precisely the class that is least organized and least able to articulate its interests: the largely female and nonwhite competitive labor sector. In areas where illegal immigrants concentrate, the situation is further confused by the fact that the apparent economic opposition between undocumented and domestic minority workers is tempered by cultural, ethnic and language affinities. To this day, many local unions and ethnic organizations are not certain whether they should oppose and denounce illegal immigrants, embrace them as part of the same community, or adopt some intermediate attitude.

In principle, the Administration's proposals appear progressive for they would strengthen the bargaining hand of domestic workers in the competitive sector, while forcing Mexico and other exporting countries to face their reality without the safety valve of emigration. Out of that situation, presumably, significant structural changes in the direction of equality might result. The configuration of class forces just outlined suggests, however, that the border enforcement clause will be difficult to maintain without a parallel program of regulated access to immigrant labor. On the other hand, border enforcement may be possible in the short run because the amnesty program, also part of the Administration's plan, would turn undocumented workers already in the country into a *de facto* immigrant contract labor force. What we must recognize, however, is that once this group is absorbed the same pressures can be expected to reassert themselves.

Neither the needs of employers of low-wage labor in the United States nor the class structure of Mexican society are likely to change significantly in the near future. The American state, at the center of the contemporary world economy, makes decisions affecting different sectors of American society not only directly but indirectly, through their repercussions in other nations integrated into the same system. It is in this sense that what appears on the surface as "foreign policy" is still domestic policy if we see it from the vantage point of the reality of the international economic system. The U.S. government cannot reasonably ignore the serious threats to political and economic stability that would be posed *in Mexico* by strict enforcement of the border. It can no more do so than ignore the opposition of a politically powerful sector of domestic employers. Despite the apparent intentions of the Administration and the probable eventual support of organized labor, it is not likely that the program as conceived will survive.

International labor migration thus represents a process remarkable for the contradictions between its determinants and the policy measures formulated to control it. The flow of illegal immigration is not an autonomous phenomenon of peripheral countries, but originates in the character of their externally shaped development. The economic hegemony exercised by the United States over these countries produces patterns of industrialization within them which increase rather than decrease the pressure on their working classes. Conversely the evolution of the world economy has produced an increasing reliance on foreign sources of cheap labor in the advanced capitalist nations. Precisely because these laborers have been made redundant in their own countries, they can be hired cheaply to counterbalance high wages for the domestic working class. Attempts to prevent such long run structural processes by administrative decisions to "close the border" or reduce the size of the "traditional" rural sector in the nations from which such workers flow are just alternative forms of official fantasy. Policies thus far formulated to deal with illegal immigration highlight the continuing gap between the reality of an internationalized political economy and the national standpoint from which its consequences are interpreted. Flows of capital and of labor are interrelated, international, and influenced by profit and wage levels and by persisting trends in the shares of wealth available to various social classes in the constituent nations of the world economy.

NOTES

Paper presented at the session on "Undocumented Mexican Workers" meetings of the Society for the Study of Social Problems, San Francisco, September 1978. This is a modified version of a statement originally delivered at the hearings on "Undocumented Workers: Implications for U.S. Policy in the Western Hemisphere" held by the U.S. House Subcommittee on Inter-American Affairs, Washington, DC, July 26, 1978. The data are part of the project "Latin American Immigrant Minorities in the United States," supported by grants MH 27666-03 from the National Institute of Mental Health and SOC 77-22089 from the National Science Foundation.

REFERENCES

Alba, Francisco. 1978 "Mexico's International Migration as a Manifestation of its Development Pattern." *International Migration Review* 12 (Winter).

Bach, Robert L. 1978a. "Foreign Policy Implications of Recent Trends in Mexican Immigration." Testimony presented before the Committee on International Relations, U.S. House of Representatives, May 24.

———. 1978b. "Mexican Immigration and the American State." *International Migration Review* 12 (Winter).

Briggs, Vernon M. 1978. "Labor Market Aspects of Mexican Migration to the United States in the 1970s." Pp. 204–225 in Stanley R. Ross (ed.), *Views Across the Border: The United States and Mexico.* Albuquerque: University of New Mexico Press.

Buroway, Michael. 1976. "The Functions and Reproduction of Migrant Labor: Comparative Material from Southern Africa and the United States." *American Journal of Sociology* 81 (March).

Cornelius, Wayne A. 1978. "Mexican Migration to the United States: Causes, Consequences, and U.S. Responses." Center for International Studies, Migration and Development Group, Massachusetts Institute of Technology (July).

Cornelius, Wayne A., and Juan Diez-Canedo. 1976. "Mexican Migration to the United States: The View from Rural Sending Communities." Center for International Studies, Migration and Development Group, Massachusetts Institute of Technology (June).

Cumberland, Charles. 1968. *Mexico: The Struggle for Modernity.* New York: Oxford University Press.

Dinerman, Ina R. 1978. "Patterns of Adaptation among Households of U.S.-bound Migrants from Michoacan, Mexico." *International Migration Review* 12 (Winter).

Eckstein, Susan. 1977. *The Poverty of Revolution: The State and the Urban Poor in Mexico.* Princeton, NJ: Princeton University Press.

Economic Commission for Latin America (ECLA). 1974. "Economic Survey of Latin America, Part 3." United Nations Document E/CN.12/974/Add.3

Marshall, Ray. 1975. "Economic Factors Influencing the International Migration of Workers." Paper presented at the Conference on Contemporary Dilemmas of the Mexican-United States Border, San Antonio, The Weatherhead Foundation.

North, David S., and Marion F. Houstoun. 1976. "The Characteristics and Role of Illegal Aliens in the U.S. Labor Market: An Exploratory Study." Mimeo. Washington, DC: Linton and Co.

Office of the U.S. Attorney General. 1978. "Illegal Immigration: President's Program." Mimeo. Washington, DC (February).

Portes, Alejandro. 1977. "Why Illegal Migration? A Structural Perspective." Latin American Immigration Project Occasional Papers, Duke University.

———. 1978. "Towards a Structural Analysis of Illegal Immigration." *International Migration Review* 12 (Winter).

Portes, Alejandro, and D. Frances Ferguson. 1977. "Comparative Ideologies of Poverty and Equity: Latin America and the United States." In I. L. Horowitz (ed.), *Equity, Income, and Policy: Comparative Studies in Three Worlds of Development.* New York: Praeger.

Samora, Julian. 1971. *Los Mojados: The Wetback Story.* Notre Dame, IN: University of Notre Dame Press.

Santibañez, Enrique. 1930. *Ensayo Acerca de la Immigración Mexicana a Estados Unidos.* San Antonio: The Clegg Co.

Stoddard, Ellwyn R. 1976. "A Conceptual Analysis of the 'Alien Invasion': Institutionalized Support of Illegal Mexican Aliens in the U.S." *International Migration Review* 10 (Summer).

United Nations. 1974. "Report on the World Social Situation—Social Trends in the Developing Countries, Latin America, and the Caribbean." U.N. Document E/CN.5/512/Add.1, 1974.

Urquidi, Victor L. 1974. "Empleo y Explosion Demografica." *Demografia y Economia* 8(2).

Vaupel, James, and Joan Curhan. 1977. *The World's Multinational Enterprises: A Sourcebook of Tables.* Boston: Harvard Business School.

Womack, John. 1968. *Zapata and the Mexican Revolution.* New York: Vintage Books.

Airborne Migrants Study Urged

POPULATION REFERENCE BUREAU

How many immigrants enter the United States each year? Among demographers concerned with the issue, conventional wisdom sets the probable annual total of net migration—legal and illegal—at between 500,000 and 600,000, says University of Pennsylvania researcher Daniel R. Vining, Jr., in a recent report.

Most demographers would agree with Ansley Coale's 1972 conclusion that continued immigration at current, fairly substantial levels does not imply indefinitely continued growth of the American population, Vining declares.

But new evidence on the size of net migration into the United States fails to support this view, he points out in "Net Migration by Air: A Lower-Bound on Total Net Migration into the United States," in which he identifies the airborne component of this net flow.

The excess of arrivals over departures, as reported by *U.S. International Air Travel Statistics* (USIATS), currently exceeds a million persons a year—a figure obviously inconsistent with current estimates of the total of net arrivals in the United States. Using additional statistics collected by individual airports and the International Air Transport Association, Vining arrives at a lower estimate of between 500,000 and 700,000 net airborne arrivals, a number significantly higher than the standard 400,000 net legal migrants per year used by the Census Bureau in its population estimates, and uncomfortably close to the 800,000 upper-limit consensus of demographers—a consensus which also includes net migration by sea and land.

A minute proportion—less than 1 percent—of the United States's 500 million annual border crossings are by sea. Precise numbers of those who come by land—about 95 percent of the total—are simply unknowable, given the length and light policing of U.S. borders. Even if land movement in and out of the United States were channeled through official border crossing points, Vining notes, the data would still be inadequate since no effort is made to record departures *from* the United States at these points.

Movement by air, by contrast, is both significant (more than 30 million arrivals and departures by air were recorded in 1978) and, with minor exceptions, well documented in both directions.

The following table from Vining's study shows arrivals, departures, and "stayers" from 1959 through 1978, as recorded by USIATS. "The excess of arrivals over departures is not

Passengers Arrived in U.S. and Departed from U.S., by Air, 1959–1978, in Thousands

Year	Arrivals (A) '000	Departures (D) '000	Net (A−D) '000
1959	2,118.7	1,945.3	173.4
1960	2,357.6	2,218.9	138.7
1961	2,609.5	2,344.8	264.7
1962	2,816.3	2,547.2	269.1
1963	3,302.4	3,053.2	249.2
1964	3,962.7	3,694.4	268.3
1965	4,614,9	4,381.1	233.8
1966	5,496.1	5,093.0	403.1
1967	6,450.6	6.005.2	445.4
1968	7.415.9	6,744.5	671.4
1969	8,654.2	7,950.5	703.7
1970	9,863.5	9,096.1	767.4
1971	11,034.9	9,749.3	1,285.6
1972	13,255.2	11,764.6	1,490.6
1973	13,935.6	12,273.6	1,662.2
1974	13,558.8	12,497.3	1,061.5
1975	13,249.7	12,578.2	671.5
1976	13,964.3	13,136.2	828.1
1977	14,700.6	13,804.0	896.6
1978	16,954.9	15,795.6	1,159.3

Note: Data exclusive of passengers between Canada and the United States and between the British Virgin Islands and the Virgin Islands of the United States, military personnel, crewmen, and travelers between the United States and its possessions, as reported to INS by air carrier, pursuant to Code of Federal Regulation 8 CRF 1.1 §231.1 and §231.2

Sources: *Passenger Travel between the U.S. and Foreign Countries by Sea and Air, 1959 to 1975* (U.S. Immigration and Naturalization Service, Washington, DC); *U.S. International Air Travel Statistics, 1976 to 1978* (Transportation Systems Center, U.S. Department of Transportation, Cambridge, Massachusetts).

only consistently positive, as one would expect, but also astoundingly large," he notes. "In recent years net arrivals have fluctuated around one million passengers per year, more than double the official legal total net migration of 400,000 and not greatly below the total natural increase of the American population."

Data published by the International Air Transport Association (IATA) reflect considerably lower net arrival figures, Vining reports, but IATA data, in addition to covering smaller passenger totals, do not include several charter airlines and exclude Miami-Europe and San Juan-Europe passenger traffic. Various other factors complicate the collection of air passenger data. For example, while the Immigration and Naturalization Service assures that proper forms are filled out on all arriving flights, both chartered and scheduled, as all passengers must go through customs, there is less interest in departing passengers, and in contrast to many other countries, there are no exit controls at U.S. airports.

Vining's findings, however, indicate that net U.S. migration by air alone is somewhere between a half-million and 700,000 annually—and that these figures may even be on the low side.

When such large populations are involved, demographers point out, even small errors in numbers can lead to serious errors in net figures. But at the very least, Vining concludes, the USIATS statistics should dispel the complacency with which many demographers have treated immigration as a source of U.S. population growth. "It seems obvious that the first course of action in the face of these figures would be to press for an independent estimate of arrival and departure rates by air in the United States, through a random sample of international flights," he adds. "Such a study would not seem to pose any technical problems to the profession, and the benefits of such an independent study would certainly justify its relatively modest costs."

32
Refugees: The New International Politics of Displacement

KATHLEEN NEWLAND

The saga of Indochina's "boat people" is the most dramatic, though not the most massive, refugee crisis of recent years. It, more than any other situation, has served to focus the eyes of the world on the plight of modern-day refugees. As 1979 came to an end with nearly 300,000 "boat people" still in refugee camps scattered around the perimeter of the South China Sea, many observers dubbed it "the year of the refugee." Few imagined that 1980 would equally merit the title, with an outpouring of refugees to match the previous year's, or that 1981 would open with the grim promise of yet another season of displacement.

There are currently about 16 million refugees adrift in the stormy seas of world politics.[1] No one predicts a quick reduction in their numbers, and it is easy to pinpoint several troubled regions capable of producing additional thousands at the drop of a hat—or the squeeze of a trigger. The scale, the complexity, and the presistence of the problem call for an almost unprecedented degree of cooperation among nations.

A fundamental change of approach to the problem of refugees may also be required. Refugee crises have been treated as aberrations in world politics: self-contained, sporadic, unpredictable upheavals bearing no relation to each other. They are treated in much the same manner as natural disasters. Yet it is becoming discouragingly clear that the presence of refugees is in fact characteristic of violent confrontation today. Because the world has become more densely populated—with half again as many people today as there were in 1960—the odds are higher that large numbers of people will be caught in the cross fire wherever shooting starts. Rivalry over land and resources has intensified, spurred by the need to satisfy the requirements and aspirations of growing populations. And poverty holds more people than ever in its grip, providing a fertile breeding ground for tensions that can erupt into violence between or within countries. Even the search for solutions to these basic problems can lead to refugee-producing conflict, as ideological disputes over development strategies degenerate into shooting matches. In El Salvador, for example, the government is opposed by both the left and the right on the thorny subject of land reform. In most armed disputes in today's world the line between the military and political aspects of the contest has blurred, placing noncombatants in the front lines. Control over civilian populations is a tactic as well as an objective of modern warfare.

The ancient themes of human greed, betrayal of popular will, lust for power, ethnic hatred, and so forth combine with economic strains that have more recently emerged to ensure that the eighties will be a "decade of refugees" unless great foresight and cooperation are brought to bear. No nation is entirely immune to the effects of today's millions of displaced people. Some leaders may be unmoved by humanitarian considerations, but even they can hardly be indifferent to the continuing potential for instability that the homeless represent. A handful of national leaders believe that they can benefit from such instability. It is the responsibility of the whole community of nations to convince these few how dangerous and futile such a notion is in a crowded, complex, and highly interdependent age.

There is really no such thing as preventive action specific to refugee problems. Prevention lies in the larger realm of maintaining global stability, peacefully resolving disputes, recognizing human rights and ameliorating the economic preconditions of violence—all, obviously, long-term propositions. In the meantime, however, the global community can do much to oil the wheels of humanitarian relief mechanisms. It can also work to improve its ability to anticipate conflicts that have a high potential for generating refugees, and thereby be better prepared to meet needs for both relief and mediation.

WHO IS A REFUGEE?

Coping with refugees is made doubly complicated by the difficulty of defining the term. Who is a refugee? There is no comprehensive international document that establishes a definition recognized by all countries. The closest thing is the United Nations 1951 Convention Relating to the Status of Refugees, as amended by the 1967 Protocol Relating to the Status of Refugees. The Convention and Protocol define a refugee as a person who "owing to well-founded fear of being persecuted for reasons of race, religion, nationality, membership of a particular social group or political opinion, is outside the country of his nationality and is unable or, owing to such fear, is unwilling to avail himself of the protection of the country."[2] Also included were stateless people who would not or could not remain in the places where they had been living—citizens, for example, of countries that had ceased to exist in the aftermath of World Wars I or II.

The technical and sometimes tiresome question of who is and who is not a refugee has enormous significance for the displaced people themselves. The answer determines the degree of support and protection the individuals receive as well as the long-term resolution of their plight. The fundamental right that refugee status gives people is the right not to be sent back against their will to the country from which they have fled: the right, in legal parlance, of "non-refoulement." Nations that ratify the U.N. Convention and Protocol obligate themselves not to expel refugees from their territory without due process of law, and, if grounds for expulsion are found, to give the refugee time to seek legal admission to another country of asylum. The obligations of the host country also include issuing identity papers and travel documents, allowing refugees at least the same civil rights as those enjoyed by other legal immigrants, and facilitating as far as possible the refugees' assimilation and naturalization.

Those governing the countries that people flee from often dispute the validity of refugees' claims, calling them bandits, guerrilla fighters, or simply illegal but voluntary migrants. The current regimes in Afghanistan, Kampuchea (formerly Cambodia), and Vietnam have used these arguments as defense against charges of violating their own citizens' basic human rights.

Countries on the receiving end of refugee flows have also been known to dispute claims of refugee status, sometimes out of apprehension over the heavy obligations a nation must bear when large numbers of homeless people descend. Thailand, for example, did not accord refugee status to most of the Kampucheans who fled across its border in 1979. The Kampucheans were, therefore, unprotected by international law, which would have shielded them from involuntary repatriation. Indeed, in June of 1979, Thailand—inundated with starving people and fearful of its own border security—forced more than 40,000 Kampucheans back across the border. Many of them died or were killed in the fighting between the forces of Heng Samrin and Pol Pot. After great international outcry over this episode, Thailand subsequently declared on open-door policy to all Kampucheans seeking asylum. But it still did not officially recognize them as refugees.[3]

The U.N. Convention of 1951 was formulated in the specific context of postwar Europe, when millions of displaced people affected by boundary shifts and changes of government existed in a legal limbo. The Convention sought to define the rights of these individuals, as well as the obligations of states that found themselves host to refugees from whom return to their own countries was likely to constitute at least a prison sentence—if not a death warrant. The task was conceived as a one-time obligation; in fact, the Convention as written applied only to victims of "events occuring before 1 January 1951," and nations were given the option of applying its provisions only to Europe. Once the refugees of World War II were taken care of, if was thought, the job would be finished.

The limits of time and geography incorporated in the 1951 Convention proved with time to be serious constraints on the world's ability to deal collectively with refugee problems. New situations kept arising that generated additional refugees—such as Algeria's war for independence from France and the breaking in 1954 of that colonial tie, and the 1956 uprising in Hungary. Since World War II, the vast majority of refugees have originated in Africa, Asia, and Latin America. (See Table 32.1.) The 1967 Protocol extended the scope of the Convention by eliminating the provision that only victims of pre-1951 events were cov-

Table 32.1. Major Sources and Locations of Refugees, 1980

Country of Origin	Refugees	Main Countries of Asylum
	(number)	
Africa		
Angola	178,000	Zaire, Zambia
Burundi	154,500	Tanzania
Chad	100,000	Cameroon
Equatorial Guinea	115,000	Gabon, Cameroon
Ethiopia	1,954,000	Somalia, Sudan, Djibouti
Namibia	36,000	Angola
Rwanda	175,000	Uganda, Burundi, Tanzania, Zaire
Uganda	105,000	Sudan, United Kingdom, Zaire
Western Sahara	50,000	Algeria
Zaire	69,000	Uganda, Angola
Asia		
Afghanistan	1,700,000	Pakistan, Iran
Indochina (Kampuchea, Laos, Vietnam)	983,000	United States, People's Republic of China, Canada, Australia, France[a]
Pakistan	55,000	Bangladesh
People's Republic of China	183,500	Hong Kong, Macao, United States
Philippines	90,000	Malaysia
Tibet	78,000	India, Nepal, Bhutan, Switzerland
Europe		
Bulgaria	60,000	Turkey
Hungary	27,000	United Kingdom
USSR	66,000	United States, Israel
Latin America		
Argentina	266,000	Italy, Spain, Brazil
Chile	76,000	Venezuela, Argentina
Cuba	120,000	United States
El Salvador	20,000	Honduras
Haiti	41,000	Dominican Republic, United States[b]
Middle East		
Iraq	30,000	Iran
Palestine	1,757,000	Jordan, Gaza Strip, West Bank, Lebanon, Syria
Internally Displaced		
Cyprus	193,000	
Ethiopia	850,000	
East Timor	200,000	
Kampuchea	4,000,000	
Laos	1,000,000	
Lebanon	1,000,000	

Source: U.S. Committee for Refugees, *1980 World Refugee Survey*, and author's estimates based on recent news reports.

[a]Countries of permanent resettlement.

[b]The total number of Haitians in these countries is much larger; this figure is the U.S. Committee on Refugees' estimate of the number of political refugees among Haitian migrants.

ered and by removing the geographic limitation, except where ratifiers of the Convention specifically chose to retain it.

The Convention and Protocol Relating to the Status of Refugees remain the most comprehensive legal instruments that deal with refugees, but their coverage is far from complete. Several factors limit them. Most important, they are only binding on governments that ratify them. So far, out of more than 150 countries in the world, only 78 have ratified one or the other.[4] Second, the U.N. instruments were designed with the individual refugee in mind, the man or woman with solid reason to believe that his or her government is determined to violate that person's basic human rights because of some particular characteristic of the individual. But many displaced people have less sharply defined, though still well-founded, fears. The simple, realistic fear of being in the way of opposing fighters is one powerful reason to flee, for example, though it has nothing to do with individual traits. Third, the Convention and Protocol apply only to people who are outside the boundaries of their own nation. Internally displaced people cannot be helped by them. And finally, international protection and support for refugees ceases as soon as they return home or acquire new nationalities, or as soon as the crisis that caused them to flee is resolved. The material needs of the displaced may continue, however, for some time after they technically ceased to be refugees.

The limited scope of the Convention and Protocol has, in practice, been overcome by several means. Many countries abide by the general terms of these international agreements even though they have not actually signed the documents. Much of international law is uncodified, and the terms of the U.N. instruments have entered into that body of customary law. They therefore have a moral force that goes beyond the binding commitments of the ratifying nations.

The definition of a refugee now extends beyond the persecuted individual to whole groups of people fleeing from dangerous circumstances. An important instrument in accomplishing this was the Organization of African Unity's Convention on Refugees, adopted by the OAU in 1969. The OAU agreement incorporated the earlier definition of a refugee and added to it "every person who, owing to external aggression, occupation, foreign domination or events seriously disturbing public order in either part or the whole of his country of origin or nationality, is compelled to leave his place of habitual residence in order to seek refuge in another place outside his country of origin or nationality." Only eighteen countries have ratified the OAU Convention, but its expanded definition has attained considerable force in custom and practice.[5]

Along with recognizing groups of refugees, the United Nations has authorized its executor in refugee affairs, the U.N. High Commissioner for Refugees, to assist people who are displaced within their own country's borders. And UNHCR may continue helping repatriated refugees until they can reconstruct their livelihoods at home. All these measures together have helped develop international mechanisms to respond to the needs of today's displaced people.[6]

The United Nations and OAU definitions of refugees are, necessarily, legalistic ones. They classify as refugees those who live unprotected by the laws of a nation and who therefore have no recourse if their rights are violated. People who leave their homeland without any right to enter another inhabit a legal no-man's-land. There is no one to issue passports if they need to travel, no agency to give them work permits, no courts to hear their grievances, and so forth—except to the extent that governments other than their own, operating according to internationally established standards, agree to protect the refugees' interests.

Neither the United Nations nor any of its member nations accord refugee status to people who flee from intolerable economic conditions; unless those conditions are a direct product of war. In fact, the statute of the U.N. High Commissioner for Refugees specifically states that "reasons of a purely economic character may not be invoked" in claiming refugee status.[7] Gauging the motives of an asylum-seeker is a delicate business and has been the basis of many disputes over the legal status of would-be refugees. A protracted lawsuit against the U.S. government on behalf of Haitians who came to the United States without official sanction illustrates the argument over definitions at its most difficult.

The Haitians, most of whom arrived by sea in dangerous boats, claimed political asylum but were said by the U.S. Government to be economically motivated migrants. International convention, of course, acknowledges a moral obligation to admit bona fide refugees for asylum until repatriation or resettlement can be arranged. Denial of entry to a migrant, however, is a legitimate expression of national sovereignty.

The Haitian case was aruged with particular vehemence because it coincided with the acceptance in the United States of nearly 120,000 Cuban émigrés, only a minority of whom met the conventional requirements for political asylum. The case was settled with a compromise that allowed both Cubans and Haitians to remain in the country but denied them refugee status. Both groups were ambiguously classified as "entrants" and received less federal assistance for resettlement that refugees would have been given. But their chief goal, and the basic right they would have had as refugees, was achieved: they avoided being deported to the country from which they had fled.[8]

The distinction between political and economic refugees often is hazy, especially when the government of a particular country views those who attempt to leave it as potential troublemakers or even traitors. In the Soviet Union and Cuba, for example, people who apply for exit visas often suffer harassment from the authorities. By the very act of attempting to emigrate, perhaps for economic reasons, people may make themselves politically suspect and therefore subject to persecution.

The international community is held back from a generous response to the plight of economic refugees by the sheer scale of the problem. The roughly 16 million political refugees seem to strain resources and goodwill to the breaking point. Yet there are many more would-be "economic refugees." Already, an estimated 20 million people have left their homes to seek work in other countries. The pool of possible migrants is vast: more than 350 million people worldwide are unemployed or severely underemployed.[9] This reservoir of deprivation and frustration carries an explosive potential that could turn millions more into political refugees.

In the rather imprecise universe of international law and custom, the definition of a refugee is constantly evolving. Every conflict that uproots people is the product of a unique set of political, economic, geographical, and social circumstances. The framework that allows the international community to deal with the displaced in a coherent way must be constantly stretched to fit particular cases. There are, however, common threads that run through many refugee crises. Understanding them can make the definitional problems easier, and may even point the way toward more lasting solutions to the plight of all refugees.

ALTERNATIVES FOR REFUGEES

The task that the international community has taken on in concerning itself with refugees is, as the Deputy U.N. High Commissioner put it, "to see that those who become refugees cease to be refugees within a reasonable time."[10] There are three basic routes to this end: voluntary repatriation, settlement in the country of first asylum, or resettlement in a third country. The first of these, in which refugees return home of their own free will, is ideal both for the refugees themselves and for the countries and institutions that work with them. Logistically and psychologically it is the easiest solution, but politically it may be the most difficult. It requires, as a starting point, that the problem that drove people from their homeland be resolved. Material support for the returnees may also be needed, at least until they can reestablish their livelihoods.

Despite the difficulties, there have been many successful cases of voluntary repatriation during the past decade. The most massive case involved the return of more than 10 million Bengalis to the new nation of Bangladesh in 1972. These refugees fled to India during the war of independence and subsequent Indo-Pakistani war. Caring for them during their exile was a monumental humanitarian task, involving almost all the U.N. agencies and private voluntary organizations concerned with refugees, as well as bilateral assistance from many countries. Between March 1971 and March 1972, more than [U.S.] $430 million was spent on the refugees, of which over half was provided by the Indian Government.[11]

When the war ended in December 1971, after the intervention of the Indian army, authorities of the Indian and Bangladesh Governments and of the UNHCR began to organize the refugees' return. In January 1972, more than 200,000 people crossed the Bangladesh border every day. In less than four months, the ten million had gone home and the refugee camps were closed. As UNHCR officials later noted, the experience held "useful lessons for the year—and the crises—to come."[12]

These lessons were put to good use throughout the seventies with smaller scale repatriation efforts in Angola, Burma, Guinea-Bissau, and Mozambique, and more recently in Nicaragua and Zimbabwe. With the defeat of the Somoza regime in Nicaragua, most of the 200,000 people who fled to neighboring countries returned. The negotiated settlement of hostilities in Zimbabwe made possible the return to their homes of over a million people who either had been displaced within Zimbabwe or had left the country during the years of fighting. As a mid-1980 about 120,000 had returned from nearby nations, half of them with international assistance. The UNHCR established a [U.S.] $22 million program to help with the repatriation.[13]

Permanent settlement outside the home country is regarded as a poor second to voluntary repatriation, but in many cases it is the only practical alternative. Some refugees flee with no expectation of returning, such as the "boat people" from Vietnam or Jewish émigrés from the Soviet Union. Others leave thinking that they will return to their homes, but slowly establish livelihoods and roots in the countries of asylum. The ease and speed of resettlement is greatly affected by location. Many refugees make permanent homes in the first place they reach: often a neighboring country where climate, culture, and perhaps even ethnicity are similar to the refugees' place of origin. Many of the Afghan refugees encamped in the northwest province of Pakistan are ethnic Pathans, as are the province's natives, for example, and almost all of Somalia's refugees from Ethiopia are ethnic Somalis.[14]

Settlement in the country of first asylum

often involves delicate political, social, and economic questions. In a racially heterogeneous society, for example, an influx of refugees may upset a delicate balance among groups—a fear that in 1979 prompted Malaysian authorities to refuse for a time to give even temporary asylum to ethnic Chinese fleeing Vietnam. Often, countries of first asylum face a huge struggle to meet the basic needs of their own citizens, so that supporting additional displaced people represents an awesome burden. Somalia, one of the poorest countries in the world, hosts about 1.5 million refugees, 90 percent of whom are women and children. Approximately one of every three residents of Somalia is a refugee.[15]

The presenece of refugees raises what may already be a high level of tension between neighboring countries. Fighters often mingle among refugee populations, using the camps for rest and medical treatment, and sometimes for recruitment. Vietnamese and Kampuchean troops of the Heng Samrin Government have crossed the Thai border several times to attack alleged guerrilla strongholds among the refugee camps.[16] And the more than one million Afghan refugees in Pakistan are suspected by the current regime in Kabul of being mere camouflage for guerrilla attacks against its rule. Pakistan cannot help but feel vulnerable to the kind of attacks from Afghanistan that were regularly visited on Mozambique, a country of asylum for both refugees and freedom fighters, by white-ruled Zimbabwe before the 1980 settlement there.

The welcome that a country of first asylum extends to refugees depends on a complex set of considerations: the strength or fragility of the receiving country's economy, the compatibility of the refugees with the local population, the speed and generosity of the international community's response to the need for humanitarian assistance, the political stability of the host government, and the foreign policy stance of that government toward the conflict that produced the refugees. The last of these can be crucial, for it can determine whether refugees from a particular country are looked upon as allies or enemies, victims or pawns. The government of Somalia, for example, has welcomed the Somali refugees from Ethiopia with open arms, and not just because of ethnic ties. Somalia has long laid claim to the Ogaden region from which the refugees come.[17] If the Ogaden Somalis eventually win their fight for self-determination, it is very likely that they would choose to merge with Somalia.

By contrast, the governments of Southeast Asian countries have accepted refugees from Kampuchea, Laos, and Vietnam for temporary asylum with nervous reluctance. The leaders of Indonesia, Malaysia, the Philippines, Thailand, and other countries in the region have discharged huge responsibilities toward hundreds of thousands of refugees, but are sure that they have nothing to gain from the situation and have no inherent responsibility for it. Indeed, they greatly fear its destabilizing effect on the entire area. Singapore's representative at a foreign ministers' meeting in 1979 described Vietnam's policy of forced explusion as "organized arson, intended to ignite the whole region."[18] The refugees, unwitting agents of this policy, have found a cool reception from neighboring countries.

Cultural expectations may also play a part in attitudes toward refugees. President Nyerere of Tanzania called upon the African tradition of hospitality at a regional conference on refugee problems in 1979 when he pointed out that "the refugees of Africa are primarily an African problem, and an African responsibility."[19]

Table 32.2. Third-Country Resettlement of Indochinese Refugees, 1975–July 1980

Resettlement Country	Refugees Resettled
	(number)
Argentina	1,281
Australia	39,464
Austria	1,136
Belgium	3,282
Canada	60,625
Denmark	1,570
France	66,245
Hong Kong	9,368
Italy	2,486
Japan	557
Malaysia	2,142
Netherlands	3,022
New Zealand	2,825
Norway	1,931
People's Rep. of China	265,554[a]
Spain	508
Sweden	1,727
Switzerland	7,192
United Kingdom	10,721
West Germany	14,297
Other	1,798
Total	497,731
United States	388,802
World Total	886,533

Source: U.S. Coordinator for Refugee Affairs, "Overview,"

[a]Includes 263,000 direct from Vietnam reported by the People's Republic of China.

Tanzania, like some other African nations, has set aside land for the permanent settlement of refugees who have come from neighboring states.

For many refugees, neither repatriation nor settlement in the first country they reach is a possibility. The costly and time-consuming process of relocating in a third country then becomes necessary. The largest and most dramatic instance of third-country resettlement in the past decade is the ongoing case of the Indochinese "boat people" and their counterparts who have fled Kampuchea, Laos, and Vietnam by land. More than 1.5 million people have left their homes since 1975. Approximately 130,000 went directly to the United States during the first year, and about 266,000 Vietnamese of Chinese origin found first and permanent asylum in the People's Republic of China in the late seventies. More than 680,000 Indochinese have been relocated indirectly, stopping first in other countries of the region to await resettlement. Of these, two-thirds eventually settled in the United States. The governments next most generous with offers of resettlement have been France, Canada, and Australia.[20] (See Table 32.2.)

The drama of the spring and summer of 1979, when nearly 60,000 Indochinese refugees arrived each month in countries of first asylum, has calmed. But the exodus has not stopped nor have all the refugees found permanent homes. In August 1980, there were 230,000 Indochinese waiting in regional refugee camps for permanent settlement. The Office of the U.S. Coordinator for Refugee Affairs emphasized then that "resettlement needs are virtually as pressing as they were one year ago."[21]

If none of the three basic solutions to homelessness can be arrived at, the remaining alternative for refugees is grim. For some groups, flight from war or persecution has turned into lives, even generations, of exile. The most prominent such case is of course that of the Palestinians, most of whom were displaced over thirty years ago and are still awaiting a durable solution. Nearly two million have the status of refugees. But the Palestinians are not alone. Tens of thousands of Tibetans have remained stateless in India since 1959, and many still dream of returning to an independent Tibet. Some observers fear that the ethnic Somali refugees from Ethiopia who now reside in Somalia will become another long-term community of exiles.

The bitter experience of prolonged uprootedness certainly scars those who live through it. Their suffering is an enduring reproach to the international system that has been unable—or in some cases unwilling—to devise a stable solution to the refugee problem.

NOTES

1. United States Committee for Refugees, *1980 World Refugee Survey* (New York: 1980).
2. United Nations, Convention Relating to the Status of Refugees, Geneva, 28 July 1951, as amended by the Protocol Relating to the Status of Refugees, New York, 31 January 1967.
3. "Cambodians: Saving an 'Endangered Species'," *Christian Science Monitor,* November 19, 1980.
4. United Nations High Commissioner for Refugees (UNHCR), *UNHCR: The Last Ten Years* (Geneva: 1980).
5. Organization of African Unity, Convention Governing the Specific Aspects of Refugee Problems in Africa, 10 September 1969; Emmanuel K. Dadzie, Göran Melander, and Peter Nobel, "Report of the Seminar Legal Aspects on the African Refugee Problem," in Göran Melander and Peter Nobel, eds., *African Refugees and the Law* (Uppsala, Sweden: Scandinavian Institute of African Studies, 1978).
6. UNHCR, *The Last Ten Years.*
7. United Nations, General Assembly, Statute of the Office of the United Nations High Commissioner for Refugees, 14 December 1950.
8. Office of the U.S. Coordinator for Refugee Affairs, "Report to the Congress Regarding Cuban and Haitian Entrants," Washington, DC, September 1980.
9. Kathleen Newland, *International Migration: The Search for Work* (Washington, DC: Worldwatch Institute, December 1979).
10. Dale de Haan, "UNHCR and a Task Which Grows," in U.S. Committee for Refugees, *1980 World Survey.*
11. UNHCR, *The Last Ten Years.*
12. Ibid.
13. Office of the U.S. Coordinator for Refugee Affairs, "Overview of World Refugee Situation." Washington, D.C., August 1980.
14. Ibid.
15. United States Committee for Refugees, "Who Helps the World's Refugees?," New York, October 1980.

16. "Blow-up on a Touchy Border," *Asiaweek,* January 16, 1981.
17. Göran Melander, *Refugees in Somalia* (Uppsala, Sweden: Scandinavian Institute of African Studies, 1980).
18. "Refugees Island Proposals From an Island Refuge," *The Economist,* July 7, 1979.
19. Julius Nyerere, speech presented at the Panafrican Conference on Refugees, Arusha, Tanzania, May 7–17, 1979, as quoted in *UNHCR News,* October/November 1979.
20. U.S. Coordinator for Refugee Affairs, "Overview."
21. Ibid.

33

The Urbanization of the Human Population

KINGSLEY DAVIS

Urbanized societies, in which a majority of the people live crowded together in towns and cities, represent a new and fundamental step in man's social evolution. Although cities themselves first appeared some 5,500 years ago, they were small and surrounded by an overwhelming majority of rural people; moreover, they relapsed easily to village or small-town status. The urbanized societies of today, in contrast, not only have urban agglomerations of a size never before attained but also have a high proportion of their population concentrated in such agglomerations. In 1960, for example, nearly 52 million Americans lived in only 16 urbanized areas. Together these areas covered less land than one of the smaller counties (Cochise) of Arizona. According to one definition used by the U.S. Bureau of the Census, 96 million people—53 percent of the nation's population—were concentrated in 213 urbanized areas that together occupied only 0.7 percent of the nation's land. Another definition used by the bureau puts the urban population at about 70 percent. The large and dense agglomerations comprising the urban population involve a degree of human contact and of social complexity never before known. They exceed in size the communities of any other large animal; they suggest the behavior of communal insects rather than of mammals.

Neither the recency nor the speed of this evolutionary development is widely appreciated. Before 1850 no society could be described as predominantly urbanized, and by 1900 only one—Great Britain—could be so regarded. Today, only 65 years later, all industrial nations are highly urbanized, and in the world as a whole the process of urbanization is accelerating rapidly.

Some years ago my associates and I at Columbia University undertook to document the progress of urbanization by compiling data on the world's cities and the proportion of human beings living in them; in recent years the work has been continued in our center—International Population and Urban Research—at the University of California at Berkeley. The data obtained in these investigations . . . shows the historical trend in terms of one index of urbanization: the proportion of the population living in cities of 100,000 or larger. Statistics of this kind are only approximations of reality, but they are accurate enough to demonstrate how urbanization has accelerated. Between 1850 and 1950 the index changed at a much higher rate than from 1800 to 1850, but the rate of change from 1950 to 1960 was twice that of the preceding 50 years! If the pace of increase that obtained between 1950 and 1960 were to remain the same, by 1990 the fraction of the world's people living in cities of 100,000 or larger would be more than half. Using another index of urbanization—the proportion of the world's population living in urban places of all sizes—we found that by 1960 the figure had already reached 33 percent.

Clearly the world as a whole is not fully urbanized, but it soon will be. This change in human life is so recent that even the most urbanized countries still exhibit the rural origins of their institutions. Its full implications for man's organic and social evolution can only be surmised.

In discussing the trend—and its implications insofar as they can be perceived—I shall use the term "urbanization" in a particular way. It refers here to the proportion of the total population concentrated in urban settlements, or else to a rise in this proportion. A common mistake is to think of urbanization as simply the growth of cities. Since the total population is composed of both the urban population and the rural, however, the "proportion urban" is a function of both of them. Accordingly, cities can grow without any urbanization, provided that the rural population grows at an equal or a greater rate.

Historically, urbanization and the growth of

cities have occurred together, which accounts for the confusion. As the reader will soon see, it is necessary to distinguish the two trends. In the most advanced countries today, for example, urban populations are still growing, but their proportion of the total population is tending to remain stable or to diminish. In other words, the process of urbanization—the switch from a spread-out pattern of human settlement to one of concentration in urban centers—is a change that has a beginning and an end, but the growth of cities has no inherent limit. Such growth could continue even after everyone was living in cities, through sheer excess of births over deaths.

The difference between a rural village and an urban community is of course one of degree; a precise operational distinction is somewhat arbitrary, and it varies from one nation to another. Since data are available for communities of various sizes, a dividing line can be chosen at will. One convenient index of urbanization, for example, is the proportion of people living in places of 100,000 or more. In the following analysis I shall depend on two indexes: the one just mentioned and the proportion of population classed as "urban" in the official statistics of each country. In practice the two indexes are highly correlated; therefore either one can be used as an index of urbanization.

Actually the hardest problem is not that of determining the "floor" of the urban category but of ascertaining the boundary of places that are clearly urban by any definition. How far east is the boundary of Los Angeles? Where along the Hooghly River does Calcutta leave off and the countryside begin? In the past the population of cities and towns has usually been given as the number of people living within the political boundaries. Thus the population of New York is frequently given as around eight million, this being the population of the city proper. The error in such a figure was not large before World War I, but since then, particularly in the advanced countries, urban populations have been spilling over the narrow political boundaries at a tremendous rate. In 1960 the New York-Northeastern New Jersey urbanized area, as delineated by the Bureau of the Census, had more than 14 million people. That delineation showed it to be the largest city in the world and nearly twice as large as New York City proper.

As a result of the outward spread of urbanites, counts made on the basis of political boundaries alone underestimate the city populations and exaggerate the rural. For this reason our office delineated the metropolitan areas of as many countries as possible for dates around 1950. These areas included the central, or political, cities and the zones around them that are receiving the spillover.

This reassessment raised the estimated proportion of the world's population in cities of 100,000 or larger from 15.1 percent to 16.7 percent. As of 1960 we have used wherever possible the "urban agglomeration" data now furnished to the United Nations by many countries. The United States, for example, provides data for "urbanized areas," meaning cities of 50,000 or larger and the built-up agglomerations around them.

It is curious that thousands of years elapsed between the first appearance of small cities and the emergence of urbanized societies in the nineteenth century. It is also curious that the region where urbanized societies arose—northwestern Europe—was not the one that had given rise to the major cities of the past: on the contrary, it was a region where urbanization had been at an extremely low ebb. Indeed, the societies of northwestern Europe in medieval times were so rural that it is hard for modern minds to comprehend them. Perhaps it was the nonurban character of these societies that erased the parasitic nature of towns and eventually provided a new basis for a revolutionary degree of urbanization.

At any rate, two seemingly adverse conditions may have presaged the age to come: one the low productivity of medieval agriculture in both per-acre and per-man terms, the other the feudal social system. The first meant that towns could not prosper on the basis of local agriculture alone but had to trade and to manufacture something to trade. The second meant that they could not gain political dominance over their hinterlands and thus become warring city-states. Hence they specialized in commerce and manufacture and evolved local institutions suited to this role. Craftsmen were housed in the towns, because there the merchants could regulate quality and cost. Competition among towns stimulated specialization and technological innovation. The need for literacy, accounting skills and geographical knowledge caused the towns to invest in secular education.

Although the medieval towns remained small and never embraced more than a minor fraction of each region's population, the close connection between industry and commerce that they fostered, together with their emphasis on technique, set the stage for the ultimate breakthrough in urbanization. This breakthrough came only with the enormous growth in productivity caused by the use of inanimate energy and machinery. How difficult it was to achieved the transition is agonizingly apparent from statistics showing that even with the conquest of the New World the growth of urbanization during three postmedieval centuries in Europe was barely perceptible. I have assembled population estimates at two or more dates for 33 towns and cities in the sixteenth century, 46 in the seventeenth and 61 in the eighteenth. The average rate of growth during the three centuries was less than .6 percent per year. Estimates of the growth of Europe's population as a whole between 1650 and 1800 work out to slightly more than 0.4 percent. The advantage of the towns was evidently very slight. Taking only the cities of 100,000 or more inhabitants, one finds that in 1600 their combined population was 1.6 percent of the estimated population of Europe; in 1700, 1.9 percent, and in 1800, 2.2 percent. On the eve of the industrial revolution Europe was still an overwhelmingly agrarian region.

With industrialization, however, the transformation was striking. By 1801 nearly a tenth of the people of England and Wales were living in cities of 100,000 or larger. This proportion doubled in 40 years and doubled again in another 60 years. By 1900 Britain was an urbanized society. In general, the later each country became industrialized, the faster was its urbanization. The change from a population with 10 percent of its members in cities of 100,000 or larger to one in which 30 percent lived in such cities took about 79 years in England and Wales, 66 in the United States 48 in Germany, 36 in Japan and 26 in Australia. The close association between economic development and urbanization has persisted: . . . in 199 countries around 1960 the proportion of the population living in cities varied sharply with per capita income.

Clearly modern urbanization is best understood in terms of its connection with economic growth, and its implications are best perceived in its latest manifestations in advanced countries. What becomes apparent as one examines the trend in these countries is that urbanization is a finite process, a cycle through which nations go in their transition from agrarian to industrial society. The intensive urbanization of most of the advanced countries began within the past 100 years; in the underdeveloped countries it got under way more recently. In some of the advanced countries its end is now in sight. The fact that it will end, however, does not mean that either economic development or the growth of cities will necessarily end.

The typical cycle of urbanization can be represented by a curve in the shape of an attenuated *S*. Starting from the bottom of the *S*, the first bend tends to come early and to be followed by a long attenuation. In the United Kingdom, for instance, the swiftest rise in the proportion of people living in cities of 100,000 or larger occurred from 1811 to 1851. In the United States it occurred from 1820 to 1890, in Greece from 1879 to 1921. As the proportion climbs above 50 percent the curve begins to flatten out; it falters, or even declines, when the proportion urban has reached about 75 percent. In the United Kingdom, one of the world's most urban countries, the proportion was slightly higher in 1926 (78.7 percent) than in 1961 (78.3 percent).

At the end of the curve some ambiguity appears. As a society becomes advanced enough to be highly urbanized it can also afford considerable suburbanization and fringe development. In a sense the slowing down of urbanization is thus more apparent than real; an increasing proportion of urbanites simply live in the country and are classified as rural. Many countries now try to compensate for this ambiguity by enlarging the boundaries or urban places; they did so in numerous censuses taken around 1960. Whether in these cases the old classification of urban or the new one is erroneous depends on how one looks at it; at a very advanced stage the entire concept of urbanization becomes ambiguous.

The end of urbanization cannot be unraveled without going into the ways in which economic development governs urbanization. Here the first question is: Where do the urbanites come from? The possible answers are few: The proportion of people in cities can rise because rural settlements grow larger and are reclassified as towns or cities; because the excess of births over deaths is greater in the city than in the country, or because people move from the country to the city.

The first factor has usually had only slight influence. The second has apparently never been the case. Indeed, a chief obstacle to the growth of cities in the past has been their excessive mortality. London's water in the middle of the nineteenth century came mainly from wells and rivers that drained cesspools, graveyards and tidal areas. The city was regularly ravaged by cholera. Tables for 1841 show an expectation of life of about 36 years for London and 26 for Liverpool and Manchester, as compared to 41 for England and Wales as a whole. After 1850, mainly as a result of sanitary measures and some improvement in nutrition and housing, city health improved, but as late as the period 1901 to 1910 the death rate of the urban counties in England and Wales, as modified to make the age structure comparable, was 33 percent higher than the death rate of the rural counties. As Bernard Benjamin, a chief statistician of the British General Register Office, has remarked: "Living in the town involved not only a higher risk of epidemic and crowd diseases . . . but also a higher risk of degenerative disease—the harder wear and tear of factory employment and urban discomfort." By 1950, however, virtually the entire differential had been wiped out.

As for birth rates, during rapid urbanization in the past they were notably lower in cities than in rural areas. In fact, the gap tended to widen somewhat as urbanization proceeded in the latter half of the nineteenth century and the first quarter of the twentieth. In 1800 urban women in the United States had 30 percent fewer children than rural women did; in 1840, 38 percent and in 1930, 41 percent. Thereafter the difference diminished.

With mortality in the cities higher and birth rates lower, and with reclassification a minor factor, the only real source for the growth in the proportion of people in urban areas during the industrial transition was rural-urban migration. This source had to be plentiful enough not only to overcome the substantial disadvantage of the cities in natural increase but also, above that, to furnish a big margin of growth in their populations. If, for example, the cities had a death rate a third higher and a birth rate a third lower than the rural rates (as was typical in the latter half of the nineteenth century), they would require each year perhaps 40 to 45 migrants from elsewhere per 1,000 of their population to maintain a growth rate of 3 percent per year. Such a rate of migration could easily be maintained as long as the rural portion of the population was large, but when this condition ceased to obtain, the maintenance of the same urban rate meant an increasing drain on the countryside.

Why did the rural-urban migration occur? The reason was that the rise in technological enhancement of human productivity, together with certain constant factors, rewarded urban concentration. One of the constant factors was that agriculture uses land as its prime instrument of production and hence spreads out people who are engaged in it, whereas manufacturing, commerce and services use land only as a site. Moreover, the demand for agricultural products is less elastic than the demand for services and manufactures. As productivity grows, services and manufactures can absorb more manpower by paying higher wages. Since nonagricultural activities can use land simply as a site, they can locate near one another (in towns and cities) and thus minimize the fraction of space inevitably involved in the division of labor. At the same time, as agricultural technology is improved, capital costs in farming rise and manpower becomes not only less needed but also economically more burdensome. A substantial portion of the agricultural population is therefore sufficiently disadvantaged, in relative terms, to be attracted by higher wages in other sectors.

In this light one sees why a large flow of people from farms to cities was generated in every country that passed through the industrial revolution. One also sees why, with an even higher proportion of people already in cities and with the inability of city people to replace themselves by reproduction, the drain eventually became so heavy that in many nations the rural population began to decline in absolute as well as relative terms. In Sweden it declined after 1920, In England and Wales after 1861, in Belgium after 1910.

Realizing that urbanization is transitional and finite, one comes on another fact—a fact that throws light on the circumstances in which urbanization comes to an end. A basic feature of the transition is the profound switch from agricultural to nonagricultural employment. This change is associated with urbanization but not identical with it. The difference emerges particularly in the later stages. Then the availability of automobiles, radios, motion pictures and electricity, as well as the reduction of the workweek and the workday, mitigate the disadvantages of living in the country. Concurrently the expanding size of cities makes them more difficult to live in. The population classed as "rural" is accordingly enlarged, both from cities and from true farms.

For these reasons the "rural" population in some industrial countries never did fall in absolute size. In all the industrial countries, however, the population dependent on agriculture—which the reader will recognize as a more functional definition of the nonurban population than mere rural residence—decreased in absolute as well as relative terms. In the United States, for example, the net migration from farms totaled more than 27 million between 1920 and 1959 and thus averaged approximately 700,000 a year. As a result the farm population declined from 32.5 million in 1916 to 20.5 million in 1960, in spite of the large excess of births in farm families. In 1964, by a stricter American definition classifying as "farm families" only those families actually earning their living from agriculture, the farm population was down to 12.9 million. This number represented 6.8 percent of the nation's population; the comparable figure for 1880 was 44 percent. In Great Britain the number of males occupied in agriculture was at its peak, 1.8 million, in 1851; by 1961 it had fallen to .5 million.

In the later stages of the cycle, then, urbanization in the industrial countries tends to cease. Hence the connection between economic development and the growth of cities also ceases. The change is explained by two circumstances. First, there is no longer enough farm population to furnish a significant migration to the cities. (What can 12.9 million American farmers contribute to the growth of the 100 million people already in urbanized areas?) Second, the rural nonfarm population, nourished by refugees from the expanding cities, begins to increase as fast as the city population. The effort of census bureaus to count fringe residents as urban simply pushes the definition of "urban" away from the notion of dense settlement and in the direction of the term "nonfarm." As the urban population becomes more "rural," which is to say less densely settled, the advanced industrial peoples are for a time able to enjoy the amenities of urban life without the excessive crowding of the past.

Here, however, one again encounters the fact that a cessation of urbanization does not necessarily mean a cessation of city growth. An example is provided by New Zealand. Between 1945 and 1961 the proportion of New Zealand's population classed as urban—that is, the ratio between urban and rural residents—changed hardly at all (from 61.3 percent to 63.6 percent) but the urban population increased by 50 percent. In Japan between 1940 and 1950 urbanization actually decreased slightly, but the urban population increased by 13 percent.

The point to be kept in mind is that once urbanization ceases, city growth becomes a function of general population growth. Enough farm-to-city migration may still occur to redress the difference in natural increase. The reproductive rate of urbanites tends, however, to increase when they live at lower densities, and the reproductive rate of "urbanized" farmers tends to decrease; hence little migration is required to make the urban increase equal the national increase.

I now turn to the currently underdeveloped countries. With the advanced nations having slackened their rate of urbanization, it is the others—representing three-fourths of humanity—that are mainly responsible for the rapid urbanization now characterizing the world as a whole. In fact, between 1950 and 1960 the proportion of the population in cities of 100,000 or more rose about a third faster in the underdeveloped regions than in the developed ones. Among the underdeveloped regions the pace was slow in eastern and southern Europe, but in the rest of the underdeveloped world the proportion in cities rose twice as fast as it did in the industrialized countries, even though the latter countries in many cases broadened their definitions of urban places to include more suburban and fringe residents.

Because of the characteristic pattern of urbanization, the current rates of urbanization in underdeveloped countries could be expected to exceed those now existing in countries far advanced in the cycle. On discovering that this is the case one is tempted to say that the underdeveloped regions are now in the typical stage of urbanization associated with early economic development. This notion, however, is erroneous. In their urbanization the underdeveloped countries are definitely not repeating past history. Indeed, the best grasp of their present situation comes from analyzing how their course differs from the previous pattern of development.

The first thing to note is that today's underdeveloped countries are urbanizing not only more rapidly than the industrial nations are now but also more rapidly than the industrial nations did in the heyday of their urban growth. The difference, however, is not large. In 40 underdeveloped countries for which we have data in recent decades, the average gain in the proportion of the population urban was 20 percent per decade; in 16 industrial countries, during the decades of their most rapid urbanization (mainly in the 19th century), the average gain per decade was 15 percent.

This finding that urbanization is proceeding only a little faster in underdeveloped countries than it did historically in the advanced nations may be questioned by the reader. It seemingly belies the widespread impression that cities throughout the nonindustrial parts of the world are bursting with people. There is, however, no contradiction. One must recall the basic distinction between a change in the proportion of the population urban, which is a ratio, and the absolute growth of cities. The popular impression is correct: the cities in underdeveloped areas are growing at a disconcerting rate. They are far outstripping the city boom of the industrializing era in the nineteenth century. If they continue their recent rate of growth, they will double their population every 15 years.

In 34 underdeveloped countries for which we have data relating to the 1940s and 1950s, the average annual gain in the urban population was 4.5 percent. The figure is remarkably similar for the various regions: 4.7 percent in seven countries of Africa, 4.7 percent in 15 countries of Asia and 4.3 percent in 12 countries of Latin America. In contrast, in nine European countries during their period of fastest urban population growth (mostly in the latter half of the nineteenth century) the average gain per year was 2.1 percent. Even the frontier industrial countries—the United States, Australia—New Zealand, Canada and Argentina—which received huge numbers of immigrants, had a smaller population growth in towns and cities: 4.2 percent per year. In Japan and the U.S.S.R. the rate was respectively 5.4 and 4.3 percent per year, but their economic growth began only recently.

How is it possible that the contrast in growth between today's underdeveloped countries and yesterday's industrializing countries is sharper with respect to the absolute urban population than with respect to the urban share of the total population? The answer lies in another profound difference between the two sets of countries—a difference in total population growth, rural as well as urban. Contemporary underdeveloped populations have been growing since 1940 more than twice as fast as industrialized populations, and their increase far exceeds the growth of the latter at the peak of their expansion. The only rivals in an earlier day were the frontier nations, which had the help of great streams of immigrants. Today the underdeveloped nations—already densely settled, tragically impoverished and with gloomy economic prospects—are multiplying their people by sheer biological increase at a rate that is unprecedented. It is this population boom that is overwhelmingly responsible for the rapid inflation of city populations in such countries. Contrary to popular opinion both inside and outside those countries, the main factor is not rural-urban migration.

This point can be demonstrated easily by a calculation that has the effect of eliminating the influence of general population growth on urban growth. The calculation involves assuming that the total population of a given country remained constant over a period of time but that the percentage urban changed as it did historically. In this manner one obtains the growth of the absolute urban population that would have occurred if rural-urban migration were the only factor affecting it. As an example, Costa Rica had in 1927 a total population of 471,500, of which 88,600, or 18.8 percent, was urban. By 1963 the country's total population was 1,325,200 and the urban population was 456,600, or 34.5 percent. If the total population had remained at 471,500 but the percentage urban had still risen from 18.8 to 34.5, the absolute urban population in 1963 would have been only 162,700. That is the growth that would have occurred in the urban population if rural-urban migration had been the only factor. In actuality the urban population rose to 456,600. In other words, only 20 percent of the rapid growth of Costa Rica's towns and cities was attributable to urbanization per se; 44 percent was attributable solely to the country's general population increase, the remainder to the joint operation of both factors. Similarly, in Mexico between 1940 and 1960, 50 percent of the urban population increase was attributable to national multiplication alone and only 22 percent to urbanization alone.

The past performance of the advanced countries presents a sharp contrast. In Switzerland between 1850 and 1888, when the proportion urban resembled that in Costa Rica recently, general population growth alone accounted for only 19 percent of the increase of town and city people, and rural-urban migration alone accounted for 60 percent. In France between 1846 and 1911 only 21 percent of the growth in the absolute urban population was due to general growth alone.

The conclusion to which this contrast points is that one anxiety of governments in the underdeveloped nations is misplaced. Impressed by the mushrooming in their cities of shantytowns filled with ragged peasants, they attribute the fantastically fast city growth to rural-urban migration. Actually this migration now does little more than make up for the small difference in the birth rate between city and countryside. In the history of the industrial nations, as we have seen, the sizable difference between urban and rural birth rates and death rates required that cities, if they were to grow, had to have an enourmous influx of people from farms and villages. Today in the underdeveloped countries the towns and cities have only a slight disadvantage in fertility, and their old disadvantage in mortality not only has been wiped out but also in many cases has been reversed. During the nineteenth century the urbanizing nations were learning how to keep crowded populations in cities from dying like flies. Now the lesson has been learned, and it is being applied to cities even in countries just emerging from tribalism. In fact, a disproportionate share of public health funds goes into cities. As a result throughout the nonindustrial world people in cities are multiplying as never before, and rural-urban migration is playing a much lesser role.

The trends just described have an important implication for the rural population. Given the explosive overall population growth in underdeveloped countries, it follows that if the rural population is not to pile up on the land and reach an economically absurd density, a high rate of rural-urban migration must be maintained. Indeed, the exodus from rural areas should be higher than in the past. But this high rate of internal movement is not taking place, and there is some doubt that it could conceivably do so.

To elaborate I shall return to my earlier point that in the evolution of industrialized countries the rural citizenry often declined in absolute as well as relative terms. The rural population of France—26.8 million in 1846—was down to 20.8 million by 1926 and 17.2 million by 1962, notwithstanding a gain in the nation's total population during this period. Sweden's rural population dropped from 4.3 million in 1910 to 3.5 million in 1960. Since the category "rural" includes an increasing portion of urbanites living in fringe areas, the historical drop was more drastic and consistent specifically in the farm population. In the United States, although the "rural" population never quite ceased to grow, the farm contingent began its long descent shortly after the turn of the century; today it is less than two-fifths of what it was in 1910.

This transformation is not occurring in contemporary underdeveloped countries. In spite of the enormous growth of their cities, their rural populations—and their more narrowly defined agricultural populations—are growing at a rate that in many cases exceeds the rise of even the urban population during the evolution of the now advanced countries. The poor countries thus confront a grave dilemma. If they do not substantially step up the exodus from rural areas, these areas will be swamped with underemployed farmers. If they do step up the exodus, the cities will grow at a disastrous rate.

The rapid growth of cities in the advanced countries, painful though it was, had the effect of solving a problem—the problem of the rural population. The growth of cities enabled agricultural holdings to be consolidated, allowed increased capitalization and in general resulted in greater efficiency. Now, however, the underdeveloped countries are experiencing an even more rapid urban growth—and are suffering from urban problems—but urbanization is not solving their rural ills.

A case in point is Venezuela. Its capital, Caracas, jumped from a population of 359,000 in 1941 to 1,507,000 in 1963; other Venezuelan towns and cities equaled or exceeded this growth. Is this rapid rise denuding the countryside of people? No, the Venezuelan farm population increased in the decade 1951 to 1961 by 11 percent. The only thing that declined was the amount of cultivated land. As a result the agricultural population density became worse. In 1950 there were some 64 males engaged in agriculture per square mile of cultivated land: in 1961 there were 78. (Compare this with 4.8 males occupied in agriculture per square mile of cultivated land in Canada, 6.8 in the United States, and 15.6 in Argentina.) With each male occupied in agriculture there are of course dependents. Approximately 225 persons in Venezuela are trying to live from each square mile of cultivated land. Most of the growth of cities in Venezuela is attributable to overall population growth. If the general population had not grown at all, and internal migration had been large enough to produce the actual shift in the proportion in cities, the increase in urban population would have been only 28 percent of what it was and the rural population would have been reduced by 57 percent.

The story of Venezuela is being repeated virtually everywhere in the underdeveloped world. It is not only Caracas that has thousands of squatters living in self-constructed junk houses on land that does not belong to them. By whatever name they are called, the squatters are to be found in all major cities in the poorer countries. They live in broad gullies beneath the main plain in San Salvador and on the hillsides of Rio de Janeiro and Bogotá. They tend to occupy with implacable determination parks, school grounds and vacant lots. Amman, the capital of Jordan, grew from 12,000 in 1958 to 247,000in 1961. A good part of it is slums, and urban amenities are lacking most of the time for most of the people. Greater Baghdad now has an estimated 850,000 people; its slums, like those in many other underdeveloped countries, are in two zones—the central part of the city and the outlying areas. Here are the *sarifa* areas, characterized by self-built reed huts; these areas account for about 45 percent of the housing in the entire city and are devoid of amenities, including even latrines. In addition to such urban problems, all the countries struggling for higher living levels find their rural population growing too and piling up on already crowded land.

I have characterized urbanization as a transformation that, unlike economic development, is finally accomplished and comes to an end. At the 1950 to 1960 rate the term "urbanized world" will be applicable well before the end of the century. One should scarcely expect, however, that mankind will complete its urbanization without major complications. One sign of trouble ahead turns on the distinction I made at the start between urbanization and city growth per se. Around the globe today city growth is disproportionate to urbanization. The discrepancy is paradoxical in the industrial nations and worse than paradoxical in the nonindustrial.

It is in this respect that the nonindustrial nations, which still make up the great majority of nations, are far from repeating past history. In the nineteenth and early twentieth centuries the growth of cities arose from and contributed to economic advancement. Cities took surplus manpower from the countryside and put it to work producing goods and services that in turn helped to modernize agriculture. But today in underdeveloped countries, as in present-day advanced nations, city growth has become increasingly unhinged from economic development and hence from rural-urban migration. It derives in greater degree from overall population growth, and this growth in nonindustrial lands has become unprecedented because of modern health techniques combined with high birth rates.

The speed of world population growth is twice what it was before 1940, and the swiftest increase has shifted from the advanced to the backward nations. In the latter countries, consequently, it is virtually impossible to create city services fast enough to take care of the huge, never-ending cohorts of babies and peasants swelling the urban masses. It is even harder to expand agricultural land and capital fast enough to accommodate the enormous natural increase on farms. The problem is not urbanization, not rural-urban migration, but human multiplication. It is a problem that is new in both its scale and its setting, and runaway city growth is only one of its painful expressions.

As long as the human population expands, cities will expand too, regardless of whether urbanization increases or declines. This means that some individual cities will reach a size that will make nineteenth-century metropolises look like small towns. If the New York urbanized area should continue to grow only as fast as the nation's population (according to medium projections of the latter by the Bureau of the Census), it would reach 21 million by 1985 and 30 million by 2010. I have calculated that if India's population should grow as the U.N. projections indicate it will, the largest city in India in the year 2000 will have between 36 and 66 million inhabitants.

What is the implication of such giant agglomerations for human density? In 1950 the New York–Northeastern New Jersey urbanized area had an average density of 9,810 persons per square mile. With 30 million people in the year 2010, the density would be 24,000 per square mile. Although this level is exceeded now in parts of New York City (which averages about 25,000 per square mile) and many other cities, it is a high density to be spread over such a big area; it would cover, remember, the suburban areas to which people moved to escape high density. Actually, however, the density of the New York urbanized region is dropping, not increasing, as the population grows. The reason is that the territory covered by the urban agglomeration is growing faster than the population: it grew by 51 percent from 1950 to 1960, whereas the population rose by 15 percent.

If, then, one projects the rise in population and the rise in territory for the New York urbanized region, one finds the density problem solved. It is not solved for long, though, because New York is not the only city in the region that is expanding. So are Philadelphia, Trenton, Hartford, New Haven, and so on. By 1960 a huge stretch of territory about 600 miles long and 30 to 100 miles wide along the Eastern seaboard contained some 37 million people. (I am speaking of a longer section of the seaboard than the Boston-to-Washington conurbation referred to by some other authors.) Since the whole area is becoming one big polynucleated city, its population cannot long expand without a rise in density. Thus persistent human multiplication promises to frustrate the ceaseless search for space—for ample residential lots, wide-open suburban school grounds, sprawling shopping centers, one-floor factories, broad freeways.

How people feel about giant agglomerations is best indicated by their headlong effort to escape them. The bigger the city, the higher the cost of space; yet, the more the level of living rises, the more people are willing to pay for low-density living. Nevertheless, as urbanized areas expand and collide, it seems probable that life in low-density surroundings will become too dear for the great majority.

One can of course imagine that cities may cease to grow and may even shrink in size while the population in general continues to multiply. Even this dream, however, would not permanently solve the problem of space. It would eventually obliterate the distinction between urban and rural, but at the expense of the rural.

It seems plain that the only way to stop urban crowding and to solve most of the urban problems besetting both the developed and the underdeveloped nations is to reduce the overall rate of population growth. Policies designed to do this have as yet little intelligence and power behind them. Urban planners continue to treat population growth as something to be planned for, not something to be itself planned. Any talk about applying brakes to city growth is therefore purely speculative, overshadowed as it is by the reality of uncontrolled population increase.

34
Urbanization in Latin America

JORGE E. HARDOY

Every year until the close of the 1970 to 1985 period, a population estimated at 8,766,000 persons will be incorporated into the cities of Latin America. Every year between 1985 and the year 2000, a population estimated at 11 million to 12 million persons will be absorbed into these same cities and into other new cities that may be built. This accelerated urban growth is due to the persistence of a high rate of natural population increase and to migrations from rural areas to the main metropolitan areas and medium-sized cities. These data and these characteristics of Latin American urbanization have been analyzed on numerous occasions.

Latin American urbanization is principally peripheral or coastal, with Mexico and Central America the exceptions to this norm. In South America and the Antilles, urbanization is concentrated in extremely small coastal areas, and the main cities are ports or are located near the principal ports of each country. The main conurbations of each country are coastal: the industrial belt between Buenos Aires and Rosario; the São Paulo–Rio de Janeiro, Santiago–Valparaíso, Lima–Callao, and Caracas–La Guayra complexes; the metropolitan areas of Montevideo, Recife, Salvador, and Porto Alegre in South America; and the Havana metropolitan area in the Antilles. Among the urban clusters in Latin America having more than one million inhabitants, only the metropolitan areas of Mexico and Colombia are located in the interior of the continent.

The origin of the peripheral concentration of urbanization in Latin America dates from the beginning of the sixteenth century, when the Spanish and Portuguese formulated their objectives in occupying these lands. When the Spanish arrived, they found two great indigenous political experiments in America—the Aztec confederation and the Inca empire—which radiated outward from the interior to the coast. They constituted the culmination of a process begun two thousand years before, a process that took place in complete independence from influences external to the continent. But the course of the European conquest and colonization of Latin America was different. Rapid establishment of fortified trading posts and, later, cities, permitted at the same time territorial control and exploitation of natural and human resources, as well as commercial, cultural, and administrative links between the new colonies and Lisbon and, through Sevilla and Cádiz, the Spanish crown. With the exception of Montevideo, all metropolitan areas that had more than one million inhabitants in 1960 were founded in the sixteenth century.

The passage of time accentuated the peripheral course of colonization. Independence from the old Spanish and Portuguese colonies accomplished nothing more than increasing the dependence of the new republics upon European industrial powers and the United States, with the consequent primacy of the principal colonial centers. Railroad and highway networks accentuated this historical tendency. A national model was formed of one or two centers in close contact with external markets and with the European and U.S. interests that determined each country's economic policy, and a periphery made up of a scarcely evolved interior. Contact of each Latin American country with the outside world was achieved through the capital city, and only occasionally through two or three cities. This situation persists. Argentina's external image is provided by Buenos Aires, Uruguay's by Montevideo, Peru's by Lima, Brazil's by Rio de Janeiro and São Paulo, Mexico's by Mexico City, and thus successively. This identification of a nation with its principal city is even stronger in less populous and smaller countries in which the capital is possibly the only city and the only market of any magnitude. These single cities and their metropolitan areas are the centers of political and economic power, finance, the most important cultural activities and universities, and, in general, the main trade ports. This concentration of function and power in extremely limited land areas only widens the breach between the developed and underdeveloped regions of each country.

Not only are contemporary Latin American cities larger and more complex than those of ten or thirty years ago, but also their links within their own national space are closer and more varied. The void that characterized each nation's territory during the nineteenth century and, in certain cases, well into the twentieth century, was finally filled with railroad lines and/or highways and/or airlines, and was also partially populated in the face of demographic pressure and the discovery and exploitation of new natural resources of greater external demand. Gradually, national urban systems expanded, and contacts among the cities of these systems increased. Isolation of the cities from each other decreased, as did the isolation of rural areas which, in zones most closely linked to these cities, were affected by the expansion of urban culture. On the other hand, underdevelopment, poverty, and differences in income and opportunities among regions and among various socioeconomic sectors of the population did not decrease. Neither were basic problems of conservation, health, education, housing, stable employment, and salaries solved for a majority of the population.

In spite of the lack of employment, housing, and urban services, in spite of the fact that the physical environment resulting from this accelerated, fragmented, and spontaneous urbanization deteriorates rapidly, and in spite of the fact that urban life does not permit large sectors of the population to enjoy spiritual and material goods, present-day Latin American cities are serving a greater number of inhabitants in improved fashion. These inhabitants find in the cities sources of employment, opportunities for education and recreation, modes of living together, and general progress, which formerly did not exist and which still do not exist in rural areas and small cities. Thus one could say that urbanization has facilitated improved education and sanitary levels, higher levels and better distribution of income, and a more open attitude on the part of growing percentages of the population toward political, cultural, and technological innovations. Possibly, unemployment and underemployment in the main industrial cities of each Latin American country are presently less than or the same as a generation ago. Possibly, proximity to centers of technical and higher education permits at least some children of working-class families to receive more adequate training. But where and when will it be possible to attempt technical solutions to human problems which persist and worsen, problems such as injustice, violence, and the humiliations imposed upon the population by a system which values profit, superfluity, competition, power, and ostentation at the cost of social justice, harmonious cooperative living, and satisfaction of basic necessities?

There is great variation, not only in the present degree of urbanization of each Latin American country, but also in present rates of urbanization and in urban potential. For example, Uruguay is a country in which 81 percent of the population lives in centers of 2,000 inhabitants or more (about 50 percent lives in the capital city, Montevideo), and the country has an extremely low rate of demographic growth. Since Uruguay is small in size and underpopulated, natural growth of its population, completely channeled into the cities, does not signify very great pressure quantitatively: barely 46,000 per year during the 1970–1985 period. On the other hand, Brazil must absorb about 3,300,000 new inhabitants per year. This is due to the fact that Brazil is not highly urbanized and has an extremely high rate of demographic growth. As a consequence, Brazil's urban population is growing at a rate of 5.67 percent per year, and in certain metropolitan areas the annual rate approaches 10 percent. Argentina, Chile, and Cuba are closer to the Uruguayan case, while Ecuador, certain Central American countries, Paraguay, and Bolivia, all of which are still predominantly rural, have an urbanistic potential that in the long run, on a percentage basis, will surpass even that of Brazil, as well as of Mexico, Colombia, and Peru.

Until a few decades ago, the majority of the world's large metropolitan areas grew because they were industrial centers of world, national, or regional importance. But there is ample evidence that the accelerated process of current urbanization is taking place in less-developed economies without simultaneous industrialization. In Latin America, even though there is a correlation by country and, in fact, by region within each country, in urbanization, per capita income, energy consumption, and percentage of gross national product produced by the industrial sector, it is also clear that the developed, industrialized, and urbanized countries of Latin America do not maintain correlations of the type estimated to exist in countries with more highly developed economies.

In other words, in Latin America, urbanization has not been accompanied by simultaneous and adequate industrialization, or by better distribution of opportunity, income, and consumption. Nor has it been accompanied by the rates of demographic growth already observed for decades in the developed countries. This precarious situation is becoming more acute, since the tertiary sector, already highly supercharged in relation to the development of each Latin American country, is not in a position to provide the employment necessary to maintain by itself an extremely large urban population.

To create employment and provide housing, urban services, and community facilities for a new urban population which, like Latin America's, increases by more than 8.5 million people per year, requires extremely large investment and operating costs. Yet little is known about this entire process. The situation, as I explained earlier, is substantially different in Brazil and Uruguay, both extreme cases. In general, however, it seems that few Latin American countries are in position, in the short and medium run, to provide housing, urban services, and facilities, to say nothing of employment, to the new urban population if present criteria and values are maintained. Here, once again, the possibilities of Argentina and Bolivia, which in this aspect are extreme cases, are also very different. My own conclusion is that, given the present power structure, there is no solution to the urban problem of Latin America, just as there is no solution to its development. In part this is due to the fact that, for historical reasons that not only have been maintained but that also appear to be increasing, the Latin American countries are organized as primary, export economies. There are too many powerful internal and external interests in almost all Latin American countries for this situation not to continue. The infrastructure networks and the spatial structure within each country, aspects that may be analyzed on any map and with statistical data, confirm this conclusion. In part this is due to the fact that for internal and external reasons it is difficult for national movements with broad popular participation to arise, movements that could shake the peoples of Latin America out of an apathy that is nothing more than a reflection of ancestral exploitation. These same interests have been careful to see that these movements do not take root, or have weakened them. Yet, in Latin America, the search is continuing for new initiatives, new ideas and experiences, permitting conscious affirmation of the collective responsibility of the peoples of Latin America and of the necessity of self-determination and participation.

The existing Latin American urban situation can be dealt with only through a broad, coordinated, and revolutionary approach of general scope for each country and particular focus for each city. It involves the definition of policies, elaboration of plans, and coordination of programs and investment. It involves the simultaneous action of creating and executing, restating the concepts of property and inheritance of material goods, denouncing an aristocratic society and a power structure that bases perpetuation of political control *(continuismo)* and, as a consequence, exploitation of poverty upon the control of wealth and justice.

There is hardly a municipal administration in Latin America that enjoys the financial resources, political power, technical personnel, and knowledge of existing problems to direct the growth of its particular city in an orderly manner. It is a fact that municipal governments do not have planning organisms of adequate technical competence, or, if they do exist, local planning agencies are unable to pressure similar organisms at the national regional, and provincial levels. National governments and intermediate decision-making levels—provinces, states, or departments—have delayed in recognizing this situation, and still do not face it with concrete action.

Gradually, the Latin American governments have embraced economic planning as a means of governmental action. Even though it has been far from effective, in certain countries it has been accepted. Nevertheless, social and spatial aspects of development have not enjoyed equal attention, and no Latin American country to date has attempted to incorporate urban policies at the national and regional levels. The private sector in turn has profited from this situation, and its activities have been instrumental in increasing the disorderly and speculative character of current urbanization in the face of the passive attitude of the public sector.

Information and research are required in order to make adequate decisions, and it is safe to say that research into Latin American urban problems is still insufficient. Information gathered by censuses undertaken by different levels of government is fragmentary and highly diverse. A large portion is of little use for serious urban studies. Basic information is also lacking regarding transportation, investment, consumption, labor, the housing and land market, etc. Many advances have been made during the past ten years, but it has still been difficult to elicit broad interest from economists, sociologists, anthropologists, and political scientists, and only a few lawyers and groups of architects and engineers have become involved. Technological research directed at urban problems is nonexistent. More notable advances are achieved in conceptual clarification than in the research that would serve to determine policy. This should not surprise us from a continent that dedicates more money to promoting the sale of frequently unnecessary products and artifacts than to urban studies, or that spends on armaments a sum that could satisfy 50 percent of the annual housing demand caused by natural population increase.

The precarious nature of the construction industry is significant for an urban population with the previously mentioned characteristics. Even in the most economically and technically advanced countries of Latin America, the construction industry has only recently begun to apply the techniques and systems that have revolutionized other industries. In addition, methods to achieve the rapid and well-coordinated construction of cities are not used since other essential preconditions do not exist. Traditional construction systems persist in Latin America. Heavy industrialism has recently been applied to construction, but its action will continue to be shackled if the diffused system of individual credit applying to isolated housing units is not overcome, fragmentation of urban land is not checked, and construction programs in urban services and facilities are not better coordinated. All of this contributes to the costly and chaotic panorama of Latin American urban development.

Urbanization of the magnitude and tendencies of Latin American would constitute a threat to any industrialized and economically developed country or region. If it is faced by less-developed countries that for the moment have precarious sources of investment, scarce technical resources, and low technological levels, it assumes crisis characteristics. While it is possible to determine what is wrong, it is more difficult to define an urban strategy of national scope, and much more difficult to transform this strategy into plans and programs for subsequent implementation. To date, the passivity with which Latin American governments have faced the growth of cities, and the unilateral physical approach with which they believed they could solve their problems, have not been entirely overcome. In addition, private enterprise has failed to solve the problems posed by economic development, population growth, and urbanization, areas in which it could collaborate by creating new employment, providing housing and urban services, and maintaining an adequate environment, among other contributions. On the other hand, backed by the prevailing power structure, private enterprise has used the giddy process of urbanization and the growing demand for land, housing, and urban services for speculative ends, distorting prices and creating situations that are extremely difficult or costly to overcome.

The future model of the Latin American city without adequate financing is difficult to predict. Many factors influence a country's spatial structure. Similarly, incorporation of new technologies or the adoption of new (for Latin America) social concepts regarding the right to property or the redistribution of power may also affect a city's internal structure. Thus, predictions are subject to great error and drastic change in each Latin American country's sociopolitical organization. In addition, how can such rapid urbanization be financed without investment resources, which are often diverted to what is considered more dynamic investment?

One way is to reduce the costs of urbanization, without lowering the standards permitting a housing unit and complementary urban services to last at least fifty years. This may in part be achieved by massively financed projects with technology appropriate to each country's stage of development. The latter requires avoiding dispersing credit in an isolated manner, advancing the technology employed in transportation and communications and construction, and developing land in logical sizes and locations. Another way of reducing costs is to recover the added value (produced by urbanization) for the benefit of society and not for speculators or fortunate owners. Still another way is to perfect the technique of building makeshift housing, given that such housing is an inescapable fact at the moment, in order to improve its habitability and facilitate its construction in areas already provided with urban services and community facilities. The three formulas suggested, implemented in the short run, are based upon the premise that there is no adequate solution to urban development without an energetic, continuous, and visionary land acquisition policy that would permit order and deter speculation, and without state control of the factors that have carried Latin American cities to their present state.

As foreshadowed above, state control of land for future urban expansion is a guarantee that the city will be reconditioned at levels still difficult to foresee and will incorporate technologies that in the developing countries are still entirely too costly. It is, in addition, the road to abolishing unjust divisions by socioeconomic level caused by the land and rental market, which has exploited existing regulations and codes. Nevertheless, socialization of urban and suburban land is only a precondition, though perhaps the most important, for a national solution to the problem of needed urban transformation. Yet the latter may not be begun without an economy that serves the entire society.

My concept of a city built for the entire population, which for the moment lacks the required investment resources, is concerned more properly with environmental, social, and economic issues than with architecture. I do not wish to suggest that aesthetics are forgotten. It is simply necessary to adopt less individualistic, less monumental aesthetics, combined with adequate use of the natural landscape. This could be the city in less developed countries for many years. It should not, however, serve as an excuse for the improvised, though partially ostentatious city of the socioeconomic classes which has caused the current misery of a majority of the population. Above all, it should not be the city of extremes so evident in Latin America today.

35
The Migration Turnaround: End of a Phenomenon?

ANTHONY AGRESTA

The Migration Turnaround, a phrase used to describe the net movement of migrants from the metropolitan to the nonmetropolitan United States during the 1970s, represents a reversal of historic patterns. Prior to 1970 metropolitan areas had been growing at a faster rate than their nonmetropolitan counterparts. The Turnaround was not expected in a nation that had been becoming more urban with each passing decade.

Social scientists, politicians and city planners have long recognized the problems of rapid metropolitan growth: rising metro crime, city overcrowding, escalating unemployment, poverty and pollution. But with the onset of the Migration Turnaround, the ruralization of America (or the decentralization of urban areas at the very least) had begun.

According to the latest census data it appears that this reversal was a temporary characteristic of the 1970s. Metropolitan America's growth is faster once again. Slackening migration away from the metropolitan areas played a key role in this "return to normalcy."

DEFINITIONS OF URBAN-NESS

The Census Bureau's detailed criteria defining what constitutes urban, rural, metropolitan, and nonmetropolitan has changed over the decades. The term metropolitan is synonomous with Standard Metropolitan Statistical Area or SMSA, (recently revised to MSA[1]). Counties are the building blocks of the SMSA. The SMSA includes contiguous counties if the counties meet certain criteria and are "socially and economically integrated with the central city."[2] This group of counties must have at least one city of 50,000 inhabitants or "twin cities" whose combined population totals at least 50,000. New England, where cities and towns, not counties, are the components of SMSAs, is an exception to the rule.

An urbanized area, defined by the Census Bureau in 1950, differs from a SMSA in a number of ways. An urbanized area is comprised of one or more central cities and an urban fringe. Urbanized areas are not defined by county limits. The urbanized area can be thought of as the core of the SMSA, which can include some rural territory (i.e., a remote part of an SMSA's county that does not meet density requirements or urban fringe criteria). SMSAs can and often do include suburban development.

Nonmetro areas which gained net migrants during the Turnaround did so for a number of reasons. Job opportunities have traditionally been an influential pull factor in a migrant's decision to move. As cities became decentralized and job opportunities increased in nonmetro counties, the numbers of metro to nonmetro migrants increased. However, motivations for moving during the Turnaround became less economic in nature. Certain rural counties were perceived by the migrants as more attractive in their amenities or quality-of-life. Migrants to nonmetro areas emphasized the importance of noneconomic factors in their decisions to move, according to Calvin Beale and Linda Swanson.[3]

THE TURNAROUND'S TURNAROUND

The onset of the Eighties appears to have marked an end to the Turnaround. Between 1980 and 1982 metropolitan areas gained almost 4.1 million inhabitants in contrast with the nonmetropolitan areas' increase of 1 million. Table 35.1 compares metro and nonmetro average annual percent changes for two periods. While nonmetropolitan America grew at an average rate of 1.34 percent annually in the 1970s, this has dropped substantially to 0.83 percent between 1980 and 1982. The South and West continue to grow at a much faster pace. Although the data do not depict across-

Table 35.1. Metropolitan and Nonmetropolitan Annual Average Percent Change by Region, 1970–1980, 1980–1982.

Region	Metropolitan		Nonmetropolitan	
	1980–1982	1970–1980	1980–1982	1970–1980
United States	1.04	1.00	0.83	1.34
North	0.09	0.08	0.17	0.77
Northeast	0.11	−0.10	0.29	0.94
New England	0.29	0.23	0.77	1.45
Middle Atlantic	0.06	−0.19	0.01	0.65
North Central	0.07	0.26	0.13	0.71
East North Central	−0.11	0.18	0.01	0.92
West North Central	0.70	0.55	0.29	0.47
South	2.01	1.96	1.04	1.53
South Atlantic	1.79	1.93	1.02	1.70
East South Central	0.70	1.34	0.41	1.37
West South Central	2.95	2.33	1.68	1.44
West	1.88	2.04	2.14	2.65
Mountain	2.70	3.45	2.37	2.70
Pacific	1.67	1.72	1.83	2.59

Source: Richard L. Forstall and Richard A. Engels, "Growth of Nonmetropolitan Areas Slows," Bureau of the Census, Press Release, March 16, 1984.

Note: Metropolitan Statistical Areas are as defined by the Office of Management and Budget effective June 30, 1984.

the-board decreases in nonmetro growth (nonmetro growth in the West South Central did experience a slight increase between the two periods), the results indicate a slowing of nonmetropolitan growth and the revival of metropolitan area growth in the 1980s. Those leaving metro areas for nonmetro areas are classified as in-migrants, while out-migrants are defined as those leaving nonmetro areas for metro areas. By subtracting the out-migration rate from the in-migration rate the net migration rate is computed. The nonmetropolitan population at the end of the interval serves as the denominator for both rates. Ideally, a base population at the beginning of the interval would be used, but when computing for a period as short as one year, using end of the interval figures should not result in any significant change. Positive net rates indicate a preponderance of migrants from metro areas over those leaving nonmetro areas (more in-migrants than out-migrants).

LEAVING THE METROPOLIS

Differences in net migration rates between the periods is a likely explanation for the changes in growth patterns. A comparison of net migration rates for a one year interval in the middle of the Migration Turnaround (1975 to 1976) and rates for an interval in the early 1980s (1982 to 1983) clearly shows that the flow of migrants to rural America is not as strong in the early 1980s as it was during the Turn-

Table 35.2. Net Migration Rates per 1,000 Population by Age and Sex for Nonmetropolitan Areas of the United States, 1982–1983 and 1975–1976

Age	Males		Females	
	1982–1983	1975–1976	1982–1983	1975–1976
16–24	−10.99	−8.21	−18.08	−12.47
25–34	+2.43	+20.10	+0.35	+11.22
35–44	+4.12	+6.69	−1.55	+5.24
45–64	+5.07	+9.07	+2.30	+9.73
65+	−0.14	+9.10	+1.11	+4.85

Source: Series P-20, No. 393, Geographic Mobility: March 1982–March 1983 and Series P-20. No. 305, Geographic Mobility: March 1975–March 1976.

Note: Both of these volumes use the 1970 Census Bureau definition of SMSA.

around. Table 35.2 provides this comparison, showing that net migration rates for the mid-year interval of the migration Turnaround indicate a net movement of migrants to nonmetropolitan areas. This is true for both males and females except those age 16 to 24.

The picture of metropolitan mobility changed dramatically by the early 1980s. By 1982 to 1983, a near balance of people migrating between metro and nonmetro areas had occurred. The Migration Turnaround may have been a phenomenon restricted to the 1970s. If indications of its presence still exist today, it is safe to say that the phenomenon is past its heydey.

Whether or not metropolitan areas will grow at a faster pace through the remaining years of this decade is not known. In any case, the ramifications of augmented metropolitan growth are potentially significant ones. Because of this, the need to monitor the urbanization or ruralization of the United States will always be of great concern to demographers.

NOTES

1. As of June 30, 1983, the Office of Management and Budget redefined metropolitan criteria. The term SMSA was changed to MSA (Metropolitan Statistical Area) with different standards applying. For explanation of these criteria see Richard L. Forstall and Maria Elena Gonzalez, "Twenty Questions: What You Should Know About the New Metropolitan Areas," in *American Demographics,* April 1984.
2. Census of the Population: 1970, Volume 1, Characteristics of the Population. Part A *Number of Inhabitants.* Washington DC: U.S. Government Printing Office, 1972, pp. xii–xiii.
3. Linda L. Swanson and Calvin L. Beale, "Patterns and Variations of the Flow of Metropolitan Migrants to Nonmetropolitan Counties, 1975–1980," Economic Research Service Publication, Washington, DC: U.S. Department of Agriculture, 1983, pp. 4–6.

36
Sun Belt Growth: Not What It Seems?

CARL HAUB

Unless one had just arrived in the United States from an extended sojourn on a remote island, it would be difficult not to know about that elusive geographic entity, the "Sun Belt." Everyone "knows" that the Frost Belt of the North, with its plethora of abandoned factories, is being forsaken by hordes of migrants seeking the good life of the Sun Belt. The traditional industries of the North, reeling from competition from Japan, have been unable to support continued population growth as people head for the new, "high-tech" and short-sleeve areas of the South and West. This would, at least, be the impression one would get from today's literature and media.

To be sure, there are many sound reasons for such an impression. Since 1980, over 90 percent of total U.S. population growth has been in the Sun Belt. In the 821 days between April 1, 1980, and July 1, 1982, during which the Frost Belt states lost an estimated 1 million persons via migration, the Sun Belt gained about 2.3 million. Thus, one might glean a rather dichotomous picture of U.S. population change.

But to really understand current U.S. demography, it is necessary to take a closer look at what is actually happening in the Sun Belt. First, contrary to the picture of westward and southward heading "hordes," not all Sun Belt states have net immigration; in fact, more than a third have net *out*-migration. Second, it may well be that higher fertility in the Sun Belt will prove to be a more important factor in future growth than the arrival of new residents. Finally, there is the eternal problem of the definition of the "Sun Belt"—just where is it?

Let's tackle the last problem first. A March 1981 issue of *American Demographics* pointed to at least half a dozen definitions of the Sun Belt: one definition included Missouri, while another excluded the Gulf states of Alabama, Louisiana, and Mississippi! Most typical, however, is use of the Census Bureau's two large Regions, the South and West, as a convenient grouping. This choice, it should be noted, takes in all states from Delaware to Florida as well as such Mountain states as Idaho and Montana.

Defining the Sun Belt as the Census Bureau's South plus West is really only justified by its ease. Other definitions require often lengthy regroupings of data. Demographer Calvin Beale of the Department of Agriculture has analyzed U.S. migration trends by ignoring state boundaries and creating 26 regions using county-level data. These economically and socially interrelated areas, such as the Southern Corn Belt and Northern Pacific Coast, make much more sense than the two part Sun Belt-Frost Belt categorization and give a truer picture of population change. For the purposes of this chapter, however, we will stay with the more common "Sun Belt," the South and West.

The next point to set straight is the impression that all Sun Belt states are receiving heavy in-migration. In fact, 12 of the 29 Sun Belt states actually lost population by migration from 1980 to 1982 (see Table 36.1). These states range from Delaware and Maryland in the northern areas of the Sun Belt to the Gulf States of Alabama and Mississippi and the Pacific states of Oregon and Hawaii. In the meantime, a majority of Frost Belt states (14 out of 21) were experiencing outmigration, just as expected, but this outward flow was concentrated in only four states (Indiana, Illionis, Michigan, and Ohio).

One note is necessary on the estimates of migration themselves. The Census Bureau derives them by a combination of methods which uses such indicators as changes in school enrollment, tax returns, state of intended residence of immigrants from abroad, resident births and deaths, and Medicare records. Estimates are subject to some error, which the Bureau continually evaluates. Thus, the estimate of −1,000 outmigration for Hawaii cannot be taken completely on face value; it is possible that there was actually a small amount of net migration into Hawaii.

Table 36.1. States Ranked by Migration Rate per 1,000 Population, 1980–1982, with Absolute Migration Numbers Shown
(Sunbelt States shown in boldface)

Rank and State	Rate	Number
1. **Nevada**	78	62,000
2. **Florida**	62	601,000
3. **Texas**	47	667,000
4. **Alaska**	45	18,000
5. **Wyoming**	34	16,000
6. **Oklahoma**	31	95,000
7. **Colorado**	28	82,000
8. **Arizona**	27	75,000
9. **California**	23	535,000
10. New Hampshire	18	17,000
11. **Georgia**	13	71,000
12. **New Mexico**	12	16,000
12. **Louisiana**	12	51,000
12. **Utah**	12	17,000
15. **Virginia**	11	61,000
16. **North Carolina**	10	57,000
17. **Washington**	7	29,000
17. **South Carolina**	7	21,000
UNITED STATES	6	1,257,000
19. Connecticut	5	17,000
20. Rhode Island	4	4,000
21. North Dakota	3	2,000
22. Massachusetts	1	7,000
22. New Jersey	1	8,000
24. Kansas	0	—
24. **Tennessee**	0	−1,000
26. **Hawaii**	−1	−1,000
27. **Delaware**	−2	−1,000
28. **Alabama**	−3	−12,000
28. **Maryland**	−3	−13,000
30. Wisconsin	−4	−17,000
30. New York	−4	−65,000
30. **Montana**	−4	−3,000
30. Maine	−4	−5,000
34. Minnesota	−6	−23,000
34. Vermont	−6	−3,000
34. Missouri	−6	−31,000
37. Pennsylvania	−7	−88,000
38. Nebraska	−8	−13,000
38. **Idaho**	−8	−8,000
40. **Mississippi**	−9	−23,000
41. **West Virginia**	−12	−23,000
41. **Arkansas**	−12	−27,000
43. **Oregon**	−13	−33,000
44. **Kentucky**	−14	−50,000
45. Illinois	−15	−171,000
45. Ohio	−15	167,000
47. Iowa	−18	−53,000
48. Indiana	−19	−107,000
49. South Dakota	−22	−15,000
50. Michigan	−33	−305,000

Table 36.2. States Ranked by Births per 100 Deaths, 1980–1982
(Sunbelt States shown in boldface)

State	Birth/Death Ratio
1. **Alaska**	550
2. **Utah**	522
3. **Hawaii**	373
4. **Wyoming**	329
5. **New Mexico**	300
5. **Idaho**	300
7. **Colorado**	270
8. **Texas**	256
9. **Arizona**	240
10. **Nevada**	238
11. North Dakota	233
11. **Louisiana**	233
13. **California**	225
14. **Washington**	215
15. **Montana**	213
16. Minnesota	208
17. South Dakota	207
18. **South Carolina**	205
18. **Georgia**	205
20. **Mississippi**	200
21. **Oregon**	198
22. Kansas	190
23. Michigan	189
24. Nebraska	188
24. **Oklahoma**	188
26. **Virginia**	187
27. Wisconsin	185
28. Illinois	184
UNITED STATES	184
29. Indiana	183
30. **Delaware**	182
30. **Maryland**	182
30. New Hampshire	182
33. Vermont	180
34. **Alabama**	177
35. **Kentucky**	175
36. Ohio	174
37. **North Carolina**	173
37. Iowa	173
39. **Tennessee**	169
40. **Arkansas**	164
41. Missouri	159
42. Maine	154
43. **West Virginia**	149
44. Connecticut	148
45. New York	144
46. New Jersey	143
47. Rhode Island	133
47. Pennsylvania	133
49. **Florida**	129
50. Massachusetts	128

Note: Data for Tables 36.1 and 36.2 from *Current Population Reports, Series* P-25, No. 927. Rates based on 1980 Census population.

The figures in the table tell us several things about the Sun Belt/Frost Belt trends. On both the losing side and the gaining side, the phenomenon is really only found in a few states. On the receiving side, California, Florida, and Texas stand out. It is these three states that have largely given the Sun Belt its reputation as a magnet for migration; they account for just under 80 percent of the Sun Belt's migration gain. On the losing side, Indiana, Illinois, Michigan, and Ohio account for three-fourths of the Frost Belt's loss. As for the other 43 states, they are presently gaining or losing migrants at a very modest rate.

So much for the present. What of the future? Migration patterns can be volatile and today's given can be tomorrow's old news. The oil shortage of the 1970s caused an unprecedented demand for coal causing rapid population growth in the Appalachian coal areas. But, with the stabiliziation of oil prices, those areas, such as West Virginia, are now losing population. In the future, limited water supplies cast doubt upon just how long rapid population growth can continue in the Southwest. In addition, states attractive to large numbers of migrants often take some steps to discourage too many new residents. While direct action to stop migration is unconstitutional (as Hawaii found out a few years ago), state or local action on zoning, housing permits, sewer moratoriums and the like can effectively discourage growth. And, in other states, environmental groups are becoming alarmed at infringement of wilderness areas.

One notable difference does stand out between the Sun Belt and the Frost Belt, however, and that is the relative youth of the population and the difference in that part of population growth caused by natural increase (the surplus of births over deaths). This situation is not likely to change very quickly in the near future since it depends on a state's age structure, and any change in a state's age structure is likely to occur only very slowly. Therefore, during the 1980s, we can expect greater growth due to births than migrants in the Sun Belt compared to the Frost Belt.

The "birth-death ratio" in Table 36.2 is simply the number of births per 100 deaths in each state from 1980 to 1982. While some of the difference among states on this measure is caused by variation in birth rates among the states, it is also due to the younger age structure of many Sun Belt states. (The younger a population, the lower the crude death rate, generally speaking.) Some northern states, where births are now only about one-third higher than deaths, will probably decline in population if these rates continue, as their populations age. The majority of states have fertility below the level needed for long-term "replacement" of the population (about two children per woman), but in the Sun Belt both higher levels of actual fertility and generally younger population ensure population growth due to fertility alone, at least for the 1980s.

So, the Sun Belt/Frost Belt phenomenon, upon closer inspection, illustrates that there are often more factors underlying many demographic trends than indicated by the "obvious." While migration certainly contributes its share to U.S. population change, only a small number of states are affected in a significant way and migration trends themselves can be quite changeable. Perhaps the ultimate difference between the two areas will prove to be their differences in fertility.

37
Cross-National Comparison of Population Density

ALICE TAYLOR DAY
LINCOLN H. DAY

Many uses of the concept of human population density generate more heat than light.

Although the inadequacy of population density as an indicator of social conditions has long been recognized by geographers, the concept is still being used for this purpose by various government officials, economists, journalists, and demographers. Exponential growth in urban areas—as well as less, although still very substantial, growth in population generally—has spurred a new interest in population density and, with this interest, an unfortunate temptation toward spurious generalization about levels of crowding and their impact on peoples in different countries around the world.

Yet the measurements of population density remains much too rudimentary to warrant the inferences about physical and social conditions currently being based upon it: and, moreover, the concept of population density is, itself, often misconstrued, particularly with reference to two types of interpretation: (i) the possibilities the concept offers for comparing conditions of life in countries with marked differences in population size, cultural patterns, and levels of income and consumption and (ii) the conclusion that can be drawn from density levels concerning a nation's population-carrying capacity—that is, the capacity of a society to sustain varying numbers of people in the present and future at given levels of living and patterns of life.

MISUSES OF THE CONCEPT

The use of density levels to support a variety of political and social positions is an old story. "Unfavorable" comparisons of the average population density of one country with those of other countries, for example, has been resorted to both by governments in support of expansionist foreign policies and by historians and social scientists in at least partial explanation of war.[1] The cases of pre-World War II Germany, Japan, Italy, and Poland are notable examples.

More recently, density has been used in support of ideological positions concerning the general questions of the social significance of population growth. Three such orientations can be distinguished. On the one hand is the view that the physical and mental well-being of the human species is seriously threatened by present levels of population density and the rises in density forecast for the future. Those holding this view are often biologists whose studies of animals[2,3] have, predictably, led them to conclude that there are limits to the extent to which human beings can absorb the impact of high population density without developing markedly pathological patterns of response. This view generally discounts the importance of cultural and social factors in mediating the actual experience of density and takes, in addition, a somewhat jaundiced view of what future developments in technology might contribute to mitigating what are perceived as being predominately negative consequences of continued population growth.[4]

At the other extreme is the view that present and predicted levels of density are entirely within manageable limits. To those of this persuasion—who often have an ideological ax, religious or economic, to grind—man is a creature either of few needs or of infinite adaptability. Projecting astronomical increases in population (often far in excess of those most serious students of population believe are possible), persons with this orientation appear to deny, first, that there are any necessarily deleterious consequences in a high level of human density and, second, that there are any ultimate limits to human expansion—whether physical, ecological, or social. The nonchalance about population density and population growth inherent in this view seems to stem from a touching faith in the power of technology to make life livable under any conceivable conditions of density—or, for that matter, of environmental artificiality.[5]

A third orientation, one adhered to by a number of government officials, economists, journalists, and even demographers, involves the recognition of the existence of limits and some concern about population trends. But this awareness and concern does not serve as a stimulus to action to halt population increase because of a counterbalancing fear of what are presumed to be the consequences both of the goal of a nongrowing society and of the steps necessary to achieve such a state of equilibrium.[6–8] The result is a wait-and-see approach to population growth—at least for the present, and at least for the United States.

Our discussion of the misuses of the density concept will be confined to this third orientation. The first has received ample comment and continues to be reviewed critically, while the second—in the light of accumulating evidence of already substantial disruption of ecosystems all over the world—hardly merits serious consideration. But the third is still relatively free of critical comment and, in any case, is the most important of the three, if only because of the number of its adherents and, particularly, the influential positions they occupy.

The major misuse of the population density concept in this third orientation is in comparing the average density of the United States with that of other countries and then deriving from these comparisons conclusions about the relative capacity of the United States to sustain additions to its population. Typical is the following observation by a well-known economist and former member of President Eisenhower's Council of Economic Advisors [6,p.70]:

> The charge of overpopulation could hardly have been addressed to a more inappropriate country. By any international standard, the United States is underpopulated. Per square mile, our population is minimal compared with that of European countries which seem able to maintain reasonable standards of public cleanliness, decorum, and social efficiency.

In a similar vein are the following selections, quoted, respectively, from the chief of the population division, U.S. Bureau of the Census[9], a prominent economist-demographer[8:p.471]; the editors of *Nature*[10: p.29]; and a liberally published journalist, frequently referred to by his fellow journalists as an "expert" on population[11, pp.18–23]:

> Australia with its smaller population in an area almost as large as that of the United States is also concerned with pollution and traffic jams. The problems of pollution, traffic, crime, and delinquency are no worse in England, France, or Holland than in the United States, despite the fact that they are much more densely settled than this country.
>
> The density of population is 4.5 times greater in France, 10 times greater in the United Kingdom, and 30 times greater in the Netherlands than in the United States; yet pollution, traffic jams, and delinquency are no worse in those countries than here. Even if our population rose to a billion, its average density would not be very high by European standards.
>
> Who will say the crowded Netherlands are more violent than the uncrowded United States?
>
> [The] population [of the United States] is distributed over 3,615,123 square miles of land, for a density of about 55 persons per square mile. In terms of density, this makes the United States one of the most sparsely populated nations in the world. As measured by density, Holland is about 18 times as "crowded" (at 975 persons per square mile), England is 10 times as dense (588 persons per square mile), scenic Switzerland seven times as dense (382), tropical Nigeria three times as dense (174), and even neighboring Mexico beats us out with 60 persons per square mile. The United States by international standards, is not a very "crowded" country.

Such statements, effectively illustrating at the most general level what Ehrlich and Holdren have dubbed the "Netherlands Fallacy,"[12] demonstrate a failure to view the density of an area within its particular environmental, social, and demographic context. First, they make invidious comparisons on the basis of average measures, comparisons that not only exclude or obscure any distinctive patterns of settlement within the areas under consideration, but also involve units of remarkably different geographic dimensions; they ignore the fact that, far from being self-sufficient, the populations of these countries depend for their maintenance upon large amounts of resources and vast areas of land outside their borders. Second, although giving lip service to the significance of cultural differences, these statements make startling inferences about population-carrying capacity on the basis of an exceedingly crude measure embodying none of the cultural elements that might significantly differentiate among the units being compared. Third, they reach conclusions about the importance of population density without considering other elements in the demographic context. They do not consider, for example, the number and proportion of the population exposed to different levels of density, probable trends in the size and geographic location of the population, or population size itself as a factor determining the impact of different levels of density. As we propose to show, isolated from consideration of these contextual elements, the numerical measurement of population density is meaningless.

INADEQUACIES IN MEASUREMENT

The simple man:land ratio is but a crude average and is affected by the type of area unit that is used in enumerating and tabulating the population data from which it is calculated. Because the size and definition of these units of area can vary within countries and regions and across national boundaries, comparisons between different areas are difficult even on a strictly geographic basis. Moreover, because the man:land ratio emphasizes total area rather than the pattern of human settlement, and because it is but an average of the number of people in a given area, it blurs the density picture in two distinct, although related, ways: possibly significant variations in density levels within an area are neglected, and no insight whatever is afforded into the actual human experience of density—that is, into the rate, nature, and quality of the contact among individuals in the population under consideration; the various meanings these contacts have for the individuals affected; and the needs that are created, met, and frustrated. Although there have been many studies touching on how the experience of density varies in the context of folk and urban,[13] poor and rich societies,[14] much of this discussion is on the level of personal observation. Yet, even where there has been an attempt to study systematically the impact of the physical density of human beings by controlling for various psychological, social, and cultural characteristics of individuals and groups, the link between numerical density and various indicators of possible impact (such as those for different levels of social disorganization) remains frustratingly obscure.[15]

But the major flaw is geographical in nature: the tendency to dwell on the man:land ratio in measuring population density masks the very unevenness of settlement, the pattern of concentration and dispersion that effectively distinguishes the unique characteristics of density in one country or area from those in another.[16,17] Data on the distribution of the population (that is, on the proportion living in places of various sizes) and on the typical patterns of land use and zoning can suggest much more about the probable impact of density than can any indicator that merely averages numbers of people within a given unit of area. Figure 37.1 illustrates very simply a few of the markedly different ways in which the same numbers of people can be distributed within geographic areas of equal size.

A further illustration of the significance of unevenness of settlement with respect to actual levels of density within an area can be obtained by doing nothing more than altering the sizes of the areas used to calculate man:land ratios. For example, comparing only portions of the land area of the United States with the land areas of similar size in European countries is enough to produce a more realistic picture of the relative densities. In terms of overall crude density, many American states are comparable to some of the most densely populated countries of Europe (Table 37.1), and the average densities of various combinations of contiguous American states also match those of selected European countries of comparable size (Table 37.2).

Moreover, while the United States has a low average population density [57 per square mile (1 square mile = 2.59 square kilometers) in 1970] compared with most European countries, an unusually large proportion of its total population lives in very dense metropolitan regions. The sheer number and proportion of Americans living and working in giant metro-

Figure 37.1. Patterns of variation in concentration and dispersion in areas of equal population density.

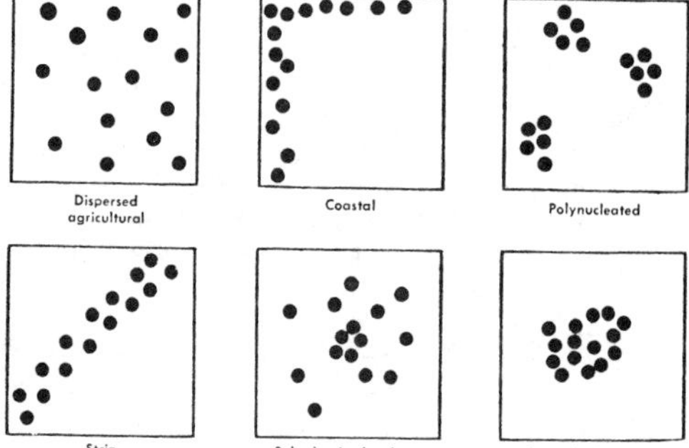

Table 37.1. Areas and Population Densities of Selected European Countries and American States (1 square mile = 2.59 square kilometers)

State or Country	Area, Including Inland Water* (10^2 square miles)	Population Density (persons per square mile) 1970	1960
United States	3615.1	57	50
New Jersey	7.8	915	774
Netherlands	15.8(13.0)†	826 (1002)†	728 (886)†
Belgium	11.8	822	777
Rhode Island	1.2	780	708
Massachusetts	8.3	689	624
Federal Republic of Germany	95.7	622	556
United Kingdom (excluding Northern Ireland)	88.8	611	577
Connecticut	5.0	606	506
Italy	116.3	461	427
Maryland	10.6	371	293
New York	49.6	368	339
Denmark	16.6	296	275
Delaware	2.1	266	217
Pennsylvania	45.4	260	250
France	211.2	240	216
Austria	32.4	229	218

Sources: *Demographic Yearbook, 1963* (United Nations, New York, 1963),[32] table 1, pp. 123–141; table 2, pp. 106–118); Bureau of the Census, *Statistical Abstract of the United States 1971* (Government Printing Office, Washington, DC, 1971), table 11, pp. 12–13 and table 263, p. 164.

*Inland waters were included in the calculation of U.S. state population density figures, thereby giving them a lower average density than would have been obtained if land area alone had been used. It was felt that waterways are used by a population in many ways (e.g., recreation, transportation, source of food, living space, esthetic enjoyment) and therefore should be included in the calculation of a ratio that is used to indicate the amount of area that a population has to meet its needs.

†Excluding inland waters.

politan regions are large, even by the standards of highly urbanized Europe (Table 37.3). Comparing the most highly industrialized and and urbanized countries of Western Europe to 17 contiguous American states of equivalent area, we find, for example, that the proportion of the population in places of 1 million or more inhabitants is much higher in the American area than in Western Europe (50 percent versus 32 percent), that the nonurban proportion is much lower (14 percent versus 26 percent), and that the proportion employed in agriculture is substantially smaller (1 percent in the American area versus 5 percent in Western Europe).

Of course, the proportion of the population

Table 37.2. Areas and Population Densities of Selected European Countries and Contiguous American States of Equivalent Size, 1970 (1 square mile = 2.59 square kilometers).

Country or Area	Area, Including Inland Waters (10^2 square miles)	Population Density (persons per square mile)
New York, Pennsylvania, Ohio, Indiana, Illinois	228.8	246
France	211.2	240
Massachusetts, Rhode Island, Connecticut	14.4	659
Switzerland	15.9	394
Denmark	16.6	296
New York	49.6	363
Greece	50.9	175

Sources: *Demographic Yearbook 1963* (United Nations, New York, 1963), table 1, pp. 123–141; (table 2, pp. 106–118),[32] Bureau of the Census, *Statistical Abstract of the United States 1971* (Government Printing Office, Washington, DC, 1971), table 11, pp. 12–13 and table 263, p. 164.

Table 37.3. Statistics on Selected Conditions in Western Europe and in 17 Contiguous American States of Equivalent Area (1 square mile = 2.59 square kilometers)

Conditions in 1970	Western Europe[a] (494,669 square miles)[17] Number	(%)	17 Contiguous States[b] (483,602 square miles)[38] Number	(%)
Total				
Total	201,700,000[37]	99.9	101,958,000[39]	99.9
In metropolitan areas:				
2,000,000+	39,224,000[40]	19.4	44,761,000[41]	43.9
1,500,000–1,999,999	13,941,000[42]	6.9	[40]	
1,000,000–1,499,999	10,693,000[40]	5.3	6,324,000[41]	6.2
500,000–999,999	14,719,000[40]	7.3	11,706,000[41]	11.4
100,000–499,999	31,930,000[40]	15.8	14,069,000[41]	13.8
In other urban areas (with fewer than 100,000 inhabitants)	38,010,000[42]	18.8	10,584,000[43]	10.4
Nonurban	53,183,000[44]	26.4	14,514,000[45]	14.2
Persons employed in agriculture	10,273,000[46]	5.1	1,371,000[47]	1.3
Ratio: persons employed in agriculture to nonurban population	.193		.094	
Passenger automobiles in use	46,286,000[48]		42,546,000[49]	
Passenger automobiles in use per person	0.229		0.417	
Passenger miles of railroad traffic (millions)	93,685[50]		5,954[51]	
Miles of high-speed motorways (with limited access and multiple-level intersections)	5,397[52]		25,369[53]	
Miles of high-speed motorways per 100 square miles of area	1.09		5.25	

[a]Austria, Belgium, France, Federal Republic of Germany, Netherlands, Switzerland, Luxembourg, United Kingdom, Denmark.

[b]Massachusetts, Rhode Island, Connecticut, New York, New Jersey, Pennsylvania, Delaware, Maryland, District of Columbia, Virginia, West Virginia, Ohio, Kentucky, Michigan, Illinois, Wisconsin, Indiana.

living in urban areas of a particular size, although an improvement over a crude man:land ratio, still reveals relatively little about either actual levels of physical density or the psychological or sociological effects of density on the inhabitants of these areas.[18] Urban physical structures and the patterns of their use and function will vary notably from one society to another, and it is these, in combination with population size, that will determine the actual operating pattern of human density.

It has been suggested that some of the limitations of the simple man:land ratio could be overcome by using a so-called "population potential ratio," the computation of which would combine the man:land ratio of a particular location with the man:land ratios of the surrounding areas, each weighted according to its distance from the location selected.[16,19] As a rough measure of spatial distribution, such a ratio has some theoretical usefulness: but, because its calculation would seem to require small geographic units of essentially equal size, it would be difficult to apply in any actual situation. Nor would it contribute much to an understanding of how different levels of density actually affect the people experiencing them, for it is, after all, still only a measure of physical, relationship.

In addition to taking account of such geographic conditions as the pattern of settlement and the proportion of the population living in agglomerations of various sizes, a realistic treatment of population density should also take into account the fact that the spatial separation of people has an internal as well as an external dimension. The population density of different areas can be differentiated not only according to the pattern of concentration and dispersion, but also according to the characteristics of persons within housing units. Although discussion of population density is almost exclusively carried on in terms of what may be termed "external," or areal, density (the number of persons per unit of area), it must be recognized that, from the standpoint of the actual human experience of density, consideration should be given also to the existence of what may be termed "internal," or "dwelling," density (the number of persons per unit of housing space).[19] In evaluating the social effects of density levels in different areas, it would seem important to gauge the relationship between these two types of density. Variation in the amount of surrounding space and in the degree of accessibility to that space (whether that space is public or private, for example) may well produce variation in the response to a given level of dwelling density. So far, however, the conclusions to be drawn from the studies of the social consequences of various combinations of internal and external human densities are, at best, ambiguous.[20]

A further problem in the measurement of population density, one referred to earlier, concerns the determination of the actual relation between levels of density and observed variations in human behavior. The investigator studying the significance of density in human life will frequently find it difficult to abstract the effects of different types and levels of density from the effects of conditions often associated with them, such as socioeconomic status, type of housing, or quality of the natural environment. Are the higher rates of physical and social pathology at the city's core a consequence of the higher density of the area, as some have claimed,[21] or of the concentration there of persons who, because of their position in society, are more susceptible to such disorders—the poor, the black, and the new arrivals from a totally different kind of environment, for example.[19] (Or is such pathology, perhaps, a reflection of differences in reporting or law enforcement?)

DENSITY AND POPULATION-CARRYING CAPACITY

These unresolved difficulties in defining and measuring population density have not discouraged generalizations for the purpose of judging potential population-carrying capacity. To observe, for example, that "Even if our population rose to a billion, its average density would not be very high by European standards," or that "By any international standard the United States is underpopulated," implies not only that our population lives at a level of density that is low in comparison with that of European nations, but also that—even in the face of substantial additions to our numbers—Americans are afforded by this presumably low density the option of being better able to meet the requirements of a more comfortable, less crowded existence. Yet, a number of studies suggest that human response to a given level of density is related not only to the degree of intensity of physical contact, but also to social organization, values, and life-styles, to the individual's status and class position within his society, and to personal and social expectations regarding a desirable way to live.[3,22,23] One example (see Table 37.3) of such differences in life-style between the United States and European countries is the private automobile, which has been a far more pervasive feature of the American scene than of the European. As a result, the American urban life-style is characterized by the single-family, detached house, the growing ubiquity of the high-speed roadway, and the virtual monopoly by the private automobile of the means of mass transit. All of this has led to the development around American cities of an "urban field," involving extensive functional specialization among component areas and considerable dispersion—commonly over a radius of 25 to 50 miles (1 mile = 1.6 kilometers) from the central business and commercial area[24]—of the major activities defining an urban entity. European cities, on the other hand, reflecting their pre-automobile and more complex pattern of urban development, are ordinarily characterized by denser populations within the central city and by a greater mixture of economic, residential, and recreational functions throughout the city itself.[25] One consequence of this is that urban neighborhoods in Europe tend to display more variety than do their American counterparts—variety, for example, in the visual stimuli they afford and in the demographic and social characteristics of their inhabitants.[26] This greater residential clustering that still characterizes European cities, despite the recent increase in automobile ownership, may also foster readier access to public space and a wider range of public amenities: public telephones, public toilets, parks, places to sit down, shade trees, cafes accessible to pedestrians, and public transportation.

Although most European countries have average rural densities substantially higher than those in the United States,[27] there is in Europe a decidedly sharper distinction between the end of the city and the beginning of the country. In addition, rural settlement in Europe lends to be concentrated in small villages, while in the United States it is commonly dispersed over the countryside in the form of low-density settlements of persons who are in terms of life-style, not rural but urban and who, because of their distance from urban centers, are highly dependent upon the private automobile for travel to shops and services, recreational facilities, and places of employment. A partial indication of the extent to which nonurban settlement is actually part of the urban field may be seen in Table 37.3, which shows the ratio of the proportion of the population employed in agriculture to the proportion of the population living in nonurban areas to be twice as high in Western Europe as in the 17 contiguous states (.193 versus .094)—and this with a total nonurban proportion nearly twice as high in Western Europe as in the U.S. area (26.4 percent versus 14.2 percent).

Even though changes are occurring—largely in response to increased automobile ownership—the urban field surrounding the typical European city remains much less extensive than that surrounding its American counterpart. Moreover, in the expansion of metropolitan regions in the United States, more and more areas in the vicinity of urban centers that were once low-density and rural in character are becoming higher density and urban in character.[28] With this change, the possibility of temporary escape from urban life, the possibility of access to a variety of land uses and types, has receded ever farther from the urban dweller's grasp. The opportunity to move rapidly between urban and rural environments has faded as the two have blended together, and as they have done so over an ever-wider area. In today's heavily industrialized societies, with their widespread use of the automobile, the extension of moderate density over larger and larger regions may well pose greater difficulties for long-term social and environmental management than would the conditions typical of preindustrial societies, and still prominent in Europe, in which pockets of high density are distributed among areas of low settlement and low intensity of human use. It is by no means unlikely that the level of "felt" density—that is, the level of density people perceive—is higher in the United States than in Europe as a result of the expansion of homogeneous suburbs and the consequent reduction in access to rural environments, even though most residential man:land ratios are lower. In terms of congenial living patterns, the optimum situation may well be one of access to a variety of density and use patterns rather than simple high or low density as such.[29]

CONDITIONS AFFECTING CARRYING CAPACITY

Differences in patterns of settlement, reflecting differences in cultural values and social organization, must be reckoned with in assessing the levels of density to which a population is exposed and the quality of its experience of this density. As Michelson has summarized it[22,p.157]: "density figures bear only indirect relations to the actual spatial situations that confront individuals. . . . It is not the number of people per acre but rather the nature of the separation of these people from each other and from nonresidential land uses that comprises the physical agent of health or pathology." Thus, when comparing the effective population-carrying capacities of different countries, the significant consideration would seem to be how a given set of cultural values, social patterns, and demographic and environmetnal conditions supports or undermines a people's capacity to adjust to a given spatial arrangement and to changing patterns of settlement in this era of rapid and extensive unbanization.

We briefly identify six facets of the American situation that seem at least as pertinent to our capacity as a nation to cope with changing patterns of population growth and concentration as is the fact of our numerically low, overall average density. The significance of these conditions lies, of course, in the way they interact with one another. Other industrialized countries may have a number of similar features, but it is the synergistic blend of these conditions in the American setting, rather than any single factor, that will be the prime determinant of our capacity to develop a satisfactory and harmonious relation among populations, resources, and social exigencies.

Size

One condition setting the United States apart from European countries, as regards its capacity to adjust to further population increase, is the enormous size of its current population. The social and environmental significance of sheer numerical size continues to be ignored. Population density and population size, although related in many ways, have quite different implications for human well-being and for the management of social and environmental affairs. Thus, for example, ten persons smoking in a small room constitutes something of a pollution problem; ten persons smoking in each of 100 small rooms, even more of a pollution problem; and, given the impact of scale on the complexity of social organization and the vulnerability of the environment to burgeoning human intrusion, ten smokers in each of 1,000 small rooms, a substantially greater order of management difficulty and environmental menace. Although the density of smokers is the same within each of the small rooms, the fact that in any given society there is only one such room or 1,000 such rooms will eventually reflect back on the conditions within the rooms themselves, deepening the problems associated with pollution and pollution control.

Yet in the quotations cited below as illustrative of what we earlier termed the wait-and-see approach, population density is first dismissed as a matter of little consequence to the generation of social problems in industrialized countries, and then the conclusion is reached, on the basis of this, that sheer numbers and current growth rates are also of no major concern to these countries. The reasoning is that since even countries of relatively low average density, like Australia, have their share of environmental problems, it is population distribution, not population size as such, that is the major demographic determinant of social difficulties.[8,p.470]

> Australia has a population of less than 12 million in an area more than 80 percent that of the United States, Yet Sydney has problems of smog, water pollution, and traffic jams. In fact, most of the social and economic problems ascribed to our excessive population in the United States or to its excessive rate of growth are affected more by how our population has chosen to distribute itself than by its size. The problems arise from excessive concentration in the metropolitan areas, not from excessive total numbers.

And again[30,p.8]:

> We must clearly distinguish between population problems associated with growth and those associated with distribution. There is no question that we can manage very well for a number of decades with a 1 percent rate of growth. There is, however, a dilemma regarding population distribution in that no one knows quite what to do.

Such conditions as these underrate the importance of size in three ways of major significance to both social organization and environmental conditions: (i) in the numbers exposed to different levels of population concentration, (ii) in the numbers contributing to the consumption and depletion of natural resources, and (iii) in the numbers added to a nation and to the world by percentage growth rates applied to population bases of often markedly different magnitude.

The few examples below suggest something of the significance that differences in the magnitude of numbers may have for the scale of difficulties faced by the United States as compared with individual European countries. In 1970, 82.3 million Americans lived in 31 conurbations of at least 1 million persons, while in all of Europe (30 countries, the Soviet Union excluded) it was 96.0 million persons in 43 such places. In the Netherlands, there was a total of 2.4 million persons living in but two conurbations of this size.[31] With virtually identical growth rates (1 percent) between 1969 and 1970, the population of the Netherlands increased by 150,000; that of the United States, by 2,190,000.[32,table4,pp.126–135] In 1972, there were more Americans receiving assistance under the federal Aid to Dependent Children program than there are people in the whole of the Netherlands.[33] The sheer size and numerical increase of the American population, and of that portion living in metropolitan areas, can hardly help but render more difficult in the United States than in the Netherlands—or, for that matter, Australia—the many complex tasks necessary to maintain a highly urbanized, technological society.

Emphasis on Local Government

A second important element in American adjustment to growth is the widespread emphasis on the autonomy of local political units and the persistent reluctance to undertake regional planning. While allocation to local units of responsibility for the execution of many social tasks undoubtedly has a number of desirable features, it also serves in many ways to exacerbate the problems associated with large numbers. Not only does size tend to generate tensions and conflicts between the central authority and subordinate units, but it also encourages local units to pursue their own interests at the expense of those of the central government or the nation as a whole. For example, although the ratio of suburban to central city populations has altered dramatically over the last few decades, spreading over much larger regions problems connected with water supply and sewage disposal, health and environmental pollution, police and fire protection, and planning and development, suburbanites continue to hold out for small governmental consolidation.[34] Meanwhile, the number of autonomous and semi-autonomous units within commuting distance of metropolitan centers continues to multiply, dividing among numerous governmental units many problems that are actually indivisible and that, if they admit of any solution at all, must be handled on a regional, or even national, basis.

Privatism

Related to this preference for local autonomy is the American emphasis on private, rather than social, provision for human needs—particularly those for space, recreation, transportation, and respite from the intensity of urban life. Displaying a reluctance, if not a downright unwillingness, to be taxed for community purposes, Americans, if they are among the fortunate, seek to avoid the competition for space and facilities in public areas by purchasing their own privacy: large lots, large houses, second homes in the country, swimming pools, waterfront properties, campsites in the mountains. Combined with our American view of land as an abundant commodity to be bought and sold on the open market, such privatism has helped produce random urban sprawl, the progressive loss of public space in and near large metropolitan centers, and the unplanned use of the environment for narrowly individual purposes. Most northern Europenan countries, with a longer tradition of national planning and an apparently deeper sense of the value of land, have assigned to government the right to lay down final, binding regulations in matters of dispute over public versus private interests. Whether or not they are actually more public-spirited, willing to bear the costs of community projects and to take a long-term, collective view of the planning process[35], northern Europenas do seem better equipped by their culture (and their laws) than do Americans by theirs to undertake the collective effort of planning both for future changes in the size and density of population and for the careful husbanding of national resources.

Affluence and the Nonaffluent

A fourth condition affecting the capacity of Americans to incorporate increasing numbers into the social-fabric is our affluence. This may enrich the lives of million of Americans, but the costs of our unusually high levels of personal wealth are becoming evident in two important ways: in the ravages of the environment caused by the highest per capita ownership of machines in the world and in the ravages of our social order caused by the continuing existence of an undereducated, underskilled, underpaid, and underprivileged minority. The inability of this substantial minority to obtain relief from the urban environment through the private route is not matched by social mechanisms adequate to ensure the meeting of their needs through public resources instead. At the same time, the latitude allowed private expenditure—in the purchase and use of land and water, for example—decreases the opportunities of this group still further. The large gap in the wealth and life chances of different Americans increases the pressures of urban densities and presents grave obstacles to any effort to plan a more socially viable pattern of population distribution within our metropolitan areas.[24]

Heterogeneity

In addition to vast differentials in wealth, Americans, as compared with Europeans, are characterized by an unusual degree of heterogeneity with respect to ethnicity and race, religion, cultural background, life-styles, and social status. Combined with the size, concentration, and emphasis on individualism of our population, this diversity makes for a pluralism of outlooks that renders more difficult the achievement of any consensus concerning national goals and the means to their fulfillment.[36]

The Growth Ethos

Finally, woven through these other cultural and environmental factors is the tenacious American emphasis on growth—a heritage of the unusually favorable combination of space, abundant resources, and rapid industrialization with which we began our history as an independent nation. Adherence to the growth ethos is reflected in many aspects of American life and continues to be vigorously fostered through the speeches of political candidates, advertising, government policies, business development, and hyperbole about technological solutions. Moreover, we have, as a nation, become increasingly dependent on general economic growth—rather than on any equalization of actual levels of living—as the principal means of improving the position of that nonaffluent, discontented (or potentially discontented) segment of our society which is deemed so threatening to the stability of our social order. For Americans, adherence to the growth ethos would seem to be another constraint on effecting those changes in attitudes and ways of life that seem to be necessary to meet the requirements of the more crowded, less abundant conditions of the future.

SUMMARY AND CONCLUSIONS

The unresolved difficulties associated with defining and measuring population density strictly circumscribe the scope and nature of the conclusions that can be properly derived from differentials in man:land ratios. Any conclusions about human density will have meaning only to the extent that they are based on a recognition that this density must be viewed in both static and dynamic terms and that if cannot be isolated, in analysis, from either the social and cultural setting, the demographic characteristics of the population, or the broader processes of social change within the society. In and of itself, the familiar man:land ratio says more about area than it does about either the human experience of density or the relation of population to resources. This ratio is therefore essentially meaningless as an indicator of comparative conditions of life among different countries and different geographic regions. The mere fact of having a relatively low average population density, thus, does not automatically entitle a nation to complacency about its ability to adjust readily to future population change, either in terms of growth in numbers or in the geographic location of its people.

NOTES AND REFERENCES

1. M. Weiner, in *Rapid Population Growth: Consequences and Policy Implications* (National Academy of Sciences, Office of the Foreign Secretary Study Committee, Johns Hopkins Press, Baltimore, 1971), pp. 567–617; F. C. Wright, *Population and Peace* (International Institute of Intellectual Cooperation, League of Nations, Paris, 1939), pp. 35–39.
2. J. B. Calhoun, *Sci. Amer.* 206, 139 (February 1962).
3. E. T. Hall, *The Hidden Dimension* (Doubleday, Garden City, NY, 1969).
4. F. H. Bormann, *Yale Alumni Mag.* 33, 38 (1970); J. Harte and R. H. Socolow, in *Patient Earth,* J. Harte and R. H. Socolow, Eds. (Holt, Rinehart & Winston, New York, 1971), pp. 259–320; L. H. Day and A. T. Day, *Too Many Americans* (Houghton Mifflin, Boston, 1964), pp. 206–225.
5. C. Clark, *Nature* 181, 1235 (1957); S. D. Kohn, *N.Y. Times Mag.* (26 July 1970), P. 26.
6. H. C. Wallich, *Newsweek* (29 June 1970), p. 70.
7. ———, ibid. (24 January 1972), p. 62; *New York Times* (12 February 1972), p. 29.
8. A. J. Coale, *Pop. Index* 34 (1968); *Life* (19 May 1972), p. 47.
9. C. Taeuber, "The people of the United States at the beginning of the 1970's," address delivered at Mount Holyoke College (13 January 1971).
10. Editorial, *Nature,* as quoted in *New York Times* (5 February, 1972), p. 29.
11. B. Wattenberg, *New Repub.* (4 and 11 April 1970), p. 18.
12. P. R. Ehrlich and J. P. Holdren, *Science* 171, 1212 (1971).
13. P. M. Hauser, in *The Study of Urbanization,* P. M. Hauser and L. Schnore, Eds. (Wiley, New York, 1965), pp. 491–517.
14. N. Keyfitz, in *Population Crisis,* S. Reid and D. Lyon, Eds. (Scott Foresman, Glenview, IL, 1972), pp. 112–117.
15. O. R. Galle, W. R. Gove, J. M. McPherson, *Science* 176, 23 (1972).
16. O. D. Duncan, *Pop. Stud.* 11 (No. 1) 27 (1957).
17. F. J. Monkhouse and H. R. Wilkinson, *Maps and Diagrams: Their Compilation and Construction* (Methuen, London, 1971), p. 321; W. A. Hance, *Population, Migration, and Urbanization in Africa* (Columbia Univ. Press, New York, 1970), pp. 43–49.
18. M. Halbwachs, *Population and Society: Introduction to Social Morphology* (Free Press, Glencoe, IL., 1960), pp. 97, 105.
19. D. M. Heer, *Society and Population* (Prentice-Hall, Englewood Cliffs, NJ, 1968), pp. 31–34.
20. R. C. Schmitt, *J. Amer. Inst. Plann.* 32, 38 (1966).
21. I. L. McHarg, *Design with Nature* (Doubleday, Garden City, NY, 1971), pp. 187–195.
22. W. Michelson, *Man and His Urban Environment: A Sociological Approach* (Addison-Wesley, Reading, Mass. 1970).
23. R. Sommer, *Personal Space* (Prentice-Hall, Englewood Cliffs, NJ, 1969).
24. B. J. L. Berry, in *Research and the 1970 Census,* A. L. Ferriss, Ed. (Southern Regional Demographic Group, Oak Ridge Associated Universities, Oak Ridge, TN, 1971), pp. 151–157.
25. M. W. Mikesell, in *The International Atlas* (Rand-McNally, Chicago, 1969), pp. xxiii–liv.
26. A. E. Parr, *Centen. Rev.* 14, 177 (Spring 1970).
27. K. Davis, *World Urbanization* 1950–1970 (Institute of International Studies, Univ. of California, Berkeley, 1969), vol. 1, pp. 247–263.
28. M. Cooper, *Patterns of Population in Connecticut: 1880–1970* (Institute for Social and Policy Studies, Yale Univ., New Haven, Conn. 1972).
29. J. Jacobs, *Death and Life of Great American Cities* (Random House, New York, 1961); J. D. Freeman, in *The Impact of Civilization on the Biology of Man,* S. V. Boyden, Ed. (Australian National Univ. Press, Canberra, 1970), pp. 154–158.

30. H. P. Miller, *Population, Pollution, and Affluence* (selection No. 36, Population Reference Bureau, Washington, DC, 1971).
31. American figures calculated from (n. 32, table 8, pp. 432–479) (with the same adjustments for the 17-state area used in Table 3 of this article, plus the following for the rest of the United States: Oxnard-Ventura added to the Los Angeles standard metropolitan statistical area (SMSA); Gary-Hammond-East Chicago to the Chicago; Fort Worth to the Dallas; and Tacoma to the Seattle-Everett); European figures from K. Davis (n. 27, table E, pp. 163–233).
32. *Demographic Yearbook 1970* (United Nations, New York, 1970).
33. J. Welsh, *N.Y. Times Mag.* (7 January 1973). p. 14.
34. A. H. Hawley and B. G. Zimmer, *The Metropolitan Community: Its People and Government* (Sage, Beverly Hills, Calif. no date).
35. A. Bailey, *The Light in Holland* (Knopf, New York, 1970): G. A. Wissink, "Metropolitan planning problems in the Netherlands," paper No. 24, prepared for United Nations Group of Experts on Metropolitan Planning and Development (Stockholm, September 1961); P. Hall, *The World Cities* (McGraw-Hill, New York, 1966), pp. 95–122.
36. U.S. Commission on Population Growth and the American Future, *Population and the American Future* (Government Printing Office, Washington, DC, 1972), pp. 12–16.
37. See *Demographic Yearbook 1970* (n. 32, table 2, pp. 106–118).
38. Bureau of the Census, *Statistical Abstract of the United States* 1971 (Government Printing Office, Washington, DC, 1971), table 263, p. 164.
39. ———, *Census of Population: 1970*, vol. 1, *Characteristics of the Population,* Part A, *Number of Inhabitants,* section 1, "Alabama-Mississippi" (Government Printing Office, Washington, DC, 1971), table 41, pp. 1-206–1-212.
40. Calculated from K. Davis (n. 27, table E, pp. 163–233).
41. Calculated from (n. 19, table 36, pp. 1-189–1-190). To achieve closer conformity with actual conditions, certain SMSA's were conbined: (i) Newark, Paterson-Clifton-Passaic, Jersey City, Stamford, and Norwalk SMSAs combined with New York SMSA; (ii) Gary–Hammond-East Chicago with Chicago; (iii) Lorain-Elyria with Cleveland; (iv) Hamilton-Middletown with Dayton; (v) New Britain and Bristol with Hartford; (vi) Petersburg-Colonial Heights with Richmond; (vii) Scranton with Wilkes-Barre-Hazelton SMSA; (viii) Lowell and Nashua with Lawrence-Haverhill SMSA.
42. Calculated as the difference between total population and the sum of the population in the other component.
43. Includes population in SMSAs of fewer than 100,000 inhabitants. Calculated as the difference between the total population and the sum of the population in the other components.
44. Calculated from K. Davis (n 27. table A, pp. 57–82).
45. Calculated from n. 39. To achieve closer conformity to actual conditions, this is defined as the rural population outside SMSAs.
46. International Labour Office, *Yearbook of Labour Statistics* (International Labour Office, Geneva, 1972) table 2, pp. 44–301; table 3, pp. 314–338. Data for Luxembourg, Denmark, and Switzerland are for 1966, 1970, and 1960, respectively, and relate to persons *economically active* in agriculture, rather than actually *employed* in agriculture.
47. Department of Agriculture, *Agricultural Statistics 1971* (Government Printing Office, Washington, DC, 1971), table 649, p. 453. This figure maximizes farm employment by including farm operators doing 1 or more hours of farm work and members of their families working 15 or more hours during survey week without cash wages, and all persons doing farm work for pay during the survey weeks. There is one survey week in each month, and the figure given is the average.
48. *Statistical Yearbook 1971* (United Nations, New York, 1971), table 148, p. 416.
49. Department of Transportation and Federal Highway Administration, *Highway Statistics 1970* (Government Printing Office, Washington, DC, 1971), p. 33.
50. See *Statistical Yearbook 1971* (48, table 146, pp. 398–401).
51. Bureau of Economics, Interstate Commerce Commission, *Transport Economics: Monthly Comment* (March-April 1972), p. 7. Data are for the Eastern District, which consists of all 17 states except Wisconsin, Kentucky, and Virginia and includes three additional ones—Vermont, New Hampshire, and Maine.
52. Economic Commission for Europe, *Annual Bulletin of Transport Statistics for Europe 1969* (United Nations, New York, 1970), table 11, pp. 43–47.
53. Calculated from Federal Highway Administration data (n. 49, table SM-2, p. 157; table SM-11, p. 163; table INT-11, p. 193). The figure given is the sum of mileage on high-speed motorways in the following categories: state primary highway system, interstate in and defense highways, and toll roads not part of the state or federal system.

38

Density-Intensity: A Theory of Crowding

JONATHAN L. FREEDMAN

While conditions of high density, either in a neighborhood or within one's own dwelling, obviously have substantial effects on how one lives, they do not appear to have generally negative consequences. Under more controlled circumstances, research demonstrates that people can function quite well even when very crowded and isolated for considerable periods of time. Indeed, at least within the limits used in these studies, increasing the density has, if anything, positive effects—reducing hostility and stress. Density has also been shown to have no effect on performance on a wide variety of tasks, thus making it seem highly unlikely that it produces stress in the usual sense of the word. Most provocatively, a series of studies has found that density sometimes does affect aggressiveness and interpersonal feelings, but that these effects are different for males and females. Furthermore, the direction of the differences is not consistent—males responding negatively to high density in some experiments and positively in others, with females also showing both tendencies. This recent work indicates that crowding can affect interpersonal behavior but that its effects are quite complex, depending on other factors in the situation. Because of the lack of consistency, it seems doubtful that males and females have basically different reactions to density. Rather, a more general principle is necessary to explain all of the diverse results.

I propose that crowding by itself has neither good effects nor bad effects on people but rather *serves to intensify the individual's typical reactions to the situation.* If he ordinarily would find the circumstances pleasant, would enjoy having people around him, would think of the other people as friends, would in a word have a positive reaction to the other people, he will have a more positive reaction under conditions of high density. On the other hand, if ordinarily he would dislike the other people, find it unpleasant having them around, feel aggressive toward them, and in general have a negative reaction to the presence of the other people, he will have a more negative reaction under conditions of high density. And if for some reason he would ordinarily be indifferent to the presence of other people, increasing the density will have little effect one way or the other. Thus, people do not respond to density in a uniform way, they do not find it either always pleasant or always unpleasant. Rather, their response to density depends almost entirely on their response to the situation itself. Density acts primarily to make this response, whatever it is, stronger.

This difference between high- and low-density situations is more obvious under some circumstances than others, but it almost always exists. Consider a few examples. Six people riding in a bus will have practically no interactions unless they know each other to begin with. They will sit in separate seats, probably spacing themselves around the bus so that there are even several seats between them. They need not touch each other in any way, talk to each other, meet each other's eyes, or even look at each other very much. The same six people riding in a minibus would have to sit near each other, probably touch occasionally, almost certainly look at each other. They can perhaps still avoid talking, but clearly there is some minimal level of interaction due to the lack of space. And finally, if the same six people share a car, they will be touching throughout the ride, will have to look at each other unless they deliberately avoid it, and there will be strong pressure to interact more directly. It is, of course, possible to share a car with five other people and never interact, but even if the people do not know each other to begin with, the chances are that there will be some social interaction. The physical proximity due to the high density makes the presence of the other people much more important and almost forces some kind of interaction. Furthermore, if the other people are unpleasant in some way—perhaps frightening or obnoxious—being with them should be more unpleasant in a car than in a minibus, which should in turn be more unpleasant than being in the large bus. Whereas if the other people are particularly pleasant, it should be most enjoyable being with them in the car and least enjoyable being in the large bus.

Imagine a cocktail party with thirty people in either a large or small room. When the room is large and the density correspondingly low, the level of interaction trends to be much less intense and intimate. People may be scattered around the room in small clumps, talking to only one or two other people. Although these interactions may be fine, the impact of the party as a whole is relatively slight. There is not the feeling of an exciting, stimulating party. Under these circumstances, if the other people at the party are not particularly pleasant, it is fairly easy to avoid interacting with them; if they are pleasant, it is somewhat more difficult to interact with them than if the room is smaller. Instead of being forced into close proximity where interactions necessarily occur, one must seek out a person to talk to. This does not, of course, prevent interactions, but it does make them somewhat harder and probably more diffuse. Under these circumstances people will usually crowd together in one corner of the room, or as so often happens at parties, in the kitchen. In this way, they increase the density so as to liven up the party.

In the small room with high density, avoiding interactions is virtually impossible. Everyone is in close proximity to everyone else, they find themselves face-to-face with other people, there is a high level of interaction that does not exist in the larger room. If the other people are unpleasant, it is still necessary to interact with them; if they are pleasant, one does not have to make a great effort to interact. This means that the characteristics of the other people are much more important in the small than in the large room.

Once again, this is a familiar experience for most people. Assuming that the people at the party are congenial, it is almost inevitable that the party will be better if there is fairly high density. Parties in large empty rooms are always unexciting and disappointing. In small rooms, as long as it is a good group of people, the party tends to be more successful. In fact, most good hosts and hostesses know that one ingredient in a good party is the right number of people for the size of the room. If it is going to be a stimulating, exciting party, there cannot be too few people relative to the amount of space. Of course, there is some limit to the number of people that can squeeze into a room, but within a broad range, the higher the density, the more exciting and stimulating a party will be.

Obviously, just as with sound, at some point there is such intense crowding that it becomes unpleasant, but even at this level the effect is due primarily to such factors as physical discomfort, odors, and lack of freedom to move. The mere experience of being with many people in a small amount of room is not negative; it only becomes so when it is associated with these other, clearly negative factors—and that occurs only at extremes such as occur in packed subways. Even an extremely crowded party, with very little space available, rarely reaches this level of density. The essential point is that unless this "breakpoint" is reached, density itself is not unpleasant but rather depends on the situation, and operates by intensifying reactions to the other people.

How does this theory apply to our finding that men respond negatively to crowding and women respond positively? It is likely that for most men in our society, entering a room full of other men in a formal, scientific setting is a somewhat threatening experience. Men typically think of other men as rivals, are suspicious of other men, and in particular are prepared to have to prove themselves or to compete with other men. When they arrive and find all other men in the room, their natural response is one of suspicion, defensiveness, and perhaps even mild hostility. Certainly, their competitive feelings tend to be aroused by a group of other men, particularly when they are then asked to play games or take part in a discussion. Accordingly, the men tend to have a somewhat negative, hostile reaction to the other men in the situation. According to the density-intensity theory, this negative response should be strengthened by high density. Thus, the men would be expected to be somewhat suspicious and hostile in the low-density condition and to become more so when density is increased.

Although there is no good evidence for this speculation, it seems probable that most women in our society have a less competitive and hostile reaction to a group of other women. There are undoubtedly great variations in this, but it does seem as if women compete less with each other (at least openly), are less suspicious of each other, and feel less that they have to prove themselves in the presence of other women than men do with other men. In fact, most women probably respond to a group of other women as a potentially interesting, intimate, friendly group. Therefore, when they enter a room full of other women, their responses are generally somewhat on the positive side, and these responses should be more positive under conditions of high density than under conditions of low density.

Finally, when the sexes are mixed, the situation is much more ambiguous, and neither men nor women have clearly positive or negative responses to the group. Therefore, increasing the density will not make their response either more positive or more negative, since they are mixed to begin with. Probably some subjects have a positive response to a mixed sex group and others have a negative, and therefore increasing the density will not have any overall effect.

One study that showed clearly the opposite pattern was conducted by Loo and involved young children who knew each other. This is quite a different situation. Presumably the general tendency for all of the children was to be friendly. Very little fighting occurred in any condition, and even that was not terribly serious. In these circumstances, increasing the density would be expected to intensify the generally friendly feelings and reduce the amount of aggressiveness. Indeed, that is exactly what happened. The boys, who were the only ones doing any fighting, did less of it when crowded than when not crowded. The girls did no fighting under low density, and increasing the density had no effect. These results can thus be explained in the same terms as the others.

The one result that we cannot explain is that by Marshall and Heslin, who found men more positive when crowded in same-sex or mixed groups, with women being more positive when crowded in a mixed group but more negative when crowded in a same-sex group. This is certainly baffling, since the situation sounds similar to ours and the results are almost exactly opposite. The finding is probably due to specific variation in the circumstances and the people who served as subjects, but we freely admit having no clue as to the critical factors.

Finally, an experiment by Griffitt and Veitch found generally negative effects of high density for all subjects. In this study, people were seated in rooms in such a way that they did not face each other. They were not introduced, did not interact in any way, and merely carried out some individual tasks. It was not a social situation in the usual sense of the word, since there was no interaction. In addition, it was probably fairly unpleasant regardless of condition since the tasks were dull, the seating arrangement unnatural, and the rooms bare and uncomfortable. Under these circumstances, everyone should have a somewhat negative reaction, and increasing the density should, if anything, intensify that response.

Thus, with the exception of the Marshall and Heslin study, all of the results are consistent with the density-intensity theory. The idea that density intensifies the typical social reaction provides a plausible explanation of all the findings. Naturally, since these explanations are offered after the results are obtained, there is no proof they are correct, but it is important that the theory can account for these diverse findings fairly easily.

A series of experiments were designed specifically to test this theory. The theory states that any response to other people—whether positive or negative—should be strengthened by increasing density. Whatever the response is under low density, it should become stronger under high density. Therefore, in order to test the theory, it is necessary to set up a situation in which the social interaction is deliberately made either pleasant or unpleasant, and then to vary the density. Then, for men, women, or mixed-sex groups, the situation that was deliberately made pleasant should be more pleasant under high density, and the unpleasant situation should be more unpleasant. If this occurs regardless of the sex of the participants, it would disprove the idea that there are innate differences in the response of the sexes to crowding, and would strongly support the theory.

In one study participants were told that we were interested in public speaking. Each person in the group would be required to give a short talk, which the rest of the group would then criticize. We provided a short speech so that the participants did not actually have to make up their talk, as we were afraid that some shy members of the group might find the situation very upsetting if they had to come up with a talk themselves. But all they had to do was read over our little speech and then deliver it to the group. No one seemed particularly upset by this, although naturally, some gave the talk better than others. The key point of the study was that for half of the groups the criticisms were all supposed to be positive. We told the subjects that we were interested in only constructive criticism, that while they listened they should concentrate on the good aspects of the presentation, should write down only what they thought were the best qualities of the speaker, and should tell him only good things about what he had done. For the other groups, all of the comments were supposed to be negative. We said that we were interested only in finding problems with the speech, that the subjects should write down only what they thought were the weaknesses of the presentation, and that they should tell the speaker only bad things about how he had performed.

Picture the situation. In one case, the speaker was surrounded by a group all of whom were going to say good things to him. No matter what he did, no matter how he faltered, or how nervous he was, all he was going to hear were positive comments. This surely is a positive situation. In particular, the social interactions are all going to be pleasant. In the other situation, the speaker was surrounded by a group all of whom were concentrating on negative aspects of his performance. No matter what he did, no matter how well he performed, no matter how brilliantly he gave his speech, all he was going to hear were negative comments. This certainly is an unpleasant situation, with the social interactions all being negative.

The positive situation and the negative situation were both done in large and small rooms. The participants were either comfortably arranged in a large room or were crowded together in a small room. Thus, there was either a pleasant or an unpleasant social situation under conditions of high and low density. Naturally all of the participants should find the positive situation more pleasant than the negative situation regardless of the size of the room. The key point is that the reactions—whether pleasant or unpleasant—will be more intense in the small rooms than in the large rooms.

This is exactly what happened. Being criticized was, of course, more negative than being praised, and the subjects responded accordingly. In the positive-criticism condition the participants liked giving the ratings more and found the experience more enjoyable and more pleasant than in the negative-criticism condition. This was true regardless of the size of the room.

More important is the effect of room size. First, there was no overall effect of density. On no measure of attitude toward the other people or the session as a whole did the large and small rooms differ appreciably, nor was there any consistency in the direction of the small differences that did occur. As usual, crowding by itself did not produce any substantial effects.

However, as predicted by our theory, room size did interact with the pleasantness of the experience. There was a consistent pattern, with the participants in the small room giving more positive ratings than those in the large room under the positive conditions. For example, in rating the speeches when only positive comments were given, they were more positive in the high-density condition than in the low-density; when only negative comments were given, they were more negative under high-density conditions. This was true of almost every measure taken—the positive group in the small room was more positive than the positive group in the large room, and the negative group in the small room was more negative than the negative group in the large room. Clearly, increasing density intensified both positive and negative reactions.

It is important to note that this occurred for all-female groups and for mixed-sex groups, although it was somewhat weaker when the sexes were mixed. Remember that in previous studies it was found that all-female groups responded positively to crowding, suggesting that perhaps females have a general tendency to like high-density situations. The present finding in which females respond more positively under high density when the experience is generally positive and more negatively under high density when the experience is generally negative makes it seem unlikely that women have an innate or learned positive response to crowding. It appears rather that both sexes respond in roughly the same way to density, intensifying their reactions to social situation.

Since we did not have all-male groups in this first study, we conducted another experiment in order to demonstrate the effect with groups composed only of men. This study was similar to the first one except that we used a slightly different method of making the situation positive or negative. In this case, the groups worked on complicated problems together in either a large or a small room. The problems consisted of transforming one word into another by changing one letter at a time, being certain that each change produced an acceptable English word. For example, *gold* could be changed to *lead* in the order *gold, goad, load, lead.* The group was given fifteen problems of this kind, one at a time, and allowed a minute to solve each. The difficulty was varied, some problems requiring only two to four steps, others five or six.

The key factor was that we arranged the problems so that some groups could solve all or most of them while other groups could solve only a few. This was done by varying the percentage of difficult problems, half of the groups getting all easy ones and half getting seven easy and eight difficult ones. Accordingly, those groups that we wanted to do well solved twelve or thirteen of the problems, while the other groups solved only five to seven. Thus, some of the groups experienced "success" while others experienced "failure." We reasoned that working together and succeeding would be a pleasant, rewarding, and generally positive interaction, while working together and failing would be unpleasant and negative. As before, we expected that either response would be stronger in the small, crowded room than in the larger, uncrowded room.

Sure enough, the results were very similar to the previous ones. First, the crowded groups were actually somewhat more positive overall than the uncrowded ones. Combining the success and failure groups, those in the small rooms tended to like each other more and feel that the other people were friendlier. Although the size of the room did not produce powerful effects, those that did appear indicate that, if anything, higher density made the experience more pleasant.

The important result for the present purpose is that the small room produced stronger responses than the large room. The failure groups in the small room found the experiment more boring, less lively, and generally a worse experience than those in the large room, while the success groups were in all these cases more positive in the small than the large room. There were no appreciable effects in the opposite direction. Thus, as in the first study, increasing the density magnified the effect of success and failure. It did this for all-male groups even though the previous work suggested that men tend to have negative responses to high density. This finding therefore provides further support for the density-intensity theory. It also directly contradicts two alternative ideas—that people generally react negatively to high density (indeed, whatever overall effects of density occurred showed it to be positive rather than negative) and that men and women have qualitatively different responses to density. We have now seen that all-male, all-female and mixed-sex groups all show the intensification effect.

A third study, conducted by Ilene Staff repeated the first one with a few important variations. Once again, people gave short speeches while others made either positive or negative criticisms. However, in half of the conditions, these criticisms were made by the other people in the room while in half they were made by observers in another room. In other words, half of the groups were giving each other positive or negative comments while half received comments only from outsiders. This raises the critical question of whether the intensification effects previously demonstrated are specific to the reactions to the other people in the room or are more general.

According to the theory, the effect should be quite specific. Increasing density makes other people a more important factor in the individual's life space. His responses to them will accordingly be stronger. But density is largely irrelevant to external factors. The people who are watching through a window and rating the individual are no more important just because there is less space in the room. Similarly, the effect of any other external factor such as the weather outside, noise, or a person threatening to deliver electric shocks should be independent of the level of density within the room. The increasing density should magnify responses to the other people in the room but not to external observers. When the pleasantness of the situation depends on interactions within the room (when the subjects are giving positive or negative ratings), the degree of density should intensify the individual's reaction; when the pleasantness is due to external factors (when outsiders are giving ratings), no intensification should occur.

That is exactly what happened. This time with mixed-sex groups only, the results of the original study were repeated and were even stronger. The members of the positive-comment group responded more positively to each other and to the experiment as a whole in the small than in the large room, while the negative comment groups showed the opoosite pattern. When comments came from outside the room, no such effects occurred. There were no consistent differences due to room size. Thus, this study reinforces the findings of the previous ones and also provides the first evidence that the effect is limited to the group itself—reactions to external people are not intensified just because the individuals are crowded.

Our research on the effects of crowding on humans leads us to two conclusions which we hold with some confidence. First, high density does not generally have negative effects on people. This is based on the following pieces of evidence:

1. In the real world, there is no relationship between crowding and pathology. With income and other factors controlled, cities

and neighborhoods that have many people per square mile have no higher rates of crime, illness, infant mortality, venereal disease, suicide, mental illness, or any other pathology than comparable areas with relatively few people per square mile. Similarly, cities and neighborhoods in which the people have little space in their houses or apartments have no more pathology than those in which people have more space. If crowding had generally negative effects, surely they would show up in this kind of survey.

2. People who are put in very small rooms and isolated from the world for periods up to twenty days manage to function quite well. The recent use of the space lab demonstrates that three men can live cooped up in a tiny vehicle performing complex tasks and get along with each other for months. In addition, the few studies in which density was varied actually found less hostility when there was less space. Although all of these studies, as well as the space program, involved unusual circumstances and participants, they certainly indicate that humans are able to cope with high density. Once again, if there were any innate or generally negative reaction to high density, it would be expected to show up in some way in this work.
3. Controlled experiments in which density is explicitly varied have not found negative effects of high density. With one exception, those studies that did find overall effects of density found people responding more positively under high than low density. More important, most experiments have not produced any overall effects of density. There is no evidence from this body of work that crowding causes either stress or arousal. It does not affect task performance, it does not make people more anxious or nervous, and it certainly does not make the experience more unpleasant. If density does have generally negative effects, they should have appeared in these careful experiments.

Therefore, it appears reasonably safe to conclude that high density does not have a generally negative effect on humans. Neither long-term exposure to vast numbers of people in a small space (cities), nor lives spent in cramped and crowded dwellings, nor short-term exposure to very high levels of density in space platforms, isolation chambers, or experimental laboratories causes people to respond negatively. Humans show no hint of territoriality in the sense of reacting aggressively to a lack of space. People will naturally do their best to defend their property from incursions, whether the property be a home, a country, or even a seat on a bus, but they show no hint of territoriality in the sense of an instinctive aggressive response to a lack of space. Whatever the effects on other animals, humans simply do not react negatively to high density per se.

Our second conclusion concerning the effects of crowding on humans is that high density makes other people a more important stimulus and thereby intensifies the typical reaction to them. Experiments have shown complex effects of density. Sometimes males respond negatively while females repond positively, but sometimes the opposite pattern prevails; sometimes both sexes show the same response. My associates and I designed our recent experiments to show that whatever the interpersonal situation, higher density will cause the individual's reaction to be stronger. We showed that positive situations elicited more positive reactions under high than low density, while negative situations produced more negative reactions under high density. This finding can also account for most of the seeming inconsistencies of earlier findings.

A great deal more research, writing, and discussion is necessary to be certain of these conclusions. There are many serious investigators who still need to be convinced, and of course, the common lore that crowding is bad will take a long time to change. But I feel that the evidence is now very strong on the first point and reasonably powerful on the second. While some changes will undoubtedly occur in our understanding of how density affects humans, I think that the two conclusions presented here will turn out to be substantially correct. Crowding is not generally negative and it does intensify reactions to other people.

PART VI

POPULATION STRUCTURE

Through the dynamic processes of fertility, mortality, and migration, the human population is constantly in a state of change. Yet at any given instant in time, it has an identifiable *structure,* which on the global or international level usually changes relatively slowly and, in the short term, (if we know about the population composition and rates of fertility, mortality, and migration) predictably. For example, we have a fairly good idea of how many children in the United States will be in each grade in school five years from now, how many women will be in their childbearing years, how many elderly there will be, based on current numbers of people at given ages and our admittedly imperfect knowledge of rates of death and migration. Population dynamics and population structure are intimately related; each influences the other. There are three major aspects of population structure: size, concentration, and composition.

Population size is considered, usually indirectly, throughout this book. Without this most basic datum, we cannot calculate birth or death rates, growth rates, rates of migration, population density, or levels or rates of urbanization. Despite its crucial importance, population size is unknown (the polite word is "estimated") in most years for most countries and subnational units. Sometimes war prevents an accurate count of the population, or results in such rapid population change that any such count becomes obsolete before it is published, as in Kampuchea in the early 1980s. Sometimes censuses are very few and far between, as in China. Sometimes there has never been a census in a less developed country (LDC), as in Ethiopia, and sometimes, even where there is a census at regular intervals in a more developed country (MDC), there are problems in undercounting a substantial proportion of the population, as in the United States (Cole, 1979; see also Part VII, especially Chapter 46, in this book). Population size has enormous implications for policy. How much food and clothing do we need to produce? How many dwelling units need to be constructed? How many classrooms and teachers do we need? What are the different impacts on pollution and natural resources of stabilizing the population at its current size as opposed to having it double in the next thirty years? Without a modest acquaintance with the population size, these questions cannot be answered, and failure to answer them can be disastrous for public policy and, in a market economy, for privately owned businesses and corporations as well.

Population concentration is intimately linked to migration, and is therefore considered in Part V of this book. One measure of population concentration is population density, the number of people in a given area. (Residential density, the number of people per dwelling or per unit of floor space, is also an aspect of concentration at a microsocial level.) Another aspect of population concentration is urbanization, which as Davis (Chapter 33) notes is both a structure (the percent of the population in urban areas) and a process (the migration of people to urban areas). Population concentration also has important implications for policy. Where people are located determines where services—schools, medical facilities, mass transportation—are most needed. Different patterns of population concentration may have different implications for the impact of the population on, for example, the environment. A given population, evenly spread out over a given land area, may not generate a major pollution problem, while the same population, concentrated into a single urban center (leaving the rest of the land area relatively uninhabited) may generate serious problems of pollution, whether from human and animal wastes in cities in some LDCs and in MDCs in the past, or from automobile exhausts in contemporary cities.

The third major aspect of population structure is population composition. The most important compositional variables are age and sex, because these have such major impacts on fertility (only women can bear children) and mortality (see Part III, especially Chapter 16). One measure of sex composition is the *sex ratio,* the ratio of males to females in the population at a given time:

$$\text{Sex ratio} = 100 \times \text{number of males/number of females}$$

Sex ratios may be computed for specific age groups, for example, infants under one year of age or people over age 65. As suggested in Part IV (see particularly Chapter 29) and Part III (introduction), sex ratios may contain or reflect important information about the status of women in a society. Although the sex composition of a population may vary considerably at the local level (see the example in Weeks, 1981:185), it tends not to vary a great deal for national populations as a whole (see, e.g., World Bank, 1981:168–169). Insofar as it does vary, however, it has very important implications for fertility, and also important implications concerning mortality and the status of women.

There is considerable variation in the age structure of national populations. As we note in the section on mortality (Part III), there is enough difference in the age structures of more developed countries (MDCs) and some less developed countries (LDCs) to give the LDCs lower death rates than the MDCs, even though the risk of dying is higher in the LDCs for every age group. The discrepancy arises because a higher proportion of the population in the MDCs is in the older, higher-risk age groups. In other words, the *median age* or average age in MDCs is higher than that in the LDCs. In Chapter 39, Coale examines the relationship between population dynamics and the age structure of a population. In particular, he looks at the relationship between average age and fertility and mortality, and comes to conclusions that are sometimes surprising. What do you think would happen in a typical LDC if the death rate declined—would the average age of the population get higher or lower? Read Coale's classic paper, and think again.

A convenient way of representing the age-sex structure of a population is the use of an *age-sex pyramid.* The age-sex pyramid is divided vertically into males and females, with females conventionally on the right and males on the left side of the pyramid. Horizontally, the pyramid is divided into *cohorts* or age groups, groups of people born around the same time. For analytical purposes, cohorts may vary in length (e.g., one, five, or ten-year cohorts), but the use of ten-year cohorts is fairly common. In part, this reflects inaccuracies in age reporting. For example, there is a tendency to round to the nearest five or ten years in reporting age (Shryock and Siegel, 1976:115–119). An ex-

Figure VI.I. Population Pyramids for France. (Source: adapted from Pressat, 1969:174.)

1851 Males		1851 Females	1959 Males		1959 Females
*	80–89	*	*	80–89	**
**	70–79	**	**	70–79	****
****	60–69	****	****	60–69	*****
*****	50–59	******	*******	50–59	*******
******	40–49	*******	*****	40–49	*******
*******	30–39	********	********	30–39	**********
*********	20–29	**********	******	20–29	********
***********	10–19	***********	*********	10–19	**********
************	00–09	************	**********	00–09	***********

ample of an age-sex pyramid is given in Figure VI.1, and in the insert between Chapters 39 and 40.

The age-sex pyramids above are reflections of a population's history. In 1851, the pyramid is similar to that of a contemporary less developed country, broad at the base, narrow at the top, almost perfectly triangular in shape. This reflects a situation in which relatively high fertility and mortality prevail. (Notice how structure reflects the dynamic processes of the past.) The proportion of the population that is female is slightly higher than that which is male, but this is apparent only upon close inspection of the pyramid. In the second pyramid, inward bulges reveal the impact of two world wars, and the more rectangular shape is characteristic of a more developed country with lower birth and death rates. The preponderance of females over males is more obvious, expecially in the cohorts affected by the two wars fought on French soil.

In contrast to the French pyramids, which mirror the past, the pyramids in the insert following Chapter 39 adumbrate the future as well as the past of the U.S. population. Three cohorts are represented in these pyramids: the small "good times" cohort, born in the Depression (around the 1930s), whose parents had low fertility; the "baby boom" cohort of the period after World War II (mostly in the 1950s, with some in the late 1940s and some in the early 1960s), a large cohort whose parents had higher than average fertility; and the "baby bust" cohort of the 1970s. Two of these cohorts, the 1930s and 1950s cohorts, have already entered adulthood, and are compared by Harter in Chapter 40. Harter shows the importance of cohort size for the impact of that cohort on both the individuals of which the cohort is comprised and for the society in general.

Independently of the cohort into which you were born, your chronological age will have a major impact on how (and whether) you live. Moreover, the proportion of people in different age groups, particularly the oldest age groups, can have a substantial impact on society. In Chapter 41, Preston provides a counterpoint to the Coale article by looking at the consequences, rather than the causes, of an aging population. He looks at some of the consequences of growing older in the United States, and of the increasing average

age of the U.S. population. Both give cause for concern. The elderly are disproportionately poor and in need of health care, a problem compounded by the bias of the medical profession toward the treatment of *acute* diseases (which are characteristically short in duration and which can be cured) rather than the *chronic* diseases (long-term, generally incurable diseases, which gradually take their toll on the individual) common among the elderly (Barberis, 1980; Soldo, 1980). Yet the economic status of the elderly has improved more than that of any other group in the United States since the inception of the Social Security program under Franklin Roosevelt. Children in the United States, by contrast, are more likely to be in poverty, more likely to commit suicide, and less likely to to benefit from public welfare programs in 1980 than a decade earlier. The advantage that the elderly have over children is both relative and absolute.

With the exclusion of many of the elderly from participation in most economically productive work through mandatory retirement regulations, and with the inevitable increases in the proportion of the elderly in society, either those who are employed will have an increased burden in supporting the elderly, or the elderly, most of them on limited, fixed incomes, may find it increasingly difficult to survive. As the large baby-boom cohort ages, political struggles over such programs as social security and medicare become even more likely, and the probability increases that children and the elderly, two economically dependent groups in the United States, may be thrust into an unwilling competition for public financial support. Preston raises grave and important questions about priorities for future public spending in America.

SOCIOECONOMIC COMPOSITION OF THE POPULATION

While age and sex composition have enormous impacts on the society, population composition covers a much broader range of variables. What percent of the population are wealthy or impoverished, black or white, Protestant or Catholic, literate or illiterate, married or unmarried, employed or unemployed? A great deal could be (and has been) written on each of these variables and on others besides. All of them have impact on the life chances of individuals. In the section on mortality, for example, the impacts of wealth and poverty (Chapter 15) and of marital status (Chapter 16) on life itself were considered.

We have selected two additional compositional characteristics for inclusion in this part. Farley (Chapter 42), using data from the 1970 and 1980 censuses, looks at the size and growth of minority populations in the United States. (Written before 1985, the chapter refers to a 1985 mid-decade census that was planned, but never taken because of budget cuts.) He also looks at evidence of both improvement and continued inequality in the status of minority groups in economics, politics, education, and health. In particular, he finds that the impact of past racism and of present institutional structures still acts to preserve existing inequality among racial groups and to hinder progress towards more equal treatment and status for minority groups.

The second compositional characteristic we consider is education. More precisely, our concern here is with the impact of age structure on education. Zajonc (Chapter 43) documents the relationships among intelligence, scholastic achievement, birth order, and family size. Although a number of other reasons were proposed for academic decline, most could be discounted because they (1) were just as evident when test scores were increasing as when they were declining, as for example in the case of the spread of television, or (2) they coincided with the first part of the decline, but not with the subsequent continuation of the decline, as for example racial composition of test takers, or (3) they simply were not correlated with the trends in the test score declines at all (Menard, 1981). Three exceptions, which could conceivably have explained the entire trend up to 1980, were drug use, the quality of teaching, and the confluence model of intelligence upon which Zajonc based his analysis.

Zajonc's article, first written in 1976, predicted that Scholastic Aptitude Test (SAT) scores, which had been declining for a decade previous to that date, would continue to decline until 1979 to 1980, then increase. As of this writing, 1980 marks the last year of the test score decline. For 1980 and 1981, SAT scores were identical; they increased in 1982, stayed the same in 1983, then increased again in 1984 (College Board, 1984). Based on correlations between drug arrests and self-reported drug use (Flanagan and McLeod, 1983; Metropolitan Life Insurance Company, 1984), changes in drug use cannot explain the increase in test scores. As Weeks (1986:127) notes, both the College Board and the Secretary of Education attributed this change to improvements in the quality of education. It would be difficult, perhaps impossible, to document any increase in the quality of education, and none was apparently detected when the first test score increases were occurring; that was when we were being warned that we were "A Nation At Risk" (National Commission on Excellence in Education, 1983). It would be surprising if the teaching profession, as represented by the National Education Association, wanted to claim credit for the test score increases. Indeed, in 1977, arguing that such tests had little to do with the quality of education (and perhaps much to do with the quality of the students), the NEA recommended "the elimination of group standardized intelligence, aptitude, and achievement tests" (National Education Association, 1977). On the basis of predictiveness alone, a strong case can be made for Zajonc's explanation of the decline and subsequent rise in achievement test scores. Zajonc's model additionally explains why, toward the end of the period of SAT score declines, test scores were increasing at the elementary level (Menard, 1981).

FOR FURTHER READING

1. Landon Y. Jones. 1984. *Great Expectations* (New York: Ballantine) details the impact of cohort size on the life-cycle social experiences of the cohort in a very readable, entertaining book on the baby-boom generation.

2. Roland Chilton and Adele Spielberger. 1971. "Is Delinquency Increasing? Age Structure and the Crime Rate," Social Forces 49(3): 487–493. The impact of population structure on rates of juvenile delinquency.

3. Reynolds Farley. 1984. *Blacks and Whites: Narrowing the Gap?* (Cambridge, MA: Harvard University). Detailed analysis of differences between American blacks and

whites regarding education, employment, income, residential and school segregation, and family welfare. Includes a "Scorecard on Black Progress." For the more advanced reader.

4. Robin Morgan. 1984. *Sisterhood is Global* (Garden City, NY: Anchor). Demographic and social data and narratives from sixty-eight countries document the status of women around the world, the meanings and functions of reproduction, and the complex relationships between reproduction and the status of women. An important handbook, relevant to several other sections (e.g., fertility, population theory) as well.

5. B. D. Miller. 1981. *The Endangered Sex.* (Ithaca, NY: Cornell University). A study of gender stratification in India. Demonstrates that higher death rates for females are the consequence of gender-based division of labor as well as the traditional preference for sons.

39
How a Population Ages or Grows Younger

ANSLEY J. COALE

The age of the whole human population could, I suppose, be measured from the moment the species originated, and the age of a national population could be measured from the country's "birthday." The age (in this sense) of the human population has been estimated as at least 100,000 and no more than a million years, and the age of national populations ranges from several thousand years for Egypt or China to a year or so for some of the emerging nations of Africa.

In this chapter, however, when we speak of the age of a population we refer to the age of its members, and to be precise we should use the term *age distribution* of a population—how many persons there are at each age—rather than the age of a population. The only way a single age can be given for a group of persons is by using some sort of average. A *young* population, then, is one that contains a large proportion of young persons, and has a low average age, while an *old* population has a high average age and a large proportion of old people.

The ages of various national populations in the world today are very different, and in many countries the present age distribution differs markedly from the past.

The oldest populations in the world are found in Northwestern Europe. In France, England, and Sweden, for example, 12 percent of the population is over 65, and half of the population in these countries is over 33, 36, and 37 respectively. The youngest population are found in the underdeveloped countries—those that have not incorporated modern industrial technology in their economies—the population of Asia, Africa and Latin America. Half of the population of Pakistan is under 18 years, of the Congo under 20 years, and of Brazil under 19 years. The proportion over 65 in Brazil is less than one-fourth what it is in France. The proportion of children under 15 is twice as great in Pakistan as in England. Paradoxically enough, the oldest nations—China, India and Egypt—have very young populations.

The highly industrialized countries all have older populations than the underdeveloped countries, and also older populations than they did fifty to a hundred years ago. Since 1900 the median age has risen in England from 24 to 36, in the United States from 23 to 30, in Japan from 23 to 26, and in Russia from 21 to 27. In the underdeveloped countries, however, the age distributions have changed only slightly, and they have, if anything, become slightly younger. In Taiwan, for example, the median age has declined from 21 to 18 since 1915.

What accounts for these differences and these trends in the age distribution of populations? One obvious factor to consider is migration. A famous spa has an old population because old people come there for the cure, and university towns like Princeton have young populations because young people come there to study. But the age distribution of most national populations is not much affected by migration, especially today when almost everywhere international migration is restricted.

Whether a national population is young or old is mainly determined by the number of children women bear. When women bear many children, the population is young; when they bear few, the population is old.

The effect of fertility (as the rate of childbearing can be called) on the age distribution is clearest when a population continuously subject to high fertility is compared to one continuously subject to low fertility. The high-fertility population has a larger proportion of children relative to adults of parental age as a direct consequence of the greater frequency of births. Moreover, by virtue of high fertility a generation ago, today's parents are numerous relative to *their* parents, and hence the proportion of old people is small. Conversely, the population experiencing a prolonged period of low fertility has few children relative to its current parents, who in turn are not numerous relative to *their* parents. Prolonged high fertility produces a large proportion of children, and a small proportion of the aged—a population with a low average age. On the other hand, prolonged low fertility produces a small proportion of children and a large proportion of the aged—a high average age.

It is the small number of children born per woman that explains the high average age now found in industrialized western Europe, and the high birth rate of the underdeveloped countries that accounts for their young populations. The increase in average age and the swollen proportion of old people in the industrialized countries are the product of the history of falling birth rates that all such countries have experienced.

Most of us would probably guess that populations have become older because the death rate has been reduced, and hence people live longer on the average. Just what is the role of mortality in determining the age distribution of a population? The answer is surprising—mortality affects the age distribution much less than does fertility, and in the opposite direction from what most of us would think. Prolongation of life by reducing death rates has the perverse effect of making the population somewhat younger. Consider the effect of the reduction in death rates in the United States, where the average duration of life has risen from about 45 years under the mortality conditions of 1900 to about 70 years today. Had the risks of death prevailing in 1900 continued unchanged, and the other variables—rates of immigration and rates of childbearing per mother—followed the course they actually did, the average age of the population today would be greater than it is: the proportion of children would be less and the proportion of persons over 65 would be greater than they are. The reduction of the death rate has produced, in other words, a younger American population.

These statements seem scarcely credible.

Does not a reduction in the death rate increase the average age at death? Are there not more old people as a result of reduced mortality than there would be with the former high death rates? How then can it be said that a reduction in the death rate makes a population younger?

It is true that as death rates fall, the average age at which people die is increased. But the average age of a population is the average age of living persons, not their average age at death. It is also true, as we all immediately realize, that as death rates fall, the number of old persons in a population increases. What we do not so readily realize is that reduced mortality increases the number of *young* persons as well. More survive from birth to ages 1, 10, 20, and 40, as well as more living to old age. Because more persons survive to be parents, more births occur.

The reason that the reduced death rates, which prolong man's life, make the population younger is that typical improvements in health and medicine produce the greatest increases in survivorship among the young rather than the old.

There is one kind of reduction in death rates that would not affect the age distribution of the population at all, that would lead to the same proportion of population at every age as if mortality had not changed. This particular form of reduced mortality is one that increases the chance of surviving one year by a certain amount—say one-tenth of 1 percent—at every age. The result would be one-tenth of a percent more persons at age 1, 5, 10, 60, and 80—at every age—than there would have been had death rates been unaltered. Because there would be one-tenth percent more parents, there would also be one-tenth percent more births. Therefore the next year's population would be one-tenth percent larger than it would otherwise have been, but the proportion of children, of young adults, of the middle-aged, and of the aged would not be altered—there would be one-tenth percent more of each.

Reductions in mortality of this singular sort that would not affect the age of the population at all are not found in actual human experience. However, there has been a tendency for persons at all ages to share some of the increased chances of survival, and the effect of reduced death rates on the age distribution has consequently been small—much smaller than the effect of reduced birth rates—in countries where both fertility and mortality have changed markedly.

As the average duration of life has risen from lower levels to 65 or 70 years, the most conspicuous advances in survivorship seem always to have occurred in infancy and early childhood. It is for this reason that reduced mortality has had the effect of producing a younger population, although the effect has usually been obscured by the much more powerful force of a falling birth rate that has occurred at the same time. Thus the population of the United States has actually become *older* since 1900, because of falling fertility; but falling mortality (with its tendency to produce a younger population) has prevented it from becoming older still.

The younger-population effect of reduced mortality is not an inevitable feature of all increases in length of life. The countries with the greatest average duration of life have by now about exhausted the possibility of increasing survivorship in a way that makes for a younger population. In Sweden today 95 percent survive from birth to age 30, compared to 67 percent in 1870. At best, survivorship to age 30 in Sweden could approach 100 percent. No important increase in population at younger ages would result. If there are further major gains in the chances of prolonged life in Sweden, they must occur at older ages, and if they occur, will make the population older.

Every individual inexorably gets older as time passes. How old he gets depends on how long he avoids death. President Eisenhower remarked after his retirement that he was glad to be old, because at his age, if he were not old, he would be dead.

Populations, on the other hand, can get older or younger. They get older primarily as the result of declining fertility, and younger primarily as the result of rising fertility.

The most highly industrialized countries have all experienced a decline of fertility of about 50 percent since their preindustrial phase, and they all have older populations than they used to have. In France and the United States, for example, the number of children each woman bore declined for more than a century, reaching a minimum just before World War II. In each country during this period the population became progressively older. In fact, the "aging" of the population continued for a time after fertility had passed its minimum. Between 1800 and 1950 the median age of the French population rose from 25 to 35 years, and in the United States in the same interval the median age increased from 16 to 30. In both countries there has been a substantial recovery in fertility during the past 25 years from the low point reached in the 1930s. This rise in fertility has produce the first decrease in median age recorded in the statistics of either nation. Between 1950 and 1960 the median age in France fell from 35 to 33, and in the United States from 30.2 to 29.6.

This reversal in the trend toward an older population in the United States has been accompanied by a more pronounced reversal in the way proportions of children were changing. The long-term decline in fertility in the United States meant that the proportion of children to adults steadily shrank from about 0.85 children (under 15) per adult (over 15) in 1800 to 0.33 per adult in 1940. By 1960 the proportion had rebounded to 0.45 children per adult. In fact, the increase in the *number* of children in the population between 1950 and 1960—more than 15 million—was greater than the increase between 1900 and 1950.

The abrupt reversal of the long-term trend toward an older population has meant the first increase in the relative burden of child dependency in the history of the United States. The very productive American economy can certainly afford to support this burden, but it has not been painless. The extremely rapid increase in the number of children in the past decade has required the construction of many new schools and the training of many teachers. In some communities where foresight, willingness to pay increased taxes, or resources were inadequate, schools have been overcrowded and the quality of instruction has suffered.

The countries that have not undergone intensive industrialization have experienced no major changes in fertility, no trends of sustained decline and recovery such as occurred in France and the United States. Rather they have experienced a largely unbroken sequence of high birth rates. There has been in consequence little change in the age composition of underdeveloped areas. All have 40 percent or more under age 15, only 2 to 4 percent over 65, and a median age of 20 years or less.

The age distributions of the industrialized countries on the one hand and of the preindustrial countries on the other are ironically mismatched with what each sort of country seems best equipped to accommodate. As we have noted before, the contrast in age of population is striking. In Pakistan or Mexico nearly one person of every two a visitor might encounter would be a child, and only two or three of every hundred would be old (over 65); while in England only one in four would be a child and about one in eight would be old. In the industrialized countries where the proportion of the aged is so large, the importance of the family in the predominantly urban environment has diminished, and consequently the role of respected old patriarch or matriarch has nearly vanished. The wealthy industrial countries can readily afford to support a sizable component of old people but have not in fact always done so adequately. The aging of their populations has been accompanied by a weakening or a disappearance of the traditional claims of the aged on their descendants for material support and, perhaps more tragically, by a weakening or disappearance of recognized and accepted position for old people in the family.

In the underdeveloped countries, on the

other hand, the relatively few old people are accorded traditional respect and whatever economic support their families have to offer, and hence the aged are less subject to special economic and social deprivation.

Because of extremely young age distributions, adults in the impoverished underdeveloped countries must support a disproportionately large dependent-child population—twice as great a burden of dependency per adult in the working ages of 15 to 65 as in typical industrialized countries—a burden these poor countries can scarcely afford. The enormous proportion of children makes it extraordinarily difficult, where incomes are extremely low, to provide adequate shelter, nourishment, and education for the young.

Moreover, the preindustrial countries can expect no relief from dependency as a result of the spectacular drop in death rates now occurring. Unless fertility declines, this drop in mortality will only make the populations younger, adding to the already extreme burden of dependent children.

In sum, it is the industrialized countries that, better able to afford a high burden of child dependency, have only half the proportion of children found in underdeveloped areas, and that, having abandoned the institutions giving a meaningful role to the aged, have four times the proportion of the elderly found in preindustrial countries.

The last question considered in this brief survey of the age of populations is the past trend in age distribution from man's origin to the present, and what alternative trends may possibly develop in the future.

The human population as a whole has always been and is now a young population, consisting of at least 40 percent children, and have a median age of no more than about 20 years, because the overall human birth rate has always been about 40 per 1,000 or higher. It is almost certain that until perhaps two hundred years ago all sizable national or regional populations likewise were young, with about the same age characteristics as the population of the world.

These statements can be made with confidence, even though no reliable records of the age distribution of the world, or of world birth rates, or even records of many national populations exist for most of man's history. We can be confident that the world's populatin has always been young because until the last two centuries it was not possible for any population to achieve low mortality for any sustained period, and any population with a low birth rate would therefore have become extinct.

It is simply not possible for a possible for a population to have a birth rate much below its death rate for a prolonged period, as can be shown by the following example. The population of the world has grown from about one-quarter billion to about three billion since the time of Julius Caesar—it has been multiplied by about twelve. But the average annual rate of increase has been very little—about 1 per 1,000 per year. If the world birth rate has averaged 40 per 1,000 (a reasonable guess), the world death rate by logical necessity has averaged 39 per 1,000. A world birth rate only 2 points lower (38 instead of 40 per 1,000) would have led to an annual *decrease* of 1 per 1,000, and the current population would be only one-twelfth instead of twelve times the population of Caesar's day. A birth rate of 35—that of England or the United States in 1880—would have reduced the 250 million of two thousand years ago to less than one hundred thousand today.

The industrialized countries have been able to reduce their birth rates without having their populations shrink drastically because they first reduced their death rates. Beginning in the late eighteenth century some countries made preliminary steps in the improvement in living conditions and sanitation that has continued until today, and in the latter half of the nineteenth century there began the remarkable development of modern medicine and public health that so greatly extended the average duration of life in the industrially more advanced countries.

In the past few decades modern medical techniques and public health methods have been introduced into the underdeveloped countries, causing an extraordinary drop in death rates, and since birth rates have not changed, the growth of world population has sharply accelerated so that it is now 2 percent per year.

Just as it is not possible for a population to maintain for long a birth rate much below its death rate, because such a population would shrink to extinction, it is not possible to maintain for long a birth rate much *above* a death rate, because then the population would grow to a physically impossible size. For example, had the current 2 percent rate of growth existed since the time of Caesar, the population of the world would have been multiplied by about 135 quadrillion instead of twelve, and there would be more than 30,000 times the entire world's current population on each square mile of land area on the earth. Starting with today's three billion persons, it would take only about 650 years for a 2 percent rate of increase to produce one person per square foot, and about twice that long to produce a total that would outweigh the earth.

In short, the present combination of a high world birth rate and a moderate and rapidly falling death rate can only be temporary. The only combinations that can long continue are birth and death rates with the same average levels.

If man chooses to continue the high birth rate that he has always had, the human population will remain a young one—but in the long run it can remain young only by returning to the high death rate and short average life it has always had. Sustained geometric increase is impossible.

If, on the other hand, mankind can avoid nuclear war, and bring the fruits of modern technology, including prolonged life, to all parts of the world, the human population must become an old one, because only a low birth rate is compatible in the long run with a low death rate, and a low birth rate produces an old population. In fact, if the expectation of life at birth of 70 years—now achieved or exceeded in many industrialized countries—becomes universal, the average number of children born per woman must decline to about two from five or more in the underdeveloped areas, slightly more than three in the United States, and some two and a half in Europe. Such a decline in fertility would give the whole world as old a population as any country has had to date—only about 21 percent under 15, at least 15 percent over 65, and as many persons over 36 as under.

A world population with the age composition of a health resort is a mildly depressing prospect. Such a population would presumably be cautious, conservative, and full of regard for the past. A young, vigorous, forward-looking population perhaps appears more attractive, but in the long run the world can keep its youth only by tolerating premature death.

We find at the end, then, that although the birth rate determines how old a population is, the death rate determines what the average birth rate in the long run must be. If prolonged life produces by its direct effects a younger population, it is nevertheless compatible only with an older population.

Progress of Depression Cohort, Baby Boom Cohort, and Baby Bust Cohort Through U.S. Population Age-Sex Pyramid: 1960–2050.

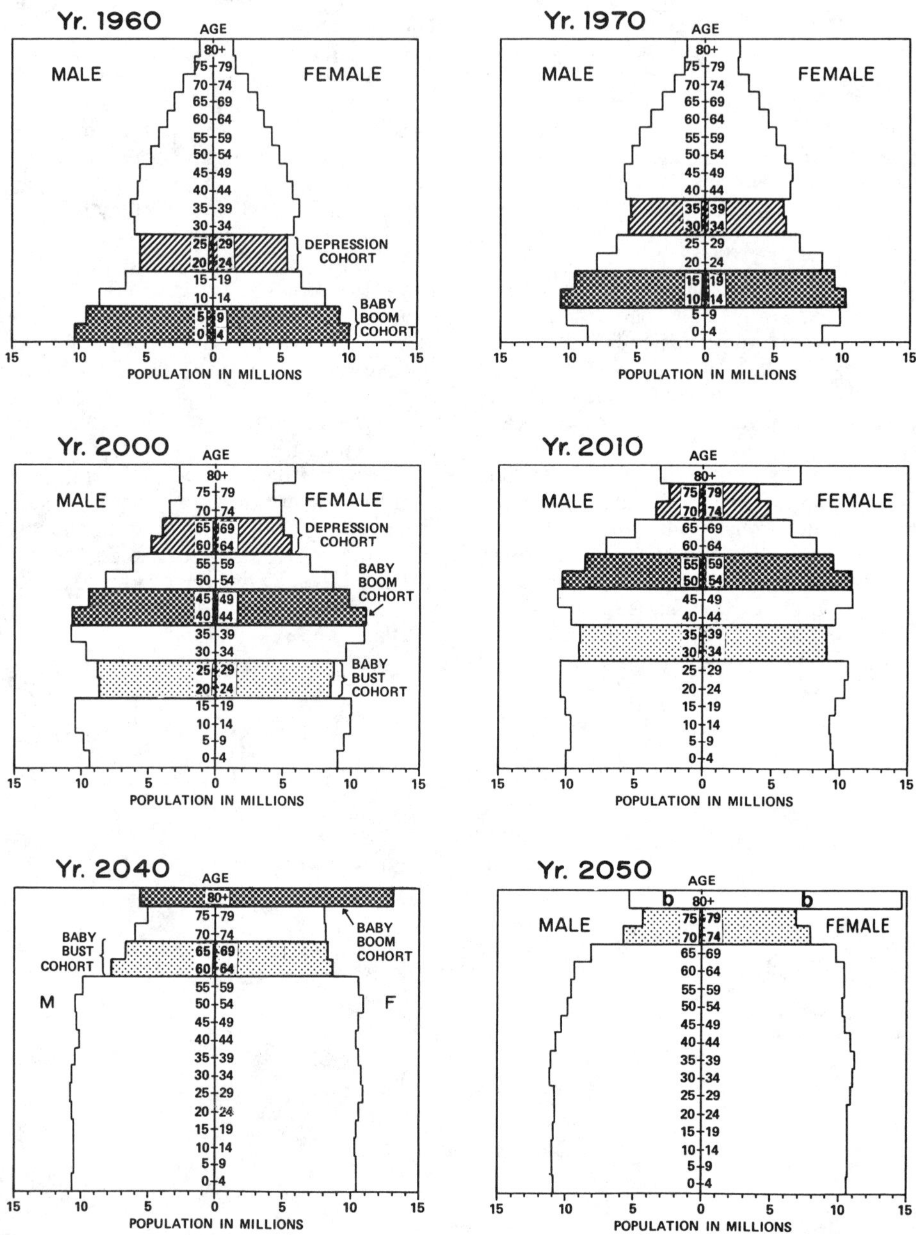

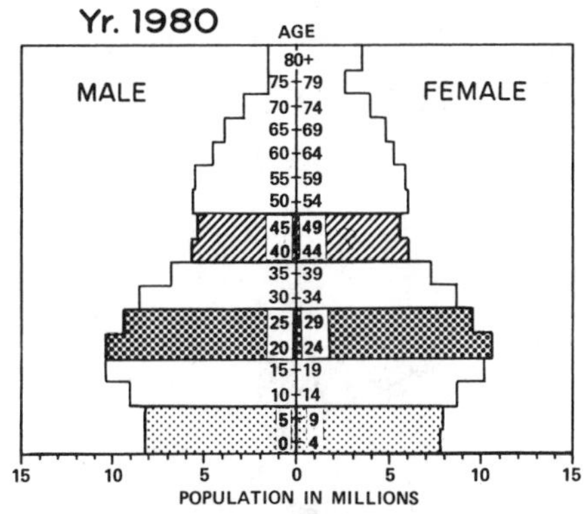

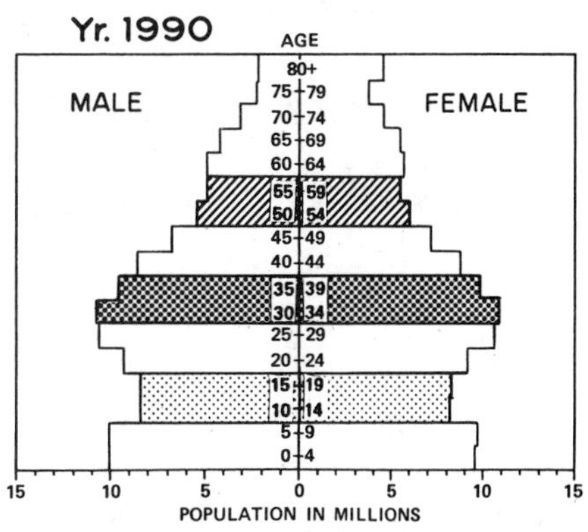

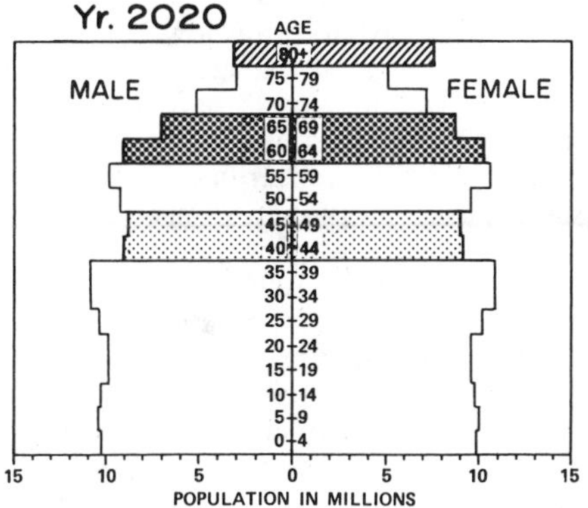

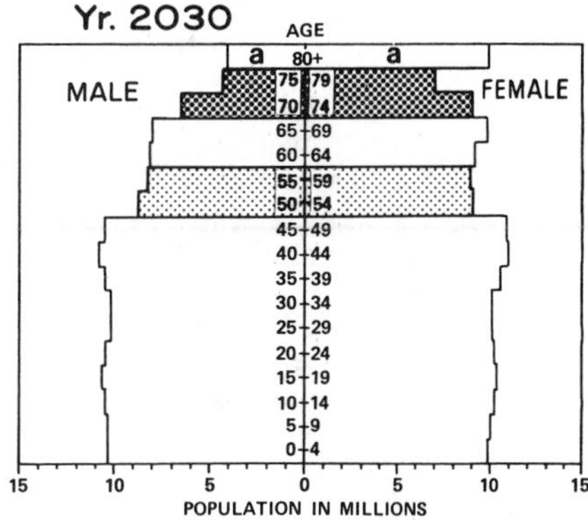

DEPRESSION COHORT
PERSONS BORN 1930 – 39

BABY BOOM COHORT
PERSONS BORN 1950 – 59

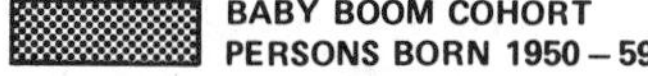

BABY BUST COHORT
PERSONS BORN 1970 – 79

Sources: 1960-1970: U.S. Bureau of the Census, *1970 U.S. Census of Population: General Population Characteristics, United States Summary*, Vol. I, PC(1)-B1, 1972, Table 52;. and 1980-2050: Special unpublished tabulations prepared by Leon F. Bouvier for the Select Commission on Immigration and Refugee Policy, 1980

[a] Includes survivors of Depression cohort.
[b] Includes survivors of baby boom cohort.

Note: 1980-2050 projections assume a total fertility rate rising to 2.0 births per woman by 1985 and constant thereafter; life expectancy at birth rising to 72.8 years for males and 82.9 years for females by 2050; net immigration constant at 750,000 persons per year.

40

The "Good Times" Cohort of the 1930s: Sometimes Less Means More (and More Means Less)

CARL L. HARTER

Many of the things we do or need in life are age specific. We go to elementary school between the ages of 6 and 14, so that is the age at which we need an elementary teacher and a school building. Most of us leave our parents and set up our own home between the ages of 18 and 25, so that age range is when we need our first job and a house or apartment of our own. From several months before birth (the need for an obstetrician) to several days after death (the need for a mortician), our lives are filled with age-specific activities and needs. How much of each age-specific need is required or expected at any one time is determined by the number of us who are at each age.

Obviously the number of persons who are at any particular age is related to the number of births that occurred that many years previously. In demographic jargon, persons who share the same year of birth are referred to as the "birth cohort" for that year. In common usage, however, the "birth" portion of the term is dropped and only the word "cohort" is used. For example, the 1936 cohort means all persons born in the calendar year 1936, and the 1930s cohort means all persons born between January 1, 1930, and January 1, 1940. Technically the term cohort can be applied to any group whose members have some demographic characteristic in common, such as the same year of first marriage, same year of first parenthood, same year of death, etc.; but, unless otherwise specified, cohort is used to refer to a group who are the same age—a birth cohort.

Once the birth year is past, births can no longer be used to increase the cohort size—one cannot enter a group by birth at age 5 or 25 or 50. Accordingly, the original size of cohorts in any nation can only be changed by deaths or migration. With each passing year deaths diminish the absolute size of each cohort; but in the United States—indeed in most of the developed world—age-specific death rates before 50 years or so are quite low and stable, and hence deaths at these ages do not alter the relative size of cohorts or even account for much absolute decrease in their size. For the past quarter of a century in the United States, for example, more than 98 percent of the people who reached age 5 were still alive at age 20.

Both the absolute and relative size of cohorts in any nation could be affected by international migration, the people who leave and enter a country. A host of social-economic-political factors can differentially stimulate members of certain cohorts to want to leave their country and/or to enter a specific country. In actual practice, however, most nations have very low annual rates of immigration and emigration. Since most nations have policies that restrict the number and the type of persons who can enter, we are not likely to see any large international migrations in the near future.

"BABY BOOMERS" GROW UP

Thus, if international migration does not significantly increase or decrease the size of a cohort at any age and if deaths do not differentially affect cohorts, then the original size of birth cohorts is the main factor that determines how many people there will be at each age each year. So in a very real sense, the number of people retiring in 1977 is related to what happened sixty five years ago—to the number of births that occurred in 1912—just as the number of youngsters entering junior high school this year was predetermined 13 years ago by the number of births that occurred in 1964.

In this "age of relativity" the absolute power

or value of something does not always increase or decrease as the absolute number or cost or size of that thing increases or decreases. For example, a society with 250 million people will not necessarily be "better off" than a society with only 50 million, nor will a family with ten members necessarily be "better off" than a family of four. We tend to be more concerned with how developed a nation is, compared to other nations, than we are with how many people it has, or with how well off a family is compared to other families, than we are with how large the family is.

There are instances, though, in which the absolute size or number of something is an important consideration. Using a boat and a lake as an analogy, neither a small, slow boat, nor a fast, large boat will be affected by a calm lake, but the different boats will have vastly different effects on the lake; A small, slow boat will hardly cause ripples on the lake whereas a large or fast boat will create high waves. On the other hand, a very rough lake will be largely unaffected by either small or large boats, but the boats in turn will be differentially affected by the rough lake: The small boat will be tossed to and fro by the lake while the large boat will more likely be able to weather the storm. In some respects an age cohort and a society have this boat-lake relationship to each other.

When a particular age group accounts for only a small proportion of the population, that age group will probably not create many "ripples" or "waves" in the society. But if that same age group, at some later date, accounts for a considerably larger proportion of the total population, it may "rock the boat" of society. In discussing the political consequences of population change, for example, Dr. Myron Weiner, Professor of Political Science at MIT, has pointed out that "It is necessary to distinguish between the political role of a particular age group when it constitutes a small portion of the population and its role when its numbers have sharply increased."[1] In 1970, Dr. George H. Brown, then Director of the Bureau of the Census, indicated that one-third of our nation's total population increase between 1970 and 1985 would be in the 25–34 age group, and as a consequence "By 1985 we may expect to see more young leaders in government, private industry and politics than ever before."[2] This increase in young leaders by 1985 is expected because their cohort constituency, the "baby boom" cohorts born after World War II, are much larger than the young adult cohorts were in 1970. In 1970 some 25 million (12 percent) Americans were aged 25 to 34, but by 1985 almost 40 million (17 percent) Americans will be 25 to 34.[3] Not only will the cohort increase by about 15 million in just 15 years, but by 1985 every sixth American will be between 25 and 35 whereas in 1970 every eighth American was in that age group.

Since these "baby boomers" constitute an increasing proportion of the voting population, we can expect them to have an increasingly significant say-so in the running of the "ship of state." At the same time, though, they have created some "stormy seas" or "tidal waves" for society. As Dr. Robert C. Cook, past president of PRB, has commented, "Wherever these children have gone, from kindergarten to college, into massive developments of three- and four-bedroom houses, into the labor market, their progress has caused a shaking of heads over crowding, split school sessions, bulldozing of green acres, and job openings."[4]

There are also instances in which a big increase in the size of a cohort can lead to seemingly contradictory conditions. For example, during the debate beween the presidential candidates on September 23, 1976, the Republican candidate stated that more people were currently employed than ever before in our history. In apparent contradiction, the Democratic candidate said that the number of unemployed people was larger than ever before and the unemployment rate was at one of the highest points since the Great Depresssion. Actually both candidates were correct, and one of the phenomena responsible for these curious employment statistics is the baby boom cohorts. Those large cohorts (plus an increase in the proportion of women seeking jobs) have now reached "employment age" and have greatly increased the size of the labor force (a term which includes the employed plus the unemployed who are seeking employment). In a recent report on the aging of the baby boom cohorts, Denis F. Johnston, Director of the Social Indicators Project in the Office of Management and Budget, points out that in the ten years prior to 1964, the labor force was increasing by about 880,000 per year, but in the ten years from 1964 to 1974 when the baby boom cohorts began entering the job market, the annual net growth of the labor force nearly doubled—to about 1,740,000 per year.[5] Many of these new job seekers are finding employment, but in the absence of sufficient new jobs to provide work opportunities for all of those large cohorts recently entering the labor force, we have seen increases both in the total number employed (some 88 million) and in the total number unemployed (some 7.5 million).

Since we know that the original size of a birth cohort has a direct bearing on the amount of future age-specific needs and activities of that cohort, it should be possible for people and societies to prepare to provide for those various needs and activities. In many case, however, it takes years of lead time for a society to develop the jobs or services required to meet the specific needs generated by each cohort. And the problems become greatly compounded if there are large year-to-year or decade-to-decade changes in the number of people at each age. For example, the slightly more than 3.5 million births in 1950 required x number of pediatricians between 1950 and 1960, but the slightly more than 4.3 million births in 1960 required x plus 18 percent pediatricians between 1960 and 1970. Since it takes at least ten years from the time a student decides to become a physician until he or she is a practicing pediatrician, in order to have had enough pediatricians for the 1960 cohort, some students in the 1950s would have had to anticipate (or hope) that there would be enough children for them to take care of when they finished their training. In 1970 the number of births (3.7 million) declined to about the 1950 level, so the extra pediatricians required in the sixties are no longer needed in the seventies.

Year-to-year or decade-to-decade fluctuations in the size of successive cohorts can indeed make it difficult for businesses, educational institutions, or any group to make long-range plans. Yet such fluctuation seems to be occurring. In his 1969 discussion of an emerging fertility pattern in the United States, Professor Norman Ryder, who was then at the University of Wisconsin, stated that "The future of fertility is likely to be increasingly bound up with questions of fluctuation rather than of trend."[6] In his discussion of future populations in 1972, Professor Nathan Keyfitz of the University of Chicago indicated that the more developed nations "will have an endless series of ups and downs in their births. . . ."[7] More recently Professor Ronald Lee of the University of Michigan has provided evidence suggesting that the fluctuations in U.S. fertility in the twentieth century may represent fertility control cycles that peak about every forty years or every other generation.[8] At any rate, fluctuations in cohort size make it difficult to anticipate how many teachers or jobs or houses, etc., will be required at some future date.

Sometimes business or governmental managers can correctly anticipate the number of people who will be needing age-specific services or doing age-specific activities. But even with such foresight these managers will often not accept the risk of guessing wrong, particularly if the risk involves investing a lot of money or time. Instead, they wait until the anticipated a demand or need arrives and then attempt to meet it. As a consequence, when cohorts are followed by ever larger cohorts, there are always demands or needs that, at least temporarily, remain unmet or unfilled.

THE "GOOD TIMES" COHORT

There is however, a cohort of currently middle-aged Americans—the 1930s cohort—that is smaller, not larger, than the cohort that preceded it. We might therefore consider whether being fewer in number has made the cohort members' life easier—a case, perhaps, in which "less means more." By virtue of their smaller number, the thirties cohort, upon encountering each important life cycle event, have experienced relative abundance—a legacy from the larger cohort that preceded them. Thus, this cohort, born during the "bad times" of the 1930s, have received advantages and "good times" at every new period in their life.

The stage was set for this relatively small "good times" cohort in the following way. For a century and a half preceding the 1930s, the country's fertility rate declined steadily—in each decade women on the average had fewer children than did women in the previous decades. Nonetheless, each decade always saw more babies produced than the decade before, as fertility (production), though declining, was still considerably above replacement level. The result was that when the female babies of each decade grew up and produced their own children, in their numbers they more than made up for the lower production per woman, so that total production was always greater than before. Immigration also added to the ranks of the producers, which helped to push total production each decade higher than production in the previous decade.

Throughout our nation's history each generation has tended to be larger than its predecessors. In keeping with the "bigger means better" philosophy that prevailed in business and industry and in keeping with the "expansion" psychology that accompanied the settling of the nation and the growth of cities, we generally viewed population growth and ever-larger cohorts as more or less natural. Until the 1930s our whole history had been one of more and ever more. Every decade had more people at each age or stage in life than the previous decade; there were more first graders, more high schoolers, more college students, more young adults seeking their first jobs, more young marrieds needing their own homes, more middle-aged adults to climb occupational career ladders, more old folks to provide for, and finally, even more deaths which called for more mortuaries and cemeteries. This relentless increase in the size of birth cohorts meant that we could never really catch up with their needs. We produced more pediatricians, or schools, or jobs, or houses, or cemeteries; but there was a seemingly never-ending supply of larger cohorts followed by even larger ones. With each cohort needing a larger supply than the one just before it, there was never quite enough for everyone.

But all that changed with the cohort born in the 1930s. For the first time we had a decade in which there were fewer births than in the decade that preceded it. For example, as indicated in Figure 40.1, the number of children age 5 in 1940 (the 1935 cohort) was about 25 percent less than it had been ten years earlier. For the first time in our history we had smaller cohorts following larger cohorts instead of the other way around.

What advantages have the thirties cohort enjoyed because of their fewer numbers? For one thing, compared to their immediate predecessors, they have needed less from society. They did not find overcrowded delivery rooms, insufficient classrooms, burgeoning universities, scarce job offers, a big housing shortage. With their fewer numbers, they have also had greater opportunity for career mobility. Relatively speaking, in all their important life cycle events the 1930s cohort has "had it made."

In 1950 when the thirties cohort was age 11 to 20, there were about a quarter million fewer 15-year-olds than there had been in 1940 (Figure 40.1). Insofar as the number of high-school classrooms, glee clubs, athletic teams, debate squads, class officers, etc., had not diminished, then the 1950 15-year-old had a greater chance

Figure 40.1. Comparisons of cohorts ages 5, 15, 25, and 35 for each decade from 1880 to 1970 in the U.S.

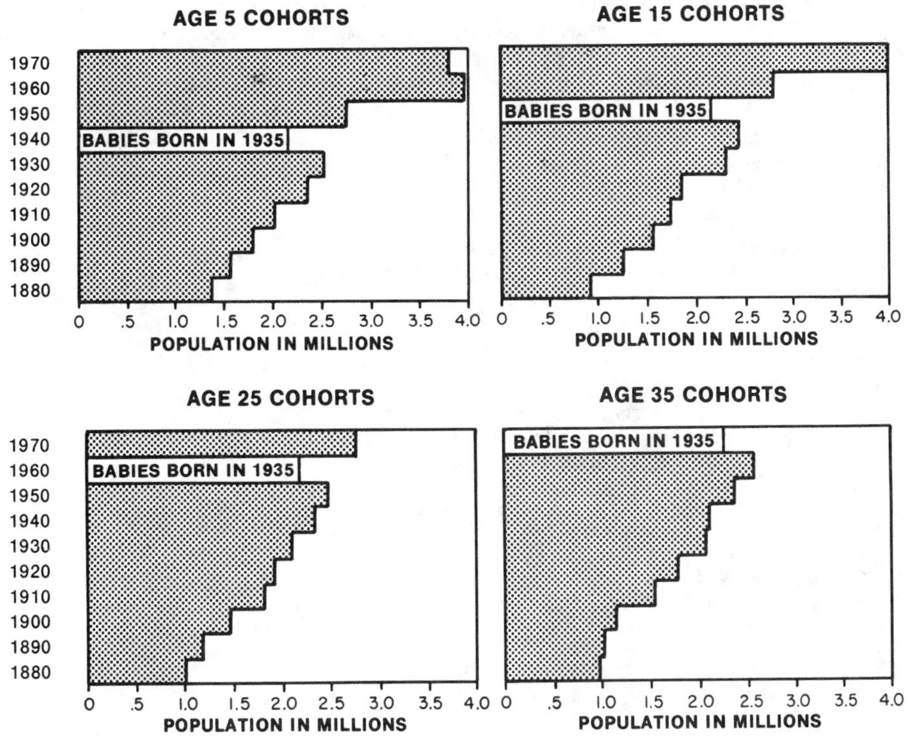

than did the 1940 15-year-old of being in a smaller-size class, of being a class officer, of being a member of the glee club and athletic team and debate squad, etc. Similarly in 1960, when the thirties cohort was 21 to 39, they required fewer new jobs and housing units than did their predecessors ten years earlier.

At their current age of 37 to 46 the thirties cohort are presumably in their most productive years—in positions of seniority, decision making, and leadership. (Parenthetically, we might well ask if the cohort's uninterrupted "good times" have prepared them to make appropriate decisions and provide the leadership required by the greatly increased cohorts of the forties and fifties—the "baby boomers"—who are following in their shadow.) Even at this middle-age stage in their life, the thirties cohort may largely escape a problem encountered by those a decade or two older than they. Technological unemployment and job obsolescence have been serious problems for persons who were trained for the pre-World War II and pre-Sputnik vocations. The thirties cohort, however, was the first cohort to be trained in the modern postwar era. While they may now be beginning to feel some job insecurity from the host of precocious young adults nipping at their heels, the thirties cohort with their modern training, relatively small number, and advanced seniority, are reasonably assured of more than subsistence income and positions until they retire some twenty to thirty years from now.

Even at retirement the thirties cohort will probably still have relatively "good times." In the United States today the largest age concentration of poor people are those in retirement—the 65s and over. Inflation continues to render them ever poorer when they live on fixed income retirement plans, and Social Security benefits (a program which began during the bad times of the 1930s) seem inadequate to keep up with the cost of living. Nevertheless, during the next twenty years there will be more people retiring each year then the year before, and by 1995 about one of every eight Americans will be age 65 or older.

Perhaps this landslide of retirees during the next twenty years will stimulate a variety of programs to assist the elderly so that retirees will indeed have some gold for their "golden years." If so, by the time the cohort of the thirties retires, during 1995 to 2005, they will once again have benefitted from the trials and tribulations of the larger cohort that preceded them.

The cohort of the thirties began life during bad times, but by being fewer in number than the cohort they followed, they have had the advantage of experiencing relatively good times throughout their lives. Similarly the past decade in this nation also produced a cohort some 17 percent smaller than the one which preceded it. Thus perhaps another advantaged cohort is on its way through life, and the good times of the thirties cohort will not have been a once and only occurrence.

NOTES AND REFERENCES

1. Weiner, Myron, "Political Demography: An Inquiry into the Political Consequences of Population Change," in Roger Revelle (ed.), *Rapid Population Growth: Consequences and Policy Implications* (Baltimore: Johns Hopkins Press for the National Academy of Sciences, 1971), p. 582.
2. Brown, George H., "1985, " *PRB Selection* No. 34 (November, 1970), p. 5.
3. U.S. Bureau of the Census, *Current Population Reports,* Series P-25, No. 601, "Projections of the Population of the United States: 1975 to 2050," (U.S. Government Printing Office, Washington, DC, 1975), pp. 8–9.
4. *PRB Population Profile,* "Marriage Gaps and Gains," (June 26, 1967), p. 4.
5. Johnston, Denis F., "The Aging of the Baby Boom Cohorts," *Statistical Reporter,* No. 76-9, (Government Printing Office, Washington, DC, March 1976), pp. 161–165.
6. Ryder, Norman B., "The Emergence of a Modern Fertility Pattern: United States, 1917–66," in S. J. Behrman, Leslie Corsa, Jr., and Ronald Freedman (eds.), *Fertility and Family Planning: A World View* (Ann Arbor: The University of Michigan Press, 1969), p. 116.
7. Keyfitz, Nathan, "On Future Population," *Journal of the American Statistical Association,* Vol. 67 (June 1972), p. 361.
8. Lee, Ronald, "The Formal Dynamics of Controlled Populations and the Echo, the Boom and the Bust," *Demography,* Vol. II (November 1974), pp. 563–585.

41

Children and the Elderly: Divergent Paths For America's Dependents

SAMUEL H. PRESTON

In 1957, the total fertility rate in the United States reached a postwar peak of 3.68 children per women (U.S. National Center for Health Statistics, 1976:4). In the two decades that followed, it fell to half of its 1957 value, and seems to have reached a temporary plateau at a figure of about 1.8 children per women. This sharp fertility decline led to a decline in the number of children under age 15 in the United States by about 7 percent between 1960 and 1982 and to a reduction of 28 percent in the proportion of the population under age 15 (U.S. Bureau of the Census, 1984b:33; 1975:15).

Very different forces were at work at the other end of the age scale. The number of people aged 65 and over increased by 54 percent between 1960 and 1980 (U.S. Bureau of the Census, 1982a:25). Reasons for the growth of this age segment are more complex. Somewhat more than half of the growth is attributable to the fact that the cohorts over age 65 in 1980 were already larger in childhood than were the earlier cohorts. Their relative size underwent little change as the cohorts aged into the preretirement years and their relation was projected to continue largely unchanged into the elderly years.[1] In 1971, the U.S. Census Bureau projected that the population aged 65 and over would grow by 17.6 percent between 1971 and 1981, only slightly faster than the projected growth (in the intermediate series) of 14.7 percent for the whole population (U.S. Bureau of the Census, 1971). But in fact the elderly population grew by 28.4 percent during this period, an increase of 61 percent greater than expected. Between 1971 and 1981, the elderly population of the United States grew faster than the population of India.

What caused this unanticipated growth spurt is, of course, a very rapid decline in old age mortality. The Census Bureau's 1971 projection anticipated a life expectancy of 72.2 years in the year 2000. But already by 1982 life expectancy was 74.5 years, having increased more than twice as much in 10 years as it was expected to increase in 30 (U.S. National Center for Health Statistics, 1983a:15).

So we have passed through several decades of abrupt demographic change. The child population has declined and the elderly population has spurted. Both of these developments were in the main unanticipated.

Most demographers would probably expect such a rapid change in age structure to have favorable consequences for children and troubling ones for the elderly. Fewer children should mean less competition for resources in the home as well as greater availability of social services earmarked for children, especially public schooling. The sharp rise in the number of elderly persons should put enormous pressure on resources directed towards the older ages, such as medical care facilities, nursing homes, and social security funds. At least this view would be characteristic of those who see the world through a Malthusian lens and find the main social drama to be the pressure of numbers on some kind of inelastic resource.

My thesis is that exactly the opposite trends have occured in the relative well-being of our two groups of age dependents and that demographic factors have not only failed to prevent this outcome but have, in many ways, encouraged it. Conditions have deteriorated for children and improved dramatically for the elderly and demographic change has been intimately involved in these developments.

EVIDENCE OF CHANGE IN THE RELATIVE STATUS OF DEPENDENTS

First, let's examine some evidence on changes in the relative welfare of children and the elderly. The job is much easier for the elderly because they are routinely included in our data collection systems and are distinguished in most tabulations. We gather very little information on children, however, and only in the last few years have we come to recognize this deficiency.

Probably the indicator of well-being on which different ages are most readily compared over time is the percentage who live in poverty. We obviously cannot compare personal incomes of the two groups but we can compare incomes in the families with whom they reside relative to some standard of minimal need. The basic standard used by the Census Bureau is an income level three times the cost of the Economy Food Plan as determined by the Department of Agriculture. Families with money incomes less than three times this amount are said to be in poverty. Some allowance is made for scale economies in larger families.

Figure 41.1 shows the percentage living in poverty, by age, in 1982 and 1970, one of the first years in which age breakdowns are available.[2] Clearly, the relation between poverty and age has changed dramatically. Although it is U-shaped in both years, the right arm dominates in 1970 and the left arm in 1982. The incidence of poverty among the elderly was double the national incidence in 1970 but by 1982 the proportion of the elderly living in poverty had actually fallen below the national average. The incidence of poverty among children under 14 in 1982 is 56 percent greater than among the elderly, whereas in 1970 it was 37 percent less. It's no mystery that the main factor in the reduction of poverty among the elderly is the expansion of social security benefits. It's been calculated that 56 percent of the elderly would have been in poverty in 1978 had it not been for such income transfers (Danziger and Gottschalk, 1983:746). The rise in child poverty appears all the more remarkable in view of the greatly increased propensity of their mothers to contribute to family income: 48.7 percent of mothers with children under age six in intact families were in the labor force in 1982, versus only 18.6 percent in 1960 (U.S. Bureau of the Census, 1983a:414).

Figure 41.1. Percentage living in poverty by age 1970 and 1982.

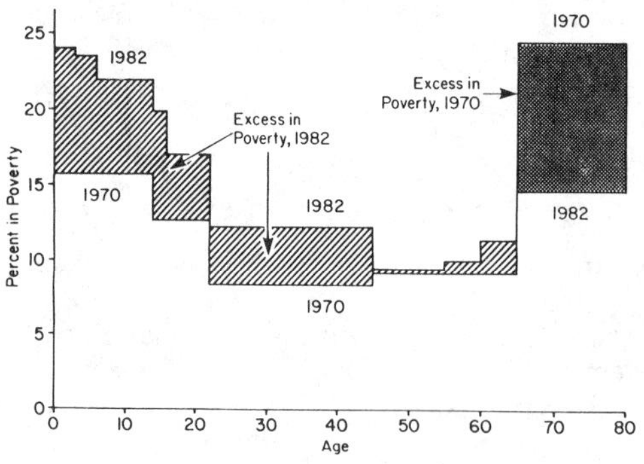

The measure of poverty incidence has been criticized on several grounds. One is that its not an indicator of welfare or well-being because people can chose to have more children at the same income level, thereby simultaneously increasing their welfare and impoverishing themselves (Pollak and Wales, 1979). While this argument clearly pertains to adults, it has no relevance to children. If they are poor, it's not because they choose to be. A more important objection is that poverty measures include only money income and neglect many in-kind transfers such as food stamps and Medicare. Most of these transfers have increased over the past several decades. But allowance for these would make the disparity in trend even sharper. A recent Census Bureau study estimated that the market value of noncash benefits grew from $6 billion in 1965 to $98 billion in 1982 (U.S. Bureau of the Census, 1984a:XI). The large majority of this increase was in the form of medical benefits and the principal beneficiaries were the elderly. Their incidence of poverty for 1982 is 14.6 percent before the allowance for noncash benefits at market value but only 3.5 percent after the allowance.

The equivalent reduction for children under 6 is from 23.8 percent to 17.2 percent, a figure still higher than the *unadjusted* national figure (U.S. Bureau of the Census, 1984a). So Figure 41.1 actually understates the degree to which child poverty has increased relative to that of the elderly. The comparisons also fail to account for tax payments or for the imputed value of owner-occupied housing, factors that several studies have shown to benefit the elderly disproportionately (U.S. Bureau of the Census, 1984b:30; Coe, 1976). The elderly are not oblivious to their improved status. A 1982 Gallup poll found that 71 percent of those aged 65 and over reported themselves as being highly satisfied with their standard of living, far and away the highest satisfaction level of any age group (Gallup, 1983a:18–19).

Figure 41.2 replaces an economic indicator with a social one, but the story is much the same. Suicide rates in 1960 to 1961 rose steadily with age, increasing by a factor of about five between ages 15 to 24 and 65+. By 1981 to 1982, however, the age gradient is very much weaker. Instead of increasing by five beyond age 15 to 24, suicide rises by less than one-half.[3] The reduced suicide rate among the elderly reflects what is apparently a widescale improvement in their psychological well-being. In 1957, 22 percent of people over 64 scored very high on a scale of psychological anxiety, compared to only 9.5 percent of persons 21 to 29; but by 1976 scores on the same test among the elderly had fallen and among young adults had risen to a common value of 15.5 percent (Veroff et al., 1981:354).

Suicide among children is very rare, although the trend is upward. But the few other available indicators of children's emotional well-being, collected by Zill and Peterson (1982), generally suggest that some deterioration has occurred. For example, the U.S. Health Examination Survey has asked parents whether "anything had ever happened to seriously upset or disturb your child." The percentage answering yes rose from 27 percent in 1963 to 1965 to 37 percent in 1976; the major reason for the deterioration was apparently a rise in family disruption and marital discord. Zill and Peterson conclude from this and the few other available time series that child stress has increased, primarily as a result of the rise in family disruption.

When we turn to public expenditure patterns, recently reviewed by Bane et al. (1983), the trends are less clear cut. They find that, per member of the recipient group, expenditure on the elderly was three times the expenditure per child in 1960 and remained three times greater in 1979. Both grew very rapidly during this period, so that the absolute gain was three times larger for the elderly. (They include public spending on higher education in their calculations; since this was one of the fastest growing components of expenditure on "children," the growth in spending would be less rapid for the child population below age 18.)

Figure 41.2. Age-specific death rates from suicide in 1960–1961 and 1981–1982.

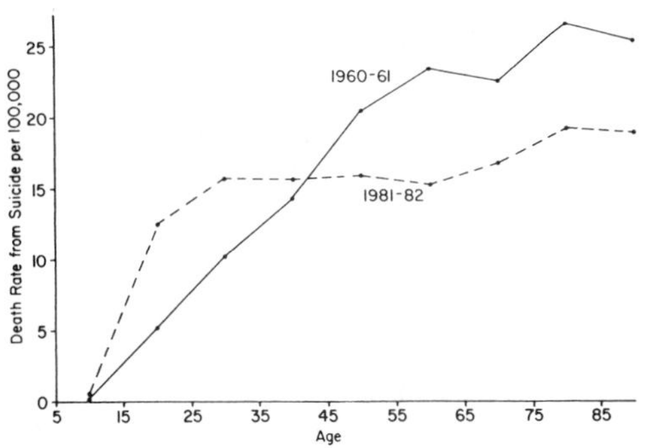

However, since 1979 there has been a sharp break with this pattern as many public programs benefitting children have been rolled back while programs targeted to the elderly have been maintained or expanded. One arena in which children and the elderly compete directly is Medicaid, which provides medical services for poor persons. Children's share of Medicaid payments dropped from 14.9 percent in 1979 to 11.9 percent in 1982 despite a rise in the child proportion among the eligible (Children's Defense Fund, 1984a). The Aid to Families with Dependent Children (AFDC) program has been sharply cut back. In 1979, there were 72 children in AFDC for every 100 children in poverty, but there were only 52 per 100 in 1982 (Children's Defense Fund, 1984a). Meanwhile, between those same years expenditures on Medicare and Medicaid rose by $32 billion, or by 63 percent (Davis, Karen, 1983). Medicare outlays alone rose from $3.4 billion in 1967 to $57.4 billion in 1983 and are projected to rise to $112 billion in 1988 (Congress of the United States, 1983).

The Office of Management and Budget recently began estimating the fraction of federal benefits that are directed towards the elderly. The elderly received $44 billion in federal dollars in 1971 and $217 billion in 1983, some $7,700 per capita (U.S. Bureau of the Census, 1983a:376). The benefits were a smaller item than national defense in 1971 and a larger item in 1983 (U.S. Bureau of the Census, 1983a:343). The total federal expenditure on all the major child-oriented programs—AFDC, Head Start, food stamps, child nutrition, child health, and all federal aid to education—is about $36 billion in 1984, only one-sixth of federal expenditure on the elderly (compiled from Children's Defense Fund, 1984b, Appendices). Per child, federal expenditure on these programs was only 9 percent of per capita expenditure on the elderly. Trends in state and local spending do not appear to have offset the age trends in federal spending (American Federation of State, County, and Municipal Employees, 1984).

The recent changes in public expenditure patterns are not simply some aberrant product of the Reagan administration. The cutback in children's programs began under Carter and has had Congressional support and the support of the American voting public.[4] Reagan himself proposed large cuts in Social Security benefits in 1981 and 1982 which were soundly defeated in Congress (Chin, 1983). Research funding is a microcosm of national trends. The National Institute of Education's (NIE's) budget in fiscal year 1981 was $65.6 million, close to that of the National Institute of Aging's (NIA's) $75.6 million. In fiscal year 1984, the Education budget is down to $48.2 million, while Aging has risen to $112.3 million. The Administration's proposal for 1984 called for a cut of at least 10 percent in extramural funding of NIA but this was overturned by Congress, which provided at 25 percent increase in funds. The Administration's proposed reduction for NIE was accepted (Consortium of Social Science Assocations, 1983).

These disparate trends in levels of public expenditure are exaggerated by disparate trends in the apparent effectiveness of public expenditure. The largest portion of public expenditure directed towards children takes the form of public schooling. Reports from commission after commission in the past year have concluded that the quality of our educational products has eroded. The best publicized indicator is the decline in Scholastic Aptitude Test scores. The sum of verbal and mathematics scores declined by 90 points between 1963 and 1980 and seems to have leveled off subsequently (Lerner, 1983). The most authoritative examination of this trend, the Wirtz Commission report of 1977, concluded that most of the decline in earlier years was attributable to compositional factors—different groups taking the test—and most of the decline in later years was real (Advisory Panel on the Scholastic Aptitude Test Score Decline, 1977). Over the period they reviewed, slightly more than half of the decline was real. As evidence, they point to sharp declines since 1970 among all major groups, including high school valedictorians. They also conclude that the decline has been underestimated by 8 to 12 points because the tests have gotten easier. Trends in scores on most other standardized tests, achievement as well as aptitude, are also typically downwards, especially in science and math, and especially among high school students (National Assessment of Educational Progress, 1978, 1981; Lerner, 1983).

At the same time that school performance has been declining, a smaller fraction of children are completing high school. The high school graduation rate dropped from 76.3 percent in 1965 to 73.6 percent in 1980 (U.S. House of Representatives, 1983:22). In contrast, 95 percent of Japanese teenagers now graduate from high school, and because of a longer school day and school years the Japanese graduate will have spent roughly four full years more in school than will an American graduate (Task Force on Education for Economic Growth, 1983). One analyst cited by the National Commission on Excellence in Education (1983:11) asserted that, "For the first time in the history of our country, the educational skills of one generation will not surpass, will not equal, will not even approach those of their parents."

While education is the principal public service provided children, health care is the principal public service provided to the elderly. For other ages of course, it is not a public service but is primarily privately arranged. However, for the elderly, 69 percent of medical care bills are paid with public monies. The total amount of public outlay for health in 1984 per person above 64 is estimated by the Congressional Budget Office to be $2,948 (Congress of the United States, 1983:19 to 20).

One indicator of the success of these expenditures is mortality rates. We have already heard evidence that old age mortality has fallen dramatically. But so, too, has mortality fallen among children, one of the few benign trends for the group. In order to compare the gains of the groups, we need a proper measuring rod. Every well-trained demographer knows that we have such a device in the form of model life tables, which indicate how much change typically occurs in age-specific death rates per unit change in life expectancy at birth. So we can examine recent mortality change in the United States to see how much improvement is implied at each age, using the "West" model (Coale et al., 1983). Figure 41.3 presents the results for female changes between 1968 and 1980.[5] If recent changes had been "normal"—that is, in accord with commonly observed relationships among age-specific death rates—then the graph would be a horizontal line. All ages would have moved up by the same amount. Obviously, the line is not horizontal. Compared to normal standards of progress, children and young adults improved the least. The four largest gains pertain to the four age groups above 65. (The figure at age 80 should not be taken too seriously since mortality has fallen to such a low level here that it is far outside the range of the models used and extrapolation was necessary). What I find particularly intriguing about the graph is the suggestion of a discontinuity at age 65, the age at which Medicare entitlements begin. Male changes are similar, being smallest among children and young adults and reaching a peak at age 70 to 75. There is no suggestion of a discontinuity at age 65, however.

The two age groups of dependents even show different trends in their degree of dependency. Older children are more often contributing to their own support by working, while the elderly are contributing less often. Labor force participation rates of persons 16 to 17 years old rose from 37.9 percent in 1960 to 43.2 percent in 1983, while the participation rate of those 65 to 69 declined from 32.3 percent to 20.4 percent (U.S. Bureau of Labor Statistics, 1984; Miller, 1984).

Having presented some evidence on the changes in the well-being of our dependents, I'm now going to argue that demographic variables have played an important role in producing these changes through their action in three arenas, which I've labeled the family, politics, and industry.

THE FAMILY

Societies use two major means for transferring resources to dependents: direct public transfers and transfers within the family. The latter is the most important means in virtually all societies. James Morgan (1978) estimates that roughly one-third of GNP in the United States takes the form of transfers from income earners to nonearners in the same coresident family. Over time, families have relinquished more and more responsibility for support of elderly dependents to the state. In terms of residence and income, this process was nearly completed by 1960. As long ago as 1942, Parsons attributed the financial difficulties of the elderly and the political agitation on their behalf to a disappearance of a sense of obligation for their support within the conjugal family.

The situation is clearly very different for children, for whom the family remains the principal source of support. But it's not too farfetched to argue that during the period since 1960 the conjugal family has begun to divest itself of care for children in much the same way that it did earlier for the elderly. The simplest form of divestiture is not to have children in the first place, and we're doing that in record numbers. But there is also less care-taking for the children that we do have. The main proximate cause here is a disappearing act by fathers. In 1980, 18.4 percent of births were out of wedlock, which in the large majority of cases means that the father takes no enduring responsibility for the child. The figure was only 5.3 percent in 1960 (U.S. Bureau of the Census, 1983a:70; Furstenberg and Talvite, 1980). Of those children born *in* wedlock, according to Bumpass (1984), 43 percent would experience a disruption leading to the divorce of their parents before age 16 under disruption rates of 1977 to 1979, compared to only 22 percent in 1963 to 1965. Hofferth (1983) extrapolates recent disruption trends and projects that two-thirds of in-wedlock births in 1980 will experience the disruption of their parents' marriage by the time the children reach age 17.

What happens to the father after the divorce? According to Furstenberg and Nord (1982), 52 percent of children with a nonresidential father had not seen him in the past year and an additional 16 percent had seen him less than once per month. Fewer than half of the

Figure 41.3. Mortality improvements by age between 1968 and 1980 for U.S. females.

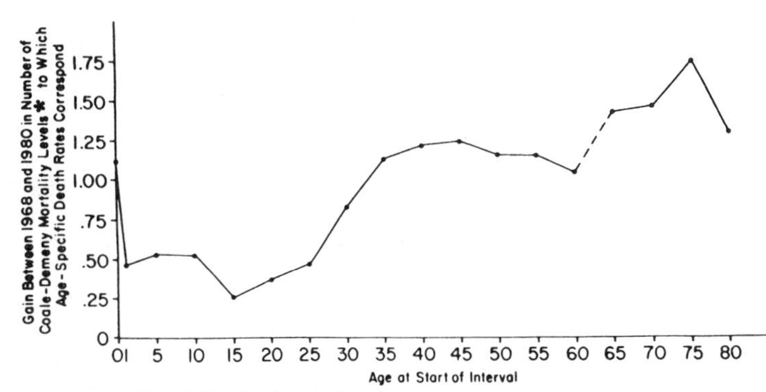

fathers made child support payments. According to a Census Bureau study for 1978, only 41.4 percent of children from a previous marriage living with the mother received child support payments from their father. A later survey of fathers found them reporting child support payments to about the same number of children, but failing to report the existence of the large majority of the children to whom they were not making payments (Cherlin et al., 1983).

Some of the children abandoned by their natural fathers will of course come to live with other adult males who support them, but this does not happen as often as commonly believed. Bane and Ellwood (1984) use Michigan's Panel Study of Income Dynamics data for 1968 to 1979 to show that 63 percent of children who enter one-parent spells in childhood are still in them at age 17. The rate of breakup after remarriage is actually higher than the rate of remarriage itself when calculations are based upon child-years of exposure.

The upshot is that economic circumstances usually deteriorate for women and children following divorce and separation. Using data from the Panel Study of Income Dynamics, Duncan and Morgan (1981) found that children whose parents divorced between 1972 and 1978 had a loss of $6,602 in annual family income between those years; 72 percent of these children had a reduction in the ratio of income to needs. A study of an earlier seven-year period in this data set found that the ratio of income to needs rose 30 percent for men who became divorced or separated and still remained in that state but declined by 7 percent for the women in this category (Hoffman and Holmes, 1976; for a recent review, see Hill, 1983.)

Obviously, these disruption patterns have something to do with the rise in child poverty. The Census Bureau figures on poverty show that 56.0 percent of children under 19 in 1982 who lived in a female-headed family without husband present lived in poverty, compared to only 13.0 percent of children in other families. The figures were similar but slightly lower in 1970. On a simple decompositional basis, 44 percent of the growth in the percentage of children in poverty between these years is attributable to the growing prevalence of female-headed households. In terms of absolute numbers, 69 percent of the growth in the number of children in poverty occurred in the category of female-headed families.[6]

The rise in marital disruption is also likely to be implicated in deteriorating psychological well-being among children, as we saw earlier. There is certainly little doubt from microlevel studies that the short-run effects are sizeable and significant (Hetherington, 1979; Hetherington et al., 1979; Kellam et al., 1977) and there is mounting evidence of substantial long-term effects, including increases in young adult suicide (Furstenberg and Allison, 1984; Furstenberg and Seltzer, 1983; Fuchs, 1983).

Family instability is also likely to be related to a minor extent to declining school achievement. A recent review of studies by Hetherington et al. (1983) concludes that both short-term and long-term deficits are associated with living in a one-parent household as a child, even after controlling the income effects that are partly produced by disruption itself. They suggest that behavioral problems are a major intervening variable (see also McLanahan, 1983).

It's tempting to push the level of explanation one step farther and try to account for the decline in marital stability itself. That is a subject better suited to encyclopedic treatment than to paragraphs in a presidential address, but I can't resist making some remarks. Some 52 percent of marriages would end in divorce according to disruption rates of 1975 to 1980 (Preston, 1983) and Kingsley Davis (1983) points out that the figure would be much higher if we counted consensual unions, some of which are reproductive. It seems incredible that we have reached this level of instability when collectively we have better health, more teeth, better odor and more orgasms. And a recent review of public opinion polls by Thornton and Freedman (1983) concludes that we are, in fact, happier with our mates of the moment. The percentage of persons saying that their marriage was either very happy or above average went from 68 percent in 1957 to 80 percent in 1976.

I think that explanations for rising instability occur at two levels. At one level are increased incentives to break up a union. We have already seen that the male's disposable income rises sharply after divorce, and his gains from divorce are greater the higher are general economic levels. Beckerians stress that higher potential earnings for women have made it more costly for them to specialize in home production and to build up marriage-specific capital, especially in the form of children. Higher incomes have also made it easier for both partners to sacrifice the scale economies attached to joint living arrangements. In effect, we can afford to buy more privacy and freedom from others' needs and expectations by establishing separate residences. Low income groups have gained incentives to split up because of expanded public programs—especially Aid to Families with Dependent Children—that penalize couples for staying together. State levels of AFDC payments have repeatedly been shown to influence disruption rates and even remarriage rates (Hutchens, 1979; Hoffman and Holmes, 1976), and evaluations of the guaranteed minimum income experiments reached similar conclusions (Hannan et al., 1977). Finally, exposure to alternative partners has increased with industrial changes that produce less sex segregation at the workplace, larger percentages in metropolitan areas, and more jobs dealing with people instead of dirt or machines.

Viewed in this light and considering only adult welfare, there is nothing problematic in the upsurge in marital disruption. We simply have greater opportunities now to act on our preferences. The lack of marriage mobility in the past is equivalent to the absence of occupational mobility in a feudal society.

These structural explanations are surely part of the story. But another part, perhaps more important, is the increased prevalence of a world view that legitimizes calculations based upon individual self-interest. Lawrence Stone, the leading family historian, refers to the rise over the past 250 years of affective individualism, the awareness of the self as unique and recognition of the right of that self to pursue selfish goals (Stone, 1982). He argues that individualism is a rare and curious ideology in human history, produced largely by the Protestant revolution and taking its most potent form when nourished by American democracy. Lesthaeghe (1983) provides strong support for the notion that ideas are playing an independent role in family change by showing that changes in marriage and divorce throughout Europe are influenced by the degree of religious secularization, independent of levels of urbanization and industrialization. One might add that it seems unlikely that any purely structural approach could explain why American divorce rates are about double those of our nearest competitors in Europe (United Nations, 1984:692–695).

Within the United States, the independent role of ideational systems for family matters is probably best represented by behavior among Mormons. The crude birth rate in Utah rose from 25.5 in 1970 to 30.1 in 1979 while the nation's was declining from 18.4 to 15.9 (Toney et al., 1983). Its TFR in 1980 was 3.22 (Population Reference Bureau, 1984:8). Utah also has (after Hawaii) the lowest divorce rate in the Pacific and Mountain region (U.S. National Center for Health Statistics, 1984a). But these rates are not a product of social and economic backwardness; Utah also has the highest educational level in the country and one of the lowest high school dropout rates (Toney et al., 1983). Obviously, we are not simply maximizing some utility function that is shared by the human community throughout time and space.

What these individualistic notions have meant for divorce is obvious. People feel less constrained by others' welfare to remain in what they consider to be a marginal marriage. Opinion polls have asked women whether they agree with the statement, "When there are children in the family, parents should stay together even if they don't get along." The percentage disagreeing with the statement rose from 51 percent in 1962 to 82 percent in 1980 (Thornton and Freedman, 1983:9). Our tendency to count only our own interests and not those of children is vividly illustrated by a recent incident in New York City, which passed a law requiring bars to warn of the dangers to the fetus of alcohol consumption by pregnant women. The local chapter of the National Organization of Women wrote a letter to Mayor Koch protesting that the bill was "protecting the unborn at the expense of women's freedom" (Sandmaier, 1983).

These two tendencies—increased incentives to divorce and increased willingness to act on those incentives in a narrowly self-interested way—are surely together responsible for the sharp rise in divorce. And there is no question that this rise has in turn made life more difficult for children, while its impact on the elderly has been muted by their prior disengagement from the conjugal family.

POLITICS

Besides the family, the state is the other major vehicle for transferring resources to dependents. Here it seems fairly obvious that the changing numbers of young and old have altered the environment for public policy decisions. In a modern democracy, public decisions are obviously influenced by the power of special interest groups, and that power is in turn a function of the size of the groups, the wealth of the groups, and the degree to which that size and wealth can be mobilized for concerted action. In all of these areas, interests of the elderly have gained relative to those of children.

It's useful to recognize that there are three sources of self-interested support for the elderly: the elderly themselves; the working-age population who are in a general sense "voting" on behalf of elderly persons who might otherwise need family support; and the working age population who are voting on behalf of themselves when they reach old age. The elderly are a very peculiar kind of special interest group, quite unlike Teamsters or Southerners or the National Rifle Association. They are a group that almost all of us can confidently expect to belong to someday. Most programs for the elderly are to some extent perceived as a social contract whereby we transfer resources to ourselves over the life cycle.

Only one of these three sources of support is available to children. Children don't vote; and adults don't vote on behalf of their own childhood, which is water over the dam. I daresay that if we passed through life backwards, adults would insist that conditions in childhood be made far more appealing.

So demographic change can clearly have a multiplier effect on political support for the elderly. The sharp mortality decline at old ages has meant more elderly voters; more working-age people with surviving parents; and an increase in the number of years that a working-age person can expect to live over 65.

The most visible and perhaps most important of these changes is the rise in the number of elderly themselves. This rise has been combined with a high degree of political participation. According to a U.S. Census Bureau (1983b) study of voting patterns in the 1982 congressional election, the highest percentage voting of any age group occurred at ages 65 to 74. Sixty-five percent of persons in this group voted, more than double the percentage at ages 20 to 29. In terms of absolute numbers, more people voted at ages 60 and over than in the swollen baby boom cohorts under 35 or in the prime child-rearing ages from 35 to 49. Once again, this age pattern reverses earlier ones: in the congressional elections of 1966, the voter participation rate above age 65 was lower than for any age between 35 and 64 (U.S. Census Bureau, 1968). The elderly also appear to be politically more knowledgeable. In a 1982 Gallup poll, 56 percent of those aged 65 and over could name their Congressional representative, the highest fraction of any age group, compared to only 30 percent among those under 30 (Gallup, 1983a:175).

The constituency for children, meanwhile, has declined both in numbers and in impact. To demonstrate the changing dependency pressures on the middle aged, I estimate from cohort fertility and life tables that the average 40-year-old couple in 1980 had nearly identical numbers of living parents and children: 2.59 parents and 2.72 children.[7] But we are still far from where we are headed if present rates of fertility and mortality were to persist: under rates of 1980, a 40-year old couple would have 2.88 living parents and 1.78 living children. It is not until age 52 that the numbers would be equal.[8] By that age, of course, most children are out of the house, and it turns out that there is *no age* in the life cycle at which the couple is expected to have more children below age 20 than it has surviving parents. The pulls and tugs of dependency concerns on the middle aged are obviously shifting, in numerical terms at least, towards the elderly.

It's not just that we have fewer children these days; parents are also less inclined to live with the ones that they've got. In 1982, only 63 percent of children under 18 were living with both of their natural parents (U.S. House of Representatives, 1983). As a result of declining fertility, residential breakups, and an aging population, only 37.1 percent of American households in 1982 contained a child under age 18 (U.S. House of Representatives, 1983). Tabulations done at the University of Pennsylvania from the 1980 Census Public Use microdata show that only 41 percent of the population aged 21 and over lives in a household with a child under 18. Equivalent figures for the 1960 and 1900 Public Use Samples are 50 percent and 59 percent.

In addition to declining numbers of parents potentially representing children among the voting-age population, parents themselves are less likely than average to vote. Among family householders with *no* children present under age 18 in the election of November 1982, 60.5 percent voted; among those whose children were all below age 6, only 38.1 percent voted (U.S. Bureau of the Census, 1983b:18). Of the votes cast in this election, only 38.4 percent belonged to people who lived in a household that had a child under 18.[9]

None of this would matter, of course, if people in different age groups and family circumstances saw public issues the same way. And there are many issues on which age differences appear to be minor. They are not even very large regarding social security, perhaps for reasons that I alluded to earlier. A 1982 Gallup poll asked people how they felt the financing crisis of social security could best be resolved. Age differences in responses were not large, although they were systematic and predictable. Elderly persons were 7 points more in favor than others of increasing current contributions from workers and employees, and 13 points more in favor of increasing the age of eligibility for the retirement cohorts to come (Gallup, 1983a).

Larger age differences seem to pertain to issues involving children. The 1983 Gallup Poll of Public Attitudes toward the Public Schools asked whether people would vote to raise taxes for schools if requested to do so by their local school system. Below age 50 the numbers were evenly split: 45 percent would favor the request and 46 percent would oppose it. At 50 and above the opponents outnumbered the supporters by 62 percent to 28 percent (Gallup, 1983b). In 1978, HUD commissioned a large Harris poll of 7,074 adults regarding the quality of community life. Respondents were asked to name the public service that they would most like to see improved. 20 percent of those 25 to 44 but only 6 percent of the elderly named the public schools. People were also asked whether the lack of child care facilities was a problem in the community. Fifty percent of those aged 25 to 34 said that it was, compared to only 19.7 percent of the elderly (U.S. Department of Housing and Urban Development, n.d.:255,713–715). While it's clear from other data that the elderly are in frequent touch with their children and grandchildren, it's also clear that they don't automatically assimilate their offspring's perceptions and concerns.

How many issues at the local or national level have turned on the changing age and family status distribution? Unfortunately, this is not a question that admits to simple answers. One possibly informative example is the passage of the Age Discrimination Act of 1975. A very detailed article in the Yale Law Journal (Schuck, 1979) documents how little careful thought went into this Act because of legislators' rush to please their powerful elderly constituents. It argues that the Act intensifies age conflict and has been interpreted by the Civil Rights Commission in such a way that the elderly gained not only at the expense of other adults but also of children.

We have talked only about the exercise of self-interest. What about altruistic motives for support of children and the elderly? These are obviously difficult to measure both in intensity and effect. A recent book by Grubb and Lazerson (1982) argues that we have drifted towards a purely self-interested and adversarial form of government and lost along the way notions of community good. Enlightened self-interest has simply become *self*-interest—looking out for number one—with particularly devastating effects for children. They argue that Americans have never had any strong sense of collective responsibility for other people's children, only private responsibility for their own. One suspects that this distinction has been strengthened by the increased availability of effective contraception, so that children are more than ever viewed as the product of a private decision. Without any sense of collective good, the obvious question is why parents shouldn't bear the costs of that voluntary decision. Since we don't choose to have parents, there is no equivalent motive to privatize their costs. A second factor probably helping to blunt any outbreak of altruistic behavior towards other people's children is that they are increasingly drawn from minorities with whom the majority may have trouble identifying. Of children under age 15, 23.6 percent are black or Spanish-origin whites, compared to 16.4 percent of persons aged 35 to 44 and only 10.8 percent of the elderly.[10] Finally, there is the very real concern that whatever public actions are taken may undermine the remaining capacity of the private family to provide for its children, might make matters worse instead of better. But while this argument may have some pertinence to AFDC programs, it seems irrelevant to public schooling, which is already overwhelmingly a public responsibility. And the "moral hazards" arguments simply appear to lack social saliency for the elderly. We appear to worry very little about whether increased benefits for them would undermine their children's willingness to care for them or lead the able-bodied to withdraw prematurely from the labor force (Bane et al., 1983). But we're scandalized by equivalent prospects for those we think of as welfare mothers.

INDUSTRY

The final and least obvious of the demographic mechanisms helping to bring about the trends described is the effect of demographic change on the major industries serving the two age groups. Education and health are two of the largest industries in the United States. Education, of course, serves primarily the young and health services are disproportionately directed towards the old. The Congressional Budget Office estimates that an elderly person will spend an average of $4,680 on health in 1984 (Congress of the United States, 1983:19). This comes to a total of $131 billion, about 4 percent of GNP.

We have already seen that the quality of products of our educational system is deteriorating and that the system is serving a somewhat smaller fraction of youth. The question is whether this deterioration is in any sense a product of the declining numbers in school. Public elementary school enrollments declined by 11 percent between 1972 to 1973 and 1982 to 1983, and secondary enrollments by 18 percent (Feistritzer, 1983: Tables 7 and 8). I believe that a persuasive case can be made that these two trends are linked.

At first blush, the evidence is all to the contrary. Expenditure per pupil in real dollars increased by 22.5 percent between 1972 to 1973 and 1982 to 1983, faster than the growth of per capita personal income. The average number of students per teacher declined from 22 to 18. The average experience level of teachers increased and a much higher fraction had Master's degrees (Feistritzer, 1983, Tables 13, 15, 34). So the quantitative indicators are favorable.

The only problem is that none of these variables has been shown to be related to student performance. Eric Hanushek (1981) has recently published a masterful review article of 130 studies of factors affecting children's performance in schools. He concludes that the only reasonably consistent findings is that smarter teachers do better in terms of evoking student achievement. Teacher effects are very large, although it's hard to say what characteristics—apart from being smart—those effects represent. Another recent review by Murname (1981) also suggests that intellectual skills of teachers are the most vital element in student performance. Both reviews conclude that physical resources, expenditures, and class size are immaterial.

So these studies focus our attention on the conditions of public school teachers. One might expect teachers to have shared in the rising pattern of school expenditure. But in fact during the 1973 to 1983 period, teachers' salaries declined from 49 percent of school expenses to only 38 percent of school expenses. Real incomes of teachers dropped by 12.2 percent during the period. Starting salaries grew more slowly than in 8 out of 9 other large fields with which teaching is routinely compared (Feistritzer, 1983:50, 73). The expenditure gap is explained by higher maintenance costs for aging buildings, higher administrative costs and higher energy costs.

Teachers have been faced not only with declining real income in the here and now but also attachment to a declining industry, so that their future earnings prospects are also diminished. These trends are surely implicated in an appalling deterioration in the quality of teachers entering the profession and a rapid outflow from the profession of those best qualified.

You already know of the decline in SAT scores nationally. The decline in SAT scores for those intending to major in education has been even faster. In 1973, education majors scored an average of 59 points below the mean on the combined SAT. By 1982, they scored 80 points lower. The average SAT score in 1982 for those intending to major in education was 394 in verbal and 419 in math (Feistritzer, 1983:88–90). This highly negative selection into the profession has been accentuated by negative selection of those who remain after entering. The 1972 National Longitudinal Survey of high school seniors enables us to compare people who left the profession to those who remained. The mean SAT score is 42 points lower for those who stayed in teaching than for those who entered and left. Altogether, continuing teachers had SAT scores that were an average of 118 points below those in the cohort who never taught (Vance and Schlechty, 1982:Tables 22–23).

The most obvious interpretation of what's been happening with regard to the teaching profession is that the demand for teachers shifted downwards because of the declining schoolaged population. This shift led to a lower wage for teachers, which induced a disproportionate number of the better teachers to leave the field or to avoid it altogether.[11] It seems likely that this tendency was reinforced by the behavior of teachers' unions, which a Rand study shows to have become increasingly concerned with issues of reduction in force and maximum class size during the 1970s as enrollments plummeted (McDonnell and Pascal, 1979:vi). Some salary increases may have been bargained away for job protection, which is a greater boon to poorer teachers with fewer opportunities elsewhere. It's also likely that greater opportunities for women in other sectors are implicated in the decline in teacher quality, especially since this decline is larger for female entrants to the profession than for male (U.S. National Center for Education Statistics, 1983:222).

If demographic factors are pertinent to teachers' salaries, then this effect ought to appear in state-level data. I've estimated simple OLS regressions to predict the change in average teacher salaries, by state, between 1972 to 1973 and 1982 to 1983. The most important factor of those examined is the growth rate in per capita income in the state, with an elasticity of about .4. The growth rate in enrollment has a positive sign in weighted and unweighted regressions and an elasticity of about .12. That is, a decline of 10 percent in enrollment is associated with about a 1.2 percent fall in teacher's salary. The coefficients are larger than their standard error, but are insignificant. The fact that they are positive and sizeable, however, is quite consistent with an interpretation of the kind that I've offered, as well as with the time series data. It is inconsistent with the Malthusian notion that school districts would translate funds liberated by falling enrollment into a search for better teachers. Quite the opposite effect seems to be working; demographic decline seems to have led to a deterioration in the salaries of teachers, which is surely implicated in their declining quality. It is interesting to note that the growth rate of the proportion over age 65 is negatively associated with the growth rate of teachers' salaries by state, with an elasticity of about −.25. States where the elderly have grown more rapidly have had larger declines in teacher salaries. Finally, states where local school districts finance a larger fraction of school expenses have had larger declines in teacher salaries.[12]

While numbers of teachers have been stagnant and salaries and quality declining, quite the opposite trends have been evident in the medical profession. Applicants to American medical schools are so outstanding that choosing among them has been described as a lottery system; even those who don't make it are so talented that we launch foreign invasions to ensure their safety. Tremendous amounts of capital have flowed into the health care industry in the past decade, to be converted into equipment and personnel who embody a never-ending stream of technical advances.[13] There can be little doubt that the growth in demand for health care services, both in terms of numbers of persons in the ages of prime use and of entitlements that were negotiated from demographic strength, have helped to produce this bloom of health for the health care industry. In turn, the health care successes have helped to generate more health care consumers by reducing mortality, a classic case of supply creating its own demand.

In short, it appears that the predominant industrial response to demographic change has been anything but classically Malthusian. The group with faster growth has been far better served by their specialized industry than the group with declining numbers. The scenario in our schools is not very different from that in certain smokestack industries, except that here the demand reduction has a demographic origin and the product is, for better or worse, the human capital of the next generation.

DISCUSSION

It is not my intention to paint the elderly as the villains of the piece. By prevailing standards, their motives and behavior are certainly no less pure than those of other groups. Their principal role here is instead that of a comparison group, the second of two dependent groups among whom demographic trends have been radically different. Feeble as it is to be dealing with an N of 2, it would be more than twice as bad to have an N of 1. But one can't simply stand on grounds of scientism and wish away the possibility that there is direct competition between the two groups. Indeed, the self-evident public resistance to higher levels of taxation and public expenditure suggests that, in the public sphere at least, gains for one group come partly at the expense of another.

The set of relationships I am proposing might on the surface appear to be exactly the opposite of those proposed by Easterlin (1980). They are not. Easterlin's arguments emphasize above all the manner in which private labor markets react to a cohort of unusual size. I am emphasizing primarily how transfers, either public or private, are related to cohort size for exactly those stages where the cohorts are out of the labor force. The arguments are quite compatible. Taken together, they suggest that the larger the role of transfers relative to earnings, and in particular the larger the role of government in the economy, the more advantageous it may be to live in a large cohort.

I have emphasized age to the almost total exclusion of sex, race, and other traditional demographic variables. How, you might ask, can we talk about the neglect of children without mentioning their abandonment by mothers heading into the labor market? The answer is that it's not at all clear that mother's work is a source of disadvantage for children, at least not as a direct determinant. Recent reviews of studies of the effect of working mothers on child development find very few and inconsistent effects, far less clear-cut than those associated with marital disruption (D'Amico et al., 1983; Heynes, 1982). Furthermore, it's obvious that women's work has become a very important contributor to children's living standards, and is the core source of support for the large numbers of children not living with their fathers. But it does seem likely, as I noted earlier, that increased earnings prospects for women have facilitated marital disruption. But so have improved opportunities for men.

With regard to race, let me just say that the main theme here is the changing status of American children, a group that includes all races. I see no particular reason for separating out the races anymore than for carrying through a distinction between Northerners and Southerners or other commonly used identifiers. For those who prefer to think of the problems in childhood as being confined to the black population—a group who for most of us constitute "other people's children"—let me just say that there is not a single trend that I've talked about that does not pertain to *both* races. Indeed, for some—declining school achievement and rising illegitimacy, for example—changes have been much faster for the white population.

SUMMARY AND CONCLUSION

Let me summarize briefly. My argument is that we have made a set of private and public choices that have dramatically altered the age profile of well-being. These choices are in an important sense joint ones involving the number of dependents we have as well as the conditions in which they live. This jointness derives from several sources. One is that the same institution—the conjugal family—remains the principal agent responsible for both childbearing and childrearing. Factors that influence the health of that institution invariably affect both numbers of and conditions for children. There was simply no way to protect children fully from the earthquake that shuddered through the American family in the past twenty years. The factors at work here are not only the objective conditions we face but also the set of values and mental constructs we elect to face them with. At the other end of the age scale, we can obviously affect the number of elderly persons as well as their circumstances by altering health programs, as we have so decisively chosen to do. A final source of jointness is that numbers themselves affect conditions. Some of these effects are largely inadvertent, as I've argued in regard to public schooling, and others seem to be very deliberate outcomes of the political process.

It's useful to step back and ask whether the mixture of numbers and conditions that we've chosen is the one that best serves us. In regard to redistributions from the working-age population to the elderly, the answer is far from obvious. There is surely something to be said for a system in which things get better as we pass through life rather than worse. The great levelling off of age curves of psychological distress, suicide and income in the past two decades might simply reflect the fact that we have decided in some fundamental sense that we don't want to face futures that become continually bleaker. But let's be clear that the transfers from the working-age population to the elderly are also transfers away from children, since the working ages bear far more responsibility for childrearing than do the elderly. And let's also recognize that the sums involved are huge. Just the increase in federal expenditures on the elderly between 1977 and 1983, if distributed among the population under age 15, would come to well over $2,000 per child. The increase in annual benefits for the elderly during this six-year period is almost exactly equal to the total amount of additional annual earnings generated by increased female labor force participation over the entire period from 1960 to 1981.[14]

While the redistribution toward the elderly is clearly a decision that a free society should be able to make, the redistributions away from children seem to be less defensible. There is no generally accepted rule in welfare economics for how children's interests ought to be represented in public decisions (d'Arge et al., 1982; Nerlove, 1974; Nerlove et al., 1984). A convenient starting place for work in the area is the assumption that each decision-making adult has children whose utility is folded into the adult's own utility function. That's a very different world from the one that we live in. When only 38 percent of voters are living with a child, the utility that we derive from other people's children would seem to be a far more salient concern than the utility that we derive from our own.

But there is more than consumption value involved. It's clear that public expenditure on children has a different character than expenditure on the elderly. Expenditure on the elderly is almost exclusively consumption expenditure, in the sense that it does not appreciably affect the future productive capacity of the economy. Most types of expenditure on children are both consumption and investment, a logic explicitly recognized in the first school law in America passed by the Massachusetts Bay Colony in 1642, "taking into consideration the great neglect of many parents in bringing up their children in learning which may be profitable to the commonwealth" (Commager, 1983). The reorientation towards the elderly is thus consistent with the declining share of GNP that is represented by savings and with dramatically rising debt service burdens on future generations.

It seems to me that we are continually faced with two questions. First, do we care about our collective future—the commonwealth—or only about our individual futures? If only our individual futures matter, then our concerns will naturally focus on ourselves as older persons and we will continue down the road we appear to be on.[15] But if we have collective concerns, we face a second and even more difficult decision about what mix of private and public childrearing responsibilities will best serve the needs of future generations. Rather than following the elderly model, at the moment we are attempting to return more and more of these responsibilities to the family. But in view of the manifest erosion in the family's ability to shoulder these responsibilities, this attempt appears to be more an answer to the first question—do we care?—than to the second—how best to proceed? The constituency for children in public decisions simply appears too feeble to fight back. In short, we may be returning responsibilities to families not because they are so strong but because they are so weak.

NOTES

Presented as the Presidential Address at the Annual Meeting of the Population Association of America, Minneapolis, Minnesota, May 3–5, 1984.

Many people contributed their ideas to this chapter. Frank Furstenberg and Susan Watkins deserve special thanks for their insights and encouragement from an early state. Other colleagues whose assistance was instrumental in improving the manuscript are Michael Aiken, Jere Behrman, P. N. Mari Bhat, Gretchen Condran, Nancy Denton, Jill Grigsby, Bob Inman, Jerry Jacobs, Doug Massey, Ann Miller, Bob Pollak, Cindi Posner, Steven Taber, Paul Taubman, and Dan Vining. Bill Butz, Don Hernandez, Paul Smith, and Jerry Jennings were helpful in supplying materials.

1. The number of children aged 0 to 19 in 1915 was 30.6 percent larger than the number of children 0 to 19 in 1895. These are the cohorts that are aged 61 to 84 in 1980 and 1960, respectively. (U.S. Bureau of the Census, 1975a:15.)
2. Sources: U.S. Bureau of the Census. Money Income and Poverty Status of Families and Persons in the United States: 1982. Current Population Reports P-60, No. 140, July 1983: Characteristics of the Low Income Population 1971. Current Population Reports P-60, No. 86. December 1972. The data plotted on Figure 41.1 are:

Age	1970 Percent in Poverty	Age	1982 Percent in Poverty
0–13	15.6	0–2	24.1
14–21	12.6	3–5	23.5
22–44	8.3	6–13	21.9
45–64	9.1	14–15	19.8
65+	24.6	16–21	17.0
All ages	12.6	22–24	12.3
		45–54	9.4
		55–59	9.9
		60–64	11.3
		65+	14.6
		All ages	15.0

3. Sources: U.S. Department of Health Education and Welfare. Public Health Service. Vital Statistics of the United States, Vol. II, Part A, 1960 and 1961; U.S. National Center for Health Statistics. Monthly Vital Statistics Reports. Vol. 31(13), October 5, 1983. The data plotted on Figure 41.2 are:

Age Group	Death Rate from Suicide per 100,000 1960–1961	1981–1982
5–14	0.25	0.50
15–24	5.15	12.50
25–34	10.15	15.85
35–44	14.30	15.60
45–54	20.50	15.90
55–64	23.40	15.25
65–74	22.50	16.80
75–84	26.95	19.25
85+	25.45	18.95

4. See especially Grubb and Lazerson (1982, p. 109). A *New York Times* poll in 1978 found very strong national support for reductions in property taxes, with "welfare and social services" the overwhelmingly preferred targets for service reductions. Respondents consistently overestimated the welfare cost component of their locality's expenses. "Poll Tax Cuts Are Widely Backed Around Nation," *New York Times:* June 28, 1978, p. 1.
5. Sources of mortality data: U.S. National Center for Health Statistics. Vital Statistics of the United States. 1968. Vol. II, Section 5. Life Tables. U.S. Government Printing Office Washington, DC; U.S. National Center for Health Statistics. Monthly Vital Statistics Report: 32. Supplement. August, 1983.
6. Data are drawn from U.S. Bureau of the Census, Money Income and Poverty Status of Families and Persons in the United States: 1982. Current Population Reports. P-60, No. 140, 1983. Table 17. The percentage of children in poverty rose from 14.9 percent to 21.3 percent between 1970 and 1982. This increase is decomposed by the conventional formula that weights changes in within-category poverty (where the categories are female-headed families and others) by the mean proportion in the category in the two years. Likewise, the change in proportions in the categories is weighted by the mean prevalence of poverty in the category. The absolute number of children in poverty increased by 2.904 million; the increase in the number of children in poverty in female-headed families was 2.007 million.
7. To estimate the number of living parents, we begin with the age distribution of fathers and mothers at the birth of their children in 1940 (Grove and Hetzel, 1968). These parents are then survived forward to 1980, one decade at a time. For each decade, mean survival rates from U.S. life tables at the beginning and end of the decade are used (Grove and Hetzel, 1968; U.S. National Center for Health Statistics, n.d.; 1983b). The procedure results in 1.54 living mothers and 1.06 living fathers for the two 40-year-old persons. The procedure assumes that there is no relationship between parents' mortality and their number of surviving offspring.

   To estimate the number of children for the couple, we use the number of children ever born to women aged 35 to 44 in "married couple families" in 1980 (U.S. Bureau of Census, 1982b:59). These children are then survived forward 12.5 years from birth by the U.S. life table of 1970 (U.S. National Center for Health Statistics, n.d.).
8. These figures are derived from a stable population corresponding to age-specific fertility and mortality rates of 1980 for males and females. The growth rate of the stable population (−.0050) is derived from female fertility and mortality. Age distributions of parents at childbirth are computed separately for males and females, and life tables are separately applied for fathers and mothers. All persons are assumed to be a member of a "couple" with a same-age spouse. The number of living children is that of the female member of the couple. National Center for Health Statistics, 1982a, 1983b.
9. Tabulations from the U.S. Bureau of the Census November, 1982 Current Population Survey Public Use Tape, performed by Nancy Denton at the University of Pennsylvania.
10. Source: U.S. Bureau of the Census (1982a:27). Ninety-five percent of Spanish-origin persons are assumed to be white.
11. This reasoning assumes that school districts are not fully capable of adapting salaries to differences in teacher quality and that higher quality teachers have on average, higher earnings opportunities in other occupations.
12. The regression equations for 50 states are the following:

    Weighted by state population:

$$\underset{}{Y = -.0149} + \underset{(.0060)}{} \; \underset{(.0964)}{.1439\, X_1} + \underset{(.1771)}{.4770X_2} - \underset{(.1630)}{.2553\, X_3} + \underset{(.0548)}{.0085X_4}$$

(.0060) (.0964) (.1771) (.1630) (.0548)

$$R^2 = .208$$

Unweighted:

$$Y = -.0069 + .1011X_1 + .4770X_2 - .2862\, X_3 - .2291X_4$$

(.0067) (.0876) (.1705) (.1640) (.0713)

$$R^2 = .449$$

Where Y = Average annual growth rate of teachers salaries, 1972 to 1973 to 1982 to 1983, in 1972 dollars
X_1 = Average annual growth rate of enrollments in public elementary and secondary schools, 1972 to 1973 to 1982 to 1983
X_2 = Average annual growth rate of per capita personal income, 1970 to 1981, in 1972 dollars
X_3 = Average annual growth rate of the proportion of population aged 65 and over, 1970 to 1981
X_4 = percentage (divided by 1000) of total school revenue derived from local sources in 1982 to 1983 (i.e., sources other than state or federal).
Data are drawn from Feistritzer (1983) and U.S. Bureau of Census (1982a).

13. A recent U.S. Office of Technology Assessment report on the biotechnology industry shows the United States to be far ahead of its international competition in this rapidly growing area, in large part because of both private and public funding advantages. The huge stock of health care entitlements amassed in the United States is probably a key underpinning of this growth and helps to explain why this is one of the few industries where American growth remains exceptional. See *Science* 223:Feb. 3, 1984:463.

14. Federal expenditures on the elderly increased from $95.7 billion in 1977 to $217.1 billion in 1983 (U.S. Bureau of the Census, 1982a, 1983a), or by $121.4 billion. There were 51.4 million children below age 15 in 1982 (U.S. Bureau of the Census, 1983a), for a ratio of $2,364 per child.

The comparison with female earnings, a theme first suggested by Davis and van den Oever (1981), is done in the following way. Women workers in 1981 earned an average of $8,300 and there were 51.94 million women working, so that they earned a total of $431.102 billion (U.S. Bureau of the Census, 1983c:189). The female labor force participation rate in 1981 (aged 16+) was 52.1 percent and in 1960, 37.7 percent (U.S. Bureau of the Census, 1982a:377). The withdrawal of women back to their participation rate of 1960 would therefore have cost the economy, as a first order approximation,

$$\frac{14.4}{52.1}(\$431.1 \text{ billion}) = \$119.2 \text{ billion}$$

in 1981. So the increase in elderly benefits, in this crude calculation, exceeds slightly the total amount of added earnings of women over a period more than three times as long.

15. Children's status may still improve when we realize that our social security system is jeopardized by worker shortages, a realization that dominates population policy concerns in Europe (McIntosh, 1983).

REFERENCES

Advisory Panel on the Scholastic Aptitude Test Score Decline. 1977. On Further Examination. Report of the Advisory Panel on the Scholastic Aptitude Test Score Decline. New York: College Examination Board.

American Federation of State, County, and Municipal Employees, AFL-CIO. 1984. State of the States. American Federation of State, County, and Municipal Employees. Washington, DC.

Bane, M. J., J. Boatright Wilson and N. Baer. 1983. "Trends in Public Spending on Children and Their Families." Pp. 109–144 in R. R. Nelson and F. Skidmore (eds.) *American Families and the Economy.* Washington, DC: National Academy Press.

———, and D. T. Ellwood. 1984. *The Dynamics of Children's Living Arrangements.* Harvard University: Unpublished manuscript.

Bumpass, L. 1984. "Children and Marital Disruption: A Replication and Update," *Demography* 21:71:82.

Cherlin, A., J. Griffith and J. McCarthy. 1983. "A Note on Maritally Disrupted Men's Reports of Child Support in the June 1980 Current Population Survey." *Demography* 20:358–390.

Children's Defense Fund. 1984a. *American Children in Poverty.* Washington, DC: Children's Defense Fund.

———. 1984b. A Children's Defense Budget. Washington, DC: Children's Defense Fund.

Chin, A. 1983. "Social Security—A Retrospective Look at Decisions for Complex Futures." Rand Paper Series. April. P-6876.

Coale, A. J., P. Demeny and B. Vaughn. 1983. *Regional Model Life Tables and Stable Populations.* New York: Academic Press.

Coe, R. D. 1976. "The Sensitivity of the Incidence of Poverty to Different Measures of Income: School-Aged Children and Families." Pp. 357–409 in G. J. Duncan and J. N. Morgan (eds.) *Five Thousand American Families—Patterns of Economic Progress.* Vol. IV. Ann Arbor: Institute for Social Research, University of Michigan.

Commager, Henry Steele. 1983. "The Measure of Higher Education." *The Rotarian.* September: 30–35.

Congress of the United States. Congressional Budget Office. 1983. Changing the Structure of Medicare Benefits: Issues and Options. Washington, DC.

Consortium of Social Science Associations. 1983. COSSA Washington Update. Vol. II(23). Dec. 16, 1983. Washington, DC.

D'Amico, R. J., R. J. Haurin, and F. L. Mott. 1983. "The Effects of Mothers' Employment on Adolescent and Early Adult Outcomes of Young Men and Women." Pp. 130–219 in Cheryl D. Hayes and Sheila B.

Kamerman (eds.) *Children of Working Parents: Experiences and Outcomes.* Washington, DC: National Academy Press.

Danziger, S., and P. Gottschalk. 1983. "The Measurement of Poverty Implications for Antipoverty Policy." *American Behavioral Scientist* 26:739–756.

d'Arge, R. C., W. D. Schulze, and D. S. Brookshire. 1982. "Carbon Dioxide and Intergenerational Choice." *American Economic Review* 72:251–256.

Davis, Karen. 1983. "Health Care's Soaring Costs," *New York Times.* Aug. 26, 1983:D2.

Davis, K., and P. van den Oever. 1981. "Age Relations and Public Policy in Industrial Society." *Population and Development Review* 7:1–19.

Davis, K. 1983. "The Future of Marriage." *Bulletin of the American Academy of Arts and Sciences* 36:15–43.

Duncan, G. J., and J. N. Morgan. 1981. "Persistence and Change in Economic Status and the Role of Changing Family Circumstances." Pp. 1–44 in M. S. Hill, D. H. Hill, and J. N. Morgan (eds.) *Five Thousand American Families—Patterns of Economic Progress.* Vol. IX. Ann Arbor: Institute for Social Research. University of Michigan.

Easterlin, R. A. 1980. *Birth and Fortune: The Impact of Numbers on Personal Welfare.* New York: Basic Books.

Feistritzer, C. E. 1983. *The Condition of Teaching: A State by State Analysis.* Princeton, NJ: The Carnegie Foundation for the Advancement of Teaching.

Fuchs, V. 1983. *How We Live.* Cambridge: Harvard University Press.

Furstenburg, F., and K. Gordon Talvite. 1980. "Children's Names and Paternal Claims." *Journal of Family Issues* 1:31–57.

Furstenburg, F., and C. Nord. 1982. "Parenting Apart: Patterns of Childrearing after Marital Disruption." Paper presented to Annual Meeting of the American Sociological Association, San Francisco.

Furstenburg, F. and P. Allison. 1984. Unpublished results from their analysis of the National Survey of Children.

Furstenburg, F. and J. A. Seltzer. 1983. "Divorce and Child Development." Paper presented to the American Ortho-psychiatric Association Panel on Current Research in Divorce and Remarriage, April 8, Boston.

Gallup, G. H. 1983a. *The Gallup Poll: Public Opinion, 1982.* Wilmington, DE: Scholarly Resources.

———. 1983b. "The 15th Annual Gallup Poll of the Public's Attitudes Toward the Public Schools." *Phi Delta Kappan* 65:33–47.

Grove, R. D., and A. M. Hetzel. 1968. Vital Statistics Rates in the United States, 1940–60. National Center for Health Statistics. Washington, DC: U.S. Government Printing Office.

Grubb, W. N., and M. Lazerson. 1982. *Broken Promises: How Americans Fail Their Children.* New York: Basic Books.

Hannan, M. T., N. Brandon Tuma, and L. P. Groeneveld. 1977. "A Model of the Effect of Income Maintenance on Rates of Marital Dissolution: Evidence from the Seattle and Denver Income Maintenance Experiments." Stanford Research Institute Center for the Study of Welfare Policy Research: Memorandum 44.

Hanushek, E. A. 1981. "Throwing Money at Schools." *Journal of Policy Analysis and Management* 1:19–41.

Hetherington, E. M., M. Cox, and R. Cox. 1979. "Play and Social Interaction in Children Following Divorce." *Journal of Social Issues* 35:26–49.

Hetherington, E. M. 1979. "Divorce: A Child's Perspective." *American Psychologist* 34:851–858.

Hetherington, E. M., K. A. Camara, and D. L. Featherman. 1983. "Achievement and Intellectual Functioning of Children in One-Parent Households." Pp. 205–284 in J. T. Spence (ed.) *Achievement and Achievement Motives.* San Francisco: W. H. Freeman and Co.

Heynes, B. 1982. "The Influence of Parents' Work on Children's School Achievement." Pp. 229–267 in S. B. Kamerman and C. D. Hayes (eds.) *Families That Work: Children in a Changing World.* Washington, DC: National Academy Press.

Hill, M. S. 1983. "Trends in the Economic Situation of U.S. Families and Children: 1970–1980." Pp. 9–58 in R. R. Nelson, and F. Skidmore (eds.). *American Families and the Economy.* Washington, DC: National Academy Press.

Hofferth, S. 1983. Updating Children's Life Course. Center for Population Research, National Institute of Child Health and Human Development. Washington, DC. Unpublished.

Hoffman, S., and J. Holmes. 1976. "Husbands, Wives, and Divorce." Pp. 23–75 in G. J. Duncan and J. N. Morgan (eds.) *Five Thousand American Families—Patterns of Economic Progress.* Vol. IV. Ann Arbor: Institute for Social Research. The University of Michigan.

Hutchens, R. M. 1979. "Welfare, Remarriage, and Marital Search." *The American Economic Review* 69:369–379.

Kellam, S. G., M. E. Ensminger, and R. J. Turner. 1977. "Family Structure and the Mental Health of Children." *Archives of General Psychiatry* 34:1012–1022.

Lerner, B. 1983. "Test Scores as a Measure of Human Capital." Pp. 70–99 in R. B. Cattell (ed.) *Intelligence and National Achievement.* Washington, DC: The Cliveden Press for the Institute for the Study of Man.

Lesthaeghe, R. 1983. *A Century of Demographic and Cultural Change in Western Europe. A Sociological Interpretation.* Brussels: Unpublished manuscript, Vrije Universiteit.

McDonnell, L., and A. Pascal. 1979. *Organized Teachers in American Schools.* Santa Monica: Rand Corporation. February. R-2407-NIE.

McIntosh, A. 1983. *Population Policy in Western Europe: Responses to Low Fertility in France, Sweden, and West Germany.* Armonk, NY: M. E. Sharpe.

McLanahan, S. 1983. "Family Structure and the Reproduction of Poverty. University of Wisconsin Institute for Research on Poverty." Discussion Paper 720-83.

Michael, R. T. 1983. "Consequences of the Rise in Female Labor Force Participation Rates: Questions and Probes." Economics Research Center, NORC. Discussion Paper Series 83-8.

Miller, A. 1984. "Tables of U.S. Labor Force Participation Rates by Age and Sex." University of Pennsylvania: Unpublished manuscript.

Morgan, J. N. 1978. Intra-Family Transfers Revisited: "The Support of Dependents Inside the Family." Pp. 347–365 in G. J. Duncan and J. N. Morgan (eds.) *Five Thousand American Families—Patterns of Economic Progress.* Vol. VI. Ann Arbor: Institute for Social Research, The University of Michigan.

Murname, R. J. 1981. "Interpreting the Evidence on School Effectiveness." *Teachers College Record* 83:19–35.

National Assessment of Education Progress. 1978. *Three National Assessments of Science: Changes in Achievement, 1969–77.* Denver, CO: Education Commission of the States.

———. 1981. *Three National Assessments of Reading: Changes in Performance,* 1970–1980. Denver, CO: Education Commission of the States.

National Commission on Excellence in Education. 1983. "A Nation at Risk: The Imperative for Educational Reform. Report to the Secretary of Education, United States Department of Education." Washington, DC: United States Department of Education.

Nerlove, M. 1974. "Household and Economy: Toward a New Theory of Population and Economic Growth," *Journal of Political Economy* 82:200–218. Part II.

Nerlove, M., A Razin, and E. Sadka. 1984. "Some Welfare Theoretic Implications of Endogenous Fertility." Presented to Conference on the Economics of the Family. University of Pennsylvania. April 12–13.

Parsons, T. 1942. "Age and Sex in the Social Structure of the United States." *American Sociological Review* 7:604–616.

Population Reference Bureau. 1984. Intercom (February).

Pollak, R., and T. J. Wales, 1979. "Welfare Comparisons and Equivalence Scales." *American Economic Review* 69:216–221.

Preston, S. H. 1983. "Estimation of Certain Measures in Family Demography Based Upon Generalized Stable Population Relations." Presented to IUSSP Conference on Family Demography: Methods and Their Applications. New York: Population Council, Dec. 12–14.

Sandmaier, M. 1983. "Drink Can Hurt Pregnant Women." *Philadelphia Inquirer* Dec. 16, 1983:27A.

Schuck, P. H. 1979. "The Graying of Civil Rights Law: The Age Discrimination Act of 1975." *The Yale Law Journal* 89:27–93.

Stone, L. 1982. "The Historical Origins of the Modern Family." The Fifth Annual O. Meredith Wilson Lecture in History. Published by the Department of History, University of Utah, Salt Lake City.

Task Force on Education for Economic Growth. 1983. *Action for Excellence: A Comprehensive Plan to Improve Our Nation's Schools.* Denver: Education Commission of the States.

Thornton, A. and D. Freedman. 1983. "The Changing American Family." *Bulletin of the Population Reference Bureau* 38:1–44.

Toney, M. B., W. Stinner, and B. Bolesonkhi. 1983. "Residence Exposure and Fertility Expectations of Young Mormon and Nonmormon Women in Utah." Logan, Utah: Unpublished manuscript, Department of Sociology, Utah State University.

U.N. Statistical Office. 1984. *1982 Demographic Yearbook.* New York: United Nations.

U.S. Bureau of the Census. 1968. Current Population Reports. Series P-20. No. 174. Washington, DC: U.S. Government Printing Office.

———. 1971a. *Current Population Reports.* Series P-25 No. 470. Washington, DC: U.S. Government Printing Office.

———. 1975. *Historical Statistics of the United States from Colonial Times to 1970. Part I.* Washington, DC: U.S. Government Printing Office.

———. 1982a. *Statistical Abstract of the United States, 1982–83.* Washington, DC: U.S. Government Printing Office.

———. 1982b. *Current Population Reports.* Series P-20 No. 375. Washington, DC: U.S. Government Printing Office.

———. 1983a. *Statistical Abstract of the United States,* 1984. Washington, DC: U.S. Government Printing Office.

———. 1983b. *Current Population Reports.* Series P-20. No. 383. Washington, DC: U.S. Government Printing Office.

———. 1983c. *Current Population Reports.* Series P-60 No. 137. Washington, DC: U.S. Government Printing Office.

———. 1984a. "Estimates of Poverty Including the Value of Noncash Benefits: 1979 to 1982." Technical Paper No. 51. Washington, DC: U.S. Government Printing Office.

———, 1984b. *Current Population Reports.* Series P-23 No. 132. Washington, DC: U.S. Government Printing Office.

U.S. Bureau of Labor Statistics. 1984. *Employment and Earnings.* Vol. 31(2) January.

U.S. Department of Housing and Urban Development. n.d. *The 1978 Community Life Data Book.* Washington, DC.

U.S. House of Representatives, Select Committee on Children, Youth, and Families. 1983. "U.S. Children and Their Families: Current Conditions and Recent Trends." Ninety-Eighth Congress. First Session. May. Washington, DC.

U.S. National Center for Education Statistics. 1983. *The Condition of Education. 1983 Edition.* Washington, DC: U.S. Government Printing Office.

U.S. National Center for Health Statistics. n.d. Vital Statistics of the United States, 1970. Vol. II Section 5, Life Tables.

———. 1976. Fertility Tables by Birth Cohorts by Color. United States, 1917–1973. Rockville, Md.: Department of Health, Education, and Welfare.

———. 1982a. Monthly Vital Statistics Report. Vol. 31(8), Supplement. Nov. 30.

———. 1983a. Monthly Vital Statistics Report. Vol. 31(13). Oct. 5.

———. 1983b. Monthly Vital Statistics Report. Vol. 32(4), Supplement. August 11.

———. 1984a. Monthly Vital Statistics Report. Vol. 32(9) Supplement.

Vance, V. S., and P. C. Schlechty. 1982. *The Structure of Teaching Occupation and the Characteristics of Teachers: A Sociological Interpretation.* Chapel Hill: Unpublished manuscript. University of North Carolina.

Veroff, J., E. Douvan, and R. A. Kukla. 1981. *The Inner American: A Self-Portrait from 1957 to 1976.* New York: Basic Books, Inc.

Zill, N., and J. Peterson. 1982. *Trends in the Behavior and Emotional Well-Being of U.S. Children.* Washington, DC: Child Trends. Manuscript prepared for 1982 Annual Meeting of American Association for the Advancement of Science, Washington, DC.

42

The Status of Majority and Minority Groups in the United States Today

JOHN E. FARLEY

MINORITY GROUPS

Blacks

Blacks are the largest minority group in the United States. According to the 1980 Census, there are 26.5 million black people in the United States, which constitutes 11.7 percent of the total population (U.S. Bureau of the Census, 1981: 1). For a variety of reasons, this estimate is probably somewhat low. The 1970 census, for example, apparently missed 7 to 8 percent of the black population; the 1960 census, 8 to 9 percent (U.S. Bureau of the Census, 1979a:10). All indications are that this undercount has been reduced in the 1980 census, though it certainly has not been completely eliminated. It is believed that the 1980 census missed about 5 percent of the black population. Thus, it is possible that the true black population at the beginning of the 1980s may exceed 27 million, or 12 percent of the total population.

Today, as in the past, the majority of black people in the United States live in the South. According to the 1970 Census, 53 percent of the black population lived in the South (U.S. Bureau of the Census, 1979a). (See Fig. 42.1.) That was the lowest percentage recorded by any census up to that time, reflecting the long period of black migration out of the South from the late nineteenth century to the mid-twentieth century (U.S. Bureau of Census, 1979a). All indications are that this black out-migration from the South ended in the early 1970s, and that since then, more black people have moved into than out of the South. Many who had previously moved out of the South have returned in recent years (Biggar, 1979:29). Consequently, the 1980 Census also showed that 53 percent of the black population lived in the South (U.S. Bureau of the Census, 1981:1). This reversal has occurred for several reasons. First, as it became apparent that the North was not the racial paradise that many southern blacks once believed it was, many black migrants found it very sensible to return to the South, where many of their families still resided and where the mores, life style, and, undoubtedly, the weather and climate were more familiar to them. Another important factor is the general nationwide pattern of jobs and population moving toward the Sun Belt. During the past decade economic growth has been greater in the South than in the North, and blacks, as well as others, have moved South to take advantage of the newly created opportunities. Indeed, the white population has also experienced substantial net migration into the South during the 1970s. In addition, there was also net black migration into the West during the middle and late 1970s (Biggar, 1979:29).

The remainder—somewhat less than half—of the black population that lives outside the South is fairly evenly spread across the Northeast and Midwest, with a smaller but growing number in the West. In 1980, 18.3 percent of black people in the United States lived in the Northeast, 20.1 percent in the North Central states (Midwest), and 8.5 percent in the West (U.S. Bureau of the Census, 1981:6).

The black population is highly urbanized. Although it was more rural than the population as a whole during the early twentieth century, today it is more urban. As of 1978, 75 percent of all blacks in the United States lived in metropolitan areas, compared to 66 percent of all whites (U.S. Bureau of the Census, 1979b:34). The black population is particularly concentrated in the large industrial cities of the Great Lakes and Northeast regions, as well as the cities in the South (though there are more rural blacks in the South than anywhere else). Compared to the population as a whole, the black population is much more highly concentrated in large central cities and much less sub-

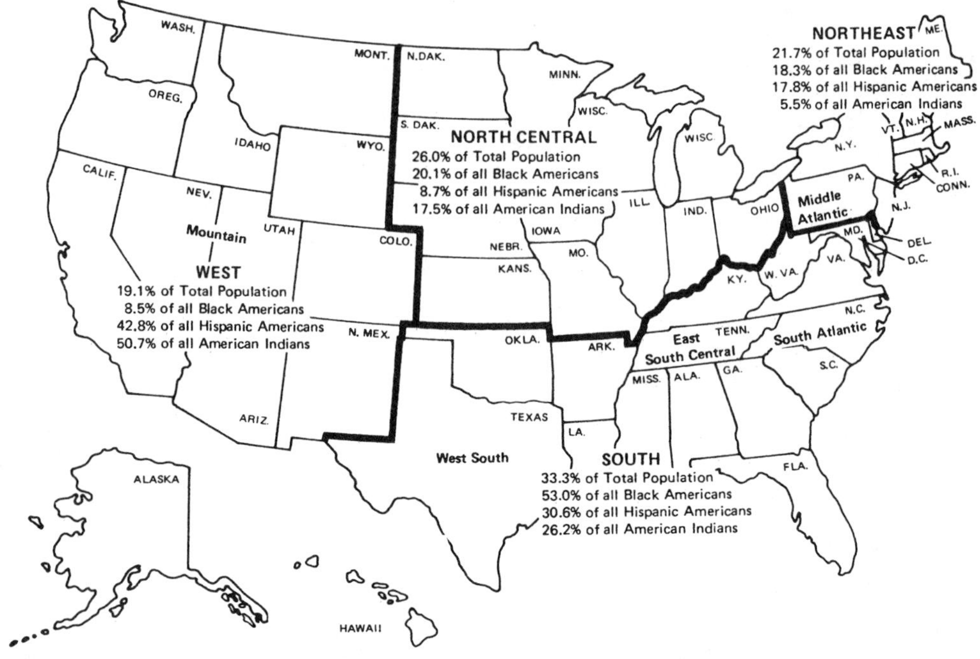

Figure 42.1. Geographic distribution of minority groups in the United States, 1980. U.S. Bureau of the Census, 1981, p. 6.

urbanized. Over half (55 percent) of all blacks live in central cities. In the total population, only 28 percent live in central cities, and 39 percent in suburbs (U.S. Bureau of the Census, 1979b:34). Although relatively few blacks live in suburbs (only about 5 percent of all suburbanites are black), black migration from the city to the suburbs has increased somewhat during the 1970s.

A final important observation can be made about the black population of the United States: It is younger than the population as a whole. In 1978, 37.9 percent of the black population was under eighteen years of age. This compares to 29.6 percent for the total population and 28.4 percent for the white population. The median age of the black population in 1980 was 24.9—five years younger than the median age for the total population, 30.0 (U.S. Bureau of the Census, 1981:3).

Hispanic Americans

The second largest minority group in the United States is Hispanic Americans, also known as Latinos or as Americans of Spanish origin (the Census Bureau's term). This umbrella label covers at least four distinct groups: Mexican-Americans, or Chicanos; Puerto Ricans; Cuban Americans; and Central and South Americans. There are also a number of Hispanic Americans who do not fit neatly into any of these categories. Table 42.1 presents Census Bureau estimates of the number of Hispanic Americans in 1979. As can be seen in the table, these estimates indicate a total of about twelve million Americans of Spanish origin, a majority of whom are Mexican-Americans. The total Hispanic population, according to this estimate, is about 5.5 percent of the U.S. population. More recent data from the 1980 census indicate that the Hispanic population as of 1980 is 14.6 million, or 6.4 percent of the United States population, though a breakdown by group was not available as of this writing. As is the case with Census Bureau statistics on blacks, it is known that these estimates are lower than the actual Spanish-origin population. For a number of reasons, including language barriers and the existence of some illegal immigration from Latin American countries in recent years, the underestimate of the Spanish population is probably greater than the underestimate of the black population, though there

Table 42.1. Americans of Spanish Origin

Group	1978 Population in Millions	Percent of Total Spanish Origin
Chicanos	7.326	60.6%
Puerto Ricans	1.748	14.5
Cuban Americans	.794	6.6
Central and South American	.840	7.0
Other Spanish origin	1.371	11.4
Total	12.079	100.0

Source: U.S. Bureau of the Census, 1980a, p. 1.

is some disagreement on its exact size. There is little doubt, however, that the census figure is significantly below the true figure for persons of Spanish origin. It has been estimated, for example, that as many as 5 to 8 million persons of Spanish origin may be illegally present in the United States (St. Louis Post Dispatch, 1978; Des Moines Register, 1978), though some demographers regard these estimates as too high because they do not consider return migration out of the United States by illegal immigrants. In any case, there is little doubt that some of these illegal immigrants have tried to avoid being counted in the census for fear of detection, which in turn has caused the census figures to be lower than the actual Hispanic population. In spite of the illegal immigration, it should be stressed that the great majority of persons of Spanish origin in the United States are present legally; most are U.S. citizens, and some have lived in the United States for generations. If we correct for the census undercount of the Hispanic population, it appears likely that the true Hispanic population of the United States is in excess of 15 million, and possibly as high as 18 or 19 million.

The Hispanic population is one of the fastest-growing population groups in the United States, partly because Latinos have a relatively high birth rate, and partly because their immigration rate, both legal and illegal, has been among the highest of any group in recent years. Officially, the Hispanic population increased by about 50 percent between 1970 and 1980, and the actual rate of growth may have been even higher. Most experts believe that by sometime in the 1990s the Hispanic population will exceed the black population, making Latinos the nation's largest minority group.

The Hispanic population is even more urban than the black population. In 1978, fully 85 percent of the Spanish-origin population lived in metropolitan areas (U.S. Bureau of the Census, 1979c). Though there is some variation among the various groups, all Hispanic groups are over 80 percent urban. Although many people associate them with agricultural labor, 81 percent of all Mexican-Americans live in metropolitan areas. This percentage is higher than that of either the white or black population. Like blacks, Latinos are heavily concentrated in central cities; 51 percent of all Americans of Spanish origin lived in central cities in 1978, a figure that is almost as high as that for blacks and well above the figure for whites. Hispanic Americans are more suburbanized than blacks but less suburbanized than whites; 34 percent of the Hispanic population lived in suburbs in 1978 (U.S. Bureau of the Census, 1979b).

The Chicano population is heavily concentrated in five Southwestern states: California, Texas, Arizona, New Mexico, and Colorado; 60 percent of all Hispanic Americans and 87 percent of all Chicanos live in these five states (U.S. Bureau of the Census, 1979c). There are, however, also sizable concentrations of Mexican-Americans in several midwestern and northeastern states; Illinois and Michigan are notable examples.

The Puerto Rican population is heavily concentrated in the urban Northeast, particularly the New York City area. As a result of this concentration, 11.4 percent of the total Latino population lives in New York State, giving it the third largest Latino population of any state, behind only California and Texas (U.S. Bureau of the Census, 1981:6). There are also sizable Puerto Rican populations in several other northeastern cities; Boston is a notable example.

The Cuban-American population, largely refugees from the Castro government and their descendants, is heavily concentrated in Florida, particularly the Miami area. According to the 1980 Census, over 850,000 Hispanic persons lived in Florida, the fourth largest total of any state. There are, however, also sizable numbers of Cuban-Americans in some parts of the Northeast.

As a whole, Latinos are one of the youngest ethnic groups in the United States. As of 1978, 42 percent of all Hispanic Americans were less than 18 years old, which is a higher proportion than for blacks and about a time and a half as high as for whites. The median age of Hispanic Americans in 1980 was 23.2, about seven years younger than for the American population as a whole (U.S. Bureau of the Census, 1981:3).

Indian People

Up-to-date and detailed statistics are more difficult to obtain for Indian people, because their relatively small numbers make it impossible to obtain reliable data on them from the Census Bureau's ongoing Current Population Surveys, the major source of current data on black and Hispanic Americans. The main source of data on Indian people is the U.S. Census, which has been taken every ten years but is now tentatively planned for every five years, with the first mid-decade census planned for 1985, depending on funding. According to the 1970 census, the Indian and Alaskan native population was about 793,000 (U.S. Bureau of the Census, 1972). By 1980, this population had risen to 1.4 million, or 0.6 percent of the U.S. population. In part this represents real growth, but much of the increase is probably the result of people of mixed parentage classifying themselves as Indian rather than white—the census determines race on the basis of self reports. In recent years, people of mixed parentage have increasingly come to think of themselves as Indian. The 1.4 million total today reflects substantial and real growth in the Indian population from a low point of around 250,000 just before the turn of the century (Driver, 1969). It is, however, no more than and probably substantially *less* than the Native American population prior to the decimation of the native population by warfare and, especially, European diseases that followed the arrival of whites on the continent (Driver, 1969; Dobyns, 1966; Kroeber, 1939).

In 1980, 50.7 percent of the Indian population lived in the West, 26.2 percent in the South, 17.5 percent in the North Central states, and 5.5 percent in the Northeast. However, just three states, Oklahoma, California, and Arizona, account for fully 37 percent of the Indian population (U.S. Bureau of the Census, 1981:6). (The regional distribution of all three minority groups we have discussed is illustrated in Fig. 42.1.)

American Indians are the only minority group that is *less* urbanized than the population as a whole. In 1970 fewer than half, 45 percent, of Indian people in the United States lived in urban areas; 55 percent lived in rural areas. Today, a majority of Indian people may live in urban areas; there was considerable urbanization between the 1960 and 1970 censuses and probably some further urbanization during the 1970s.

Not only are Indian people more rural than any other group, they also frequently become less permanently linked to the city even when they do move there. Urban Indians frequently live in cities near the reservation where they grew up. They tend to maintain close ties with the reservation, often remaining active in its cultural, social, and religious affairs. They also return to the reservation frequently for weekend visits and are visited by friends who still live on the reservation (Steele, 1972, 1975). Urban Indians also oftentimes view their residence in the city as a temporary sojourn and return to the reservation after a period of living in the city.

The Indian population is probably the youngest of any major American racial or ethnic group. As of the 1980 Census, 43.8 percent of all Indian people in the United States were under twenty. The median age of Native Americans was 23.0 (U.S. Bureau of the Census, 1981:3).

Blacks, Latinos, and Indian People as Minority Groups

We have said that the three major groups we have been discussing are those that best fit the definition of minority group. We will explore the present-day status of these groups later in this chapter, but it is important to note that these three groups, more than any others, today have less than their proportionate share of virtually all resources in American society. They have less wealth and lower incomes, less education, and less political power. They are accorded lower social status and live shorter lives than any other groups in American society. Although there are some other groups that suffer low status in *some* of these areas, these are the only groups that, *on the whole* (there are many individuals who are exceptions to the general pattern) suffer low status across the board in *all* of these areas.

GROUPS WITH INTERMEDIATE STATUS

There are a number of racial and ethnic groups in the United States whose status in some ways is that of a minority group but in other ways is not. These groups are near, or even in some cases above, the overall societal norm in some areas, such as income or education. However, each has in the past been or is now subject to widespread discrimination in American society. Furthermore, each of these groups has, to a large degree, been excluded from the upper echelons of American corporate power structure, or what Mills (1956) has called the power elite. Among these groups are the various Asian-American groups, Jewish Americans, and a variety of "white ethnic" groups of eastern and southern European origin. We shall have more to say about the status of these groups later in this chapter; here we shall present general information about the numbers and geographic distribution of these groups.

Asian-Americans

The three largest Asian-American groups in the United States, as of the 1970 Census, were Japanese-Americans, Chinese-Americans, and Filipino-Americans. The 1970 populations of the various Asian-American groups are shown in Table 42.2.

These populations are heavily concentrated in the West, particularly in the states of California and Hawaii. Over half of each of the three groups live in these two states. There is also a large concentration of Chinese-Americans in New York State, with a Chinese population of over 80,000. Lesser but substantial numbers (over 10,000) of the other two groups are also found in New York State and of all three groups in Illinois. Overall, in 1980, 59.5 percent of Asian-Americans lived in the West, 16.0 percent in the Northeast, 13.4 percent in the South, and 11.1 percent in the Midwest (U.S. Bureau of the Census, 1981:6).

By 1980, a fourth group, Vietnamese Americans, had become numerous due to the large influx of refugees from Vietnam during the 1970s, growing rapidly to a population of several hundred thousand. This large-scale immigration of Vietnamese, along with substantial immigration among other groups, led to an increase in the population of Asians and Pacific Islanders to 3.4 million, or 1.5 percent of the U.S. population—about double the 1970 total (U.S. Bureau of the Census, 1981:6).

All Asian-American groups are highly urban. Fully 97 percent of all Chinese-Americans live in urban areas. Among Japanese-Americans, the corresponding figure is 89 percent, and among Filipinos, 86 percent (Office of Special Concerns, 1974). Chinese-Americans predominantly live in central cities rather than suburbs; just over two thirds of all Chinese-Americans live in central cities. Four urban areas account for the majority of the Chinese-American population: San Francisco–Oakland, New York City, Honolulu, and Los Angeles–Long Beach. Most of these urban Chinese-Americans live in the central-city neighborhoods known as the Chinatowns. In addition to the cities mentioned, Chicago and Boston also have sizable Chinatowns.

Compared to the Chinese, Japanese-Americans and Filipino-Americans are more suburbanized, but more of them live in central cities than anywhere else. About 48 percent of each of these groups live in central cities, compared to 28 percent of the total population (Office of Special Concerns, 1974).

Japanese-Americans are, on the average, older than the population as a whole, with a median age of 32.4. Chinese and Filipino Americans, on the other hand, are somewhat younger than the population as a whole, with median ages of 26.7 and 26.1 respectively (U.S. Bureau of the Census, 1973:593–594).

Although the majority of Asian-Americans fit into one of the groups discussed above, there are some who do not. There were, for example, about 71,000 Korean-Americans living in the United States as of the 1970 Census (U.S. Bureau of the Census, 1973:594).

Table 42.2. 1970 Population of Asian-American Groups (to nearest 1000)

Japanese-Americans	591,000
Chinese-Americans	435,000
Filipino-Americans	343,000

Source: U.S. Bureau of the Census, 1972.

Jewish Americans

Accurate data on Jewish Americans and other white ethnic groups are more difficult to obtain and less reliable than data on the other groups we have been discussing. The Census does not ask people their religion, and only incomplete data (first- and second-generation immigrants) were obtained on nationality before the 1980 census.

The best guess is that the Jewish population of the United States is slightly above 6 million, or 3 percent of the U.S. population (Goren, 1980:571). This is about half the world's Jewish population. The U.S. Jewish population is growing less rapidly than the population as a whole because of its relatively low birth rate.

The Jewish population is highly urbanized. In 1957, the last year for which good data are available, 96 percent of all Jewish Americans lived in urban areas (U.S. Bureau of the Census, 1958). In particular, a sizable proportion lives in the Greater New York City metropolitan area. This is reflected in the regional distribution of Jewish Americans: About 64 percent of them live in the Northeast. The remainder are somewhat evenly distributed through the Midwest, South, and West.

Eastern and Southern European "White Ethnics"

The term "white ethnics" is applied to a wide variety of groups from eastern and southern Europe. As a general rule, these groups have immigrated to the United States somewhat more recently than the groups from northern and western Europe. The bulk of the eastern and southern European migration arrived after 1900, during the early part of the twentieth century. Much of the Italian population, for example, came in one decade, 1901 to 1910. In contrast, immigration from Ireland peaked in the 1850s and immigration from Germany peaked in the 1880s (Thomlinson, 1976).

The eastern and southern European "white ethnics" include, among others, Italian, Polish, Greek, Russian, Hungarian, Czechoslovakian, and Ukrainian Americans. A 1972 survey by the Census Bureau indicated that the largest of these groups was Italian-Americans, with a population of about 8.8 million. Next came Polish-Americans at 5.1 million, and Russian-Americans at 2.2 million (U.S. Bureau of the Census, 1973b). Many of the latter group are also Jewish. Although this survey did not cover Greek-Americans, membership in the Greek Orthodox Church—nearly 2 million in 1977 (Jacquet, 1979)—is suggestive of the size of that group.

The majority of these ethnic groups are concentrated in the Northeast and in the Great Lakes states. This is reflected in 1970 statistics, which show that in Massachusetts, New York, Rhode Island, Connecticut, and New Jersey, 30 percent or more of the population was of foreign stock (U.S. Bureau of the Census, 1972:472). Eastern and southern Europeans also make up a substantial portion of the population in Illinois, Michigan, Wisconsin, and the northern parts of Ohio and Indiana. For the most part, these ethnic groups are highly urban; they are heavily concentrated in the large industrial cities of the above-mentioned regions.

A final important characteristic of these groups is that they generally belong to religions outside the Protestant majority in the United States. The majority of eastern and southern Europeans are Catholic. This is particularly true for Italians and Poles, though a sizable portion of the latter are Jewish. A large part of the Russian-American population also is Jewish; much of the remainder is Russian Orthodox. The various Slavic groups tend to belong to one of the Eastern Orthodox churches, as do Greek Americans, who typically belong to the Greek Orthodox Church.

WHITES FROM WESTERN AND NORTHERN EUROPE: A DOMINANT GROUP WITHIN A DOMINANT GROUP

In contemporary America the groups that most clearly fit the definition of majority or dominant group are whites from western and northern Europe. Certainly whites as a whole are in a dominant position relative to blacks, Chicanos, American Indians and, to a lesser degree, Asian-Americans. Within that white population, however, the most advantaged groups are those from western and northern Europe. The largest and most established among these groups are the English, Scots, and Welsh, who totaled 29.5 million, or 14.4 percent of the population in 1972. Nearly as large a group are the Germans, who totaled 25.5 million, or 12.5 percent of the population. The Irish, who numbered 16.4 million, make up 8 percent of the population. Combined, these three groups are over one third of the U.S. population (U.S. Bureau of the Census, 1973).

There are other, smaller, groups that also are of northern and western European origin; among these are Americans of French, Dutch, and Scandinavian (Swedish, Norwegian, and Danish) origin.

As a general rule, these groups immigrated earlier than most of the eastern and southern Europeans, though Scandinavians are something of an exception in this regard. Partly because of this, these groups tend to be more assimilated into American society and less conscious of ethnicity than other groups we have discussed, though some ethnic awareness persists in all American ethnic groups and may be on the rise in many.

The British groups (English, Scots, Welsh), a sizable proportion of the Germans, and the Scandinavians and Dutch are predominantly Protestant. These are the groups that form the core of the so-called WASP (white Anglo-Saxon Protestant) population. Most of the rest of the Germans and the majority of the Irish are Catholic, although there are many Irish, particularly in the South, who belong to fundamentalist Protestant churches.

For the most part, these groups are quite widely distributed geographically. The most notable exceptions are the Scandinavian groups, which are largely concentrated in the upper Midwest.

As we have indicated, these groups are generally in a dominant socioeconomic position. They tend to have relatively high economic, educational, and occupational levels, and relatively low rates of poverty, though there is some variation by both nationality and religion. Data from large scale surveys by the National Opinion Research Center indicate, for example, that among eleven white Catholic and Protestant ethnic groups, the four highest occupational prestige ratings were among British Protestants, Irish Catholics, German Catholics, and German Protestants in that order (Greeley, 1977:60). In urban areas outside the South, Scandinavian Protestants also ranked close to these four groups (Greeley, 1977:61; see also Greeley, 1974).

EVIDENCE OF IMPROVEMENT IN MINORITY STATUS

There are some social indicators that suggest substantial improvement in the status of minorities between about 1940 and 1980. Some of the trends are fairly recent; others have been under way since around World War II.

One indication of improved status among minorities can be seen in their occupational structure. One indicator of a group's occupational status is the number or proportion of group members who hold professional or managerial positions. Among blacks the number of persons in professional occupations more than tripled between 1960 and 1975. The number of blacks in management positions increased by about two and one-fourth times. Among whites, people in professional occupations increased by only about one and two-thirds times; people in managerial positions, by about one and one-fourth times (U.S. Department of Commerce, 1977:377). In other words, the number of blacks in high-status jobs grew at a relatively faster rate than did the number of whites in such jobs. Latinos, too, experienced a more rapid growth in high status jobs than did whites during this period (Moore, 1976:64; U.S. Bureau of the Census, 1979:26). Thus, by the late 1970s, a substantially higher proportion of the black and Latino populations held high-status occupations in the United States than ever before, though that proportion was still lower for both blacks and Latinos than it was for whites.

Among those who are employed, the gap in individual incomes between minorities and whites has declined substantially over the past thirty years. In 1950, for example, the median income of employed black males was around 60 percent of the median income of employed white males. By 1975 it was nearly 75 percent—a substantial closing of the gap (U.S. Department of Commerce, 1977:459; U.S. Bureau of the Census, 1979a; Freeman, 1978). In 1975 the income of employed black women was nearly as high as that of employed white women—97 percent, according to Freeman. In the early 1950s it was only about half as high. If we focus on the subgroup of *young* workers who have just recently *finished college,* the gap has been practically eliminated. As an example of this, black male college graduates between the ages of twenty-five and twenty-nine earn 93 percent as much as comparable white males (Freeman, 1978:59).

In the area of political representation, there is also evidence of substantial minority gain. Between 1970 and 1977, the number of black elected officials in the United States more than tripled, rising from around 1,300 in 1970 to over 4,500 in 1979 (U.S. Bureau of the Census, 1979f). This figure includes 162 black mayors (Hamilton, 1978). Among the major cities that have elected black mayors are Los Angeles, Detroit, Washington, Atlanta, New Orleans, and Birmingham, Alabama—the city that had been a national symbol of resistance to black rights during the early 1960s. During the 1970s two states, Arizona and New Mexico, elected Chicano governors. Between 1965 and 1973 the number of Spanish-surnamed legislators in five southwestern states nearly doubled, increasing from thirty-five to sixty-six (Moore, 1976:156). In 1981, San Antonio became the first major city to elect a Chicano mayor. Thus, it is clear that both blacks and Chicanos have made very substantial gains in political representation during the past ten to fifteen years.

Finally, it is important to reiterate that deliberate racial discrimination is today illegal and less common than in the past. This in itself is a dramatic change, considering that as recently as thirty years ago, such discrimination was not only legal and widespread but, in some parts of the country, required by law. This decline in deliberate discrimination has, as we have indicated, been accompanied by some rather dramatic reductions in prejudice in the population.

It seems clear from these data, then, that in at least some areas there *has* been substantial improvement in the status of minority group members in America. An important factor in this improvement has been the rise of minority group social movement. . . .

Despite these apparent gains, some hard questions must still be asked. First, we must ask, despite whatever progress has occurred, how much inequality and racism still persists? More specifically, what is the standing of minorities relative to that of whites in America today? The fact that minorities have gained in certain areas does not necessarily mean either that they have caught up or that *all* minority group members have gained at all. Finally, we must ask what is the absolute level of living among minorities today? We shall turn to these questions in the next section.

EVIDENCE OF CONTINUING MAJORITY-MINORITY INEQUALITY

Economics

Despite the progress we have seen among some segments of the minority population, the overall picture today continues to be one of serious majority-minority inequality in the economic arena. One important indicator of economic well-being is median family income. The median family income for all white, black, and Spanish-origin families in 1978 is shown in Table 42.3. These data clearly show that, whatever gains have been made, the income of Latinos and, even more so, blacks, remains substantially below that of whites. Indeed, the figure for blacks represents only a small gain relative to whites over the past forty years: In the 1940s median family income for blacks was about 50 percent of what it was for whites. Today, it is about 59 percent.

Another indicator of the economic position of a group is the proportion of its members who are below the federally defined poverty level (approximately $6,200 for a family of four, $3100 for a single individual in 1977, but adjusted for inflation annually). In 1977, 8.9 percent of the white population, but 31.3 percent of the black population and 22.4 percent of the Spanish-origin population had incomes below the poverty level (U.S. Bureau of the Census, 1979e). In other words, black people are more than three times as likely as white people to be poor, and Latinos are about two and a half times as likely as Anglos to be poor. Recent statistics are not available for Indian people, but the 1970 Census indicated that in 1969, 39 percent of the Indian population had incomes below the poverty level—a higher percentage than any of the other groups.

A final indicator of economic status is the unemployment rate. Here, too, substantial inequalities are evident. For 1980 the unemployment rate for whites was 6.3 percent. For blacks and other races, it was 14.1 percent. For Hispanic Americans, it was 10.1 percent (Wescott and Bednarzik, 1981:7). Among Indians on reservations in 1973 the unemployment rate was 38 percent. Thus, we see that the unemployment rate for blacks is more than twice as high as for whites; for Latinos, nearly twice as high, and, for reservation Indians, considerably higher, though recent data are not available.

In general, black unemployment has been about twice as high as white unemployment since the end of World War II. Prior to that time, during the 1920s and 1930s, blacks and whites had very similar unemployment rates (Wilson, 1978). However, since the war there has been a drastic reduction in the number of low-skill, low-pay, dead-end jobs that many blacks had occupied. In general, a sizable seg-

Table 42.3. Median Family Income, 1978: Whites, Blacks, and Persons of Spanish Origin

	Median Family Income	Percent of White Median Family Income
White	$18,368	—
Black	10,879	58.6
Spanish Origin	12,566	68.4

Source: U.S. Bureau of the Census, 1980b.

ment of the black population has continued to be excluded from the opportunity to learn skills necessary for better jobs, and the disappearance of the unskilled jobs has left many of those individuals unemployed (Wilson, 1978).

The problem of minority unemployment becomes even greater if we focus on particular segments of the minority population. Among young black urban males, for example, the unemployment rate is believed to be in the range of 40 percent to 50 percent.

Taken as a whole, these economic data indicate that very substantial inequalities between whites and minorities persist. While a segment of the black and Hispanic population today enjoys relatively high incomes and good jobs, another large segment of the minority population can only be described as trapped at the bottom of the socioeconomic structure. For this group things are not getting better; indeed, relative to everyone else they are probably getting worse. If we examine the minority population as a whole, two conclusions appear evident. First, among the black and Hispanic populations there is increasing stratification and a growing gap between a segment that is relatively well-off and another segment that is impoverished and struggling for survival. Second, if we take the overall minority population, the *average* economic positions of blacks, Latinos, and Indians remain substantially lower than the average position of whites, and the average positions have improved only marginally relative to the position of whites.

Political Representation

As we have seen earlier in this chapter, the political representation of black and Hispanic Americans has risen dramatically during the past decade. Nonetheless, the political representation of these groups remains well below their share of the population. In 1977, for example, there were sixteen blacks in the U.S. House of Representatives, and one in the U.S. Senate (Hamilton, 1978). These figures work out to about 4 percent and 1 percent, respectively, for a group that makes up nearly 12 percent of the population. In the Congress elected in 1978, there were still sixteen blacks in the House but none in the Senate—the only black senator was defeated in his reelection campaign. Overall, the total number of black elected officials is less than 1 percent of all elected officials (Joint Center for Political Studies, 1977). In 1980 there were still no black governors, and no black person had ever been elected President or Vice President or even received the Democratic or Republican nomination for either of these offices.

Among Hispanic Americans, the underrepresentation is even greater. In California, for example, 16 percent of the population is Chicano, but only 5 percent of the state legislature seats and 2 percent of all elected officials in the mid-1970s were Chicano. It is thus evident that for Chicanos, as for blacks, recent gains in political representation have not yet approached a share of representation proportionate to the group's population.

Education

Data on the educational attainment in 1979 for whites, blacks, and Americans of Spanish Origin are shown in Tables 42.4, 42.5, and 42.6. Table 42.4 shows median years of school completed—a good overall measure of a group's educational status. These data indicate that in the population over 25, there is a gap of a little more than half a year between the median black position and the median white position, and more than a two-year gap between Latinos and whites. However, if we add younger adults to the total and look at everyone over 18, the gap decreases to less than half a year for blacks and a year and a half for Latinos. This would appear to suggest that despite substantial educational inequality among the total population, the gap is decreasing among younger adults who have recently come through the educational system. This is confirmed by looking at the third column of Table 42.4, which shows that among young adults only (ages 20 to 24), the gap is only three-tenths of a year for blacks and half a year for Latinos. Thus, inequality in the *amount* of education has been greatly reduced (though not eliminated) among young

Table 42.4. Median Years of School Completed by Age, for Whites, Blacks, and Americans of Spanish Origin, 1979

	Age		
	25+	18+	20–24
White	12.5	12.5	12.8
Black	11.9	12.1	12.5
Spanish origin	10.3	11.3	12.3

Source: U.S. Bureau of the Census, 1980c, pp. 23–27.

Table 42.5. Percent High School Graduates by Age, for Whites, Blacks, and Americans of Spanish Origin, 1979

	Age		
	25+	18+	20–24
White	69.7	71.5	85.7
Black	49.4	53.6	75.0
Spanish Origin	42.0	45.7	61.7

Source: U.S. Bureau of the Census, 1980c, pp. 23–27.

black and Hispanic Americans who have recently come through the educational system. This pattern is confirmed in Table 42.5, which shows the percentage of the three groups who have graduated from high school. The intergroup gap is great when we look at the whole adult population, particularly those 25 and over who would have graduated by 1970 or 1971. Among *young* adults, however, the gap is again reduced but not eliminated. Note that Hispanic young adults, in particular, remain well below white young adults on this measure. Black young adults are also behind but not by as much.

The figures on college graduation indicate less improvement in the standing of blacks and Latinos relative to whites. While the proportion of college graduates among the younger population *relative to* the population over 25 shows somewhat more gain among blacks than among whites, the proportion of college graduates among young blacks (25 to 29) remains only about half as high as among whites the same age. Among Latinos the picture is even more dismal. The percentage of Latinos between the ages of 25 and 29 who have completed four years of college is barely higher than the percentage for all Latinos over 25, and relative to the figures for the white population in the same age group, it is lower.

Table 42.6. Percent of Population with Four or More Years of College by Age, for Whites, Blacks, and Americans of Spanish Origin, 1977

	Age	
	25+	25–29
White	17.2	24.3
Black	7.9	12.4
Spanish Origin	6.7	7.3

Source: U.S. Bureau of the Census, 1980c, pp. 23–27.

Data on current college enrollment are also instructive. In 1978, about 10.4 percent of U.S. college students were black. This is a substantial improvement over the statistics for years past: in 1974, 9.2 percent were black; in 1972, 8.9 percent; and, in 1966, only 4.7 percent (U.S. Bureau of the Census, 1980d; U.S. Bureau of the Census, 1979f). Nonetheless, blacks are still underrepresented among college students, since the college age population is 12.9 percent black (U.S. Bureau of the Census, 1980e). In addition, blacks are overrepresented in the less prestigious colleges and universities, and black enrollment actually fell during the late 1970s at a number of major state universities. Among Hispanic Americans, the underrepresentation is even greater; only 3.8 percent of U.S. college students were Hispanic in 1978 (U.S. Bureau of the Census, 1980d), despite that group's substantially larger representation in the college age population.

These data indicate that, while there has been some improvement in educational attainment in the black and Hispanic populations, serious inequalities remain. Among younger blacks and Latinos, particularly, the educational gap with whites has closed but not disappeared. However, these data suggest that, even in the younger population, there are far fewer college graduates among blacks than among whites. The gap is even greater among Hispanic Americans. Furthermore, there have been only modest gains among the black population and apparently none at all among the Latino population.

Unfortunately, data of this nature are not available for American Indians. All indications are, however, that the problem of unequal education is at least as great for Indian people as for blacks and Latinos. In the late 1960s fewer than half of all Indian youths entering high school were finishing. This would probably indicate high school graduation rates significantly lower than for either black or Hispanic Americans.

Of course, statistics about educational attainment cannot begin to tell the whole story about how well or poorly any group is being served by the educational system. Quality of education is as important as quantity, and even statistics showing that young blacks' educational levels are becoming closer to those of whites say nothing about the issue of educational quality. We know, for example, that black students are underrepresented in prestigious private colleges and major state universities and overrepresented in community colleges and smaller regional or commuter state colleges and universities. . . .

Health and Mortality

So far, we have seen evidence of continuing serious racial and ethnic inequality in the areas of economics, political representation, and education. In such situations, there is always the risk that such information will be seen by some as just so many more statistics in a world where we are daily bombarded by more and more statistics. However, one area, probably more than any other, shows the human dimension—and indeed the human tragedy—of racial and ethnic inequality. In the United States today, the racial or ethnic group to which one belongs even partially determines how long that person will live. It also influences the amount that person can expect to be ill in his or her lifetime and the likelihood that one or more of his or her children will die in infancy. These differences exist not because of biological racial differences, but rather because of social inequalities associated with race or ethnicity. We turn now to the grim statistics.

On the average, black Americans live about five years less than white Americans. In 1976 the male life expectancy for whites was 69.7 years; for blacks and other races 64.1 years, a gap of 5.6 years. Among females the figures are 77.3 for whites and 72.6 for blacks and other races, a difference of 4.7 years (U.S. Department of Health, Education and Welfare, 1978). Recent data are not available for American Indians, but the 1970 life expectancy for Indians (male and female) was 64.9. If the Indian life expectancy has followed the general trend in the population, it would be a year or two higher today, around 66 or 67. This would be 6 or 7 years less than among the population as a whole.

Infant mortality is also higher among minority groups than it is among whites. The infant mortality rate (number of deaths per year to infants under one year old per thousand live births) was 13.3 for whites in 1976, but 25.5—nearly twice as high—for blacks (U.S. Department of Health, Education and Welfare, 1978). Among American Indians the rate is slightly lower than among black Americans—23.8 in 1971; probably a little lower today (National Center for Health Statistics, 1976).

In addition to living shorter lives and experiencing a greater risk of infant death, members of minority groups experience more illness on the average than do whites. In 1976, black Americans, on the average, experienced 23.3 days of restricted activity due to illness, and Hispanic Americans, 20.3 days. White Americans averaged 17.6 days (National Center for Health Statistics, 1976). If we consider only bed disability, we find a similar pattern. The average number of bed disability days was 9.9 for blacks and 9.3 for Latinos, but only 6.6 for whites (National Center for Health Statistics, 1976).

SUMMARY AND CONCLUSION

We have seen in the preceding pages that very serious racial and ethnic inequalities remain in the United States. It is true that racial and ethnic prejudice and deliberate discrimination have decreased considerably over the past two or three decades, though they have certainly not disappeared. It is true that increasing numbers of black and Hispanic Americans have attained middle-class status, and that some are wealthy and/or highly educated. However, there are still large segments of the black, Hispanic, and American Indian populations who have not shared in the progress and who are trapped at the bottom of the socioeconomic ladder. For them, things are not getting better; indeed, in some ways they are getting worse. Consequently, the overall position of the minority population remains one of substantial disadvantage. In some cases, the gap between the minority populations as a whole and the white population has narrowed only slightly.

The facts in this chapter carry some important implications about the social forces influencing majority-minority relations in America today. Considering the considerable decrease in deliberate discrimination, it would appear that *open and deliberate* acts of discrimination are probably not the main cause of continuing racial and ethnic inequality in America *today.* Rather, today's continuing inequality would appear to be largely the result of two factors. The first is the continuing effects of past discrimination. This discrimination has left a large portion of the minority population—particularly the "underclass," which is near or below the poverty level—without the resources necessary to enjoy a reasonable level of living or to offer one's children much chance for upward mobility. The second factor involves a host of institutional, social, and economic processes that have the *effect* (though often not the intention) of maintaining and sometimes worsening the racial and ethnic inequalities in our society. These processes, which are the legacy of past discrimination and exploitation, impact particularly heavily on the "underclass." Because these processes are so institutionalized and because some advantaged segments of the population benefit from them, there is frequently fierce resistance to any attempts to alter them in a way that would bring about greater equality.

REFERENCES

Biggar, Jeanne C. 1979. "The Sunning of America: Migration to the Sunbelt." *Population Bulletin* 34(1).

Des Moines Register. 1978. "Latinos Likely to Become Dominant Minority in U.S." by Michael Kilian. Copyright 1977, *Chicago Tribune,* January 1, 1978.

Freeman, Richard. 1978. "Black Economic Progress Since 1964." *The Public Interest* 52:52–68.

Goren, Arthur A. 1980. "Jews." Pp. 571–598 in Stephan Thernstrom, Ann Orlov, and Oscar Handlin, eds. *Harvard Encyclopedia of American Ethnic Groups.* Cambridge, MA: Harvard University Press.

Greeley, Andrew M. 1977. *The American Catholic: A Social Portrait.* New York: Basic Books.

———. 1974. *Ethnicity in the United States: A Preliminary Reconnaissance.* New York: John Wiley and Sons.

Hamilton, Charles V. 1978. "Blacks and Electoral Politics." *Social Policy* 9:21–27.

Jacquet, Constant H., Jr., ed. 1979. *Yearbook of American and Canadian Churches, 1979.* Nashville: Abington Press.

Joint Center for Political Studies. 1977. *National Roster of Black Elected Officials,* Vol. 7. Washington, DC: Joint Center for Political Studies.

Mills, C. Wright. 1956. *The Power Elite.* New York: Oxford University Press.

Moore, Joan W., with Harry Pachon. 1976. *Mexican Americans.* Englewood Cliffs, NJ: Prentice-Hall.

National Center for Health Statistics. 1976. *Health Characteristics of Minority Groups.* Washington, DC: U.S. Government Printing Office.

Office of Special Concerns. Office of the Assistant Secretary, U.S. Department of Health, Education, and Welfare. 1974. *A Study of Selected Socioeconomic Characteristics of Ethnic Minorities Based on the 1970 Census. Volume II: Asian-Americans.* Washington, DC: U.S. Government Printing Office.

St. Louis Post Dispatch. 1978. "Social Progress Slow for Chicanos." by Pete Herrera, United Press International. October 31, 1978.

Thomlinson, Ralph. 1976. *Population Dynamics: Causes and Consequences of World Population Change,* second edition. New York: Random House.

U.S. Bureau of the Census. 1981. *1980 Census of Population.* Age, Sex, Race, and Spanish Origin of the Population by Regions, Divisions, and States: 1980. (Report Number PC80-51-1.) Washington, DC: U.S. Government Printing Office.

———. 1980a. *Current Population Reports: Population Characteristics.* "Persons of Spanish Origin in the United States: March 1979." Series P-20, Number 364. Washington, DC: U.S. Government Printing Office.

———. 1980b. *Current Population Reports: Consumer Income.* "Money Income of Families and Persons in the United States: 1978." Series P-60, Number 123. Washington, DC: U.S. Government Printing Office.

———. 1980c. *Current Population Reports: Population Characteristics.* "Educational Attainment in the United States: March 1979 and 1978." Series P-20, Number 356. Washington, DC: U.S. Government Printing Office.

———. 1980d. *Current Population Reports: Population Characteristics.* "Field of Study of College Students: October, 1978." Series P-20, Number 351. Washington, DC: U.S. Government Printing Office.

———. 1980e. *Current Population Reports: Population Estimates and Projections.* "Estimates of the Population of the United States by Age, Sex, and Race: 1976 to 1978." Washington, DC: U.S. Government Printing Office.

———. 1979a. *The Social and Economic Status of the Black Population in the United States: An Historical View, 1970–1978.* Current Population Reports, Special Studies, Series P-23, Number 80. Washington, DC: U.S. Government Printing Office.

———. 1979b. *Current Population Reports: Population Characteristics.* "Population Profile of the United States: 1978." Series P-20, Number 336. Washington, DC: U.S. Government Printing Office.

———. 1979c. *Current Population Reports: Population Characteristics.* "Persons of Spanish Origin in the United States: March, 1978." Series P-20, Number 339. Washington, DC: U.S. Government Printing Office.

———. 1979d. *Current Population Reports: Consumer Income.* "Money Income in 1977 of Families and Persons in the United States." Series P-60, Number 118. Washington, DC: U.S. Government Printing Office.

———. 1979e. *Current Population Reports: Consumer Income.* "Characteristics of the Population Below the Poverty Level: 1977." Series P-60, Number 119. Washington, DC: U.S. Government Printing Office.

———, 1979f. *Current Population Reports: Population Characteristics.* "School Enrollment: Social and Economic Characteristics of Students: October, 1978." Series P-20, Number 346. Washington, DC: U.S. Government Printing Office.

———. 1973. *Current Population Reports: Population Characteristics.* "Characteristics of the Population by Ethnic Origin: March, 1972 and 1971." Series P-20, Number 249. Washington, DC: U.S. Government Printing Office.

———. 1972. *1970 Census of Population.* "General Social and Economic Characteristics: United States Summary." PC(1)-C1. Washington, DC: U.S. Government Printing Office.

U.S. Department of Commerce. 1977. *Social Indicators 1976.* Washington, DC: U.S. Government Printing Office.

U.S. Department of Health, Education, and Welfare. 1978. *Health—United States 1978.* Washington, DC: U.S. Government Printing Office.

Wescott, Diane W., and Robert W. Bednarzik. 1981. "Employment and Unemployment: A Report on 1980." *Monthly Labor Review 104(2):4–14.*

Wilson, James Q. 1978. *Varieties of Police Behavior: The Management of Law and Order in Eight Communities.* Cambridge, MA: Harvard University Press.

43

Family Configuration and Intelligence

R. B. ZAJONC

Variations in scholastic aptitude scores parallel trends in family size and the spacing of children.

In 1962 the average Scholastic Aptitude Test score of high school seniors was 490. In 1975 it barely surpassed 450. This decline has been steady over the last 12 years, and it appears to be continuing. Some educational authorities blame it on television, on the erosion of interest in language skills, or on a widespread craving for freedom of expression that is at odds with disciplined learning, but there is no evidence to support any of these opinions. Nor is there any evidence that the decline in SAT averages is due to the rising numbers of poor and minority students who have taken the tests. In fact, the proportion of such students remained stable in the last several years while SAT scores continued to decrease.[1]

In all likelihood a number of diverse conditions converged to precipitate the decline. In this paper, however, the focus is entirely on one set of such factors, those associated with changing family patterns. I shall try to show generally that variations in aggregate intelligence scores are closely associated with variations in patterns of family configuration, and that these aggregate family factors are deeply implicated in the declining SAT scores as a special case of a general phenomenon that manifests itself also in a variety of national, ethnic, regional, racial, and sex differences in intellectual test performance. For the purpose of this argument, I will first summarize a recent theoretical analysis that specifies the conditions under which family configuration may foster or impede intellectual growth. I will then examine some relevant empirical findings, and finally return to the special case of the SATs.

Table 43.1 is based on a study by Breland[2] in which the averages of nearly 800,000 candidates on the National Merit Scholarship Qualification Test (NMSQT) were examined as a function of family size and birth order. Five features of these results are of particular significance: (i) NMSQT scores generally decline with increasing family size; (ii) within each family size they decline with birth order; (iii) the rate of decline decreases with successive birth orders; (iv) there is a discontinuity for the only child, who scores below a level that would be expected had intelligence declined monotonically with increasing family size; (v) twins have comparatively low scores.

Such effects of birth order and family size on intellectual test performance have been recently explicated in a theory called the confluence model.[3] In this model, Markus and I try to capture the effects of the immediate intellectual environment on intellectual growth, and to specify how individual differences emerge in the social context of the family. The basic idea of the confluence model is that within the family the intellectual growth of every member is dependent on that of all the other members, and that the rate of this growth depends on the family configuration. Different family configurations constitute different intellectual environments. "Intellectual environment" can be thought of in this context as being some function of the average of the absolute intellectual levels of its members. Note that we are not considering IQ, which is a quantity relative to age, but rather an absolute quantity such as mental age. If the intellectual environment is conceived as an average of all the members' absolute "contributions," then it changes continually as the children develop, and it manifests the most dramatic changes when there is an addition to or departure from the family. Of course, abrupt changes in the environment need not have immediate effects.

The confluence model defines intellectual growth of the individual as a function of his age and represents changes in the rate of this growth by a parameter α_τ which is a function of the intellectual environment in the family at time τ. The following examples illustrate, in a simplified form, the dependence of intellectual growth on the changing family configuration. For the purpose of these examples consider the

Table 43.1. Mean Scores on the National Merit Scholarship Qualification Test, 1965, by Place in Family Configuration.[2]

Family Size	Birth Order 1		2	3	4	5
1	103.76					
2	106.21		104.44			
3	106.14		103.89	102.71		
4	105.59		103.05	101.30	100.18	
5	104.39		101.71	99.37	97.69	96.87
Twins		98.04				

absolute intellectual levels of the parents to be 30 arbitrary units each, and of the newborn child to be zero. Thus, the intellectual environment at the birth of the first child has an average value of 20. Suppose the second child is born when the intellectual level of the firstborn reaches 4. The second born then enters into an environment of $(30 + 30 + 4 + 0)/4 = 16$. (Note that since the intellectual environment is an average of the absolute intellectual levels of all family members, the individual is included as a part of his own environment.) If a third child is born when the intellectual level of the firstborn has reached, say, 7 and that of the secondborn is at 3, the family intellectual environment will then be reduced to 14.

These examples illustrate a number of significant consequences that the confluence model predicts. It might appear from these examples that intellectual environment should decline with birth order. That is not so. In itself birth order is not an important variable. The model predicts that its effects are mediated entirely by the age spacing between siblings. Observe that if the second child is not born until the first reaches an intellectual level of 24, for example, then the newborn enters an environment of $(30 + 30 + 24 + 0)/4 = 21$, which is more favorable than the one of 20 entered by the firstborn. Hence, with large enough age gaps between siblings (allowing sufficient time for the earlier born to mature), the negative effects of birth order can be nullified and even reversed.

In principle, the negative effects of family size can also be overcome by age spacing between children. If each child were to be born only after its predecessors reached maturity (to take an extreme example), each successive sibling would enter a progressively more favorable environment, and the average intellectual levels would increase with family size. Of course, older children tend to leave home eventually. Furthermore, biological constraints set limits on the covariation of family size and spacing. Demographic data show that birth intervals invariably decline as family size increases.

The examples above deal only with environment at birth. The confluence model considers the intellectual growth process over time and evaluates all changes in the rates of family members' growth that are caused by the resulting changes in intellectual environment.[4]

The growth parameter α_τ represents an important aspect of this analysis, for it reflects all significant changes in the individual's intellectual environment. But it also reflects the confluent nature of intellectual development within the family context. The intellectual development of all family members is affected by the common familial intellectual milieu. Therefore α_τ is the same for all members at the point in family history τ, a feature of the model which underscores the mutuality of intellectual influences among family members. It may be noted that the later these influences occur in the individual's life, the smaller is their effect.[5]

Representing intellectual environment as some function of the average absolute intellectual levels within the family is obviously a simplification of what is an enormously complex process. Clearly, intellectual growth will not be greatly enhanced by a highly favorable environment if there is no interaction between the child and the people around him. The influence of the parents' and siblings' intellectual levels on the child's growth is necessarily mediated by diverse processes of social interaction that vary from family to family. Ideally the parameter α_τ should represent not only the intellectual levels of the family members but also the amount of time each family member spends with the child. The nature of social interaction in the home also influences intellectual growth; a game of tag may not be as conducive to the development of intelligence as a game of chess. This sort of articulation of the parameter α_r is impracticable at present, not only because of the formal complexity that it would entail but also because we do not yet know how various forms of social interaction contribute to intellectual growth. It will be shown, however, that even though the confluence model ignores much of the richness of the social processes that mediate intellectual growth, it leads to a variety of empirically supported inferences about differences in intellectual test performance among individuals and groups.

FAMILY SIZE

In addition to Breland's study of NMSQT candidates, there are three other studies in which the intellectual test performance of large populations was examined for its relationship to the sort of family variables that, according to the confluence model, influence intellectual development. The earliest of these was carried out in Scotland on 70,000 school children.[6] The more recent ones come from France[7] and the Netherlands[8] and report data for 100,000 and 400,000 individuals respectively. They are summarized in Figure 43.1. To make them roughly comparable, all the averages have been converted into standard deviation units [$X' = (X - \overline{X})/\sigma$, where X's are cell means and $\overline{X}$'s and σ's are the means and the standard deviations of the samples]. There are a number of interesting similarities and differences among the four samples which can be understood if we analyze them in terms of the confluence model.

All four sets of data, even though they are derived from different tests of intellectual performance, different age groups, different cohorts, and different countries, indicate that intellectual level generally declines with family size. Even in the NMSQT sample, which consists of promising students, there is decline with family size. As a result of the selective factor, however, the effect is attenuated in that sample. In others the effect is quite substantial. In the French and Scottish samples the difference between the IQs of children from the smallest and the largest families is about one standard deviation (15 points).

It is well known that family size differs across socioeconomic strata and so does intellectual test performance. The possibility that socioeconomic factors mediated these results must be considered. Three socioeconomic levels (SES) were differentiated in the Dutch sample, six in the French. Both sets of data (Fig. 43.2) reveal that intellectual performance declines with increasing family size independently of SES. In the French sample the partial correlation between family size and IQ was −.45. In fact, it appears that SES contributes to the family size effects only a little, for the correlation rises to only −.47 when SES is allowed to vary freely. Needless to say, socioeconomic status does affect intelligence scores, a fact that is clear from Figure 43.2. The partial correlation between them is .66.

BIRTH ORDER AND SPACING OF SIBLINGS

It is strikingly apparent in Figure 43.1 that in the Dutch and American samples intellectual test performance declines with birth order whereas in the French and Scottish there is no such decline.[9] According to the confluence model, the effects of birth order are totally mediated by the age gaps between successive children, hence these differences in the effects of birth order must be associated with differences in age gaps.

While there is no specific and direct empirical information about age gaps in the four samples, information about national averages in these countries taken from census data can be used. Unfortunately, data on birth intervals are not collected uniformly. (In Scotland no such data were tabulated at all in 1936, when the children in the Scottish sample were born.) Hence, comparisons with regard to birth intervals must rely on indirect indices.

One reliable correlate of birth intervals is, of course, birthrate. When birthrate is high or rising, intervals between successive births are normally quite short; during a period of low or declining birthrate they are longer. For the Dutch subjects (who were born in 1944 to 1946) the corresponding birthrate was rising, from 24.0 in 1944 to 30.2 in 1946. The birthrate in the United States in the year 1948, when most of the NMSQT respondents were born, was 24.2 and also rising. For the French cohorts, however, the birthrate averaged over the years of their births was 18.2 and declining, and the Scottish birthrate in 1936 was 17.9 and declining as well.[10] Hence the differences in intellectual performance associated with birth order (Fig. 43.1) are entirely consistent with the pattern of differences in birthrates in the four countries. Where birth order is least detrimental to intellectual performance, namely in Scotland, is also where birthrate is lowest.

National averages for intervals between suc-

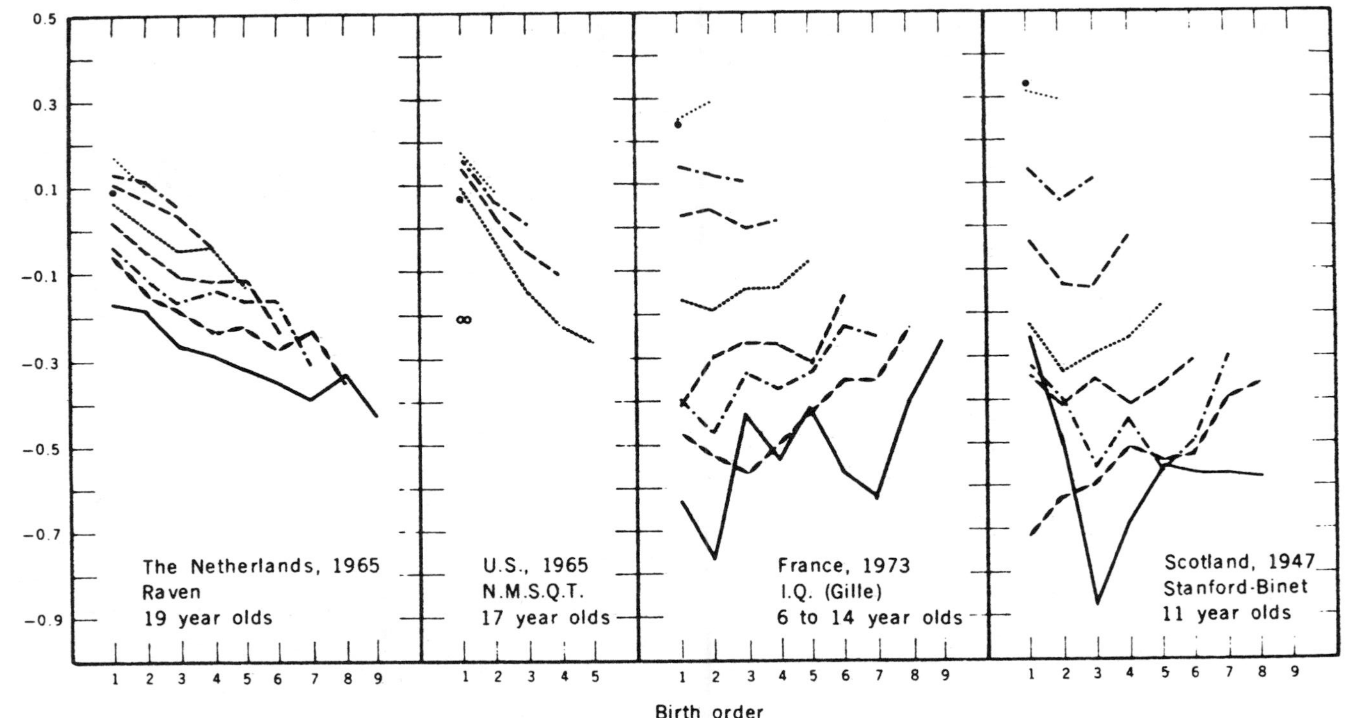

Figure 43.1. Intellectual performance of four large populations, plotted as function of birth order and family size. Separate curves in each graph represent different family sizes, which can be read from the last birth order on each curve. Solid circles represent only children. The double open circle in the U.S. data represents twins. The years show when data were collected. The means of the Dutch, American, French, and Scottish data sets are 2.82, 102.5, 99.2, and 36.74 respectively. The corresponding standard deviations are 1.43, 21.25, 14.53, and 16.10.

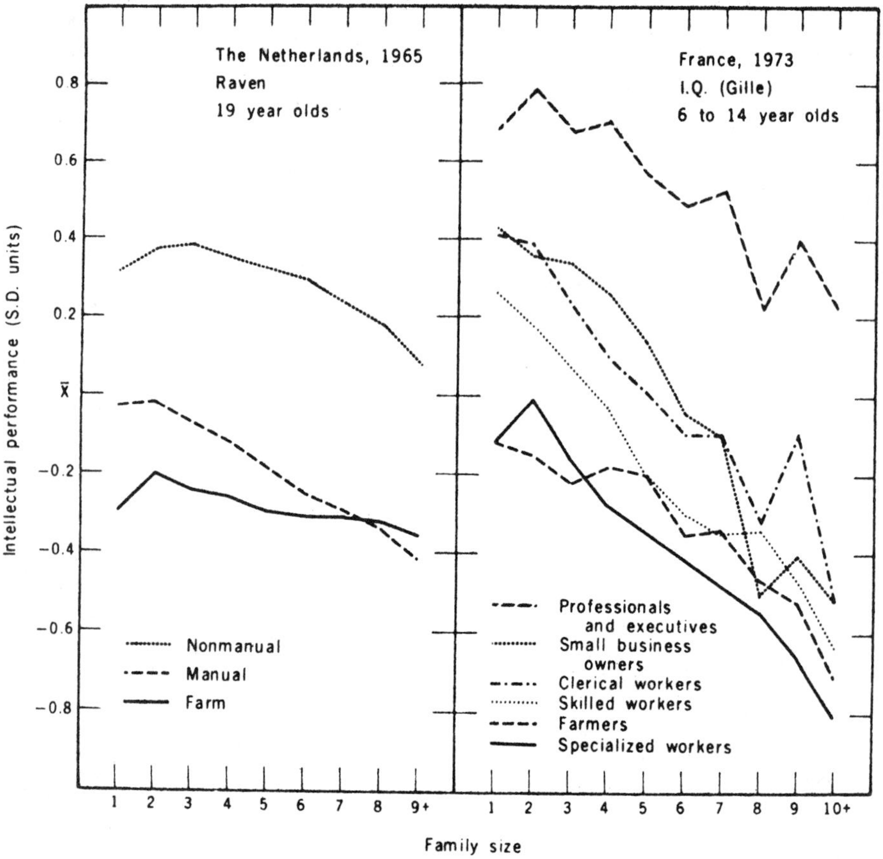

Figure 43.2. Relation of family size and socioeconomic status to intellectual performance in the Netherlands and in France.

cessive births in completed families, that is, families known to have had their last children, have been collected only recently, and they are available for the cohorts from which the French sample was drawn.[11] The intervals for completed families of two to six children are reproduced in Figure 43.3. They are generally quite long. For some of the points in Figure 43.3 comparable data are available from U.S. births of about 1959[12] and from Dutch births of about 1944, both estimated from data on births since marriage tabulated by birth order.[13] The American and Dutch intervals are considerably shorter than the French. For example, the intervals between the first and second births in American and Dutch two-child families were 45.7 and 44.6 months respectively; the French interval was over 60 months. The intervals between the second and third births in American and Dutch three-child families

Figure 43.3. Intervals between successive children in completed French families of two to six children, according to a 1962 survey.[11]

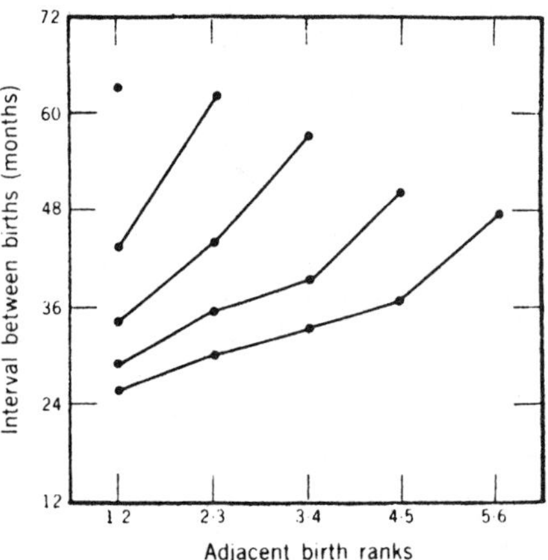

were 45.8 and 47.0 months, again more than one year shorter than in the French. Hence the pattern of differences in birth order effects (Fig. 43.1) is paralleled by a pattern of differences in birth intervals in the four countries such as the confluence model leads us to expect. For the Dutch and American cohorts, in which there is a general decline in intellectual performance with birth order, birth intervals seem generally to be short. For the French and Scottish samples, which do not show such a decline, they are substantially longer.

An interesting trend is observed in Figure 43.3; each successive child appears to be separated from the preceding sibling by an increasingly longer gap. Last children, therefore, come after the longest gap. This trend may explain why there is a quadratic component in the birth order curves shown in Figure 43.1, and why there seems to be in some cases an upswing in intelligence for later-born children.[14]

One other important factor no doubt contributed to the pattern of results in the French and Scottish birth order data. These scores come from children 6 to 14 years of age and 11 years of age respectively. Obviously, children of those ages who are among the eldest in large families cannot be very widely separated in age from their siblings. The youngest in large families, however, can come from sibships with large or small gaps, hence there is no reason to suppose that the gaps of the later-born children differed from the national averages, which we noted were relatively high. If the short age gaps of earlier-born children depress their intellectual performance, their advantage in order of birth could be nullified. Longer gaps between later-born children in these samples may compensate for the depressing effects of late birth order. Together, these factors would produce a pattern of birth order effects such as was found in the French and Scottish samples. These considerations suggest that the differences in birth order effects among the four national samples in Figure 43.1 are associated with differences in age gaps.

There is some other more direct information which indicates that children with large age gaps between them and their younger siblings attain higher intellectual levels than children close in age to younger siblings. In a family of two children, for example, the larger the age separation the longer the older child can remain in an environment undiluted by the presence of an intellectually immature sibling. Long birth intervals give older children the benefits of being in a small family for a longer period of time and during an early phase of growth, which is sensitive to environmental effects. It is also to the advantage of the younger child to postpone its birth, because the later it arrives the more mature will be the environment which it enters at birth and in which it will develop. Higher IQs for pairs of widely spaced children than for closely spaced pairs were indeed found by Tabah and Sutter.[15] More recently, an extensive study of perinatal effects[16] found that children born after long intervals score four points higher on the Stanford-Binet scale than children born after shorter intervals, a difference that was independent of the socioeconomic status of parents.

EVIDENCE FROM TWINS

Twins score consistently and substantially lower on intelligence tests and other tests of intellectual performance than do nontwins. For example, in the National Merit Scholarship sample[2] twins achieved an average score of 98.0, singly born children an average of 102.57. Tabah and Sutter[15] report an average IQ of 89.2 for twins and 101.2 for singly born children among French 6- to 12-year-olds. Other studies agree with these findings.[17,18] Record, McKeown, and Edwards[19] found an average verbal reasoning score of 95.7 for twins and 91.6 for triplets, which are deficits of .30 and .58 S.D. unit. Admittedly, biological factors may be involved here, but deficits for twins and larger multiple births would also be expected according to the confluence model. Twins have of course the shortest possible gaps between successive siblings. Thus, a family with two singly born children and a family with twins represent quite different intellectual environments. For twins who are the first offspring the intellectual environment at birth is $(30 + 30 + 0 + 0)/4 = 15$. In a two-child family the environment of the firstborn is 20, and it must be higher than 15 at the birth of the second child because $(30 + 30 + x + 0)/4 > 15$, since $x > 0$. Hence, with other factors constant, the intellectual environment for twins must necessarily be lower than for either of two singly born siblings.

Perhaps the most important evidence of environmental effects on the intellectual growth of twins comes from another aspect of the Record-McKeown-Edwards study.[19] It follows from the confluence model that the intellectual performance of twins who were separated early in life should be higher than of twins reared to-

Table 43.2. Mean Verbal Reasoning Scores and Mean Birth Weights of Twins, by Fate of their Co-twins [Data from[19]]

	Twins Whose Co-twins					
	Were Stillborn, or Died in First Four Weeks			Survived		
Sex	*N*	Verbal Reasoning Score	Birth Weight (kg)	*N*	Verbal Reasoning Score	Birth Weight (kg)
Males	85	98.2	2.34	967	93.9	2.58
Females	63	99.3	2.22	948	96.5	2.45
Both sexes	148	98.7	2.29	1924	95.2	2.52

gether. Record et al. report that twins whose co-twins were stillborn or died within four weeks achieve nearly the same average intelligence as nontwins. Table 43.2 reproduces these data together with the average birth weights of the subjects. The fact that the birth weights of twins who both survive are higher than of those of whom one dies early suggests that physiological factors, for example oxygen deficiency, that are postulated as explaining the relatively low intelligence of multiple-birth children may have been exaggerated.[20]

PARENTAL ABSENCE

It follows directly from the confluence model that a one-parent home constitutes an inferior intellectual environment and should result in intellectual deficits, and that early loss of a parent should produce greater deficits than a loss occurring at a later age. In most studies of this effect the absent parent is the father, and their results agree with these inferences.[16,21,22] For example, fatherless students scored in the fifty-fifth percentile on the American College Entrance Examination test, while a comparable group from intact homes scored in the sixty-fifth percentile.[23] A recent extensive study of desegregation[24] found children from intact homes scoring 100.64 (S.D. 15.05) on a combined mathematical and verbal achievement test, and children from single-parent homes 95.37 (S.D. 13.95)—a difference of one-third of a standard deviation. Other studies show similar effects.[25–29] Differences in intelligence and in intellectual performance found between children from fatherless homes and from intact homes are greater the longer the father's absence and the younger the child when loss of the parent occurred.[25–27] Interestingly, the most severe deficits are often in the quantitative skills.[22,26] It appears also that, in comparison with other causes of loss of parent, death may have an especially depressing effect on intellectual performance.[30] Although being deprived of a parent is generally accompanied by stress in the home from other sources, such as marital conflict or bereavement, intellectual deficits occur even when the father's absence is temporary and free from these stressful correlates. Children of men in the service,[26] for example, and children whose fathers are frequently absent or not readily available because of their occupation, show substantial intellectual and academic lags.[25] Restoration of adult presence has beneficial effects. Remarriage of the remaining parent, especially if it occurs early in the child's life, results in improved intellectual performance.[30]

Many of the cited studies did not control for socioeconomic factors such as sharp drops in income due to fathers' absence. But deficits in the intellectual test performance of fatherless children are also found when comparisons are made within a single socioeconomic stratum.[16] For example, Carlsmith's subjects[26] were all Harvard undergraduates whose fathers had been in military service; absence of these fathers would not have caused appreciable drop in income. Santrock[30] found similar deficits in samples of white lower-class children.

ONLY AND LAST CHILDREN

In all four sets of data in Figure 43.1 the only child shows a distinct discontinuity with the family size effect; that is, only children score below a level that would be expected if intelligence increased monotonically with decreasing family size. The discontinuity is fairly pronounced. In three out of the four samples, the only children have lower averages than children from families of two, and in the American and the Dutch data lower than from families of three.

A possible explanation may be that only children have fewer opportunities to be teachers. Children with siblings, especially the older children, show their brothers and sisters how to hold a bat or skip rope, help them tie their shoes, explain to them the meanings of new words and rules of new games, warn them about what may get them into trouble, divulge what they may get away with, spot errors and ineptitude and offer critique. One who has to explain something will see from the other's reactions whether the explanation was well understood, and be prompted to improve the explanation, with the consequence that his or her own understanding of the matter is improved. An active participation in an intellective process is decidedly more instructive than a passive participation.[31] Only children do not usually have the chance to serve as such intellectual resources.

Viewing the only child from this perspective makes him or her seem like a lastborn child rather than an anomalous firstborn, which has been the usual characterization.[32] The last child also is usually a nonteacher, since he is unlikely to have skills or information that his older siblings might require. It is interesting that the last child, in at least one of the sets of data in Figure 43.1, like the only child creates a discontinuity in the observed patterns. The discontinuity of the last child, however, is with respect to the effects of birth order. In the Dutch sample the last child declines more than other children, and this decline occurs in all family sizes. In the Dutch data the discontinuity for the last child is equivalent in magnitude to the discontinuity for the only child.[33] Altus[34] reports Scholastic Aptitude Test data from the University of California at Santa Barbara that also fit the foregoing pattern. In two-child families the decline from the first to the second (that is, last) was 20.1 (over one-sixth of a standard deviation). In three-child families the decline from the first to the second child was only 2.1 SAT points, but from the second to the last child was 21.9 points.

The nonteacher deficit can be counteracted in the case of last children. The last child who is born many years after the birth of the next to the last enters an environment of intellectually more mature children—a condition that may overcome the nonteacher handicap. Recall that in France, where lastborns tended to show an upswing rather than a decline (Figure 43.1), intervals for last children were especially long (Figure 43.3). Intervals for last children are also longer than for earlier ones in the United States.[12] Moreover, the teacher role is not entirely closed off to last children, for there must be some occasions when they, too, can serve as resources. For only children the nonteacher handicap cannot be offset or diminished in these ways. The only children should, therefore, produce a consistent discontinuity in the overall family size effect, whereas the discontinuity of the last children in the effect of birth order should be less consistent because of its vulnerability to the effects of spacing. Where the gaps are known to be especially long, as in France, the inordinate drop for the last child disappears (Figure 43.1).

If we consider the effects of gaps together with the nonteacher deficit, then the first child represents an interesting case. As was suggested above, a large gap will allow the firstborn to remain in an "undiluted" environment for a longer period of time and hence benefit his or her intellectual development. But during all this time the child must continue to suffer the nonteacher handicap, which may obliterate the favorable effects of an undiluted environment. The trade-off value between the two opposing factors is not known at present. However, since last children have nothing to lose from the postponement of their arrival, they should show greater beneficial effects of large gaps than should first children. Breland[2] reports just such findings for the NMSQT sample. In two-child families, firstborns with large gaps scored .18 S.D. unit and those with short gaps .17 S.D. unit above the mean of the entire sample. In these families, however, secondborn children with long age separations scored .12 unit above the mean and those with short gaps only .04 S.D. unit. In three-child families the pattern was similar.

In general, it would be expected, according to the confluence model, that the larger the interval between adjacent siblings the more likely that the birth-order effect would be reversed, so that the younger child might surpass the older in intellectual attainment. Breland's data are based on observations of individuals who come from different families. Other studies on the effects of age gaps also utilize subjects whose siblings' intelligence scores are not known. There are very few such studies and they show conflicting results.[35] Most informative would be within-family differences in IQ and their relation to differences in age gaps. One report[36] that meets this criterion contains intelligence scores of a small number of entire families. The percentages of pairs of adjacent siblings in which the elder surpassed the younger in IQ were computed in each of four categories of age gaps. These were 59.2, 54.9, 51.6, and 51.1 percent for gaps of 12.24, 36, and 48 or more months respectively.

NATIONAL, REGIONAL, ETHNIC, AND RACIAL DIFFERENCES

There are by now a large number of studies reporting differences in intellectual test performance among different national, regional, and ethnic groups. Some investigators have attempted to find genetic explanations but most of these differences have, in fact, gone unexplained. It is clear that these differences share at least one factor: variations in family configuration. Setting aside the important question of whether the various tests used are appropriate measures of intellectual ability in different populations, we may consider whether the national, regional, ethnic, and racial differences in test performance can perhaps be better understood on the basis of differences in family configuration of populations. For example, in 1960 the American white family contained on the average 2.27 children, the American black family 3.05. White and black families also differ in the length of intervals between children. In the white population the average intervals between the first and second child, the second and third, and the third and fourth were 26.7, 31.8, and 30.6 months respectively. The corresponding figures for the black population were 23.1, 23.0, and 22.3. The IQs of children born to older mothers are consistently higher.[35] It is interesting, therefore, that the white mother is on the average nearly three years older when she bears her first child than is the black mother. Yet another important aspect of family configuration is the presence of adults in the home; we noted above that the absence of a parent has a depressing effect on intellectual development. Among white Americans, in 1960, 1968, 1970, and 1974 there were respectively 6.1, 7.7, 7.8, and 10.4 percent of households with only the mother present. The comparable figures for black households are 19.8, 27.6, 29.3, and 37.8.[37] It would be surprising if these differences in family configuration between whites and blacks were not seriously implicated in the differences sometimes found between these groups in intellectual test performance.

The evidence examined thus far has involved comparisons of intellectual test performance of the individuals' own family patterns. Studies that compare test performance of national or ethnic groups do not as a rule contain family pattern data of their own respondents. However, since they are sampled from populations whose characteristic patterns of family configuration are often known or can be estimated, the association between family factors and intellectual test performance can be examined indirectly. For example, the average IQs of 5504 children of various ethnic backgrounds in the United States[38] have a correlation with family size in the respective ethnic groups that varies between −.49 and −.69, depending on what demographic index is used to estimate family size.[39] A recent international study obtained measures of reading comprehension for three age groups of school children in a number of countries.[40] In Figure 43.4 reading comprehension scores of one of the age groups (ten-year-olds) is plotted against birthrates in these countries. The intellectual performance scores were obtained in 1971 to 1972; the birthrates are those of 1961 to 1962. The relationship of these scores with the corresponding birthrates is quite strong, and it is nearly as strong in the other age groups.

Figure 43.4. Reading comprehension scores and birth rates (per 1000 population) in 13 countries.[40]

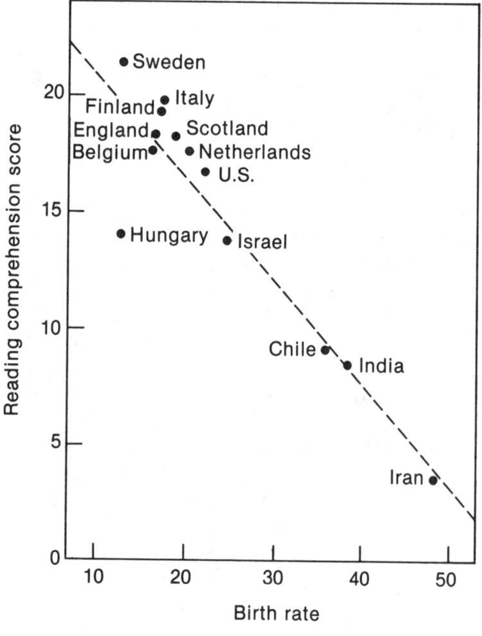

Table 43.3. Average Order of Live Births in France in 1962 and Average Intelligence of French Children Tested in 1973, by Region[4]

Region	Mean Order of Births	Mean IQ	$\frac{X - \bar{X}}{\sigma}$
Picardie-Champagne	3.09	96.5	−.19
Nord	3.08	97.7	−.10
Normandie	3.01	98.7	−.03
Poitou-Centre	2.90	98.1	−.08
Bourgogne-Lorraine	2.86	99.8	.05
Bretagne-Loire	2.82	96.5	−.19
Limousin-Auvergne	2.70	97.5	−.12
Alsace-Strasbourg	2.68	98.6	−.04
Sud-Ouest	2.52	99.1	−.01
Sud-Est	2.42	101.1	.13
Région Parisienne	2.27	102.9	.25

The French survey referred to earlier[7] reports clear differences in IQ among children from different regions of the country. These are paralleled by differences in family configuration. Table 43.3 shows both the average IQ in each region and another aggregate index of family configuration—average order of births—which combines two important factors of intellectual environment, family size and birth rank. In many countries birth records include information about the mother's previous pregnancies and that information is summarized in demographic yearbooks. Average order of births can be readily calculated from these reports.[41] High values of average order of births for a given year indicate that children born that year have on the average more older siblings and come from larger families. The association between this index and average IQ is clearly evident.

There are, of course, other important differences among groups, regions, and countries besides those in birth rates, order of births, and family size. Differences in economic resources, educational opportunities, linguistic habits, and literacy rates, for example, would contribute to these differences in intellectual performance scores. It is not being argued here that variation in family pattern is the only factor implicated in the intellectual differences.

SEX DIFFERENCES

The sort of confounding with socioeconomic or genetic factors which obscures the source of the association between family pattern and regional or ethnic differences in intelligence is totally absent with respect to sex differences. In the United States, the Scholastic Aptitude Test scores of males have tended to be somewhat higher on the average than those of females. In the speculation about factors that might account for sex differences in SATs the possible contribution of family configuration has been thus far overlooked. There are two consistent differences between the positions of males and females in the family configuration. First, the intervals following male births are somewhat longer than those following female births,[42] probably because of parental preference for male offspring. Second, females are more likely to come late in the sibship than are males.[43] This difference in the average order of births of the two sexes is quite small, but in the United States, for example, it has occurred without exception for at least the last twenty-eight years. A preference regarding the sex of offspring cannot explain this second difference. There are more fetal deaths among males than among females. Also, fetal deaths are more likely to occur in later pregnancies.[44] These two factors could combine to produce the consistent sex differences in aggregate birth order.

If sex differences in SAT's are associated with differences in the kinds of family environments that surround males and females, then the magnitudes of sex differences in SAT's should be systematically related to the magnitudes of sex differences in the order of births. In Fig. 43.5 this association (with both differences expressed in ratios) is shown for years in

Figure 43.5. Differences in mean SAT scores of males and females (expressed in ratios) and their relation to sex differences in average orders of live births (also expressed as ratios).

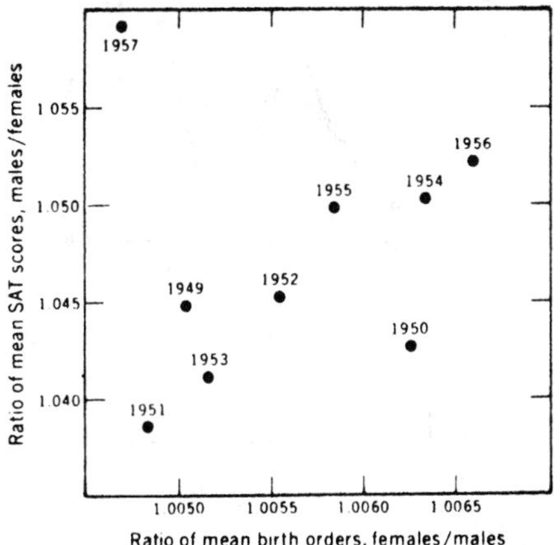

which SAT data were published by sex. Except in 1957, the relation between the two ratios is quite strong. In the large NMSQT sample[2] the pattern is similar: males achieved an average score of 103.45 and females 101.28, a ratio of 1.021. The ratio of birth orders in that sample, female/male, was 1.013. Since the female high school students who take SATs (or the NMSQT) come from the same populations as the male, economic, regional, or linguistic differences could not have contributed to this relationship.

TRENDS IN FAMILY CONFIGURATION

Return now to the marked decline in SAT scores. As with sex differences, short temporal trends in these scores cannot be attributed to socioeconomic factors, let alone to genetic effects. The proportion of poor and minority students remained fairly stable in the period of declining scores.[1] Moreover, if the decline in scores were due to increases in the numbers of poor and minority students taking the tests, the main change in the distribution of the scores would be an increase in the proportion of low scorers, without any changes in the absolute numbers of high scorers. That has not been the case. In 1972, for example, there were 53,794 high school seniors with verbal SAT scores of over 650 (two SDs above the mean). In 1973, when the mean verbal score dropped by 8 points, only 39,779 seniors had such scores.[1]

High school seniors for whom average SAT scores are known were born between 1940 and 1957, and the scores can be compared with the corresponding average birth orders of children born in those years (Fig. 43.6). Except in the World War II years, the association is close indeed.[45] During the war years there was considerable fluctuation in birthrate and thus in average orders of births. Also, the proportion taking SATs was smaller among those cohorts than it is today. But even for the wartime cohorts SAT scores reflect birth order fluctuations to some extent. After 1946 the two trends are virtually parallel. For some recent years the

Figure 43.6. Average order of live births in the United States, 1939 to 1969, and average SAT scores for the first 18 cohorts. Future SAT averages are predicted to lie within the shaded area.

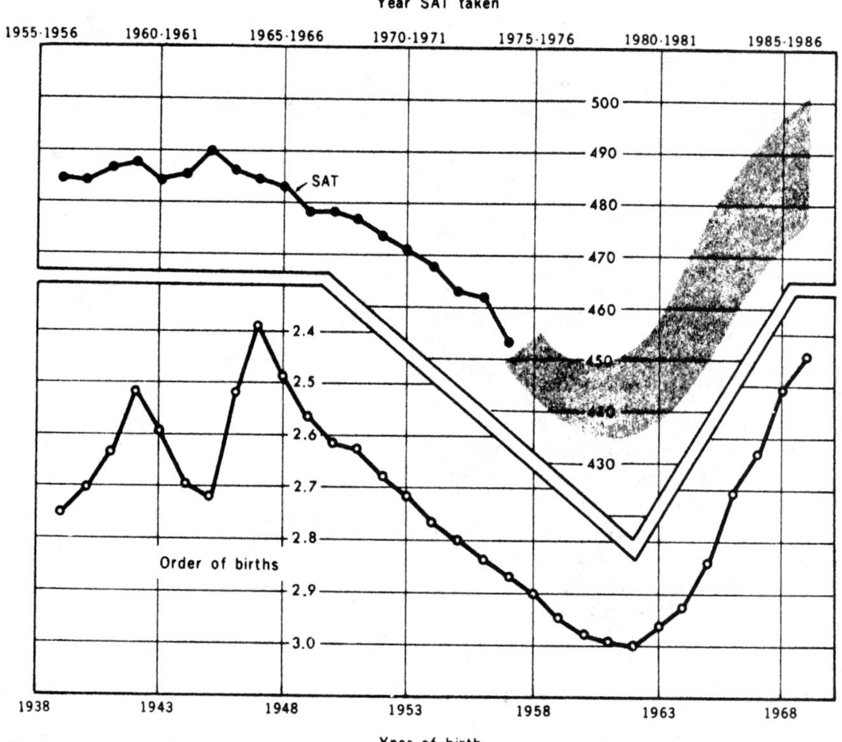

number of high school students with SAT scores above 500 is known. When we compare the percentage of such students with the percentage of firstborns in the respective cohorts (Fig. 43.7) the correspondence is also quite striking.

As may also be seen in Figure 43.6, in 1962 the average birth order begins to rise markedly. Of the 1947 births 42 percent were first children. In 1962 only 27 percent were first children, but the proportion has been steadily increasing, and last year's births include as large a proportion of firstborns as did the 1947 births. Children born in 1963 will be taking the SAT's in 1980. If average orders of births are reliable predictors of SAT scores, in 1980 ± 2 years the alarming downward trend should be reversed. This prospect can be partially verified on younger children, for scores on school tests of children born around 1963 should begin showing increments now. Temporal changes in test scores of Iowa children born between 1953 and 1967, together with aggregate orders of births in that state, are shown in Figure 43.8.[46] There is indeed a rise in scholastic performance which begins exactly with the children born in 1962, when birth orders begin to rise. Similar trends are observed among third-, sixth-, and ninth-graders in New York State (Figure 43.9). That state established a testing program in 1966, at which time a "reference point" was chosen for each of the three grades. The percentages of pupils who surpassed that reference point in reading skills (Fig. 43.9) parallel the changing average order of live births of the cohorts.[47] Beginning with

Figure 43.7. Percentage of SAT scores above 500, 1966 to 1974, and percentage of firstborns in the corresponding cohorts.

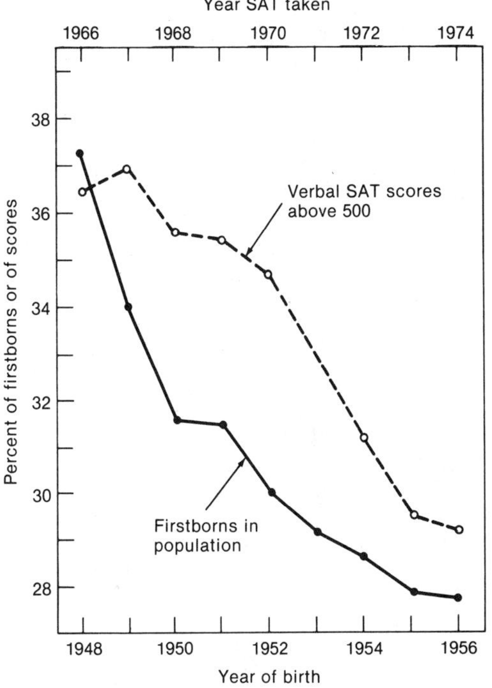

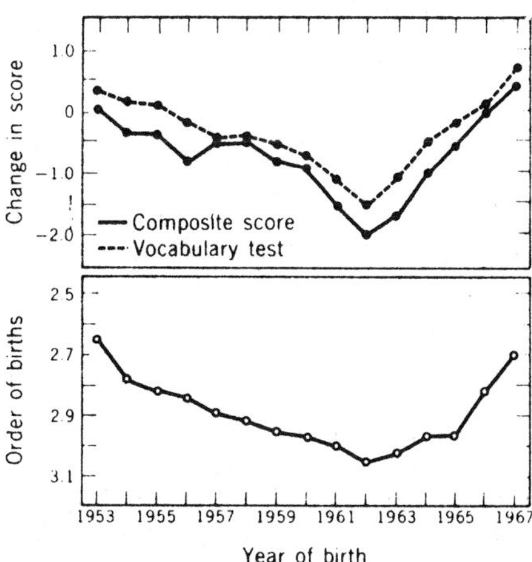

Figure 43.8. Average order of live births in Iowa, 1953 to 1967, and changes in Iowa Basic Skills scores of these cohorts (grades 3 to 8). In the Iowa Basic Skills Testing Program 1965 was designated as the base year, and all scores are reported as deviations from the 1965 average score [46].

Figure 43.9. Average order of live births in New York State, 1952 to 1966, and percent of third-, sixth-, and ninth-grade pupils who surpassed 1966 reference point in reading skill [47].

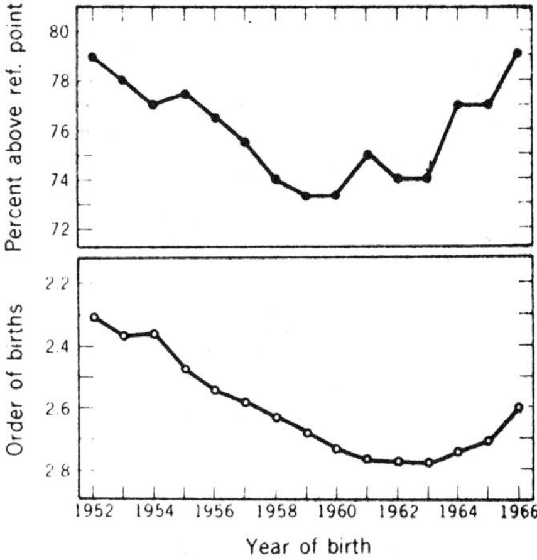

children born in 1963 there is a definite rise in test scores which is coincidental with the sharp reversal in birth trends. Several other states have also reported rising test scores recently in lower elementary grades.

SUMMARY AND CONCLUSION

A variety of findings reveal the impact of family configuration on intelligence: (i) Intellectual performance increases with decreasing family size. (ii) Children born early in the sibship perform better on intelligence tests than later children when intervals between successive births are relatively short. (iii) Long inter-sibling spacing appears to cancel the negative effects of birth order and in extreme cases to reverse them. (iv) In general, long intervals enhance intellectual growth. (v) The adverse effects of short intervals are reflected in the typically low IQ's of children of multiple births. (vi) In the special case of only children, the benefits of a small family are apparently counteracted by the lack of opportunities to serve as teachers to younger children. (vii) Last children suffer that handicap too. (viii) Absence of a parent is associated with lower intellectual performance by the children. (ix) Temporal changes in family patterns such as birthrates, average orders of births, intervals between children, and family size are reflected in temporal changes in aggregate measures of intellectual performance. (x) Differences in family patterns between different countries, between different regions of the same country, and between ethnic or racial groups are also associated with differences in aggregate intellectual performance. (xi) Males and females differ in average birth order, and this difference is reflected in aggregate intellectual performance scores.

The pattern of these diverse data is consistent with the analysis of intellectual development based on the confluence model. Of course, not all variation in intelligence is accounted for by variation in family configuration. For example, in the United States the large decline in SAT scores (over one-third S.D. in 12 years) cannot be a function of changes in family configuration alone because it is considerably larger than we would expect on the basis of a simple extrapolation from the four national samples in Figure 43.1. Nor is all of the sex difference in SAT scores accounted for by the sex difference in orders of births. It should not be overlooked, however, that the average birth orders in these data are based on entire cohorts, whereas SATs were taken by only 25 percent of the children in these cohorts.

Nor is it claimed that the confluence model generates a unique interpretation of all these facts. For each of them one could probably supply another reasonable explanation. The intellectual deficit of twins could have a biological basis, for example, and the higher intelligence of twins who lost their co-twins may involve unknown genetic factors. The drop in SATs may be due to a general decline in intellectual interests, and the lower intelligence scores of children living in one-parent homes may be due to a history of conflict or stress. Future research will shed light on these questions. At the moment, however, the confluence model has the advantage of parsimony. And because it makes rather specific predictions, it can be readily verified.

Lest premature implications be drawn from this paper for family planning, education, population growth, or composition of day care centers, another word of caution is called for. IQ isn't everything. Large families may contribute to growth in attributes other than intelligence: social competence, moral responsibility, or ego strength, for example. These or similar family effects are still to be verified, however.

What contribution can the confluence model make to the controversy between the hereditarian and the environmentalist view of intelligence? Clearly, on the basis of the empirical evidence now available, we cannot evaluate the relative importance of the two factors, and the controversy will not be resolved until we know precisely how these factors influence intellectual development. Hereditarians lack information about genetic loci that might transmit intelligence, and environmentalists have not been able to identify the critical features of the environment that generate intellectual effects.[48] And the two groups suffer equally from ambiguities about what abilities intelligence tests are assumed to measure in different populations.[49] Generally, the environmental case has relied more on attacking the inadequacies of the genetic position than on positive evidence that would establish the role of environmental factors in intellectual development. Moreover, the hereditarian view has had the advantage of a formal model—the polygenic model of parent-offspring resemblance[50]—while up to now there has been no parallel formalization of environmental effects.

Some specific derivations with implications for the analysis of genetic effects on intelligence follow directly from the confluence model. Such analysis utilizes estimates of heritability, some of which involve comparisons between correlations of the intelligence of twins and correlations of the intelligence of nontwin siblings. According to the confluence model, such comparisons must suffer from a confounding with birth intervals. The age gap for twins is, of course, constant at zero, whereas age gaps between other siblings vary. If variations in birth intervals affect the early and the later children differentially (as seems to be the case), heritability indices based on sibling correlations without regard to birth intervals are inaccurate. Similarly, parent-offspring correlations, which are also parts of heritability estimates, are inaccurate if they do not control for birth order, birth intervals, and family size. If there is in fact a close relation between IQ of parents and of children, and if family factors influence the intercept of the corresponding regression line, then combining over birth order and family size simply adds variance around all the points of the regression line and thus attenuates the over-all coefficient. Third, the interpretation of the close intellectual similarity of separated twins may have underestimated the contribution of environmental factors. According to the confluence model, placing twins in two separate environments makes these environments more similar. If two families of the same size adopt twins (or two other individual who do not differ in mental age), the average intellectual levels of these families will be necessarily more similar after adoption than previously. These effects may be quite small. Nevertheless, in inferences about genetic effects drawn from adoption studies the influence that the foster child may have on the foster family environment should be considered.

While aggregate data support the confluence model in a variety of ways, its full usefulness can only be determined when its predictions are tested against a substantial sample of family configurations, examined repeatedly over a period of several years. From such data the relation of the environmental variables that it specifies to the total IQ variance in the sample can be measured. Since it is sometimes asserted that as much as 86 percent of this variance is genetically determined, it would be of some interest to establish just how much can be assigned to environmental factors when the analysis begins with them. Judging from the consistency and magnitude of some of the effects reviewed here, it would be surprising if the variables specified by the confluence model did not account for more than the small fraction allowed by heritability analysis to environmental factors and to error. When we have calculated the variance in IQ that is associated with the environmental variables of family size, birth rank, birth intervals, parental absence, and presence of other adults in the home, and with the portion of the parent-offspring covariation that has no genetic bases, the interplay of genetic and environmental forces in intellectual performance will be better understood.

NOTES AND REFERENCES

1. S. A. McCandless, paper presented at the western regional meeting of the College Entrance Examination Board, San Francisco, 1975.
2. H. M. Breland, *Child Dev.* 45, 1011 (1974).
3. R. B. Zajonc and G. B. Markus, *Psychol. Rev.* 82, 74 (1975).
4. Absolute intellectual level M_t attained by a given child at age t is assumed to develop as a sigmoid function of age. The only child grows according to the function $f(t) = \alpha_1[1 - \exp(-k^2t^2)]$, where α_1, the intellectual environment in the family at birth of the child, is a function of the average of the intellectual levels of all family members including the newborn child, and k is an arbitrary constant that varies with the type of intellectual ability examined or with the scale used for its measurement. The first child of a larger family also grows according to the function $f(t)$ until a sibling is born, at which time the firstborn will shift from $f(t)$ to some other function, $g(t) = \alpha_2[-\exp(-k^2t^2)]$, where α_2 is the new intellectual environment that coincides with the birth of the second child. If there is another child still later, the intellectual growth of the firstborn would change to yet another function, $h(t) = \alpha_3[1 - \exp(-k^2t^2)]$, and so on. If the second child is born when the first is t_1 years old, we can estimate the firstborn's absolute intellectual level M at t_2 from the sum of the two functions $f(t)$ and $g(t)$, where the first is evaluated from age t_0 to age t_1 and the second from t_1 to t_2.

$$M_{12} = f(t)\Big|_{t_0}^{t_1} + g(t)\Big|_{t_1}^{t_2} = \alpha_1[1 - \exp(-k^2t_1^2)] + \alpha_2[1 - \exp(-k^2t_2^2)] - \alpha_2[1 - \exp(-k^2t_1^2)]$$

5. In social and developmental psychology, environmental effects have been generally treated as independent of the individual. Such an approach simplifies analysis, but it is decidedly a misrepresentation of reality. Perhaps when the individual-environment interaction is examined at a fixed point in time an independence of this sort may be assumed. However, when developmental processes and changes over time are involved, specific features of the individual-environment interdependence must be incorporated in the analysis, for if at one time individual A influences the state of individual B, and if later B's state affects the state of A, then A's initial state affects A via changes in B.

   Moreover, treating the environment and the individual as independent units not only violates intuitive notions of social reality, it also leads to inaccurate theoretical implications. If the confluence model did not include the individual in calculating his or her own intellectual environment, later-born children would always be predicted to have environments superior to those of earlier-borns. For example, at the birth of the second child the environment of the firstborn would be $(30 + 30 + 0)/3 = 20$ and of the secondborn $(30 + 30 + x)/3 > 20$, because $x > 0$. This advantage of the secondborn would continue throughout the growth process, and a negative birth order effect would invariably be predicted, a theoretical result that is in clear conflict with data in Table 1 and with other results which will be reviewed below.
6. *The Trend of Scottish Intelligence* (Univ. of London Press, London, 1949); the data used in this article were computed from pp. 101–117.
7. *Enquête Nationale sur le Niveau Intellectuel des Enfants d'Age Scolaire* (Institut National d'Etudes Demographiques, Paris, 1973); the data used in this article are from pp. 25–115.
8. Dutch data in this article were recomputed from L. Belmont and F. A. Marolla, *Science* 182, 1096 (1973).
9. It was conflicting results of this type which prompted some scholars to doubt whether birth order deserves "the heavy investment needed to carry out any more definitive studies" [C. Schooler, *Psychol. Bull.* 78, 161 (1972)].
10. *Demographic Yearbook* (United Nations Publications, New York, 1954), pp. 252–261; ibid. (1965), pp. 276–299. Birthrates are births per 1000 population.
11. J. C. Deville, *Enquête de 1962* (Institut National de la Statistique et des Etudes Economiques, Paris, 1962). The tables were supplied by L. Henry, Institut National d'Etudes Demographiques. Very similar results are reported for 1954 by J. Magaud and L. Henry, *Population* 23, 879 (1968).
12. Bureau of the Census, *Current Population Reports,* Series P-20, No. 108 (Government Printing Office, Washington, DC, 1961), pp. 46–48.
13. *Mouvement de la Population* (Institut National de la Statistique et des Etudes Economiques, Paris, 1967), p. 260; ibid. (1969), pp. 159, 212, 266. The Dutch data were supplied by H. G. Moors and were calculated by G. B. Markus.
14. The quadratic trend is amplified by averaging sigmoid function assumed here to represent intellectual growth.
15. L. Tabah and J. Sutter, *Ann. Hum. Genet.* 19, 120 (154).
16. S. H. Broman et al., *Preschool IQ: Prenatal and Early Developmental Correlates* (Erlbaum, Hillsdale, NJ, 1975).
17. H. L. Koch, *Twins and Twin Relations* (Univ. of Chicago Press, Chicago, 1966).
18. R. B. McCall, M. I. Appelbaum, P. S. Hogarty, *Monogr. Soc. Res. Child Dev.* 38, 1 (1973); S. N. Mehrotra and T. Maxwell, *Popul. Stud.* 3, 295 (1949); L. L. Thurstone and R. L. Jenkins, *J. Educ. Psychol.* 20, 641 (1929).
19. R. G. Record, T. McKeown, J. H. Edwards, *Ann. Hum. Genet. Soc.* 34, 11 (1970).
20. Prematurity of birth, which is common in twins, was found by Koch (n.17) to be unrelated to twin intelligence. Premature twins were not lower on any of the intellectual performance measures than full-term twins.
21. H. B. Biller, *Parental Deprivation* (Lexington Books, Toronto, 1974).
22. D. B. Lynn, *The Father: His Role in Child Development* (Brooks-Cole, Monterey, CA, 1974).
23. B. Sutton-Smith, B. G. Rosenberg, F. Landy, *Child Dev.* 39, 1213 (1968).
24. H. B. Gerard and N. Miller, *School Desegregation* (Plenum, New York, in press).
25. R. W. Blanchard and H. B. Biller, *Dev. Psychol.* 4, 301 (1971).
26. L. Carlsmith, *Harv. Educ. Rev.* 34, 3 (1964).
27. F. Landy, B. G. Rosenberg, B. Sutton-Smith, *Child Dev.* 40, 941 (1969).
28. E. E. Lessing, S. W. Zagorin, W. Nelson, *J. Genet. Psychol.* 117, 181 (1970).
29. Note that the early intellectual environment of twins $[(30 + 30 + 0 + 0)/4 = 15]$ is equivalent to that of the single child in a one-parent home $[(30 + 0)/2 = 15]$. It is interesting, therefore, and supportive of the confluence model, that the deficits in test scores of twins and of children from one-parent homes are similar in magnitude.
30. J. W. Santrock, *Child Dev.* 43, 455 (1972).
31. E. Burnstein, *Psychol. Monogr.* 76, No. 35 (1962); F. I. M. Craik and R. S. Lockhart, *J. Verb. Learn. Verb. Behav.* 11, 671 (1972); R. B. Zajonc, *J. Abnorm. Soc. Psychol.* 67, 96 (1960).
32. J. Sadger, *Fortschr. Med.* 29, 601 (1911); S. Schachter, *Am. Sociol. Rev.* 28, 757 (1963).

33. See (n.3, p. 81). The handicap of the lastborn is represented by a separate parameter λ in the confluence model (n.3, p.86).
34. W. D. Altus, *J. Consult. Psychol.* 29, 202 (1965).
35. V. G. Cicirelli, *Child Dev.* 38, 481 (1967); B. G. Rosenberg and B. Sutton-Smith, *Dev. Psychol.* 1, 661 (1969). A factor that complicates the effects of birth intervals is mother's age at birth of child. Intelligence scores show an increase with maternal age (n.16) that is independent of the effects of birth order [R. G. Record, T. McKeown, J. H. Edwards, *Ann. Hum. Genet.* 33, 61 (1969)]. The relation between the effects of mother's age and birth interval, however, remains to be determined.
36. M. C. Outhit, *Arch. Psychol.* 149, 1 (1933).
37. R. Farley and A. Hermalin, *Am. Sociol. Rev.* 36, 1 (1971). Data for 1970 and 1974 are from an unpublished study by the same authors.
38. N. D. M. Hirsch, *Genet. Psychol. Monogr.* 1, 231 (1926).
39. Family sizes were computed from *16th Census of the United States* (Government Printing Office, Washington, DC, 1940), pp. 127–128, 135–136.
40. Data on reading comprehension are from R. L. Thorndike, *Reading Comprehension Education in Fifteen Countries* (Wiley, New York, 1973), birth rates from *Demographic Yearbook,* (United Nations Publications, New York, 1962 to 1964). The data were plotted against birth rates rather than against average orders of births because the latter figures were not available for three of the countries.
41. Order of live births was computed from *Mouvement de la Population* (Institut National de la Statistique et des Etudes Economiques, Paris, 1969, pp. 535–536. Average order of live births is

$$\Sigma(B_i i)/\Sigma B_i$$

where B_i is the number of live births of the order i. Eighth and later births were combined letting $(i \geqq 8) = 10$.
42. M. P. Schutzenberger, *Sem. Hôp. Paris* 26, 4458 (1950); G. Wyshak, *J. Biosoc. Sci.* 1, 337 (1969).
43. M. S. Teitelbaum, *J. Biosoc. Sci.* 2, Suppl., 61 (1970).
44. J. N. Norris and J. A. Heady, *Lancet* 268 (1955).
45. Birthrates show very similar relationships with SAT trends. For example, the correlation of SAT scores with crude birthrate (births per 1000 population) over the last 18 years is −.61 and with fertility (births per 1000 women of childbearing age) −.71. Minnesota collects scholastic aptitude tests from high school juniors. Over the last 13 years the association between those scores and birth orders in the state was equally high. The scores are in E. O. Swanson, *Student Counseling Bureau Reviews,* vol. 25 (Student Counseling Bureau, University of Minnesota, Minneapolis, 1973), pp. 69–72. The average orders of live births in Minnesota come from *Vital Statistics of the United States,* 1943 to 1955 (Bureau of the Census, Washington, DC, 1945, 1946; Government Printing Office, Washington, DC, 1947 to 1957).
46. These figures were computed from data supplied by W. E. Coffman, Director, Iowa Testing Programs. The figures supplied for 1973 and 1974 had been interpolated from 1972 and 1975. Orders of live births for Iowa were computed from *Vital Statistics of the United States,* 1953 to 1964 (Government Printing Office, Washington, DC, 1955 to 1966).
47. These figures were averaged from data supplied by V. A. Taber, Director, Division of Educational Testing, State University of New York, Albany.
48. L. Erlenmeyer-Kimling and L. F. Jarvik, *Science* 142, 1477 (1963); J. Hirsch, *Educ. Theory* 25, 3 (1975); C. Jencks et al., *Inequality: A Reassessment of the Effects of Family and Schooling in America* (Basic Books, New York, 1972); A. R. Jensen, *Harv. Educ. Rev.* 39, 1 (1969); D. Layzer, *Science* 183, 1259 (1974); J. A. Rondal, *Psychol. Belg.* 14, 149 (1974); S. Scarr-Salapatek, *Science* 174, 1285 (1971); P. Urbach, *Brit. J. Phil. Sci.* 25, 99 (1974).
49. T. A. Cleary, L. G. Humphreys, S. A. Kendrick, A. Wesman, *Am. Psychol.* 30, 15 (1975); L. J. Cronbach, ibid., p. 1; D. Wechsler, ibid., p. 135.
50. C. Burt, *Brit. J. Psychol.* 57, 137 (1966).
51. This research was supported by grant 1-R01 HD08986-01 from the National Institute of Child Health and Human Development. This chapter was completed while I held a fellowship at the Center for Advanced Study in the Behavioral Sciences. I am grateful to Patricia B. Gurin, Gregory B. Markus, Richard E. Nisbett, Howard Schuman, Beth Shinn, and especially Hazel J. Markus for their helpful comments and critique. I also thank Benno G. Fricke, Harold B. Gerard, Albert A. Hermalin, Louis Henry, Sam McCandless, Hein G. Moors, and E. W. Swanson for allowing me to have data they collected and for directing me to important sources of other data, and to Louis Gottfried, David Reames, and David Ravid for their assistance in tabulating some of the results reported here.

PART VII

POPULATION RESEARCH

The study of populations is called demography. The major areas of concern are fertility, mortality, and migration as well as important related characteristics of populations such as age, gender, race, religion, and marital status. In its broadest sense, population research is carried out by a variety of practitioners using the methods of their particular fields such as history, sociology, anthropology, geography, economics, psychology, biology, ecology, or mathematics. Here the goal is often to design policies for, predict, or understand the causes and consequences of demographic phenomena. Ecologists might be interested in the carrying capacity of an area; geographers might want to devise land-use patterns for new settlements; social scientists might want to understand the economic, psychological, or cultural reasons for bearing children; and epidemiologists might want to study the relationship between industrial wastes and infant mortality. This book contains examples of several different types of population studies, including social demography, historical demography, and economic demography.

In its narrower meaning, population research is called formal demography. Much of the effort of demographers goes to preparing the data that will be used in population studies, through endeavors such as a census; the collection of "vital statistics" through surveys or registration systems for birth, death, marriage, and divorce; and in some countries, though not the United States, the registration of internal migration.

In *The Methods and Materials of Demography,* Shryock and Siegel et al. (1973, 1976) have provided a most comprehensive and detailed discussion and critique of demographic data, its collection, and the methods of formal demography. In many countries, particularly the LDCs, demographic data collection systems are so inadequate (or nonexistent) that it is necessary to supplement them with surveys and to apply very elaborate methods of estimation for even basic figures such as the crude death rate. The United Nations (1983) has been primarily responsible for the dissemination of these methods. Haupt and Kane (1978) have prepared an easy-to-follow handbook of the most common demographic terms and methods.

Demographic methods fall into four categories: description, dynamics, estimation, and projection or forecasting. Description includes a detailing of the size, distribution, causes of death, and characteristics of a population at a particular time (see Part VI). Population dynamics is concerned with changes in a population over time which are usually expressed in annual rates such as for births, deaths, migration, marriage, divorce, morbidity (illness), and growth. These rates may be crude, for example, births per 1,000 population, or highly refined, such as births per 1,000 married women aged thirty-five with two previous births and husband present. The more refined a rate, the more information it provides, but it also requires more descriptive data and therefore is more subject to error.

Estimates are made in the absence of data. For example in the United States where a census is taken every ten years the denominator of demographic rates (total population or specific subgroups) must be estimated between censuses, whereas the data for the numerators are collected through ongoing and quite complete registration systems for variables such as births, deaths, and marriages. It is difficult to estimate the size of a local population, and even more difficult to estimate the size of subgroups, especially if the community is experiencing considerable migration. School registration, Social Security receipts, new driver's licenses, and utility hookups may be used to make estimates of migration, population, or subgroups. Another technique is to monitor housing and weight each type by an average household size (usually obtained through a survey) to reach a total population estimate (Watkins, 1984). Often communities are quite surprised by the results of the next census. Yet even parts of a census are estimates because some questions are given only to samples, and because of editing and imputation procedures, which "can also destroy all evidence that particular data are of poor quality and should be used with caution or should not be used at all" (Banister, 1980:1).

Population forecasts and projections are attempts to predict the future. They range from the simple extrapolation of the current situation, for example, the doubling time discussed in the introduction to Part I, to elaborate simulation models of global systems such as those discussed in Part III. In either case, they are totally dependent upon assumptions regarding the unknown. Both the period total fertility rate and life expectancy are forecasts based on the assumption of stable age-specific birth or death rates.

Throughout this book issues regarding the quality of demographic data have been raised. Accuracy and coverage are of concern. In some cases the quality of data is so poor or definitions so varied (for example, what constitutes an urban area) that the data should only be taken as an estimate and not used for any but rough comparison with other units or with the same unit across time. Nevertheless, demographic data are usually reported with several decimal places and analyzed with methods that require interval-level data (equally spaced numbers) even when it might be better to treat them as ordinal (rank order) numbers. The qualifications and footnotes associated with sources of demographic data (e.g., World Bank, 1984; Population Reference Bureau, 1984a) are testimonies to these problems. An announcement that world population growth has declined by 0.3 percent should not be taken too seriously. In the part introductions for this book, we too have been guilty, for the sake of convenience, of using demographic data as if it were quite accurate.

Another important issue is the interpretation of demographic data and their use as social indicators by giving them meaning far beyond that for which they were intended. As discussed in Part II, it maybe appropriate to use the crude death rate (deaths per 1,000 population in a year) as an indicator of the general level of health or risk of dying, but it should not be used for comparisons of populations with different age structures. The Soviet infant mortality controversy, also discussed in Part II, is an example of how demographic data may be given multiple interpretations or may be misused—in this case to serve political ends.

Data regarding fertility, mortality, migration, population distribution, and population structure have already been discussed in their respective sections. The quality of vital statistics were discussed in Chapters 17 and 18. Regarding the accuracy of migration statistics, see Chapter 31 and the insert that follows it. The chapters in this section are concerned with total population as estimated by the U.S. census (Chapters 44 and 45), the projection of local population growth and the "statistical backwardness" of the United States (Chapters 46 and 47). These aspects of demography, it will be seen, are highly controversial. Moreover, they refer to the most fundamental measurement in demography: population size.

Chapter 44 is an elementary introduction to the decennial census of the United States. The U.S. Census Bureau explains how the census is used, particularly for political apportionment and for decisions on the distribution of federal funds. The chapter continues with a description of how the census is taken and deals with issues which include the right to privacy and the completeness of the census. Chapter 44 is somewhat more optimistic and complimentary to the Census Bureau than Chapter 45, in which demographer Philip Hauser examines the census undercount in detail. Hauser notes the federal suits leveled against the Census Bureau by cities which assert that the census has undercounted their populations. Such an undercount, as implied by the Census Bureau in Chapter 44, can result in political underrepresentation and loss of federal funds, so the reasons for the lawsuits are readily apparent. Hauser concludes by suggesting alternative methods that may be used to adjust the census for differential undercounting.

In Chapter 46, Lee et al. describe the United States as a "backward nation" with regard to population statistics. By comparison with other more developed countries, the United States collects less information less frequently, with the result that extensive estimation is necessary. As Lee et al. note, for large populations like that of the United States, or California or New York, this is much less a problem than for smaller populations like those of Nevada or smaller areas within states. Even for national populations, however, projections may be problematic. One would think that projections of the elderly population, in particular, could be made with a fair degree of precision (after all, they have already been born and we have some idea of age-specific death rates), but as Preston (Chapter 41) documents, even national projections of the U.S. elderly population between 1971 and 1981 were off by 61 percent. The crucial factor here is that social, economic, and demographic processes change over time in ways that may not be predictable, leading to what the Population Reference Bureau (in the insert before Chapter 7) calls "demographic surprises" like the baby boom in the 1950s and the migration turnaround in the 1970s.

In the final chapter, Moen examines a case study of problems in population projection, then extends the analysis to the problem of population projection for small areas generally. Boom and bust cycles, the need for more detailed data, and standard but faulty assumptions about market conditions are among the pitfalls that population forecasters face when attempting to project or predict future population characteristics, especially at the local level. Our final note, then, is one of caution: Although population forecasts can be made, sometimes with surprisingly high accuracy (especially in the short term and for large populations), they need to be continually updated as the conditions upon which they were based change over time.

FUR FURTHER READING

1. Henry S. Schryock, Jacob S. Siegel, and associates. 1976. *The Methods and Materials of Demography,* condensed edition by Edward G. Stockwell (New York: Academic Press). The standard tome on demographic methods, definitely for the more advanced (and determined) student.

2. Roland Pressat. 1972. *Demographic Analysis* (Chicago: Aldine). For the more advanced student, shorter but in some respects more technical than Schryock and Siegel.

3. Nathan Keyfitz. 1968. *Introduction to the Mathematics of Population* (Reading, MA: Addison-Wesley). For those who survived Schryock and Siegel, Pressat, and four semesters of calculus.

4. For a brief, readable summary of demographic measures at the elementary level, see Arthur Haupt and Thomas T. Kane. 1978. *Population Handbook.* Or 1980. *Population Handbook: International Edition* (both Washington, DC: Population Reference Bureau).

5. Andrei Rogers. 1985. *Regional Population Projection Models* (Beverly Hills, CA: Sage). Also for advanced readers, a review of population projection techniques. Development of theory and step-by-step instructions for multiregional, multistate population projections which take age and interregional migration into account. A large step beyond conventional demographic accounting methods.

6. There are several sources of demographic and related data, the most important of which are the annual *World Population Data Sheet* of the Population Reference Bureau, the annual *Demographic Yearbook* of the United Nations, and the annual *World Development Report* of the World Bank and the many country, regional, and global studies of the United Nations. For the United States, there are the U.S. Bureau of the Census and the U.S. Center for Health Statistics. The most readable source is the annual U.S. Statistical Abstracts, published by the Census Bureau. Some of this material is very advanced. Also, see Ruth L. Sivard. 1985. *Women . . . A World Survey* (Washington, DC: World Priorities) for extensive data on women.

44
Why Have a Census?

U.S. BUREAU OF THE CENSUS

A Pennsylvania newspaper once told of a census taker's interview with an elderly woman who lived in the mountains and knew nothing about the census.

"Every ten years," the census taker explained, "the government tries to find out how many people there are in the United States."

"Lordy, honey," the woman replied, "I sure don't know."

Neither would anyone else without a systematic count of the population, or census.

The Constitution of the United States requires a census every ten years, but the census is not an American invention. Civilized nations have been counting their people for centuries. In ancient Egypt, people had to list their names, addresses, occupations—even their scars—every fourteen years. One Roman ruler decreed that anyone who didn't answer the census honestly and completely was liable to forfeit all possessions, be whipped, and sold into slavery. Today at least 125 nations around the world conduct censuses.

Why? The answer is sound management.

To function productively and efficiently as a society we must know about ourselves—our numbers, certainly, but also our locations, conditions, problems and needs. Facts and figures on such aspects of our lives are imperative for sound self-management. Our needs for such facts and figures increase as our society grows larger, becomes more complex, and changes more quickly.

THE CENSUS HELPS REPRESENT YOU IN GOVERNMENT

The census is essential to representative government in our Nation, for it helps assure that every person is fully represented in Congress.

The Constitution provides that each state shall be entitled to two seats in the U.S. Senate and at least one seat in the House of Representatives, regardless of population. The remainder of the 435 House seats are reapportioned among the states every ten years on the basis of their population using census counts.

If there were no other reasons for the census, this one alone would justify the enumeration every decade and make it extremely important for everyone to be counted.

Also, within each state the census helps assure balanced representation. Under the one-person, one-vote principle established by the Supreme Court in the 1960s, states are required to achieve a high degree of equality in the number of persons in congressional districts. Some state courts permit deviations of not more than 1 percent from the average population of election districts in that state.

Moreover, to assure balanced representation, many states also use census statistics for redrawing their own legislative districts. The law now requires the Census Bureau to provide data to every state for this purpose.

Every citizen should seek to be counted by the census so that he or she can be sure of being properly represented in our government.

GOVERNMENT PLANNING, GOVERNMENT SHARING

The census helps guide the allocation throughout the Nation of billions of dollars in federal funds. Included in the sharing of federal revenue with state and local governments and the distribution of grants-in-aid for the support of more than 100 programs, totaling about $50 billion annually.

Census data are useful for:

- Determining whether a particular government program is needed, and why.
- Deciding where the program would be carried out.
- Determining how the program should be operated.
- Managing the program.

Almost every question in the census questionnaire is aimed toward helping to fulfill these needs.

GOVERNMENT PROGRAMS DEPEND ON CENSUS INFORMATION

The following are a few of the federal programs that rely on census population and housing data in the distribution of funds to local areas—your communities:

Employment and Training
Health Services
Mental Health Centers
Housing and Community Development
Vocational Education
General Revenue Sharing
Educationally Deprived Children
Federal Aid to Highways
Special Programs for the Elderly
Water and Waste Disposal
State Reading Improvement Program
Nutrition for the Elderly
Unemployment Insurance
Alcohol and Drug Abuse
Headstart
Handicapped Children
Community Action Programs
Vocational Rehabilitation
Student Loans
Highway Safety
Agricultural Research
Energy Research and Development
Airport and Airway Development
Summer Programs for Disadvantaged Youth
Land and Water Conservation
Cooperative Extension Service
Law Enforcement Assistance
Rural Development
Industrial Development
Emergency School Aid
Anti-Recession Assistance
Summer Youth Recreation
Indian and Native American Employment
Comprehensive Employment and Training Act (CETA)
Senior Community Service Employment Program
Public Library Construction and Services

At the state level, census information guides the distribution of additional billions of dollars in state government funds to local jurisdictions. Thus participation in the census by every resident helps assure that his or her community will receive a fair share of federal and state funds.

RELATED USES OF CENSUS INFORMATION

How census facts and figures influence planning, management, and funding requirements can be illustrated by the Nutrition Program for the Elderly. Congress initiated the program on the basis of population information on the national numbers and needs of elderly persons. Funding was to be based on state populations of people over sixty years of age. The census provides the answers, and most recently, $242 million was distributed among the participating states in 1978.

State and local governments have also used the census to determine where the nutrition program is most needed. For instance, in Indianapolis the Mayor's Task Force on Aging asked the Census Bureau to pinpoint the twenty small areas of the city with the highest concentrations of senior citizens. The Bureau supplied the data, and by the following year nutrition centers for the elderly had opened to serve each of those twenty locations.

Following are a few more samples of the value of census information:

- Census data were used in choosing a new location for, and laying out an entire Pennsylvania village—Nelson Township—when the old site had to be abandoned because of a flood control project.
- In Maine, census statistics were used to obtain federal funds for a winterization program to help low-income people with weatherstripping, insulation assistance and fuel payments.
- In Dallas, a local business owner studied census information while trying to decide whether to open an expensive private restaurant and club in the Red Bird Shopping Center.
- In Stamford, Connecticut, city leaders studied census statistics before deciding where to locate a new fire station.
- In Pennsylvania, Foodarama Supermarkets use census data when determining where to open new grocery stores.
- In Maryland, church leaders studied census

population figures before deciding to establish a new Presbyterian church in Edgewood.

- In Fort Smith, Arkansas, Mrs. McKeever's fourth-grade class relied upon census data to estimate how much energy America's fourth graders could save in a year.
- In Central Falls, Rhode Island, local officials found census statistics helpful in obtaining Federal funds to open the Blackstone Valley CAP Health Center.
- In San Francisco, transportation planners will use census information when selecting bus routes, subway stops, and highways that need widening.
- In San Antonio, Texas, bankers studied census data while deciding whether to open a new bank in the Ingram Park Mall.
- In Albany, Georgia, officials used census figures to help prove the need for expanding the Palmyra Nursing Home.
- In Spartanburg, South Carolina, citizens used census statistics to help obtain Federal money to convert Old Evans Junior High into a social services and senior citizens center.
- In many States, census statistics help Boy Scout leaders project how many boys might be joining the Scouts and how many camps would be needed to accommodate them.

HOW THE CENSUS WILL BE TAKEN

The challenge of the census will be to gather an estimated 3.3 billion items of information from more than 220 million people in approximately 80 million households spread over 3.6 million square miles of territory—all within a short period of time. Obviously, a tremendous amount of careful planning and coordination are required to reach so many people effectively.

To save time and enhance the convenience of answering the census, the mail will be used extensively. The system will work this way:

On March 28, 1980, every household will receive, through the mail, a census questionnaire. About 90 percent of the households, including those in more populous areas, will be asked to fill out the questionnaires and to return them by mail in postage-free envelopes.

The remaining 10 percent of the Nation's households will be asked to complete the questionnaires and hold them for census takers to pick up personally. This will occur in more sparsely settled areas. Sending out census enumerators in such regions will help to assure that a questionnaire is obtained from every household.

In Puerto Rico, the Virgin Islands, Guam, American Samoa, the Commonwealth of the Northern Mariana Islands, parts of Alaska, and the Trust Territory of the Pacific Islands, census takers will be used in various procedures to call on households.

THE QUESTIONNAIRE

During the first census in 1790—when the population was about four million—some people complained to President George Washington that the census was seeking information that was none of the government's business. Some people still feel that way.

Actually, almost every question posed by the census is important to federal and local governmental programs designed to benefit you, your neighbors and your community. Not one question is included out of simple curiosity. Most questions provide answers that guide national and local government programs.

Decisions on the specific questions in the 1980 questionnaire were made following five years of research among thousands of users and potential users of census information. This work involved local meetings in 70 cities in all 50 states and coordination with members of Congress, other governmental officials, the governors of the states, national minority interests, and the Census Bureau's nine advisory committees.

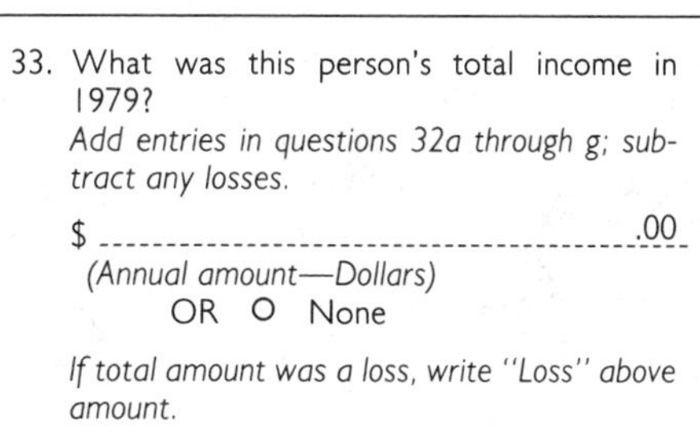
33. What was this person's total income in 1979?
Add entries in questions 32a through g; subtract any losses.

$ ______________________ .00
(Annual amount—Dollars)
OR O None

If total amount was a loss, write "Loss" above amount.

People often wonder why a particular question must be asked. Actually, every question has its purpose—such as this and other income questions, used as criteria of need by the government programs shown here: General revenue sharing; Aid to Families with Dependent Children; CETA jobs; Industrial development grants; Drug abuse prevention grants; School Breakfast program; Urban and rural community action programs; Race, sex discrimination in hiring and pay.

Each and every question has one or multiple purposes, and each question is important.

The questions are simple. Many people will be able to answer the short form in fifteen to twenty minutes; the long form will typically take about forty-five minutes to complete. Accompanying each questionnaire will be an instruction sheet providing easily understood guidance on filling out the questionnaire. All anyone will need is a pencil to fill in the appropriate circle beside each question or write in a word or two.

But—again in the interest of saving the public's time and tax dollars—all 80 million households will not be asked all of the census questions. There will be, in fact, two questionnaires. One will contain only nineteen questions, the other posing an additional forty-six questions. Nationally, about one in six households, selected at random, will receive the longer form, although in some small communities half the households will receive it. The remaining five-sixths of the households will receive the short form.

THE RIGHT TO PRIVACY

Every person's answers to the 1980 census are confidential, by federal law. That is an assurance the Census Bureau makes to everyone. The only people who can see individual answers are Census Bureau workers under oath not to reveal them. The penalty would be a fine up to $5,000 and/or five years in jail. Permanent modern laws about census confidentiality have been in effect since 1929, and the Census Bureau has never violated those laws or even been seriously accused of doing so.

No individual names or addresses provided on the 1980 census questionnaires will be entered into any computer, and Social Security numbers are not requested. No outsider—not even another federal agency—is given access to census answers which identify a specific person. The Census Bureau publishes summary statistics that do not reveal facts about a particular person or household.

After the census questionnaires have been microfilmed, the questionnaires themselves are shredded, dissolved in acid, and recycled as paper pulp. The microfilm will be kept for seventy-two years under lock and key at a special Bureau facility in Pittsburg, Kansas, where there are no computers, not even for the most innocent purposes. In the year 2052, the microfilms from the 1980 census will be made public for the purposes of historical research.

The Census Bureau has never broken its promise, backed by law, to respect the confidentiality of census data, though that promise has sometimes been put to the test:

- Fifty years ago, the Secretary of State asked the Census Bureau for data about specific farms in the State of Washington, where clouds of sulfur dioxide from a Canadian smelter damaged crops. An international tribune was investigating the incident. Request denied.
- Some thiry years ago, the Attorney General requested census information about certain people in connection with a rising concern about sabotage and foreign infiltrators. Request denied.
- Five years ago, a major corporation asked a U.S. District Court judge to order that census information about its competitors be made available as courtroom evidence. Request denied.

TABULATING THE 1980 CENSUS

What happens to the millions of census questionnaires after people have answered and returned them?

Step by step, here are the highlights of the processing procedures:

- Following a review for completeness at one of the 409 district offices, your questionnaire will be shipped to one of three processing centers—Jeffersonville, Indiana; New Orleans, Louisiana; or Laguna Niguel, California.
- With a special camera at one of these three centers, a microfilm will be made of your questionnaire. Your address and phone number are face down during this process, so they are not microfilmed.
- The microfilm then goes to an optical scanner that will "read" your answers and transmit this information electronically to the Census Bureau's computers in Suitland, Maryland. The optical scanner is sensitive only to the circles you will have checked. It cannot transmit handwriting so your name is electronically prevented from being passed on to a computer. As noted earlier, your name and address never go into any computer.
- Now the computers add up the raw statistics on population and other matters, state by state.
- Population counts of the states must be presented to the President by January 1, 1981, for purposes of congressional reapportionment. Counts for all counties, cities, and other recognized subdivisions must be given

to each state by April 1, 1981, for use in redistricting.

TOWARD A COMPLETE AND ACCURATE COUNT

It is always the aim of the census to try to count every U.S. resident, even though an absolutely perfect count is impossible.

For many years, the Census Bureau has heavily invested in time, money, facilities, and research into the development of continually improved techniques for conducting the census, with notable results.

What is called the "undercount" of the population, first estimated by the Bureau on its own initiative about thirty years ago, has lessened appreciably in the more recent censuses. In 1950, the undercount was shown to be 3.3 percent of the total population. In 1960 it was reduced to 2.7 percent, and in 1970 it fell to 2.5 percent.

After the 1970 census the Bureau undertook the greatest effort in its history to help assure, in 1980, a count as complete as possible. The Bureau is especially concerned about reducing differentials in the undercount among minorities and regions of the Nation. The 1980 plans call for:

- Improvements in the canvassing by the census takers of their assigned areas, and tighter quality control on the canvassing.
- Greater use of information sources such as driver's licenses to help identify, locate, and be sure everyone is counted.
- Special techniques for locating and counting persons traveling in the United States and migrant workers.
- More careful checking of individual questionnaires with respect to persons living in or visiting a household.
- Improved methods for the compilation of mailing lists, and for reviewing and checking the lists, to be sure everyone receives a questionnaire by mail.

Minority Programs

Special programs, some going back several years, are aimed toward the counts of the minority elements of the population. These include Black, Spanish origin, Asian and Pacific American people, American Indians, Eskimos, and Aleuts.

The Bureau's Minority Statistics Program informs minority groups of the value of census data about themselves, aids them in using such data, and gains their advice and cooperation in improving the quality of minority statistics.

The National Services Program carries out a nationwide communication task with exhibits and workshops aimed at informing and gaining the support of large minority-interest groups.

The Community Services Program includes some 200 specialists who conduct educational and promotional work with neighborhood, citywide, state, and regional organizations, fostering grass-roots support for the census.

Local Programs

Because of the importance of participation in the census by State and local governments, the Census Bureau has established two major nationwide activities as further steps to help insure complete and accurate counts of the population and housing—the Local Review Program and Complete Count Committees. Both activities will focus on the approximately 39,000 governmental units throughout the Nation.

The Local Review Program will invite the assistance of local government officials in spotting possible errors in the precensus counts of addresses and, after the census, in the statistical totals for their areas. The latter review will be accomplished while census workers are still in the field, permitting verification of any recommended changes.

The Complete Count Committees will consist of citizens appointed by the principal elected officials in the States, counties and municipalities. Their purpose, in conjunction with local government activities, will be to encourage public cooperation with the census.

YOUR HELP IS NEEDED

The requirement for accuracy and completeness in the 1980 census is greater than at any time in our history. Thus, more than for any prior census, the Census Bureau is seeking widespread support.

The more important benefits of this census effort will not be just more accurate statistics as such. Rather, the benefits extend to all the uses of census facts and figures in guiding both our private enterprise system and our federal, state, and local government programs, which affect you and your family every day and will directly influence the future well-being of the entire country.

You can help both yourself and your country by cooperating fully with the census.

45
THE U.S. CENSUS UNDERCOUNT

PHILIP M. HAUSER

BACKGROUND

Prior to the 1940 Census of Population, the officials of the U.S. Bureau of the Census, largely nonprofessionals, insisted that the census canvass counted everybody in the nation. Beginning with the 1940 census and the increasing professionalization of the census staff, not only was it publicly acknowledged by the bureau that there was a net undercount of the population, but also efforts were made within the bureau to measure the undercount. Such efforts, some in cooperation with demographers and statisticians outside the bureau, discovered that the undercount differed by sex, age, race, ethnicity, and geographic area.

In the United States, undercounts have political as well as statistical significance. That is, under provisions of the U.S. Constitution differential population undercounts affect representation in the U.S. House of Representatives and in state and local legislative bodies and, under various federal grant programs, also affect the distribution of funds to states and localities—funds that reach over $50 billion for fiscal year 1980.

Census publications report that, based on bureau research, the 1950 population census failed to enumerate 3.3 percent of the population, the 1960 census, 2.7 percent, and the 1970 census, 2.5 percent. Translated into absolute numbers the 1970 census failed to enumerate some 5.3 million persons.

Census publications have also reported differential underenumeration. Differential undercounts by sex for the same three censuses were:

	1950	1960	1970
Males	3.8%	3.3%	3.3%
Females	2.8	2.2	1.8

Differential undercounts by the age of the person also occurred. In general the underenumeration was greater for the age groups of greater mobility—those in their late teens, in their twenties and thirties. Undercounts were smaller for the less mobile younger and older age groups.

The census undercount, as reported by the bureau, also varied by race as follows:

	1950	1960	1970
White	2.5%	2.0%	1.9%
Black and other	9.7	8.1	6.9
Black alone	—	8.0	7.7

It may be seen that, although completeness of enumeration improved somewhat over the years, the undercount of blacks for each of the censuses was about four times that of whites.

The degree of underenumeration can become very high when a "worst case" example is observed. Reflecting the combined adverse effects of sex, age, and race on completeness of enumeration, census demographers have estimated that black males twenty-eight years of age were undercounted by 22 percent in the 1970 census. Thus, only 78 percent of twenty-eight-year-old black males were counted for purposes of congressional apportionment or for the allocation of federal funds based on population distribution.

For technical reasons it has not been possible to obtain as reliable estimates of underenumeration by ethnicity of the population as by sex, age, and race. This follows because the estimation procedures, which will be further explained below, involve measurements of fertility, mortality, and net migration. Such data have not been available in the United States by ethnicity. Nevertheless, some studies have been made by census personnel on the underenumeration of persons of Hispanic origin—the second largest minority group in the United States. The conclusion reached was that persons of Spanish origin were undercounted at a rate between that of the white and black populations, but at a rate closer to that of blacks than of whites.

It is also relatively difficult to measure undercount by geographic areas within the nation. But it is estimated, for example, that in the 1970 census the undercount in the South was greater than in the North. The reason for this, it is held, is that the South has a larger proportion of blacks than the North, is more rural, and has more poverty. It is harder to obtain accurate listings of households in rural than in urban areas, and poverty is characterized by inferior housing, which is often more difficult to locate.

Since the components involved in the estimation of census undercounts are subject to error, so are the measurements of the undercounts. When better statistics on emigration from the United States became available, the Bureau of the Census in 1980 revised the estimate of 1970 census underenumeration. The revised measurement of the 1970 net undercount was 2.3 percent, down from the original estimate of 2.5 percent. In absolute numbers, the 1970 census undercount was reduced from 5.3 million persons to 4.7 million. Although net underenumeration was lowered in the revised measurement, the differences between black and white undercounts remained large. Black males of all ages in the revised data were undercounted by 10.1 percent compared with 2.1 percent for white males; and black females were undercounted by 5.3 percent compared with 0.9 percent for white females.

THE DISPUTE

The known census differential underenumeration of persons by race led to the filing of lawsuits in the federal district courts in Detroit and in New York City claiming that the greater census undercounts of blacks and persons of Spanish origin deprived blacks and Hispanics of equitable representation in the U.S. House of Representatives and in state and local legislative bodies and discriminated against political areas with relatively large proportions of blacks and Hispanics in the allocation of federal funds based on population distribution. The plaintiffs asked the courts to require the adjustment for differential undercounts of the 1980 census statistics for use for purposes of reapportionment and for the allocation of funds.

The federal district courts in Detroit and in New York City found in favor of the plaintiffs and forbade the Bureau of the Census to publish its 1980 population census counts without adjustment for differential underenumeration. The Bureau appealed to the U.S. Supreme Court, as a result of which the prohibition to publish was removed but the substantive issue was not resolved.

The Bureau's appeal to the U.S. Courts of Appeal on the substantive issue remained unaffected. However, the appelate courts in due course overturned the district court decisions on legalistic grounds, also without adjudication of the substantive issue (the validity of the adjustments requested by the plaintiffs). In consequence, it is still possible that either through rehearings in the courts of appeal or in the U.S. Supreme Court the adjustment of the census data for differential undercounts for reapportionment and fund allocation purposes may still be required, if not for the 1980 census, then for subsequent censuses.

At the time of the court proceedings, the magnitude of the 1980 census undercounts had not been determined, nor had the population totals been compiled. However, it was acknowledged by census officials that differential undercounts were likely. As the 1980 census count of the total U.S. population became known, to the surprise of demographers in the Bureau of the Census, and of other demographic experts, the total population figure was about 5 million greater than had been anticipated by the bureau.

The Bureau of the Census had, as for prior censuses, prepared estimates of the 1980 population for the United States as a whole. In earlier censuses the error of closure—the difference between the estimated population and the census counts—was a fraction of 1 percent. In 1980 the error of closure was unprecedently high, 4.8 million persons or 2.13 percent. Moreover, the greater than expected number was very close to the estimated net underenumeration in the 1970 census population. Thus, it was possible, even if unlikely, that the 1980 census was the most complete census ever conducted in the United States and that no underenumeration had occurred. This possible explanation, however, was short lived. Bureau of the Census evaluation of possible undercount, required by the district courts, led to preliminary measurement of the 1980 census undercount. The preliminary finding, despite the unexpectedly large total population figure, disclosed that there was differential underenumeration by sex, age, and race in the 1980 census as in prior censuses. Moreover, it became apparent that the unexpectedly high total population figure was in all probability attributable to the increase in illegal aliens who entered the nation across the Mexican border with the United States. For example, California and Texas, states bordering Mexico, each had over a million more persons according to the 1980 census count than had been expected in published bureau projections. Other states in the path of Mexican immigration also had higher population counts than had been projected by the bureau.

THE BUREAU OF THE CENSUS POSITION

The Census Bureau, with increasing professionalization since 1940, not only acknowledged that there was a differential undercount but also commenced studies to measure and improve census coverage. For the 1980 census the bureau had introduced a number of procedures to increase the completeness of enumeration, especially for the population elements that had in the past been most undercounted.

In response to the lawsuits in Detroit and New York, the bureau took the position that there was no adequate basis for making adjustments for differential underenumeration—that there were no methods that would meet bureau professional standards. Also, as Dr. Barbara A. Bailar states in explaining the stand of the bureau, "Adjustment for apportionment purposes was not considered because it was the view of the bureau that federal statutes prohibited adjustment for that purpose and that the time constraints would not permit it."

Table 45.1 Census Bureau Estimates of Net Undercount of the Population by Age, Sex, and Race, 1980

	Black		White and Other Races	
Age	Male	Female	Male	Female
All ages	7.5	2.1	−0.5	−1.7
Under 5 years	9.2	8.7	−0.6	−0.8
5 to 9 years	5.9	5.5	−0.5	−0.5
10 to 14 years	1.1	0.9	−1.8	−1.7
15 to 19 years	−0.7	−1.0	−2.0	−2.0
20 to 24 years	7.2	1.6	−2.2	−2.9
25 to 34 years	11.6	1.4	−0.4	−2.3
35 to 44 years	16.1	3.2	1.6	−0.6
45 to 54 years	15.1	2.5	1.5	−1.8
55 to 64 years	6.2	0.4	—	−2.5
65 to 74 years	−4.3	−5.6	−1.5	−2.6
75 years and over	0.5	4.7	−0.7	0.1

Source: Passel, J. S., J. S. Siegel and J. G. Robinson, "Coverage of the National Population by Age, Sex, and Race in the 1980 Census: Preliminary Estimates by Demographic Analysis," presented at the American Statistical Association Meeting, Detroit, August 10–13, 1981.

Note: A munus sign indicates a net overcount.

As discussed in Dr. Bailar's paper, the bureau documented its position with, among others, the following conclusions:

1. There is now no satisfactory measure of the undercount.
2. There is no satisfactory way to distribute the undercount to local areas.
3. There are a variety of models that could be used to distribute the undercount and no way to compare or evaluate them.
4. Uses for census data vary which make different needs for adjustment.
5. Adjustment of population counts alone is not satisfactory to most users who want adjustment.
6. Adjustment for an undercount of the size and distribution of the 1970 undercount would not change apportionment, but using estimates that have sampling variances or biases could lead to incorrect changes in apportionment.
7. Most units of government would lose money if adjusted population counts were used in funding formulas such as that used in revenue sharing.

REBUTTAL

The above conclusions were based on competent statistical analyses that are worth reading but that are based on premises that could become irrelevant if it were decided by the courts that considerations of equity required by the Constitution were paramount. In other words, if the premise of the bureau had been that it was incumbent upon it to get as close to the truth in the census counts as possible, given the differential undercounts, plans and procedures for the 1980 census would have been different, and the ingenuity and statistical virtuosity displayed by the bureau in the Bailar paper could have been marshalled to make the required adjustments.

It is true that, given the bureau's plans and procedures for the conduct of the 1980 census, it was not possible to measure differential underenumeration and make adjustments in time to meet the statutory dates for publication (January 1, 1981, for the United States as a whole and April 1, 1981, for the states and localities). However, in testimony I submitted as a witness in the U.S. district court in Detroit, I outlined a method which could have achieved the measurement of undercount and adjustment in time to meet the statutory dates.

Furthermore, the court itself could have, and offered to, set aside the dates, which were established by Congress, if they prohibited compliance with constitutional requirements. The court took the position that constitutional mandates superseded legislative provisions, and the argument of the bureau that the statutory dates could not be met became irrelevant.

The bureau's decision not to adjust the counts for differential undercount was not based on the statistics to be obtained subsequent to the census taking but, rather, on prior assumptions that precluded a concerted effort to measure the 1980 census undercount and to make the adjustments. The high variances reported by Bailar in the analyses that show the shakiness of possible adjustments are based on procedures that the bureau has followed and not on alternative procedures. If it became established that present census disregard of differential underenumeration violates the Constitution of the United States, the bias would represent the basis for devising new procedures with potentially smaller variances.

In addition to this consideration several other assumptions of the Bureau of the Census can be challenged. For example, Dr. Bailar's position that most government units would lose by adjustments for differential underenumeration has some lamentable implications. Since it is known that the minority populations—blacks and Hispanics—tend to be concentrated in urban places, especially inner-city zones, it should be expected that adjustments for differential underenumeration would adversely affect a large number of other governmental units. Should the large number of other governmental units, although adversely affected, be permitted to deprive minority populations of their constitutional rights? Moreover, would not the large number of governmental units adversely affected, without adjustment be getting more than their just shares of representatives and federal funds? Furthermore, the minority population numbers adversely affected by differential undercount are much more important than the number of governmental units.

The bureau's preliminary finding that the 1980 census undercount was smaller than that in earlier censuses does not negate the fact that the differential undercount has remained substantially the same and it is the differential undercount, still considerable, that creates the political problem.

Also an issue in the adjustment problem is the advisability of making "synthetic" adjustments for local areas. Synthetic adjustment employs the national or large-area underenumeration measurements in making adjustments for smaller areas. Synthetic adjustment, opposed by the bureau, although it admittedly could create error for some areas, would come closer to the "truth" across the board, and it would certainly decrease the bias in census statistics adversely affecting the constitutional rights of the most underenumerated population elements. In all likelihood errors produced by synthetic adjustments would be minor compared with the errors in the unadjusted underenumerated populations.

Another questionable element in the bureau's position as given in Bailar's paper is that "uses for census data vary which make different needs for adjustment." This statement fails to recognize that the consideration of equity as required by the Constitution is the major use of the census and overrides all other possible uses. Moreover, the adjustments for differential undercount affect only the statistics on numbers of people and not necessarily the mass of data involving characteristics of the population emanating from the total computer output, much of which is not even published. Without question differential underenumeration also distorts the characteristics statistics, but whether the total census output should be adjusted is an independent question not involving the legal and constitutional issues.

Next, the Census Bureau has agreed that several different measurements of undercount are possible and that since there is no objective way to determine which is best, none should be used. This position ignores what may be a crucial question. The question is whether any or all of the alternative measurements get closer to the truth than the raw unadjusted census counts. Indeed, if any or all of the potential measurements of undercount do get closer to the truth, then, given the consideration of equity and justice, some measurement should be used for adjustment for underenumeration. It is unconscionable for the bureau, in a matter involving equity and justice, not to use a statistic which is known to be closer to the truth just because it does not know if this is the best statistic available. And there is a valid solution to this problem.

Which of the several measurements should be used? One possibility, if no better decision can be made, is to use an average of the measurements. The bureau uses the averaging of alternative measurements routinely in its estimate of unemployment in the Current Population Survey measurements of the labor force.

Such a procedure is justified if all of the alternatives have a high likelihood of being closer to the truth.

Still another alternative is to have the bureau technicians most conversant with the technical details determine the method to be used. If this is done it becomes necessary, of course, as for the other alternatives, legally to fix this responsibility upon the bureau and to protect it as far as possible from legal challenges to the method chosen.

Finally, in respect to the points enumerated by Dr. Bailar, the calculations demonstrating that the adjustments called for, using the 1970 undercount measurements, would not change apportionment but that sampling errors might erroneously affect the apportionment is speculative and fails to consider the impact of differential undercount adjustments over the long run.

UNDERCOUNT MEASUREMENT

In brief, there are three basic methods used, or that could be used, in making undercount measurements. In addition, these methods can be used in various combinations. The first, and most widely used for measurement of national undercounts, is "demographic analysis." Second is the "matching method"—comparison of decennial census returns with sample surveys or with relevant official records to obtain net undercount. Third is the use of multiple regression techniques to obtain the effect of administrative variables, among others, including enumerator impact, on underenumeration. For each of these methods of determining completeness of enumeration, the synthetic method described earlier can be used to obtain undercount statistics for small areas from undercount statistics for larger areas. Each of these measurement methods has definite limitations.

For the United States as a whole the accuracy of the demographic analysis method is dependent on the accuracy of the components on which it is based—fertility, mortality, and net immigration into the United States. Moreover, the demographic analysis method for measurement of states and smaller areas is dependent also on net internal migration. Although reasonably precise measurements are available on fertility and mortality for the nation as a whole, the data for emigration have been quite defective and, therefore, so also are the data for net immigration. For measurement of net undercount for areas smaller than the nation as a whole, statistics on net internal migration are subject to considerable error. The correction of the undercount measurement in the 1970 census after more accurate data were obtained on emigration is an example of the way error in a component of demographic analysis can affect the measurement of underenumeration.

The matching method is also subject to error on several counts. First it is, of course, dependent on the accuracy of the listings with which the census returns are compared and with the validity of the matching process itself. When the census returns are compared with sample surveys conducted by the bureau there is also involved a correlation error—the error resulting from both operations, that is, the census and the sample survey, missing the same persons. In such matching it is taken for granted that the sample survey coverage is more complete than that of the census because of the more intensive and repetitive procedures in the sample surveys.

Census experience has indicated that the demographic analysis method provides a greater measurement of undercount than the matching method. But the demographic analysis method cannot produce measurement of undercount by ethnicity because the information for the required components—fertility, mortality, and migration—are not available by ethnic group.

The matching method may be used to obtain measurements for different elements of the population by sex and age and such other characteristics for which information is available on both the census and the listings with which it is matched. For example, the census reports for persons sixty-five years old and over can be matched with persons sixty-five and over receiving Social Security pensions, names of infants can be matched to birth certificates, and men turning eighteen can be matched to registration for potential military service. The matching can, of course, provide estimates of both census misses and, in reverse, of numbers missed in the listings with which the census names are matched. A technique is available, the Chandrasekar-Deming Technique, for estimating what both listings may have missed.

To compensate for the understatement of undercount obtained by the matching method, I have suggested that the measurements obtained for characteristics other than sex, age, and race (i.e., ethnicity) be adjusted by the ratios of the demographic analysis measurements to the measurements obtained through the matching method. That is, the undercount for Hispanics resulting from the matching method could be adjusted by the ratio of the undercount by demographic analysis for blacks to the undercount by the matching method for blacks.

Less utilized but increasingly being studied are the possibilities of the regression method. This method involves analysis of measurement of undercount as obtained by the other two methods as related to other factors such as the characteristics of the population and the characteristics of various elements involved in the administration of the census. The latter could include such items as quality of the enumerators by various criteria available to the Census Bureau (such as cooperation of respondents as measured by proportion of refusals or incomplete responses). The equations resulting could then be used to obtain measurements of undercount for subareas of the nation based on the variables used in the regressions.

It should be observed that the multiple regression method as well as matching method could produce measurements of census undercount by geographic area.

A major issue in the litigation in re the undercount has been focused on the manner in which national or large geographic area measurements of undercount could be distributed to smaller localities. The simplest way is, of course, provided by the synthetic method, aspects of which have already been discussed. It may be noted here, however, that regression analysis can also be used to distribute larger area measurements of undercount. For example, the national measurement for undercount of Hispanics, as obtained from the proposed synthesis of the demographic analysis and matching methods, could be related to other variables in regression equations and provide a basis for distributing the national measurement of undercount to subareas of the nation in accordance with local differences in the variables used in the regression equation.

CONCLUDING OBSERVATIONS

The United States has now conducted twenty decennial population censuses as required by the Constitution to provide the bases for apportioning representatives in the U.S. House of Representatives among the states. In all probability each of these twenty censuses failed to achieve 100 percent completeness in coverage. Yet it was not until the 1980 census that lawsuits were filed in federal courts alleging that the census failed to count members of minority racial and ethnic groups as completely as others, and claiming that, in consequence, the constitutional rights of such minority groups were being violated.

Although the Bureau of the Census since at least 1940 has acknowledged that the population censuses did not count everybody and that there were differences in the degree of completeness in coverage for various elements of the population, neither the executive nor the legislative branches of the government required that the census counts be adjusted for differential undercount. It should not be surprising in view of the growing restiveness of minority population groups and increased political action as manifest in the civil rights movement, that representatives of such groups, in the pursuit of equity in legislative representation and in the apportionment of federal funds, appealed to the third branch of the U.S. government, the federal judiciary, for relief.

As has been reported above, the problems posed by the differential undercount in the population census are complex, legally and statistically. Although no adjustments have yet been required by the courts for the 1980 census counts, the substantive issue is still unresolved and may yet be adjudicated. Thus, even if the 1980 census counts are not adjusted, it is still possible that population counts in future censuses may have to be adjusted for apportionment and financial purposes.

BIBLIOGRAPHICAL NOTES

The most comprehensive and succinct document containing the position of the Bureau of the Census is: Barbara A. Bailar and Nathan Keyfitz, "Issues in Adjusting for the 1980 Census Undercount," paper presented at the general methodology lecture, American Statistical Association Meeting, Detroit, August 10–13, 1981. The paper contains relevant technical references.

Other materials drawn upon for this chapter, some of which are in the bibliography of the Bailar-Keyfitz paper, are:

America's Uncounted People. 1972. Edited by Carole W. Parsons. Report of the Advisory Committee on Problems of Census Enumeration. Washington, DC: National Academy of Sciences.

Coale, Ansley J. and Zelnick, Melvin. 1963. *New Estimates of Fertility and Population in the United States: A Study of Annual White Births from 1855 to 1960 and of Completeness of Enumeration in the Censuses from 1880 to 1960.* Princeton: Princeton University Press. This is an early paper on the measurement of underenumeration.

U.S. Bureau of the Census. 1980. *Current Population Reports.* Series P-25, No. 870. "Estimates of the Population of the United States, by Age, Race, and Sex: 1976 to 1979." U.S. Government Printing Office, Washington, DC. See especially appendix tables A1 and A2.

———. 1979. *Current Population Reports.* Series P-25, No. 796. "Illustrative Projections of State Populations by Age, Race, and Sex: 1975 to 2000." U.S. Government Printing Office, Washington, DC.

———. 1979. *Current Population Reports.* Series P-23, No. 82. "Coverage of the Hispanic Population of the United States in the 1970 Census: A Methodological Analysis." By Jacob S. Siegel and Jeffrey S. Passel. U.S. Government Printing Office, Washington, DC.

———. 1976. *Current Population Reports.* Series P-23, No. 62. "Concepts and Methods Used in Labor Force Statistics Derived from the Current Population Survey." U.S. Government Printing Office, Washington, DC. See page 10, "Composite Estimate," for technique of averaging two diverse sources of labor force statistics.

———. 1974. 1970 Census of Population and Housing, Evaluation and Research Program. Series PHC(E)-4. "Estimates of Coverage of Population by Sex, Race, and Age: Demographic Analysis." U.S. Government Printing Office, Washington, DC, p. 9.

Young (Mayor of the City of Detroit) v. Klutznick (U.S. Secretary of Commerce) and Barabba (Director of the Bureau of the Census). 652 *Federal Reporter* 617. Sixth U.S. Circuit Court of Appeals. 15 June 1981. Includes review of district court decision and minority judge opinion in the three to two reversal of the district court.

For an update of the legal situation since this article was written, see the materials relating to the plaintiffs' petition to the U.S. Supreme Court for adjudication of the substantive issue, particularly the publication "In the Supreme Court of the United States, October Term, 1981; Young (Mayor, City of Detroit) and City of Detroit v. Baldridge (Secretary of Commerce) and Chapman (Director, Bureau of the Census); Petition for a Writ of Certiorari to the United States Court of Appeals for the Sixth Circuit" and the companion publication "Petitioners' Appendix to Petition for a Writ of Certiorari to the United States Court of Appeals for the Sixth Circuit."

46
Trends and Prospects

EVERETT S. LEE
HAROLD F. GOLDSMITH
MICHAEL GREENBERG
DONALD B. PITTENGER

POPULATION ACCOUNTING IN THE UNITED STATES AND OTHER COUNTRIES

Though the United States was the first country to develop a continuing system of population accounting, it has lagged behind many of the advanced countries in the collection of data on population and housing. The most important information to be collected by any nation is the number, characteristics, distribution, and living conditions of its people. For maximum usefulness these data must be accurate and timely. One would suppose that any one of the more developed countries would set up a system that would provide the requisite data at frequent intervals and make certain they were valid. Indeed most of the developed countries do just that and, except for a few of the poorest or most isolated, the less developed countries, in the interest of development, are setting up censuses or population registers. Of course, we too take a census, but it is taken once in ten years and most of the questions are addressed to a sample of the population. From that sample, some of the most important characteristics of the population are estimated. Thus, the process of estimation begins with the census itself, and involves the imputing of missing items or even "missing persons," and the inflation of the sample to represent total population. For small areas some items are deleted for reasons of sampling variability as well as privacy. Utilizing primarily censuses and periodic sample surveys, the Bureau has amassed useful and relatively accurate data. However, despite the enviable record of the Bureau of the Census, it cannot hope to achieve the levels of completeness and accuracy that are commonly obtained by most of the advanced countries, especially those with small, homogeneous populations. Americans do not welcome the small intrusion into their privacy that the census entails, though it comes but once in ten years, and some groups are actively hostile to it. By contrast, the Dutch think it necessary to maintain in a central register current data on every inhabitant, and the Japanese are so impressed with the usefulness of carefully assembled data that they annually celebrate a holiday known as Statistics Day.

Population registers, as they are found in Sweden, Denmark, the Netherlands, West Germany, Israel, and a number of other countries, include items on each individual along with data on parents, spouse, and children. People are entered in the register at birth with date of birth, sex, and parentage noted. Additional items are entered later—for example, religion, marriage, divorce, education, and occupation. A person migrating from one community to another takes out a migration certificate, one copy of which is sent to the community of destination and another accompanies the migrant. At the destination, the migrant reports to the proper office, which notifies the community of origin that he has arrived. The migrant is then entered on the register at the new community and removed from the register of origin. Thus, from birth to death, a frequently, updated and detailed record is maintained for each person.

In these countries, it is a simple matter to determine the population of each small area at any time. Nevertheless, several countries with population registers also take censuses. These are used to check on the population register and to gather data not obtainable from the register. In keeping with the desire for timely data, these countries usually take censuses at much shorter intervals than we do. Five years is a common intercensal period.

Population registers and frequent censuses indicate the lengths to which other countries are willing to go to avoid the uncertainties we tolerate in regard to population. Of course, we too have long been aware of the need for more frequent information about our people. President Grant, a statesman seldom applauded for his acuity, noted in his Fourth Annual Message to the Congress that "The interval at present established between the Federal census is so long that the information obtained at the decennial period as to the material condition, wants and resources of the nation is of little practical value after the expiration of the first half of that period" (Richardson, 1969). Indeed, one of the few distinctions of the Grant administration was that it was the first to recommend a five-year interval between censuses. Grant was aware, of course, of the political implications, and suggested that the middecade census be "divested of all political character and no reapportionment of Congressional representation be made under it" (Richardson, 1969).

In contrast to the ten-year intervals that separate censuses of population and housing are the four-year intervals between agricultural censuses and the five-year intervals between censuses of business. However, the Constitution requires a reapportionment of the House of Representatives after each census, and the extension of the "one man—one vote" requirement to states and cities or even counties has greatly increased the political impact of the census by threatening party control at the local level. To reapportion the House of Representatives and to make the now required changes in state and other political entities is a formidable task, one that few would want to undertake frequently.

For these and other reasons, mostly economic, the mid-decade census, which was scheduled to begin in 1985, will not be conducted. At best there will be a sample survey larger than the usual Current Population Survey, but far too small to provide data for small areas. However, it will provide control totals for larger areas against which included small areas can be checked. It can also be used to improve estimates of characteristics that are difficult to assess in small areas. More and more, we are forced to the realization that the proper allocation of health and other resources depends upon the distribution of different kinds of people, and when census and register data are not available we are forced to make estimates. Larger and better surveys of population and housing, as envisioned at middecade, will not obviate the need for data for small areas. Thus, instead of reducing the demand for estimates for small areas, the reliable information obtained for larger areas from such surveys will stimulate the demand for small area estimates.

THE LONG HISTORY OF POPULATION ESTIMATION IN THE UNITED STATES

The practice of estimating population has an old and honored history in the United States. It began with the estimation of population for the states, spread to large cities, was eventually undertaken for counties, and now is done for those thousands of places that are incorporated or otherwise can claim federal or state funds. Often, there have been protests against the practice, yet at each level of aggregation, estimates have proven useful and feasible, taking into account, of course, the absolute and proportional errors that can be tolerated.

When the founding fathers drew up the Constitution of the United States, they realized that regular censuses (population registers were not considered, though the church registers that were their prototypes were already in existence in Scandinavian countries) were necessary for democracy, for how else could proportional representation be maintained. But in order to set up the House of Representatives it was necessary to estimate the population of the states separately for the free and the slaves—the latter being counted as three-fifths of a person for the purpose of representation and the imposition of direct taxes. These estimates were made quite informally by delegates at the convention, and were used to apportion the sixty-five members of the first House of Representatives. Made in 1787, they can be compared with the counts made three years later at the first census. Even without making an allowance for differential growth of the states over the intervening three years, the estimates look very good. Indeed, the number of representatives accorded any one state would not have changed by more than one; Virginia or North Carolina might have gained a representative and Georgia might have lost one (Bureau of the Census, 1976).

Thus, almost 200 years ago the populations of the United States could be estimated well enough for the purpose of establishing representation in the Congress. Undoubtedly we could still do as well, if we accepted the risk that minor over- or underestimation for a particular state could result in the gain or loss of one representative. Such a result can depend upon a very small number when the necessary adjustments are made to avoid giving a state a fraction of a representative. Indeed, it is not improbable that estimates for the states would result in no more misallocation of representatives than does a census. This illustrates another and a major use of population estimates. They are the basis for challenging or correcting a census count.

It is an old story for cities to estimate their populations and challenge decennial census counts. Sometimes the challenges were based on nothing more than casual or biased observations, but on occasion they were carefully constructed. As early as 1890, in the *Special Reports of the 1900 Census,* the Bureau addressed itself to the reliability of existing methods of estimating population. Maintaining that "the results of the Federal census, giving the population of the several states and territories, are accepted without challenge both by the Congress and by the country," the Bureau nevertheless noted that "the accuracy of the figures for the population of a city is sometimes disputed or denied" (Bureau of the Census, 1906).

Admitting that such challenges were often made in good faith, the Bureau set out to examine the data upon which estimates were based and the methodology by which they were prepared. The following ways of estimating total population were listed:

1. Assume the same annual rate of growth as occurred between the two previous censuses.
2. Apply some ratio to the number of voters in an election.
3. Apply some ratio to the number of children in school or counted in school censuses.
4. Apply some ratio to the number of persons listed in city or other directories.

For a sample of seventy-eight cities the Bureau experimented with each of these methods and found them all wanting. Noting that in more than half of the cities the rate of growth for 1890 to 1900 differed by 18 percent or more from that for the previous intercensal period, the Bureau dismissed simple extrapolation. Votes cast in an election were found to be highly variable from one city to another, and within cities from time to time. Furthermore, the increase in the number of voters did not run parallel with the increase in population. The number of children discovered in school censuses were seldom taken with sufficient accuracy to be good bases for population estimates.

City directories were dismissed as always resulting in overestimates. Quoting James A. Garfield, who in turn was quoting Samuel Johnson, the Bureau said: "To count is a modern practice; the ancient method was to guess and where numbers are guessed they are always magnified" (Bureau of the Census, 1906). The Bureau preferred that cities not make estimates, but if they must it suggested arithmetic extrapolation. For that practice the rationale was that it generally gave the best results, at least in the short run, for the cities studied. Interestingly, this technique tends to underestimate where rates of growth are sustained or increased.

SCIENCE OR ART

It still remains embarrassingly true that a simple, disingenuous method will sometimes yield better estimates than elaborate, presumably sophisticated methods. The modern successor to arithmetic or geometric extrapolation is a multiple regression that typically uses such data as school enrollment, motor vehicle registration, resident births, resident deaths, and sales taxes. Undoubtedly, the results of such regressions now in use will be reviewed after the 1980 Census to see if different factors would have given better results. Such techniques have the advantage of relative simplicity and complete empiricism. Furthermore, the collection of data and calculations can be turned over to clerks.

Unfortunately, estimating populations is something like weather forecasting. Standard sets of data can be used in specified ways, but improved forecasts can be made by people who have long-time knowledge of a particular area and understand the special ways in which local weather varies from standard patterns. In many cases the final step in making the best estimate for a local area is not science but art—the tailoring of mechanically obtained results to fit local conditions and make them consonant with estimates for neighboring or encompassing areas. In this regard much progress has been made in recent years. The cooperative program that the Bureau of the Census has set up with the states and the checking of initial returns from the 1980 Census by local authorities are important steps toward achieving a consistent and improved program for local estimates.

But there are problems in any cooperative arrangement no matter how cheerfully entered into, as any husband and wife will attest. In particular, there is the tendency, noted by Samuel Johnson, to overestimate the population. This springs from the usual definition of growth as good, and a willingness to accept increases rather than decreases. In many cases, the purpose of the estimate is to prove that certain monies should be forthcoming or to set the stage for action that will not be taken if growth is lagging. It is all too easy to resolve matters of doubt in favor of growth. For example, Earle Klay found that county commissioners in Florida were almost universally convinced that their counties were growing at about the same rate as the state when, in fact, they were growing much more slowly (Klay, 1974).

ACCEPTABLE ERROR

Almost as harmful to the progress of science as carelessness in measurement is overemphasis on precision, a striving for accuracy in nonsignificant digits. Just as one may need to measure distance to the nearest kilometer or the nearest centimeter, one must be content with population counts to the nearest million or the nearest hundred, depending upon the purpose for which we use the figures. And, if one is wise, one will copy the engineer who estimates the heaviest traffic to which a bridge will be subjected and then build in an additional factor of safety. On the whole, we are accustomed to living with moderate uncertainty, but when it comes to population there is a tendency to be uncomfortable with the slightest suggestion of error. The census, thanks to the high standards that have been maintained throughout its existence and the emphasis we put on equal representation, is almost sacrosanct and the merest suggestion of error comes as a shock.

In fact, the census is intended to count every soul from the last infant to be born to those still expiring. Estimates, however, are another matter. They cannot be exact and we must admit to a variety of biases. Thus we must face the question of acceptable error. Usually we measure error as a percentage difference from an actual census or some other type of count, either of which may be flawed. As we might expect on purely statistical grounds as well as on the basis of available data, percentage errors tend to increase as the size of the areas for which estimates are made decrease. For the United States we may expect the error to be minor, probably no more than the usual undercount of 3 percent or so. For states it will vary a great deal but generally in relation to size. For California and New York the percentage error should be small, but for Nevada or Montana it could be large. Similar considerations apply to counties; the larger the county, the less the percentage error. For these areas we have evaluations of estimates, published after censuses, which go back three decades, but for areas below the county level we have had no major evaluations.

If we had evaluations of estimates for small areas, they would undoubtedly show quite large percentage errors. This, of course, is to be expected because of the data on which they are based and because of statistical variation. This we must accept but we should raise the question as to how much error is acceptable and what kinds of errors are most acceptable. For example, when we evaluate population estimates for states and counties we hope to find that the average error is small—the nearer to zero the better. Additionally, we would like to find about the same number of estimates that were high as low but clustered closely around the average error.

An important question is that of percentage versus numerical error. For many small areas, the percentage errors in population estimates will seem large, say 20 percent. But is a 20 percent error crucial for a little populated area? Would it matter very much if the estimated population of Living County, Texas, were 50 percent higher than the population enumerated in the 1980 Census? That would be an error of something less than 50 people in a quite extensive county. For areas with large populations, the percentage error is usually the most meaningful statistic; a 1 percent error for California represents a large number of people and could cost the state hundreds of thousands of dollars. On the other hand, an error of 10,000 is a negligible matter for the state.

Very little thought has been given to the dispersion of error around the mean. Indeed, we will doubtless find different mean errors and different dispersions of errors around the mean not only for different techniques of estimation, but also for areas of different size, location, or composition when the same method of estimation is used. Therefore, we must continue to ask ourselves not only how widely applicable the technique may be and the magnitude of the error to be expected, but also whether the technique will have a greater or lesser spread of error for different size or type of places.

Donald Pittenger, who has had long experience with population estimates for small areas, has listed several criteria against which the different methods should be assessed. The first is accuracy, the second is cost, the third is the detail obtainable, and last, but by no means least, is privacy. Utilizing these criteria, and comparing the census and various methods of estimation against population registers, which are generally up to date, and permit balance sheets of population to be made at any time, the population registers' accuracy is very good and the cost may be moderate. There is, however, the key question of privacy. With population registers, the state can follow the individual through life, even through generations. The registers are always available for the use of the state, and sometimes they are open to the general public. To Americans the possibility of the invasion of privacy and the misuse of records by the state has precluded population registers in this country, but the continuing and mounting invasion by illegal immigrants may soon force such a system. Indeed, there may be no other way to protect ourselves.

Furthermore, since we are not willing to face the cost and political implications of a quinquennial census, we must consider expansion of the Current Population Survey, regularly conducted by the Bureau of the Census, from which estimates of population and population characteristics are made for the nation, its regions, the combination of metropolitan areas, and sometimes for states. It is not unlikely that the sample size for these surveys will be expanded and that estimates can and will be made regularly for states and agglomerations of equal population. Unfortunately, such surveys will not provide estimates for small areas. Obviously, we shall continue to need and make estimates for small areas. Moreover, as concern for the environment mounts because of differential change in population characteristics or production, the need for timely and accurate information about the number and characteristics of population in small areas will mount.

REFERENCES

Klay, W. E. 1974. "A Comparative Analysis of Florida County Commissioners: Attitudes and Perceptions about Local Population Changes: Some Political, Demographic, and Economic Dimensions." M.A. thesis, University of Georgia.

Richardson, J. D. (ed.). 1969. *Compilation of the Messages and Papers of the Presidents 1789–1897,* 8:203.

U.S. Bureau of the Census, 1976. *Historical Statistics of the United States: Colonial Times to 1970,* 6:1085. Washington, DC: Government Printing Office.

———. 1906. *Special Report: Supplementary Analysis and Derivative Tables, 12th Census of the United States, 1900.* Washington, DC: Government Printing Office.

47

Voodoo Forecasting: Technical, Political, and Ethical Issues Regarding the Projection of Local Population Growth

ELIZABETH W. MOEN

Exxon Goes Synthetic

On April 2, 1981, the president of Exxon Corporation, U.S.A., told a Colorado School of Mines audience that the United States could develop a 15 million barrel per day (b/d) synthetic fuel industry within the next thirty years. According to Randall Meyer, "Some processes for producing . . . shale oil and intermediate BTU gas made from coal—are *technically proven* and generally thought to be *economically competitive* with oil imports at current world prices" (Meyer, 1981:7, my emphasis). Meyer went on to predict that this synthetic fuel industry would require a capital investment of $850 billion in "today's dollars" or over $3 trillion in "spent dollars," directly employ nearly 900,000 people, and bring to the energy resource counties of Northwest Colorado—which in 1980 had a population of 183,257—over one and a half million people.

Just eight months earlier Exxon had paid Atlantic Richfield $300 million for its 60 percent ownership in the Colony Oil Shale Project. Tosco Corporation (an energy company primarily engaged in oil refining) held the other 40 percent of the project, which at that time was expected to produce 46,000 b/d by 1985. At about the same time, Exxon released its now-famous White Paper, upon which Meyer's speech was based, which concluded that Colorado and Utah should have an 8 million b/d shale oil industry. The shale would be dug from a series of "rolling" open pit mines, each one three-and-a-half miles long, two miles wide, and a half-mile deep. Each mine would employ 22,000 miners and 8,000 operators. Exxon predicted that 600,000 b/d would be produced by 1990, and 1.5 million b/d by 1995. (For rationale and details, see Exxon, 1980.) The rest is history:

March 1982: Colony announces it will sell its first barrel in 1986 or 1987 (Tosco, 1982).

April 12: Information is leaked from Washington, D.C., that Colony cost estimates are up from $3 billion to $5 billion (*Western Colorado Report,* 4/12/82).

April 28: Citing a cost estimate of $6 billion, Exxon Board of Directors decides to stop funding its share of Colony (*Denver Post,* 5/9/82).

April 30: Randall Meyer breaks the news to Tosco executives (*Denver Post,* 5/9/82).

May 2: Tosco exercises its option to sell its 40 percent share to Exxon and thereby closes the project. In Western Colorado this day is known as Black Sunday (*Denver Post,* 5/9/82).

May 3: Workers arriving for the 5:00 A.M. shift are told they are out of work. Over 2,000 workers representing an $85 million payroll are laid off by Colony contractor Brown and Root. Estimates of total jobs lost range from 4,000 to 10,000 (*Denver Post,* 5/9/82). Workers begin to prematurely "finish" Battlement Mesa, Exxon's 1,563 acre housing development for Colony workers, which was to have had 7,300 dwelling units and a population of 25,000 by 1995. Many of the 2,000 residents prepare to leave to seek work elsewhere.

July 27: *Rocky Mountain News* announces, "Mobil urges massive plan for oil shale."

The Necessity and Impossibility of Population Forecasting

Boom and bust cylces are not new to the United States, and they are not confined to rural resource communities. Recently, however, much more attention has been paid to the consequences of these cycles. The first catalyst was the National Environmental Protection Act (Council on Environmental Quality, 1979) which requires impact assessments for large projects done on federal land or funded with federal money. A large proportion of the economic, environmental, and social impact assessments are based on population projections. Attention was also drawn by media and research reports to rapidly increasing rates of social problems in resource "boom towns" (e.g., Gilmore and Duff, 1975; Cortese and Jones, 1977; McKeown and Lantz, n.d.). Often these communities did not know how much growth would occur and/or when it would occur, and/or were not able to prepare for expected growth in time. Consequently, high priority has been given to the refinement of population projection methods. To date it has been a futile task.

In this chapter I argue that such efforts are misplaced. The failure of population projections lies less in the methods employed than in the ways projections are used and in the inability to obtain key data. The argument is developed via examples drawn primarily from two studies of planning related to energy production in Colorado (for details see Moen, 1980; Lillydahl et al., 1982) All unreferenced quotes and data come from interviews conducted during these studies. In the concluding section, an alternative method of population forecasting is suggested.

THE PROBLEM

Demographers who know enough to forecast migration also know better.

Peter Morrison

The importance of population projections to impact assessment, planning, and resource allocation cannot be overemphasized. In fact, for " . . . many planners and decision makers the magnitude of population impacts is synonymous with the magnitude of all impacts" (Leistritz and Murdock, 1981:63). In subnational areas characterized by low rates of natural increase, population baseline estimates and subsequent projections are determined by the most mercurial and most difficult to measure population dynamic—internal migration. As Leistritz and Murdock (1981:82) point out, "Unlike mortality or fertility patterns where some theoretical limits can be set, for migration the range of possible values and the reasons for changes in direction from in- to out- or out-to inmigration are not well understood." The problem of estimating and predicting in- and outmigration becomes especially serious when an area is experiencing or is supposed to experience rapid, large-scale economic development. Difficulties are compounded even further when economic growth and change are based upon volatile markets, uncertain technologies, and "footloose" industries.

Projection methods and models for subnational areas have been reviewed by Kunofsky (1982), Leistritz and Murdock (1981), Chalmers and Anderson (1977), Sanderson and O'Hare (1977), Pittenger (1976), Shryock and Siegel (1976) and Morrison (1975), among others.[2] The failure of such forecasting even in the best of circumstances is well known. Calling population projections "informed guesses," Morrison (cited in Kunofsky, 1982:1) claims that forecasters have "doggedly clung to their art . . . accumulating so notorious a record of inaccuracy as to make one wonder why they keep at it." "The answer," he claims, " . . . is simple: someone has to." Showing little faith in his trade, Keyfitz (1981:579) makes the following disclaimer: "Demographers can no more be held responsible for inaccuracy in forecasting population 20 years ahead than geologists, meteorologists, or economists when they fail to announce earthquakes, cold winters or depressions 20 years ahead." (Also see Ascher, 1978 and 1981, regarding the failure of *all* the forecasting efforts—economic, energy, transportation, technological, and population—that affect energy production and energy production communities.) Compounding the problem, if there has not been a recent census, the forecast's baseline population estimate may also be quite inaccurate (e.g., Lee and Goldsmith, 1982).

What, then, are communities to do when faced with the possibility of rapid growth? If they do not prepare adequately and in advance (which may require 10 years), they will likely become examples of the classic boom town, which not only has high rates of social problems but also high rates of population turnover and low levels of worker productivity (Gilmore and Duff, 1975). On the other hand, if communities over-prepare, they may be left with high levels of unemployment, failing businesses, unpaid loans, empty housing, and excess infrastructure and capital facilities to pay for and maintain.

An ideal population projection method

would provide estimates of the numbers and characteristics of immigrants and outmigrants detailed enough to plan for community needs (housing, classrooms, services, etc.) and to predict subsequent growth (age-gender distributions, age-specific birth and death rates). If energy production facilities will require a large number of employees, then the community and the state need to know:

- How many energy jobs will there be?
- How many and what kind of additional jobs will be generated by the energy jobs?
- How many employees will move in from out of state?
- How many jobs will go to the local residents?
- How many employees will move in from within the state?
- Where will the newcomers live—in the energy community itself or elsewhere?
- How long will the newcomers stay?
- Will those who leave need replacements?
- When they leave, will they leave the state?
- If they remain in the state, will they go to another energy community?
- How many employees will commute?
- Will they commute from within or without the state?
- Will newcomers and commuters spend their salaries in the energy community?
- What will the newcomer workers be like (age, sex, race, marital status)?
- How many of those who are married will bring their families along?
- How many children will they have and how old will they be?
- Will their spouses or children want employment too?

This task is not only formidable but, as will be shown, impossible even in a highly simplified form. It is formidable because it requires a great deal of up-to-date data (e.g., characteristics of workers[3] and numerous assumptions about future events, relationships among variables, and the stability of the relationships. It is impossible because the data which drive all such models—future employment or at least future activity by employers—may be withheld, misrepresented, or even unknown by industry. Consequently, projections may be highly unreliable not only in the long run but from day-to-day. This problem is not unique to energy production communities; it is merely more acute and dramatic. Problems of forecasting in the State of Colorado are given as an example.

Population Projections Before and After Exxon

In an earlier study of energy and population planning in Colorado, it was found that the projections for Region 11 (the four-county planning area in Northwest Colorado where shale oil production would occur) made by the state for its official projections, by the state for Environmental Protection Agency (EPA) water and sewer funds, and by the Region 11 Council of Governments (COG) were in considerable disagreement. Not only were they based on very different methods and assumptions (e.g., no new energy-related jobs will be filled by Colorado residents vs. no inmigration until local unemployment is very low), but also the methods and assumptions varied according to the purpose for which a projection was made (Moen, 1980). When industry uses projections as a means of furthering its own interests, the future gets even muddier.

Conventional wisdom before the Exxon White Paper held that no more than 400,000 b/d would be produced in Colorado before 2000. In 1979, the Colorado Energy Research Institute (CERI) was confident that no more than 200,000 to 300,000 b/d would be produced by 1990. In fact, according to the Colorado Department of Natural Resources, no more than 200,000 b/d could be produced unless Congress were to modify air quality regulations (Moen, 1980). Shortly after Exxon's White Paper, however, shale oil production and, consequently, population projections were revised upwards, sometimes quite dramatically. For example, CERI revised its estimate to four "scenarios" for the year 2000: extreme = 4 million b/d; high = 1,800,000 b/d; medium = 900,000 b/d; and low = 400,000 b/d. According to these scenarios, the private investment needed just for plant construction would range from $15.2 billion to almost $200 billion. Increased water consumption due to oil shale development would range from 81,000 to 868,000 acre-feet per year by 2000, and capital expenditures for the required new electrical power plants would range from $800 million to $8.8 billion. To accommodate the oil shale-related population growth of between 456,000 and 1.248 million people by 2000, there would be a need for 25,000 to 313,000 housing units, $400 million to $5.8 billion for public facilities, and annual public capital and operating budgets of $41 million to over $1 billion (Warren, 1981). Although projections were made for the 10 counties that comprise Northwest Colorado, most of this growth would occur in the four counties in Region 11.

A variety of other population projections have been made for Colorado and Region 11, before and after Exxon. The foregoing should be enough to illustrate how confusing the situation is for planners, administrators, investors, and especially local officials who are rarely in a position to evaluate the data upon which they must base their decisions regarding capital expenditure, taxation, land use regulations, and development permits.

Local Government's Dilemma

A brief look at Rio Blanco County and its county seat, Meeker, shows the double bind that counties undergoing economic development are in. The 3,264 square mile county has two towns, Meeker and Rangely, which are separated by 50 miles of narrow, winding road. In 1980, C-a and C-b, the two Colorado shale oil tracts leased from the federal government, were in operation and Multi Mineral Corporation was about to open a third shale oil tract. These projects lay halfway between Meeker and Rangely. A coal mine near Meeker was planning to expand, and there were many smaller energy resource operations throughout the county. (The Exxon–Tosco Colony project was in adjacent Garfield County, but was not expected to affect Rio Blanco's population.)

The 1980 census found 2,356 residents in Meeker and 6,255 in Rio Blanco County. In 1981, the COG forecast a 1990 population of from 13,507 to 14,179 for Meeker, and 19,060 to 25,703 for the county (Colorado West Council of Governments, 1981). However, in mid-1981, the local administrator of the highly influential Bar 70 Enterprises, which plans to create a residential, commerical and industrial development just east of Meeker that would house between 16,000 and 25,000 people, believed these forecasts to be much too low. Basing his forecasts on knowledge garnered from government and industry contacts, he predicted the Meeker area would grow to 25,000 people by the mid-1990s *without oil shale development*—because of coal, oil, gas, power plants, pipelines, water diversion projects, reservoirs, uranium, nahcolite, dawsonite, and related industries. "The plastics industries will come to coal and oil. They're going to be moving here. . . . The industries that have traditionally served energy in Appalachia and the East Coast want to come here—the parts, the machinery and so forth." Further, if shale oil were to be commerically produced, another 16,000 people would be added to the local population. He also cited a Department of Energy prediction that the area could grow to over 100,000 because of a proposed railroad to link all of the oil shale projects. "If they go for that kind of growth," he said, the town "will self-destruct in twenty years."

By the end of 1981, however, the three oil shale projects had closed and the coal mine near Meeker had all but done so.[4] Needless to say, population projections are now being revised downward, but projections do not tell the entire story. A brief review of the recent history of the C-b tract (named Cathedral Bluffs by the developers, Occidental Petroleum and Tenneco) and of Northern Coal Company will give some idea of what Rio Blanco and many other resource counties have experienced. (For greater detail, see Lillydahl et al., 1982.) The tale is summarized in Table 47.1.

Cathedral Bluff's Bluffs

The story is told by the local newspaper, the *Meeker Herald.*

10/02/80: In a public discussion, Cathedral Bluffs Oil Shale Project Representative Bob Loucks states: "A quick look at the next 10 years' employment pattern that the company expects to follow for operations, construction, and secondary workers finds an employment of 643 in 1980 to grow to 1,046 by next year. 1982's 1,777 workers will almost double to 3,340 by 1983 and expand to 4,827 by 1984." Eastern Rio Blanco School Superintendent Bob King questions Loucks' figures, asking, "What are the odds of C-b fully developing the project?" Loucks replies, "100 percent sure." *(Meeker Herald)*

04/23/81: "Oxy Denies Cutting Back." The most recent predictions by C-b increase employees to 980 by the end of 1982 and to 4,270 by 1985. Cathedral Bluffs states it plans to continue hiring. *(Meeker Herald)*

05/29/81: Twenty percent of the Cathedral Bluffs workforce is laid off. *(Meeker Herald)*

11/18/81: Cathedral Bluffs announces there are currently 650 employees on the C-b tract, there will be about 550 in a year, and in 1983 a significant increase in employment will begin which will build up to around 2,500 by 1986. (Minutes of

Table 47.1. Employment Forecasts and Actual Employment Levels, Cathedral Bluffs Oil Shale (C-b) and Northern Coal Mine, Rio Blanco County, Colorado

Date Forecast Made	Actual Employment at Time of Forecast	Employment Forecast, by Year						
		1981	1982	1983	1984	1985	1986	1987
Cathedral Bluffs Oil Shale (C-b)								
10/1980	643	1,046	1,777	3,340	4,827	7,116	8,445	9,215
04/1981	450		980			4,270		
06/1981			1,000–1,100				2,500	
11/1981	650		550					
12/1981	760		105					
01/1982	500	*	300–350 (Jan.) 12 (Fall)					
Northern Coal								
10/1981	145		225				500–900	
10/1981	124	63						
05/1982	52							
08/1982	6							

Sources: Rio Blanco County Impact Mitigation Task Force/Eastern Advisory Group minutes, personal communication with Northern Coal Mine and Cathedral Bluffs Oil Shale, and the *Meeker Herald.*

Rio Blanco County Impact Mitigation Task Force, Eastern Advisory Group, 11/18/81)

12/15/81: William McDermott, Executive Vice President of Occidental Petroleum, speaks very positively about C-b's future *(Meeker Herald)*

12/17/81: Development of the over-$4 billion C-b project is halted. Only 20 of 475 construction workers and 85 of 285 Occidental employees will be retained. *(Meeker Herald)*

A week later, the following appeared in the *Meeker Herald:*

> "After listening to years and years of talk about all the growth that was projected, the news that the company was shutting down was a shock to the community, especially after the signals the company was sending out. . . . " School Superintendent Bob King was quoted as saying, "The shutdown just reaffirms my opinion that the only certainty in the oil shale game is uncertainty." City Planner Frank Freeman said that, although he took into consideration a reduction in energy company activity, " . . . I had no idea that C-b would do what they did." (*Meeker Herald,* 12/24/81)

Just prior to C-b tract's shutdown, Rio Blanco Oil Shale and Multi Mineral Corporation both abruptly cut back their oil shale workforces and let it be known that future operations were not as definite as the community had been led to believe. (Since then, both operations have been terminated.)

Northern Coal Goes Under

Northern Coal provides another example of the futility of trying to project population growth on the basis of industries' stated plans.

01/21/81: "Major Expansion of Northern Mine Approved." Northern Coal plans to expand its two existing mines and open two new ones. The operation would cover 4,750 acres, and last 30 years, with a peak annual production of 4.25 million tons of coal. The current employment of 145 is predicted to reach 200 to 250 operational workers by 1982, and eventually over 900. *(Meeker Herald)*

04/02/81: Northern Coal President Bud Bobo reports that during a two-week marketing trip to the Orient, Northern Coal was successful in lining up coal sales and had "actually turned down prospective orders for our coal." *(Meeker Herald)*

08/20/81: "Rumors of Northern Closing Unfounded But State They Are 'Reevaluating.'" *(Meeker Herald)*

09/03/81: "Concerns Over Future of Northern Coal Grow as Company Lays Off Workers." *(Meeker Herald)*

10/01/81: "Northern to Continue Production But With Half the Workforce." Following a summer peak of 160, there are now 124 workers, which will be cut to 60–65. A soft market for coal is one of the reasons given by company officials. [Meanwhile, a large coal mine is being opened in the other end of the county.] Annual production of coal at Northern will be about 100,000 tons. *(Meeker Herald)* By the time this issue of the *Herald* was printed and put into circulation, the Northern Coal mine had been put up for sale.

08/05/82: "Bottom Line Decision Forces Northern Coal to Close Mines." Northern was "once seen as the steady employer that could help the community ride out the ups and downs of energy development." *(Meeker Herald)*

Rio Blanco County is not presented as an example of a worst case. The county is—because of its Impact Mitigation Task Force and development permit regulations—one of the best cases to be found in the country (see Lillydahl et al. 1982, for details). Because of its insistence that growth pay for itself, nearly all of the capital expenditures for expansion in the county and in Meeker were paid for by mineral severance taxes, oil shale leasing funds, prepayment of taxes, industry gifts, and development fees. Consequently, county residents were not left with high taxes or a high level of bonded indebtedness. However, in Meeker the residents were left with a water and sewer system for a population of 8,000, expanded school and municipal buildings, a swimming pool with a roof but no walls, a new tax-levying recreation district, and an overexpanded hospital that now cannot afford the minimum staff necessary for its operation. At the same time, social services—which were not funded to keep up with actual, much less expected, growth—now have growing caseloads as a result of unemployment. Public health, crisis intervention, counseling by ministers and welfare services are especially in demand. Meeker is establishing a food, baby formula, and diaper distribution center to help meet the needs of unemployed residents and the increasing number of families that pass through the area in search of work.

Private investment is another story. In all energy communities in Region 11, local stores had expanded and remodelled, and new stores, motels, restaurants, housing developments, and recreation facilities were opening. "For sale" signs are now the local logo, and half-finished buildings stand witness to the third shale oil boom/bust the area has experienced in this century.

A Better Mousetrap?

The response to the failure of forecasting in Colorado and elsewhere has been the development of increasingly complicated models that require more and more data and more and more assumptions about future events, as well as about relationships among variables and the stability of these relationships—all of which may only increase the possibility of error and the illusion of precision.

Again, Colorado provides an example. Recognizing the chaos in forecasting, Governor Richard Lamm and the Colorado Department of Natural Resources established a Cumulative Impact Task Force (CITF) (1982) which, among other things, was to develop a population and economic forecasting model that would consider energy production as a regional activity.[5] This alone is a giant step forward from the usual practice of examining each project as an isolated event and from the common implicit assumption that project workers and other impacts do not cross county lines.

The three-part CITF model is very detailed and the thought that went into it is evident from the documentation. The model begins with the Basic Activity System (BAS) component—which, like all such models, is driven by industry data or "best guesses" regarding future economic activity and employment. The BAS is an economic-demographic model of the same family as the better-known OBERS (Bureau of Economic Analysis, 1977), wherein a change in the basic employment sector (e.g., mining) is assumed to have a functional relationship to personal income, which in turn is assumed to have a functional relationship to nonbasic employment (e.g., service sector). Immigration is a function of the additional basic jobs and nonbasic income generated and the available local labor force.[6] The model developers have gone to extraordinary efforts to develop economic coefficients to represent regional trade patterns (the ratio of nonbasic employment to personal income), but since some of the coefficients were so far from the mean that they were excluded from the model, the results are rather artificial. Further, although the size of communities and, therefore, their relationships in a hypothesized economic hierarchy are taken into account in the calculation of new nonbasic jobs, economic "leakage" (purchases made outside the area) may be underestimated. Consequently, inmigration may be overestimated. A great deal of lower- and midorder shopping (e.g., groceries, clothing) and other commerce is carried out in Denver (a five hour drive if the 55 mph speed limit is exceeded), which is not included in the zone of influence. (Although it is not clear in the documentation, higher-order Denver purchases—e.g., designer clothes, washing machines, medical specialists—are said to be included in the model.) In addition, Region 11 residents also do a large volume of mail-order shopping. Moreover, the modelers assume that Meeker residents do most of their mid- to higher-order shopping in Rifle or Grand Junction (both of which are in the study area)—when in fact a substantial proportion of Meeker's shopping dollars go regularly not only to Denver but also to Vernal, Utah, which is in the study area but not linked to Meeker in the economic hierarchy. Meeker residents do higher-order shopping out of town in order to obtain higher quality goods or goods that cannot be purchased at home. But they also do a great deal of lower-order shopping out of town in order to get better prices. Moreover, going out of town to shop—even to Denver—is seen as a form of recreation and an excuse to take advantage of other urban amenities. Consequently, money that is assumed to be spent within study area towns, and thus to generate jobs within those towns, is actually spent elsewhere. (See Sanderson and O'Hare, 1977: Finsterbusch, 1980; and Leistritz and Murdock, 1981, for additional concerns regarding the estimation of nonbasic employment.)

An assumption of labor market equilibrium (and, apparently, a nearly perfect match between labor force skills and employment needs) is used to determine how many of the new jobs will be filled by new residents. It is assumed that with seven percent unemployment, outmigration will occur and that with three percent unemployment, inmigration will occur. Although these thresholds can be adjusted, the literature on energy boom towns, as well as that on rural industrialization, and the recent experiences of energy production areas suggest that in- and outmigration are not so predictable. Unemployed residents may not leave (or there may be a considerable lag time), employed residents may leave, too many or too few job seekers may arrive and those who do not find jobs may remain and join the ranks of the unemployed (Greenwood, 1975; Da Vanzo, 1978; Morrison, 1971). Prices and wages, which are not in the CITF model, also influence labor migration as much as unemployment rates do (Greenwood, 1976).

One reason migration does not respond to unemployment rates as assumed is that, contrary to the implicit assumption of the CITF model, there is a relationship between the local and national economy that influences migration (Greenwood, 1975). Consequently, in Meeker and other towns affected by the shale oil bust, unemployed workers may not leave because unemployment rates are high elsewhere. At the same time, even though no jobs are available, workers from areas with even higher unemployment rates continue to come to Meeker in search of work.

It is also assumed that local labor force participation rates will converge to projections of national labor force participation rates by 1990. However, in energy boom towns, even with low unemployment rates, local labor force participation rates do not necessarily reflect the *desire* for employment, especially among the spouses of employed newcomers (Moen et al., 1981). Summers (1976) and others have found that residents of rural communities undergoing industrialization frequently do not get the new jobs. Instead they move out, remain unemployed, or remain in lower-paying jobs. Since there is both hidden unemployment and considerable concern about rapid growth and the resulting need for capital expenditure, the model could include assumptions about training and hiring programs for local and state residents and the spouses of employed newcomers to generate higher-than-national labor force participation rates, but it does not. In fact, even though there is a high level of unemployment among minorities in Colorado and there are programs to increase minority employment in energy and construction work, the model does not include race as a variable.[7]

A County Projection Model is used as the second component. Its purpose is to age the newcomer and longtimer populations via a cohort survival technique that relies upon local demographic data and numerous assumptions about the characteristics of newcomers. Construction workers are treated separately, and their characteristics are estimated from data such as the *Construction Worker Profile* (Mountain West Research, Inc., 1975) as well as assumptions regarding a reciprocal relationship between worker and housing characteristics. Predicting housing characteristics, however, is as difficult as predicting worker characteristics. In Meeker, an off-again on-again industry-sponsored mobile home park, and the continuously shifting plans of the privately developed Bar 70 project, are only two examples. The demographic characteristics of outmigrants do not seem to be a concern of the model even though outmigration, which may be caused by dissatisfaction with the community as well as by unemployment, is likely to affect the age distribution and age-specific birth and death rates.

The third component, the Subcounty Allocation Model, is more complex than most distribution formulas. But it is also very mechanistic and does not reflect very well the great differences in values and attitudes about growth, politics, land use and development permit policies, and other growth management tools found in the communities and counties in the study area. These are what will determine to a considerable degree the location, kind, and price of housing, and even the location of industry. It was not by chance that a power plant was recently located just across the state line, in Utah, even though its coal supply is located in Rio Blanco County.

Only a sample of potential sources of error in the CITF model has been presented. The two major flaws are that its accuracy rests entirely upon the reliability of industry data and that such a complex model is premature. As Rathge, Leistritz and Smathers (1982:1) point out, "to date there exists little more than a rudimentary understanding of population dynamics with energy projects." Keyfitz (1982) has found that the problem is not limited to energy projects.

In the face of criticism, it has been argued that a model such as the CITF is very flexible and therefore many of the data, assumptions, and relationships can be changed to suit the user. The counter-argument, however, is that users do not have the necessary data and do not know the appropriate assumptions and relationships. In addition, if every user obtains a different answer, what is the point of the model?[8]

The point I am trying to make is that the CITF and similar efforts are high-tech quantitative answers to what is essentially a political and ethical problem. Consequently, it is not surprising that local governments are dropping out of the CITF as an expression of their dissatisfaction with the results of trial runs of the model. Moreover, according to the *Meeker Herald* (2/10/83:1) the local users of the CITF model are complaining that the computer runs are "becoming more involved and complex than anyone had ever realized." In addition, the political nature of the CITF is becoming evident now that industries are hiring "their own consultants to work the computer printouts from their own angle." All of this has caused one Rio Blanco County Commissioner "to once again wish out loud that he should have tried to kill the CITF program." A different mousetrap is needed.

TOWARD A SOLUTION

Review of the Problem

The problems of predicting population growth associated with economic development are severe and the consequences of error may be substantial. The major causes of error and variation among predictions are created by industry, by modelers, and by model users.

Industry's Role

Most complex, subnational forecasting methods are driven by data provided by or guessed about industry. As shown here, these data may be very unreliable. Leistritz and Murdock (1981:49) have also discussed the "substantial degree of uncertainty often associated with resource development projects." Just before the shutdown of the Colony Oil Shale project, the publisher of a regional newspaper emphasized that companies "make little effort to keep the Western Slope informed. . . . The progress of a project is usually described as inevitable until the day it is cut back or shut down. . . . A bust after a 20 year boom is bad enough. But a six-month boom–bust cycle is unacceptable" (*Western Colorado Report,* 4/12/82). Industry may be genuinely ignorant, but there are also many reasons why it might wish to distort or inflate future prospects: to intimidate the competition, to draw a larger labor force to the area, to change forecasts being done by others,[9] to obtain federal funds (e.g., from the Synthetic Fuels Board), to encourage investment in the company and in the area to be affected, and, as noted by a Rio Blanco County official, to "snow the locals." Regarding the latter, the publisher of the *Western Colorado Report* (5/10/82) told of his skepticism about Exxon's projections, which was subdued by the impression made "by top Exxon executives—distinguished, graying, trim, and well spoken," who, like many of the top executives of the major oil and coal companies, had come to Western Colorado to reassure the residents that big growth and big money were on the way:

> Despite the impressiveness of the performers and the performance, and despite the fact that we were

> surrounded by the Western Slope's cargo cult—men and women who believed that the ultimate treasure had finally fallen from the sky—we had trouble accepting the Exxon scenario. But battling against this common sense judgment was our theory of how the world works. It told us that the Exxon executives must know what they're doing. After all, you don't get to the top of an $84 billion corporation by doing silly things.

The encouragement of advance planning and development of housing, services, infrastructure, shopping centers, etc. may be especially important to industry because there is an interrelationship among living conditions, labor productivity, and labor force turnover. A decline in worker productivity (high turnover, absenteeism, and poor performance on the job) may be the result of social problems and the factors that contribute to these social problems—such as high rates of geographic mobility and dissatisfaction with housing and/or working conditions. Low worker productivity is very costly to energy companies and subsequently to the consumers of their products (Weisz, 1979; Gilmore and Duff, 1975; Lillydahl et al., 1982).

Since community development must be started years in advance of the need, industry may use inflated forecasts as a catalyst. Policies developed in Rio Blanco County may put a damper on this practice. The provision of "front end" money (direct payments and prepayment of severance and other taxes) is now being tied to development permits, so that community development can be initiated without the local residents bearing much of the cost. (See Lillydahl et al., 1982, for further discussion.)

Although suggestions that industry also be responsible for costs of a bust have not been officially implemented, the state has granted Meeker's Pioneer Hospital over $200,000 in impact mitigation funds to help cover an anticipated $300,000 deficit in fiscal 1983. According to the hospital administrator, the hospital expanded on a basis of industry projections and, now that the anticipated growth has not occurred, the hospital cannot affort to pay the minimum costs necessary to remain open.

Feelings are growing in resource communities that industries should be more responsible for their projections. Obviously, given the world economy, the oil market, and the lack of a coherent federal energy policy in the United States, energy industries cannot be held entirely responsible for their failure of prophecy. On the other hand, numerous studies of U.S. energy consumption, synthetic and nuclear fuel technology, and the relative costs of oil and shale oil should have led to extreme caution and very conservative predictions regarding the demand for energy as well as the cost of synthetic fuels and the ability to produce them (e.g., Stobaugh and Yergin, 1979; Krenz, 1980; Lovins and Lovins, 1980; Office of Technology Assessment, 1980; Kelly and Ganell, 1981; and Petersen, 1982). Participation in a process such as the CITF may encourage more realistic and reliable assessments by industry. To the extent industries have to pay for boom and bust, they may become increasingly serious about their actions and their projections.

Users

The users of forecasting models, such as state, county and local governments (who may be the designers as well), may also have reasons to influence the outcome. Population growth and distribution are deeply imbedded in politics, and projections may be used to discourage, induce, accommodate, or fund growth (Scott et al., 1975; Ascher, 1978; Moen, 1980; Kunofsky, 1982). It may be especially tempting to local governments to inflate projections when millions of dollars in energy impact mitigation funds are available. If it were accurate, the CITF could discourage what one state official described as the "incredible patronage" associated with impact mitigation funds derived from inflated projections.

In some instances, what has been called "the projection game" is played. In this case, areas that desire higher rate of population growth—or, more often, the funding that goes along with a higher rate of population growth—enter data or build assumptions into their models that will produce the desired high rates. To the extent that additional services, facilities and infrastructure attract new residents and employment, or employment is within commuting distance, the projections will become a self-fulfilling prophecy. But to the extent that such areas are competing for the same population, the services, facilities and infrastructure may be underutilized in these places and/or abandoned in others. Either way, it is wasteful and costly (Moen, 1980; Kunofsky, 1982).

Conversely, communities that expect growth may be using projections and the resulting funding as a means of protecting themselves from becoming stereotypic boom towns, that is, towns with inadequate infrastructure, housing, and services and high rates of social problems. Their problem is that they may not know what the rate, total, or timing of the growth will be. This is the dilemma faced in the extreme by resource communities.

Model Builders

Krannich and Starfield (1977) have blamed the failure of subnational demographic forecasting on demographers' lack of interest in the problem. Perhaps, as Morrison says, demographers know better. In fact, a great deal of work has been done in this area, although little of it appears in mainstream demographic journals such as *Demography*. The response, as discussed above, has been to develop increasingly complex methods rather than to investigate why simpler methods do not work. In a discussion of the goals of forecasting, Ascher (1978:2) notes that model builders may want to "... provide an image of technological sophistication" so that "the methodological elegance of the forecast would be a more important criterion [of success] than its accuracy." Noting the trend toward complexity, Pittenger (1980) advises that if the method cannot be understood by intelligent citizens it should be treated with skepticism.

Regarding the problem of accuracy, Ascher (1978:19) has found that fancy models are not necessary. Instead, he concludes that much more attention should be paid to assumptions: *"When the core assumptions are valid, the choice of methodology is either secondary or obvious"* (my emphasis). However, rather than grappling with assumptions, population projection model builders are more likely to suggest frequent updates, multiple scenarios, a range of projections, or "what ifs" (e.g., Leistritz and Murdock, 1981). The model builder may feel better having given this advice, but it will be small comfort to small towns told they *may* have to accommodate 456,000 *or* 1.248 million people within twenty years.

The Big Problem

Population forecasts are political, and forecasters—whether government, industry, or other interest groups—may have many hidden agendas. Where assumptions are required in design or in use, there cannot be a value-free or policy-free model. When values and policy are not made explicit, the entire planning process is jeopardized. Model builders, although very aware of the limitations of their methods, seem to be more interested in creating very complex tasks for computers than in acquiring accurate and up-to-date data, developing and *testing* assumptions that actually reflect reality, or making their values explicit (see Ascher, 1978, 1981; Kunofsky, 1982).

But even if forecasters were neutral and methods were perfect, forecasts would fail and communities would continue to be surprised and disappointed, because the failure of forecasting lies in the planning process itself. The problem is obvious: in this country, growth planning and management are concerned almost entirely with population growth and distribution, while employment—a major influence on population distribution and local growth (Greenwood, 1975), especially for resource communities—is generally left out of the public planning process. The result may be an impossible planning strategy because in a dynamic situation such as energy development, accurate population forecasts cannot be made without employment planning.[10]

One Solution

Forecasting and planning are ultimately moral issues: how much control should communities have over their futures? In Western Colorado, the question is now being raised:

> A giant game of musical chairs has been set in motion by the vision of Western Colorado as America's Saudi Arabia. Now many of those who set the game in motion have not only stopped the music; they are walking off with their stereo and records under their arms.... While local government has protected itself against the worst effects of a boom, we haven't taken the next step and decided whether we want that boom.... In most cases the large companies have said that the local communities can have anything they want except the choice of rejecting the project.... We do not have to continue to be colonies of Houston or Denver or Los Angeles, soaring or crashing on decisions made in distant boardrooms (*Western Colorado Report*, 5/10/82).

Forecasting/Planning Philosophies

Elsewhere (Moen, 1980) I have discussed the concepts of passive and active forecasting and planning. The forecasting methods discussed above are passive in that they attempt to predict the timing, location and rate of growth that will happen, and the community is then expected to accommodate whatever is forecast. In the absence of a real crystal ball, the best way a community, region, and state can predict and plan for population growth and change is through active projections and planning—deciding what would be desirable and then designing policies and programs to achieve that future. Population projection models would then be used more as a research tool, for example, to determine patterns of labor force participation and growth rates that would lead to a desired population growth rate and size. To the extent that communities are seen to have the right to control their growth and development, active projections are preferable for philosophical as well as methodological reasons.

If active and passive projections/planning are seen as the ideal types on a continuum of community versus industry control, then somewhere in-between is what the French call "indicative" planning. Government and industry work together so the public sector has more reliable information, the private sector is more accountable for its actions, and the values of the citizens are more explicitly considered (Brown, 1978). In the case of the many energy resources that lie under public (federal) lands and are needed by the entire country, the federal and local governments would be involved.

According to Ascher (1978:212), "The forecasting apparatus used to predict what *will* happen can be adapted to recommend what *ought* to be done.... Normative forecasting seeks to identify appropriate policy rather than assume some particular policy choices as givens." Ascher (1978:212) explains that one motivation behind the development of normative, that is, active, forecasting is "the recognition that forecasting is interwined with policy decisions" made by public or private forecast users.

Morrison's conclusion (cited in Kunofsky, 1982) that the value of forecasting is not that it provides an accurate view of the future, but that it can reveal the mechanisms of population growth and change, implies that projection models could be used more appropriately in active forecasting. Model builders would have an easier task in that they could concentrate on assumptions, data, and relationships specified by the stated goals of the user, and since policies and values would be explicit, the model builder's values and policies would no longer be inadvertently built into the method.

With active forecasting, the methods would not change radically; instead, the model would simply be run backwards. Data that formerly drove such models would become results. What were formerly results would drive the model. But the model would be simpler because many of the variables would become constants as the result of public policy decisions.

There would have to be considerable change, however, in the planning process. In order for communities to have some say in their futures, there would have to be employment planning as well as population planning. Consequently, industry would no longer be free to present grandiose schemes as certainties or to close everything down on short notice, and industry's habit of planning primarily for profits (Ascher, 1978) would have to be curtailed. Public officials would have to pay more attention to their constituents, and citizens would have to participate in the ongoing design of their futures. (Comprehensive land-use planning and zoning is one example of active forecasting and planning in common use today.)

What Might Have Happened?

In the case of oil shale, had active planning/forecasting been in place, the resource communities of Western Colorado would not have been anticipating such high rates of growth, and there would have been no sudden project closings.

Historically there has been considerable agreement among state and local officials that shale oil development should be phased to prevent rapid rates and high levels of population growth, as well as sudden economic and population decline. The general consensus in Meeker has been that the town's population should not exceed 8,000.

Second, since the federal government would have been involved in the active planning/forecasting process, there would have been a more coherent and stable energy policy for the nation. Thus, shale oil would have been evaluated more thoroughly. If it had been found a necessary and appropriate source of energy, its development would not have been left to the mercy of international and national economics and politics.

Finally, if industry had been thought to have a greater obligation to resource communities and had been held accountable for its actions, projects might not have been initiated at all, or would have been planned and pursued in a much more cautious manner. A full accounting of all the costs of shale oil production (internal and external), of the quality of the energy produced, and the potential demand for it, might have prevented what then Congress-member and now Federal Office of Management and Budget Director David Stockman (1979) has called "the senseless rush to synfuels" (Krenz, 1980; Office of Technology Assessment, 1980; Lovins and Lovins, 1980; Subcommittee on Energy Development and Applications. 1981).

Legality of Active Planning

The legal/constitutional limits to local growth control are not entirely clear because there have not been many court decisions on this issue. However, ever since the right to zone land was established in *Euclid Village v. Ambler Realty Co.* [272 U.S. 365 (1926)], the courts have strongly supported zoning as an exercise of the power to uphold the "health, safety, morals, and general welfare" of the community (Ellickson and Tarlock, 1981:38). These decisions include the right to limit the number of unrelated persons in a household [*Village of Belle Terre v. Boraas,* 416 U.S. 1 (1974)], the right to control the growth *rate* via limits on building permits [*Construction Industry Association v. City of Petaluma,* 522 F.2d 897 (9th Cir. 1975)], and even the right to exclude racial minorities as long as the exclusion has a nonracial motivation [*Village of Arlington Heights v. Metropolitan Housing Development Corporation,* 429 U.S. 252 (1977)]. On the other hand, devices to set ceilings on growth, such as by the denial of water and sewer services [*Robinson v. City of Boulder,* 547 P.2d 228 (Colorado 1976)] or a limit on total housing stock [*City of Boca Raton v. Boca Villas Corporation,* 371 So.2d 154 (Fla. App. 1979)] have been struck down. However, it is not clear that the cap per se is invalid, for evidence was lacking in these cases that the cap was necessary to protect the public welfare (for example, from shortages of water or other resources).

Regarding energy resource communities, Wyoming's Facilities Siting Act [Wyoming Statutes title 35, ch. 12], which allows communities to set limits on population growth rates associated with large projects, has not been overturned. Rio Blanco County's recent ordinance that requires industry to pay for all costs to tax-raising entities (e.g., city government, school districts, sewer service) and to provide "front end" money for housing has not even been challenged.

In sum, the courts appear fairly permissive in allowing restrictions on growth in terms of limiting the rate of growth, mitigating the negative consequences of growth, and determining the location and kind of growth (e.g., exclusion of factories). The courts have not permitted restrictions, however, that are seen to interfere with freedom of travel (i.e., absolute limits), at least when the evidence is not convincing that population growth threatens the public welfare.

It would appear, then, that local governments can limit the size of energy projects via zoning. If limitations on job supply were found to be analogous to limitations on housing supply, then limits on the rate of growth in employment (as opposed to a strict ceiling) would be constitutional. However, a state probably cannot require that residents, or residents of a certain duration, be given priority in public and private employment [*Hicklin v. Orbeck,* 437 U.S. 518 (1978); Lee (1979)].

The conclusion to be drawn from this brief review is that, while communities may not be able to exert full control over inmigration, there are legal devices available that would enable them to exert considerable control should they desire to do so (Ellickson and Tarlock, 1981; Getches, 1983).

Active forecasting would not be easy to initiate or maintain, but many surprised, disappointed, and devastated communities around the country are testimony to the worth of the effort. The publisher of the *Western Colorado Report* spoke for many communities when he wrote,

> all of us in Western Colorado are in the . . . position of medieval serfs. The knights are up in their castles jousting and figuring and making billion-dollar decisions which will have large effects on us. . . . Every now and then the knights drop the drawbridge and ride out on a foray, sometimes scattering money and jobs on our heads and sometimes riding through our crops, firing our barns, and chasing off our livestock. . . . The abrupt folding of the Colony project signals another reckless ride by knights. Western Colorado should take steps to see that it's the last such ride (*Western Colorado Report,* 04/12/82).

NOTES

I wish to thank Jane Lillydahl, Ed Marston, Peter Morrison, Michael Greenwood, Donald Pittenger, Reid Reynolds, Derek Winstanley, and an anonymous reviewer for comments on an earlier draft of this chapter, as well as Illana Gallon, Barbara Gabella, Lillian Valenzuela, and Michael Greenstein for technical and editorial assistance. Special thanks go to David Getches, University of Colorado School of Law, for advice regarding legal aspects of growth control.

1. The two research projects reported on here were carried out in the Research Program on Population Processes in the Institute of Behavioural Science, University of Colorado, Boulder. The projects were funded respectively by the Colorado Energy Research Institute and the National Institute of Mental Health. The NIMH project was funded under grant number MH33524.
2. Demographers and other predictors often make a distinction between projections and forecasts. Projections are claimed to be reliable only to the extent that the assumptions upon which they are based are indeed valid. Given the difficulty in making such assumptions (e.g., the age-specific fertility rates for 1985), a variety of assumptions may be employed to produce a range of projections. Forecasts have a connotation of certainty (Leistritz and Murdock, 1981), even though the forecaster has no more insight regarding the future than does the projectionist, and it is only assumed that the assumptions underlying a forecast will obtain. Consequently, in this paper the words forecast and projection are used interchangeably (also see Keyfitz, 1982). A problem is that local residents and officials tend to believe forecasts and projections right down to the last decimal place, and they do not want to be confronted with a range of projections—they want the "truth" about the future.
3. Many projection models for energy resource areas continue to employ the worker characteristics found in a mid-1970s survey of construction workers (Mountain West Research, 1975), even though the characteristics of these workers change as the push-pull factors change. For instance, since that survey, the demand for workers increased considerably until 1981, while the economy of other parts of the nation declined. Forecasting models which assumed the past would repeat itself could not have forecast the scenes reminiscent of *The Grapes of Wrath* that have been witnessed throughout Western Colorado and other energy production states and the accompanying increase in diversity of inmigrant job seekers.
4. Another large coal mine opened near Rangely, but because of the distance, mountain roads, and weather, few inmigrant employees will live in Meeker.
5. Only the demographic component of the model, which determines to a considerable degree the outcome of the economic component, is considered here. It should be noted that other complex forecasting models contain assumptions very different from the CITF model (e.g., Temple, 1980).
6. Economic-demographic models such as OBERS have been found to be quite inadequate (Morrison, 1975; Bureau of Economic Analysis, 1977; Population Reference Bureau, 1982), especially in rural areas undergoing economic change (Meidinger, 1978). Although the BAS is more sophisticated than OBERS and aggregates from the bottom up rather than disaggregating from the top down, it is of the same family of models.
7. I realize I am both criticizing complex models and calling for more detail. But if such models are to be used, then should they not contain details that have been identified as important?
8. Proponents of the CITF also say that it is not meant to be a forecasting model, but only a "what if" device which would enable the user to determine, for example, the capital expenditures needed if the town grew by x or y, or the revenue loss that might be incurred if industry did not fulfill its plans. These are very important functions (if the model is correct), but the distinction between "what if" and forecasting as a justification for the CITF model is unconvincing. If this model is not to be used for forecasting and planning, what is? Proponents of the CITF model also argue that it can be used for "sensitivity analyses" which would enable the identification of "crucial" variables and thereby improve the data and assumptions. To the extent that the model is seen as a method in development rather than in reliable tool, their point is well-taken.
9. For instance, one consulting firm advised the California construction industry to "develop its own population projection capability" because it is "necessary to influence the outcome of population projections at the national, state, and Bay Area level" (Kunofsky, 1982:7).
10. Some state and local governments attempt to lure employers with devices such as tax breaks or cheap land, and others use zoning and permits to try to control the rate of employment growth, but explicit policies regarding employment are rare.

REFERENCES

Ascher, W. 1978. *Forecasting: An Appraisal for Policy-Makers and Planners.* Baltimore, MD: Johns Hopkins.

Ascher, W. 1981. "The Forecasting Potential of Complex Models." *Policy Sciences* 13:247–267.

Brown, L. 1978. *The Twenty-Ninth Day.* New York: Norton.

Bureau of Economic Analysis. 1977. "Population, Personal Income, and Earnings by State: Projections to 2000." Report prepared for the Environmental Protection Agency (October). Washington, DC: U.S. Department of Commerce.

Chalmers, J. A., and E. J. Anderson. 1977. *Economic/Demographic Assessment Manual.* Denver, Colorado: Bureau of Reclamation.

Colorado Energy Research Institute (CERI). 1981. *Colorado Oil Shale Development Scenarios, 1981–2000.* Golden, CO: Colorado Energy Research Institute.

Colorado West Council of Governments. 1981. *Rio Blanco County-Wide Capital Improvements Program.* (May 15, 1981). Rifle, CO: Colorado West Council of Governments.

Cortese, C. F., and B. Jones. 1977. "The Sociological Analysis of Boom Towns." *Western Sociological Review* 8:76–90.

Council on Environmental Quality. 1979. *Regulations for Implementing the Procedural Provisions of the National Environmental Policy Act.* Washington, DC: U.S. Government Printing Office.

Cumulative Impact Task Force (CITF). 1982. Planning and Assessment Model Documentation (untitled). Revised 6/1/82. Denver, CO: Colorado State Department of Natural Resources.

Da Vanzo, J. 1978. "Does Unemployment Affect Migration? Evidence from Micro Data." *The Review of Economics and Statistics* 60:504–514.

Ellickson, R. C., and A. D. Tarlock. 1981. *Land-Use Controls: Cases and Materials.* Boston: Little, Brown & Co.

Environmental Projection Agency (EPA). 1979. "Population Projections for the State of Colorado." Transcript of Proceedings. (November 1) Denver, CO.

Exxon Corporation, U.S.A. 1980. "Energy Outlook, 1980–2000." (December) Exxon Corporation, U.S.A.

Finsterbusch, K. 1980. *Understanding Social Impacts.* Beverly Hills: Sage Publications.

Getches, David. 1983. Personal communication.

Gilmore, J. S., and M. K. Duff. 1975. *Boom Town Growth Management: A Case Study of Rock Springs–Green River, Wyoming.* Boulder, CO: Westview Press.

Greenwood, M. J. 1975. "Research on Internal Migration in the United States." *Journal of Economic Literature* 13:397–433.

Greenwood, M. J. 1976. "A Simultaneous-Equations Model of White and Nonwhite Migration and Urban Change." *Economic Inquiry* 14:1–15.

Kelly, H., and K. Ganell. 1981. *A New Prosperity: Building a Sustainable Energy Future.* (Reprint of a Solar Energy Research Institute report.) Andover, MA: Brick House.

Keyfitz, N. 1972. "On Future Population." *Journal of the American Statistical Association* 67:347–363.

———. 1981. "The Limits of Population Forecasting," *Population and Development Review* 7:579–593.

———. 1982. "Can Knowledge Improve Forecasts?" *Population and Development Review* 8:729–751.

Krannich, R. S., and G. S. Starfield. 1977. "The Application of Demography to Energy Facility Development Projects." Working Paper #39. Pennsylvania State University: Center for Environmental Policy.

Krenz, J. H. 1980. *Energy: From Opulence to Sufficiency.* New York: Praeger Publishing.

Kunofsky, J. 1982. *Handbook on Population Projections.* San Francisco, CA: The Sierra Club.

Lee, E. S., and H. F. Goldsmith, (eds.). 1982. *Population Estimates. Methods for Small Area Analysis.* Beverly Hills: Sage Publications.

Lee, Michael A. 1979. "Durational Residence Requirements for Public Employment," *California Law Review* 67:386–406.

Leistritz, F. L., and S. H. Murdock. 1981. *The Socioeconomic Impact of Resource Development: Methods for Assessment.* Boulder, CO: Westview Press.

Lillydahl, J. H., W. W. Moen, E. Boulding, K. Yount, S. Scott-Stevens, and I. Gallon. 1982. *Quality of Life, Expectations of Change, and Planning for the Future in an Energy Production Community.* Boulder, CO: Institute of Behavioral Science, University of Colorado.

Lovins, A. B., and L. H. Lovins. 1980. *Energy/War.* San Francisco, CA: Friends of the Earth.

McKeown, R. L., and A. Lantz. n.d. "Rapid Growth and Impact on Quality of Life in Rural Communities: A Case Study." Denver, CO: Denver Research Institute.

Meidinger, E. E. 1978. "Modeling the Social Impacts of Capital Projects." Presented at the International Symposium on Simulation, Modeling and Decision Making in Energy Systems (June). Montreal, Quebec.

Meyer, R. (President, Exxon Corporation, U.S.A.). (April 2, 1981). Address to the Colorado School of Mines. Exxon Reprint.

Moen, E. W. 1980. "Public Planning and the Social Costs of Energy Production: Two Futures for Colorado," in *Energy Issues in Colorado's Future.* Golden, CO: Colorado Energy Research Institute.

Moen, E. W., E. Boulding, J. Lillydahl, and R. Palm. 1981. *Women and the Social Costs of Economic Development: Two Colorado Case Studies.* Boulder, CO: Westview.

Morrison, P. 1975. *Overview of Population Forecasting for Small Areas.* Santa Monica, CA: Rand Corporation.

Morrison, P. 1971. *The Propensity to Move.* Santa Monica, CA:Rand Corporation.

Mountain West Research, Inc. 1975. *Construction Worker Profile.* Washington, DC: Old West Regional Commission.

Office of Technology Assessment (OTA). 1980. *An Assessment of Oil Shale Technologies.* Washington, DC: U.S. Government Printing Office.

Petersen, K. K. (ed.). 1982. *Oil Shale, the Environmental Challenges II.* Proceedings of an International Symposium, August 10–13, Vail, Colorado. Golden, CO: Colorado School of Mines.

Pittenger, D. B. 1976. *Projecting State and Local Populations.* Cambridge, MA: Ballinger.

Pittenger, D. B. 1977. "Population Forecasting Standards." *Demography* 14: 363–368.

Pittenger, D. B. 1980. "Some Problems in Forecasting Population for Government Planning Purposes." *American Statistician* 34:135–139.

Population Reference Bureau. 1982. "Six Demographic Surprises." *Population Bulletin* 37:33.

Rathge, R. W., F. L. Leistritz, and L. S. Smathers. 1982. "Demographic Changes Associated with Energy Development Projects." Presented at 1982 Population Association of America Annual Meeting, San Diego, California.

Sanderson, D., and M. O'Hare. 1977. *Predicting the Local Impacts of Energy Development.* Cambridge, MA: MIT Press.

Science Policy Research Division, Congressional Research Service. 1981. "Costs of Synthetic Fuels in Relation to Oil Prices." Report prepared for the Subcommittee on Energy Development and Applications of the Committee on Science and Technology, U.S. House of Representatives. Washington, DC: U.S. Government Printing Office.

Scott, R. W., D. J. Brower, and D. D. Miner (eds.). 1975. *Management and Control of Growth.* Washington, DC: Urban Land Institute.

Shryock, H. S., and J. S. Siegel. 1976. *The Methods and Materials of Demography.* New York: Academic Press.

Stobaugh, R., and D. Yergin. 1979. *Energy Future.* New York: Random House.

Stockman, D. 1979. "Why the Senseless Rush to Synfuels?" *Reader's Digest* (December):2–5.

Subcommittee on Energy Development and Applications. 1981. *Cost of Synthetic Fuels in Relation to Oil Prices.* Washington, DC: U.S. Government Printing Office.

Summers, G. F. 1976. *Industrial Invasion of Nonmetropolitan America.* New York: Praeger.

Temple, G. 1980. "Dynamic Disequilibrium Models in Local Impact Analysis." Minneapolis, Minn.: University of Minnesota, Department of Agriculture and Applied Economics.

Tosco. 1982. "Oil Shale: Colony's First Barrel to be Sold in 1986–1987," *Tosco News Update,* March 29, 1982. Denver, CO: Tosco Corporation.

Warren P. 1981. *Colorado Oil Shale Development Scenarios, 1981–2000.* Golden, CO: Colorado Energy Research Institute.

Weisz, R. 1979. "Stress and Mental Health in a Boom Town," in J. A. Davenport and J. Davenport Ill (eds.), *Boom Towns and Human Services.* Laramie, WY: University of Wyoming.

References to Introductions

Abrahamson, M. 1980. *Urban Sociology.* Second edition. Englewood Cliffs, NJ: Prentice-Hall.

American Association for the Advancement of Science (AAAS). 1983. "Update." *Science* #83 4(9):6.

Anderson, C. 1976. *The Sociology of Survival.* Homewood, IL: Dorsey.

Antonovsky, A., and J. Berstein. 1977. "Social Class and Infant Mortality." *Social Science and Medicine* 11 (May):453–470.

Appleman, P. 1976. *Thomas Robert Malthus: An Essay on the Principle of Population.* New York: Norton.

Banister, J. 1980. "Use and Abuse of Census Editing and Imputations." *Asian and Pacific Census Forum* 6(3):1–2, 16–18, 20.

Banks, J. S., and O. Banks. 1969. *Feminism and Family Planning in Victorian England.* New York: Schocken.

Barberis, M. 1980. "America's Elderly: Policy Implications." *Policy Supplement to Population Bulletin* 35(4). Washington, DC: Population Reference Bureau.

Beale, C. L., and G. V. Fuguitt. 1978. "The New Pattern of Nonmetropolitan Population Change." Pp. 157–177 of K. E. Taeuber, L. L. Bumpass, and J. A. Sweet (eds.) *Social Demography.* New York: Academic Press.

Bean, F. D., and T. A. Sullivan. 1985. "Confronting the Problem." *Society* (May/June):67–73.

Becker, G. S. 1960. "An Economic Analysis of Fertility." *Demographic and Economic Change in Developed Countries.* Princton, NJ: Princeton University.

———. 1981. *A Treatise on the Family.* Cambridge, MA: Harvard University.

Ben-Porath, Y. (ed.). 1982. "Income Distribution and the Family." *Population and Development Review.* Supplement to volume 8.

Birdsall, N. 1980. "Population Growth and Poverty in the Developing World." *Population Bulletin* 35(5). Washington, DC: Population Reference Bureau.

Bondestram, L., and S. Bergstrom (eds.). 1980. *Poverty and Population Control.* New York: Academic.

Bongaarts, J., O. Frank, and R. Lesthaeghe. 1984. "The Proximate Determinants of Fertility in Sub-Saharan Africa." *Population and Development Review* 10(3):511–537.

Bongaarts, J., and R. G. Potter. 1983. *Fertility, Biology, and Behavior.* New York: Academic.

Boserup, E. 1981. *Population and Technological Change.* Chicago: University of Chicago.

Bourgeois-Pichat, J. 1983. "Review of *Levels and Trends of Mortality Since 1950* by the United Nations and the World Health Organization." *Population and Development Review* 9(2):361–372.

Brown, G. F. 1984. "United Nations International Conference on Population, Mexico City, 6–13 August 1984." *Studies in Family Planning* 15(6):296–302.

Brown, L. 1981. *Building a Sustainable Society.* New York: Norton.

Brown, L. R., W. Chandler, C. Flavin, S. Postel, L. Stark, and E. Wolf. 1984. *State of the World 1984.* New York: Norton.

Bulatao, R. A. 1979. *On the Nature of the Transition in the Value of Children.* Honolulu: East-West Center.

Balatao, R. A., and J. T. Fawcett. 1983. *Influences on Childbearing Intentions Across the Fertility Career: Demographic and Socioeconomic Factors and the Value of Children.* Honolulu: East-West Population Institute.

Cain, M. T. 1978. "The Household Life Cycle and Economic Mobility in Rural Bangladesh." *Population and Development Review* 4(3):421–438.

Caldicott, H. 1980. *Nuclear Madness.* New York: Bantam.

Caldwell, J. C. 1982. *Theory of Fertility Decline.* New York: Academic.

Caldwell, J. C., P. H. Reddy, and P. Caldwell. 1985. "Education Transition in Rural South India." *Population and Development Review* 11(1):29–51.

Chandler, W. U. 1984. "Improving World Health: A Least Cost Strategy." Worldwatch Paper 59. Washington, DC: Worldwatch Institute.

———. 1985a. "Energy Productivity: Key to Environmental Protection and Economic Progress." Worldwatch Paper 63. Washington, DC: Worldwatch Institute.

———. 1985b. "Investing in Children." Worldwatch Paper 64. Washington, DC: Worldwatch Institute.

Clark, C. 1967. *Population Growth and Land Use.* New York: St. Martin's.

Coale, A. J. 1985. "Nuclear War and Demographers' Projections." *Population and Development Review* 11(3):483–493.

Cole, J. P. 1979. *Geography of World Affairs.* New York: Penguin.

College Board. 1984. *National Report on College-Bound Seniors, 1984.* Princeton, NJ: College Entrance Examination Board.

Commission on Population Growth and the American Future. 1972. *Population and the American Future.* Washington, DC: U.S. Government Printing Office.
Commoner, B. 1972. *The Closing Circle.* New York: Bantam.
Corbett, J. 1983. "Nuclear War and Crisis Relocation Planning: A View from the Grass Roots." *Impact Assessment Bulletin* 2(4):23–33.
Covey, H. C., and S. Menard. 1983. "Crime in the Region of Colorado Affected by Energy Resource Development." *Journal of Research in Crime and Delinquency* 20:110–125.
————. 1984. "Response to Rapid Social Change: The Case of Boomtown Law Enforcement." *Journal of Police Science and Administration* 12:164–169.
Crewdson, J. 1983. *The Tarnished Door: The New Immigrants and the Transformation of America.* New York: Times Books.
Daly, H. 1980. *Economics, Ecology, Ethics.* San Francisco: Freeman.
Davis, C., and M. Feshbach. 1980. *Rising Infant Mortality in the USSR in the 1970s.* Series P-95, No. 74. Washington, DC: U.S. Bureau of the Census.
Davis, K., and J. Blake. 1956. "Social Structure and Fertility." *Economic Development and Cultural Change* 5(April):211–235.
Davis, S. H. 1977. *Victims of the Miracle: Development and the Indians of Brazil.* Cambridge: Cambridge University.
Demerath, N. J. 1976. *Birth Control and Foreign Policy: The Alternatives to Family Planning.* New York: Harper & Row.
Durham, W. H. 1979. *Scarcity and Survival in Central America: Ecological Origins of the Soccer War.* Stanford, CA: Stanford University Press.
Easterlin, R. A. 1969. "Towards a Socio-Economic Theory of Fertility." Pp. 127–151 of S. J. Behrman, L. Corsa, and R. Freedman (eds.), *Fertility and Family Planning: A World View.* Ann Arbor: University of Michigan Press.
Eberstadt, N. 1981. "The Health Crisis in the USSR." *New York Review of Books* 28(2):23–29.
————. 1984. "A Comment." *Population and Development Review* 10(1):91–98.
Eckholm, E. P. 1977. *The Picture of Health.* New York: Norton.
————. 1979. "The Dispossessed of the Earth: Land Reform and Sustainable Development." Worldwatch Paper 30. Washington, DC: Worldwatch Institute.
Ehrlich, P. R. 1968. *The Population Bomb.* New York: Ballantine.
Ehrlich, P. R., L. Bilderback, and A. R. Ehrlich. 1979. *The Golden Door.* New York: Ballantine.
Eitenger, L., and D. Schwarz (eds.). 1981. *Strangers in the World.* Bern: Hans Huber.
Espenshade, T. J. 1977. "The Value and Cost of Children." *Population Bulletin* 32(1). Washington, DC: Population Reference Bureau.
European Parliament. 1984. "Resolution on the Need for Community (EEC) Measures to Promote Population Growth in Europe." *Population and Development Review* 10(3):569–570.
Faaland, J. (ed.). 1982. *Population and the World Economy in the 21st Century.* New York: St. Martin's.
Feshbach, M. 1984. "A Comment." *Population and Development Review* 10(1):91–98.
Flanagan, T. J., and M. McLeod. 1983. *Sourcebook of Criminal Justice Statistics, 1982.* Washington, DC: U.S. Government Printing Office.
Forrester, J. W. 1971. *World Dynamics.* Cambridge, MA: Wright-Allen.
Freedman, R. 1963. "Norms for Family Size in Underdeveloped Areas." *Proceedings of the Royal Society* 159:220–245.
————. 1979. "Theories of Fertility Decline: A Reappraisal." *Social Forces* 58:1–17.
Garcia, R. 1981. *Drought and Man: The 1972 Case History.* New York: Pergamon.
Gardner, R. W., B. Robey, and P. C. Smith. 1985. "Asian Americans: Growth, Change, Diversity," *Population Bulletin* 40(4). Washington, DC: Population Reference Bureau.
Geiger, H. J. 1980. "Addressing Apocalypse Now: The Effects of Nuclear Warfare as a Public Health Concern." *American Journal of Public Health* 70(9):958–961.
George, S. 1979. *Feeding the Few.* Washington, DC: Institute for Policy Studies.
Gimenez, M. E. 1980. "Feminism, Pronatalism, and Motherhood." *International Journal of Women's Studies* 3(3):215–240.
Gold, R. 1985. *Ranching, Mining, and the Human Impact of Natural Resource Development.* New Brunswick, NJ: Transaction.
Goliber, T. J. 1985. "Sub-Saharan Africa: Population Pressures on Development." *Population Bulletin* 40(1). Washington, DC: Population Reference Bureau.
Gordon, L. 1976. *Woman's Body, Woman's Rights.* New York: Grossman.
Greer, T. H. 1972. *A Brief History of Western Man.* New York: Harcourt Brace Jovanovich.
Hardin, G. 1974. "Living on a Life Boat." *BioScience* 24:561–568.
Haupt, A., and T. Kane. 1978. *Population Handbook.* Washington, DC: Population Reference Bureau.
Higgins, G. M., A. H. Kassam, L. Naiken, G. Fischer, and M. M. Shah. 1983. *Potential Population Supporting*

Capacities of Lands in the Developing World. Rome: United Nations Food and Agricultural Organization.

Hughes, B. 1985. *World Futures.* Baltimore: John Hopkins.

Hutchinson, E. P. 1981. Legislative History of American Immigration Policy 1798–1965. Philadelphia: University of Pennsylvania.

Jejeebhoy, S. J. 1984. "The Shift from Natural to Controlled Fertility." *Studies in Family Planning* 15(4):191–198.

Jones, C. 1984. "Racism or Xenophobia or Cultural Incompatibility." *Migration Today* 33:4–6.

Jones, E., and F. W. Grupp. 1983. "Infant Mortality Trends in the Soviet Union." *Population and Development Rview* 9(2):213–246.

———. 1984. "Rejoinder." *Population and Development Review* 10(1):98–102.

Kahn, H. 1982. *The Coming Boom: Economic, Political, and Social.* New York: Simon and Schuster.

Keely, C. B. 1979. *U.S. Immigration: A Policy Analysis.* New York: The Population Council.

———. 1982. "Illegal Immigration." *Scientific American* 246(3):41–47.

Kelley, A. C., and J. G. Williamson. 1984. "Population Growth, Industrial Revolutions, and the Urban Transition." *Population and Development Review* 10(3):419–441.

Kenan, G. 1982. "On Nuclear War." *The New York Review of Books* 29(1):8–12.

King, T., with R. Cuca, R. Gulhati, M. Hossain, E. Stern, P. Visaria, K. C. Zacharia, G. Zafros, B. M. Burke, B. Newlon, and R. Repetto. 1974. *Population Policies and Economic Development.* Baltimore: Johns Hopkins Press.

Kleinman, D. S. 1980. *Human Adaptation and Population Growth: A Non-Malthusian Perspective.* Montclair, NJ: Allanheld, Osmun.

Knodel, J., N. Havonon, and A. Pramualratana. 1984. Fertility Transition in Thailand: A Qualitative Analysis." *Population and Development Review* 10(2):297–328.

Kocher, J. E. 1973. *Rural Development, Income Distribution, and Fertility Decline.* New York: The Population Council.

Kutzik, A. J. 1981. "Infant Mortality in the Soviet Union/Anti-Sovietism in the United States." *New World Review* 49(4):20–27.

LaRoque, G. R. 1983. "America's Nuclear Ferment." *The Defense Monitor* XII(3):1–6, 8.

Lang, J. S., and S. Mukherjee. 1984. "India's Tragedy—A Warning Heard Around the World." *U.S. News and World Report* (Dec. 17):25–26.

London, J., and G. F. White. 1984. *The Environmental Effects of Nuclear War.* Boulder, CO: Westview.

Mamdani, M. 1972. *The Myth of Population Control.* New York: Monthly Review.

Mass, B. 1976. *Population Target.* Brampton, Ontario: Charters Publishers.

Mauldin, W. P., and B. Berelson. 1978. "Conditions of Fertility Decline in Developing Countries, 1965–1975." *Studies in Family Planning* 9(5):89–147.

Mauldin, W. P., N. Choucri, F. W. Notestein, and M. Teitelbaum. 1974. "A Report on Bucharest." *Studies in Family Planning* 5(12):357–395.

McEvedy, C., and R. Jones. 1978. *Atlas of World Population History.* New York: Penguin.

Meadows, D. H. 1985. "Charting the Way the World Works." *Technology Review* 88(2):54–64.

Meadows, D. H., D. L. Meadows, J. Randers, and W. W. Behrens III. 1972. *The Limits to Growth.* New York: E. P. Dutton.

Meek, R. L. (ed.). 1971. *Marx and Engels on the Population Bomb.* Berkeley: Ramparts Press.

Menard, S. 1981. "The Test Score Decline: An Analysis of Available Data." Pp. 183–209 of B. E. Mercer and S. C. Hey (eds.) *People in Schools: A Reader in the Sociology of Learning and Teaching.* Cambridge, MA: Schenkman.

———. 1983. "Fertility, Development, and Family Planning." Studies in Comparative International Development XVIII(3):75–100.

———. 1986. "A Research Note on International Comparisons of Inequality of Income." *Social Forces* 64(3):778–793.

Menard, S., and H. C. Covey. 1984. "The Impact of Rapid Population Growth and Energy Development on Court Workloads." *Social Science Journal* 21:111–122.

Merton, R. K. 1961. "The Role of Genius in Scientific Advance." *New Scientist* 259:306–308.

Mesarovic, M., and E. Pestel. 1974. *Mankind at the Turning Point.* New York: E. P. Dutton.

Metropolitan Life Insurance Company. 1984. "Alcohol and Other Drug Abuse Among Adolescents." *Statistical Bulletin* 65(1):4–13.

Michaelson, K. L. (ed.). 1981. *And The Poor Get Children: Radical Perspectives on Population Dynamics.* New York: Monthly Review.

Miller, B. D. *The Endangered Sex.* Ithaca, NY: Cornell University.

Miller, C. A. 1985. "Infant Mortality in the U.S." *Scientific American* 253(1):31–37.

Moen, E. W. 1977. "Third World Women, World Population Growth: A Case of Blaming the Victim?" *Journal of Scoiology and Social Welfare* (Sept.) 1186–1202.

Moen, E., E. Boulding, J. Lillydahl, and R. Palm. 1981. *Women and the Social Costs of Economic Development.* Boulder: Westview.

Morgan, R. 1984. *Sisterhood is Global.* Garden City, NY: Anchor.

Morris, J. K. 1966. "Professor Malthus and His Essay." *Population Bulletin* 22(1). Washington, DC: Population Reference Bureau.

Morrison, P. A., and J. P. Wheeler. 1976. "Rural Renaissance in America? The Revival of Population Growth in Remote Areas." *Population Bulletin* 31(3). Washington, DC: Population Reference Bureau.

Mumford, S. D. 1984. *American Democracy and the Vatican: Population Growth and National Security.* Amherst, NY: Humanist Press.

Murdoch, W. W. 1980. *The Poverty of Nations.* Baltimore: John Hopkins.

Nathanson, C. A. 1977. "Sex Roles as Variables in Preventive Health Behavior." *Journal of Comminity Health* 3(2):142–155.

National Commission on Excellence in Education. 1983. *A Nation At Risk: The Imperative for Educational Reform.* Washington, DC: U.S. Department of Education.

National Education Association. 1977. "NEA Resolution on Standardized Tests." *Today's Education* 66(March–April):55.

New Directions for Women. 1985. "Data Shows Women's Health Up in Smoke." *New Directions for Women* (Jan./Feb.):4.

Newland, K. 1981. "Infant Mortality and the Health of Societies." Worldwatch Paper 47. Washington, DC: Worldwatch Institute.

Omran, A. R. 1977. "Epidemiologic Transition in the U.S." *Population Bulletin* 32(2). Washington, DC: Population Reference Bureau.

Peterson, R. W. 1985. "Abortions Worldwide Increase as Result of U.S. Aid Policies." Reprinted from *New York Times.* Boulder Daily Camera (March 28):8.

Petras, E. M. 1981. "The Global Labor Market in the Modern World Economy." Pp. 44–63 of M. M. Kritz, C. B. Keely, and S. M. Tomasi (eds.), *Global Trends in Migration: Theory and Research on International Population Movements.* New York: Center for Migration Studies.

Piotrow, P. T. 1980. *World Population: The Present and Future Crisis.* New York: Foreign Policy Association.

Population Reference Bureau. 1982. "U.S. Population: Where We Are; Where We're Going." *Population Bulletin* 37(2). Washington, DC: Population Reference Bureau.

———. 1983. *World Population Data Sheet, 1984.* Washington, DC: Population Reference Bureau.

———. 1984a. *World Population Data Sheet, 1984.* Washington, DC: Population Reference Bureau.

———. 1984b. "How Many Illegals in the 1980 Census." *Population Today* 12(7/8):10.

———. 1984c. "Report from Mexico City." *Population Today* 12(10):2, 8–12.

———. 1985a. "Singapore Promotes Selective Sterilization." *Population Today* 13(2):5.

———. 1985b. "U.S. Ends Aid to IPPF." *Population Today* 13(2):7.

Prescott, D. M. and A. S. Flexer. 1982. *Cancer: The Misguided Cell.* Sunderland, MA: Sinauer.

Pressat, R. 1972. *Demographic Analysis.* Chicago: Aldine.

Preston, S. H. (ed.). 1978. *The Effects of Infant and Childhood Mortality on Fertility.* New York: Academic Press.

———. 1982. *Biological and Social Aspects of Mortality and the Length of Life.* Liege: Ordina.

Quale, G. R. 1966. *Eastern Civilizations.* New York: Appleton-Century-Crofts.

Raloff, J. 1983. "Beyond Armageddon." *Science News* 124 (November 12):314–317.

Repetto, R. 1979. *Economic Equality and Fertility in Developing Countries.* Baltimore: Johns Hopkins.

Retherford, R. 1975. *Changing Sex Differentials in Mortality.* Westport, CT: Greenwood.

Salas, R. M. 1974. *Population Assistance and the UNFPA.* New York: United Nations Fund for Population Activities.

———. 1984. *Population: The Mexico Conference and the Future.* New York: United Nations Fund for Population Activities.

Scheer, R. 1982. *With Enough Shovels.* New York: Random House.

Schell, J. 1982. *The Fate of the Earth.* New York: A. A. Knopf.

Sherris, J. D., and G. Fox. 1983. "Infertility and Sexually Transmitted Disease: A Public Health Challenge." *Population Reports,* Series L, No. 4.

Shryock, H. S., J. S. Siegel, and associates. 1973. *The Methods and Materials of Demography.* Volumes I and II. Washington, DC: U.S. Government Printing Office.

———. 1976. *The Methods and Materials of Demography.* Condensed edition by E. G. Stockwell. New York: Academic.

Simon, J. L. 1974. "Population Growth May Be Good for the LDCs in the Long Run." *Economic Development and Cultural Change* 24(Jan.):309–338.

———. 1981. *The Ultimate Resource.* Princeton: Princeton University.

Simon, J. L., and H. Kahn. 1984. *The Resourceful Earth.* New York: Basil Blackwell.

Soldo, B. J. 1980. "America's Elderly in the 1980s." *Population Bulletin* 35(4). Washington, DC: Population Reference Bureau.

Soni, V. 1983. "Thirty Years of the Indian Family Planning Program: Past Performance, Future Prospects." *International Family Planning Perspectives* 9(2):35–45.

Stycos, J. M. 1974. "Demographic Chic at the U.N." *Family Planning Perspectives* 6(3):160–164.

Szymanski, A. 1982. "On the Uses of Disinformation to Legitimate the Revival of the Cold War: Health in the USSR." *Science and Society* XLV(4):453–474.

Teitelbaum, M. S. 1974. "Population and Development: Is a Consensus Possible?" *Foreign Affairs* (53):742–760.

———. 1980. "Right Versus Right: Immigration and Refugee Policy in the U.S." *Foreign Affairs* 59(1):21–59.

Tinbergen, J. 1976. *RIO: Reshaping the International Order.* New York: E. P. Dutton.

Turco, R. P., O. B. Toon, T. P. Ackermen, J. B. Pollack, and C. Sagan. 1984. "The Climate Effects of Nuclear War." *Scientific American* 251(2):33–43.

Tsui, A. O., and D. J. Bogue. 1978. "Declining World Fertility: Trends, Causes, Implications." *Population Bulletin* 33(4). Washington, DC: Population Reference Bureau.

ul Haq, M. 1981. *The Poverty Curtain.* New York: Norton.

United Nations. 1977. *World Statistics in Brief.* New York: United Nations.

———. 1979. *Trends and Characteristics of International Migration Since 1950.* New York: United Nations.

United Nations, Department of International Economic and Social Affairs. 1983. *Manual X: Indirect Techniques for Demographic Estimation.* New York: United Nations.

United Nations Food and Agricultural Organization (FAO). 1983. *World Food Report.* Rome: United Nations.

United Nations and World Health Organization. 1982. *Levels and Trends of Mortality Since 1950.* New York: United Nations.

U.S. Department of Commerce. 1984. *Statistical Abstracts of the United States, 1982–1983.* Washington, DC: U.S. Government Printing Office.

Verbrugge, L. M. 1976. "Sex Differentials in Morbidity and Mortality in the U.S." *Social Biology* 23 (Winter):275–296.

Watkins, J. 1984. "The Effect of Residential Structure Variation on Dwelling Unit Enumeration from Aerial Photographs." *Photogrammetric Engineering and Remote Sensing* 50(11):1599–1607.

Weeks, J. R. 1981. *Population.* Second edition. Belmont, CA: Wadsworth.

———. 1986. *Population.* Third edition. Belmont, CA: Wadsworth.

Weir, D., and M. Shapiro. 1981. *Circle of Poison.* San Francisco: Institute for Food and Development Policy.

Weisbord, R. G. 1973. "Birth Control and the Black American: A Matter of Genocide?" *Demography* 10(4):571–590.

Weston, H. B. (ed.). 1984. *Toward Nuclear Disarmament.* Boulder, CO: Westview.

Williamson, N. E. 1977. *Sons or Daughters: A Cross Cultural Survey of Parental Preferences.* Beverly Hills, CA: Sage.

World Bank. 1980. *World Development Report 1980.* New York: Oxford.

———. 1981. *World Development Report 1981.* New York: Oxford.

———. 1982. *World Development Report 1982.* New York: Oxford.

———. 1984. *World Development Report 1984.* New York: Oxford.

World Resources Institute. 1984. *The Global Possible: Resources, Development, and the New Century.* Washington, DC: World Resources Institute.

Wulf, D., and P. Willson. 1984. "Global Politics in Mexico City." *Family Planning Perspectives* 16(5)228–232.

Yu, E., and W. T. Liu. 1980. *Fertility and Kinship in the Philippines.* Notre Dame, IN: University of Notre Dame.

Zolberg, A. 1984. "Review of *The Tarnished Door: The New Immigrants and the Transformation of America,* by John Crewdson." *Population and Development Review* 10(3):558–561.

Name Index

Subject Index